Everyman, I will go with thee,
and be thy guide

THE EVERYMAN
LIBRARY

*The Everyman Library was founded by J. M. Dent
in 1906. He chose the name Everyman because he wanted
to make available the best books ever written in every
field to the greatest number of people at the cheapest possible
price. He began with Boswell's 'Life of Johnson';
his one-thousandth title was Aristotle's 'Metaphysics',
by which time sales exceeded forty million.*

*Today Everyman paperbacks remain true to
J. M. Dent's aims and high standards, with a wide range
of titles at affordable prices in editions which address
the needs of today's readers. Each new text is reset to give
a clear, elegant page and to incorporate the latest thinking
and scholarship. Each book carries the pilgrim logo,
the character in 'Everyman', a medieval morality play,
a proud link between Everyman
past and present.*

RESTORATION PLAYS

Edited by
ROBERT G. LAWRENCE
University of Victoria, Canada

EVERYMAN
J. M. DENT · LONDON
CHARLES E. TUTTLE
VERMONT

First published in Everyman 1912
Augmented edition including *The Man of Mode,* 1932
Revised edition, including re-edited text of
The Provoked Wife, 1932
Reprinted 1980, 1983, 1985 and 1988
This Edition 1994
Reprinted 1995, 1997

J. M. Dent
Orion Publishing Group,
Orion House, 5 Upper St Martin's Lane,
London WC2H 9EA
and
Charles E. Tuttle Co. Inc.
28 South Main Street,
Rutland, Vermont 05701, USA

Typeset at The Spartan Press Ltd, Lymington, Hants

Printed in Great Britain by
The Guernsey Press Co. Ltd, Guernsey, C.I.

British Library Cataloguing in Publication Data
is available upon request.

ISBN 0 460 87432 2

CONTENTS

NOTE ON THE AUTHORS AND EDITOR

WILLIAM CONGREVE (1670–1729)
JOHN DRYDEN (1631–1700)
GEORGE ETHEREGE (1636–c. 1691)
GEORGE FARQUHAR (c. 1677–1701)
THOMAS OTWAY (1652–1685)
JOHN VANBRUGH (1664–1707)
WILLIAM WYCHERLEY (1641–1715)

Biographical information on these playwrights can be found at the front of each play.

ROBERT G. LAWRENCE is Professor Emeritus at the University of Victoria, Victoria, B. C., Canada. He has edited other volumes in the Everyman's Library and has published articles on Canadian literature and theatre. He has taught in several Canadian universities, specialising in 16–18th century drama, and later in Canadian theatre and literature.

HISTORICAL CHRONOLOGY

Year	Event
1618–48	Thirty Years War
1625	Death of James I; accession of Charles I
1628	Petition of Right
1629–40	Charles I rules without Parliament
1620–	John Evelyn, *Diary*
1706	
1631	John Dryden born
1636	George Etherege born
1640	The Short Parliament
1640–53	The Long Parliament
1641	William Wycherley born
1642–6,	Civil Wars
1648,	
1649–51	
1649	Charles I beheaded in January
	Rump Parliament proclaims Commonwealth
1650	Introduction of coffee to England, leading to the establishment of coffee houses
1652–4,	Three Dutch wars
1664–7,	
1672–4	
1652	Thomas Otway born
1653–9	The Protectorate; Oliver Cromwell Lord Protector (dies September 1658)
1658–9	Son Richard Cromwell Lord Protector from September until May

THEATRICAL AND CULTURAL CHRONOLOGY

_____

Year   _Event_

1642   Puritan animosity and anti-royalist sentiments force closing
            of London theatres (September); some provincial theatres
            remain open
1642–60   Plays surreptitiously performed or at least tolerated; Sir
            William Davenant, for example, offers 'private'
            entertainments 1655–60, notably his opera _The Siege of
            Rhodes_, 1656 ff.

Year	Event
1660	Restoration of the Monarchy in May; Charles II ascends the throne Charles II marries Princess Catherine of Braganza (Portugal) – no legitimate children
1660–9	Samuel Pepys, *Diary*
1662	Act of Uniformity, establishing the Anglican faith exclusively
1664	John Vanbrugh born
1665–6	Great Plague; *c.* 70,000 deaths in London amongst a population of *c.* 500,000. Theatres closed June 1665–October 1666
1666	Great Fire of London
1670	William Congreve born
1672	Also 1687 and 1688. Declarations of Indulgence to Catholics and Dissenters

Year	Event
1660	(February/March–August) Three theatres open in London, until suppressed.

Charles II authorises only two theatrical troupes, the King's Company and the Duke's Company. The former perform briefly at the Cockpit (or Phoenix) Theatre. The playhouses built or rebuilt after 1660 have roofs, changeable scenery, curtains, proscenium arches, and female performers

(November) The King's Company, managed by Thomas Killigrew (1612–83, courtier, playwright), are briefly at the Red Bull, St John Street, Clerkenwell, then at Gibbons's Tennis Court, Vere Street, near Lincoln's Inn Fields. (Thomas Killigrew was succeeded in 1677 by his son Charles)

The Duke's Company (patron, the Duke of York, brother of Charles II, later James II), managed by Sir William Davenant (1606–68, playwright, poet, poet laureate), opens at Salisbury Court, near the Strand. (Lady Henrietta Maria Davenant and others manage her late husband's theatres during son Charles's minority, to 1673)

1661	The Duke's Company move to the Duke's Theatre, the newly rebuilt Lisle's Tennis Court, Lincoln's Inn Fields
1662	Killigrew's patent from Charles II specifies that all female roles are to be played by women, not boys; English actresses have, however, been appearing on public stages since December 1660
1663	Killigrew and the King's Company open first Theatre Royal, Bridges Street, near Catherine Street and Drury Lane
1668	John Dryden, *An Essay of Dramatic Poesy*
1671	John Dryden, *Marriage à la Mode* The Duke's Company transfer to the new Dorset Garden Theatre
1672	Theatre Royal burns; in February the King's Company move to Lisle's Tennis Court, until recently occupied by the Duke's Company

Year	Event
1673	Test Act, requiring loyalty to Anglican faith
1674–82	Earl of Shaftesbury Whig leader; promoted Duke of Monmouth, illegitimate son of Charles II, as heir
c. 1677	George Farquhar born
1678	Titus Oates's Popish Plot (October), based on a false rumour that Catholics intend to kill Charles II and many Protestants
1679	Habeas Corpus Act
1681–5	Charles II rules without Parliament
1683	Rye House Plot to assassinate Charles II and James, Duke of York
1685	Death of Charles II (February); succeeded by Catholic brother James II
1685–8	Reign of James II
1685	Unsuccessful rebellion of Duke of Monmouth
	Bloody Assizes
	Thomas Otway dies
1688	Glorious Revolution, deposition of James II
1688–94	Joint reign of William and Mary, the elder (Protestant) daughter of James II; after her death (1694), William (III) reigns, dies 1702 – no children
1689	Act of Toleration, giving greater religious liberty
	Bill of Rights, which qualifies powers of the king (who must be a Protestant) and strengthens Parliament
c. 1692	George Etherege dies

Year	Event
1674	Killigrew opens the second Theatre Royal, Drury Lane, designed by Wren, on the same site as the earlier Theatre Royal
1675	William Wycherley, *The Country Wife*
1676	William Wycherley, *The Plain Dealer*
	George Etherege, *The Man of Mode*
1678	John Dryden, *All for Love*
1682	The King's Company fails as a result of Thomas and Charles Killigrew's mismanagement; it is absorbed by Charles Davenant's Duke's Company as the United Company, utilising from November 1682 both the Theatre Royal (drama) and the Dorset Garden Theatre (opera)
	Thomas Otway, *Venice Preserved*
1693	United Company taken over by Christopher Rich and Sir Thomas Skipworth
	William Congreve, *The Old Bachelor*

Year   *Event*

1697   Treaty of Ryswick

1700   John Dryden dies
1701   Act of Settlement, nominating to the throne successively
            Anne, younger (Protestant) daughter of James II, and her
            cousin Sophia of Hanover
1701–13   War of the Spanish Succession
1702–14   Reign of Queen Anne – no surviving children

1707   Act of Union, joining England and Scotland
            George Farquhar dies

1714–27   Reign of George I
1715   William Wycherley dies
1726   John Vanbrugh dies
1729   William Congreve dies

Year	Event
1694	William Congreve, *The Double Dealer*
	Thomas Betterton and other Davenant actors secede from United Company (the remnants of which remain at the Theatre Royal), to establish a rival company, in April 1695, at the Lisle's Tennis Court, which they rebuild
1695	William Congreve, *Love for Love*
1696	John Vanbrugh, *The Relapse*
1697	John Vanbrugh, *The Provoked Wife*
	William Congreve, *The Mourning Bride*
1698	Jeremy Collier, *A Short View of the Immorality and Profaneness of the English Stage*
1700	William Congreve, *The Way of the World*
1705	William Congreve and Sir John Vanbrugh (designer) open the Queen's Theatre in the Haymarket, with frequent presentations by Betterton's company
1706	George Farquhar, *The Recruiting Officer*
1707	George Farquhar, *The Beaux Stratagem*
1708	Betterton's company and Rich's company reunite, playing at Drury Lane and the Queen's Theatre

INTRODUCTION

ANGELICA . . . The great secret for keeping matters right in wedlock is never to quarrel with your wives for trifles; for we are but babies at best and must have our playthings, our longings, our vapours, our frights, our monkeys, our china, our fashions, our washes, our patches, our waters, our tattle, and impertinence; therefore I say 'tis better to let a woman play the fool than provoke her to play the devil.

George Farquhar, *Sir Harry Wildair* (London, 1701), IV, iv

The five comedies and two tragedies in this newly-edited volume are amongst the most interesting and enduring plays of the Restoration period (1660–*c*. 1710). Between the Puritan closing of the theatres in 1642 and the accession of Charles II in 1660, the interregnum dominated by Oliver Cromwell, dramatic activity almost ceased. The restoration of the monarchy was enthusiastically welcomed, but both social and theatrical conditions had changed during the eighteen-year period of turmoil. Almost all the pre-Civil War theatres had been destroyed, and an uncertain society was in search of new values. (A steady flow of moralistic criticism of drama during the decades of the Restoration shows that Puritan attitudes still existed.) The two new theatres licensed to open after the reinstatement of the monarchy were almost wholly controlled by the Court for many years and catered for the first decade or so principally to aristocratic tastes and audiences. Gradually, as Samuel Pepys and other observers noted, higher percentages of citizens, merchants, students, housewives, clerks and servants attended the theatre. The proscenium arch, painted scenery and the appearance of women in female roles were distinctive features of the new era in drama.

Theatrical activity in the early 1660s consisted largely of adaptations and revivals (Shakespeare, Beaumont, Fletcher, Shirley, Brome, etc.); however, after the interruption caused by the Plague, 1665, and the Great Fire, 1666, the types of drama most characteristic of the Restoration period firmly established themselves: the comedy of manners, historical tragedy, and heroic plays.[1] Wycherley's *The Country Wife* (1675) and Etherege's *The Man of Mode* (1676) are attractive examples of the early comedy of manners; whilst Vanbrugh's *The Provoked Wife* (1697), Congreve's *The Way of the World* (1700), and Farquhar's *The Beaux Stratagem* (1707) represent an evolving and climaxing sophistication of this form, with a few hints of the later sentimental comedy. The five comedies in this volume appear regularly in modern theatres around the world. Dryden's *All for Love* (1677) and Otway's *Venice Preserved* (1682) are tragedies of sufficient interest and power to be staged occasionally in recent times.

In 1660 King Charles II granted licences to two theatrical organisations: the King's Company, which performed at the first Theatre Royal, Bridges Street, from 1663 and at the second Theatre Royal, Drury Lane, from 1674, and the Duke's Company (with James, Duke of York, as its patron), which performed at Lincoln's Inn Fields from 1661 and later at Dorset Garden. (Earlier both companies had acted at other locations.) *The Country Wife* and *All for Love* were first staged by the King's Company, *The Man of Mode* and *Venice Preserved* by the Duke's.

After a financial crisis the two companies joined forces in 1682, continuing mainly at the Theatre Royal as the United Company until 1695. Then Thomas Betterton and other actors left, to establish a new company at the Lincoln's Inn Fields theatre, where *The Provoked Wife* and *The Way of the World* were first presented. In 1705 this troupe moved to the Haymarket,[2] to open the new Queen's Theatre, designed and constructed by architect John Vanbrugh. *The Beaux Stratagem* was first seen here in 1707.

In 1698 a French visitor, Henri Misson, wrote about theatrical London:

There are two theatres at London (a third [at Lincoln's Inn Fields] is lately opened), one large and handsome, where they sometimes act

---

[1] The melodramatic extravagances of heroic drama – such as Roger Boyle, the Earl of Orrery's *The Tragedy of Mustapha* (1665), John Dryden's *The Conquest of Granada* (1670–71), and Nathaniel Lee's *Sophonisba* (1675) – did not long survive their own period on stage, and heroic drama is not therefore included in this anthology.

[2] There were complaints that this theatre was a long distance from the town. The Haymarket was then used for the sale of hay and straw, the nearest habitation being at the village of Charing. At the Haymarket 'the air was so pure and clear that the washer-women dried their linen by spreading it upon the grass in the fields' [G. Thornbury, *Old and New London, Illustrated* (London, 1873–8), IV, p. 217]

operas and sometimes plays; the other something smaller, which is only for plays. The pit is an amphitheatre, filled with benches without backboards and adorned and covered with green cloth. Men of quality, particularly the younger sort, some ladies of reputation and virtue, and abundance of damsels that hunt for prey, sit all together in this place, higgledy-piggledy, toy, play, hear, hear not. Farther up, against the wall, under the first gallery and just opposite to the stage, rises another amphitheatre, which is taken up by persons of the best quality, among whom are generally very few men. The galleries, whereof there are only two rows, are filled with none but ordinary people, particularly the upper one.

[*Memoirs and Observations in his Travels over England*, London, 1719, cited in *Restoration and Georgian England, 1660–1788*, ed. D. Thomas (Cambridge, England, 1989), p. 72]

Some plays in this volume include references to prices of admission to the theatres, with indications of the implicit social gradations. A place in a box cost four shillings, the pit two shillings and sixpence, the middle gallery one shilling and sixpence (here the Pinchwifes sit – *The Country Wife*, I, i, and II, i – 'amongst the ugly people', because the husband does not wish his young and pretty wife to be ogled by the gallants in the pit), and the top gallery one shilling.

At this time plays were performed only in the afternoons, beginning about 3.00 p.m. or later. The stages were lit by candles. *The Country Wife* illustrates one lighting convention in action: in Act IV, scene i, Pinchwife extinguishes a candle to create make-believe darkness in a room; Mrs Pinchwife then makes use of this 'blackout' to disguise herself as Alithea and be taken to meet Horner. The dialogue attempts some degree of realism as Pinchwife gropes in the apparent darkness: 'Mrs Margery, where are you?' . . . 'Come, sister, where are you now?'

Contemporary techniques for effecting scene changes are illustrated in several of these plays: a series of painted panels on either side of the central performance area were slid in and out on grooves to create different settings. For example, the first episode of Act III in *The Country Wife* takes place in the Pinchwifes' lodgings; at its conclusion 'the scene changes to the New Exchange'. (The play has six other examples of this method of scene modification.)[3]

[3] A few stage directions in other plays in this volume illustrate similar Restoration scene changing. See Richard Southern, *Changeable Scenery, its Origin and Development in the British Theatre* (London, 1952).

The 'comedy of manners' is a term of convenience embracing many aspects of Restoration dramatic form and style. Such dramas had in common an interest in contemporary social customs and relationships, almost invariably with a realistic urban setting, usually London, because here were to be found the Court, the aristocracy and the largest audiences. The principal subjects were love, courtship and marriage. Few earlier plays had offered as sustained an analysis (or dissection) of contemporary marital relationships. Several dramas illustrate the tentative movements towards feminine emancipation from traditional restrictions. The topic of marriage was very closely linked to morality, with explicit or implicit consideration of behaviour appropriate to the married state.

The tragedies too concern themselves with this subject. *All for Love* looks back seventeen centuries, as John Dryden contrasts the morally-sanctioned union of Antony and Octavia and the illicit relationship between Antony and Cleopatra, considering why and how the world was well lost. The historical events behind Otway's *Venice Preserved* took place almost within living memory; the play combines a study of political events in Venice and their effect on the fictional marriage of Jaffeir and Belvidera.

The action of the comedies in the volume is contemporaneous with their presentation between 1675 and 1707; they set in sharp contrast the marriages arranged for dynastic or mercenary reasons (the Sullen and Brute unions are the most notorious examples) and those marriages based on genuine affection, such as the unions of Young Bellair and Emilia, and Mirabell and Millamant.

Some Restoration comedies combine information and entertainment, being largely uncritical, perhaps bemused, depictions of the *mores* of upper-class society; others are more satiric, with an emphasis on the disjunctions between appearance and reality, on the distinctions between true wits and false wits, and on the unattractive human traits of affectation, hypocrisy, selfishness, vanity, sexual aggressiveness. Many of these plays show the influence of Thomas Hobbes, who saw laughter as a symptom of superiority, and who interpreted human motivations primarily in terms of aggression and the need for power over others. Façades are important, and the mask is a frequent satiric symbol or image. Remarkably, considering the interest in both political and religious affairs evident in the poetry and prose of the day, references to such topics are infrequent in Restoration comedy.

Although these humorous plays are fictions, they convey a vigorous sense on stage of the daily activities of a tiny percentage of the population of London (some 500,000 people) between 1675 and

1707. The five playwrights give little attention to the English nobility, concentrating on a sampling from the lower edge of the aristocracy, a score or so of the dilettante men and women able to live at leisure in considerable luxury from inherited wealth or property. (Sir Jasper Fidget, in *the Country Wife*, a modern entrepreneur, is an exception; his large income derives from commercial and political projects.) Some take their way of life securely for granted; others abuse their wealth and position, and are ridiculed by the dramatists.

The social satire here is directed especially towards knights and their ladies, following a long English theatrical tradition.[4] One thinks of Sir Jasper and Lady Fidget, Lady Wishfort, Sir Fopling Flutter, Lady Fanciful, and Sir John Brute; however, a few, like Lady Brute, Lady Bountiful, and Sir Charles Freeman, earn their creators' approbation. Restoration theatregoers were as curious about the activities and antics of the gentry as people today are about the real or fabricated lives of the rich, famous, or notorious, as depicted on stage and television. Some eighteenth-century playgoers thought that they saw themselves imitated on stage; others believed that they could identify real people behind the performers.

Money is an important subject in these comedies and in *Venice Preserved*. The stage characters are sometimes ambitious for greater wealth or are threatened by a loss of it. It often dominates marital arrangements. Mr Fainall, in *The Way of the World*, concentrates most of his attention and ambition on money. Sir Fopling Flutter, in *The Man of Mode*, is an amusing extraordinary example of conspicuous consumption: he is accompanied by six attendants and a page, is the possessor of a caléche drawn by at least four horses, and his life is dominated by clothes, perukes and shoes. His mind is occupied wholly by his class-conscious social activities, like attendance at royal levées and couchées, and the memory of his social triumphs in Paris. Lady Fanciful, in *The Provoked Wife*, engages in a similarly extravagant way of life.

Restoration comedies incorporated much realism; four of those included here have many factual details of London life (the fifth, *The Beaux Stratagem*, is provincial in tone, with settings divided between a Lichfield coaching inn and an aristocratic home). The dramatists allude to identifiable London streets, parks, taverns and the New Exchange. This large building in the Strand, housing many business enterprises, comparable to a modern shopping centre, is utilised in many plays set in London. In *The Atheist* (1683), Thomas Otway communicates its social importance. Courtice is speaking:

[4]In *The Country Wife* Sparkish claims that he has no wish ever to be a knight 'for fear of being knighted in a play and being dubbed a fool' (III, ii).

Methinks this place looks as it were made for loving; the lights on each hand of the walk look stately, and then the rustling of silk petticoats, the din and chatter of the pretty parti-coloured parrots that hop and flutter from one side to t'other puts every sense upon its proper office and sets the wheels of nature finely moving. (II, i)

The speeches and actions of servants contribute much to the true-to-life vitality evident on Restoration comic stages. Many of these men and women have a vigorous independence of spirit that owes something to Ben Jonson and ultimately to classical Greek comedy. Servants like Handy, Razor, Cherry, Pert and Busy are memorable for their outspokenness (they have revealing names, as is usual in Restoration comedy). There is an unforgettable realism in Lady Wishfort's description of her maid Foible's earlier career; she was a poverty-stricken purveyor of used clothing and trinkets ('threepennyworth of small ware') from a street stall (*The Way of the World*, V, i).

In the two tragedies included here, the sense of actuality is, of course, less immediate and intense. Contemporary reports make clear that the public were very much attracted to stage depictions of the historical past, as in *Venice Preserved*, in which the events had taken place only seven decades before, and in *All for Love*, almost two thousand years earlier.

As well, Restoration comedy reveals ambivalent attitudes towards France: a combination of admiration, leading to sincere emulation, and criticism, leading to satire. After the execution of King Charles I, in 1649, the years of exile in France of his heir, Charles II, and his Court powerfully affected the widespread adoption in England of French values and manners subsequent to the regeneration of the monarchy in 1660. Writing satirically in 1675, William Wycherley centred the plot of *The Country Wife* on the gossip that Horner contracted a venereal disease in France. A year later, in *The Man of Mode*, George Etherege described how Sir Fopling Flutter 'went to Paris a plain, bashful English blockhead, and is returned a fine, undertaking French fop' (IV, i). The same play ridicules the English vogue for French opera and ballet (II, i). Similarly, the *précieuse* pretensions of Madamoiselle and her English mistress, Lady Fanciful, in *The Provoked Wife* are derided, and incidental criticism of French manners and taste occurs in other comedies. On the more serious side, John Dryden has some pointed comments on French literary criticism (The Preface to *All for Love*, pp. 218–20). English critics were familiar with the plays of Jean Baptiste Molière, and English playwrights imitated them.

In its own period Restoration comedy was often attacked for encouraging immorality, most notoriously by the Reverend Jeremy Collier in *A Short View of the Immorality and Profaneness of the English Stage* (1698). He and other contemporary reviewers contributed to the decline of Restoration drama, as did important changes in the tastes of theatre audiences. The middle class was growing in wealth and power, and by the end of the seventeenth century the wives of merchants and gentry became the principal theatregoers and arbiters of taste and moral attitudes. They tended to be Puritan in philosophy. As well, they approved of the sentimental comedy of playwrights like Colley Cibber (*Love's Last Shift*, 1696) and Sir Richard Steele (*The Conscious Lovers*, 1722); this kind of drama was indebted to the comedy of manners, as were subsequently the plays of Sheridan and Goldsmith.

Tragedy of the Restoration period was sternly moral and retributive in its emphasis. It leaned heavily on the past for plots and techniques, although it was somewhat more domestic in nature than earlier English tragedy. Restoration tragedies were written either in old-fashioned rhyme or in generally sententious blank verse. Both *All for Love* and *Venice Preserved* reveal some influences of heroic drama, but they are less rhetorical and sensational than most tragedies of the period; however, critics have questioned Dryden's sentimental introduction of Octavia and her children and Otway's inclusion of the Nicky-Nacky scenes and the bloody apparitions of Jaffeir and Pierre. The ethical and moral problems which both plays raise are still relevant; they accentuate the conflict between duty and inclination in domestic contexts, human frailty being the primary cause of the tragic outcomes. The fact that fewer than one-quarter of the new plays written during the Restoration were tragedies indicates that contemporary tastes ran more to heroic drama and comedy, perhaps as a reaction to the violence, stresses, and real-life tragedies of the Civil War, 1642–51.

The Restoration Court coterie which had given both comedy and tragedy so much early impetus disintegrated after the death of King Charles II in 1685. James II and his successor, Mary II, reigned for too short a time to leave any real mark on English culture, whilst the dour William III, Mary's co-regent, and Queen Anne, who succeeded him in 1702, had no interest in the theatre.

Any survey of Restoration drama impresses by its vitality. Both tragedy and comedy are full of dynamic people, actively, even obsessively, pursuing their objectives and creating conflicts as well as harmonious relationships, often in the form of the witty love game or duel, in passionate, sophisticated dialogue. Restoration comedy especially has contributed several unforgettably vivid characters to a permanent gallery of English originals: Lady Wishfort, Millamant, Mirabell, Sir Fopling Flutter, Jack Pinchwife, Mrs Sullen, Aimwell and Archer, amongst others. The characters of Restoration drama are mirrors of the ways of their world, vividly revealing over three centuries later the tastes and attitudes of the times, with, in the tragedies, glimpses of an earlier past as seen through Restoration eyes. These plays are relevant still because the political relationships between rulers and ruled and the social *cum* marital relationships between men and women bring these seven dramas close to comparable preoccupations in the present century.

Each of these plays was published shortly after its first stage presentation in London; the earliest editions, except for *The Man of Mode* and *Venice Preserved*, include on the Dramatis Personae pages the names of the major performers. Almost all of them are identified, with notes on their careers and other biographical information, in *The London Stage 1660–1800* . . . , Part I: 1660–1700, ed. W. Van Lennep (Carbondale, Ill., 1965); Part 2: 1700–1729, ed. E. L. Avery, 2 vols., (Carbondale, Ill., 1960) and P. Highfill, Jr., *et al.*, *A Biographical Dictionary of Actors [and] Actresses* . . . *in London 1660–1800*, 16 vols. when completed (Carbondale, Ill., 1973–). Where performers' names have been recorded in the Dramatis Personae of the earliest editions of these dramas, a note identifies the most familiar form of forenames and surnames.

The text of each play in this collection is based on the earliest published version, using British Library, London, copies. Spelling has been conservatively modernised, retaining the seventeenth-century form when it conveys a distinctive tone or pronunciation (as 'huswife').[5] Punctuation has been made uniform, to make for easy reading (Restoration playwrights and compositors used the colon and semicolon erratically); original commas have been retained when they seemed to suggest the rhythms of an actor's speech. Common nouns have the initial letter in lower case type. Parentheses enclose stage directions located within speeches in the original text; square brackets set off material added by the editor for clarity of speech or action. Speech headings, with a few exceptions, are as in the quarto editions. In verse this volume uses -'d, to indicate the past tense of verbs, except where the metre of a line requires -ed. In prose, -ed

[5] 'Mrs', often pronounced 'Mistress', was used in the seventeenth century as a courtesy title for both married and unmarried women. 'Mr' was often pronounced 'Master'.

appears throughout. Reprints of the earliest published versions of these plays are available in Scolar editions and *Three Centuries of Drama: English 1500–1800* [Readex Microprint] (New York, 1955–66).

Extensive explanatory notes at the bottom of the pages of play texts will assist readers outside Britain who do not have easy access to reference tools dealing with seventeenth-century allusions to people, places and little-known literary works. A bibliography of significant books and articles follows this introduction to the Restoration period, and individual bibliographies of important research materials relating to the seven plays appear after the separate introductions to them.

ROBERT G. LAWRENCE

BIBLIOGRAPHY

K. Lynch, *The Social Mode of Restoration Comedy*. New York, 1926.

J. H. Smith, *The Gay Couple in Restoration Comedy*. Cambridge, Mass., 1948.

T. Fujimura, *The Restoration Comedy of Wit*. Princeton, 1952.

J. H. Wilson, *All the King's Ladies: Actresses of the Restoration*. Chicago, 1958.

N. Holland, *The First Modern Comedies; the Significance of Etherege, Wycherley, and Congreve*. Cambridge, Mass., 1959.

P. F. Vernon, 'Marriage of Convenience and the Moral Code of Restoration Comedy'. *Essays in Criticism*, 12 (October 1962), 370–87.

C. O. McDonald, 'Restoration Comedy as Drama of Satire: an Investigation into Seventeenth-Century Aesthetics'. *Studies in Philology*, 61 (July 1964), 522–44.

A. H. Scouten, 'Notes toward a History of Restoration Comedy'. *Philological Quarterly*, 45 (January 1966), 62–70.

E. Miner, ed., *Restoration Dramatists: a Collection of Critical Essays* (Twentieth-Century Views). Englewood Cliffs, N. J., 1966.

E. Rothstein, *Restoration Tragedy: Form and Process of Change*. Madison, Wisc., 1967.

V. O. Birdsall, *Wild Civility; the English Comic Spirit on the Restoration Stage*. Bloomington, Ill., 1970.

R. D. Hume, 'Diversity and Development in Restoration Comedy 1660–1679'. *Eighteenth Century Studies*, 15 (Spring 1972), 365–97.

H. Hawkins, *Likeness of Truth in Elizabethan and Restoration Drama*. Oxford, 1972.

G. Marshall, *Restoration Serious Drama*. Norman, Okla., 1975.

R. D. Hume, *The Development of English Drama in the Late Seventeenth Century*. Oxford, 1976.

S. S. Kenny, 'Perennial Favorites: Congreve, Vanbrugh, Cibber, Farquhar, and Steele'. *Modern Philology*, 73 (May 1976), S4–11.

M. L. McDonald, *The Independent Woman in the Restoration Comedy of Manners*. Salzburg, 1976.

J. D. Canfield, 'Religious Language and Religious Meaning in Restoration Comedy'. *Studies in English Literature 1500–1900*, 20 (Summer 1980), 385–406.

H. Love, 'Who Were the Restoration Audience'? *The Yearbook of English Studies*, 10 (1980), 21–44.

L. Brown, *English Dramatic Form, 1660–1760, an Essay in Generic History*. New Haven, 1981.

P. Malekin, '"Imparadist in One Anothers Arms" or "The Ecclesiastical Mousetrap": Marriage in Restoration Comedy' (Chapter 14), *Liberty and Love, English Literature and Society 1640–88*. London, 1981.

R. D. Hume, *The Rakish Stage: Studies in English Drama, 1660–1800*. Carbondale, Ill., 1983.

J. Powell, *Restoration Theatre Production*. London, 1984.

J. Milhous and R. D. Hume, *Producible Interpretations: Eight English Plays 1675–1707*. Carbondale, Ill., 1985.

J. L. Styan, *Restoration Comedy in Performance*. Cambridge, Eng., 1986.

R. M. Weber, *The Restoration Rake-Hero: Transformations in Sexual Understanding in Seventeenth-Century England*. Madison, Wisc., 1986.

E. Burns, *Restoration Comedy: Crises of Desire and Identity*. Basingstoke, 1987.

D. Hughes, 'Naming and Entitlement in Wycherley, Etherege, and Dryden'. *Comparative Drama*, 21 (Fall 1987), 259–89.

J. Peters, '"Things govern'd by words": Late Seventeenth-century Comedy and Reformers'. *English Studies*, 68 (1987), 142–53.

H. C. Knutson, *The Triumph of Wit: Moliere and Restoration Comedy*. Columbus, Ohio, 1988.

R. Markley, *Two-Edg'd Weapons: Style and Ideology in the Comedies of Etherege, Wycherley, and Congreve*. Oxford, 1988.

J. Pearson, *The Prostituted Muse: Images of Women and Women Dramatists*. New York, 1988.

E. Howe, *The First English Actresses: Women and Drama 1660–1700*. Cambridge, Eng., 1992.

B. Corman, *Genre and Generic Change in English Comedy, 1660–1710*. Toronto, 1993.

William Wycherley
THE COUNTRY WIFE
1675

The Country Wife
a comedy,
acted at the Theatre Royal.
Written by Mr Wycherley.

Indignor quicquam reprehendi, non quia crasse
Compositum illepideve putetur, sed quia nuper:
Nec veniam Antiquis, sed honorem & praemia posei.[1]
HORACE.

London,
Printed for Thomas Dring, at the Harrow,
at the corner of Chancery Lane in Fleet Street,
1675

---

[1] I am offended that any work is blamed, not because it is supposed gross or inelegant in style, but because modern, and that people demand not only indulgence for the ancients but honour and rewards.

Horace, *Epistles*, II, 1, 76–78.

BIOGRAPHY

Wycherley was born in Shropshire in 1641; he studied in France and briefly at the Inner Temple, London, and at Queen's College, Oxford. He was a courtier and poet, was involved in a series of law suits, and was briefly in military service. As a playwright he wrote *Love in a Wood* (1671), *The Gentleman Dancing-Master* (1672), *The Country Wife* (1675) and *The Plain Dealer* (1676). He married the widowed Countess of Drogheda in 1679 (she died *c.* 1685) and later Elizabeth Jackson a few days before his death 31 December 1715. He was imprisoned for debt during several months of 1685–86. The ambitious Alexander Pope attached himself to the poet-playwright 1704–15.

INTRODUCTION

This is Wycherley's third and most popular play, and Harry Horner, the unmarried man-about-town posing as a eunuch, would seem to be the centre of the action in his efforts to seduce Margery Pinchwife, Lady Fidget, Mrs Squeamish and Mrs Dainty Fidget. Horner is certainly Wycherley's most memorable creation in the play; frank about his self-interest, he accepts, exposes and takes advantage of a cynical, hypocritical, short-sighted world.[1]

Margery Pinchwife, the 'country wife' of the title, is also pivotal in at least one of the play's three plots – the familiar story of a suspicious old man endeavouring vainly to protect his young wife from the attention of gallants. She is also a confidante of her sister-in-law, Alithea, and later, disguised as Alithea, she has, unconsciously, several roles to play in the drama's two other plots involving Sparkish and Horner. The country wife proves to be no more virtuous than Lady Fidget's pseudo-virtuous 'gang', but the playwright sets her naivete against the dominant hypocrisy of the 'women of honour'.

Margery is attracted to Horner early on, thanks in part to Pinchwife's inept revelations about Horner's interest in her; like her husband, she has not heard the rumour that Horner is a eunuch.[2] With skilful dramatic irony, Wycherley brings Margery and Horner together by means of two disguises in sequence, the gulled husband abetting both meetings. Whilst this relationship is developing, Horner

[1] One assumes, without confirming evidence, that Horner and his friends are young; however, Charles Hart, the actor in the King's Company who first played Horner in 1675, was in his late forties. Possibly Wycherley thought of Horner as an aging roué, a contemporary of Pinchwife, then forty-nine; Pinchwife was first performed by Michael Mohun, aged about fifty-nine.

[2] Pinchwife's ignorance of Horner's much-publicised impotence is plausible. He has just come up from the country, he does not now move in Horner's social circle, and he is sufficiently disliked by those in the know that they are unlikely to enlighten him.

is actively preparing for his seduction of Lady Fidget, by reassuring her privately that he is normal sexually; this plot too is helped along by an obtuse husband, the businessman baronet.

At the same time as all this is happening, Horner himself wants the rumour (which he invented) that he is a eunuch to spread – for, as he explains to the slow-witted Dr Quack, husbands will trust an impotent man in their wives' bedrooms, and sexually available women will pointedly ignore or reject a seemingly useless male. The possibilities for dramatic irony here are large, since all members of the audience and some people on stage know that Horner is as sexually vital as ever, whilst a number of characters believe, largely on the authority of Dr Quack, he is a eunuch. A contemporary commonplace, venereal disease, is supposed to have made Horner impotent, which adds verisimilitude to his myth.

Pursuing his goal, Horner does make a considerable sacrifice in social acceptability; Act III, Scene ii, illustrates how in the box at the theatre the impotent man is held in contempt, 'shoved and ill-used' by society women. Presumably he intends his new role to last indefinitely, because dropping the 'act' in public would probably exclude him from the society that had once accepted him, especially the husbands, who would in the event believe they had been victimised.

Once Wycherley has clearly established two plots, involving two married couples, the Fidgets and the Pinchwifes, he introduces a third, which centres on the preparations for the wedding of Alithea and Sparkish. Sparkish, on the fringes of Horner's sophisticated social world, has little in common with Fidget or Pinchwife, except in having a fine potential for being tricked. (With a very apt and sharp-edged satire, Wycherley defines the character of Sparkish early in the drama by having him describe his stylish, distracting behaviour in the playhouse. In small ways he anticipates Sir Fopling Flutter in *The Man of Mode*.)

This dupe has a rival for the possession of Alithea, not in Horner, who is interested in more promiscuous women, but in Horner's friend, Frank Harcourt.[3] This rivalry should be no contest, given the evidence of Sparkish's failings and Harcourt's virtues, were it not for Alithea's extraordinary loyalty to her ridiculous fiancé, engendered by her sense of honour (the word appears eighty-two times in the play).

As the highest-ranking woman in the play, Lady Fidget should have the strongest sense of honour. Within five minutes of the opening of the action, she asks Horner, 'Would you wrong my honour'? But it quickly becomes evident that her aristocratic honour is a sham; as soon as she

---

[3] For dramatic convenience, Harcourt and Alithea meet for the first time in Act II, Scene i, even though Alithea has been living in town.

learns that Horner is not impotent (II, i), she enthusiastically advances the cuckolding of Sir Jasper, a process climaxing in the notable 'china' scene (IV, iii).[4] He believes his honour to be secure, convinced as he is of Horner's impotence.

Likewise Pinchwife's honour is in danger from the rake's interest in the countryman's young and pretty bride, and he is equally oblivious to the hazard: 'She's an innocent creature, has no dissembling in her' (IV, iii). Unconscious of honour, Margery is very different from the worldly Lady Fidget, and only gradually, during her first visit to London, does Margery arrive at a small degree of social awareness as she tastes the pleasures of the town and Horner's sexuality. Even Sparkish has an underdeveloped sense of honour; when he feels that Harcourt has disparaged his 'parts', the fop is willing to draw his sword, if Pinchwife will back him.

As these sexual games take their course, Alithea's sense of honour persuades her to remain loyal to Sparkish and resist the sincere courting of Harcourt. Some readers, scholars and theatregoers have found Alithea's virtue unconvincing and exaggerated. They point to Sparkish's obtuseness, vanity and preposterousness, but, as she sensibly indicates, an honourable lady of that period could not casually end an engagement to a man without suffering social opprobrium (II, i). She is, for the moment, 'stuck with' Sparkish, and it would, in any event, be rash of her to yield to the flattery of a casual man-about-town. Fortuitously, as a result of complex and skilful plotting, Alithea is ultimately freed from Sparkish without having to compromise her sense of honour (he rudely rejects her because the misguided Pinchwife has convinced him that she has formed an attachment to Horner).

Disguise, both as a theme and stage prop, is central in the play. By the end of the fast-paced action (encompassing a Wednesday and a Thursday) it is evident that almost every character habitually wears a disguise of some kind: Horner as eunuch, Sparkish as wit, Pinchwife as man who knows the town, Sir Jasper as shrewd manipulator of people, Lady Fidget as woman of honour and so on. Two characters, Margery and Harcourt, assume actual disguises and a third, Alithea, seems to appear as herself when the person who comes on stage is actually Margery wearing her sister-in-law's cloak. Disguise, gullibility and hypocritical honour are also associated with impotence, a pervasive

---

[4]The equivocal references to china in this episode have an echo in Wycherley's *The Plain Dealer* (1676): the puritanical Mrs Olivia Trifle speaks of *The Country Wife* as this 'hideous' and 'filthy' play, objecting to the use of the name 'Horner' and stating that the ambiguities connected with 'china' have forced her to dispose of all the china in her apartment (II, i, 395–456).

theme; all the men, except Harcourt, are deficient in one way or another.

Wycherley's serious analyses of marriage in the late seventeenth century are relieved and vitalised by the enormous amount of fun he provides through language and action. (His clever choice of characters' names directs audience attitudes – Horner creates horns, the Fidgets are restless, Sparkish is a would-be fop and wit, Pinchwife cruel, Quack a physician, Alithea represents 'truth'.) The play is full of dramatic irony as Horner assumes his disguise, as Lady Fidget and Margery Pinchwife endeavour, in quite different ways, to trick their husbands (Margery's persuading her husband to carry her love letter to Horner is a triumph of dissimulation), and as Sparkish, equally confident, throws his fiancée in the direction of Harcourt.

With remarkable skill, Wycherley has the trio of male gulls present and active on stage during the three seduction scenes associated with each: Sir Jasper participates in the 'china' scene, Pinchwife unknowingly leads his disguised wife towards Horner at the New Exchange and Sparkish presents his fiancée on their wedding day to his rival Frank Harcourt disguised as a clergyman, Frank's mythical twin brother Ned. The three male dupes represent three different aspects of Restoration society: Sir Jasper is the aggressive entrepreneur of the business world, Pinchwife the rough countryman, with a similar interest in money, and Sparkish the urban fop with an independent income.

However, Wycherley's clever mixture of disguise and affectation, honour and adultery, loyalty and hypocrisy works its way out in five acts in a manner not wholly satisfying to every reader and viewer: *The Country Wife* concludes with Horner and Lady Fidget apparently triumphant; Sir Jasper remains a self-satisfied, credulous ass; Sparkish has lost Alithea, but is unlikely to grieve long; and Pinchwife, not knowing that he is a cuckold, will continue to prevail over a likeable country wife, foiled in her naive attempt to exchange an old husband for a dynamic lover.

Harry Horner has dominated much of both action and theme, but it is important to observe that he is perhaps not entirely triumphant. Early in the relationship between Horner and Lady Fidget, during the often-overlooked bargaining scene (II, i), she asks about betrayal: what if he should tattle about her indiscretion? She regards him (with heavy irony) as 'truly a man of honour'. First concerned about her own honour, she is somewhat comforted when Horner reassures her that if he were to reveal his affair with her nobody would believe him; with his reputation, the world would assume he were lying about any relationship with any woman.

What is only hinted at in the scene is the other side of this coin: the risk to Horner should Lady Fidget, 'upon any future falling-out', reveal that he is no eunuch. Horner's present role as an impotent man will be forever vulnerable to betrayal by Lady Fidget, Dainty Fidget or Biddy Squeamish. Any one of them could betray him anonymously, perhaps through a servant; many men and women would believe such a story.

While in the beginning Horner hoped to enlarge his sexual horizons (I, i), perhaps by Act v he has in fact trapped himself into being limited to these three females, who, jealous of each other, could threaten to expose him ('Sister sharers, let us not fall out . . . Harry Common, I hope you can be true to three . . .' – v, iv). In the denouement of the play he is within seconds of being exposed by Margery ('To my certain knowledge . . .', she says; 'Stop her mouth!' cries Mrs Squeamish.)

Like many twentieth-century plays, *The Country Wife* ends in ambivalence, an unresolved conflict between old values and new. In older plays of the seventeenth century, all of the participants who violate social mores are punished and the virtuous rewarded. In the decades immediately following the Puritan regime, morality was by no means as clear-cut as it had been earlier; Wycherley and other playwrights of the Restoration saw men and women as they were, less than well-intentioned, subject to the temptations of vanity, hypocrisy and sexuality, especially when inhibited (as they saw it) by old-fashioned conventions and by wholly unsatisfactory marital partners. The ambivalence is pronounced in attitudes towards Lady Fidget: within traditional morality she is bound to be loyal to her husband; however, her disloyalty draws some sympathy from modern readers and audiences as she describes the 'indifference' of 'men of quality' and how she and her colleagues 'lie untumbled and unasked for' whilst men like Sir Jasper constantly pursue City schemes.

Ambivalence also surrounds the country wife; at the end of Act v she seems trapped indefinitely in old Pinchwife's country estate, yet her circumstances have changed since she left home a few days earlier. Her innocent eyes have been opened by Horner and his London associates, and her creator hints that her 'dear bud' will be unable to control her as he once did. With her new-found ability to lie, Margery can be expected to nag her self-deluding husband into making a return visit to London.

There is an ambiguity in Horner's perhaps-enviable playboy philandering; it may prove to be transient and unsatisfying. Alithea and Harcourt are, conversely, both almost unsullied, estimable characters; however, they are not universally applauded. Perhaps their only fault is a lack of vivacity, the vitality of Millamant and Mirabell in the later *The Way of the World*. Harcourt is an undynamic hero; he wins Alithea almost by default, because Sparkish shows himself to be a jealous fool, ending Alithea's delusions about him.

The readers of this play, who are able to peruse it at leisure, especially appreciate Wycherley's artistry – his skill in structure and unity, his occasionally rough, colloquial language, his use of metaphors, aphorisms, maxims and *doubles enrendres* (notably involving words like 'sign', 'honour' and 'china'). Several of the characters (Sir Jasper, Lady Fidget, Sparkish, and Horner) pride themselves on their facility with language; it often leads them into trouble.

Wycherley cannot be said to have been a wholly original playwright; however, in this drama he owes only a general indebtedness to Terence (*Eunuchus*, 162 BC), Molière (*L'École des Maris*, 1661, *L'École des Femmes*, 1662), Thomas Duffett (*The Spanish Rogue*, 1674), and a few other contemporary dramatists.

The Country Wife, the third of Wycherley's four plays, was immediately popular, holding the boards until 1766, when it was supplanted by David Garrick's bowdlerised, sentimental adaptation, *The Country Girl*. Wycherley's play has been revived frequently in the twentieth century; particularly relevant today is its criticism of growing commercialism in every aspect of life.

BIBLIOGRAPHY

The Country Wife

R. A. Zimbardo, *Wycherley's Drama: a Link in the Development of English Satire*. New Haven, 1965.

D. M. Vieth, 'Wycherley's *The Country Wife*: An Anatomy of Masculinity'. *Papers on Language and Literature*, 2 (Fall 1966), 335–50.

R. S. Wolper, 'The Temper of *The Country Wife*'. *Humanities Association Bulletin*, 18 (Spring 1967), 69–74.

P. Malekin, 'Wycherley's Dramatic Skills and the Interpretation of *The Country Wife*'. *Durham University Journal*, N. S. 31 (December 1969), 32–40.

K. M. Rogers, *William Wycherley*. New York, 1972.

W. Freedman, 'Impotence and Self-destruction in *The Country Wife*'. *English Studies*, 53 (October 1972), 421–31.

C. A. Hallett, 'The Hobbesian Substructure of *The Country Wife*'. *Papers on Language and Literature*, 9 (Fall 1973), 380–95.

W. R. Chadwick, *The Four Plays of William Wycherley*. The Hague, 1975.

A. Kaufman, 'Wycherley's *Country Wife* and the Don Juan Character'. *Eighteenth Century Studies*, 9 (Winter 1975), 216–31.

M. E. Novak, 'Margery Pinchwife's "London Disease": Restoration Comedy and the Libertine Offensive of the 1670's'. *Studies in the Literary Imagination*, 10 (Spring 1977), 1–23.

G. Beauchamp, 'Amorous Machievellism of *The Country Wife*'. *Comparative Drama*, 11 (Winter 1977–8), 316–30.

B. E. McCarthy, *William Wycherley: a Biography*. Athens, Ohio, 1979.

R. D. Hume, 'William Wycherley: Text, Life, Interpretation'. *Modern Philology*, 78 (May 1981), 399–415.

D. Duncan, 'Mythic Parody in *The Country Wife*'. *Essays in Criticism*, 31 (October 1981), 299–312.

H. W. Matalene, 'What Happens in *The Country Wife*'. *Studies in English Literature 1500–1900*, 22 (Summer 1982), 395–411.

H. Weber, 'Horner and his Women of Honour: the Dinner Party in *The Country Wife*'. *Modern Language Quarterly*, 43 (June 1982), 107–20.

J. Harwood, *Critics, Values, and Restoration Comedy*. Carbondale, Ill., 1982.

H. Love, 'The Theatrical Geography of *The Country Wife*'. *Southern Review* (Adelaide), 16 (November 1983), 404–15.

J. Thompson, *Language in Wycherley's Plays*. University, Alabama, 1984.

E. Sedgwick, 'Sexualism and the Citizen of the World: Wycherley, Sterne, and Male Homosocial Desire'. *Critical Inquiry*, 11 (December 1984), 226–45.

D. Payne, 'Reading the Signs in *The Country Wife*'. *Studies in English Literature 1500–1900*, 26 (Summer 1986), 403–19.

A. Rayner, 'Wycherley's Aphorism: Delight in Dystopia'. A. Rayner, *Comic Persuasion: Moral Structure in British Comedy from Shakespeare to Stoppard*. Berkeley, 1987.

M. Neill, 'Horned Beasts and China Oranges: Reading the Signs in *The Country Wife*'. *Eighteenth Century Life*, n. s. 12 (May 1988), 3–17.

H. Burke, 'Wycherley's "Tendentious Joke": The Discourse of Alterity in *The Country Wife*'. *The Eighteenth Century: Theory and Interpretation*, 29 (Fall 1988), 227–41.

W. Marshall, 'Wycherley's Great Stage of Fools: Madness and Theatricality in *The Country Wife*'. *Studies in English Literature 1500–1900*, 29 (Summer 1989), 409–29.

P. Thompson, 'The Limits of Parody in *The Country Wife*'. *Studies in Philology*, 89 (Winter 1992), 100–14.

PROLOGUE

SPOKEN BY MR HART

Poets,[1] like cudgell'd bullies, never do
At first or second blow submit to you;
But will provoke you still,[2] and ne'er have done
Till you are weary first with laying on.
The late so-baffl'd scribbler[3] of this day,
Though he stands trembling, bids me boldly say
What we before most plays are us'd to do,
For poets out of fear first draw[4] on you;
In a fierce prologue the still pit defy,
And, ere you speak, like Castril[5] give the lie.
But though our Bayeses'[6] battles oft I've fought,
And with bruis'd knuckles their dear conquests bought;
Nay, never yet fear'd odds upon the stage,
In prologue dare not hector with the age;
But would take quarter from your saving hands,
Though Bayes within all yielding countermands,
Says you confederate wits no quarter give;
Therefore his play shan't ask your leave to live.
Well, let the vain, rash fop, by huffing so,
Think to obtain the better terms of you;
But we, the actors, humbly will submit,

[1] *Poets* i.e. playwrights.
[2] *still* repeatedly.
[3] *scribbler* Wycherley himself, whose play immediately preceding *The Country Wife*, *The Gentleman Dancing Master*, had been withdrawn after only six performances in 1672.
[4] *draw* draw a sword.
[5] *Castril* 'The Angry Boy', Jonson, *The Alchemist*, 1610.
[6] *Bayeses'* a name for any playwright, deriving from 'Bayes' as a nickname for John Dryden, satirised in *The Rehearsal*, 1671, by Villiers and others.

Now and at any time to a full pit;
Nay, often we anticipate your rage,
And murder poets for you on our stage.
We set no guards upon our tiring-room,
But when with flying colours there you come,
We patiently, you see, give up to you
Our poets, virgins, nay, our matrons too.

THE PERSONS

MR HORNER	Mr [Charles] Hart
MR HARCOURT	Mr Kenaston[1]
MR DORILANT	Mr Lydal[2]
MR PINCHWIFE	Mr [Michael] Mohun
MR SPARKISH	Mr Haynes[3]
SIR JASPER FIDGET	Mr [William] Cartwright
MRS MARGERY PINCHWIFE	Mrs Bowtel[4]
MRS ALITHEA	Mrs [Elizabeth] James
MY LADY FIDGET	Mrs Knep[5]
MRS DAINTY FIDGET	Mrs Corbet[6]
MRS SQUEAMISH	Mrs Wyatt
OLD LADY SQUEAMISH	Mrs [Margaret] Rutter
WAITERS, SERVANTS, [A PARSON,] *and* ATTENDANTS	
A BOY	
A QUACK	Mr Schotterel[7]
[CLASP]	
LUCY, ALITHEA's *maid*	Mrs Cory[8]

The Scene London

[1]Edward Kynaston.   [2]Edward Lydall.
[3]Joseph Haines.   [4]Elizabeth Bowtell.
[5]Elizabeth Knepp, a friend of Pepys (*Diary*, 6 December 1665–2 February 1669 *passim*).   [6]Mary Corbett.
[7]Robert Shatterell.   [8]Katherine Corey.

THE COUNTRY WIFE

Act One

SCENE ONE

[Horner's lodging]

Enter HORNER, QUACK *following him at a distance*

HORN. (*Aside*) A quack is as fit for a pimp as a midwife for a bawd; they are still but in their way both helpers of nature. – [*Aloud*] Well, my dear doctor, hast thou done what I desired?

QUACK. I have undone you forever with the women, and reported you throughout the whole town as bad as an eunuch, with as much trouble as if I had made you one in earnest.

HORN. But have you told all the midwives you know, the orange-wenches at the playhouses, the City husbands, and the old fumbling keepers[1] of this end of the town, for they'll be the readiest to report it?

QUACK. I have told all the chambermaids, waiting-women, tire-women,[2] and old women of my acquaintance; nay, and whispered it as a secret to 'em, and to the whisperers of Whitehall; so that you need not doubt 'twill spread, and you will be as odious to the handsome young women as –

HORN. As the smallpox. Well, –

QUACK. And to the married women of this end of the town as –

HORN. As the great ones;[3] nay, as their own husbands.

QUACK. And to the City dames, as Aniseed Robin,[4] of filthy and contemptible memory; and they will frighten their children with your name, especially their females.

HORN. And cry, 'Horner's coming to carry you away'! I am only afraid 'twill not be believed. You told 'em it was by an English-French disaster,[5] and an English-French surgeon, who has given me

[1] *keepers* supporters of mistresses.

[2] *tire-women* ladies' maids.

[3] *great ones* the great pox, syphilis.

[4] *Aniseed Robin* a notorious London hermaphrodite, c. 1600–50, who sold aniseed water in the streets.

[5] *English-French disaster* a venereal disease, the pox. 'French', as used later in the play, generally had such a connotation.

at once not only a cure, but an antidote for the future against that damned malady, and that worse distemper, love, and all other women's evils?

QUACK.   Your late journey into France has made it the more credible, and your being here a fortnight before you appeared in public, looks as if you apprehended the shame, which I wonder you do not. Well, I have been hired by young gallants to belie 'em t'other way; but you are the first would be thought a man unfit for women.

HORN.   Dear Mr Doctor, let vain rogues be contented only to be thought abler men than they are; generally 'tis all the pleasure they have, but mine lies another way.

QUACK.   You take, methinks, a very preposterous way to it, and as ridiculous as if we operators in physic should put forth bills to disparage our medicaments, with hopes to gain customers.

HORN.   Doctor, there are quacks in love as well as physic, who get but the fewer and worse patients for their boasting; a good name is seldom got by giving it one's self; and women, no more than honour, are compassed by bragging. Come, come, doctor, the wisest lawyer never discovers[6] the merits of his cause till the trial; the wealthiest man conceals his riches, and the cunning gamester his play. Shy husbands and keepers, like old rooks,[7] are not to be cheated but by a new unpractised trick; false friendship will pass now no more than false dice upon 'em; no, not in the City.

Enter BOY

BOY.   There are two ladies and a gentleman coming up.   [*Exit*]

HORN.   A pox! Some unbelieving sisters[8] of my former acquaintance, who, I am afraid, expect their sense should be satisfied of the falsity of the report.

Enter SIR JASPER FIDGET, LADY FIDGET *and* MRS DAINTY FIDGET

No – this formal fool and women!

QUACK.   His wife and sister.

SIR JASP.   My coach breaking just now before your door, sir, I look upon as an occasional[9] reprimand to me, sir, for not kissing your hands, sir, since your coming out of France, sir; and so my disaster, sir, has been my good fortune, sir; and this is my wife and sister, sir.

HORN.   What then, sir?

SIR JASP.   My lady and sister, sir. – Wife, this is Master Horner.

LADY FID.   Master Horner, husband!

---

[6]*discovers* reveals.   [7]*rooks* sharpers.
[8]*sisters* women reputedly loose.   [9]*occasional* timely.

SIR JASP. My lady, my Lady Fidget, sir.

HORN. So, sir.

SIR JASP. Won't you be acquainted with her, sir? – (*Aside*) So, the report is true, I find, by his coldness or aversion to the sex; but I'll play the wag with him. – [*Aloud*] Pray salute my wife, my lady, sir.

HORN. I will kiss no man's wife, sir, for him, sir; I have taken my eternal leave, sir, of the sex already, sir.

SIR JASP. (*Aside*) Ha, ha, ha! I'll plague him yet. – [*Aloud*] Not know my wife, sir?

HORN. I do know your wife, sir; she's a woman, sir, and consequently a monster, sir, a greater monster than a husband, sir.

SIR JASP. A husband! How,[10] sir?

HORN. So, sir; (*Makes horns*) but I make no more cuckolds, sir.

SIR JASP. Ha, ha, ha! Mercury,[11] Mercury!

LADY FID. Pray, Sir Jasper, let us be gone from this rude fellow.

MRS DAIN. Who, by his breeding, would think he had ever been in France?

LADY FID. Foh! He's but too much a French fellow, such as hate women of quality and virtue for their love to their husbands, Sir Jasper; a woman is hated by 'em as much for loving her husband as for loving their money. But, pray, let's be gone.

HORN. You do well, madam; for I have nothing that you came for. I have brought over not so much as a bawdy picture, new postures,[12] nor the second part of the *École des Filles*,[13] nor –

QUACK. (*Apart to* HORNER) Hold, for shame, sir! What d'ye mean? You'll ruin yourself forever with the sex –

SIR JASP. Ha, ha, ha! He hates women perfectly, I find.

MRS DAIN. What pity 'tis he should!

LADY FID. Ay, he's a base, rude fellow for't. But affectation makes not a woman more odious to them than virtue.

HORN. Because your virtue is your greatest affectation, madam.

LADY FID. How, you saucy fellow! Would you wrong my honour?

HORN. If I could.

LADY FID. How d'ye mean, sir?

SIR JASP. Ha, ha, ha! No, he can't wrong your ladyship's honour, upon my honour. He, poor man – hark you in your ear [*Whispers*] – a mere[14] eunuch.

---

[10]*How* Indeed.

[11]*Mercury* quicksilver; then used in the treatment of venereal diseases.

[12]*new postures* probable allusions to an edition of Pietro Aretino's *Sonetti Lussuriosi*, 1524, with engravings of Marc Raimondi, based on indecent drawings of Giulio Romano (Jules Romain).

[13]*École des Filles* a pornographic book by Michel Mililot or Millot, 1655 or a later edition. Pepys was familiar with it (*Diary*, 13 January, 8 and 9 February 1668).

[14]*mere* complete, absolute.

LADY FID.   Oh, filthy French beast! Foh! Foh! Why do we stay? Let's be gone; I can't endure the sight of him.

SIR JASP.   Stay but till the chairs[15] come; they'll be here presently.[16]

LADY FID.   No, no.

SIR JASP.   Nor can I stay longer. 'Tis, let me see, a quarter and half quarter of a minute past eleven. The Council[17] will be sat; I must away. Business must be preferred always before love and ceremony with the wise, Mr Horner.

HORN.   And the impotent, Sir Jasper.

SIR JASP.   Ay, ay, the impotent, Master Horner! Ha, ha, ha!

LADY FID.   What, leave us with a filthy man alone in his lodgings?

SIR JASP.   He's an innocent man now, you know. Pray stay; I'll hasten the chairs to you. Mr Horner, your servant; I should be glad to see you at my house. Pray come and dine with me, and play at cards with my wife after dinner; you are fit for women at that game yet, ha, ha! – (*Aside*) 'Tis as much a husband's prudence to provide innocent diversion for a wife as to hinder her unlawful pleasures; and he had better employ her than let her employ herself. – [*Aloud*] Farewell.

HORN.   Your servant, Sir Jasper.   *Exit* SIR JASPER

LADY FID.   I will not stay with him, foh! –

HORN.   Nay, madam, I beseech you stay, if it be but to see I can be as civil to ladies yet as they would desire.

LADY FID.   No, no, foh! You cannot be civil[18] to ladies.

MRS DAIN.   You as civil as ladies would desire?

LADY FID.   No, no, no! Foh, foh, foh!

                        Exeunt LADY FIDGET *and* MRS DAINTY FIDGET

QUACK.   Now I think I, or you yourself rather, have done your business with the women.

HORN.   Thou art an ass. Don't you see already, upon the report and my carriage,[19] this grave man of business leaves his wife in my lodgings, invites me to his house and wife, who before would not be acquainted with me out of jealousy?

QUACK.   Nay, by this means you may be the more acquainted with the husbands, but the less with the wives.

HORN.   Let me alone. If I can but abuse the husbands, I'll soon disabuse the wives. Stay – I'll reckon you up the advantages I am like

[15]*chairs* sedan chairs.

[16]*presently* immediately.

[17]*Council* Privy Council.

[18]*civil* polite, decent, with a *double entendre*; see *The Provoked Wife*, IV, ii, p. 462.

[19]*carriage* behaviour.

to have by my stratagem: first, I shall be rid of all my old acquaintances, the most insatiable sorts of duns, that invade our lodgings in a morning; and next to the pleasure of making a new mistress is that of being rid of an old one, and of all old debts. Love, when it comes to be so, is paid the most unwillingly.

QUACK. Well, you may be so rid of your old acquaintances; but how will you get any new ones?

HORN. Doctor, thou wilt never make a good chemist,[20] thou art so incredulous and impatient. Ask but all the young fellows of the town if they do not lose more time, like huntsmen, in starting the game than in running it down. One knows not where to find 'em; who will or will not. Women of quality are so civil, you can hardly distinguish love from good breeding, and a man is often mistaken; but now I can be sure that she that shows an aversion to me loves the sport, as those women that are gone, whom I warrant to be right.[21] And then the next thing is, your women of honour, as you call 'em, are only chary of their reputations, not their persons; and 'tis scandal they would avoid, not men. Now may I have, by the reputation of an eunuch, the privileges of one, and be seen in a lady's chamber in a morning as early as her husband; kiss virgins before their parents or lovers; and may be, in short, the *passe-partout*[22] of the town. Now, doctor.

QUACK. Nay, now you shall be the doctor; and your process is so new that we do not know but it may succeed.

HORN. Not so new neither; *probatum est*,[23] doctor.

QUACK. Well, I wish you luck and many patients, whilst I go to mine.

Exit

Enter HARCOURT *and* DORILANT

HAR. Come, your appearance at the play yesterday has, I hope, hardened you for the future against the women's contempt and the men's raillery; and now you'll abroad as you were wont.

HORN. Did I not bear it bravely?

DOR. With a most theatrical impudence, nay, more than the orange-wenches show there, or a drunken vizard-mask,[24] or a great-bellied[25] actress; nay, or the most impudent of creatures, an ill[26] poet; or what is yet more impudent, a secondhand critic.

[20]*chemist* alchemist.
[21]*right* promiscuous.
[22]*passe-partout* master key.
[23]*probatum est* it has been proved.
[24]*vizard-mask* prostitute.
[25]*great-bellied* pregnant; see also *The Way of the World*, v, i, p. 555.
[26]*ill* inferior.

HORN.   But what say the ladies? Have they no pity?

HAR.   What ladies? The vizard-masks, you know, never pity a man when all's gone, though in their service.

DOR.   And for the women in the boxes, you'd never pity them when 'twas in your power.

HAR.   They say 'tis pity but all that deal with common women should be served so.

DOR.   Nay, I dare swear they won't admit you to play at cards with them, go to plays with 'em, or do the little duties which other shadows of men are wont to do for 'em.

HORN.   Who do you call shadows of men?

DOR.   Half-men.

HORN.   What, boys?

DOR.   Ay, your old boys, old *beaux garçons*, who, like superannuated stallions, are suffered to run, feed, and whinny with the mares as long as they live, though they can do nothing else.

HORN.   Well, a pox on love and wenching! Women serve but to keep a man from better company. Though I can't enjoy them, I shall you the more. Good fellowship and friendship are lasting, rational, and manly pleasures.

HAR.   For all that, give me some of those pleasures you call effeminate too; they help to relish one another.

HORN.   They disturb one another.

HAR.   No, mistresses are like books. If you pore upon them too much, they doze[27] you, and make you unfit for company; but if used discreetly, you are the fitter for conversation by 'em.

DOR.   A mistress should be like a little country retreat near the town; not to dwell in constantly, but only for a night and away, to taste the town the better when a man returns.

HORN.   I tell you, 'tis as hard to be a good fellow, a good friend, and a lover of women, as 'tis to be a good fellow, a good friend, and a lover of money. You cannot follow both, then choose your side. Wine gives you liberty, love takes it away.

DOR.   Gad, he's in the right on't.

HORN.   Wine gives you joy; love, grief and tortures, besides the surgeon's. Wine makes us witty; love, only sots. Wine makes us sleep; love breaks it.

DOR.   By the world he has reason, Harcourt.

HORN.   Wine makes —

DOR.   Ay, wine makes us — makes us princes; love makes us beggars, poor rogues, egad — and wine —

[27]*doze* confuse.

HORN. So, there's one converted. – No, no, love and wine, oil and vinegar.[28]

HAR. I grant it; love will still be uppermost.

HORN. Come, for my part, I will have only those glorious, manly pleasures of being very drunk and very slovenly.

Enter BOY

BOY. Mr Sparkish is below, sir. [*Exit*]

HAR. What, my dear friend! A rogue that is fond of me only, I think, for abusing him.

DOR. No, he can no more think the men laugh at him than that women jilt[29] him, his opinion of himself is so good.

HORN. Well, there's another pleasure by drinking I thought not of: I shall lose his acquaintance because he cannot drink; and you know 'tis a very hard thing to be rid of him, for he's one of those nauseous offerers at wit who, like the worst fiddlers, run themselves into all companies.

HAR. One that, by being in the company of men of sense, would pass for one.

HORN. And may so to the short-sighted world, as a false jewel amongst true ones is not discerned at a distance. His company is as troublesome to us as a cuckold's when you have a mind to his wife's.

HAR. No, the rogue will not let us enjoy one another, but ravishes our conversation, though he signifies no more to't than Sir Martin Mar-all's[30] gaping and awkward thrumming upon his lute does to his man's voice and music.

DOR. And, to pass for a wit in town, shows himself a fool every night to us that are guilty of the plot.

HORN. Such wits as he are, to a company of reasonable men, like rooks[31] to the gamesters, who only fill a room at the table, but are so far from contributing to the play that they only serve to spoil the fancy of those that do.

DOR. Nay, they are used like rooks too, snubbed, checked, and abused; yet the rogues will hang on.

HORN. A pox on 'em, and all that force nature, and would be still what she forbids 'em! Affectation is her greatest monster.

HAR. Most men are the contraries to that they would seem. Your bully, you see, is a coward with a long sword; the little humbly-fawning physician, with his ebony cane, is he that destroys men.

---

[28]*oil and vinegar* which do not mix.   [29]*jilt* deceive.

[30]*Sir Martin Mar-all* In Dryden's *Sir Martin Mar-all*, 1667, he serenades his mistress in mime whilst his hidden servant plays and sings (Act v). Sir Martin fails to stop when Warner does.   [31]*rooks* fools.

DOR. The usurer, a poor rogue possessed of mouldy bonds and mortgages; and we they call spendthrifts are only wealthy, who lay out his money upon daily new purchases of pleasure.

HORN. Ay, your arrantest cheat is your trustee or executor; your jealous man, the greatest cuckold; your churchman, the greatest atheist; and your noisy pert rogue of a wit, the greatest fop, dullest ass, and worst company, as you shall see; for here he comes.

Enter SPARKISH

SPARK. How is't, sparks, how is't? Well, faith, Harry, I must rally thee a little, ha, ha, ha, upon the report in town of thee, ha, ha, ha! I can't hold, i'faith! Shall I speak?

HORN. Yes, but you'll be so bitter then.

SPARK. Honest Dick and Frank here shall answer for me; I will not be extreme bitter, by the universe.

HAR. We will be bound in a ten-thousand-pound bond, he shall not be bitter at all.

DOR. Nor sharp nor sweet.

HORN. What, not downright insipid?

SPARK. Nay then, since you are so brisk and provoke me, take what follows. You must know, I was discoursing and rallying with some ladies yesterday, and they happened to talk of the fine new signs in town —

HORN. Very fine ladies, I believe.

SPARK. Said I, 'I know where the best new sign is'. — 'Where'? says one of the ladies — 'In Covent Garden', I replied — Said another, 'In what street'? — 'In Russell Street',[32] answered I. — 'Lord,' says another, 'I'm sure there was never a fine new sign there yesterday'. — 'Yes, but there was', said I again, 'and it came out of France and has been there a fortnight'.

DOR. A pox! I can hear no more, prithee.

HORN. No, hear him out; let him tune his crowd[33] awhile.

HAR. The worst music, the greatest preparation.

SPARK. Nay, faith, I'll make you laugh. — 'It cannot be', says a third lady. — 'Yes, yes', quoth I again. — Says a fourth lady, —

HORN. Look to't, we'll have no more ladies.

SPARK. No — then mark, mark now. Said I to the fourth, 'Did you never see Mr Horner? He lodges in Russell Street, and he's a sign of a man, you know, since he came out of France! Ha, ha, ha!

HORN. But the devil take me if thine be the sign of a jest.

[32]*Russell Street* Like the restaurant and the two taverns referred to in this conversation, this fashionable residential street was close to the Theatre Royal, Drury Lane.

[33]*crowd* fiddle.

SPARK. With that they all fell a-laughing till they bepissed themselves. What, but it does not move you methinks. Well, I see one had as good go to law without a witness as break a jest without a laugher on one's side. – Come, come, sparks, but where do we dine? I have left at Whitehall an earl, to dine with you.

DOR. Why, I thought thou hadst loved a man with a title better than a suit with a French trimming to't.

HAR. Go to him again.

SPARK. No, sir, a wit to me is the greatest title in the world.

HORN. But go dine with your earl, sir; he may be exceptious.[34] We are your friends and will not take it ill to be left, I do assure you.

HAR. Nay, faith, he shall go to him.

SPARK. Nay, pray, gentlemen.

DOR. We'll thrust you out if you won't. What, disappoint anybody for us?

SPARK. Nay, dear gentlemen, hear me.

HORN. No, no, sir, by no means. Pray go, sir.

SPARK. Why, dear rogues, –

DOR. No, no.   *They all thrust him out of the room*

ALL. Ha, ha, ha!

    Re-enter SPARKISH

SPARK. But, sparks, pray hear me. What, d'ye think I'll eat then with gay, shallow fops and silent coxcombs? I think wit as necessary at dinner as a glass of good wine, and that's the reason I never have any stomach when I eat alone. – Come, but where do we dine?

HORN. Even where you will.

SPARK. At Chateline's?

DOR. Yes, if you will.

SPARK. Or at the Cock?

DOR. Yes, if you please.

SPARK. Or at the Dog and Partridge?

HORN. Ay, if you have a mind to't, for we shall dine at neither.

SPARK. Pshaw! With your fooling we shall lose the new play,[35] and I would no more miss seeing a new play the first day than I would miss sitting in the wit's row;[36] therefore I'll go fetch my mistress,[37] and away.   *Exit*

    Enter PINCHWIFE

[34]*exceptious* irritated.

[35]*lose the new play* In *The Plain Dealer*, 1676, Wycherley later alluded to Mrs Trifle's unfashionable behaviour: '. . . she was seen at *The Country Wife* after the first day'.

[36]*the wits' row* in the pit.

[37]*mistress* i.e. his fiancée, Alithea.

HORN. Who have we here? Pinchwife?

PINCH. Gentlemen, your humble servant.

HORN. Well, Jack, by thy long absence from the town, the grumness of thy countenance, and the slovenliness of thy habit, I should give thee joy, should I not, of marriage?

PINCH. (*Aside*) Death! Does he know I'm married too? I thought to have concealed it from him at least – [*Aloud*] My long stay in the country will excuse my dress, and I have a suit of law that brings me up to town; that puts me out of humour. Besides, I must give Sparkish tomorrow five thousand pounds[38] to lie with my sister.

HORN. Nay, you country gentlemen, rather than not purchase, will buy anything; and he is a cracked title,[39] if we may quibble. Well, but am I to give thee joy? I heard thou wert married.

PINCH. What then?

HORN. Why, the next thing that is to be heard, is thou'rt a cuckold.

PINCH. (*Aside*) Insupportable name!

HORN. But I did not expect marriage from such a whoremaster as you, one that knew the town so much and women so well.

PINCH. Why, I have married no London wife.

HORN. Pshaw, that's all one. That grave circumspection in marrying a country wife is like refusing a deceitful, pampered Smithfield jade,[40] to go and be cheated by a friend in the country.

PINCH. (*Aside*) A pox on him and his simile! – [*Aloud*] At least we are a little surer of the breed there, know what her keeping has been, whether foiled[41] or unsound.

HORN. Come, come, I have known a clap gotten in Wales, and there are cozens,[42] justices' clerks, and chaplains in the country – I won't say coachmen. But she's handsome and young?

PINCH. (*Aside*) I'll answer as I should do. – [*Aloud*] No, no; she has no beauty but her youth, no attraction but her modesty; wholesome, homely, and huswifely, that's all.

DOR. He talks as like a grazier[43] as he looks.

PINCH. She's too awkward, ill-favoured, and silly to bring to town.

HAR. Then methinks you should bring her, to be taught breeding.

PINCH. To be taught! No, sir, I thank you. Good wives and private soldiers should be ignorant. I'll keep her from your instructions, I warrant you.

---

[38]*five thousand pounds* Alithea's dowry, a very large sum of money.

[39]*a cracked title* an unsatisfactory acquisition.

[40]*Smithfield jade* from the tradition that a horse bought in Smithfield Market, London, would likely be of dubious quality.

[41]*foiled* injured.   [42]*cozens* tricksters.

[43]*grazier* a farmer who raises cattle.

HAR. (*Aside*) The rogue is as jealous as if his wife were not ignorant.

HORN. Why, if she be ill-favoured, there will be less danger here for you than by leaving her in the country. We have such variety of dainties that we are seldom hungry.

DOR. But they have always coarse, constant, swingeing stomachs[44] in the country.

HAR. Foul feeders indeed!

DOR. And your hospitality is great there.

HAR. Open house; every man's welcome.

PINCH. So, so, gentlemen.

HORN. But prithee, why wouldst thou marry her? If she be ugly, ill-bred, and silly, she must be rich then.

PINCH. As rich as if she brought me twenty thousand pound out of this town; for she'll be as sure not to spend her moderate portion as a London baggage would be to spend hers, let it be what it would. So 'tis all one. Then, because she's ugly, she's the likelier to be my own; and being ill-bred, she'll hate conversation; and since silly and innocent, will not know the difference betwixt a man of one-and-twenty and one of forty.

HORN. Nine — to my knowledge. But if she be silly, she'll expect as much from a man of forty-nine as from him of one-and-twenty. But methinks wit is more necessary than beauty; and I think no young woman ugly that has it, and no handsome woman agreeable without it.

PINCH. 'Tis my maxim, he's a fool that marries, but he's a greater that does not marry a fool. What is wit in a wife good for but to make a man a cuckold?

HORN. Yes, to keep it from his knowledge.

PINCH. A fool cannot contrive to make her husband a cuckold.

HORN. No, but she'll club with a man that can; and what is worse, if she cannot make her husband a cuckold, she'll make him jealous, and pass for one; and then 'tis all one.

PINCH. Well, well, I'll take care for one. My wife shall make me no cuckold, though she had your help, Mr Horner. I understand the town, sir.

DOR(*Aside*) His help!

HAR. (*Aside*) He's come newly to town, it seems, and has not heard how things are with him.

HORN. But tell me, has marriage cured thee of whoring, which it seldom does?

---

[44]*swingeing stomachs* gross appetites.

HAR.   'Tis more than age can do.

HORN.   No, the word[45] is, 'I'll marry and live honest',[46] but a marriage vow is like a penitent gamester's oath, and entering into bonds and penalties to stint himself to such a particular small sum at play for the future, which makes him but the more eager; and, not being able to hold out, loses his money again, and his forfeit to boot.

DOR.   Ay, ay, a gamester will be a gamester whilst his money lasts, and a whoremaster whilst his vigour.

HAR.   Nay, I have known 'em, when they are broke and can lose no more, keep a-fumbling with the box in their hands to fool with only, and hinder other gamesters –

DOR.   That had wherewithal to make lusty stakes.

PINCH.   Well, gentlemen, you may laugh at me, but you shall never lie with my wife – I know the town.

HORN.   But prithee, was not the way you were in better? Is not keeping better than marriage?

PINCH.   A pox on't! The jades would jilt me; I could never keep a whore to myself.

HORN.   So, then you only married to keep a whore to yourself! Well, but let me tell you, women, as you say, are like soldiers, made constant and loyal by good pay rather than by oaths and covenants; therefore I'd advise my friends to keep rather than marry, since too I find, by your example, it does not serve one's turn, for I saw you yesterday in the eighteen-penny place[47] with a pretty country wench.

PINCH.   (*Aside*) How the devil! Did he see my wife then? I sat there that she might not be seen. But she shall never go to a play again.

HORN.   What, dost thou blush, at nine-and-forty, for having been seen with a wench?

DOR.   No, faith, I warrant 'twas his wife, which he seated there out of sight; for he's a cunning rogue, and understands the town.

HAR.   He blushes. Then 'twas his wife; for men are now more ashamed to be seen with them in public than with a wench.

PINCH.   (*Aside*) Hell and damnation! I'm undone, since Horner has seen her, and they know 'twas she.

HORN.   But prithee, was it thy wife? She was exceeding pretty; I was in love with her at that distance.

---

[45]*the word* the conventional phrase.   [46]*honest* chaste.

[47]*eighteen-penny place* the second or middle gallery of the theatre, the section frequented by prostitutes.

PINCH.   You are like never to be nearer to her. Your servant,
  gentlemen.   *Offers to go*
HORN.   Nay, prithee stay.
PINCH.   I cannot; I will not.
HORN.   Come, you shall dine with us.
PINCH.   I have dined already.
HORN.   Come, I know thou hast not. I'll treat thee, dear rogue; thou
  shalt spend none of thy Hampshire money today.
PINCH.   (*Aside*) Treat me! So, he uses me already like his cuckold.
HORN.   Nay, you shall not go.
PINCH.   I must; I have business at home.   *Exit*
HAR.   To beat his wife! He's as jealous of her as a Cheapside husband
  of a Covent Garden wife.[48]
HORN.   Why, 'tis as hard to find an old whoremaster without jealousy
  and the gout as a young one without fear or the pox:
        As gout in age from pox in youth proceeds,
        So wenching past, then jealousy succeeds,
        The worst disease that love and wenching breeds.   *Exeunt*

[48]*Cheapside . . . wife* as a businessman of a sophisticated, fashionable wife.

Act Two

SCENE ONE

[A room in PINCHWIFE'S *house]*

[Enter] MRS MARGERY PINCHWIFE *and* ALITHEA. PINCHWIFE
peeping behind at the door

MRS PINCH. Pray, sister, where are the best fields and woods to walk
in, in London?

ALITH. A pretty question! Why, sister, Mulberry Garden[1] and St
James's Park; and, for close[2] walks, the New Exchange.[3]

MRS PINCH. Pray, sister, tell me why my husband looks so grum here
in town, and keeps me up so close, and will not let me go a-walking,
nor let me wear my best gown yesterday.

ALITH. Oh, he's jealous, sister.

MRS PINCH. Jealous! What's that?

ALITH. He's afraid you should love another man.

MRS PINCH. How should he be afraid of my loving another man,
when he will not let me see any but himself?

ALITH. Did he not carry you yesterday to a play?

MRS PINCH. Ay, but we sat amongst ugly people. He would not let
me come near the gentry, who sat under us, so that I could not see
'em. He told me none but naughty women sat there, whom they
toused and moused. But I would have ventured, for all that.

ALITH. But how did you like the play?

MRS PINCH. Indeed, I was a-weary of the play, but I liked hugeously
the actors. They are the goodliest, properest men, sister!

ALITH. Oh, but you must not like the actors, sister.

MRS PINCH. Ay, how should I help it, sister? Pray, sister, when my
husband comes in, will you ask leave for me to go a-walking?

ALITH. *(Aside)* A-walking! Ha, ha! Lord, a country-gentlewoman's
pleasure is the drudgery of a foot-post;[4] and she requires as much

---

[1] *Mulberry Garden* a fashionable park where Buckingham Palace now stands.

[2] *close* enclosed.

[3] *New Exchange* a large, two-storied arcaded building, 1609–1737, on the south
side of the Strand, opposite Bedford Street, popular for promenades and assigna-
tions, and referred to in many Restoration plays.

[4] *foot-post* one who carries messages or letters. A similar attitude towards walking
appears in Millamant's comment, *The Way of the World*, IV, i, p. 541.

airing as her husband's horses. – But here comes your husband. I'll ask, though I'm sure he'll not grant it.

MRS PINCH.   He says he won't let me go abroad for fear of catching the pox.

ALITH.   Fie, the smallpox[5] you should say.

   Enter PINCHWIFE

MRS PINCH.   O my dear, dear bud, welcome home! Why dost thou look so fropish?[6] Who has nangered[7] thee?

PINCH.   You're a fool.   MRS PINCHWIFE *goes aside and cries*

ALITH.   Faith, so she is, for crying for no fault, poor tender creature!

PINCH.   What, you would have her as impudent as yourself, as arrant a jill-flirt, a gadder, a magpie, and, to say all, a mere[8] notorious town-woman?

ALITH.   Brother, you are my only censurer; and the honour of your family shall sooner suffer in your wife there than in me, though I take the innocent liberty of the town.

PINCH.   Hark you, mistress, do not talk so before my wife. – The innocent liberty of the town!

ALITH.   Why, pray, who boasts of any intrigue with me? What lampoon[9] has made my name notorious? What ill women frequent my lodgings? I keep no company with any women of scandalous reputations.

PINCH.   No, you keep the men of scandalous reputations company.

ALITH.   Where? Would you not have me civil? Answer 'em in a box at the plays, in the drawing-room at Whitehall, in St James's Park, Mulberry Garden, or –

PINCH.   Hold, hold! Do not teach my wife where the men are to be found. I believe she's the worse for your town-documents[10] already. I bid you keep her in ignorance, as I do.

MRS PINCH.   Indeed, be not angry with her, bud; she will tell me nothing of the town, though I ask her a thousand times a day.

PINCH.   Then you are very inquisitive to know, I find!

MRS PINCH.   Not I indeed, dear; I hate London. Our place-house[11] in the country is worth a thousand of't. Would I were there again!

PINCH.   So you shall, I warrant. But were you not talking of plays and

---

5*pox . . . smallpox* See other references, I, i, p. 15.   6*fropish* peevish.
7*nangered* angered.   8*mere* absolutely.
9*lampoon* See also *The Man of Mode*, I, i, p. 126.
10*town-documents* lessons.
11*place-house* country house.

players when I came in? – [*To* ALITHEA] You are her encourager in such discourses.

MRS PINCH.   No, indeed, dear; she chid me just now for liking the playermen.

PINCH.   (*Aside*) Nay, if she be so innocent as to own to me her liking them, there is no hurt in't. – [*Aloud*] Come, my poor rogue, but thou likest none better than me?

MRS PINCH.   Yes, indeed, but I do; the playermen are finer folks.

PINCH.   But you love none better than me?

MRS PINCH.   You are mine own dear bud, and I know you. I hate a stranger.

PINCH.   Ay, my dear, you must love me only, and not be like the naughty town-women, who only hate their husbands, and love every man else; love plays, visits, fine coaches, fine clothes, fiddles, balls, treats, and so lead a wicked town-life.

MRS PINCH.   Nay, if to enjoy all these things be a town-life, London is not so bad a place, dear.

PINCH.   How! If you love me, you must hate London.

ALITH.   [*Aside*] The fool has forbad me discovering to her the pleasures of the town, and he is now setting her agog upon them himself.

MRS PINCH.   But, husband, do the town-women love the playermen too?

PINCH.   Yes, I warrant you.

MRS PINCH.   Ay, I warrant you.

PINCH.   Why, you do not, I hope?

MRS PINCH.   No, no, bud. But why have we no playermen in the country?

PINCH.   Ha! Mrs Minx, ask me no more to go to a play.

MRS PINCH.   Nay, why, love? I did not care for going, but when you forbid me, you make me, as 'twere, desire it.

ALITH.   (*Aside*) So 'twill be in other things, I warrant.

MRS PINCH.   Pray let me go to a play, dear.

PINCH.   Hold your peace, I wo' not.

MRS PINCH.   Why, love?

PINCH.   Why, I'll tell you –

ALITH.   (*Aside*) Nay, if he tell her, she'll give him more cause to forbid her that place.

MRS PINCH.   Pray why, dear?

PINCH.   First, you like the actors, and the gallants may like you.

MRS PINCH.   What, a homely country girl? No, bud, nobody will like me.

PINCH.   I tell you, yes, they may.

MRS PINCH.   No, no, you jest. I won't believe you. I will go.

PINCH.   I tell you then, that one of the lewdest fellows in town, who saw you there, told me he was in love with you.

MRS PINCH.   Indeed! Who, who, pray, was't?

PINCH.   (*Aside*) I've gone too far, and slipped before I was aware. How overjoyed she is!

MRS PINCH.   Was it any Hampshire gallant, any of our neighbours? I promise you, I am beholding to him.

PINCH.   I promise you, you lie; for he would but ruin you, as he has done hundreds. He has no other love for women but that. Such as he look upon women like basilisks,[12] but to destroy 'em.

MRS PINCH.   Ay, but if he loves me, why should he ruin me? Answer me to that. Methinks he should not; I would do him no harm.

ALITH.   Ha, ha, ha!

PINCH.   'Tis very well; but I'll keep him from doing you any harm, or me either. But here comes company. Get you in, get you in.

MRS PINCH.   But, pray, husband, is he a pretty gentleman that loves me?

PINCH.   In, baggage, in!   *Thrusts her in and shuts the door*
         Enter SPARKISH *and* HARCOURT

[*Aside*] What, all the lewd libertines of the town brought to my lodging by this easy coxcomb! 'Sdeath, I'll not suffer it.

SPARK.   Here, Harcourt, do you approve my choice? – [*To* ALITHEA] Dear little rogue, I told you I'd bring you acquainted with all my friends, the wits and –   HARCOURT *salutes*[13] *her*

PINCH.   [*Aside*] Ay, they shall know[14] her as well as you yourself will, I warrant you.

SPARK.   This is one of those, my pretty rogue, that are to dance at your wedding tomorrow; and him you must bid welcome ever to what you and I have.

PINCH.   (*Aside*) Monstrous!

SPARK.   Harcourt, how dost thou like her, faith? Nay, dear, do not look down; I should hate to have a wife of mine out of countenance at anything.

PINCH.   [*Aside*] Wonderful!

SPARK.   Tell me, I say, Harcourt, how dost thou like her? Thou hast stared upon her enough to resolve me.

HAR.   So infinitely well that I could wish I had a mistress too, that might differ from her in nothing but her love and engagement to you.

---

[12]*basilisks* mythological creatures whose glance was believed to be fatal.
[13]*salutes* kisses.
[14]*know* punning on 'have a sexual relationship with'.

ALITH. Sir, Master Sparkish has often told me that his acquaintance were all wits and railleurs, and now I find it.

SPARK. No, by the universe, madam, he does not rally now; you may believe him. I do assure you, he is the honestest, worthiest, true-hearted gentleman – a man of such perfect honour, he would say nothing to a lady he does not mean.

PINCH. [*Aside*] Praising another man to his mistress!

HAR. Sir, you are so beyond expectation obliging that –

SPARK. Nay, egad, I am sure you do admire her extremely; I see't in your eyes. – He does admire you, madam. – By the world, don't you?

HAR. Yes, above the world, or the most glorious part of it, her whole sex; and till now I never thought I should have envied you or any man about to marry, but you have the best excuse for marriage I ever knew.

ALITH. Nay, now, sir, I'm satisfied you are of the society of the wits and railleurs, since you cannot spare your friend, even when he is but too civil to you; but the surest sign is, since you are an enemy to marriage, – for that I hear you hate as much as business or bad wine –

HAR. Truly, madam, I never was an enemy to marriage till now, because marriage was never an enemy to me before.

ALITH. But why, sir, is marriage an enemy to you now? Because it robs you of your friend here? For you look upon a friend married as one gone into a monastery, that is, dead to the world.

HAR. 'Tis indeed, because you marry him; I see, madam, you can guess my meaning. I do confess heartily and openly, I wish it were in my power to break the match; by heavens I would.

SPARK. Poor Frank!

ALITH. Would you be so unkind to me?

HAR. No, no, 'tis not because I would be unkind to you.

SPARK. Poor Frank! No, gad, 'tis only his kindness to me.

PINCH.(*Aside*) Great kindness to you indeed! Insensible fop, let a man make love to his wife to his face!

SPARK. Come, dear Frank, for all my wife there that shall be, thou shalt enjoy me sometimes, dear rogue. By my honour, we men of wit condole for our deceased brother in marriage as much as for one dead in earnest. I think that was prettily said of me, ha, Harcourt? – But come, Frank, be not melancholy for me.

HAR. No, I assure you, I am not melancholy for you.

SPARK. Prithee, Frank, dost think my wife that shall be, there, a fine person?

HAR. I could gaze upon her till I became as blind as you are.

SPARK. How, as I am? How!

HAR. Because you are a lover, and true lovers are blind, stock blind.[15]

---

[15]*stock blind* as blind as a block of wood, etc.

SPARK. True, true; but by the world, she has wit too, as well as beauty. Go, go with her into a corner, and try if she has wit. Talk to her anything; she's bashful before me.

HAR. Indeed, if a woman wants[16] wit in a corner, she has it nowhere.

ALITH. (*Aside to* SPARKISH) Sir, you dispose of me a little before your time –

SPARK. Nay, nay, madam, let me have an earnest of your obedience, or – Go, go, madam.   HARCOURT *courts* ALITHEA *aside*

PINCH. How, sir, if you are not concerned for the honour of a wife, I am for that of a sister; he shall not debauch her. Be a pander to your own wife, bring men to her, let 'em make love before your face, thrust 'em into a corner together, then leave 'em in private! Is this your town wit and conduct?

SPARK. Ha, ha, ha! A silly wise rogue [who] would make one laugh more than a stark fool! Ha, ha! I shall burst. Nay, you shall not disturb 'em; I'll vex[17] thee, by the world.

Struggles with PINCHWIFE *to keep him from* HARCOURT *and* ALITHEA

ALITH. The writings are drawn, sir, settlements made; 'tis too late, sir, and past all revocation.

HAR. Then so is my death.

ALITH. I would not be unjust to him.

HAR. Then why to me so?

ALITH. I have no obligation to you.

HAR. My love.

ALITH. I had his before.

HAR. You never had it; he wants, you see, jealousy, the only infallible sign of it.

ALITH. Love proceeds from esteem; he cannot distrust my virtue. Besides, he loves me, or he would not marry me.

HAR. Marrying you is no more sign of his love than bribing your woman,[18] that he may marry you, is a sign of his generosity. Marriage is rather a sign of interest[19] than love; and he that marries a fortune covets a mistress, not loves her. But if you take marriage for a sign of love, take it from me immediately.

ALITH. No, now you have put a scruple in my head; but in short, sir, to end our dispute, I must marry him; my reputation would suffer in the world else.

HAR. No; if you do marry him – with your pardon, madam – your

---

[16]*wants* lacks.   [17]*vex* harrass.
[18]*woman* servant.   [19]*interest* i.e. self-interest.

reputation suffers in the world, and you would be thought in necessity for a cloak.²⁰

ALITH.   Nay, now you are rude, sir. – Mr Sparkish, pray come hither; your friend here is very troublesome, and very loving.²¹

HAR.   (*Aside to* ALITHEA) Hold, hold!

PINCH.   D'ye hear that?

SPARK.   Why, d'ye think I'll seem to be jealous, like a country bumpkin?

PINCH.   No, rather be a cuckold, like a credulous cit.²²

HAR.   Madam, you would not have been so little generous as to have told him.

ALITH.   Yes, since you could be so little generous as to wrong him.

HAR.   Wrong him! No man can do't; he's beneath an injury, a bubble,²³ a coward, a senseless idiot, a wretch so contemptible to all the world but you that –

ALITH.   Hold, do not rail at him, for since he is like to be my husband, I am resolved to like him. Nay, I think I am obliged to tell him you are not his friend. – Master Sparkish, Master Sparkish!

SPARK.   What, what? – [*To* HARCOURT] Now, dear rogue, has she not wit?

HAR.   Not so much as I thought and hoped she had.   *Speaks surlily*

ALITH.   Mr Sparkish, do you bring people to rail at you?

HAR.   Madam –

SPARK.   How, no; but if he does rail at me, 'tis but in jest, I warrant: what we wits do for one another, and never take any notice of it.

ALITH.   He spoke so scurrilously of you, I had no patience to hear him; besides, he has been making love to me.

HAR.   (*Aside*) True, damned tell-tale woman!

SPARK.   Pshaw, to show his parts.²⁴ We wits rail and make love often, but to show our parts; as we have no affections, so we have no malice. We –

ALITH.   He said you were a wretch below an injury.

SPARK.   Pshaw!

HAR.   [*Aside*] Damned, senseless, impudent, virtuous jade! Well, since she won't let me have her, she'll do as good: she'll make me hate her.

²⁰*if you do . . . a cloak* i.e. the world would think you had only one reason for marrying this man, an existing pregnancy.
²¹*loving* passionate.
²²*cit* a citizen, a tradesman.
²³*bubble* dupe, fool.
²⁴*parts* talents, with a sexual innuendo.

ALITH. A common bubble –

SPARK. Pshaw!

ALITH. A coward –

SPARK. Pshaw, pshaw!

ALITH. A senseless, drivelling idiot –

SPARK. How, did he disparage my parts? Nay, then, my honour's concerned; I can't put up that, sir, by the world! Brother,[25] help me to kill him! – (*Aside*) I may draw now, since we have the odds of him. 'Tis a good occasion too, before my mistress.   *Offers to draw*

ALITH. Hold, hold!

SPARK. What, what?

ALITH. (*Aside*) I must not let 'em kill the gentleman neither, for his kindness to me. I am so far from hating him that I wish my gallant had his person and understanding. – [*To* SPARKISH] Nay, if my honour –

SPARK. I'll be thy death.

ALITH. Hold, hold! Indeed, to tell the truth, the gentleman said, after all, that what he spoke was but out of friendship to you.

SPARK. How! Say I am, I am a fool, that is, no wit, out of friendship to me?

ALITH. Yes, to try whether I was concerned enough for you; and made love to me only to be satisfied of my virtue, for your sake.

HAR. (*Aside*) Kind; however, –

SPARK. Nay, if it were so, my dear rogue, I ask thee pardon; but why would not you tell me so, faith?

HAR. Because I did not think on't, faith.

SPARK. Come, Horner does not come; Harcourt, let's be gone to the new play. – Come, madam.

ALITH. I will not go, if you intend to leave me alone in the box, and run into the pit, as you use to do.

SPARK. Pshaw! I'll leave Harcourt with you in the box to entertain you, and that's as good; if I sat in the box, I should be thought no judge but of trimmings.[26] – Come away, Harcourt; lead her down.

Exeunt SPARKISH, HARCOURT *and* ALITHEA

PINCH. Well, go thy ways for the flower of the true town fops, such as spend their estates before they come to 'em, and are cuckolds before they're married. But let me go look to my own freehold. –How!

Enter LADY FIDGET, MRS DAINTY FIDGET *and* MRS SQUEAMISH

LADY FID. Your servant, sir. Where is your lady? We are come to wait upon her to the new play.

PINCH. New play!

LADY FID. And my husband will wait upon you presently.

[25] *Brother* i.e. Pinchwife, his prospective brother-in-law.
[26] *trimmings* fashions.

PINCH. (*Aside*) Damn your civility. – [*Aloud*] Madam, by no means. I will not see Sir Jasper here till I have waited upon him at home; nor shall my wife see you till she has waited upon your ladyship at your lodgings.

LADY FID. Now we are here, sir, –

PINCH. No, madam.

MRS DAIN. Pray, let us see her.

MRS SQUEAM. We will not stir till we see her.

PINCH. (*Aside*) A pox on you all! – (*Goes to the door and returns*) She has locked the door and is gone abroad.

LADY FID. No, you have locked the door, and she's within.

MRS DAIN. They told us below she was here.

PINCH. (*Aside*) Will nothing do? – [*Aloud*] Well, it must out then. To tell you the truth, ladies, which I was afraid to let you know before, lest it might endanger your lives, my wife has just now the smallpox come out upon her. Do not be frightened, but pray be gone, ladies; you shall not stay here in danger of your lives. Pray get you gone, ladies.

LADY FID. No, no, we have all had 'em.

MRS SQUEAM. Alack, alack!

MRS DAIN. Come, come, we must see how it goes with her; I understand the disease.

LADY FID. Come!

PINCH. (*Aside*) Well, there is no being too hard for women at their own weapon, lying; therefore I'll quit the field. *Exit*

MRS SQUEAM. Here's an example of jealousy!

LADY FID. Indeed, as the world goes, I wonder there are no more jealous, since wives are so neglected.

MRS DAIN. Pshaw! As the world goes, to what end should they be jealous?

LADY FID. Foh, 'tis a nasty world.

MRS SQUEAM. That men of parts, great acquaintance, and quality should take up with and spend themselves and fortunes in keeping little playhouse creatures! Foh!

LADY FID. Nay, that women of understanding, great acquaintance, and good quality should fall a-keeping too of little creatures! Foh!

MRS SQUEAM. Why, 'tis the men of quality's fault; they never visit women of honour and reputation as they used to do; and have not so much as common civility for ladies of our rank, but use us with the same indifferency and ill-breeding as if we were all married to 'em.

LADY FID. She says true. 'Tis an arrant shame women of quality should be so slighted. Methinks birth – birth should go for something; I have known men admired, courted, and followed for their titles only.

MRS SQUEAM.   Ay, one would think men of honour should not love, no more than marry, out of their own rank.

MRS DAIN.   Fie, fie upon 'em! They are come to think cross-breeding for themselves best, as well as for their dogs and horses.

LADY FID.   They are dogs and horses for't.

MRS SQUEAM.   One would think, if not for love, for vanity a little.

MRS DAIN.   Nay, they do satisfy their vanity upon us sometimes, and are kind to us in their report, tell all the world they lie with us.

LADY FID.   Damned rascals, that we should be only wronged by 'em! To report a man has had a person, when he has not had a person, is the greatest wrong in the whole world that can be done to a person.

MRS SQUEAM.   Well, 'tis an arrant shame noble persons should be so wronged and neglected.

LADY FID.   But still 'tis an arranter shame for a noble person to neglect her own honour, and defame her own noble person with little inconsiderable fellows! Foh!

MRS DAIN.   I suppose the crime against our honour is the same with a man of quality as with another.

LADY FID.   How! No, sure, the man of quality is likest one's husband, and therefore the fault should be the less.

MRS DAIN.   But then the pleasure should be the less.

LADY FID.   Fie, fie, fie! For shame, sister! Whither shall we ramble? Be continent in your discourse, or I shall hate you.

MRS DAIN.   Besides, an intrigue is so much the more notorious for the man's quality.

MRS SQUEAM.   'Tis true nobody takes notice of a private[27] man, and therefore with him 'tis more secret; and the crime's the less when 'tis not known.

LADY FID.   You say true; i'faith, I think you are in the right on't. 'Tis not an injury to a husband till it be an injury to our honours; so that a woman of honour loses no honour with a private person, and to say truth —

MRS DAIN.   (*Apart to* MRS SQUEAMISH) So, the little fellow is grown a private person with her —

LADY FID.   But still my dear, dear honour —

Enter SIR JASPER FIDGET, HORNER *and* DORILANT

SIR JASP.   Ay, my dear, dear of honour, thou hast still so much honour in thy mouth —

HORN.   (*Aside*) That she has none elsewhere.

[27]*private* untitled.

LADY FID.   Oh, what d'ye mean to bring in these upon us?

MRS DAIN.   Foh, these are as bad as wits.

MRS SQUEAM.   Foh!

LADY FID.   Let us leave the room.

SIR JASP.   Stay, stay. Faith, to tell you the naked truth –

LADY FID.   Fie, Sir Jasper, do not use that word 'naked'.

SIR JASP.   Well, well, in short, I have business at Whitehall and cannot go to the play with you; therefore would have you go –

LADY FID.   With those two to a play?

SIR JASP.   No, not with t'other, but with Mr Horner; there can be no more scandal to go with him than with Mr Tattle or Master Limberham.

LADY FID.   With that nasty fellow? No, no.

SIR JASP.   Nay, prithee, dear, hear me.   *Whispers to* LADY FIDGET

HORN.   Ladies, –

HORNER *and* DORILANT *draw near* MRS SQUEAMISH *and* MRS DAINTY FIDGET

MRS DAIN.   Stand off.

MRS SQUEAM.   Do not approach us.

MRS DAIN.   You herd with the wits, you are obscenity all over.

MRS SQUEAM.   And I would as soon look upon a picture of Adam and Eve without fig-leaves as any of you, if I could help it; therefore keep off and do not make us sick.

DOR.   What a devil are these?

HORN.   Why, these are pretenders to honour, as critics to wit, only by censuring others; and as every raw, peevish, out-of-humoured, affected, dull, tea-drinking, arithmetical[28] fop sets up for a wit by railing at men of sense, so these for honour, by railing at the court and ladies of as great honour as quality.

SIR JASP.   Come, Mr Horner, I must desire you to go with these ladies to the play, sir.

HORN.   I, sir?

SIR JASP.   Ay, ay, come, sir.

HORN.   I must beg your pardon, sir, and theirs; I will not be seen in women's company in public again for the world.

SIR JASP.   Ha, ha, strange aversion!

MRS SQUEAM.   No, he's for women's company in private.

SIR JASP.   He – poor man – he – Ha, ha, ha!

MRS DAIN.   'Tis a greater shame amongst lewd fellows to be seen in virtuous women's company than for the women to be seen with them.

---

[28]*arithmetical* precise, fussy.

HORN. Indeed, madam, the time was I only hated virtuous women, but now I hate the other too. I beg your pardon, ladies.

LADY FID. You are very obliging, sir, because we would not be troubled with you.

SIR JASP. In sober sadness, he shall go.

DOR. Nay, if he will not, I am ready to wait upon the ladies, and I think I am the fitter man.

SIR JASP. You, sir? No, I thank you for that. Master Horner is a privileged man amongst the virtuous ladies; 'twill be a great while before you are so, he, he, he! He's my wife's gallant, he, he, he! No, pray withdraw, sir, for as I take it, the virtuous ladies have no business with you.

DOR. And I am sure he can have none with them. 'Tis strange a man can't come amongst virtuous women now but upon the same terms as men are admitted into the Great Turk's²⁹ seraglio. But heavens keep me from being an ombre³⁰ player with 'em! – But where is Pinchwife? *Exit*

SIR JASP. Come, come, man; what, avoid the sweet society of womankind? That sweet, soft, gentle, tame, noble creature, woman, made for man's companion –

HORN. So is that soft, gentle, tame, and more noble creature a spaniel, and has all their tricks: can fawn, lie down, suffer beating and fawn the more; barks at your friends when they come to see you, makes your bed hard, gives you fleas, and the mange sometimes. And all the difference is, the spaniel's the more faithful animal, and fawns but upon one master.

SIR JASP. He, he, he!

MRS SQUEAM. Oh, the rude beast!

MRS DAIN. Insolent brute!

LADY FID. Brute! Stinking, mortified, rotten French wether! To dare –

SIR JASP. Hold, an't please your ladyship. – For shame, Master Horner! Your mother was a woman – (*Aside*) Now shall I never reconcile 'em. – [*Aside to* LADY FIDGET] Hark you, madam, take my advice in your anger. You know you often want one to make up your drolling³¹ pack of ombre players, and you may cheat him easily, for he's an ill gamester,³² and consequently loves play.

---

²⁹*Great Turk* probably Murad IV, Sultan of Turkey 1623–40, notorious for his ruthlessness.

³⁰*ombre* a popular card game, for three players. See Alexander Pope, *The Rape of the Lock*, III, 27–98.

³¹*drolling* comical.

³²*gamester* literally, a card player, gambler; with *doubles entendres*, here and below, concerning sexual activity.

Besides, you know, you have but two old civil gentlemen (with stinking breaths too) to wait upon you abroad; take in the third into your service. The other are but crazy;[33] and a lady should have a supernumerary gentleman-usher,[34] as a supernumerary coach-horse, lest sometimes you should be forced to stay at home.

LADY FID.   But are you sure he loves play and has money?

SIR JASP.   He loves play as much as you, and has money as much as I.

LADY FID.   Then I am contented to make him pay for his scurrility. Money makes up in a measure all other wants in men. – (*Aside*) Those whom we cannot make hold for gallants, we make fine.[35]

SIR JASP.   (*Aside*) So, so; now to mollify, to wheedle him. – [*Aside to* HORNER] Master Horner, will you never keep civil company? Methinks 'tis time now, since you are only fit for them. Come, come, man, you must e'en fall to visiting our wives, eating at our tables, drinking tea with our virtuous relations after dinner, dealing cards to 'em, reading plays and gazettes to 'em, picking fleas out of their shocks[36] for 'em, collecting receipts,[37] new songs, women,[38] pages, and footmen for 'em.

HORN.   I hope they'll afford me better employment, sir.

SIR JASP.   He, he, he! 'Tis fit you know your work before you come into your place; and since you are unprovided of a lady to flatter and a good house to eat at, pray frequent mine, and call my wife mistress, and she shall call you gallant, according to the custom.

HORN.   Who, I?

SIR JASP.   Faith, thou shalt for my sake; come, for my sake only.

HORN.   For your sake –

SIR JASP.   Come, come, here's a gamester for you. Let him be a little familiar sometimes; nay, what if a little rude? Gamesters may be rude with ladies, you know.

LADY FID.   Yes, losing gamesters have a privilege with women.

HORN.   I always thought the contrary, that the winning gamester had most privilege with women; for when you have lost your money to a man, you'll lose anything you have, all you have, they say, and he may use you as he pleases.

SIR JASP.   He, he, he! Well, win or lose, you shall have your liberty with her.

---

[33]*crazy* infirm.

[34]*gentleman-usher* For a similar reference, see *The Man of Mode*, I, i, p. 121.

[35]*make fine* penalise.

[36]*shocks* poodles; picking fleas from dogs is alluded to in *The Way of the World*, IV, i, p. 547. Shock is Belinda's lap dog in Pope's *The Rape of the Lock*, I, 115 *passim*.

[37]*receipts* recipes.

[38]*women* female servants.

LADY FID. As he behaves himself; and for your sake I'll give him admittance and freedom.

HORN. All sorts of freedom, madam?

SIR JASP. Ay, ay, ay, all sorts of freedom thou canst take. And so go to her, begin thy new employment; wheedle her, jest with her, and be better acquainted one with another.

HORN. (*Aside*) I think I know her already; therefore may venture with her my secret for hers.   HORNER *and* LADY FIDGET *whisper*

SIR JASP. Sister, coz, I have provided an innocent playfellow for you there.

MRS DAIN. Who, he?

MRS SQUEAM. There's a playfellow, indeed!

SIR JASP. Yes, sure – What, he is good enough to play at cards, blindman's-buff, or the fool with, sometimes.

MRS SQUEAM. Foh, we'll have no such playfellows.

MRS DAIN. No, sir, you shan't choose playfellows for us, we thank you.

SIR JASP. Nay, pray hear me.   *Whispering to them*;
                    [LADY FIDGET *and* HORNER *speak apart*]

LADY FID. But, poor gentleman, could you be so generous, so truly a man of honour, as for the sakes of us women of honour, to cause yourself to be reported no man? No man! And to suffer yourself the greatest shame that could fall upon a man, that none might fall upon us women by your conversation?[39] But, indeed, sir, as perfectly, perfectly the same man as before your going into France, sir, as perfectly, perfectly, sir?

HORN. As perfectly, perfectly, madam. Nay, I scorn you should take my word; I desire to be tried only, madam.

LADY FID. Well, that's spoken again like a man of honour; all men of honour desire to come to the test. But, indeed, generally you men report such things of yourselves, one does not know how or whom to believe; and it is come to that pass, we dare not take your words, no more than your tailors,[40] without some staid servant of yours be bound with you. But I have so strong a faith in your honour, dear, dear, noble sir, that I'd forfeit mine for yours, at any time, dear sir.

HORN. No, madam, you should not need to forfeit it for me; I have given you security already to save you harmless, my late reputation being so well known in the world, madam.

LADY FID. But if upon any future falling-out, or upon a suspicion of

---

[39]*by your conversation* i.e. by association with you.

[40]*no more . . . tailors* i.e. no more than your tailors can take your word, with reference to receiving payment.

my taking the trust out of your hands, to employ some other, you yourself should betray your trust, dear sir. I mean, if you'll give me leave to speak obscenely,[41] you might tell, dear sir.

HORN. If I did, nobody would believe me. The reputation of impotency is as hardly recovered again in the world as that of cowardice, dear madam.

LADY FID. Nay then, as one may say, you may do your worst, dear, dear sir.

SIR JASP. Come, is your ladyship reconciled to him yet? Have you agreed on matters? – For I must be gone to Whitehall.

LADY FID. Why, indeed, Sir Jasper, Master Horner is a thousand, thousand times a better man than I thought him. Cousin Squeamish, sister Dainty, I can name him now. Truly, not long ago, you know, I thought his very name obscenity, and I would as soon have lain with him as have named him.

SIR JASP. Very likely, poor madam.

MRS DAIN. I believe it.

MRS SQUEAM. No doubt on't.

SIR JASP. Well, well, that your ladyship is as virtuous as any she, I know, and him all the town knows – he, he, he! Therefore, now you like him, get you gone to your business together; go, go to your business, I say, pleasure, whilst I go to my pleasure, business.

LADY FID. Come then, dear gallant.

HORN. Come away, my dearest mistress.

SIR JASP. So, so; why, 'tis as I'd have it. *Exit*

HORN. And as I'd have it.

LADY FID. Who for his business from his wife will run
       Takes the best care to have her business done. *Exeunt*

[41] *obscenely* openly.

Act Three

SCENE ONE

[PINCHWIFE'S *lodgings*]

Enter ALITHEA *and* MRS PINCHWIFE

ALITH. Sister, what ails you? You are grown melancholy.

MRS PINCH. Would it not make anyone melancholy to see you go every day fluttering about abroad, whilst I must stay at home like a poor, lonely, sullen bird in a cage?

ALITH. Ay, sister; but you came young and just from the nest to your cage, so that I thought you liked it and could be as cheerful in't as others that took their flight themselves early, and are hopping abroad in the open air.

MRS PINCH. Nay, I confess I was quiet enough till my husband told me what pure[1] lives the London ladies live abroad, with their dancing, meetings, and junketings, and dressed every day in their best gowns; and, I warrant you, play at nine-pins every day of the week, so they do.

Enter PINCHWIFE

PINCH. Come, what's here to do? You are putting the town-pleasures in her head and setting her a-longing.

ALITH. Yes, after nine-pins. You suffer none to give her those longings you mean but yourself.

PINCH. I tell her of the vanities of the town like a confessor.

ALITH. A confessor! Just such a confessor as he that, by forbidding a silly[2] ostler to grease the horse's teeth,[3] taught him to do't.

PINCH. Come, Mrs Flippant, good precepts are lost when bad examples are still before us: the liberty you take abroad makes her hanker after it, and out of humour at home. Poor wretch, she desired not to come to London; I would bring her.

ALITH. Very well.

PINCH. She has been this week in town, and never desired till this afternoon to go abroad.

[1] *pure* splendid.
[2] *silly* ignorant.
[3] *grease the horse's teeth* a variation of the ostlers' trick of putting grease on a horse's hay, so that the animal should eat less.

ALITH.   Was she not at a play yesterday?

PINCH.   Yes, but she ne'er asked me; I was myself the cause of her going.

ALITH.   Then if she ask you again, you are the cause of her asking, and not my example.

PINCH.   Well, tomorrow night I shall be rid of you; and the next day, before 'tis light, she and I'll be rid of the town and my dreadful apprehensions. – Come, be not melancholy, for thou shalt go into the country after tomorrow, dearest.

ALITH.   Great comfort!

MRS PINCH.   Pish! What d'ye tell me of the country for?

PINCH.   How's this? What, pish at the country?

MRS PINCH.   Let me alone; I am not well.

PINCH.   Oh, if that be all – What ails my dearest?

MRS PINCH.   Truly, I don't know, but I have not been well since you told me there was a gallant at the play in love with me.

PINCH.   Ha!

ALITH.   That's by my example too!

PINCH.   Nay, if you are not well, but are so concerned because a lewd fellow chanced to lie and say he liked you, you'll make me sick too.

MRS PINCH.   Of what sickness?

PINCH.   Oh, of that which is worse than the plague, jealousy.

MRS PINCH.   Pish, you jeer! I'm sure there's no such disease in our receipt-book⁴ at home.

PINCH.   No, thou never met'st with it, poor innocent. – (*Aside*) Well, if thou cuckold me, 'twill be my own fault; for cuckolds and bastards are generally makers of their own fortune.

MRS PINCH.   Well, but pray, bud, let's go to a play tonight.

PINCH.   'Tis just done; she comes from it.⁵ But why are you so eager to see a play?

MRS PINCH.   Faith, dear, not that I care one pin for their talk there; but I like to look upon the player-men, and would see, if I could, the gallant you say loves me; that's all, dear bud.

PINCH.   Is that all, dear bud?

ALITH.   This proceeds from my example!

MRS PINCH.   But if the play be done, let's go abroad, however, dear bud.

PINCH.   Come, have a little patience and thou shalt go into the country on Friday.

⁴*receipt-book* a housewife's handbook.

⁵*'Tis . . . it* i.e. the day's performance has concluded; she has missed the opportunity.

MRS PINCH. Therefore I would see first some sights to tell my neighbours of. Nay, I will go abroad, that's once.[6]

ALITH. I'm the cause of this desire too!

PINCH. But now I think on't, who was the cause of Horner's coming to my lodgings today? That was you.

ALITH. No, you, because you would not let him see your handsome wife out of your lodging.

MRS PINCH. Why, O Lord! Did the gentleman come hither to see me indeed?

PINCH. No, no. – You are not the cause of that damned question too, Mistress Alithea? – (*Aside*) Well, she's in the right of it. He is in love with my wife and comes after her – 'tis so – but I'll nip his love in the bud, lest he should follow us into the country, and break his chariot-wheel near our house, on purpose for an excuse to come to't. But I think I know the town.

MRS PINCH. Come, pray, bud, let's go abroad before 'tis late; for I will go, that's flat and plain.

PINCH. (*Aside*) So! The obstinacy already of the town-wife; and I must, whilst she's here, humour her like one. – [*Aloud*] Sister, how shall we do, that she may not be seen or known?

ALITH. Let her put on her mask.

PINCH. Pshaw, a mask makes people but the more inquisitive, and is as ridiculous a disguise as a stage-beard: her shape, stature, habit will be known, and if we should meet with Horner, he would be sure to take acquaintance with us, must wish her joy, kiss her, talk to her, leer upon her, and the devil and all. No, I'll not use[7] her to a mask, 'tis dangerous; for masks have made more cuckolds than the best faces that ever were known.

ALITH. How will you do then?

MRS PINCH. Nay, shall we go? The Exchange will be shut and I have a mind to see that.

PINCH. So – I have it: I'll dress her up in the suit we are to carry down to her brother, little Sir James. Nay, I understand the town-tricks. Come, let's go dress her. A mask? No. A woman masked, like a covered dish, gives a man curiosity and appetite, when, it may be, uncovered, 'twould turn his stomach. No, no.

ALITH. Indeed, your comparison is something a greasy[8] one; but I had a gentle gallant used to say, a beauty masked, like the sun in eclipse, gathers together more gazers than if it shined out. *Exeunt*

---

[6]*once* once for all.
[7]*use* accustom.
[8]*greasy* unpleasant.

[SCENE TWO]

The scene changes to the New Exchange

Enter HORNER, HARCOURT, *and* DORILANT

DOR. Engaged to women, and not sup with us!

HORN. Ay, a pox on 'em all!

HAR. You were much a more reasonable man in the morning, and had as noble resolutions against 'em as a widower of a week's liberty.

DOR. Did I ever think to see you keep company with women in vain?

HORN. In vain? No. 'Tis, since I can't love 'em, to be revenged on 'em.

HAR. Now your sting is gone, you looked in the box, amongst all those women, like a drone in the hive: all upon you, shoved and ill-used by 'em all, and thrust from one side to t'other.

DOR. Yet he must be buzzing amongst 'em still, like other old, beetle-headed, liquorish[9] drones. Avoid 'em and hate 'em, as they hate you.

HORN. Because I do hate 'em, and would hate 'em yet more, I'll frequent 'em. You may see by marriage, nothing makes a man hate a woman more than her constant conversation.[10] In short, I'll converse with 'em, as you do with rich fools, to laugh at 'em and use 'em ill.

DOR. But I would no more sup with women, unless I could lie with 'em, than sup with a rich coxcomb, unless I could cheat him.

HORN. Yes, I have known thee sup with a fool for his drinking; if he could set out your hand[11] that way only, you were satisfied, and if he were a wine-swallowing mouth, 'twas enough.

HAR. Yes, a man drinks often with a fool, as he tosses with a marker,[12] only to keep his hand in ure.[13] But do the ladies drink?

HORN. Yes, sir; and I shall have the pleasure at least of laying 'em flat with a bottle, and bring as much scandal that way upon 'em as formerly t'other.

HAR. Perhaps you may prove as weak a brother amongst 'em that way as t'other.

DOR. Foh, drinking with women is as unnatural as scolding with 'em. But 'tis a pleasure of decayed fornicators, and the basest way of quenching love.

[9]*liquorish* lecherous.
[10]*conversation* company.
[11]*set out your hand* gratify you.
[12]*tosses . . . marker* throws dice with a scorekeeper.
[13]*ure* practice.

HAR.　Nay, 'tis drowning love, instead of quenching it. But leave us for civil women too!

DOR.　Ay, when he can't be the better for 'em. We hardly pardon a man that leaves his friend for a wench, and that's a pretty lawful call.

HORN.　Faith, I would not leave you for 'em, if they would not drink.

DOR.　Who would disappoint his company at Lewis's[14] for a gossiping?

HAR.　Foh! Wine and women, good apart, together as nauseous as sack and sugar. But hark you, sir, before you go, a little of your advice; an old maimed general, when unfit for action, is fittest for counsel. I have other designs upon women than eating and drinking with them; I am in love with Sparkish's mistress, whom he is to marry tomorrow; now how shall I get her?

　　Enter SPARKISH, *looking about*

HORN.　Why, here comes one will help you to her.

HAR.　He? He, I tell you, is my rival, and will hinder my love.

HORN.　No; a foolish rival and a jealous husband assist their rivals' designs; for they are sure to make their women hate them, which is the first step to their love for another man.

HAR.　But I cannot come near his mistress but in his company.

HORN.　Still the better for you; for fools are most easily cheated when they themselves are accessories; and he is to be bubbled of his mistress as of his money, the common mistress, by keeping him company.

SPARK.　Who is that that is to be bubbled? Faith, let me snack;[15] I han't met with a bubble since Christmas. Gad, I think bubbles are like their brother woodcocks,[16] go out with the cold weather.

HAR.　(*Apart to* HORNER) A pox! He did not hear all, I hope.

SPARK.　Come, you bubbling rogues you, where do we sup? – Oh, Harcourt, my mistress tells me you have been making fierce love to her all the play long! Ha, ha! – But I –

HAR.　I make love to her!

SPARK.　Nay, I forgive thee, for I think I know thee, and I know her; but I am sure I know myself.

HAR.　Did she tell you so? I see all women are like these of the Exchange; who, to enhance the price of their commodities, report to their fond[17] customers offers which were never made 'em.

---

[14]*Lewis's* a London eating house.
[15]*snack* share.
[16]*woodcocks* proverbially simple birds.
[17]*fond* credulous.

HORN.   Ay, women are as apt to tell[18] before the intrigue, as men after it, and so show themselves the vainer sex. But hast thou a mistress, Sparkish? 'Tis as hard for me to believe it as that thou ever hadst a bubble, as you bragged just now.

SPARK.   Oh, your servant, sir; are you at your raillery, sir? But we were some of us beforehand with you today at the play. The wits were something bold with you, sir; did you not hear us laugh?

HORN.   Yes, but I thought you had gone to plays to laugh at the poet's wit, not at your own.

SPARK.   Your servant, sir; no, I thank you. Gad, I go to a play as to a country treat: I carry my own wine to one, and my own wit to t'other, or else I'm sure I should not be merry at either. And the reason why we are so often louder than the players is because we think we speak more wit, and so become the poet's rivals in his audience. For to tell you the truth, we hate the silly rogues; nay, so much that we find fault even with their bawdy upon the stage, whilst we talk nothing else in the pit as loud.

HORN.   But why shouldst thou hate the silly poets? Thou has too much wit to be one, and they, like whores, are only hated by each other; and thou dost scorn writing, I'm sure.

SPARK.   Yes, I'd have you to know I scorn writing; but women, women, that make men do all foolish things, make 'em write songs too. Everybody does it. 'Tis even as common with lovers as playing with fans; and you can no more help rhyming to your Phyllis[19] than drinking to your Phyllis.

HAR.   Nay, poetry in love is no more to be avoided than jealousy.

DOR.   But the poets damned your songs, did they?

SPARK.   Damn the poets! They turned 'em into burlesque, as they call it. That burlesque is a hocus-pocus trick they have got, which, by virtue of Hictius Doctius, topsy turvy,[20] they make a wise and witty man in the world a fool upon the stage you know not how; and 'tis therefore I hate 'em too, for I know not but it may be my own case, for they'll put a man into a play for looking asquint. Their predecessors were contented to make serving-men only their stage-fools, but these rogues must have gentlemen, with a pox to 'em, nay, knights; and, indeed, you shall hardly see a fool upon the stage but he's a knight. And to tell you the truth, they have kept me these six years from being a knight in earnest, for fear of being knighted in a play and dubbed a fool.

DOR.   Blame 'em not; they must follow their copy, the age.

[18]*tell* tattle.
[19]*Phyllis* conventional name for a lover in pastoral poetry and drinking songs.
[20]*Hictius . . . turvy* jugglers' jargon.

HAR.   But why shouldst thou be afraid of being in a play, who expose
yourself every day in the playhouses and as public places?

HOR.   'Tis but being on the stage, instead of standing on a bench in the
pit.

DOR.   Don't you give money to painters to draw you like?[21] And are
you afraid of your pictures at length[22] in a playhouse, where all your
mistresses may see you?

SPARK.   A pox! Painters don't draw the smallpox or pimples in one's
face. Come, damn all your silly authors whatever, all books and
booksellers, by the world; and all readers, courteous or uncourteous!

HAR.   But who comes here, Sparkish?

> *Enter* PINCHWIFE *and* MRS PINCHWIFE *in man's clothes,*
> ALITHEA, LUCY, *her maid* [*and* CLASP]

SPARK.   Oh, hide me! There's my mistress too.

> SPARKISH *hides himself behind* HARCOURT

HAR.   She sees you.

SPARK.   But I will not see her: 'tis time to go to Whitehall, and I must
not fail the drawing-room.

HAR.   Pray, first carry me, and reconcile me to her.

SPARK.   Another time. Faith, the king will have supped.

HAR.   Not with the worse stomach for thy absence. Thou art one of
those fools that think their attendance at the king's meals as necessary
as his physicians, when you are more troublesome to him than his
doctors or his dogs.

SPARK.   Pshaw, I know my interest, sir. Prithee hide me.

HORN.   Your servant, Pinchwife. – What, he knows[23] us not!

PINCH.   (*To his* WIFE *aside*) Come along.

MRS PINCH.   Pray, have you any ballads? Give me sixpenny worth.

CLASP.   We have no ballads.

MRS PINCH.   Then give me *Covent Garden Drollery*,[24] and a play or
two – Oh, here's *Tarugo's Wiles*,[25] and *The Slighted Maiden*.[26] I'll
have them.

PINCH.   (*Apart to her*) No; plays are not for your reading. Come along;
will you discover yourself?

HORN.   Who is that pretty youth with him, Sparkish?

[21]*like* accurately.

[22]*at length* at full length.

[23]*knows* acknowledges.

[24]*Covent Garden Drollery* a collection of poems, songs, ballads, etc., London,
1672.

[25]*Tarugo's Wiles* a comedy by Sir Thomas St Serfe, London, 1668.

[26]*The Slighted Maiden* a comedy by Sir Robert Stapleton, London, 1663;
ridiculed in *The Rehearsal* (staged 1671).

SPARK. I believe his wife's brother, because he's something like her;
but I never saw her but once.

HORN. Extremely handsome; I have seen a face like it too. Let us
follow 'em.

  Exeunt PINCHWIFE, MRS PINCHWIFE, ALITHEA, LUCY [*and*
  CLASP]; HORNER *and* DORILANT *following them*

HAR. Come, Sparkish, your mistress saw you and will be angry you
go not to her. Besides, I would fain be reconciled to her, which none
but you can do, dear friend.

SPARK. Well, that's a better reason, dear friend. I would not go near
her now for her's or my own sake, but I can deny you nothing; for
though I have known thee a great while, never go if I do not love thee
as well as a new acquaintance.

HAR. I am obliged to you indeed, dear friend. I would be well with
her only to be well with thee still; for these ties to wives usually
dissolve all ties to friends. I would be contented she should enjoy you
a-nights, but I would have you to myself a-days, as I have had, dear
friend.

SPARK. And thou shalt enjoy me a-days, dear, dear friend, never
stir;[27] and I'll be divorced from her sooner than from thee. Come
along.

HAR. (*Aside*) So, we are hard put to't when we make our rival our
procurer; but neither she nor her brother would let me come near
her now. When all's done, a rival is the best cloak to steal to a
mistress under, without suspicion; and when we have once got to
her as we desire, we throw him off like other cloaks.

            Exit SPARKISH, HARCOURT *following him*
      Re-enter PINCHWIFE *and* MRS PINCHWIFE, *in man's clothes*

PINCH. (*To* ALITHEA, *offstage*) Sister, if you will not go, we must
leave you. – (*Aside*) The fool her gallant and she will muster up all
the young saunterers of this place, and they will leave their dear
sempstresses to follow us. What a swarm of cuckolds and
cuckold-makers are here! – Come, let's be gone, Mistress Margery.

MRS PINCH. Don't you believe that; I han't half my bellyful of sights
yet.

PINCH. Then walk this way.

MRS PINCH. Lord, what a power of brave signs are here! Stay – the
Bull's Head, the Ram's Head, and the Stag's Head,[28] dear.

PINCH. Nay, if every husband's proper sign here were visible, they
would be all alike.

---

²⁷*stir* be upset.
²⁸*Stag's Head* Inns with these names existed in London about 1675. The
'husband's proper sign' is the horns of a cuckold.

MRS PINCH.　What d'ye mean by that, bud?

PINCH.　'Tis no matter, no matter, bud.

MRS PINCH.　Pray tell me; nay, I will know.

PINCH.　They would be all bulls', stags', and rams' heads.

Exeunt PINCHWIFE *and* MRS PINCHWIFE
Re-enter SPARKISH, HARCOURT, ALITHEA *and* LUCY, *at the
other side*

SPARK.　Come, dear madam, for my sake you shall be reconciled to
him.

ALITH.　For your sake I hate him.

HAR.　That's something too cruel, madam, to hate me for his sake.

SPARK.　Ay, indeed, madam, too, too cruel to me, to hate my friend
for my sake.

ALITH.　I hate him because he is your enemy; and you ought to
hate him too, for making love to me, if you love me.

SPARK.　That's a good one! I hate a man for loving you! If he did
love you, 'tis but what he can't help; and 'tis your fault, not his, if
he admires you. I hate a man for being of my opinion! I'll ne'er
do't, by the world.

ALITH.　Is it for your honour or mine, to suffer a man to make love
to me, who am to marry you tomorrow?

SPARK.　Is it for your honour or mine, to have me jealous? That he
makes love to you is a sign you are handsome; and that I am not
jealous is a sign you are virtuous. That, I think, is for your
honour.

ALITH.　But 'tis your honour too I am concerned for.

HAR.　But why, dearest madam, will you be more concerned for his
honour than he is himself? Let his honour alone, for my sake and his.
He, he has no honour —

SPARK.　How's that?

HAR.　But what my dear friend can guard himself.

SPARK.　O ho, that's right again.

HAR.　Your care of his honour argues his neglect of it, which is no
honour to my dear friend here; therefore, once more let his honour
go which way it will, dear madam.

SPARK.　Ay, ay. Were it for my honour to marry a woman whose
virtue I suspected, and could not trust her in a friend's hands?

ALITH.　Are you not afraid to lose me?

HAR.　He afraid to lose you, madam! No, no. You may see how the
most estimable and most glorious creature in the world is valued by
him. Will you not see it?

SPARK.　Right, honest Frank, I have that noble value for her that I
cannot be jealous of her.

ALITH.   You mistake him. He means you care not for me nor who has me.

SPARK.   Lord, madam, I see you are jealous![29] Will you wrest[30] a poor man's meaning from his words?

ALITH.   You astonish me, sir, with your want of jealousy.

SPARK.   And you make me giddy, madam, with your jealousy and fears and virtue and honour. Gad, I see virtue makes a woman as troublesome as a little reading or learning.

ALITH.   Monstrous!

LUCY.   (*Behind*) Well, to see what easy husbands these women of quality can meet with! A poor chambermaid can never have such ladylike luck. Besides, he's thrown away upon her. She'll make no use of her fortune, her blessing; none to[31] a gentleman for a pure cuckold, for it requires good breeding to be a cuckold.

ALITH.   I tell you then plainly, he pursues me to marry me.

SPARK.   Pshaw!

HAR.   Come, madam, you see you strive in vain to make him jealous of me. My dear friend is the kindest creature in the world to me.

SPARK.   Poor fellow!

HAR.   But his kindness only is not enough for me, without your favour. Your good opinion, dear madam, 'tis that must perfect my happiness. Good gentleman, he believes all I say; would you would do so! Jealous of me? I would not wrong him nor you for the world.

SPARK.   Look you there. Hear him, hear him, and do not walk away so.   ALITHEA *walks carelessly*[32] *to and fro*

HAR.   I love you, madam, so –

SPARK.   How's that? Nay, now you begin to go too far indeed.

HAR.   So much, I confess, I say, I love you, that I would not have you miserable and cast yourself away upon so unworthy and inconsiderable a thing as what you see here.
                    Clapping his hand on his breast, points at SPARKISH

SPARK.   No, faith, I believe thou wouldst not. Now his meaning is plain; but I knew before thou wouldst not wrong me nor her.

HAR.   No, no, heavens forbid the glory of her sex should fall so low as into the embraces of such a contemptible wretch, the least of mankind – my friend here. I injure him!   *Embracing* SPARKISH

ALITH.   Very well.

[29]*jealous* vehement.
[30]*wrest* misinterpret.
[31]*none to* there's no one like.
[32]*carelessly* casually.

SPARK.   No, no, dear friend, I knew it. Madam, you see he will rather wrong himself than me, in giving himself such names.

ALITH.   Do not you understand him yet?

SPARK.   Yes; how modestly he speaks of himself, poor fellow!

ALITH.   Methinks he speaks impudently of yourself, since — before yourself too; insomuch that I can no longer suffer his scurrilous abusiveness to you, no more than his love to me.   *Offers to go*

SPARK.   Nay, nay, madam, pray stay. His love to you? Lord, madam, has he not spoke yet plain enough?

ALITH.   Yes, indeed, I should think so.

SPARK.   Well, then, by the world, a man can't speak civilly to a woman now, but presently she says he makes love to her. Nay, madam, you shall stay, with your pardon, since you have not yet understood him, till he has made an *éclaircissement* of his love to you, that is, what kind of love it is. Answer to thy catechism, friend: do you love my mistress here?

HAR.   Yes, I wish she would not doubt it.

SPARK.   But how do you love her?

HAR.   With all my soul.

ALITH.   I thank him; methinks he speaks plain enough now.

SPARK.   (*To* ALITHEA) You are out[33] still. — But with what kind of love, Harcourt?

HAR.   With the best and truest love in the world.

SPARK.   Look you there then, that is with no matrimonial love, I'm sure.

ALITH.   How's that? Do you say matrimonial love is not best?

SPARK.   [*Aside*] Gad, I went too far ere I was aware. — But speak for thyself, Harcourt; you said you would not wrong me nor her.

HAR.   No, no, madam, e'en take him, for heaven's sake.

SPARK.   Look you there, madam.

HAR.   Who should in all justice be yours, he that loves you most.

Claps his hand on his breast

ALITH.   Look you there, Mr Sparkish, who's that?

SPARK.   Who should it be? — Go on, Harcourt.

HAR.   Who loves you more than women titles, or fortune fools.

Points at SPARKISH

SPARK.   Look you there, he means me still, for he points at me.

ALITH.   Ridiculous!

HAR.   Who can only match your faith and constancy in love.

SPARK.   Ay.

33*out* mistaken.

HAR.	Who knows, if it be possible, how to value so much beauty and virtue.

SPARK.	Ay.

HAR.	Whose love can no more be equalled in the world than that heavenly form of yours.

SPARK.	No.

HAR.	Who could no more suffer a rival than your absence, and yet could no more suspect your virtue than his own constancy in his love to you.

SPARK.	No.

HAR.	Who, in fine,[34] loves you better than his eyes, that first made him love you.

SPARK.	Ay. Nay, madam, faith, you shan't go till –

ALITH.	Have a care, lest you make me stay too long.

SPARK.	But till he has saluted you, that I may be assured you are friends, after his honest advice and declaration. Come, pray, madam, be friends with him.

Re-enter PINCHWIFE *and* MRS PINCHWIFE

ALITH.	You must pardon me, sir, that I am not yet so obedient to you.

PINCH.	What, invite your wife to kiss men? Monstrous! Are you not ashamed? I will never forgive you.

SPARK.	Are you not ashamed that I should have more confidence in the chastity of your family than you have? You must not teach me; I am a man of honour, sir, though I am frank[35] and free; I am frank, sir –

PINCH.	Very frank, sir, to share your wife with your friends.

SPARK.	He is an humble, menial[36] friend, such as reconciles the differences of the marriage bed. You know man and wife do not always agree; I design him for that use, therefore would have him well with my wife.

PINCH.	A menial friend! You will get a great many menial friends by showing your wife as you do.

SPARK.	What then? It may be I have a pleasure in't, as I have to show fine clothes at a playhouse the first day, and count money before poor rogues.

PINCH.	He that shows his wife or money will be in danger of having them borrowed sometimes.

SPARK.	I love to be envied, and would not marry a wife that I alone could love; loving alone is as dull as eating alone. Is it not a frank age? And I am a frank person; and to tell you the truth, it may be I love to have rivals in a wife; they make her seem to a man still but as a kept

---

[34]*in fine* in short.
[35]*frank* generous, used ironically here and below.
[36]*menial* domestic.

mistress; and so good night, for I must to Whitehall. —Madam, I hope
you are now reconciled to my friend; and so I wish you a good night,
madam, and sleep if you can, for tomorrow you know I must visit you
early with a canonical gentleman. Good night, dear Harcourt. *Exit*

HAR.   Madam, I hope you will not refuse my visit tomorrow, if it
should be earlier, with a canonical gentleman, than Mr Sparkish's.

PINCH.   This gentlewoman is yet under my care; therefore you must
yet forbear your freedom with her, sir.

Coming between ALITHEA *and* HARCOURT

HAR.   Must, sir?

PINCH.   Yes, sir, she is my sister.

HAR.   'Tis well she is, sir, for I must be her servant, sir. Madam, —

PINCH.   Come away, sister; we had been gone, if it had not been for
you, and so avoided these lewd rake-hells, who seem to haunt us.

Re-enter HORNER *and* DORILANT

HORN.   How now, Pinchwife!

PINCH.   Your servant.

HORN.   What, I see a little time in the country makes a man turn wild
and unsociable, and only fit to converse with his horses, dogs, and his
herds.

PINCH.   I have business, sir, and must mind it. Your business is
pleasure; therefore you and I must go different ways.

HORN.   Well, you may go on, but this pretty young gentleman —

Takes hold of MRS PINCHWIFE

HAR.   The lady —

DOR.   And the maid —

HORN.   Shall stay with us, for I suppose their business is the same with
ours, pleasure.

PINCH.   (*Aside*) 'Sdeath, he knows her, she carries it so sillily! Yet if he
does not, I should be more silly to discover it first.

ALITH.   Pray, let us go, sir.

PINCH.   Come, come —

HORN.   (*To* MRS PINCHWIFE) Had you not rather stay with us? —
Prithee, Pinchwife, who is this pretty young gentleman?

PINCH.   One to whom I'm a guardian. — (*Aside*) I wish I could keep her
out of your hands.

HORN.   Who is he? I never saw anything so pretty in all my life.

PINCH.   Pshaw, do not look upon him so much; he's a poor bashful
youth, you'll put him out of countenance. — Come away, brother.

Offers to take her away

HORN.   Oh, your brother!

PINCH.   Yes, my wife's brother. — Come, come, she'll stay supper for
us.

HORN.   I thought so, for he is very like her I saw you at the play with, whom I told you I was in love with.

MRS PINCH.   (*Aside*) Oh, Jeminy![37] Is this he that was in love with me? I am glad on't, I vow, for he's a curious[38] fine gentleman, and I love him already, too. – (*To* PINCHWIFE) Is this he, bud?

PINCH.   (*To his* WIFE) Come away, come away.

HORN.   Why, what haste are you in? Why won't you let me talk with him?

PINCH.   Because you'll debauch him; he's yet young and innocent, and I would not have him debauched for anything in the world – (*Aside*) How she gazes on him! The devil!

HORN.   Harcourt, Dorilant, look you here; this is the likeness of that dowdy he told us of, his wife; did you ever see a lovelier creature? The rogue has reason to be jealous of his wife, since she is like him, for she would make all that see her in love with her.

HAR.   And, as I remember now, she is as like him here as can be.

DOR.   She is indeed very pretty, if she be like him.

HORN.   Very pretty? A very pretty commendation! She is a glorious creature, beautiful beyond all things I ever beheld.

PINCH.   So, so.

HAR.   More beautiful than a poet's first mistress of imagination.

HORN.   Or another man's last mistress of flesh and blood.

MRS PINCH.   Nay, nor you jeer, sir; pray don't jeer me.

PINCH.   Come, come. – (*Aside*) By heavens, she'll discover herself!

HORN.   I speak of your sister, sir.

PINCH.   Ay, but saying she was handsome, if like him, made him blush. – (*Aside*) I am upon a rack!

HORN.   Methinks he is so handsome he should not be a man.

PINCH.   (*Aside*) Oh, there 'tis out! He has discovered her! I am not able to suffer any longer. – (*To his* WIFE) Come, come away, I say.

HORN.   Nay, by your leave, sir, he shall not go yet. – (*Aside to them*) Harcourt, Dorilant, let us torment this jealous rogue a little.

HAR., DOR.   How?

HORN.   I'll show you.

PINCH.   Come, pray let him go. I cannot stay fooling any longer. I tell you his sister stays supper for us.

HORN.   Does she? Come then, we'll all go to sup with her and thee.

PINCH.   No, now I think on't, having stayed so long for us, I warrant she's gone to bed. – (*Aside*) I wish she and I were well out of their hands. – [*To his* WIFE] Come, I must rise early tomorrow, come.

---

[37] *Jeminy* a commonplace asseveration, from Gemini, the twins, Castor and Pollox, of the zodiac.

[38] *curious* remarkably.

HORN.   Well then, if she be gone to bed, I wish her and you a good
  night. But pray, young gentleman, present my humble service to her.
MRS PINCH.   Thank you heartily, sir.
PINCH.   (*Aside*) 'Sdeath, she will discover herself yet in spite of me. –
  [*Aloud*] He is something more civil to you, for your kindness to his
  sister, than I am, it seems.
HORN.   Tell her, dear, sweet little gentleman, for all your brother
  there, that you have revived the love I had for her at first sight in the
  playhouse.
MRS PINCH.   But did you love her indeed, and indeed?
PINCH.   (*Aside*) So, so – [*Aloud*] Away, I say.
HORN.   Nay, stay. Yes, indeed, and indeed; pray do you tell her so,
  and give her this kiss from me.   *Kisses her*
PINCH.   (*Aside*) Oh heavens, what do I suffer? Now 'tis too plain he
  knows her, and yet –
HORN.   And this, and this –   *Kisses her again*
MRS PINCH.   What do you kiss me for? I am no woman.
PINCH.   (*Aside*) So; there, 'tis out. – [*Aloud*] Come, I cannot, nor will
  stay any longer.
HORN.   Nay, they shall send your lady a kiss too. Here, Harcourt,
  Dorilant, will you not?   *They kiss her*
PINCH.   (*Aside*) How, do I suffer this? Was I not accusing another just
  now for this rascally patience, in permitting his wife to be kissed
  before his face? Ten thousand ulcers gnaw away their lips. – [*Aloud*]
  Come, come.
HORN.   Good night, dear little gentleman; madam, good night;
  farewell, Pinchwife. – (*Apart to* HARCOURT *and* DORILANT) Did
  not I tell you I would raise his jealous gall?
                        Exeunt HORNER, HARCOURT *and* DORILANT
PINCH.   So, they are gone at last; stay, let me see first if the coach be at
  this door.   *Exit*
     Re-enter HORNER, HARCOURT *and* DORILANT
HORN.   What, not gone yet? Will you be sure to do as I desired you,
  sweet sir?
MRS PINCH.   Sweet sir, but what will you give me then?
HORN.   Anything. Come away into the next walk.
                Exit HORNER, *haling*[39] *away* MRS PINCHWIFE
ALITH.   Hold, hold! What d'ye do?
LUCY.   Stay, stay, hold!
HAR.   Hold, madam, hold. Let him present him; [40] he'll come
  presently. Nay, I will never let you go till you answer my question.[41]

  [39]*haling* pulling.
  [40]*present him* give him a gift.
  [41]*question* i.e. his proposition of marriage.

LUCY.   For God's sake, sir, I must follow 'em.

ALITHEA *and* LUCY, *struggling with* HARCOURT *and* DORILANT

DOR.   No, I have something to present you with too; you shan't follow them.

Re-enter PINCHWIFE

PINCH.   Where? How? What's become of —? gone! Whither?

LUCY.   He's only gone with the gentleman, who will give him something, an't please your worship.

PINCH.   Something! Give him something, with a pox! Where are they?

ALITH.   In the next walk only, brother.

PINCH.   Only, only! Where, where?

Exit and returns presently, then goes out again

HAR.   What's the matter with him? Why so much concerned? But, dearest madam, —

ALITH.   Pray let me go, sir; I have said and suffered enough already.

HAR.   Then you will not look upon nor pity my sufferings?

ALITH.   To look upon 'em, when I cannot help 'em, were cruelty not pity; therefore, I will never see you more.

HAR.   Let me then, madam, have my privilege of a banished lover, complaining or railing, and giving you but a farewell reason why, if you cannot condescend to marry me, you should not take that wretch, my rival.

ALITH.   He only, not you, since my honour is engaged so far to him, can give me a reason why I should not marry him; but if he be true, and what I think him to me, I must be so to him. Your servant, sir.

HAR.   Have women only constancy when 'tis a vice, and are, like fortune, only true to fools?

DOR.   (*To* LUCY, *who struggles to get from him*) Thou shalt not stir, thou robust creature; you see I can deal with you; therefore you should stay the rather, and be kind.

Re-enter PINCHWIFE

PINCH.   Gone, gone, not to be found! Quite gone! Ten thousand plagues go with 'em! Which way went they?

ALITH.   But into t'other walk, brother.

LUCY.   Their business will be done presently sure, an't please your worship; it can't be long in doing, I'm sure on't.

ALITH.   Are they not there?

PINCH.   No, you know where they are, you infamous wretch, eternal shame of your family, which you do not dishonour enough yourself you think, but you must help her to do it too, thou legion of bawds!

ALITH.   Good brother, —

PINCH.   Damned, damned sister!

ALITH.   Look you here, she's coming.

Re-enter MRS PINCHWIFE *in man's clothes, running, with her hat under her arm full of oranges and dried fruit,* HORNER *following*

MRS PINCH.　O dear bud, look you here what I have got, see!

PINCH.　(*Aside, rubbing his forehead*) And what I have got here[42] too, which you can't see.

MRS PINCH.　The fine gentleman has given me better things yet.

PINCH.　Has he so? – (*Aside*) Out of breath and coloured! I must hold yet.

HORN.　I have only given your little brother an orange, sir.

PINCH.　(*To* HORNER) Thank you, sir. – (*Aside*) You have only squeezed my orange, I suppose, and given it me again; yet I must have a City patience.[43] – (*To his* WIFE) Come, come away.

MRS PINCH.　Stay till I have put up my fine things, bud.

Enter SIR JASPER FIDGET

SIR JASP.　O Master Horner, come, come, the ladies stay for you; your mistress, my wife, wonders you make not more haste to her.

HORN.　I have stayed this half hour for you here, and 'tis your fault I am not now with your wife.

SIR JASP.　But, pray, don't let her know so much; the truth on't is, I was advancing a certain project to his majesty about – I'll tell you.

HORN.　No, let's go, and hear it at your house. Good night, sweet little gentleman. One kiss more; you'll remember me now, I hope.

Kisses her

DOR.　What, Sir Jasper, will you separate friends? He promised to sup with us, and if you take him to your house, you'll be in danger of our company too.

SIR JASP.　Alas, gentlemen, my house is not fit for you; there are none but civil[44] women there, which are not for your turn. He, you know, can bear with the society of civil women now, ha, ha, ha! Besides, he's one of my family; he's – he, he, he!

DOR.　What is he?

SIR JASP.　Faith, my eunuch, since you'll have it. He, he, he!

Exeunt SIR JASPER FIDGET *and* HORNER

DOR.　I rather wish thou wert his or my cuckold. Harcourt, what a good cuckold is lost there for want of a man to make him one! Thee and I cannot have Horner's privilege, who can make use of it.

HAR.　Ay, to poor Horner 'tis like coming to an estate at threescore, when a man can't be the better for't.

---

[42]*got here* the horns of a cuckold.

[43]*City patience* the self-restraint of City merchants, who were reputed to be constantly cuckolded by young gallants.

[44]*civil* respectable.

PINCH.   Come.

MRS PINCH.   Presently, bud.

DOR.   Come, let us go too. – (*To* ALITHEA) Madam, your servant. – (*To* Lucy) Good night, strapper.[45]

HAR.   Madam, though you will not let me have a good day or night, I wish you one, but dare not name the other half of my wish.

ALITH.   Good night, sir, forever.

MRS PINCH.   I don't know where to put this here, dear bud. You shall eat it; nay, you shall have part of the fine gentleman's good things, or treat, as you call it, when we come home.

PINCH.   Indeed, I deserve it, since I furnished the best part of it.

Strikes away the orange

> The gallant treats, presents, and gives the ball,
> But 'tis the absent cuckold pays for all.   *Exeunt*

[45]*strapper* a robust person.

Act Four

SCENE ONE

PINCHWIFE'S *house in the morning*

Enter ALITHEA *dressed in new clothes, and* LUCY

LUCY. Well, madam, now have I dressed you, and set you out with so many ornaments, and spent upon you ounces of essence and pulvilio,[1] and all this for no other purpose but as people adorn and perfume a corpse for a stinking second-hand grave; such, or as bad, I think Master Sparkish's bed.

ALITH. Hold your peace.

LUCY. Nay, madam, I will ask you the reason why you would banish poor Master Harcourt forever from your sight; how could you be so hardhearted?

ALITH. 'Twas because I was not hardhearted.

LUCY. No, no; 'twas stark love and kindness, I warrant.

ALITH. It was so; I would see him no more because I love him.

LUCY. Hey day, a very pretty reason!

ALITH. You do not understand me.

LUCY. I wish you may yourself.

ALITH. I was engaged to marry, you see, another man, whom my justice will not suffer me to deceive or injure.

LUCY. Can there be a greater cheat or wrong done to a man than to give him your person without your heart? I should make a conscience of it.

ALITH. I'll retrieve it for him after I am married a while.

LUCY. The woman that marries to love better will be as much mistaken as the wencher that marries to live better. No, madam, marrying to increase love is like gaming to become rich; alas, you only lose what little stock you had before.

ALITH. I find by your rhetoric you have been bribed to betray me.

LUCY. Only by his merit, that has bribed your heart, you see, against your word and rigid honour. But what a devil is this honour? 'Tis sure a disease in the head, like the megrim[2] or falling sickness,[3] that

[1] *pulvilio* perfumed powder.
[2] *megrim* migraine.
[3] *falling sickness* epilepsy.

always hurries people away to do themselves mischief. Men lose
their lives by it; women, what's dearer to 'em, their love, the life of
life.

ALITH.   Come, pray talk no more of honour, nor Master Harcourt; I
wish the other would come, to secure my fidelity to him and his right
in me.

LUCY.   You will marry him then?

ALITH.   Certainly. I have given him already my word, and will my
hand too, to make it good, when he comes.

LUCY.   Well, I wish I may never stick pin more, if he be not an arrant
natural[4] to t'other fine gentleman.

ALITH.   I own he wants the wit of Harcourt, which I will dispense
withal for another want he has, which is want of jealousy, which
men of wit seldom want.

LUCY.   Lord, madam, what should you do with a fool to your
husband? You intend to be honest, don't you? Then that husbandly
virtue, credulity, is thrown away upon you.

ALITH.   He only that could suspect my virtue should have cause to do
it; 'tis Sparkish's confidence in my truth that obliges me to be so
faithful to him.

LUCY.   You are not sure his opinion may last.

ALITH.   I am satisfied 'tis impossible for him to be jealous after the
proofs I have had of him. Jealousy in a husband – heaven defend me
from it! It begets a thousand plagues to a poor woman: the loss of
her honour, her quiet, and her –

LUCY.   And her pleasure.

ALITH.   What d'ye mean, impertinent?

LUCY.   Liberty is a great pleasure, madam.

ALITH.   I say, loss of her honour, her quiet, nay, her life sometimes;
and what's as bad almost, the loss of this town; that is, she is sent
into the country,[5] which is the last ill usage of a husband to a wife, I
think.

LUCY.   (*Aside*) Oh, does the wind lie there? – [*Aloud*] Then of
necessity, madam, you think a man must carry his wife into the
country, if he be wise. The country is as terrible, I find, to our young
English ladies, as a monastery[6] to those abroad; and on my virginity,
I think they would rather marry a London jailer than a high sheriff of
a county, since neither can stir from his employment. Formerly
women of wit married fools for a great estate, a fine seat, or the like;
but now 'tis for a pretty seat only in Lincoln's Inn Fields, St James's

---

[4]*natural* simpleton.
[5]*country* Compare *The Man of Mode*, III, i, p. 146 and v, ii, p. 200
[6]*monastery* i.e. convent.

Fields,[7] or the Pall Mall.

Enter SPARKISH, *and* HARCOURT *dressed like a parson*

SPARK. Madam, your humble servant, a happy day to you, and to us all.

HAR. Amen.

ALITH. Who have we here?

SPARK. My chaplain, faith – O madam, poor Harcourt remembers his humble service to you; and, in obedience to your last commands, refrains coming into your sight.

ALITH. Is not that he?

SPARK. No, fie, no; but to show that he ne'er intended to hinder our match, has sent his brother here to join our hands. When I get me a wife, I must get her a chaplain, according to the custom; this is his brother, and my chaplain.

ALITH. His brother?

LUCY. (*Aside*) And your chaplain, to preach in your pulpit[8] then –

ALITH. His brother?

SPARK. Nay, I knew you would not believe it. – I told you, sir, she would take you for your brother Frank.

ALITH. Believe it?

LUCY. (*Aside*) His brother! Ha, ha, he! He has a trick left still, it seems.

SPARK. Come, my dearest, pray let us go to church before the canonical hour[9] is past.

ALITH. For shame, you are abused still.

SPARK. By the world, 'tis strange now you are so incredulous.

ALITH. 'Tis strange you are so credulous.

SPARK. Dearest of my life, hear me. I tell you this is Ned Harcourt of Cambridge, by the world; you see he has a sneaking college look. 'Tis true he's something like his brother Frank; and they differ from each other no more than in their age, for they were twins.

LUCY. Ha, ha, he!

ALITH. Your servant, sir; I cannot be so deceived, though you are. But come, let's hear, how do you know what you affirm so confidently?

SPARK. Why, I'll tell you all. Frank Harcourt coming to me this morning to wish me joy and present his service to you, I asked him if he could help me to a parson. Whereupon he told me he had a brother in town who was in orders; and he went straight away and sent him you see there to me.

[7]*St James's Fields* an open area around what is now St James's Square.

[8]*pulpit* to cuckold you. See *The Man of Mode*, v, ii, p. 195.

[9]*canonical hour* when marriages might then be legally performed, between 8.00 a.m. and noon.

ALITH. Yes, Frank goes and puts on a black coat, then tells you he is Ned; that's all you have for't.

SPARK. Pshaw, pshaw! I tell you, by the same token, the midwife put her garter about Frank's neck, to know 'em asunder, they were so like.

ALITH. Frank tells you this too?

SPARK. Ay, and Ned there too; nay, they are both in a story.

ALITH. So, so; very foolish.

SPARK. Lord, if you won't believe one, you had best try him by your chambermaid there; for chambermaids must needs know chaplains from other men, they are so used to 'em.

LUCY. Let's see: nay, I'll be sworn he has the canonical smirk, and the filthy, clammy palm of a chaplain.

ALITH. Well, most reverend doctor, pray let us make an end of this fooling.

HAR. With all my soul, divine, heavenly creature, when you please.

ALITH. He speaks like a chaplain indeed.

SPARK. Why, was there not 'soul', 'divine', 'heavenly', in what he said?

ALITH. Once more, most impertinent black-coat, cease your persecution, and let us have a conclusion to this ridiculous love.

HAR. (*Aside*) I had forgot; I must suit my style to my coat, or I wear it in vain.

ALITH. I have no more patience left; let us make once an end of this troublesome love, I say.

HAR. So be it, seraphic lady, when your honour shall think it meet and convenient so to do.[10]

SPARK. Gad, I'm sure none but a chaplain could speak so, I think.

ALITH. Let me tell you, sir, this dull trick will not serve your turn; though you delay our marriage, you shall not hinder it.

HAR. Far be it from me, munificent patroness, to delay your marriage; I desire nothing more than to marry you presently, which I might do, if you yourself would; for my noble, good-natured, and thrice-generous patron here would not hinder it.

SPARK. No, poor man, not I, faith.

HAR. And now, madam, let me tell you plainly, nobody else shall marry you. By heavens, I'll die first, for I'm sure I should die[11] after it.

LUCY. [*Aside*] How his love has made him forget his function,[12] as I have seen it in real parsons!

[10]*it . . . to* These words are, with a slight variation, from the communion service, *The Book of Common Prayer*.

[11]*die* engage in sexual intercourse.

[12]*function* professional role or duty.

ALITH. That was spoken like a chaplain too! Now you understand him, I hope.

SPARK. Poor man, he takes it heinously to be refused. I can't blame him; 'tis putting an indignity upon him not to be suffered; but you'll pardon me, madam, it shan't be; he shall marry us. Come away, pray, madam.

LUCY. Ha, ha, he! More ado! 'Tis late.

ALITH. Invincible stupidity! I tell you, he would marry me as your rival, not as your chaplain.

SPARK. Come, come, madam.   *Pulling her away*

LUCY. I pray, madam, do not refuse this reverend divine the honour and satisfaction of marrying you, for I dare say he has set his heart upon't, good doctor.

ALITH. What can you hope or design by this?

HAR. [*Aside*] I could answer her, a reprieve for a day only often revokes a hasty doom. At worst, if she will not take mercy on me and let me marry her, I have at least the lover's second pleasure, hindering my rival's enjoyment, though but for a time.

SPARK. Come, madam, 'tis e'en twelve o'clock, and my mother charged me never to be married out of the canonical hours. Come, come. Lord, here's such a deal of modesty, I warrant, the first day.

LUCY. Yes, an't please your worship, married women show all their modesty the first day, because married men show all their love the first day.   *Exeunt*

SCENE TWO

The scene changes to a bedchamber [in PINCHWIFE'S *house], where appear* PINCHWIFE *and* MRS PINCHWIFE

PINCH. Come, tell me, I say.

MRS PINCH. Lord, han't I told it an hundred times over?

PINCH. (*Aside*) I would try, if in the repetition of the ungrateful[13] tale, I could find her altering it in the least circumstance; for if her story be false, she is so too. – [*Aloud*] Come, how was't, baggage?

MRS PINCH. Lord, what pleasure you take to hear it, sure!

PINCH. No, you take more in telling it I find; but speak, how was't?

MRS PINCH. He carried me up into the house next to the Exchange.

PINCH. So, and you two were only in the room!

MRS PINCH. Yes, for he sent away a youth that was there, for some

---

[13]*ungrateful* unpleasant.

dried fruit and China oranges.[14]

PINCH.   Did he so? Damn him for it – and for –

MRS PINCH.   But presently came up the gentlewoman of the house.

PINCH.   Oh, 'twas well she did; but what did he do whilst the fruit came?

MRS PINCH.   He kissed me an hundred times, and told me he fancied he kissed my fine sister, meaning me, you know, whom he said he loved with all his soul, and bid me be sure to tell her so, and to desire her to be at her window by eleven of the clock this morning, and he would walk under it at that time.

PINCH.   (*Aside*) And he was as good as his word, very punctual. A pox reward him for't!

MRS PINCH.   Well, and he said if you were not within, he would come to her, meaning me, you know, bud, still.

PINCH.   [*Aside*] So – he knew her certainly; but for this confession, I am obliged to her simplicity. – [*Aloud*] But what, you stood very still when he kissed you?

MRS PINCH.   Yes, I warrant you. Would you have had me discovered myself?

PINCH.   But you told me he did some beastliness to you, as you called it; what was't?

MRS PINCH.   Why, he put –

PINCH.   What?

MRS PINCH.   Why, he put the tip of his tongue between my lips, and so mousled me – and I said I'd bite it.

PINCH.   An eternal canker seize it, for a dog!

MRS PINCH.   Nay, you need not be so angry with him neither, for to say truth, he has the sweetest breath I ever knew.

PINCH.   The devil! You were satisfied with it then, and would do it again?

MRS PINCH.   Not unless he should force me.

PINCH.   Force you, changeling![15] I tell you no woman can be forced.

MRS PINCH.   Yes, but she may, sure, by such a one as he, for he's a proper, goodly, strong man; 'tis hard, let me tell you, to resist him.

PINCH.   [*Aside*] So, 'tis plain she loves him, yet she has not love enough to make her conceal it from me; but the sight of him will increase her aversion for me and love for him; and that love instruct her how to deceive me and satisfy him, all idiot as she is. Love![16]

[14]*China oranges Citrus aurantium*, then an exotic delicacy, believed to derive from China. Pepys paid six pence each for oranges at the Duke of York's Theatre (*Diary*, 11 May 1668).

[15]*changeling* In folklore fairies were said to steal an attractive child, exchanging it for an ugly or stupid one.

[16]*Love* i.e. Cupid.

'Twas he gave women first their craft, their art of deluding. Out of Nature's hands they came plain, open, silly, and fit for slaves, as she and heaven intended 'em; but damned Love – Well, I must strangle that little monster whilst I can deal with him. – [*Aloud*] Go fetch pen, ink, and paper out of the next room.

MRS PINCH.   Yes, bud.   *Exit*

PINCH.   Why should women have more invention in love than men? It can only be because they have more desires, more soliciting[17] passions, more lust, and more of the devil.

   Re-enter MRS PINCHWIFE

Come, minx, sit down and write.

MRS PINCH.   Ay, dear bud, but I can't do't very well.

PINCH.   I wish you could not at all.

MRS PINCH.   But what should I write for?

PINCH.   I'll have you write a letter to your lover.[18]

MRS PINCH.   O Lord, to the fine gentleman a letter!

PINCH.   Yes, to the fine gentleman.

MRS PINCH.   Lord, you do but jeer; sure you jest.

PINCH.   I am not so merry. Come, write as I bid you.

MRS PINCH.   What, do you think I am a fool?

PINCH.   (*Aside*) She's afraid I would not dictate any love to him, therefore she's unwilling. – [*Aloud*] But you had best begin.

MRS PINCH.   Indeed, and indeed, but I won't, so I won't.

PINCH.   Why?

MRS PINCH.   Because he's in town; you may send for him if you will.

PINCH.   Very well, you would have him brought to you; is it come to this? I say, take the pen and write, or you'll provoke me.

MRS PINCH.   Lord, what d'ye make a fool of me for? Don't I know that letters are never writ but from the country to London, and from London into the country? Now he's in town, and I am in town too; therefore I can't write to him, you know.

PINCH.   (*Aside*) So, I am glad it is no worse; she is innocent enough yet. – [*Aloud*] Yes, you may, when your husband bids you, write letters to people that are in town.

MRS PINCH.   Oh, may I so? Then I'm satisfied.

PINCH.   Come, begin: 'Sir', –   *Dictates*

MRS PINCH.   Shan't I say, 'Dear Sir'? – You know one says always something more than bare 'Sir'.

PINCH.   Write as I bid you, or I will write 'whore' with this penknife in your face.

[17]*soliciting* tempting.

[18]The subplot concerning Mrs Pinchwife's letters owes something to Molière's *L'École des Maris*, 1661.

MRS PINCH.   Nay, good bud – 'Sir', –   *Writes*

PINCH.   'Though I suffered last night your nauseous, loathed kisses
and embraces' – Write!

MRS PINCH.   Nay, why should I say so? You know I told you he had a
sweet breath.

PINCH.   Write!

MRS PINCH.   Let me but put out 'loathed'.

PINCH.   Write, I say!

MRS PINCH.   Well then.   *Writes*

PINCH.   Let's see, what have you writ? – (*Takes the paper and reads*)
'Though I suffered last night your kisses and embraces' – Thou
impudent creature, where is 'nauseous' and 'loathed'?

MRS PINCH.   I can't abide to write such filthy words.

PINCH.   Once more, write as I'd have you, and question it not, or I
will spoil thy writing with this. I will stab out those eyes that cause
my mischief.   *Holds up the penknife*

MRS PINCH.   O Lord! I will.

PINCH.   So, so; let's see now. – (*Reads*) 'Though I suffered last night
your nauseous, loathed kisses and embraces' – Go on: 'yet I would
not have you presume that you shall ever repeat them' – So –

                                                                              She writes

MRS PINCH.   I have writ it.

PINCH.   On then: 'I then concealed myself from your knowledge to
avoid your insolencies'.   *She writes*

MRS PINCH.   So –

PINCH.   'The same reason, now I am out of your hands' –

                                                                              She writes

MRS PINCH.   So –

PINCH.   'Makes me own to you my unfortunate, though innocent
frolic of being in man's clothes' –   *She writes*

MRS PINCH.   So –

PINCH.   'That you may for evermore cease to pursue her, who hates
and detests you' –   *She writes on*

MRS PINCH.   So – Heigh!   *Sighs*

PINCH.   What, do you sigh? – 'detests you, as much as she loves her
husband and her honour'.

MRS PINCH.   I vow, husband, he'll ne'er believe I should write such a
letter.

PINCH.   What, he'd expect a kinder from you? Come now, your name
only.

MRS PINCH.   What, shan't I say, 'Your most faithful, humble servant
till death'?

PINCH.   No, tormenting fiend! – (*Aside*) Her style, I find, would be

very soft.[19] – [*Aloud*] Come, wrap it up now, whilst I go fetch wax
and a candle; and write on the backside, 'For Mr Horner'.   *Exit*

MRS PINCH. 'For Mr Horner'. – So, I am glad he has told me his
name. Dear Mr Horner! But why should I send thee such a letter that
will vex thee and make thee angry with me? Well, I will not send it. –
Ay, but then my husband will kill me, for I see plainly he won't let me
love Mr Horner. But what care I for my husband? – I won't, so I
won't, send poor Mr Horner such a letter; but then my husband –
But oh, what if I writ at bottom my husband made me write it? – Ay,
but then my husband would see't. Can one have no shift?[20] Ah, a
London woman would have had a hundred presently. Stay! What if I
should write a letter, and wrap it up like this, and write upon't too?
Ay, but then my husband would see't – I don't know what to do. –
But yet evads[21] I'll try, so I will, for I will not send this letter to poor
Mr Horner, come what will on't. 'Dear sweet Mr Horner', – (*Writes
and repeats what she writes*) So – 'My husband would have me send
you a base, rude, unmannerly letter; but I won't, – so – 'and would
have me forbid you loving me; but I won't, – so – 'and would have
me say to you, I hate you, poor Mr Horner; but I won't tell a lie for
him', – there – 'for I'm sure if you and I were in the country at cards
together' – so – 'I could not help treading on your toe under the
table' – so – 'or rubbing knees with you, and staring in your face, till
you saw me' – very well – 'and then looking down, and blushing for
an hour together', – so – 'but I must make haste before my husband
comes; and now he has taught me to write letters, you shall have
longer ones from me, who am, dear, dear, poor Mr Horner, your
most humble friend, and servant to command till death, – Margery
Pinchwife'. Stay, I must give him a hint at bottom – so – Now wrap it
up just like t'other – so – now write, 'For Mr Horner' – But oh now,
what shall I do with it? For here comes my husband.

Re-enter PINCHWIFE

PINCH. (*Aside*) I have been detained by a sparkish coxcomb, who
pretended a visit to me; but I fear 'twas to my wife. – [*Aloud*] What,
have you done?

MRS PINCH. Ay, ay, bud, just now.

PINCH. Let's see't. What d'ye tremble for? What, you would not
have it go?

MRS PINCH. Here. – (*Aside*) No, I must not give him that; so I had
been served if I had given him this.

                        He opens and reads the first letter

[19]*soft* tender.
[20]*shift* device, plot.
[21]*evads* i.e. i'vads, i' faith.

PINCH.   Come, where's the wax and seal?

MRS PINCH.   (*Aside*) Lord, what shall I do now? Nay then, I have it. –
[*Aloud*] Pray let me see't. Lord, you think me so arrant a fool I
cannot seal a letter? I will do't, so I will.

> *Snatches the letter from him, changes it for the other, seals it, and
> delivers it to him*

PINCH.   Nay, I believe you will learn that, and other things too, which
I would not have you.

MRS PINCH.   So, han't I done it curiously:²² – (*Aside*) I think I have;
there's my letter going to Mr Horner, since he'll²³ needs have me
send letters to folks.

PINCH.   'Tis very well; but, I warrant, you would not have it go now?

MRS PINCH.   Yes, indeed, but I would, bud, now.

PINCH.   Well, you are a good girl then. Come, let me lock you up in
your chamber till I come back; and be sure you come not within
three strides of the window²⁴ when I am gone, for I have a spy in the
street. – (*Exit* MRS PINCHWIFE; PINCHWIFE *locks the door*) At
least, 'tis fit she think so. If we do not cheat women, they'll cheat us,
and fraud may be justly used with secret enemies, of which a wife is
the most dangerous; and he that has a handsome one to keep, and a
frontier town, must provide against treachery rather than open
force. Now I have secured all within, I'll deal with the foe without
with false intelligence.   *Holds up the letter. Exit*

[SCENE THREE]

The scene changes to HORNER'S *lodging*

Enter HORNER *and* QUACK

QUACK.   Well, sir, how fadges²⁵ the new design? Have you not the
luck of all your brother projectors, to deceive only yourself at last?

HORN.   No, good domine doctor, I deceive you, it seems, and others
too; for the grave matrons and old, rigid husbands think me as unfit
for love as they are; but their wives, sisters, and daughters know,
some of 'em, better things already.

QUACK.   Already!

²²*curiously* skilfully.
²³*he'll* Pinchwife will.
²⁴*three strides* Compare Corvino's strictures on Celia, Jonson, *Volpone* (1607),
II, v, 50–56.
²⁵*fadges* prospers.

HORN.   Already, I say. Last night I was drunk with half a dozen of your civil persons, as you call 'em, and people of honour, and so was made free of their society and dressing-rooms forever hereafter; and am already come to the privileges of sleeping upon their pallets, warming smocks, tying shoes and garters, and the like, doctor, already, already, doctor.

QUACK.   You have made use of your time, sir.

HORN.   I tell thee, I am now no more interruption to 'em, when they sing or talk bawdy, than a little squab[26] French page who speaks no English.

QUACK.   But do civil persons and women of honour drink and sing bawdy songs?

HORN.   Oh, amongst friends, amongst friends; for your bigots in honour are just like those in religion: they fear the eye of the world more than the eye of heaven, and think there is no virtue but railing at vice, and no sin but giving scandal. They rail at a poor, little, kept player, and keep themselves some young, modest pulpit comedian to be privy to their sins in their closets, not to tell 'em of them in their chapels.

QUACK.   Nay, the truth on't is, priests, amongst the women now, have quite got the better of us lay-confessors, physicians.

HORN.   And they are rather their patients; but –
  Enter LADY FIDGET, *looking about her*
Now we talk of women of honour, here comes one. Step behind the screen there, and but observe if I have not particular privileges with the women of reputation already, doctor, already.

[QUACK *retires*]

LADY FID.   Well, Horner, am not I a woman of honour? You see I'm as good as my word.

HORN.   And you shall see, madam, I'll not be behindhand with you in honour; and I'll be as good as my word too, if you please but to withdraw into the next room.

LADY FID.   But first, my dear sir, you must promise to have a care of my dear honour.

HORN.   If you talk a word more of your honour, you'll make me incapable to wrong it. To talk of honour in the mysteries of love is like talking of heaven or the deity in an operation of witchcraft, just when you are employing the devil: it makes the charm impotent.

LADY FID.   Nay, fie, let us not be smutty. But you talk of mysteries and bewitching to me; I don't understand you.

[26]*squab* squat and plump.

HORN. I tell you, madam, the word money in a mistress's mouth at such a nick of time is not a more disheartening sound to a younger brother[27] than that of honour to an eager lover like myself.

LADY FID. But you can't blame a lady of my reputation to be chary.

HORN. Chary! I have been chary of it already, by the report I have caused of myself.

LADY FID. Ay, but if you should ever let other women know that dear secret, it would come out. Nay, you must have a great care of your conduct; for my acquaintance are so censorious (oh, 'tis a wicked, censorious world, Mr Horner!), I say, are so censorious and detracting that perhaps they'll talk to the prejudice of my honour, though you should not let them know the dear secret.

HORN. Nay, madam, rather than they shall prejudice your honour, I'll prejudice theirs; and, to serve you, I'll lie with 'em all, make the secret their own, and then they'll keep it. I am a Machiavel in love, madam.

LADY FID. Oh, no, sir, not that way.

HORN. Nay, the devil take me, if censorious women are to be silenced any other way.

LADY FID. A secret is better kept, I hope, by a single person than a multitude; therefore pray do not trust anybody else with it, dear, dear Mr Horner.   *Embracing him*

    Enter SIR JASPER FIDGET

SIR JASP. How now!

LADY FID. (*Aside*) Oh, my husband! – Prevented[28] – and what's almost as bad, found with my arms about another man; that will appear too much! What shall I say? – [*Aloud*] Sir Jasper, come hither; I am trying if Mr Horner were ticklish, and he's as ticklish as can be. I love to torment the confounded toad; let you and I tickle him.

SIR JASP. No, your ladyship will tickle him better without me, I suppose. But is this your buying china? I thought you had been at the china-house.

HORN. (*Aside*) China-house! That's my cue, I must take it. – [*Aloud*] A pox, can't you keep your impertinent wives at home? Some men are troubled with the husbands, but I with the wives; but I'd have you to know, since I cannot be your journeyman at night, I will not be your drudge by day, to squire your wife about and be your man of straw or scarecrow only to pies[29] and jays that would be nibbling at

---

[27]*younger brother* Within the rules of primogeniture the elder or eldest son (or rarely daughter) inherited the father's estate. This is Heartfree's problem in *The Provoked Wife*, v, ii.

[28]*Prevented* Frustrated, hindered.

[29]*pies* magpies.

your forbidden fruit; I shall be shortly the hackney[30] gentleman-usher of the town.

SIR JASP. (*Aside*) He, he, he! Poor fellow, he's in the right on't, faith. To squire women about for other folks is as ungrateful an employment as to tell[31] money for other folks. – [*Aloud*] He, he, he! Be'n't angry, Horner.

LADY FID. No, 'tis I have more reason to be angry, who am left by you to go abroad indecently[32] alone; or, what is more indecent, to pin myself upon such ill-bred people of your acquaintance as this is.

SIR JASP. Nay, prithee, what has he done?

LADY FID. Nay, he has done nothing.

SIR JASP. But what d'ye take ill, if he has done nothing?

LADY FID. Ha, ha, ha! Faith, I can't but laugh, however; why, d'ye think the unmannerly toad would not come down to me to the coach? I was fain to come up to fetch him or go without him, which I was resolved not to do, for he knows china very well, and has himself very good, but will not let me see it, lest I should beg some; but I will find it out, and have what I came for yet.

HORN. (*Apart to* LADY FIDGET, *as he follows her to the door*) Lock the door, madam. – (*Exit* LADY FIDGET, *and locks the door*) – [*Aloud*] So, she has got into my chamber and locked me out. Oh, the impertinency of womankind! Well, Sir Jasper, plain dealing is a jewel; if ever you suffer your wife to trouble me again here, she shall carry you home a pair of horns; by my lord mayor, she shall; though I cannot furnish you myself, you are sure, yet I'll find a way.

SIR JASP. (*Aside*) Ha, ha, he! At my first coming in, and finding her arms about him, tickling him it seems, I was half jealous, but now I see my folly. – [*Aloud*] He, he, he! Poor Horner.

HORN. Nay, though you laugh now, 'twill be my turn ere long. O women, more impertinent, more cunning, and more mischievous than their monkeys, and to me almost as ugly! – Now is she throwing my things about and rifling all I have; but I'll get in to her the back way and so rifle her for it.

SIR JASP. Ha, ha, ha! Poor angry Horner.

HORN. Stay here a little; I'll ferret her out to you presently, I warrant.
Exit at the other door

[SIR JASPER *calls through the door to his* WIFE; *she answers from within*]

SIR JASP. Wife, my Lady Fidget, wife, he is coming in to you the back way.

[30]*hackney* hired out.
[31]*tell* count.
[32]*indecently* immodestly.

LADY FID.　Let him come, and welcome, which way he will.

SIR JASP.　He'll catch you and use you roughly and be too strong for you.

LADY FID.　Don't you trouble yourself; let him if he can.

QUACK.　(*Behind*) This indeed I could not have believed from him, nor any but my own eyes.

　　Enter MRS SQUEAMISH

MRS SQUEAM.　Where's this woman-hater, this toad, this ugly, greasy, dirty sloven?

SIR JASP.　(*Aside*) So, the women all will have him ugly. Methinks he is a comely person, but his wants make his form contemptible to 'em; and 'tis e'en as my wife said yesterday, talking of him, that a proper, handsome eunuch was as ridiculous a thing as a gigantic coward.

MRS SQUEAM.　Sir Jasper, your servant. Where is the odious beast?

SIR JASP.　He's within in his chamber, with my wife; she's playing the wag with him.

MRS SQUEAM.　Is she so? And[33] he's a clownish beast, he'll give her no quarter; he'll play the wag with her again, let me tell you. Come, let's go help her. What, the door's locked?

SIR JASP.　Ay, my wife locked it.

MRS SQUEAM.　Did she so? Let's break it open then.

SIR JASP.　No, no, he'll do her no hurt.

MRS SQUEAM.　(*Aside*) No! – But is there no other way to get in to 'em? Whither goes this? I will disturb 'em.　　*Exit at another door*

　　Enter OLD LADY SQUEAMISH

LADY SQUEAM.　Where is this harlotry, this impudent baggage, this rambling tomrigg?[34] O Sir Jasper, I'm glad to see you here. Did you not see my vile grandchild come in hither just now?

SIR JASP.　Yes.

LADY SQUEAM.　Ay, but where is she then? Where is she? Lord, Sir Jasper, I have e'en rattled myself to pieces in pursuit of her. But can you tell what she makes[35] here? They say below, no woman lodges here.

SIR JASP.　No.

LADY SQUEAM.　No? What does she here then? Say, if it be not a woman's lodging, what makes she here? But are you sure no woman lodges here?

33*And* If.
34*tomrigg* tomboy or strumpet.
35*makes* does.

SIR JASP. No, nor no man neither; this is Mr Horner's lodging.

LADY SQUEAM. Is it so? Are you sure?

SIR JASP. Yes, yes.

LADY SQUEAM. So; then there's no hurt in't, I hope. But where is he?

SIR JASP. He's in the next room with my wife.

LADY SQUEAM. Nay, if you trust him with your wife, I may with my Biddy. They say he's a merry harmless man now, e'en as harmless a man as ever came out of Italy with a good voice,[36] and as pretty, harmless company for a lady as a snake without his teeth.

SIR JASP. Ay, ay, poor man.

Re-enter MRS SQUEAMISH

MRS SQUEAM. I can't find 'em. – Oh, are you here, grandmother? I followed, you must know, my Lady Fidget hither; 'tis the prettiest lodging, and I have been staring on the prettiest pictures.

Re-enter LADY FIDGET *with a piece of china in her hand, and* HORNER *following*

LADY FID. And I have been toiling and moiling[37] for the prettiest piece of china, my dear.

HORN. Nay, she has been too hard for me, do what I could.

MRS SQUEAM. O Lord, I'll have some china too. Good Mr Horner, don't think to give other people china and me none; come in with me too.

HORN. Upon my honour, I have none left now.

MRS SQUEAM. Nay, nay, I have known you deny your china before now, but you shan't put me off so. Come.

HORN. This lady had the last there.

LADY FID. Yes indeed, madam, to my certain knowledge, he has no more left.

MRS SQUEAM. Oh, but it may be he may have some you could not find.

LADY FID. What, d'ye think if he had had any left, I would not have had it too? For we women of quality never think we have china enough.

HORN. Do not take it ill I cannot make china for you all, but I will have a roll-waggon[38] for you too, another time.

MRS SQUEAM. Thank you, dear toad.

LADY FID. (*Aside to* HORNER) What do you mean by that promise?

HORN. (*Aside to* LADY FIDGET) Alas, she has an innocent, literal understanding.

[36]*good voice* a castrato.

[37]*moiling* drudging.

[38]*roll-waggon* literally, a blue-and-white cylindrical vase of the Transitional or K'ang Hsi period; it is related to the sexual innuendo of 'china' (Wycherley, *Complete Plays*, ed. G. Weales, New York, 1967, p. 369).

LADY SQUEAM.　　Poor Mr Horner, he has enough to do to please you all, I see.

HORN.　　Ay, madam, you see how they use me.

LADY SQUEAM.　　Poor gentleman, I pity you.

HORN.　　I thank you, madam. I could never find pity but from such reverend[39] ladies as you are; the young ones will never spare a man.

MRS SQUEAM.　　Come, come, beast, and go dine with us, for we shall want a man at ombre after dinner.

HORN.　　That's all their use of me, madam, you see.

MRS SQUEAM.　　Come, sloven, I'll lead you, to be sure of you.

Pulls him by the cravat

LADY SQUEAM.　　Alas, poor man, how she tugs him! Kiss, kiss her: that's the way to make such nice women quiet.

HORN.　　No, madam, that remedy is worse than the torment; they know I dare suffer anything rather than do it.

LADY SQUEAM.　　Prithee kiss her, and I'll give you her picture in little that you admired so last night; prithee do.

HORN.　　Well, nothing but that could bribe me: I love a woman only in effigy, and good painting as much as I hate them. I'll do't, for I could adore the devil well painted.　　　*Kisses* MRS SQUEAMISH

MRS SQUEAM.　　Foh, you filthy toad! Nay, now I've done jesting.

LADY SQUEAM.　　Ha, ha, ha, I told you so.

MRS SQUEAM.　　Foh, a kiss of his —

SIR JASP.　　Has no more hurt in't than one of my spaniel's.

MRS SQUEAM.　　Nor no more good neither.

QUACK.　　(*Behind*) I will now believe anything he tells me.

Enter PINCHWIFE

LADY FID.　　O Lord, here's a man! Sir Jasper, my mask, my mask! I would not be seen here for the world.

SIR JASP.　　What, not when I am with you?

LADY FID.　　No, no, my honour — Let's be gone.

MRS SQUEAM.　　O grandmother, let's be gone; make haste, make haste. I know not how he may censure us.

LADY FID.　　Be found in the lodgings of anything like a man! Away!

Exeunt SIR JASPER FIDGET, LADY FIDGET, OLD LADY SQUEAM-ISH *and* MRS SQUEAMISH

QUACK.　　(*Behind*) What's here? Another cuckold? He looks like one, and none else sure have any business with him.

HORN.　　Well, what brings my dear friend hither?

PINCH.　　Your impertinency.

HORN.　　My impertinency! Why, you gentlemen that have got hand-

[39]*reverend* worthy of respect (used ironically).

some wives think you have a privilege of saying anything to your friends, and are as brutish as if you were our creditors.

PINCH.   No, sir, I'll ne'er trust you any way.

HORN.   But why not, dear Jack? Why diffide[40] in me thou know'st so well?

PINCH.   Because I do know you so well.

HORN.   Han't I been always thy friend, honest Jack, always ready to serve thee, in love or battle, before thou wert married, and am so still?

PINCH.   I believe so; you would be my second now, indeed.

HORN.   Well then, dear Jack, why so unkind, so grum, so strange to me? Come, prithee kiss me, dear rogue. Gad, I was always, I say, and am still as much thy servant as –

PINCH.   As I am yours, sir. What, you would send a kiss to my wife, is that it?

HORN.   So, there 'tis – a man can't show his friendship to a married man but presently he talks of his wife to you. Prithee, let thy wife alone, and let thee and I be all one, as we were wont. What, thou art as shy of my kindness as a Lombard Street alderman of a courtier's civility at Locket's![41]

PINCH.   But you are over-kind to me, as kind as if I were your cuckold already; yet I must confess you ought to be kind and civil to me, since I am so kind, so civil to you, as to bring you this: look you there, sir.

Delivers him a letter

HORN.   What is't?

PINCH.   Only a love-letter, sir.

HORN.   From whom? How! This is from your wife – Hum – and hum – *Reads*

PINCH.   Even from my wife, sir. Am I not wondrous kind and civil to you now too? – (*Aside*) But you'll not think her so.

HORN.   (*Aside*) Ha! Is this a trick of his or hers?

PINCH.   The gentleman's surprised I find. – What, you expected a kinder letter?

HORN.   No, faith, not I; how could I?

PINCH.   Yes, yes, I'm sure you did. A man so well made as you are must needs be disappointed if the women declare not their passion at first sight or opportunity.

HORN.   (*Aside*) But what should this mean? Stay, the postscript. – (*Reads aside*) 'Be sure you love me, whatsoever my husband says to the contrary, and let him not see this, lest he should come home and

---

[40]*diffide* distrust.

[41]*as shy . . . Locket's* i.e. as suspicious as a City banker or goldsmith of the motives of a gallant's treating him at this fashionable eating house at Charing Cross.

pinch me, or kill my squirrel'. It seems he knows not what the letter contains.

PINCH.   Come, ne'er wonder at it so much.

HORN.   Faith, I can't help it.

PINCH.   Now I think I have deserved your infinite friendship and kindness, and have showed myself sufficiently an obliging kind friend and husband; am I not so, to bring a letter from my wife to her gallant?

HORN.   Ay, the devil take me, thou art the most obliging kind friend and husband in the world, ha, ha!

PINCH.   Well, you may be merry, sir; but, in short, I must tell you, sir, my honour will suffer no jesting.

HORN.   What dost thou mean?

PINCH.   Does the letter want42 a comment? Then know, sir, though I have been so civil a husband as to bring you a letter from my wife, to let you kiss and court her to my face, I will not be a cuckold, sir, I will not.

HORN.   Thou art mad with jealousy. I never saw thy wife in my life but at the play yesterday, and I know not if it were she or no. I court her, kiss her!

PINCH.   I will not be a cuckold, I say; there will be danger in making me a cuckold.

HORN.   Why, wert thou not well cured of thy last clap?43

PINCH.   I wear a sword.

HORN.   It should be taken from thee, lest thou shouldst do thyself a mischief with it; thou art mad, man.

PINCH.   As mad as I am and as merry as you are, I must have more reason44 from you ere we part. I say again, though you kissed and courted last night my wife in man's clothes, as she confesses in her letter –

HORN.   (*Aside*) Ha!

PINCH.   Both she and I say you must not design it again, for you have mistaken your woman, as you have done your man.

HORN.   (*Aside*) Oh, I understand something now. – [*Aloud*] Was that thy wife? Why wouldst thou not tell me 'twas she? Faith, my freedom with her was your fault, not mine.

PINCH.   (*Aside*) Faith, so 'twas.

HORN.   Fie, I'd never do't to a woman before her husband's face, sure.

42*want* lack.

43*clap* i.e. the danger will be in my catching a venereal disease from your wife.

44*reason* explanation.

PINCH. But I had rather you should do't to my wife before my face than behind my back, and that you shall never do.

HORN. No, you will hinder me.

PINCH. If I would not hinder you, you see by her letter she would.

HORN. Well, I must e'en acquiesce then, and be contented with what she writes.

PINCH. I'll assure you 'twas voluntarily writ; I had no hand in't, you may believe me.

HORN. I do believe thee, faith.

PINCH. And believe her too, for she's an innocent creature, has no dissembling in her; and so fare you well, sir.

HORN. Pray, however, present my humble service to her, and tell her I will obey her letter to a tittle and fulfil her desires, be what they will, or with what difficulty soever I do't; and you shall be no more jealous of me, I warrant her and you.

PINCH. Well then, fare you well; and play with any man's honour but mine, kiss any man's wife but mine, and welcome. *Exit*

HORN. Ha, ha, ha, doctor.

QUACK. It seems he has not heard the report of you, or does not believe it.

HORN. Ha, ha! Now, doctor, what think you?

QUACK. Pray, let's see the letter. Hum – 'for – dear – love you –'
Reads the letter

HORN. I wonder how she could contrive it! What say'st thou to't? 'Tis an original.

QUACK. So are your cuckolds, too, originals, for they are like no other common cuckolds, and I will henceforth believe it not impossible for you to cuckold the Grand Signior[45] amidst his guards of eunuchs; that I say –

HORN. And I say for the letter, 'tis the first love letter that ever was without flames, darts, fates, destinies, lying and dissembling in't.

Enter SPARKISH, *pulling in* PINCHWIFE

SPARK. Come back; you are a pretty brother-in-law, neither go to church nor to dinner with your sister bride!

PINCH. My sister denies her marriage and, you see, is gone away from you dissatisfied.

SPARK. Pshaw, upon a foolish scruple, that our parson was not in lawful orders and did not say all the common prayer, but 'tis her modesty only, I believe. But let women be never so modest the first day, they'll be sure to come to themselves by night, and I shall have enough of her then. In the meantime, Harry Horner, you must dine

---

45 *Grand Signior* the Sultan of Turkey.

with me; I keep my wedding at my aunt's in the Piazza.[46]

HORN.   Thy wedding! What stale maid has lived to despair of a husband, or what young one of a gallant?

SPARK.   Oh, your servant, sir. This gentleman's sister then, no stale maid.

HORN.   I'm sorry for't.

PINCH.   (*Aside*) How comes he so concerned for her?

SPARK.   You sorry for't? Why, do you know any ill by her?

HORN.   No, I know none but by thee; 'tis for her sake, not yours, and another man's sake that might have hoped, I thought.

SPARK.   Another man, another man! What is his name?

HORN.   Nay, since 'tis past, he shall be nameless. – (*Aside*) Poor Harcourt, I am sorry thou hast missed her.

PINCH.   (*Aside*) He seems to be much troubled at the match.

SPARK.   Prithee, tell me. – Nay, you shan't go, brother.

PINCH.   I must of necessity, but I'll come to you to dinner.

Exit

SPARK.   But, Harry, what, have I a rival in my wife already? But with all my heart, for he may be of use to me hereafter; for though my hunger is now my sauce, and I can fall on heartily without, but the time will come when a rival will be as good sauce for a married man to a wife as an orange to veal.

HORN.   O thou damned rogue, thou hast set my teeth on edge with thy orange.

SPARK.   Then let's to dinner; there I was with you again. Come.

HORN.   But who dines with thee?

SPARK.   My friends and relations, my brother Pinchwife, you see, of your acquaintance.

HORN.   And his wife?

SPARK.   No, gad, he'll ne'er let her come amongst us good fellows; your stingy country coxcomb keeps his wife from his friends, as he does his little firkin[47] of ale, for his own drinking, and a gentleman can't get a smack on't; but his servants, when his back is turned, broach it at their pleasures, and dust it away, ha, ha, ha! Gad, I am witty, I think, considering I was married today, by the world; but come –

HORN.   No, I will not dine with you unless you can fetch her too.

SPARK.   Pshaw, what pleasure canst thou have with women now, Harry?

HORN.   My eyes are not gone; I love a good prospect yet, and will not

---

46 *Piazza* a fashionable residential area, an arcade on the north and east sides of the square of Covent Garden, designed by Inigo Jones, *c.* 1634.

47 *firkin* a cask containing nine gallons (*c.* 40 litres).

dine with you unless she does too. Go fetch her, therefore, but do not tell her husband 'tis for my sake.

SPARK. Well, I'll go try what I can do. In the meantime, come away to my aunt's lodging; 'tis in the way to Pinchwife's.

HORN. The poor woman has called for aid and stretched forth her hand, doctor; I cannot but help her over the pale[48] out of the briars.

Exeunt

SCENE FOUR

The scene changes to PINCHWIFE'S *house.* MRS PINCHWIFE
alone, leaning on her elbow. – A table, pen, ink, and paper

MRS PINCH. Well, 'tis e'en so, I have got the London disease they call love; I am sick of my husband, and for my gallant. I have heard this distemper called a fever, but methinks 'tis liker an ague; for when I think of my husband I tremble, and am in a cold sweat, and have inclinations to vomit, but when I think of my gallant, dear Mr Horner, my hot fit comes, and I am all in a fever indeed; and, as in other fevers, my own chamber is tedious to me, and I would fain be removed to his, and then methinks I should be well. Ah, poor Mr Horner! Well, I cannot, will not stay here; therefore I'll make an end of my letter to him, which shall be a finer letter than my last, because I have studied it like anything. O sick, sick!

Takes the pen and writes
Enter PINCHWIFE, *who, seeing her writing, steals softly behind*
her and, looking over her shoulder, snatches the paper from her

PINCH. What, writing more letters?

MRS PINCH. O Lord, bud, why d'ye fright me so?

She offers to run out; he stops her and reads

PINCH. How's this? Nay, you shall not stir, madam. 'Dear, dear, dear Mr Horner' – very well – I have taught you to write letters to good purpose! But let us see't. 'First, I am to beg your pardon for my boldness in writing to you, which I'd have you to know I would not have done, had not you said first you loved me so extremely, which if you do, you will never suffer me to lie in the arms of another man whom I loathe, nauseate, and detest'. – Now you can write these filthy words. But what follows? – 'Therefore, I hope you will speedily find some way to free me from this unfortunate match, which was never, I assure you, of my choice, but I'm afraid 'tis already too far gone; however, if you love me, as I do you, you will

[48]*pale* fence.

try what you can do; but you must help me away before tomorrow, or else, alas, I shall be forever out of your reach, for I can defer no longer our – our –' What is to follow 'our'? – Speak, what? Our journey into the country, I suppose! O woman, damned woman! And Love, damned Love, their old tempter! For this is one of his miracles; in a moment he can make those blind that could see, and those see that were blind, those dumb that could speak, and those prattle who were dumb before;[49] nay, what is more than all, make these dough-baked,[50] senseless, indocile animals, women, too hard for us, their politic[51] lords and rulers, in a moment. But make an end of your letter, and then I'll make an end of you thus, and all my plagues together.   *Draws his sword*

MRS PINCH.   O Lord, O Lord, you are such a passionate man, bud!
          Enter SPARKISH

SPARK.   How now, what's here to do?

PINCH.   This fool here now!

SPARK.   What, drawn upon your wife? You should never do that[52] but at night in the dark, when you can't hurt her. This is my sister-in-law, is it not? Ay, faith, e'en our country Margery (*Pulls aside her handkerchief*); one may know her. Come, she and you must go dine with me; dinner's ready, come. But where's my wife? Is she not come home yet? Where is she?

PINCH.   Making you a cuckold; 'tis that they all do, as soon as they can.

SPARK.   What, the wedding day? No, a wife that designs to make a cully[53] of her husband will be sure to let him win the first stake of love, by the world. But come, they stay dinner for us. Come, I'll lead down our Margery.

PINCH.   No, sir, go; we'll follow you.

SPARK.   I will not wag[54] without you.

PINCH.   [*Aside*] This coxcomb is a sensible[55] torment to me amidst the greatest in the world.

SPARK.   Come, come, Madam Margery.

PINCH.   No, I'll lead her my way. What, would you treat your friends with mine, for want of your own wife? (*Leads her to t'other door,*

[49]*make . . . before* Pinchwife has a faulty memory for the words of Isaiah, 35, 5–6.

[50]*dough-baked* inadequately cooked; or foolish.

[51]*politic* natural.

[52]*that* i.e. draw, in the sense of make ready for sexual intercourse.

[53]*cully* dupe.

[54]*wag* stir.

[55]*sensible* acutely felt.

and locks her in and returns) – (*Aside*) I am contented my rage should take breath.

SPARK.   I told Horner this.

PINCH.   Come now.

SPARK.   Lord, how shy[56] you are of your wife! But let me tell you, brother, we men of wit have amongst us a saying that cuckolding, like the smallpox, comes with a fear; and you may keep your wife as much as you will out of danger of infection, but if her constitution incline her to't, she'll have it sooner or later, by the world, say they.

PINCH.   (*Aside*) What a thing is a cuckold, that every fool can make him ridiculous! – [*Aloud*] Well, sir, but let me advise you, now you are come to be concerned, because you suspect the danger not to neglect the means to prevent it, especially when the greatest share of the malady will light upon your own head, for

> Hows'e'er the kind wife's belly comes to swell,
> The husband breeds[57] for her, and first is ill.   *Exeunt*

[56]*shy* suspicious.
[57]*breeds* grows cuckold's horns.

Act Five

SCENE ONE

PINCHWIFE'S *house*

Enter PINCHWIFE *and* MRS PINCHWIFE. *A table and candle*

PINCH. Come, take the pen and make an end of the letter, just as you intended; if you are false in a tittle, I shall soon perceive it, and punish you with this as you deserve. – (*Lays his hand on his sword*) Write what was to follow. Let's see – 'You must make haste, and help me away before tomorrow, or else I shall be forever out of your reach, for I can defer no longer our' – What follows 'our'?

MRS PINCH. Must all out then, bud? – Look you there, then.

MRS PINCHWIFE *takes the pen and writes*

PINCH. Let's see – 'For I can defer no longer our – wedding. Your slighted Alithea'. What's the meaning of this? My sister's name to't? Speak, unriddle.

MRS PINCH. Yes, indeed, bud.

PINCH. But why her name to't? Speak – speak, I say.

MRS PINCH. Ay, but you'll tell her then again.[1] If you would not tell her again –

PINCH. I will not. I am stunned, my head turns round. Speak.

MRS PINCH. Won't you tell her, indeed, and indeed?

PINCH. No. Speak, I say.

MRS PINCH. She'll be angry with me; but I had rather she should be angry with me than you, bud; and, to tell you the truth, 'twas she made me write the letter, and taught me what I should write.

PINCH. [*Aside*] Ha, I thought the style was somewhat better than her own. – [*Aloud*] But how could she come to you to teach you, since I had locked you up alone?

MRS PINCH. Oh, through the keyhole, bud.

PINCH. But why should she make you write a letter for her to him, since she can write herself?

MRS PINCH. Why, she said, because – for I was unwilling to do it –

PINCH. Because what? Because?

MRS PINCH. Because, lest Mr Horner should be cruel and refuse her,

---

[1] *tell her again* you'll repeat what I am telling you now.

or vain afterwards and show the letter, she might disown it, the hand not being hers.

PINCH. (*Aside*) How's this? Ha! Then I think I shall come to myself again. This changeling could not invent this lie, but if she could, why should she? She might think I should soon discover it. – Stay –now I think on't too, Horner said he was sorry she had married Sparkish; and her disowning her marriage to me makes me think she has evaded it for Horner's sake. Yet why should she take this course? But men in love are fools; women may well be so. – [*Aloud*] But hark you, madam, your sister went out in the morning, and I have not seen her within since.

MRS PINCH. Alack-a-day, she has been crying all day above, it seems, in a corner.

PINCH. Where is she? Let me speak with her.

MRS PINCH. (*Aside*) O Lord, then he'll discover all! – [*Aloud*] Pray hold, bud; what, d'ye mean to discover me? She'll know I have told you then. Pray, bud, let me talk with her first.

PINCH. I must speak with her, to know whether Horner ever made her any promise, and whether she be married to Sparkish or no.

MRS PINCH. Pray, dear bud, don't, till I have spoken with her and told her that I have told you all; for she'll kill me else.

PINCH. Go then, and bid her come out to me.

MRS PINCH. Yes, yes, bud.

PINCH. (*Pausing*) Let me see –

MRS PINCH. (*Aside*) I'll go, but she is not within to come to him. I have just got time to know of Lucy, her maid, who first set me on work, what lie I shall tell next, for I am e'en at my wit's end. *Exit*

PINCH. Well, I resolve it: Horner shall have her. I'd rather give him my sister than lend him my wife, and such an alliance will prevent his pretensions to my wife, sure. I'll make him of kin to her, and then he won't care for her.

Re-enter MRS PINCHWIFE

MRS PINCH. O Lord, bud, I told you what anger you would make[2] me with my sister.

PINCH. Won't she come hither?

MRS PINCH. No, no. Alack-a-day, she's ashamed to look you in the face, and she says if you go in to her, she'll run away downstairs, and shamefully go herself to Mr Horner, who has promised her marriage, she says; and she will have no other, so she won't.

PINCH. Did he so? Promise her marriage? Then she shall have no other. Go tell her so; and if she will come and discourse with me a

[2]*make* cause.

little concerning the means, I will about it immediately. Go. (*Exit* MRS PINCHWIFE) His estate is equal to Sparkish's, and his extraction as much better than his, as his parts are; but my chief reason is, I'd rather be of kin to him by the name of brother-in-law than that of cuckold.

Re-enter MRS PINCHWIFE

Well, what says she now?

MRS PINCH.   Why, she says she would only have you lead her to Horner's lodging; with whom she first will discourse the matter before she talks with you, which yet she cannot do; for alack, poor creature, she says she can't so much as look you in the face; therefore she'll come to you in a mask. And you must excuse her, if she make you no answer to any question of yours till you have brought her to Mr Horner; and if you will not chide her nor question her, she'll come out to you immediately.

PINCH.   Let her come. I will not speak a word to her nor require a word from her.

MRS PINCH.   Oh, I forgot: besides, she says she cannot look you in the face, though through a mask; therefore would desire you to put out the candle.

PINCH.   I agree to all. Let her make haste. – There, 'tis out. – (*Puts out the candle. Exit* MRS PINCHWIFE) My case is something better: I'd rather fight with Horner for not lying with my sister than for lying with my wife; and of the two, I had rather find my sister too forward than my wife. I expected no other from her free education, as she calls it, and her passion for the town. Well, wife and sister are names which make us expect love and duty, pleasure and comfort; but we find 'em plagues and torments, and are equally, though differently, troublesome to their keeper; for we have as much ado to get people to lie with our sisters as to keep 'em from lying with our wives.

Re-enter MRS PINCHWIFE *masked, and in hoods and scarfs, and a night-gown*3 *and petticoat of* ALITHEA'S

What, are you come, sister? Let us go then. But first let me lock up my wife. Mrs Margery, where are you?

MRS PINCH.   Here, bud.

PINCH.   Come hither, that I may lock you up: get you in. – (*Locks the door*) Come, sister, where are you now?

MRS PINCHWIFE *gives him her hand; but when he lets her go, she steals softly on to the other side of him, and is led away by him for his sister* ALITHEA

3*nightgown* dressing gown.

[SCENE TWO]

The scene changes to HORNER'S *lodging*

Enter HORNER *and* QUACK

QUACK.   What, all alone? Not so much as one of your cuckolds here nor one of their wives! They use to take their turns with you, as if they were to watch you.

HORN.   Yes, it often happens that a cuckold is but his wife's spy, and is more upon family duty when he is with her gallant abroad, hindering his pleasure, than when he is at home with her playing the gallant. But the hardest duty a married woman imposes upon a lover is keeping her husband company always.

QUACK.   And his fondness[4] wearies you almost as soon as hers.

HORN.   A pox! Keeping a cuckold company, after you have had his wife, is as tiresome as the company of a country squire to a witty fellow of the town when he has got all his money.

QUACK.   And as at first a man makes a friend of the husband to get the wife, so at last you are fain to fall out with the wife to be rid of the husband.

HORN.   Ay, most cuckold-makers are true courtiers: when once a poor man has cracked his credit[5] for 'em, they can't abide to come near him.

QUACK.   But at first, to draw him in, are so sweet, so kind, so dear, just as you are to Pinchwife. But what becomes of that intrigue with his wife?

HORN.   A pox! He's as surly as an alderman that has been bit;[6] and since he's so coy, his wife's kindness is in vain, for she's a silly innocent.

QUACK.   Did she not send you a letter by him?

HORN.   Yes; but that's a riddle I have not yet solved. Allow the poor creature to be willing, she is silly too, and he keeps her up so close –

QUACK.   Yes, so close that he makes her but the more willing, and adds but revenge to her love, which two, when met, seldom fail of satisfying each other one way or other.

HORN.   What, here's the man we are talking of, I think.

Enter PINCHWIFE, *leading in his* WIFE *masked, muffled, and in her sister's gown*

Pshaw!

4*fondness* foolishness.
5*cracked his credit* bankrupted himself.
6*bit* cheated.

QUACK.   Bringing his wife to you is the next thing to bringing a love letter from her.

HORN.   What means this?

PINCH.   The last time, you know, sir, I brought you a love letter; now, you see, a mistress. I think you'll say I am a civil man to you.

HORN.   Ay, the devil take me, will I say thou art the civilest man I ever met with, and I have known some. I fancy I understand thee now better than I did the letter. But, hark thee, in thy ear —

PINCH.   What?

HORN.   Nothing but the usual question, man: is she sound, on thy word?

PINCH.   What, you take her for a wench, and me for a pimp?

HORN.   Pshaw, 'wench' and 'pimp', paw7 words. I know thou art an honest fellow and hast a great acquaintance among the ladies, and perhaps hast made love for me rather than let me make love to thy wife.

PINCH.   Come, sir, in short, I am for no fooling.

HORN.   Nor I neither; therefore, prithee, let's see her face presently. Make her show, man. Art thou sure I don't know her?

PINCH.   I am sure you do know her.

HORN.   A pox, why dost thou bring her to me then?

PINCH.   Because she's a relation of mine —

HORN.   Is she, faith, man? Then thou art still more civil and obliging, dear rogue.

PINCH.   Who desired me to bring her to you.

HORN.   Then she is obliging, dear rogue.

PINCH.   You'll make her welcome for my sake, I hope.

HORN.   I hope she is handsome enough to make herself welcome. Prithee, let her unmask.

PINCH.   Do you speak to her; she would never be ruled by me.

HORN.   Madam, — (MRS PINCHWIFE *whispers to* HORNER) She says she must speak with me in private. Withdraw, prithee.

PINCH.   (*Aside*) She's unwilling, it seems, I should know all her indecent conduct in this business. — [*Aloud*] Well then, I'll leave you two together, and hope when I am gone, you'll agree; if not, you and I shan't agree, sir.

HORN.   [*Aside*] What means the fool? If she and I agree 'tis no matter what you and I do. *Whispers to* MRS PINCHWIFE, *who makes signs with her hand for him*8 *to be gone*

PINCH.   [*Aside*] In the meantime I'll fetch a parson, and find out Sparkish, and disabuse him. — You would have me fetch a parson,

----

7*paw* improper.   8*him* Pinchwife.

would you not? Well then, now I think I am rid of her, and shall have no more trouble with her. Our sisters and daughters, like usurers' money, are safest when put out; but our wives, like their writings,[9] never safe, but in our closets under lock and key.   *Exit*

   Enter BOY

BOY.   Sir Jasper Fidget, sir, is coming up.   [*Exit*]

HORN.   Here's the trouble of a cuckold now we are talking of. A pox on him! Has he not enough to do to hinder his wife's sport but he must other women's too? – Step in here, madam.

                          Exit MRS PINCHWIFE

   Enter SIR JASPER FIDGET

SIR JASP.   My best and dearest friend.

HORN.   [*Aside to* QUACK] The old style,[10] doctor. – [*Aloud*] Well, be short, for I am busy. What would your impertinent wife have now?

SIR JASP.   Well guessed, i'faith, for I do come from her.

HORN.   To invite me to supper! Tell her I can't come. Go.

SIR JASP.   Nay, now you are out, faith; for my lady and the whole knot of the virtuous gang, as they call themselves, are resolved upon a frolic of coming to you tonight in a masquerade, and are all dressed already.

HORN.   I shan't be at home.

SIR JASP.   [*Aside*] Lord, how churlish he is to women! – [*Aloud*] Nay, prithee, don't disappoint 'em; they'll think 'tis my fault; prithee, don't. I'll send in the banquet and the fiddles. But make no noise on't,[11] for the poor virtuous rogues would not have it known for the world that they go a-masquerading; and they would come to no man's ball but yours.

HORN.   Well, well, get you gone; and tell 'em, if they come, 'twill be at the peril of their honour and yours.

SIR JASP.   He, he, he, we'll trust you for that. Farewell.   *Exit*

HORN.   Doctor, anon you too shall be my guest,
             But now I'm going to a private feast.   *Exeunt*

SCENE THREE

The scene changes to the Piazza of Covent Garden

   Enter SPARKISH *with a letter in his hand*, PINCHWIFE *following*

SPARK.   But who would have thought a woman could have been false to me? By the world, I could not have thought it.

---

9 *their writings* usurers' documents.
10 *old style* an old-fashioned, pedantic manner.
11 *make no noise on't* don't reveal it.

PINCH.   You were for giving and taking liberty: she has taken it only, sir, now you find in that letter. You are a frank person, and so is she, you see there.

SPARK.   Nay, if this be her hand – for I never saw it.

PINCH.   'Tis no matter whether that be her hand or no; I am sure this hand, at her desire, led her to Mr Horner, with whom I left her just now, to go fetch a parson to 'em at their desire too, to deprive you of her forever, for it seems yours was but a mock marriage.

SPARK.   Indeed, she would needs have it that 'twas Harcourt himself, in a parson's habit, that married us; but I'm sure he told me 'twas his brother Ned.

PINCH.   Oh, there 'tis out; and you were deceived, not she, for you are such a frank person. But I must be gone. – You'll find her at Mr Horner's. Go, and believe your eyes.   *Exit*

SPARK.   Nay, I'll to her and call her as many crocodiles, sirens, harpies, and other heathenish names as a poet would do a mistress who had refused to hear his suit, nay more, his verses on her. – But stay, is not that she following a torch at t'other end of the Piazza? And from Horner's certainly. 'Tis so.

    Enter ALITHEA *following a torch, and* LUCY *behind*

You are well met, madam, though you don't think so. What, you have made a short visit to Mr Horner, but I suppose you'll return to him presently; by that time the parson can be with him.

ALITH.   Mr Horner and the parson, sir!

SPARK.   Come, madam, no more dissembling, no more jilting, for I am no more a frank person.

ALITH.   How's this?

LUCY.   (*Aside*) So, 'twill work, I see.

SPARK.   Could you find out no easy country fool to abuse? None but me, a gentleman of wit and pleasure about the town? But it was your pride to be too hard for a man of parts, unworthy false woman – false as a friend that lends a man money to lose; false as dice, who undo those that trust all they have to 'em.

LUCY.   (*Aside*) He has been a great bubble, by his similes,[12] as they say.

ALITH.   You have been too merry, sir, at your wedding-dinner, sure.

SPARK.   What, d'ye mock me too?

ALITH.   Or you have been deluded.

SPARK.   By you.

---

[12]*by his similes* i.e. to judge by his choice of similes, he has often been tricked.

ALITH. Let me understand you.

SPARK. Have you the confidence – I should call it something else, since you know your guilt – to stand my just reproaches? You did not write an impudent letter to Mr Horner, who I find now has clubbed with you in deluding me with his aversion for women, that I might not, forsooth, suspect him for my rival?

LUCY. (*Aside to* ALITHEA) D'ye think the gentleman can be jealous now, madam?

ALITH. I write a letter to Mr Horner!

SPARK. Nay, madam, do not deny it. Your brother showed it me just now, and told me likewise, he left you at Horner's lodging to fetch a parson to marry you to him, and I wish you joy, madam, joy, joy; and to him too, much joy; and to myself more joy, for not marrying you.

ALITH. (*Aside*) So, I find my brother would break off the match, and I can consent to't, since I see this gentleman can be made jealous. – [*Aloud*] O Lucy, by his rude usage and jealousy, he makes me almost afraid I am married to him. Art thou sure 'twas Harcourt himself, and no parson, that married us?

SPARK. No, madam, I thank you. I suppose that was a contrivance too of Mr Horner's and yours, to make Harcourt play the parson; but I would as little as you have him one now, no, not for the world; for shall I tell you another truth? I never had any passion for you till now, for now I hate you. 'Tis true, I might have married your portion, as other men of parts of the town do sometimes. And so, your servant. And to show my unconcernedness, I'll come to your wedding, and resign you with as much joy as I would a stale wench to a new cully, nay, with as much joy as I would after the first night, if I had been married to you. There's for you; and so your servant, servant. *Exit*

ALITH. How was I deceived in a man!

LUCY. You'll believe then a fool may be made jealous now? For that easiness in him that suffers him to be led by a wife will likewise permit him to be persuaded against her by others.

ALITH. But marry Mr Horner! My brother does not intend it, sure. If I thought he did, I would take thy advice and Mr Harcourt for my husband. And now I wish that if there be any over-wise woman of the town who, like me, would marry a fool for fortune, liberty, or title, first, that her husband may love play,[13] and be a cully to all the town but her, and suffer none but fortune to be mistress of his purse;

---

[13]*play* gambling.

then, if for liberty, that he may send her into the country under the conduct of some huswifely mother-in-law; and if for title, may the world give 'em none but that of cuckold.

LUCY.   And for her greater curse, madam, may he not deserve it.

ALITH.   Away, impertinent! Is not this my old Lady Lanterlu's?[14]

LUCY.   Yes, madam. – (*Aside*) And here I hope we shall find Mr Harcourt.   *Exeunt*

SCENE FOUR

The scene changes again to HORNER'S *lodgings.*
A table, banquet, and bottles

Enter HORNER, LADY FIDGET, MRS DAINTY FIDGET, *and* MRS SQUEAMISH

HORN.   (*Aside*) A pox, they are come too soon, before I have sent back my new – mistress. All that I have now to do is to lock her in, that they may not see her.

LADY FID.   That we may be sure of our welcome, we have brought our entertainment with us, and are resolved to treat thee, dear toad.

MRS DAIN.   And that we may be merry to purpose, have left Sir Jasper and my old Lady Squeamish quarrelling at home at backgammon.

MRS SQUEAM.   Therefore let us make use of our time, lest they should chance to interrupt us.

LADY FID.   Let us sit then.

HORN.   First, that you may be private, let me lock this door and that, and I'll wait upon you presently.

LADY FID.   No, sir, shut 'em only, and your lips forever; for we must trust you as much as our women.[15]

HORN.   You know all vanity's killed in me; I have no occasion for talking.

LADY FID.   Now, ladies, supposing we had drank each of us our two bottles, let us speak the truth of our hearts.

MRS DAIN. *and* MRS SQUEAM.   Agreed.

LADY FID.   By this brimmer, for truth is nowhere else to be found – (*Aside to* HORNER) not in thy heart, false man!

HORN.   (*Aside to* LADY FIDGET) You have found me a true man, I'm sure.

LADY FID.   (*Aside to* HORNER) Not every way. – But let us sit and be merry.

Sings

Why should our damn'd tyrants[16] oblige us to live
On the pittance of pleasure which they only give?

[14]*Lanterlu's* from the card game, usually called 'loo'.
[15]*women* servants.   [16]*tyrants* husbands.

We must not rejoice
With wine and with noise:
In vain we must wake in a dull bed alone,
Whilst to our warm rival the bottle they're gone.
Then lay aside charms,
And take up these arms.[17]
'Tis wine only gives 'em their courage and wit;
Because we live sober, to men we submit.
If for beauties you'd pass,
Take a lick of the glass,
'Twill mend your complexions, and when they are gone,
The best red we have is the red of the grape:
Then, sisters, lay't on,
And damn a good shape.

MRS DAIN. Dear brimmer! Well, in token of our openness and plain-dealing, let us throw our masks over our heads.

HORN. (*Aside*) So 'twill come to the glasses anon.

MRS SQUEAM. Lovely brimmer! Let me enjoy him first.

LADY FID. No, I never part with a gallant till I've tried him. Dear brimmer that makest our husbands short-sighted!

MRS DAIN. And our bashful gallants bold.

MRS SQUEAM. And, for want of a gallant, the butler lovely in our eyes. — Drink, eunuch.

LADY FID. Drink, thou representative of a husband. Damn a husband!

MRS DAIN. And, as it were a husband, an old keeper.

MRS SQUEAM. And an old grandmother.

HORN. And an English bawd, and a French surgeon.

LADY FID. Ay, we have all reason to curse 'em.

HORN. For my sake, ladies?

LADY FID. No, for our own; for the first spoils all young gallants' industry.

MRS DAIN. And the other's art makes 'em bold only with common women.

MRS SQUEAM. And rather run the hazard of the vile distemper amongst them than of a denial amongst us.

MRS DAIN. The filthy toads choose mistresses now as they do stuffs,[18] for having been fancied and worn by others.

MRS SQUEAM. For being common and cheap.

LADY FID. Whilst women of quality, like the richest stuffs, lie untumbled and unasked for.

---

[17]*these arms* the glasses; so noted in the 1675 edition.
[18]*stuffs* material for clothing.

HORN.   Ay, neat and cheap and new often they think best.

MRS DAIN.   No, sir, the beasts will be known by a mistress longer than by a suit.

MRS SQUEAM.   And 'tis not for cheapness neither.

LADY FID.   No, for the vain fops will take druggets[19] and embroider 'em. But I wonder at the depraved appetites of witty men; they use[20] to be out of the common road and hate imitation. Pray tell me, beast, when you were a man, why you rather chose to club with a multitude in a common house[21] for an entertainment than to be the only guest at a good table.

HORN.   Why, faith, ceremony and expectation are insufferable to those that are sharp bent. People always eat with the best stomach at an ordinary, where every man is snatching for the best bit.

LADY FID.   Though he get a cut over the fingers. – But I have heard that people eat most heartily of another man's meat, that is, what they do not pay for.

HORN.   When they are sure of their welcome and freedom; for ceremony in love and eating is as ridiculous as in fighting. Falling on briskly is all should be done on those occasions.

LADY FID.   Well then, let me tell you, sir, there is nowhere more freedom than in our houses, and we take freedom from a young person as a sign of good breeding, and a person may be as free as he pleases with us, as frolic, as gamesome, as wild as he will.

HORN.   Han't I heard you all declaim against wild men?

LADY FID.   Yes, but for all that, we think wildness in a man as desirable a quality as in a duck or rabbit. A tame man? Foh!

HORN.   I know not, but your reputations frightened me as much as your faces invited me.

LADY FID.   Our reputation! Lord, why should you not think that we women make use of our reputation, as you men of yours, only to deceive the world with less suspicion? Our virtue is like the statesman's religion, the Quaker's word, the gamester's oath, and the great man's honour – but to cheat those that trust us.

MRS SQUEAM.   And that demureness, coyness, and modesty that you see in our faces in the boxes at plays is as much a sign of a kind[22] woman as a vizard-mask in the pit.

MRS DAIN.   For, I assure you, women are least masked when they have the velvet vizard on.

---

[19] *druggets* cheap woollen goods.
[20] *use* are accustomed.
[21] *common house* a verbal play on 'conventional eating house' and 'brothel'.
[22] *kind* promiscuous.

LADY FID.   You would have found us modest women in our denials only.

MRS SQUEAM.   Our bashfulness is only the reflection of the men's.

MRS DAIN.   We blush when they are shamefaced.

HORN.   I beg your pardon, ladies; I was deceived in you devilishly. But why that mighty pretence to honour?

LADY FID.   We have told you. But sometimes 'twas for the same reason you men pretend business often: to avoid ill company, to enjoy the better and more privately those you love.

HORN.   But why would you ne'er give a friend a wink then?

LADY FID.   Faith, your reputation frightened us, as much as ours did you, you were so notoriously lewd.

HORN.   And you so seemingly honest.²³

LADY FID.   Was that all that deterred you?

HORN.   And so expensive – you allow freedom, you say?

LADY FID.   Ay, ay.

HORN.   That I was afraid of losing my little money, as well as my little time, both which my other pleasures required.

LADY FID.   Money? Foh! You talk like a little fellow now. Do such as we expect money?

HORN.   I beg your pardon, madam, I must confess I have heard that great ladies, like great merchants, set but the higher prices upon what they have because they are not in necessity of taking the first offer.

MRS DAIN.   Such as we make sale of our hearts?

MRS SQUEAM.   We bribed for our love? Foh!

HORN.   With your pardon, ladies, I know, like great men in offices, you seem to exact flattery and attendance only from your followers, but you have receivers²⁴ about you, and such fees to pay, a man is afraid to pass your grants.²⁵ Besides, we must let you win at cards, or we lose your hearts; and if you make an assignation, 'tis at a goldsmith's, jeweller's, or china-house, where for your honour you deposit to him,²⁶ he must pawn his to the punctual cit,²⁷ and so, paying for what you take up, pays for what he takes up.

MRS DAIN.   Would you not have us assured of our gallants' love?

MRS SQUEAM.   For love is better known by liberality than by jealousy.

---

²³*honest* virtuous.

²⁴*receivers* servants who will receive or demand bribes.

²⁵*pass your grants* accept your favours.

²⁶*deposit to him* commit to your lover.

²⁷*cit* citizen, merchant, who will demand payment punctually.

LADY FID.   For one may be dissembled, the other not. – (*Aside*) But my jealousy can be no longer dissembled, and they are telling ripe.[28] – [*Aloud*] Come, here's to our gallants in waiting, whom we must name, and I'll begin. This is my false rogue.   *Claps him on the back*

MRS SQUEAM.   How!

HORN.   (*Aside*) So, all will out now.

MRS SQUEAM.   (*Aside to* HORNER) Did you not tell me 'twas for my sake only you reported yourself no man?

MRS DAIN.   (*Aside to* HORNER) O wretch, did you not swear to me 'twas for my love and honour you passed for that thing you do?

HORN.   So, so.

LADY FID.   Come, speak, ladies: this is my false villain.

MRS SQUEAM.   And mine too.

MRS DAIN.   And mine.

HORN.   Well then, you are all three my false rogues too, and there's an end on't.

LADY FID.   Well then, there's no remedy; sister sharers, let us not fall out, but have a care of our honour. Though we get no presents, no jewels of him, we are savers of our honour, the jewel of most value and use, which shines yet to the world unsuspected, though it be counterfeit.

HORN.   Nay, and is e'en as good as if it were true, provided the world think so; for honour, like beauty now, only depends on the opinion of others.

LADY FID.   Well, Harry Common,[29] I hope you can be true to three. Swear; but 'tis to no purpose to require your oath, for you are as often forsworn as you swear to new women.

HORN.   Come, faith, madam, let us e'en pardon one another; for all the difference I find betwixt we men and you women, we forswear ourselves at the beginning of an amour, you as long as it lasts.

Enter SIR JASPER FIDGET *and* OLD LADY SQUEAMISH

SIR JASP.   O my Lady Fidget, was this your cunning, to come to Mr Horner without me? But you have been nowhere else, I hope.

LADY FID.   No, Sir Jasper.

LADY SQUEAM.   And you came straight hither, Biddy?

MRS SQUEAM.   Yes, indeed, lady grandmother.

SIR JASP.   'Tis well, 'tis well; I knew when once they were thoroughly acquainted with poor Horner, they'd ne'er be from him. You may let

---

[28]*telling ripe* ready to be told.

[29]*Harry Common* Harry Horner is now shared by all three women. Compare 'Doll Common', Jonson, *The Alchemist*.

her masquerade it with my wife and Horner, and I warrant her reputation safe.

Enter BOY

BOY. O sir, here's the gentleman come whom you bid me not suffer to come up without giving you notice, with a lady too, and other gentlemen.

HORN. Do you all go in there whilst I send 'em away; and, boy, do you desire 'em to stay below till I come, which shall be immediately.

Exeunt SIR JASPER FIDGET, LADY FIDGET, LADY SQUEAMISH, MRS SQUEAMISH *and* MRS DAINTY FIDGET

BOY. Yes, sir. *Exit*

Exit HORNER *at the other door, and returns with* MRS PINCHWIFE

HORN. You would not take my advice to be gone home before your husband came back; he'll now discover all. Yet pray, my dearest, be persuaded to go home and leave the rest to my management; I'll let you down the back way.

MRS PINCH. I don't know the way home, so I don't.

HORN. My man shall wait upon you.

MRS PINCH. No, don't you believe that I'll go at all; what, are you weary of me already?

HORN. No, my life, 'tis that I may love you long; 'tis to secure my love and your reputation with your husband; he'll never receive you again else.

MRS PINCH. What care I? D'ye think to frighten me with that? I don't intend to go to him again; you shall be my husband now.

HORN. I cannot be your husband, dearest, since you are married to him.

MRS PINCH. Oh, would you make me believe that? Don't I see every day at London here women leave their first husbands and go and live with other men as their wives? Pish, pshaw, you'd make me angry but that I love you so mainly.[30]

HORN. So, they are coming up. In again, in, I hear 'em. – (*Exit* MRS PINCHWIFE) Well, a silly mistress is like a weak place,[31] soon got, soon lost. A man has scarce time for plunder. She betrays her husband first to her gallant, and then her gallant to her husband.

Enter PINCHWIFE, ALITHEA, HARCOURT, SPARKISH, LUCY *and a* PARSON

PINCH. Come, madam, 'tis not the sudden change of your dress, the confidence of your asserverations, and your false witness there[32] shall persuade me I did not bring you hither just now; here's my

---

[30]*mainly* strongly.   [31]*place* fortification.   [32]*false witness there* Lucy.

witness, who cannot deny it, since you must be confronted. – Mr
Horner, did not I bring this lady to you just now?

HORN.   (*Aside*) Now I must wrong one woman for another's sake,
but that's no new thing with me, for in these cases I am still on the
criminal's side against the innocent.

ALITH.   Pray speak, sir.

HORN.   (*Aside*) It must be so. I must be impudent and try my luck;
impudence uses to be too hard for truth.

PINCH.   What, you are studying an evasion or excuse for her? Speak,
sir.

HORN.   No, faith, I am something backward only to speak in
women's affairs or disputes.

PINCH.   She bids you speak.

ALITH.   Ay, pray, sir, do, pray satisfy him.

HORN.   Then truly, you did bring that lady to me just now.

PINCH.   O ho!

ALITH.   How, sir?

HAR.   How, Horner?

ALITH.   What mean you, sir? I always took you for a man of honour.

HORN.   (*Aside*) Ay, so much a man of honour that I must save my
mistress, I thank you, come what will on't.

SPARK.   So, if I had had her, she'd have made me believe the moon
had been made of a Christmas pie.

LUCY.   (*Aside*) Now could I speak, if I durst, and solve the riddle, who
am the author of it.

ALITH.   O unfortunate woman! A combination against my honour –
which most concerns me now, because you share in my disgrace, sir,
and it is your censure, which I must now suffer, that troubles me, not
theirs.

HAR.   Madam, then have no trouble; you shall now see 'tis possible
for me to love too, without being jealous. I will not only believe your
innocence myself, but make all the world believe it. – (*Aside to*
HORNER) Horner, I must now be concerned for this lady's honour.

HORN.   And I must be concerned for a lady's honour too.

HAR.   This lady has her honour, and I will protect it.

HORN.   My lady has not her honour, but has given it me to keep, and I
will preserve it.

HAR.   I understand you not.

HORN.   I would not have you.

MRS PINCH.   What's the matter with 'em all? *Peeping in behind*

PINCH.   Come, come, Mr Horner, no more disputing. Here's the
parson; I brought him not in vain.

HAR.   No, sir, I'll employ him, if this lady please.

PINCH.   How! What d'ye mean?

SPARK.   Ay, what does he mean?

HORN.   Why, I have resigned your sister to him; he has my consent.

PINCH.   But he has not mine, sir; a woman's injured honour, no more than a man's, can be repaired or satisfied by any but him that first wronged it; and you shall marry her presently, or –

Lays his hand on his sword

Re-enter MRS PINCHWIFE

MRS PINCH.   O Lord, they'll kill poor Mr Horner! Besides, he shan't marry her whilst I stand by and look on; I'll not lose my second husband so.

PINCH.   What do I see?

ALITH.   My sister in my clothes!

SPARK.   Ha!

MRS PINCH.   Nay, pray now don't quarrel about finding work for the parson; he shall marry me to Mr Horner. – (*To* PINCHWIFE) For now, I believe, you have enough of me.

HORN.   [*Aside*] Damned, damned loving changeling!

MRS PINCH.   Pray, sister, pardon me for telling so many lies of you.

HAR.   I suppose the riddle is plain now.

LUCY.   No, that must be my work. – Good sir, hear me.

Kneels to PINCHWIFE, *who stands doggedly*33 *with his hat over his eyes*

PINCH.   I will never hear woman again, but make 'em all silent thus –

Offers to draw upon his WIFE

HORN.   No, that must not be.

PINCH.   You then shall go first; 'tis all one to me.

Offers to draw on HORNER, *but is stopped by* HARCOURT

HAR.   Hold!

Re-enter SIR JASPER FIDGET, LADY FIDGET, LADY SQUEAMISH, MRS DAINTY FIDGET, *and* MRS SQUEAMISH

SIR JASP.   What's the matter? What's the matter? Pray, what's the matter, sir? I beseech you communicate, sir.

PINCH.   Why, my wife has communicated,34 sir, as your wife may have done too, sir, if she knows35 him, sir.

SIR JASP.   Pshaw, with him? Ha, ha, he!

PINCH.   D'ye mock me, sir? A cuckold is a kind of a wild beast; have a care, sir.

33*doggedly* sullenly.
34*communicated* with the sense of having had a sexual relationship.
35*knows* is acquainted with, and a sexual innuendo.

SIR JASP. No, sure, you mock me, sir. He cuckold you? It can't be, ha, ha, he! Why, I'll tell you, sir, – *Offers to whisper*

PINCH. I tell you again, he has whored my wife, and yours too, if he knows her, and all the women he comes near; 'tis not his dissembling, his hypocrisy, can wheedle me.

SIR JASP. How, does he dissemble? Is he an hypocrite? Nay, then – how – wife – sister, is he an hypocrite?

LADY SQUEAM. An hypocrite? A dissembler? Speak, young harlotry, speak, how!

SIR JASP. Nay, then – Oh, my head[36] too! O thou libidinous lady!

LADY SQUEAM. O thou harloting harlotry, has thou done't then?

SIR JASP. Speak, good Horner, art thou a dissembler, a rogue? Hast thou –

HORN. Soh.[37]

LUCY. (*Apart to* HORNER) I'll fetch you off,[38] and her too, if she[39] will but hold her tongue.

HORN. (*Apart to* LUCY) Canst thou? I'll give thee –

LUCY. (*To* PINCHWIFE) Pray have but patience to hear me, sir, who am the unfortunate cause of all this confusion. Your wife is innocent, I only culpable; for I put her upon telling you all these lies concerning my mistress, in order to the breaking off the match between Mr Sparkish and her, to make way for Mr Harcourt.

SPARK. Did you so, eternal rotten tooth? Then, it seems, my mistress was not false to me; I was only deceived by you. Brother that should have been, now man of conduct, who is a frank person now, to bring your wife to her lover, ha?

LUCY. I assure you, sir, she came not to Mr Horner out of love, for she loves him no more –

MRS PINCH. Hold! I told lies for you, but you shall tell none for me, for I do love Mr Horner with all my soul, and nobody shall say me nay; pray, don't you go to make poor Mr Horner believe to the contrary; 'tis spitefully done of you, I'm sure.

HORN. (*Aside to* MRS PINCHWIFE) Peace, dear idiot.

MRS PINCH. Nay, I will not peace.

PINCH. Not till I make you.

Enter DORILANT *and* QUACK

DOR. Horner, your servant. I am the doctor's guest; he must excuse our intrusion.

QUACK. But what's the matter, gentlemen? For heaven's sake, what's the matter?

---

[36]*my head* His cuckold's horns pain him.   [37]*Soh* a sigh.
[38]*fetch you off* help you to escape.   [39]*she* i.e. Margery Pinchwife.

HORN. Oh, 'tis well you are come. 'Tis a censorious world we live in; you may have brought me a reprieve, or else I had died for a crime I never committed, and these innocent ladies had suffered with me; therefore, pray satisfy these worthy, honourable, jealous gentlemen that – *Whispers*

QUACK. Oh, I understand you. Is that all? – Sir Jasper, by heavens, and upon the word of a physician, sir – *Whispers to* SIR JASPER

SIR JASP. Nay, I do believe you truly. – Pardon me, my virtuous lady, and dear of honour.

LADY SQUEAM. What, then all's right again?

SIR JASP. Ay, ay, and now let us satisfy him too.
They whisper with PINCHWIFE

PINCH. An eunuch? Pray, no fooling with me.

QUACK. I'll bring half the surgeons in town to swear it.

PINCH. They! They'll swear a man that bled to death through his wounds⁴⁰ died of an apoplexy.

QUACK. Pray hear me, sir. Why, all the town has heard the report of him.

PINCH. But does all the town believe it?

QUACK. Pray inquire a little, and first of all these.

PINCH. I'm sure when I left the town he was the lewdest fellow in't.

QUACK. I tell you, sir, he has been in France since; pray, ask but these ladies and gentlemen, your friend Mr Dorilant. Gentlemen and ladies, han't you all heard the late sad report of poor Mr Horner?

ALL THE LADIES. Ay, ay, ay.

DOR. Why, thou jealous fool, dost thou doubt it? He's an arrant French capon.

MRS PINCH. 'Tis false, sir. You shall not disparage poor Mr Horner, for to my certain knowledge –

LUCY. Oh, hold!

MRS SQUEAM. (*Aside to* LUCY) Stop her mouth!

LADY FID. (*To* PINCHWIFE) Upon my honour, sir, 'tis as true –

MRS DAIN. D'ye think we would have been seen in his company?

MRS SQUEAM. Trust our unspotted reputations with him?

LADY FID. (*Aside to* HORNER) This you get, and we too, by trusting your secret to a fool.

HORN. Peace, madam. – (*Aside to* QUACK) Well, doctor, is not this a good design, that carries a man on unsuspected and brings him off safe?

PINCH. Well, if this were true – (*Aside*) but my wife –
DORILANT *whispers with* MRS PINCHWIFE

---

⁴⁰*wounds* received in a duel, then illegal.

ALITH.   Come, brother, your wife is yet innocent, you see; but have a care of too strong an imagination, lest, like an over-concerned, timorous gamester, by fancying⁴¹ an unlucky cast, it should come. Women and fortune are truest still to those that trust 'em.

LUCY.   And any wild thing grows but the more fierce and hungry for being kept up, and more dangerous to the keeper.

ALITH.   There's doctrine for all husbands, Mr Harcourt.

HAR.   I edify, madam, so much that I am impatient till I am one.

DOR.   And I edify so much by example, I will never be one.

SPARK.   And because I will not disparage my parts, I'll ne'er be one.

HORN.   And I, alas, can't be one.

PINCH.   But I must be one – against my will – to a country wife, with a country murrain⁴² to me!

MRS PINCH.   (*Aside*) And I must be a country wife still too, I find; for I can't, like a city one, be rid of my musty husband and do what I list.

HORN.   Now, sir, I must pronounce your wife innocent, though I blush whilst I do it; and I am the only man by her now exposed to shame, which I will straight drown in wine, as you shall your suspicion; and the ladies' troubles we'll divert with a ballad. Doctor, where are your maskers?

LUCY.   Indeed, she's innocent, sir. I am her witness; and her end of coming out was but to see her sister's wedding, and what she has said to your face of her love to Mr Horner was but the usual innocent revenge on a husband's jealousy. Was it not, madam? Speak.

MRS PINCH.   (*Aside to* LUCY *and* HORNER) Since you'll have me tell more lies – [*Aloud*] Yes, indeed, bud.

PINCH.   For my own sake fain I would all believe;
              Cuckolds, like lovers, should themselves deceive.
              But –   *Sighs*
              His honour is least safe (too late I find)
              Who trusts it with a foolish wife or friend.
                      A Dance of Cuckolds

HORN.   Vain fops but court and dress and keep a pother,
              To pass for women's men with one another;
              But he who aims by women to be priz'd,
              First by the men, you see, must be despis'd.   *Exeunt*

---

⁴¹*fancying* imagining.   ⁴²*murrain* cattle plague.

EPILOGUE

SPOKEN BY MRS KNEP

Now you the vigorous, who daily here
O'er vizard-mask in public domineer,
And what you'd do to her, if in place where;[1]
Nay, have the confidence to cry, 'Come out!'
Yet when she says, 'Lead on!' you are not stout;[2]
But to your well-dress'd brother straight turn round,
And cry, 'Pox on her, Ned, she can't be sound!'
Then slink away, a fresh one to engage,
With so much seeming heat and loving rage
You'd frighten list'ning actress on the stage,
Till she at last has seen you huffing come,
And talk of keeping in the tiring-room,
Yet cannot be provok'd to lead her home.
Next, you Falstaffs of fifty, who beset
Your buckram maidenheads,[3] which your friends get;
And whilst to them you of achievements boast,
They share the booty and laugh at your cost.
In fine, you essenc'd[4] boys, both old and young,
Who would be thought so eager, brisk, and strong,
Yet do the ladies, not their husbands, wrong;
Whose purses for your manhood make excuse,
And keep your Flanders mares[5] for show not use;
Encourag'd by our woman's man today,
A Horner's part may vainly think to play;
And may intrigues so bashfully disown
That they may doubted be by few or none;

---

[1] *where* if opportunity offers. [2]*stout* bold.
[3]*buckram maidenheads* i.e. as imaginary as the thieves in buckram garments
whom Falstaff pretended to have attacked: Shakespeare, *1 Henry IV*, II, iv, 227.
[4]*essenc'd* perfumed. [5]*Flanders mares* mistresses.

May kiss the cards at picquet, ombre, loo,
And so be thought to kiss the lady too;
But, gallants, have a care, faith, what you do;
The world, which to no man his due will give,
You by experience know you can deceive,
And men may still believe you vigorous,
But then we women — there's no cozening us.

George Etherege

THE MAN OF MODE
Or
SIR FOPLING FLUTTER

1676

The Man of Mode,
Or
Sir Fopling Flutter,
a comedy,
acted at the Duke's Theatre;
by George Etherege, Esq.
Licenced June 3, 1676
Roger L'Estrange.

London,
printed by J. Macock,
for Henry Herringman
at the sign of the Blue Anchor
in the Lower Walk of the New Exchange.
1676

BIOGRAPHY

Born in 1636, perhaps in Maidenhead; apprenticed to an attorney at Beaconsfield; briefly studied at Clement's Inn, London. Subsequently he was a poet, courtier and wit, with a small private income. He wrote *The Comical Revenge*, 1664, and *She Would if She Could*, 1668. He was for a short time a Gentleman of the Privy Chamber in Ordinary, and then a diplomat in Turkey 1668–71. Etherege wrote *The Man of Mode* in 1676. He was knighted and married in 1679, and was a diplomat at Ratisbon, Germany, 1685–89. He is thought to have died in 1692.

INTRODUCTION

The Man of Mode, Etherege's last play, is one of the finest early examples of the English comedy of manners. The word 'mode' helps to define the genre, for the play is centred on two young men, Dorimant and Fopling, who are guided by their idea of 'style' – in their dress, their ways of speaking and their relationship with women. Although the affected and superficial Sir Fopling Flutter contributes only peripherally to the plot, his role is pivotal in illustrating the play's theme, the excesses of affectation, and in showing how close Dorimant is to being another Fopling. (The play's alternative title was *Sir Fopling Flutter*.) However, while clothes are the centre of Fopling's life, to Dorimant they are incidental, and Fopling lacks discrimination, which Dorimant possesses. Yet, they have in common a liking for things superficial, and, interestingly, there is no really serious satire of Fopling's extravagances of speech, manners and taste.[1]

Dorimant, more subtle and versatile in speech than Horner in *The Country Wife*, is both an exponent of manners and the major force behind the entire action. His aggressive interest in four young women, Mrs Loveit, Emilia, Belinda and Harriet, brings out the varied aspects of his personality and creates the more obvious tensions of the play. At the same time an almost unrelated plot is working itself out through Young Bellair and Emilia, who are unaffectedly in love and anxious to marry. The two plots are casually linked by the lively and independent Harriet, presently engaged to Young Bellair, as arranged by her mother, Lady Woodvill, and his father, Old Bellair. Young Bellair is, however, already secretly betrothed to Emilia. In time parental wills

[1] John Dennis's *A Defense of Sir Fopling Flutter*, 1722, reflects an eighteenth-century controversy over *The Man of Mode*. In 1711 Richard Steele had been highly critical in *The Spectator* of the morality of Etherege's play, and in 1722 Steele produced his corrective play *The Conscious Lovers*, provoking Dennis's response, which had little to do with Sir Fopling, but is a close analysis of Etherege's intentions in the character of Dorimant.

are defeated, and in this 'modern' age the young women attach themselves to the lovers of their choice.

Although the overall structure of the play is not particularly tight, the flow from one plot to the other is always natural. The action takes place over slightly more than twenty-four hours, and the play begins after events have been set on their course. Dorimant has begun pursuing Belinda and arranging his rejection of Loveit, and Young Bellair's relationships with Emilia and Harriet have already been established. The way has been prepared for what happens next. Every scene anticipates a later situation or character revelation. The opening episode, for example, introduces a mysterious masked girl (later identified as Belinda), announces the unexpected, ominous arrival of Old Bellair and refers repeatedly to Sir Fopling Flutter, who does not appear until III, ii.

Young Bellair's 'romances' are in sharp contrast to the cynical, libertine *affaires d'amour* of Dorimant, who is trying, at one and the same time, to break off with the vain and passionate Loveit, to seduce Belinda, and to offer himself, after his own initial resistance, as a serious lover to Harriet. (He also has a casual interest in Emilia.) There are obviously several unattractive aspects of Dorimant's character which would seem to inhibit his being the hero of this comedy; however, Etherege gives to Dorimant some sincerity, tolerance, and good nature, as well as much self-interest. Dorimant's assets and liabilities are in balance throughout most of the play – the combination giving him rather more realism than most heroes of Restoration drama possess – but near the end, as Dorimant gradually removes Harriet's objections to his pursuit of her, he has to muster up all the sincerity he can to make convincing his promises of fidelity.[2] Old habits die hard; whilst Dorimant protests his devotion to Harriet in Act V, he conciliates the angry Loveit by explaining that he has gone over to Harriet only from necessity, 'to repair the ruins of my estate'. (This statement may or may not be true; Dorimant has made only one passing reference earlier to his financial circumstances; he is certainly generous enough to Foggy Nan, Tom and Molly.) He also suggests to Belinda a further meeting; she replies curtly, 'Never'. Both women have learned something important about Dorimant in two days and perhaps a lesson or two about life, and his humbling relationships with both have contributed to his maturation.

The play includes several varied characters of much interest. First there is Harriet Woodvill, who is almost certainly like no other girl

[2] In IV, i, Dorimant had abruptly terminated his enthusiastic wooing of Harriet in order to fulfil (at five o'clock in the morning) his first assignation with Belinda.

Dorimant has ever encountered. She has self-discipline (although she is in love with him), self-confidence, wit and skill at teasing this new suitor with a diabolical reputation. These characteristics in Harriet, lacking in her rivals, Loveit and Belinda, will be found later in Millamant in *The Way of the World*. It is Harriet's self-restraint that challenges Dorimant and intensifies his love for her.

It is possible that the orange-woman in *The Man of Mode* (1, i), first performed at the Duke's Theatre, is a caricature of Orange Moll (Mrs Mary Meggs), who sold oranges (at sixpence each), carried *billets doux*, and distributed gossip at the rival house, the Theatre Royal, Drury Lane. (The name of the actress who played the part of the orange-woman is unknown.) Meggs, referred to frequently by Pepys and others, held the profitable monopoly for the sale of fruit and sweetmeats from about 1663 until her death in 1691. (One of her assistants was Nell Gwynn.)

In addition, there is Medley, a professional gossip; hence Dorimant cannot trust him – 'a flea or a maggot is not made more monstrous by a magnifying glass than a story is by his telling it'. And there is perky Old Bellair, who bounces through his scenes with his verbal eccentricities. He has a degree of pretension, illustrated in his naive ambition to marry, at the age of fifty-five, the girl whom his son intends to wed. Old Bellair and the two aristocratic senior ladies on the fringes of the action provide the traditional conflict of generations. The affectations of Sir Fopling Flutter provide much stage entertainment; Mrs Loveit, his female counterpart, was more amusing to a Restoration audience than a modern one. She is a *précieuse* and a caricature of now old-fashioned female figures from the heroic dramas of the time. Sir John Vanbrugh was to draw Loveit to extremes in his Lady Fanciful (*The Provoked Wife*, 1697).

The Man of Mode is, as noted, a play about appearances. There are frequent references to mirrors, cosmetics, masks and masquerades, and one fine scene has Harriet and Young Bellair pretending to woo each other and deceiving 'the grave people', her mother and his father. (There is a similar situation in Goldsmith's *She Stoops to Conquer*, 1773.) Most of the metaphors and similes echo the artificiality or unreality; the majority have reference directly or indirectly to Dorimant via gaming, commerce, religion (used in a tongue-in-cheek manner), and in particular his role as devil. Thus the 'gilded lover' Dorimant speaks directly about: 'Love [that] gilds us over and makes us show fine things to one another for a time, but soon the gold wears off, and then the native brass appears.' More obliquely, there are a number of references to enticing fruit as Dorimant's devilish seduction schemes unfold. There are no allusions to apples in the play, but

Dorimant enjoys a fine peach, provided by the informative orange-woman, whilst he considers the possibilities of captivating Harriet; and later Belinda, seduced and abruptly dropped, has had a surfeit of nectarines.

The imagery contributes significantly to the wit and sparkle of the play, much of it conveyed in colloquial dialogue. Etherege uses key words like 'wild'/'wildness' to develop character and to point directions. The sophisticated interchanges, especially those between Dorimant and Fopling, anticipate the scintillating style of *The Way of the World*.

The Man of Mode concludes with an unanswered question, similar to that which Wycherley left at the end of *The Country Wife*: how much sincerity does Dorimant possess? He has fallen in love (as he seems to have done many times before) with Harriet, partly because she would not allow him to seduce her ('Without church security, there's no taking up there'), partly because she is both pretty and wealthy. The playwright invites reader or viewer to think about this vital young couple in a 'dismal, great rambling lone house' in the desert of Hampshire (a county then rather more isolated from London than it is today). Both Dorimant and Harriet have their reasons to return to London as soon as possible. Will they be a Millamant and a Mirabell (they exchange similar provisos), or will Dorimant revert to his former self and resume acquaintance with Loveit and Belinda? Although one likes to think that the beneficent influences of the shrewd, altogether likeable Harriet have reformed the profligate Dorimant in less than forty-eight hours, Etherege does not offer a placid, romantic ending to the play.

During the five acts Etherege made use of eleven excerpts from contemporary poets; seven (spoken by Dorimant) are from Edmund Waller (1606–87), by then regarded as old-fashioned. The playwright used these lines ironically because they reflected a rather out-of-date idealism.

Other specific influences on *The Man of Mode* are difficult to isolate. The play includes some reminders of Molière, and there is a cousinship between Dorimant and Horner, in *The Country Wife*, (1675). Audiences in 1676 may have believed that Etherege modelled characters in *The Man of Mode* on individuals whom he and they knew in London society, but there is little substantial evidence that he did so. The playwright undoubtedly drew upon the aristocratic society with which he was familiar, and the careers of some of the Restoration beaux and fops, like Sir George Hewitt, Sir Car Scroope and John Wilmot, second Earl of Rochester, would indicate that little dramatic heightening was necessary.

BIBLIOGRAPHY

The Man of Mode

D. Underwood, *Etherege and the Seventeenth-century Comedy of Manners*. New Haven, 1957.

D. Krause, 'The Defaced Angel: a Concept of Satanic Grace in Etherege's *The Man of Mode*'. *Drama Survey*, 7 (Winter 1968–9), 87–103.

P. C. Davies, 'The State of Nature and the State of War: a Reconsideration of *The Man of Mode*'. *University of Toronto Quarterly*, 39 (October 1969), 53–62.

R. D. Hume, 'Reading and Misreading *The Man of Mode*'. *Criticism*, 14 (Winter 1972), 1–11.

L. Martin, 'Past and Parody in *The Man of Mode*'. *Studies in English Literature 1500–1900*, 16 (Summer 1976), 363–76.

B. Corman, 'Interpreting and Misinterpreting *The Man of Mode*'. *Papers on Language and Literature*, 13 (Winter 1977), 35–53.

D. D. Mann, *Sir George Etherege: a Reference Guide*. Boston, 1981.

R. A. Zimbardo, 'Of Women, Comic Imitation of Nature, and Etherege's *The Man of Mode*'. *Studies in English Literature 1500–1900*, 21 (Summer 1981), 373–87.

J. Barnard, 'Point of View in *The Man of Mode*'. *Essays in Criticism*, 34 (October 1984), 285–308.

R. Weiss, 'Utopian Rhetoric in *The Man of Mode*'. *The Eighteenth Century: Theory and Interpretation*, 27 (Spring 1986), 141–61.

D. Wilkinson, 'Etherege and a Restoration Pattern of Wit'. *English Studies*, 68 (December 1987), 497–510.

A. R. Huseboe, *Sir George Etherege*. Boston, 1987.

F. Ogée, '"All the World Will be in the Park Tonight": Seeing and Being Seen in Etherege's *The Man of Mode*'. *Restoration: Studies in English Literary Culture, 1660–1700*. 13 (Fall 1989), 86–94.

S. Staves, 'The Secrets of Genteel Identity in *The Man of Mode*: Comedy of Manners vs. The Courtesy Book'. *Studies in Eighteenth-Century Culture*, 19 (1989), 117–28.

L. Berglund, 'The Language of the Libertines: Subversive Morality in *The Man of Mode*'. *Studies in English Literature 1500–1900*, 30 (Summer 1990), 369–86.

TO HER ROYAL HIGHNESS
THE DUCHESS[1]

Madam,

Poets, however they may be modest otherwise, have always too good an opinion of what they write. The world, when it sees this play dedicated to your Royal Highness, will conclude I have more than my share of that vanity. But I hope the honour I have of belonging to you will excuse my presumption. 'Tis the first thing I have produced in your service, and my duty obliges me to what my choice durst not else have aspired.

I am very sensible, madam, how much it is beholding to your indulgence for the success it had in the acting, and your protection will be no less fortunate to it in the printing; for all are so ambitious of making their court to you that none can be severe to what you are pleased to favour.

This universal submission and respect is due to the greatness of your rank and birth; but you have other illustrious qualities which are much more engaging. Those would but dazzle, did not these really charm the eyes and understandings of all who have the happiness to approach you.

Authors on these occasions are never wanting to publish a particular of their patron's virtues and perfections; but your Royal Highness's are so eminently known that, did I follow their examples, I should but paint those wonders here of which everyone already has the idea in his mind. Besides, I do not think it proper to aim at that in prose which is so glorious a subject for verse; in which hereafter, if I show more zeal than skill, it will not grieve me much, since I less passionately desire to be esteemed a poet than to be thought, Madam, your Royal Highness's most humble, most obedient, and most faithful servant,

GEORGE ETHEREGE.

[1] *Duchess* Mary of Modena, 1658–1718, Duchess of York; married James, Duke of York, 1673; queen-consort when he became King James II in 1685.

PROLOGUE

by SIR CAR SCROOPE, BARONET[1]

Like dancers on the ropes poor poets fare:
Most perish young, the rest in danger are;
This, one would think, should make our authors wary,
But, gamester-like, the giddy fools miscarry.
A lucky hand or two so tempts 'em on
They cannot leave off play till they're undone.
With modest fears a muse does first begin,
Like a young wench newly entic'd to sin;
But tickl'd once with praise, by her good will,
The wanton fool would never more lie still.
'Tis an old mistress you'll meet here tonight,
Whose charms you once have look'd on with delight;
But now of late such dirty drabs have known ye,
A muse o' the better sort's asham'd to own ye.
Nature well drawn and wit must now give place
To gaudy nonsense and to dull grimace;
Nor is it strange that you should like so much
That kind of wit, for most of yours is such.
But I'm afraid that while to France we go,
To bring you home fine dresses, dance, and show,
The stage, like you, will but more foppish grow.
Of foreign wares why should we fetch the scum,
When we can be so richly serv'd at home?
For, heav'n be thank'd, 'tis not so wise an age
But your own follies may supply the stage.
Though often plough'd, there's no great fear the soil
Should barren grow by the too-frequent toil,
While at your doors are to be daily found

---

[1] *Scroope* 1649–80; poet, courtier in the court of Charles II.

Such loads of dunghill to manure the ground.
'Tis by your follies that we players thrive,
As the physicians by diseases live;
And as each year some new distemper reigns,
Whose friendly poison helps t'increase their gains,
So among you there starts up every day
Some new unheard-of fool for us to play.
Then for your own sakes be not too severe,
Nor what you all admire at home, damn here:
Since each is fond of his own ugly face,
Why should you, when we hold it, break the glass?

DRAMATIS PERSONAE

MR DORIMANT
MR MEDLEY
OLD BELLAIR
YOUNG BELLAIR
SIR FOPLING FLUTTER
LADY TOWNLEY
EMILIA
MRS LOVEIT
BELINDA
LADY WOODVILL
HARRIET, *her daughter*
PERT *and* BUSY, *waiting-women*
A SHOEMAKER
AN ORANGE-WOMAN
THREE SLOVENLY BULLIES
TWO CHAIRMEN
MR SMIRK, *a parson*
HANDY, *a valet de chambre*
Pages, footmen, etc.

Scene: London.

THE MAN OF MODE

Act One

SCENE ONE

A dressing-room. A table covered with a toilet,[1] clothes laid ready.

Enter DORIMANT *in his gown and slippers, with a note in his hand made up, repeating verses*

DOR. Now for some ages had the pride of Spain
      Made the sun shine on half the world in vain.[2] (*Then looking on the note – For Mrs Loveit*) What a dull insipid thing is a *billet-doux* written in cold blood, after the heat of the business is over! It is a tax upon good nature which I have here been labouring to pay, and have done it, but with as much regret as ever fanatic[3] paid the Royal Aid[4] or Church Duties.[5] 'Twill have the same fate, I know, that all my notes to her have had of late: 'twill not be thought kind enough. Faith, women are i' the right when they jealously examine our letters, for in them we always first discover[6] our decay of passion. – Hey! Who waits?

Enter HANDY

HANDY. Sir.

DOR. Call a footman.

HANDY. None of 'em are come yet.

DOR. Dogs! Will they ever lie snoring abed till noon?

HANDY. 'Tis all one, sir; if they're up, you indulge 'em so, they're ever poaching after whores all the morning.

DOR. Take notice henceforward, who's wanting in his duty, the next clap he gets, he shall rot for an example. What vermin are those chattering without?

HANDY. Foggy[7] Nan, the orange-woman, and swearing Tom, the shoemaker.

---

[1] *toilet* elaborate decorated cloth for a dressing table.
[2] *Now . . . vain* Edmund Waller, 'Of a War with Spain and a Fight at Sea', *Poems*, II (London, 1901), pp. 23–27.
[3] *fanatic* dissenter, nonconformist.
[4] *Royal Aid* a tax for the benefit of royalty.
[5] *Church Duties* fees charged for various services rendered by the church.
[6] *discover* reveal.   [7] *Foggy* Fat.

DOR. Go; call in that overgrown jade with the flasket of guts before her; fruit is refreshing in a morning.   *Exit* HANDY

> It is not that I love you less
> Than when before your feet I lay.[8]

Enter ORANGE-WOMAN [*with* HANDY]

How now, Double Tripe! What news do you bring?

OR.-WOM. News! Here's the best fruit has come to town t'year; gad, I was up before four a'clock this morning, and bought all the choice i' the market.

DOR. The nasty refuse of your shop.

OR.-WOM. You need not make mouths at it; I assure you 'tis all culled ware.

DOR. The citizens buy better on a holiday in their walk to Totnam.[9]

OR.-WOM. Good or bad, 'tis all one; I never knew you commend anything. Lord, would the ladies had heard you talk of 'em as I have done. Here, bid your man give me an angel.[10]   *Sets down the fruit*

DOR. Give the bawd her fruit again.

OR.-WOM. Well, on my conscience, there never was the like of you. God's my life, I had almost forgot to tell you there is a young gentlewoman lately come to town with her mother, that is so taken with you.

DOR. Is she handsome?

OR.-WOM. Nay, gad, there are few finer women, I tell you but so, and a hugeous fortune, they say. Here, eat this peach, it comes from the stone; 'tis better than any Newington[11] you've tasted.

DOR. This fine woman, I'll lay my life, (*Taking the peach*) is some awkward, ill-fashioned country toad, who, not having above four dozen black hairs on her head, has adorned her baldness with a large white fruz, that she may look sparkishly in the forefront of the king's box at an old play.

OR.-WOM. Gad, you'd change your note quickly if you did but see her.

DOR. How came she to know me?

    [8]*It is . . . I lay* Edmund Waller, 'The Self-banished', *Poems*, i (London, 1901), p. 101.

    [9]*Totnam* Tottenham; about seven miles (ten kilometres) north of London, then popular for working-class outings. 'The suburb fools trudge to Lamb's Conduit or Totnam' (Thomas Shadwell, *The Virtuoso* [1676], v, ii, 13–14).

    [10]*angel* a gold coin then worth ten shillings (50 pence), not minted since the reign of Charles II.

    [11]*Newington* a variety of peach, from Kent.

OR.-WOM. She saw you yesterday at the Change;[12] she told me you came and fooled with the woman at the next shop.

DOR. I remember there was a mask observed me indeed. Fooled, did she say?

OR.-WOM. Ay, I vow she told me twenty things you said too; and acted with her head and with her body so like you –

Enter MEDLEY

MED. Dorimant, my life, my joy, my darling sin, how dost thou?

OR.-WOM. Lord, what a filthy trick these men have got of kissing one another! *She spits*

MED. Why do you suffer this cartload of scandal to come near you and make your neighbours think you so improvident to need a bawd?

OR.-WOM. Good, now we shall have it! You did but want him to help you. Come, pay me for my fruit.

MED. Make us[13] thankful for it, huswife; bawds are as much out of fashion as gentlemen-ushers: none but old formal ladies use the one, and none but foppish old stagers[14] employ the other. Go, you are an insignificant brandy bottle.

DOR. Nay, there you wrong her, three quarts of canary[15] is her business.

OR.-WOM. What you please, gentlemen.

DOR. To him! Give him as good as he brings.

OR.-WOM. Hang him, there is not such another heathen in the town again, except it be the shoemaker without.

MED. I shall see you hold up your hand at the bar next sessions for murder, huswife; that shoemaker can take his oath you are in fee with the doctors to sell green fruit to the gentry, that the crudities [16] may breed diseases.

OR.-WOM. Pray give me my money.

DOR. Not a penny; when you bring the gentlewoman hither you spoke of, you shall be paid.

OR.-WOM. The gentlewoman! The gentlewoman may be as honest[17] as your sisters, for aught as I know. Pray pay me, Mr Dorimant, and do not abuse me so; I have an honester way of living, you know it.

---

[12]*Change* the New Exchange, an arcaded building, with fashionable shops, in the Strand. Henry Herringman, who published Etherege's three plays, had his business there.

[13]*Make us* i.e. God make us.   [14]*stagers* veterans.

[15]*canary* a light sweet wine from the Canary Islands; mistress, whore.

[16]*crudities* undigested matter in the stomach.

[17]*honest* chaste.

MED.   Was there ever such a resty bawd?

DOR.   Some jade's tricks she has, but she makes amends when she's in good humour. Come, tell me the lady's name, and Handy shall pay you.

OR.-WOM.   I must not, she forbad me.

DOR.   That's a sure sign she would have you.

MED.   Where does she live?

OR.-WOM.   They lodge at my house.

MED.   Nay, then she's in a hopeful way.

OR.-WOM.   Good Mr Medley, say your pleasure of me, but take heed how you affront my house. God's my life, 'In a hopeful way'!

DOR.   Prithee, peace! What kind of woman's the mother?

OR.-WOM.   A goodly grave gentlewoman. Lord, how she talks against the wild young men o' the town! As for your part, she thinks you an arrant devil; should she see you, on my conscience she would look if you had not a cloven foot.

DOR.   Does she know me?

OR.-WOM.   Only by hearsay; a thousand horrid stories have been told her of you, and she believes 'em all.

MED.   By the character, this should be the famous Lady Woodvill and her daughter Harriet.

OR.-WOM.   [*Aside*] The devil's in him for guessing, I think.

DOR.   Do you know 'em?

MED.   Both very well; the mother's a great admirer of the forms and civility of the last age.

DOR.   An antiquated beauty may be allowed to be out of humour at the freedoms of the present.[18] This is a good account of the mother; pray, what is the daughter?

MED.   Why, first she's an heiress, vastly rich.

DOR.   And handsome?

MED.   What alteration a twelvemonth may have bred in her I know not, but a year ago she was the beautifulest creature I ever saw; a fine, easy, clean shape; light brown hair in abundance; her features regular; her complexion clear and lively; large wanton[19] eyes; but above all, a mouth that has made me kiss it a thousand times in imagination, teeth white and even, and pretty pouting lips, with a little moisture ever hanging on them, that look like the Provence[20] rose fresh on the bush, ere the morning sun has quite drawn up the dew.

---

[18]*antiquated . . . present* Compare Lady Wishfort, *The Way of the World*, III, i, p. 525.

[19]*wanton* roguish.

[20]*Provence* more correctly Provins, a town in northeast France, noted for roses.

DOR. Rapture, mere[21] rapture!

OR.-WOM. Nay, gad, he tells you true; she's a delicate creature.

DOR. Has she wit?

MED. More than is usual in her sex, and as much malice. Then she's as wild as you would wish her, and has a demureness in her looks that makes it so surprising.

DOR. Flesh and blood cannot hear this and not long to know her.

MED. I wonder what makes her mother bring her up to town; an old doting keeper[22] cannot be more jealous of his mistress.

OR.-WOM. She made me laugh yesterday; there was a judge came to visit 'em, and the old man, she told me, did so stare upon her, and when he saluted her smacked so heartily; who would think it of 'em?

MED. God-a-mercy, a judge!

DOR. Do 'em right; the gentlemen of the long robe have not been wanting by their good examples to countenance the crying sin o' the nation.

MED. Come, on with your trappings; 'tis later than you imagine.

DOR. Call in the shoemaker, Handy.

OR.-WOM. Good Mr Dorimant, pay me; gad, I had rather give you my fruit than stay to be abused by that foul-mouthed rogue; what you gentlemen say, it matters not much, but such a dirty fellow does one more disgrace.

DOR. Give her ten shillings, and be sure you tell the young gentlewoman I must be acquainted with her.

OR.-WOM. Now do you long to be tempting this pretty creature. Well, heavens mend you!

MED. Farewell, Bog.[23] *Exeunt* ORANGE-WOMAN *and* HANDY Dorimant, when did you see your *pis aller*,[24] as you call her, Mrs Loveit?

DOR. Not these two days.

MED. And how stand affairs between you?

DOR. There has been great patching of late, much ado; we make a shift to hang together.

MED. I wonder how her mighty spirit bears it.

DOR. Ill enough, on all conscience; I never knew so violent a creature.

MED. She's the most passionate in her love and the most extravagant in her jealousy of any woman I ever heard of. What note is that?

---

[21]*mere* asbsolute.   [22]*keeper* a man who supports a mistress.
[23]*Bog* Corpulent person.   [24]*pis aller* last resource.

DOR.   An excuse I am going to send her for the neglect I am guilty of.

MED.   Prithee read it.

DOR.   No; but if you will take the pains you may.

MED.   (*Reads*) 'I never was a lover of business, but now I have a just reason to hate it, since it has kept me these two days from seeing you. I intend to wait upon you in the afternoon, and in the pleasure of your conversation forget all I have suffered during this tedious absence'. This business of yours, Dorimant, has been with a vizard[25] at the playhouse; I have had an eye on you. If some malicious body should betray you, this kind note would hardly make your peace with her.

DOR.   I desire no better.

MED.   Why, would her knowledge of it oblige you?

DOR.   Most infinitely; next to the coming to a good understanding with a new mistress, I love a quarrel with an old one; but the devil's in't, there has been such a calm in my affairs of late, I have not had the pleasure of making a woman so much as break her fan, to be sullen, or forswear herself these three days.

MED.   A very great misfortune. Let me see. I love mischief well enough to forward this business myself; I'll about it presently,[26] and though I know the truth of what you've done will set her a-raving, I'll heighten it a little with invention, leave her in a fit o' the mother,[27] and be here again before you're ready.

DOR.   Pray stay; you may spare yourself the labour; the business is undertaken already by one who will manage it with as much address, and I think with a little more malice than you can.

MED.   Who i' the devil's name can this be?

DOR.   Why the vizard, that very vizard you saw me with.

MED.   Does she love mischief so well as to betray herself to spite another?

DOR.   Not so neither, Medley. I will make you comprehend the mystery: this mask, for a further confirmation of what I have been these two days swearing to her, made me yesterday at the playhouse make her a promise before her face utterly to break off with Loveit; and because she tenders my reputation, and would not have me do a barbarous thing, has contrived a way to give me a handsome occasion.

MED.   Very good.

DOR.   She intends, about an hour before me, this afternoon to make

[25]*vizard* mask, with the implication of 'prostitute'.
[26]*presently* immediately.   [27]*mother* hysteria.

Loveit a visit, and (having the privilege, by reason of a professed friendship between 'em) to talk of her concerns.

MED.   Is she a friend?

DOR.   Oh, an intimate friend!

MED.   Better and better; pray proceed.

DOR.   She means insensibly[28] to insinuate a discourse of me, and artificially[29] raise her jealousy to such a height that, transported with the first motions of her passion, she shall fly upon me with all the fury imaginable as soon as ever I enter; the quarrel being thus happily begun, I am to play my part, confess and justify all my roguery, swear her impertinence and ill-humour make her intolerable, tax her with the next fop that comes into my head, and in a huff march away; slight her, and leave her to be taken by whosoever thinks it worth his time to lie down before her.

MED.   This vizard is a spark, and has a genius[30] that makes her worthy of yourself, Dorimant.

        Enter HANDY, SHOEMAKER, *and* FOOTMAN

DOR.   You rogue there, who sneak like a dog that has flung down a dish, if you do not mend your waiting I'll uncase[31] you, and turn you loose to the wheel of fortune. Handy, seal this, and let him run with it presently.   *Exeunt* HANDY *and* FOOTMAN

MED.   Since you're resolved on a quarrel, why do you send her this kind note?

DOR.   To keep her at home in order to the business – (*To the* SHOEMAKER) How now, you drunken sot?

SHOEM.   'Zbud, you have no reason to talk; I have not had a bottle of sack of yours in my belly this fortnight.

MED.   The orange-woman says your neighbours take notice what a heathen you are, and design to inform the bishop and have you burned for an atheist.

SHOEM.   Damn her, dunghill! If her husband does not remove her, she stinks so the parish intend to indict him for a nuisance.

MED.   I advise you like a friend, reform your life; you have brought the envy of the world upon you by living above yourself. Whoring and swearing are vices too genteel for a shoemaker.

SHOEM.   'Zbud, I think you men of quality will grow as unreasonable as the women; you would engross[32] the sins o' the nation; poor folks can no sooner be wicked but they're railed at by their betters.

---

[28]*insensibly* gradually.   [29]*artificially* skilfully.
[30]*genius* character.   [31]*uncase* strip you (of livery).
[32]*engross* monopolise.

DOR. Sirrah, I'll have you stand i' the pillory for this libel!

SHOEM. Some of you deserve it, I'm sure; there are so many of 'em that our journeymen nowadays, instead of harmless ballads, sing nothing but your damned lampoons.[33]

DOR. Our lampoons, you rogue?

SHOEM. Nay, good master, why should not you write your own commentaries as well as Caesar?

MED. The rascal's read, I perceive.

SHOEM. You know the old proverb: ale and history.[34]

DOR. Draw on my shoes, sirrah.

SHOEM. Here's a shoe —

DOR. Sits with more wrinkles than there are in an angry bully's forehead.

SHOEM. 'Zbud, as smooth as your mistress's skin does upon her. So, strike your foot in home. 'Zbud, if e'er a *monsieur* of 'em all make more fashionable wear, I'll be content to have my ears whipped off with my own paring knife.

MED. And served up in a *ragoût* instead of coxcombs to a company of French shoemakers for a collation.

SHOEM. Hold, hold! Damn 'em. Caterpillars![35] Let 'em feed upon cabbage. Come, master, your health this morning, next my heart now.[36]

DOR. Go, get you home, and govern your family better; do not let your wife follow you to the alehouse, beat your whore, and lead you home in triumph.

SHOEM. 'Zbud, there's never a man i' the town lives more like a gentleman with his wife than I do. I never mind her motions,[37] she never inquires into mine; we speak to one another civilly, hate one another heartily, and because 'tis vulgar to lie and soak[38] together, we have each of us our several[39] settle-bed.[40]

DOR. Give him half a crown.

MED. Not without[41] he will promise to be bloody drunk.

[*Enter* HANDY]

---

[33]*lampoons* Lampoons and satires, in manuscript and print, were very popular.

[34]*ale and history* 'Truth is in ale as in history'.

[35]*Caterpillars* parasites.

[36]*your health ... now* He asks for a gratuity in order sincerely to drink Dorimant's health.

[37]*motions* activities.   [38]*soak* drink.

[39]*several* separate.   [40]*settle-bed* a bench that may be converted into a bed.

[41]*without* unless.

SHOEM. Tope's the word i' the eye of the world, for my master's honour, Robin.[42]

DOR. Do not debauch my servants, sirrah.

SHOEM. I only tip him the wink; he knows an alehouse from a hovel. *Exit* SHOEMAKER

DOR. My clothes, quickly.

MED. Where shall we dine today?

Enter YOUNG BELLAIR

DOR. Where you will; here comes a good third man.

Y. BELL. Your servant, gentlemen.

MED. Gentle sir, how will you answer this visit to your honourable mistress? 'Tis not her interest you should keep company with men of sense, who will be talking reason.

Y. BELL. I do not fear her pardon, do you but grant me yours for my neglect of late.

MED. Though you've made us miserable by the want of your good company, to show you I am free from all resentment, may the beautiful cause of our misfortune give you all the joys happy lovers have shared ever since the world began.

Y. BELL. You wish me in heaven, but you believe me on my journey to hell.

MED. You have a good strong faith, and that may contribute much towards your salvation. I confess I am but of an untoward[43] constitution, apt to have doubts and scruples, and in love they are no less distracting than in religion; were I so near marriage, I should cry out by fits as I ride in my coach, 'Cuckold, Cuckold', with no less fury than the mad fanatic does 'Glory' in Bethlem.[44]

Y. BELL. Because religion makes some run mad, must I live an atheist?

MED. Is it not great indiscretion for a man of credit, who may have money enough on his word, to go and deal with Jews who for little sums make men enter into bonds and give judgments?[45]

Y. BELL. Preach no more on this text; I am determined, and there is no hope of my conversion.

---

[42]*Tope . . . Robin* Familiarly addressed to Robin (probably Handy) with a gesture of raising a glass: 'The whole world should be willing to drink Dorimant's health'.

[43]*untoward* wayward.

[44]*mad fanatic* Evidently a reference to Oliver Cromwell's former servant, Daniel, who became insane and was put in Bethlehem Hospital, London, *c.* 1650. See M. Prior, 'A Dialogue between Oliver Cromwell and his Porter', *Literary Works* (Oxford, 1959), 1, 655–63.

[45]*give judgments* give certificates for the formal assignment of chattels as security.

DOR. (*To* HANDY, *who is fiddling about him*) Leave your unnecessary fiddling; a wasp that's buzzing about a man's nose at dinner is not more troublesome than thou art.

HANDY. You love to have your clothes hang just, sir.

DOR. I love to be well dressed, sir, and think it no scandal to my understanding.

HANDY. Will you use the essence, or orange-flower water?

DOR. I will smell as I do today, no offence to the ladies' noses.

HANDY. Your pleasure, sir.   [*Exit* HANDY]

DOR. That a man's excellency should lie in neatly tying of a ribbon or a cravat! How careful's nature in furnishing the world with necessary[46] coxcombs.

Y. BELL. That's a mighty pretty suit of yours, Dorimant.

DOR. I am glad 't has your approbation.

Y. BELL. No man in town has a better fancy[47] in his clothes than you have.

DOR. You will make me have an opinion of my genius.

MED. There is a great critic, I hear, in these matters, lately arrived piping hot from Paris.

Y. BELL. Sir Fopling Flutter, you mean.

MED. The same.

Y. BELL. He thinks himself the pattern of modern gallantry.

DOR. He is indeed the pattern of modern foppery.

MED. He was yesterday at the play, with a pair of gloves up to his elbows and a periwig more exactly curled than a lady's head newly dressed for a ball.

Y. BELL. What a pretty lisp he has!

DOR. Ho! That he affects in imitation of the people of quality of France.

MED. His head stands for the most part on one side, and his looks are more languishing than a lady's when she lolls at stretch in her coach or leans her head carelessly against the side of a box i' the playhouse.

DOR. He is a person indeed of great acquired follies.

MED. He is like many others, beholding to his education for making him so eminent a coxcomb; many a fool had been lost to the world had their indulgent parents wisely bestowed neither learning nor good breeding on 'em.

Y. BELL. He has been, as the sparkish word is, brisk upon the ladies already; he was yesterday at my Aunt Townley's, and gave Mrs Loveit a catalogue of his good qualities under the character of a

[46]*necessary* predestined.   [47]*fancy* taste.

complete gentleman, who, according to Sir Fopling, ought to dress well, dance well, fence well, have a genius for love letters, an agreeable voice for a chamber, be very amorous, something discreet, but not over-constant.

MED.   Pretty ingredients to make an accomplished person.

DOR.   I am glad he pitched upon Loveit.

Y. BELL.   How so?

DOR.   I wanted a fop to lay to her charge, and this is as pat as may be.

Y. BELL.   I am confident she loves no man but you.

DOR.   The good fortune were enough to make me vain, but that I am in my nature modest.

Y. BELL.   Hark you, Dorimant. With your leave, Mr Medley; 'tis only a secret concerning a fair lady.

MED.   Your good breeding, sir, gives you too much trouble; you might have whispered without all this ceremony.

Y. BELL.   (*To* DORIMANT) How stand your affairs with Belinda of late?

DOR.   She's a little jilting baggage.

Y. BELL.   Nay, I believe her false enough, but she's ne'er the worse for your purpose; she was with you yesterday in a disguise at the play.

DOR.   There we fell out, and resolved never to speak to one another more.

Y. BELL.   The occasion?

DOR.   Want of courage to meet me at the place appointed. These young women apprehend loving as much as the young men do fighting at first; but once entered, like them too, they all turn bullies straight.

Enter HANDY

HANDY.   (*To* YOUNG BELLAIR) Sir, your man without desires to speak with you.

Y. BELL.   Gentlemen, I'll return immediately. *Exit* YOUNG BELLAIR

MED.   A very pretty fellow this.

DOR.   He's handsome, well-bred, and by much the most tolerable of all the young men that do not abound in wit.

MED.   Ever well-dressed, always complaisant, and seldom impertinent; you and he are grown very intimate, I see.

DOR.   It is our mutual interest to be so: it makes the women think the better of his understanding and judge more favourably of my reputation; it makes him pass upon some for a man of very good sense, and I upon others for a very civil person.

MED.   What was that whisper?

DOR.   A thing which he would fain have known, but I did not think it fit to tell him; it might have frighted him from his honourable intentions of marrying.

MED.   Emilia, give her her due, has the best reputation of any young woman about the town who has beauty enough to provoke detraction; her carriage is unaffected, her discourse modest, not at all censorious nor pretending, like the counterfeits of the age.

DOR.   She's a discreet maid, and I believe nothing can corrupt her but a husband.

MED.   A husband?

DOR.   Yes, a husband; I have known many women make a difficulty of losing a maidenhead who have afterwards made none of making a cuckold.

MED.   This prudent consideration, I am apt to think, has made you confirm poor Bellair in the desperate resolution he has taken.

DOR.   Indeed, the little hope I found there was of her, in the state she was in, has made him by my advice contribute something towards the changing of her condition.

   Enter YOUNG BELLAIR

Dear Bellair, by heavens, I thought we had lost thee; men in love are never to be reckoned on when we would form a company.

Y. BELL.   Dorimant, I am undone; my man has brought the most surprising news i' the world.

DOR.   Some strange misfortune is befallen your love.

Y. BELL.   My father came to town last night, and lodges i' the very house where Emilia lies!

MED.   Does he know it is with her you are in love?

Y. BELL.   He knows I love, but knows not whom, without some officious sot has betrayed me.

DOR.   Your Aunt Townley is your confidante and favours the business.

Y. BELL.   I do not apprehend any ill office from her; I have received a letter, in which I am commanded by my father to meet him at my aunt's this afternoon; he tells me further he has made a match for me, and bids me resolve to be obedient to his will or expect to be disinherited.

MED.   Now's your time, Bellair; never had lover such an opportunity of giving a generous proof of his passion.

Y. BELL.   As how, I pray?

MED.   Why, hang an estate, marry Emilia out of hand, and provoke your father to do what he threatens; 'tis but despising a coach, humbling yourself to a pair of galoshes,48 being out of countenance

---

48*galoshes* originally country shoes with leather uppers and wooden soles.

when you meet your friends, pointed at and pitied wherever you go by all the amorous fops that know you, and your fame will be immortal.

Y. BELL. I could find in my heart to resolve not to marry at all.

DOR. Fie, fie! That would spoil a good jest and disappoint the well-natured town of an occasion of laughing at you.

Y. BELL. The storm I have so long expected hangs o'er my head and begins to pour down upon me; I am on the rack, and can have no rest till I'm satisfied in what I fear. Where do you dine?

DOR. At Long's[49] or Locket's.[50]

MED. At Long's let it be.

Y. BELL. I'll run and see Emilia, and inform myself how matters stand; if my misfortunes are not so great as to make me unfit for company, I'll be with you. *Exit* BELLAIR

Enter a FOOTMAN *with a letter*

FOOT. (*To* DORIMANT) Here's a letter, sir.

DOR. The superscription's right: 'For Mr Dorimant'.

MED. Let's see: the very scrawl and spelling of a true-bred whore.

DOR. I know the hand; the style is admirable, I assure you.

MED. Prithee read it.

DOR. (*Reads*) 'I told a you you dud not love me, if you dud, you would have seen me again ere now; I have no money, and am very mallicolly; pray send me a guynie to see the operies. Your servant to command, Molly'.

MED. Pray let the whore have a favourable answer, that she may spark it in a box and do honour to her profession.

DOR. She shall, and perk up[51] i' the face of quality. Is the coach at door?

HANDY. You did not bid me send for it.

DOR. Eternal blockhead! (HANDY *offers to go out*) Hey, sot.

HANDY. Did you call me, sir?

DOR. I hope you have no just exception to the name, sir?

HANDY. I have sense, sir.

DOR. Not so much as a fly in winter. – How did you come, Medley?

MED. In a chair.

FOOT. You may have a hackney coach if you please, sir.

---

[49]*Long's* Two London taverns had this name, one in the Haymarket, the other in Covent Garden.

[50]*Locket's* a famous ordinary at Spring Garden, near Charing Cross, frequented by Etherege; the proprietor was Adam Locket. Referred to in *The Provoked Wife*, II, i, p. 424; *The Way of the World*, III, i, p. 524; and other contemporary plays.

[51]*perk up* put on airs.

DOR. I may ride the elephant[52] if I please, sir; call another chair, and let my coach follow to Long's.

Exeunt singing, 'Be calm, ye great parents', etc.[53]

[52]*elephant* Elephants were then popular in private menageries.
[53]*Be . . . parents, etc.* from the song beginning 'My lord, great Neptune, for my sake . . .' in the final episode of Act v of Thomas Shadwell's operatic version of *The Tempest*, 1674.

Act Two

SCENE ONE

[LADY TOWNLEY'S *house*]

Enter my LADY TOWNLEY *and* EMILIA

LADY TOWN. I was afraid, Emilia, all had been discovered.

EMIL. I tremble with the apprehension still.

LADY TOWN. That my brother should take lodgings i' the very house where you lie!

EMIL. 'Twas lucky we had timely notice to warn the people[1] to be secret; he seems to be a mighty good-humoured old man.

LADY TOWN. He ever had a notable smirking way with him.

EMIL. He calls me rogue, tells me he can't abide me, and does so bepat me.

LADY TOWN. On my word you are much in his favour then.

EMIL. He has been very inquisitive, I am told, about my family, my reputation, and my fortune.

LADY TOWN. I am confident he does not i' the least suspect you are the woman his son's in love with.

EMIL. What should make him then inform himself so particularly of me?

LADY TOWN. He was always of a very loving temper himself; it may be he has a doting fit upon him; who knows?

EMIL. It cannot be.

Enter YOUNG BELLAIR

LADY TOWN. Here comes my nephew. Where did you leave your father?

Y. BELL. Writing a note within. Emilia, this early visit looks as if some kind jealousy would not let you rest at home.

EMIL. The knowledge I have of my rival gives me a little cause to fear your constancy.

Y. BELL. My constancy! I vow –

EMIL. Do not vow – Our love is frail as is our life, and full as little in our power; and are you sure you shall outlive this day?

Y. BELL. I am not; but when we are in perfect health 'twere an

---

[1] *the people* servants.

idle thing to fright ourselves with the thoughts of sudden death.

LADY TOWN. Pray, what has passed between you and your father i' the garden?

Y. BELL. He's firm in his resolution, tells me I must marry Mrs Harriet, or swears he'll marry himself and disinherit me; when I saw I could not prevail with him to be more indulgent, I dissembled an obedience to his will which has composed his passion, and will give us time, and I hope opportunity, to deceive him.

Enter OLD BELLAIR *with a note in his hand*

LADY TOWN. Peace, here he comes.

O. BELL. Harry, take this, and let your man carry it for me to Mr Fourbe's[2] chamber, my lawyer, i' the Temple.[3]

[*Exit* YOUNG BELLAIR]

(*To* EMILIA) Neighbour, adod, I am glad to see thee here; make much of her, sister, she's one of the best of your acquaintance. I like her countenance and her behaviour well; she has a modesty that is not common i' this age, adod, she has.

LADY TOWN. I know her value, brother, and esteem her accordingly.

O. BELL. Advise her to wear a little more mirth in her face, adod, she's too serious.

LADY TOWN. The fault is very excusable in a young woman.

O. BELL. Nay, adod, I like her ne'er the worse, a melancholy beauty has her charms; I love a pretty sadness in a face which varies now and then, like changeable colours, into a smile.

LADY TOWN. Methinks you speak very feelingly, brother.

O. BELL. I am but five-and-fifty, sister, you know, an age not altogether insensible! (*To* EMILIA) Cheer up, sweetheart, I have a secret to tell thee may chance to make thee merry; we three will make collation together anon; i' the meantime, mum;[4] I can't abide you; go, I can't abide you.

Enter YOUNG BELLAIR

Harry, come, you must along with me to my Lady Woodvill's. I am going to slip the boy at a mistress.

Y. BELL. At a wife, sir, you would say.

O. BELL. You need not look so glum, sir; a wife is no curse when she brings the blessing of a good estate with her; but an idle town flirt, with a painted face, a rotten reputation, and a crazy fortune, adod, is the devil and all; and such a one I hear you are in league with.

---

[2]*Mr Fourbe's* a fourbe is a cheat.

[3]*Temple* The Chambers of benchers and barristers were located in the Inner and Middle Temple, formerly headquarters of the Knights Templar.

[4]*mum* be mum.

Y. BELL.   I cannot help detraction, sir.

O. BELL.   Out a pize[5] o' their breeches, there are keeping fools enough for such flaunting baggages, and they are e'en too good for 'em. (*To* EMILIA) Remember night, go, you're a rogue, you're a rogue; fare you well, fare you well; come, come, come along, sir.

Exeunt OLD *and* YOUNG BELLAIR

LADY TOWN.   On my word, the old man comes on apace; I'll lay my life he's smitten.

EMIL.   This is nothing but the pleasantness of his humour.

LADY TOWN.   I know him better than you; let it work, it may prove lucky.

Enter a PAGE

PAGE.   Madam, Mr Medley has sent to know whether a visit will not be troublesome this afternoon?

LADY TOWN.   Send him word his visits never are so.   [*Exit* PAGE]

EMIL.   He's a very pleasant man.

LADY TOWN.   He's a very necessary man among us women; he's not scandalous i' the least, perpetually contriving to bring good company together, and always ready to stop up a gap at ombre;[6] then he knows all the little news o' the town.

EMIL.   I love to hear him talk o' the intrigues; let 'em be never so dull in themselves, he'll make 'em pleasant i' the relation.

LADY TOWN.   But he improves things so much one can take no measure of the truth from him. Mr Dorimant swears a flea or a maggot is not made more monstrous by a magnifying glass than a story is by his telling it.

EMIL.   Hold, here he comes.

Enter MEDLEY

LADY TOWN.   Mr Medley.

MED.   Your servant, madam.

LADY TOWN.   You have made yourself a stranger of late.

EMIL.   I believe you took a surfeit of ombre last time you were here.

MED.   Indeed I had my bellyful of that termagant Lady Dealer. There never was so insatiable a carder; an old gleeker[7] never loved to sit to't like her. I have played with her now at least a dozen times till she's worn out all her fine complexion, and her tour[8] would keep in curl no longer.

---

[5] *Out a pize* Old Bellair's usual imprecation; perhaps 'a pox'.

[6] *ombre* a popular card game, for three players. See Pope, *The Rape of the Lock*, III, 27–98.

[7] *gleeker* a player of gleek, a card game for three persons.

[8] *tour* headdress.

LADY TOWN.   Blame her not, poor woman; she loves nothing so well as a black ace.

MED.   The pleasure I have seen her in when she has had hope in drawing for a matadore!⁹

EMIL.   'Tis as pretty sport to her as persuading masks off is to you to make discoveries.

LADY TOWN.   Pray, where's your friend, Mr Dorimant?

MED.   Soliciting his affairs; he's a man of great employment, has more mistresses now depending¹⁰ than the most eminent lawyer in England has causes.

EMIL.   Here has been Mrs Loveit, so uneasy and out of humour these two days.

LADY TOWN.   How strangely love and jealousy rage in that poor woman!

MED.   She could not have picked out a devil upon earth so proper to torment her; he has made her break a dozen or two of fans already, tear half a score points¹¹ in pieces, and destroy hoods and knots¹² without number.

LADY TOWN.   We heard of a pleasant serenade he gave her t'other night.

MED.   A Danish serenade,¹³ with kettledrums and trumpets.

EMIL.   Oh, barbarous!

MED.   What,¹⁴ you are of the number of the ladies whose ears are grown so delicate since our operas,¹⁵ you can be charmed with nothing but *flutes douces*¹⁶ and French hautboys.¹⁷

EMIL.   Leave your raillery and tell us, is there any new wit come forth, songs or novels?

MED.   A very pretty piece of gallantry by an eminent author called

---

⁹*matadore* one of the winning cards in ombre; they included the two black aces.
¹⁰*depending* pending.   ¹¹*points* pieces of lace.
¹²*knots* bows of ribbon.
¹³*a Danish serenade* 'The King doth wake tonight . . . and as he drains his draughts of Rhenish down/The kettledrum and trumpet thus bray out . . .' (*Hamlet*, I, iv, 8–11).
¹⁴*What* Indeed.
¹⁵*our operas* No doubt an allusion to operatic versions of *Macbeth*, by William Davenant (1673), *The Tempest*, by Thomas Shadwell (1674), and the operas *Psyche*, also by Shadwell (1674), and *Ariadne*, by Pierre Perrin (1674).
¹⁶*flutes douces* recently introduced to England, similar to recorders.
¹⁷*hautboys* oboes.

The Diversions of Brussels,[18] very necessary to be read by all old
ladies who are desirous to improve themselves at questions and
commands,[19] blindman's buff, and the like fashionable recreations.

EMIL. Oh, ridiculous!

MED. Then there is *The Art of Affectation*,[20] written by a late beauty
of quality, teaching you how to draw up your breasts, stretch up
your neck, to thrust out your breech, to play with your head, to toss
up your nose, to bite your lips, to turn up your eyes, to speak in a silly
soft tone of a voice, and use all the foolish French words that will
infallibly make your person and conversation charming, with a
short apology at the latter end, in the behalf of young ladies who
notoriously wash[21] and paint, though they have naturally good
complexions.

EMIL. What a deal of stuff you tell us!

MED. Such as the town affords, madam. The Russians, hearing the
great respect we have for foreign dancing, have lately sent over some
of their best baladines, who are now practising a famous ballet
which will be suddenly[22] danced at the Bear Garden.[23]

LADY TOWN. Pray forbear your idle stories, and give us an account
of the state of love as it now stands.

MED. Truly there has been some revolutions in those affairs, great
chopping and changing among the old, and some new lovers, whom
malice, indiscretion, and misfortune have luckily brought into play.

LADY TOWN. What think you of walking into the next room, and
sitting down before you engage in this business?

MED. I wait upon you, and I hope, though women are commonly
unreasonable, by the plenty of scandal I shall discover, to give you
very good content, ladies.   *Exeunt*

[18]*The Diversions of Brussels* Medley ridicules Richard Flecknoe's *A Treatise of
the Sports of Wit* (1675), a serious account of a gathering of intellectual ladies near
Brussels, 1650, and their diversions during seven days of earnest debate (R. S. Cox,
Jr., 'Richard Flecknoe and *The Man of Mode*', M.L.Q., 29 (March 1968), 183–89.

[19]*questions and commands* a game involving ridiculous questions and commands.

[20]*The Art of Affectation* a title (like *The Diversions of Brussels*) invented by
Medley, ridiculing serious books like Hannah Woolley's *The Gentlewoman's
Companion*, 1675.

[21]*wash* use cosmetic washes.   [22]*suddenly* soon.

[23]*The Russians . . . Bear Garden* Medley is probably using mythical Russian male
ballet dancers to hit at the contemporary popularity in England of visiting French
theatrical and ballet companies, implying, with hyperbole, that they were as inept as
dancing or baited bears.

SCENE TWO

[MRS LOVEIT's *house*]

Enter MRS LOVEIT *and* PERT. MRS LOVEIT *putting up a letter,
then pulling out her pocket-glass and looking in it*

LOV.   Pert.

PERT.   Madam.

LOVE.   I hate myself, I look so ill²⁴ today.

PERT.   Hate the wicked cause on't, that base man Mr Dorimant, who
makes you torment and vex yourself continually.

LOV.   He is to blame, indeed.

PERT.   To blame to be two days without sending, writing, or coming
near you, contrary to his oath and covenant! 'Twas to much purpose
to make him swear. I'll lay my life there's not an article but he has
broken: talked to the vizards i' the pit, waited upon the ladies from
the boxes to their coaches, gone behind the scenes and fawned upon
those little insignificant creatures the players; 'tis impossible for a
man of his inconstant temper to forbear, I'm sure.

LOV.   I know he is a devil, but he has something of the angel yet
undefaced in him, which makes him so charming and aggreeable
that I must love him, be he never so wicked.

PERT.   I little thought, madam, to see your spirit tamed to this degree,
who banished poor Mr Lackwit but for taking up another lady's fan
in your presence.

LOV.   My knowing of such odious fools contributes to the making of
me love Dorimant the better.

PERT.   Your knowing of Mr Dorimant, in my mind, should rather
make you hate all mankind.

LOV.   So it does, besides himself.

PERT.   Pray, what excuse does he make in his letter?

LOV.   He has had business.

PERT.   Business in general terms would not have been a current²⁵
excuse for another; a modish man is always very busy when he is in
pursuit of a new mistress.

LOV.   Some fop has bribed you to rail at him. He had business; I will
believe it, and will forgive him.

PERT.   You may forgive him anything, but I shall never forgive him
his turning me into ridicule, as I hear he does.

LOV.   I perceive you are of the number of those fools his wit has made
his enemies.

PERT.   I am of the number of those he's pleased to rally, madam; and

²⁴*ill* ugly.   ²⁵*current* acceptable.

if we may believe Mr Wagfan and Mr Caperwell, he sometimes makes merry with yourself too among his laughing companions.

LOV.   Blockheads are as malicious to witty men as ugly women are to the handsome; 'tis their interest, and they make it their business to defame 'em.

PERT.   I wish Mr Dorimant would not make it his business to defame you.

LOV.   Should he, I had rather be made infamous by him than owe my reputation to the dull discretion of those fops you talk of.

Enter BELINDA

Belinda!   *Running to her*

BEL.   My dear.

LOV.   You have been unkind of late.

BEL.   Do not say unkind, say unhappy!

LOV.   I could chide you; where have you been these two days?

BEL.   Pity me rather, my dear, where I have been so tired with two or three country gentlewomen, whose conversation has been more insufferable than a country fiddle.

LOV.   Are they relations?

BEL.   No, Welsh acquaintance I made when I was last year at St Winifred's;[26] they have asked me a thousand questions of the modes and intrigues of the town, and I have told 'em almost as many things for news that hardly were so when their gowns were in fashion.

LOV.   Provoking creatures, how could you endure 'em?

BEL.   (*Aside*) Now to carry on my plot; nothing but love could make me capable of so much falsehood; 'tis time to begin, lest Dorimant should come before her jealousy has stung her. (*Laughs, and then speaks on*) I was yesterday at a play with 'em, where I was fain to show 'em the living, as the man at Westminster does the dead:[27] that is Mrs Such-a-one, admired for her beauty; this is Mr Such-a-one, cried up for a wit; that is sparkish Mr Such-a-one, who keeps reverend[28] Mrs Such-a-one, and there sits fine Mrs Such-a-one, who was lately cast off by my Lord Such-a-one.

LOV.   Did you see Dorimant there?

BEL.   I did, and imagine you were there with him and have no mind to own it.

LOV.   What should make you think so?

BEL.   A lady masked in a pretty *déshabillé*,[29] whom Dorimant entertained with more respect than the gallants do a common vizard.

LOV.   (*Aside*) Dorimant at the play entertaining a mask! O heavens!

---

[26]*St Winifred's* a miraculous shrine and well at Holywell, Wales.
[27]*dead* For a fee, guides at Westminster Abbey took visitors around the tombs.
[28]*reverend* worthy of respect.   [29]*déshabillé* negligent style.

BEL.   (*Aside*) Good.

LOV.   Did he stay all the while?

BEL.   Till the play was done, and then led her out, which confirms me it was you.

LOV.   Traitor!

PERT.   Now you may believe he had business, and you may forgive him too.

LOV.   Ungrateful, perjured man!

BEL.   You seem so much concerned, my dear, I fear I have told you unawares what I had better have concealed for your quiet.

LOV.   What manner of shape had she?

BEL.   Tall and slender, her motions were very genteel; certainly she must be some person of condition.

LOV.   Shame and confusion be ever in her face when she shows it!

BEL.   I should blame your discretion for loving that wild man, my dear; but they say he has a way so bewitching that few can defend their hearts who know him.

LOV.   I will tear him from mine, or die i' the attempt.

BEL.   Be more moderate.

LOV.   Would I had daggers, darts, or poisoned arrows in my breast, so I could but remove the thoughts of him from thence!

BEL.   Fie, fie! Your transports are too violent, my dear. This may be but an accidental gallantry, and 'tis likely ended at her coach.

PERT.   Should it proceed further, let your comfort be, the conduct Mr Dorimant affects will quickly make you know your rival, ten to one let you see her ruined, her reputation exposed to the town; a happiness none will envy her but yourself, madam.

LOV.   Whoe'er she be, all the harm I wish her is, may she love him as well as I do, and may he give her as much cause to hate him!

PERT.   Never doubt the latter end of your curse, madam.

LOV.   May all the passions that are raised by neglected love –jealousy, indignation, spite, and thirst of revenge – eternally rage in her soul as they do now in mine!   *Walks up and down with a distracted air*
    Enter a PAGE

PAGE.   Madam, Mr Dorimant –

LOV.   I will not see him.

PAGE.   I told him you were within, madam.

LOV.   Say you lied, say I'm busy, shut the door; say anything.

PAGE.   He's here, madam.
    Enter DORIMANT

DOR.   They taste of death who do at heaven arrive,
       But we this paradise approach alive.[30]

[30]*They . . . alive* Edmund Waller, 'Of Her Chamber', *Poems*, 1 (London, 1901), p. 26.

(*To* LOVEIT) What, dancing the galloping nag[31] without a fiddle?
(*Offers to catch her by the hand; she flings away and walks on*) I
fear this restlessness of the body, madam, (*Pursuing her*) proceeds
from an unquietness of the mind. What unlucky accident puts you
out of humour: a point ill-washed, knots spoiled i' the making up,
hair shaded awry, or some other little mistake in setting you in
order?

PERT.   A trifle, in my opinion, sir, more inconsiderable than any you
mention.

DOR.   O Mrs Pert, I never knew you sullen enough to be silent; come,
let me know the business.

PERT.   The business, sir, is the business that has taken you up these
two days; how have I seen you laugh at men of business, and now to
become a man of business yourself!

DOR.   We are not masters of our own affections; our inclinations
daily alter. Now we love pleasure, and anon we shall dote on
business; human frailty will have it so, and who can help it?

LOV.   Faithless, inhuman, barbarous man!

DOR.   Good, now the alarm[32] strikes. –

LOV.   Without sense of love, of honour, or of gratitude! Tell me – for I
will know – what devil, masked she was, you were with at the play
yesterday?

DOR.   Faith, I resolved as much as you, but the devil was obstinate
and would not tell me.

LOV.   False in this as in your vows to me! You do know.

DOR.   The truth is, I did all I could to know.

LOV.   And dare you own it to my face? Hell and furies!

Tears her fan in pieces

DOR.   Spare your fan, madam; you are growing hot and will want it
to cool you.

LOV.   Horror and distraction seize you, sorrow and remorse gnaw
your soul, and punish all your perjuries to me!   *Weeps*

DOR.   So thunder breaks the cloud in twain,
          And makes a passage for the rain.[33]   *Turning to* BELINDA
Belinda, you are the devil that have raised this storm; you were at the
play yesterday, and have been making discoveries to your dear.

BEL.   You're the most mistaken man i' the world.

DOR.   It must be so, and here I vow revenge, resolve to pursue

[31]*galloping nag* probably a country dance.
[32]*alarm* call to arms.
[33]*So . . . rain* Matthew Roydon, 'An Elegy, or Friend's Passion, for his Astrophell'
(a tribute to Sidney) in *The Phoenix Nest*, 1593 (R. Howarth, 'Untraced Quotations
in Etherege', *Notes and Queries*, 158 (30 June 1945), p. 281.

and persecute you more impertinently than ever any loving fop did his mistress, hunt you i' the Park,[34] trace you i' the Mall,[35] dog you in every visit you make, haunt you at the plays and i' the drawing room, hang my nose in your neck, and talk to you whether you will or no, and ever look upon you with such dying eyes till your friends grow jealous of me, send you out of town, and make the world suspect your reputation. (*In a lower voice*) At my Lady Townley's when we go from hence.

He looks kindly on BELINDA

BEL. [*Aside*] I'll meet you there.

DOR. [*Aside*] Enough.

LOV. Stand off, you sha' not stare upon her so.

Pushing DORIMANT away

DOR. [*Aside*] Good! There's one made jealous already.

LOV. Is this the constancy you vowed?

DOR. Constancy at my years! 'Tis not a virtue in season; you might as well expect the fruit the autumn ripens i' the spring.

LOV. Monstrous principle!

DOR. Youth has a long journey to go, madam. Should I have set up my rest at the first inn I lodged at, I should never have arrived at the happiness I now enjoy.

LOV. Dissembler, damned dissembler!

DOR. I am so, I confess; good nature and good manners corrupt me. I am honest in my inclinations, and would not, were't not to avoid offence, make a lady a little in years believe I think her young, wilfully mistake art for nature, and seem as fond of a thing I am weary of as when I doted on't in earnest.

LOV. False man!

DOR. True woman!

LOV. Now you begin to show yourself!

DOR. Love gilds us over and makes us show fine things to one another for a time, but soon the gold wears off, and then again the native brass appears.

LOV. Think on your oaths, your vows and protestations, perjured man.

DOR. I made 'em when I was in love.

LOV. And therefore ought they not to bind? Oh, impious!

DOR. What we swear at such a time may be a certain proof of a present passion; but to say truth, in love there is no security to be given for the future.

---

34 *Park* either Hyde or St James's Park.
35 *Mall* an avenue on the north side of St James's Park, a popular promenade.

LOV.   Horrid and ungrateful! Begone and never see me more.

DOR.   I am not one of those troublesome coxcombs who, because
they were once well received, take the privilege to plague a woman
with their love ever after. I shall obey you, madam, though I do
myself some violence.   *He offers to go and* LOVEIT *pulls him back*

LOV.   Come back, you sha' not go. Could you have the ill-nature to
offer it?

DOR.   When love grows diseased, the best thing we can do is to put it
to a violent death; I cannot endure the torture of a lingering and
consumptive passion.

LOV.   Can you think mine sickly?

DOR.   Oh, 'tis desperately ill! What worse symptoms are there than
your being always uneasy when I visit you, your picking quarrels
with me on slight occasions, and in my absence kindly listening to
the impertinences of every fashionable fool that talks to you?

LOV.   What fashionable fool can you lay to my charge?

DOR.   Why, the very cock-fool of all those fools, Sir Fopling Flutter.

LOV.   I never saw him in my life but once.

DOR.   The worse woman you, at first sight to put on all your charms,
to entertain him with that softness in your voice and all that wanton
kindness in your eyes you so notoriously affect when you design a
conquest.

LOV.   So damned a lie did never malice yet invent. Who told you this?

DOR.   No matter. That ever I should love a woman that can dote on a
senseless caper, a tawdry French ribbon, and a formal cravat!

LOV.   You make me mad.

DOR.   A guilty conscience may do much; go on, be the game-mistress
o' the town, and enter [36] all our young fops as fast as they come from
travel.

LOV.   Base and scurrilous!

DOR.   A fine mortifying reputation 'twill be for a woman of your
pride, wit, and quality!

LOV.   This jealousy's a mere pretence, a cursed trick of your own
devising; I know you.

DOR.   Believe it and all the ill of me you can. I would not have a
woman have the least good thought of me that can think well of
Fopling. Farewell; fall to, and much good may [it] do you with your
coxcomb.

LOV.   Stay, oh, stay, and I will tell you all.

DOR.   I have been told too much already.   *Exit* DORIMANT

LOV.   Call him again.

PERT.   E'en let him go, a fair riddance.

[36]*enter* initiate.

LOV.   Run, I say; call him again. I will have him called.

PERT.   The devil should carry him away first, were it my concern.

Exit PERT

BEL.   He's frightened me from the very thoughts of loving men. For heaven's sake, my dear, do not discover what I told you; I dread his tongue as much as you ought to have done his friendship.

Enter PERT

PERT.   He's gone, madam.

LOV.   Lightning blast him!

PERT.   When I told him you desired him to come back, he smiled, made a mouth at me, flung into his coach, and said –

LOV.   What did he say?

PERT.   'Drive away'; and then repeated verses.

LOV.   Would I had made a contract to be a witch when first I entertained this greater devil, monster, barbarian; I could tear myself in pieces. Revenge, nothing but revenge can ease me; plague, war, famine, fire, all that can bring universal ruin and misery on mankind; with joy I'd perish to have you in my power but this moment.   *Exit* LOVEIT

PERT.   Follow, madam; leave her not in this outrageous passion.

PERT *gathers up the things*

BEL.   He's given me the proof which I desired of his love:
But 'tis a proof of his ill-nature too;
I wish I had not seen him use her so.
I sigh to think that Dorimant may be
One day as faithless and unkind to me.   *Exeunt*

Act Three

SCENE ONE

LADY WOODVILL's *lodgings*

Enter HARRIET *and* BUSY, *her woman*

BUSY. Dear madam, let me set that curl in order.

HAR. Let me alone, I will shake 'em all out of order.

BUSY. Will you never leave this wildness?

HAR. Torment me not.

BUSY. Look, there's a knot falling off.

HAR. Let it drop.

BUSY. But one pin, dear madam.

HAR. How do I daily suffer under thy officious fingers!

BUSY. Ah, the difference that is between you and my Lady Dapper! How uneasy she is if the least thing be amiss about her!

HAR. She is indeed most exact; nothing is ever wanting to make her ugliness remarkable.

BUSY. Jeering people say so.

HAR. Her powdering, painting, and her patching[1] never fail in public to draw the tongues and eyes of all the men upon her.

BUSY. She is indeed a little too pretending.

HAR. That women should set up for beauty as much in spite of nature as some men have done for wit!

BUSY. I hope, without offence, one may endeavour to make oneself agreeable.

HAR. Not when 'tis impossible. Women then ought to be no more fond of dressing than fools should be of talking. Hoods and modesty, masks and silence, things that shadow and conceal: they should think of nothing else.

BUSY. Jesu, madam, what will your mother think is become of you? For heaven's sake, go in again.

HAR. I won't.

BUSY. This is the extravagant'st thing that ever you did in your life, to leave her and a gentleman who is to be your husband.

---

[1]*patching* Wearing small patches, usually of black silk, on the face was a contemporary fad.

HAR.   My husband! Hast thou so little wit to think I spoke what I
       meant when I overjoyed her in the country with a low curtsey and
       'What you please, madam, I shall ever be obedient'?
BUSY. Nay, I know not, you have so many fetches.[2]
HAR.   And this was one to get her up to London; nothing else, I assure
       thee.
BUSY. Well, the man, in my mind, is a fine man.
HAR.   The man indeed wears his clothes fashionably, and has a pretty
       negligent way with him, very courtly and much affected; he bows,
       and talks, and smiles so agreeably as he thinks.
BUSY. I never saw anything so genteel.
HAR.   Varnished over with good breeding, many a blockhead makes a
       tolerable show.
BUSY. I wonder you do not like him.
HAR.   I think I might be brought to endure him, and that is all a
       reasonable woman should expect in a husband; but there is duty i'
       the case, and like the haughty Merab,
               I find much aversion in my stubborn mind,
               Which is bred by being promis'd and design'd.[3]
BUSY. I wish you do not design your own ruin! I partly guess your
       inclinations, madam. That Mr Dorimant –
HAR.   Leave your prating, and sing some foolish song or other.
BUSY. I will; the song you love so well ever since you saw Mr
       Dorimant.

Song

               When first Amintas charm'd my heart,
               My heedless sheep began to stray;
               The wolves soon stole the greatest part,
               And all will now be made a prey.

               Ah, let not love your thoughts possess,
               'Tis fatal to a shepherdess;
               The dang'rous passion you must shun,
               Or else, like me, be quite undone.

HAR.   Shall I be paid down by a covetous parent for a purchase? I need
       no land; no, I'll lay myself out[4] all in love. It is decreed –
       Enter YOUNG BELLAIR

   [2]*fetches* tricks.
   [3]*I find . . . design'd* a paraphrase of lines about Merab, the eldest daughter of Saul,
in A. Cowley, *Davideis*, Book III, lines 625–26, in *Poems* (Cambridge, 1905),
p. 341.
   [4]*lay myself out* exert myself.

Y. BELL.   What generous resolution are you making, madam?

HAR.   Only to be disobedient, sir.

Y. BELL.   Let me join hands with you in that.

HAR.   With all my heart; I never thought I should have given you mine so willingly. Here I, Harriet –

Y. BELL.   And I, Harry –

HAR.   Do solemnly protest –

Y. BELL.   And vow –

HAR.   That I with you –

Y. BELL.   And I with you –

BOTH.   Will never marry.

HAR.   A match!

Y. BELL.   And no match! How do you like this indifference now?

HAR.   You expect I should take it ill, I see.

Y. BELL.   'Tis not unnatural for you women to be a little angry [if] you miss a conquest, though you would slight the poor man were he in your power.

HAR.   There are some, it may be, have an eye like Bartholomew,⁵ big enough for the whole fair, but I am not of the number, and you may keep your gingerbread; 'twill be more acceptable to the lady whose dear image it wears, sir.

Y. BELL.   I must confess, madam, you came a day after the fair.

HAR.   You own then you are in love.

Y. BELL.   I do.

HAR.   The confidence is generous, and in return I could almost find in my heart to let you know my inclinations.

Y. BELL.   Are you in love?

HAR.   Yes, with this dear town, to that degree I can scarce endure the country in landscapes and in hangings.⁶

Y. BELL.   What a dreadful thing 'twould be to be hurried back to Hampshire!

HAR.   Ah, name it not!

Y. BELL.   As for us, I find we shall agree well enough. Would we could do something to deceive the grave people!

HAR.   Could we delay their quick proceeding, 'twere well; a reprieve is a good step towards the getting of a pardon.

Y. BELL.   If we give over the game we are undone; what think you of playing it on booty?⁷

---

⁵*Bartholomew* Bartholomew Cokes, in Jonson's *Bartholomew Fair* (1614, and frequently revived during the Restoration) was carried away by enthusiasm for gingerbread and other gewgaws at the Fair.

⁶*hangings* tapestries, etc.

⁷*playing it on booty* deliberately to lose in a game in order to trick a victim later.

HAR.   What do you mean?

Y. BELL.   Pretend to be in love with one another; 'twill make some dilatory excuses we may feign pass the better.

HAR.   Let us do't, if it be but for the dear pleasure of dissembling.

Y. BELL.   Can you play your part?

HAR.   I know not what it is to love, but I have made pretty remarks[8] by being now and then where lovers meet. Where did you leave their gravities?

Y. BELL.   I' the next room; your mother was censuring our modern gallant.

Enter OLD BELLAIR *and* LADY WOODVILL

HAR.   Peace! Here they come. I will lean against this wall and look bashfully down upon my fan, while you, like an amorous spark, modishly entertain me.

LADY WOOD.   Never go about to excuse 'em; come, come, it was not so when I was a young woman.

O. BELL.   Adod, they're something disrespectful.

LADY WOOD.   Quality was then considered, and not rallied by every fleering[9] fellow.

O. BELL.   Youth will have its jest, adod it will.

LADY WOOD.   'Tis good breeding now to be civil to none but players and Exchange women;[10] they are treated by 'em as much above their condition as others are below theirs.

O. BELL.   Out a pize on 'em! Talk no more; the rogues ha' got an ill habit of preferring beauty, no matter where they find it.

LADY WOOD.   See your son and my daughter; they have improved their acquaintance since they were within.

O. BELL.   Adod, methinks they have; let's keep back and observe.

Y. BELL.   Now for a look and gestures that may persuade 'em I am saying all the passionate things imaginable.

HAR.   Your head a little more on one side, ease yourself on your left leg, and play with your right hand.

Y. BELL.   Thus, is it not?

HAR.   Now set your right leg firm on the ground, adjust your belt, then look about you.

Y. BELL.   A little exercising will make me perfect.

HAR.   Smile, and turn to me again very sparkish.

Y. BELL.   Will you take your turn and be instructed?

HAR.   With all my heart.

Y. BELL.   At one motion play your fan, roll your eyes, and then settle a kind look upon me.

---

[8]*remarks* observations.   [9]*fleering* impudent.

[10]*Exchange women* clerks in shops in the New Exchange, the Strand.

HAR.   So.

Y. BELL.   Now spread your fan, look down upon it, and tell the sticks with a finger.

HAR.   Very modish!

Y. BELL.   Clap your hand up to your bosom, hold down your gown; shrug a little, draw up your breasts, and let 'em fall again gently, with a sigh or two, etc.

HAR.   By the good instructions you give, I suspect you for one of those malicious observers who watch people's eyes and from innocent looks make scandalous conclusions.

Y. BELL.   I know some, indeed, who, out of mere love to mischief, are as vigilant as jealousy itself, and will give you an account of every glance that passes at a play and i' the Circle.[11]

HAR.   'Twill not be amiss now to seem a little pleasant.

Y. BELL.   Clap your fan then in both your hands, snatch it to your mouth, smile, and with a lively motion fling your body a little forwards. So. Now spread it; fall back on the sudden, cover your face with it, and break out into a loud laughter. Take up, look grave, and fall a-fanning of yourself. Admirably well acted.

HAR.   I think I am pretty apt at these matters.

O. BELL.   Adod, I like this well.

LADY WOOD.   This promises something.

O. BELL.   Come, there is love i' the case, adod there is, or will be; what say you, young lady?

HAR.   All in good time, sir; you expect we should fall to and love, as gamecocks fight, as soon as we are set together; adod, you're unreasonable!

O. BELL.   Adod, sirrah,[12] I like thy wit well.

Enter a SERVANT

SERV.   The coach is at the door, madam.

O. BELL.   Go, get you and take the air together.

LADY WOOD.   Will not you go with us?

O. BELL.   Out a pize. Adod, I ha' business and cannot. We shall meet at night at my sister Townley's.

Y. BELL.   (*Aside*) He's going to Emilia. I overheard him talk of a collation.   *Exeunt*

---

[11]*the Circle* the Ring, a fashionable promenade at the north edge of Hyde Park.

[12]*sirrah* sometimes addressed to a woman, seriously or in jest.

SCENE TWO

[LADY TOWNLEY'S *house*]

Enter LADY TOWNLEY, EMILIA *and* MR MEDLEY

LADY TOWN.   I pity the young lovers we last talked of; though, to say truth, their conduct has been so indiscreet they deserve to be unfortunate.

MED.   You've had an exact account, from the great lady i' the box down to the little orange-wench.

EMIL.   You're a living libel, a breathing lampoon; I wonder you are not torn in pieces.

MED.   What think you of setting up an office of intelligence for these matters? The project may get money.

LADY TOWN.   You would have great dealings with country ladies.

MED.   More than Muddiman[13] has with their husbands.

Enter BELINDA

LADY TOWN.   Belinda, what has been become of you? We have not seen you here of late with your friend Mrs Loveit.

BEL.   Dear creature, I left her but now so sadly afflicted.

LADY TOWN.   With her old distemper, jealousy?

MED.   Dorimant has played her some new prank.

BEL.   Well, that Dorimant is certainly the worst man breathing.

EMIL.   I once thought so.

BEL.   And do you not think so still?

EMIL.   No. indeed!

BEL.   O Jesu!

EMIL.   The town does him a great deal of injury, and I will never believe what it says of a man I do not know again, for his sake.

BELL.   You make me wonder!

LADY TOWN.   He's a very well-bred man.

BEL.   But strangely ill-natured.

EMIL.   Then he's a very witty man.

BEL.   But a man of no principles.

MED.   Your man of principles is a very fine thing indeed!

BEL.   To be preferred to men of parts by women who have regard to their reputation and quiet. Well, were I minded to play the fool, he should be the last man I'd think of.

MED.   He has been the first in many lady's favours, though you are so severe, madam.

---

[13]*Muddiman* Henry Muddiman, 1629–92, editor of a series of newsletters particularly popular in the provinces: *The Parliamentary Intelligencer*, renamed *The Kingdom's Intelligencer* (1659–63), *The Oxford Gazette* (1665–67), *The London Gazette* (1667–present).

LADY TOWN. What he may be for a lover I know not, but he's a very pleasant acquaintance, I am sure.

BEL. Had you seen him use Mrs Loveit as I have done, you would never endure him more.

EMIL. What, he has quarrelled with her again?

BEL. Upon the slightest occasion; he's jealous of Sir Fopling.

LADY TOWN. She never saw him in her life but yesterday, and that was here.

EMIL. On my conscience, he's the only man in town that's her aversion; how horribly out of humour she was all the while he talked to her!

BEL. And somebody has wickedly told him –

EMIL. Here he comes.

Enter DORIMANT

MED. Dorimant! You are luckily come to justify yourself. Here's a lady –

BEL. Has a word or two to say to you from a disconsolate person.

DOR. You tender your reputation too much, I know, madam, to whisper with me before this good company.

BEL. To serve Mrs Loveit, I'll make a bold venture.

DOR. Here's Medley, the very spirit of scandal.

BEL. No matter.

EMIL. 'Tis something you are unwilling to hear, Mr Dorimant.

LADY TOWN. Tell him, Belinda, whether he will or no.

BEL. (*Aloud*) Mrs Loveit –

DOR. Softly, these are laughers; you do not know 'em.

BEL. (*To* DORIMANT, *apart*) In a word, you've made me hate you, which I thought you never could have done.

DOR. In obeying your commands.

BEL. 'Twas a cruel part you played! How could you act it?

DOR. Nothing is cruel to a man who could kill himself to please you; remember, five o'clock tomorrow morning.

BEL. I tremble when you name it.

DOR. Be sure you come.

BEL. I sha' not.

DOR. Swear you will.

BEL. I dare not.

DOR. Swear, I say.

BEL. By my life, by all the happiness I hope for –

DOR. You will.

BEL. I will.

DOR. Kind.

BEL. I am glad I've sworn; I vow I think I should ha' failed you else.

DOR.   Surprisingly kind! In what temper did you leave Loveit?

BEL.   Her raving was prettily over, and she began to be in a brave way of defying you and all your works. Where have you been since you went from thence?

DOR.   I looked in at the play.

BEL.   I have promised, and must return to her again.

DOR.   Persuade her to walk in the Mall this evening.

BEL.   She hates the place and will not come.

DOR.   Do all you can to prevail with her.

BEL.   For what purpose?

DOR.   Sir Fopling will be here anon; I'll prepare him to set upon her there before me.

BEL.   You persecute her too much; but I'll do all you'll ha' me.

DOR.   (*Aloud*) Tell her plainly, 'tis grown so dull a business I can drudge on no longer.

EMIL.   There are afflictions in love, Mr Dorimant.

DOR.   You women make 'em, who are commonly as unreasonable in that as you are at play;[14] without the advantage be on your side, a man can never quietly give over when he's weary.

MED.   If you would play without being obliged to complaisance, Dorimant, you should play in public places.

DOR.   Ordinaries[15] were a very good thing for that, but gentlemen do not of late frequent 'em; the deep play is now in private houses.

                                        BELINDA *offering to steal away*

LADY TOWN.   Belinda, are you leaving us so soon?

BEL.   I am to go to the Park with Mrs Loveit, madam. *Exit* BELINDA

LADY TOWN.   This confidence[16] will go nigh to spoil this young creature.

MED.   'Twill do her good, madam. Young men who are brought up under practising lawyers prove the abler counsel when they come to be called to the bar themselves.

DOR.   The town has been very favourable to you this afternoon, my Lady Townley; you use to have an *embarras* of chairs and coaches at your door, an uproar of footmen in your hall, and a noise of fools above here.

LADY TOWN.   Indeed my house is the general rendezvous and, next to the playhouse, is the common refuge of all the young idle people.

EMIL.   Company is a very good thing, madam, but I wonder you do not love it a little more chosen.

LADY TOWN.   'Tis good to have an universal taste; we should love wit, but for variety be able to divert ourselves with the extravagancies of those who want it.

[14]*play* gambling.   [15]*Ordinaries* taverns or eating-houses.
[16]*confidence* intimacy.

MED.   Fools will make you laugh.

EMIL.   For once or twice; but the repetition of their folly after a visit or two grows tedious and insufferable.

LADY TOWN.   You are a little too delicate, Emilia.

Enter a PAGE

PAGE.   Sir Fopling Flutter, madam, desires to know if you are to be seen.

LADY TOWN.   Here's the freshest fool in town, and one who has not cloyed you yet. Page!

PAGE.   Madam.

LADY TOWN.   Desire him to walk up.   [*Exit* PAGE]

DOR.   Do not you fall on him, Medley, and snub him. Soothe him up in his extravagance; he will show the better.

MED.   You know I have a natural indulgence for fools and need not this caution, sir.

Enter SIR FOPLING FLUTTER, *with his page after him*

SIR FOP.   Page, wait without. [*Exit* PAGE] Madam, (*To* LADY TOWNLEY) I kiss your hands. I see yesterday was nothing of chance; the *belles assemblées* form themselves here every day. Lady, (*To* EMILIA) your servant. Dorimant, let me embrace thee; without lying, I have not met with any of my acquaintance who retain so much of Paris as thou dost – the very air thou hadst when the marquis mistook thee i' the Tuileries, and cried '*Hé, Chevalier!*' and then begged thy pardon.

DOR.   I would fain wear in fashion as long as I can, sir; 'tis a thing to be valued in men as well as baubles.

SIR FOP.   Thou art a man of wit, and understand'st the town; prithee let thee and I be intimate. There is no living without making some good man the confidant of our pleasures.

DOR.   'Tis true, but there is no man so improper for such a business as I am.

SIR FOP.   Prithee, why hast thou so modest an opinion of thyself?

DOR.   Why, first, I could never keep a secret in my life, and then there is no charm so infallibly makes me fall in love with a woman as my knowing a friend loves her. I deal honestly with you.

SIR FOP.   Thy humour's very gallant, or let me perish; I knew a French count so like thee.

LADY TOWN.   Wit, I perceive, has more power over you than beauty, Sir Fopling, else you would not have let this lady stand so long neglected.

SIR FOP.   (*To* EMILIA) A thousand pardons, madam; some civility's due, of course, upon the meeting a long absent friend. The *éclat* of so much beauty, I confess, ought to have charmed me sooner.

EMIL. The *brillant* of so much good language, sir, has much more power than the little beauty I can boast.

SIR FOP. I never saw anything prettier than this high work on your *point d'Espagne.*[17]

EMIL. 'Tis not so rich as *point de Venise.*

SIR FOP. Not altogether, but looks cooler and is more proper for the season. Dorimant, is not that Medley?

DOR. The same, sir.

SIR FOP. Forgive me, sir; in this *embarras* of civilities I could not come to have you in my arms sooner. You understand an equipage[18] the best of any man in town, I hear.

MED. By my own you would not guess it.

SIR FOP. There are critics who do not write, sir.

MED. Our peevish poets will scarce allow it.

SIR FOP. Damn 'em, they'll allow no man wit who does not play the fool like themselves and show it! Have you taken notice of the *calèche*[19] I brought over?

MED. Oh, yes! 'T has quite another air than th'English makes.

SIR FOP. 'Tis as easily known from an English tumbril[20] as an Inns of Court man[21] is from one of us.

DOR. Truly, there is a *bel air* in *calèches* as well as men.

MED. But there are few so delicate to observe it.

SIR FOP. The world is generally very *grossier* here, indeed.

LADY TOWN. He's very fine.

EMIL. Extreme proper.

SIR FOP. A slight suit I made to appear in at my first arrival, not worthy your consideration, ladies.

DOR. The pantaloon is very well mounted.

SIR FOP. The tassels are new and pretty.

MED. I never saw a coat better cut.

SIR FOP. It makes me show long-waisted, and, I think, slender.

DOR. That's the shape our ladies dote on.

MED. Your breech, though, is a handful too high in my eye, Sir Fopling.

SIR FOP. Peace, Medley; I have wished it lower a thousand times, but a pox on't, 'twill not be.

LADY TOWN. His gloves are well fringed, large and graceful.

---

[17]*point d'Espagne* Spanish lace.
[18]*equipage* a carriage and horses, with attendants.
[19]*calèche* a light carriage with a collapsible top, only recently introduced to England.
[20]*tumbril* dung cart.   [21]*Inns of Court man* a lawyer.

SIR FOP. I was always eminent for being *bien ganté*.[22]

EMIL. He wears nothing but what are originals of the most famous hands in Paris.

SIR FOP. You are in the right, madam.

LADY TOWN. The suit?

SIR FOP. Barroy.[23]

EMIL. The garniture?[24]

SIR FOP. Le Gras.

MED. The shoes?

SIR FOP. Piccar.

DOR. The periwig?

SIR FOP. Chedreux.[25]

LADY TOWN *and* EMIL. The gloves?

SIR FOP. Orangerie. You know the smell, ladies. Dorimant, I could find in my heart for an amusement to have a gallantry with some of our English ladies.

DOR. 'Tis a thing no less necessary to confirm the reputation of your wit than a duel will be to satisfy the town of your courage.

SIR FOP. Here was a woman yesterday –

DOR. Mistress Loveit.

SIR FOP. You have named her.

DOR. You cannot pitch on a better for your purpose.

SIR FOP. Prithee, what is she?

DOR. A person of quality, and one who has a rest[26] of reputation enough to make the conquest considerable. Besides, I hear she likes you too.

SIR FOP. Methought she seemed, though, very reserved and uneasy all the time I entertained her.

DOR. Grimace and affectation. You will see her i' the Mall tonight.

SIR FOP. Prithee let thee and I take the air together.

DOR. I am engaged to Medley, but I'll meet you at St James's and give you some information upon the which you may regulate your proceedings.

SIR FOP. All the world will be in the Park[27] tonight. Ladies, 'twere pity to keep so much beauty longer within doors and rob the Ring of all those charms that should adorn it. – Hey, page!

Enter page

---

[22]*bien ganté* well gloved.

[23]*Barroy* not identified; perhaps 'Barri', and may be related to *drap-de-berry*, a woollen cloth from Berry, France (*The Way of the World*, III, i, p. 529).

[24]*garniture* trimmings. [25]*Chedreux* the inventor of a style of peruque.

[26]*rest* remnant. [27]*the Park* i.e. Hyde Park.

See that all my people be ready. (*Goes out again*) Dorimant, *au
revoir*.[28]   *Exit* SIR FOPLING

MED.   A fine-mettled coxcomb.

DOR.   Brisk and insipid.

MED.   Pert and dull.

EMIL.   However you despise him, gentlemen, I'll lay my life he passes
for a wit with many.

DOR.   That may very well be; nature has her cheats, stums[29] a brain,
and puts sophisticate[30] dulness often on the tasteless multitude for
true wit and good humour. Medley, come.

MED.   I must go a little way; I will meet you i' the Mall.

DOR.   I'll walk through the garden thither. (*To the Women*) We shall
meet anon and bow.

LADY TOWN.   Not tonight; we are engaged about a business the
knowledge of which may make you laugh hereafter.

MED.   Your servant, ladies.

DOR.   *Au revoir*! as Sir Fopling says.

                              Exeunt MEDLEY *and* DORIMANT

LADY TOWN.   The old man will be here immediately.

EMIL.   Let's expect[31] him i' the garden.

LADY TOWN.   Go, you are a rogue.

EMIL.   I can't abide you.   *Exeunt*

SCENE THREE

The Mall

Enter HARRIET *and* YOUNG BELLAIR, *she pulling him*

HAR.   Come along.

Y. BELL.   And leave your mother?

HAR.   Busy will be sent with a hue and cry after us; but that's no
matter.

Y. BELL.   'Twill look strangely in me.

HAR.   She'll believe it a freak of mine and never blame your manners.

Y. BELL.   What reverend acquaintance is that she has met?

---

[28]*au revoir* The first edition, 1676, gives 'a Revoir' here and 16 lines below,
perhaps reflecting Fopling's affected or inaccurate pronunciation. Elsewhere in the
play the spelling and punctuation may suggest his use of the French language.

[29]*stums* to renew fermentation temporarily in dull wine by adding must
(unfermented or partly fermented grape juice).

[30]*sophisticate* adulterated.

[31]*expect* await.

HAR.   A fellow-beauty of the last king's time,[32] though by the ruins
you would hardly guess it.   *Exeunt*
　　Enter DORIMANT *and crosses the stage*
　　Enter YOUNG BELLAIR *and* HARRIET

Y. BELL.   By this time your mother is in a fine taking.[33]

HAR.   If your friend Mr Dorimant were but here now, that she might
find me talking with him.

Y. BELL.   She does not know him, but dreads him, I hear, of all
mankind.

HAR.   She concludes if he does but speak to a woman she's undone; is
on her knees every day to pray heav'n defend me from him.

Y. BELL.   You do not apprehend[34] him so much as she does.

HAR.   I never saw anything in him that was frightful.

Y. BELL.   On the contrary, have you not observed something extreme
delightful in his wit and person?

HAR.   He's agreeable and pleasant, I must own, but he does so much
affect being so, he displeases me.

Y. BELL.   Lord, madam, all he does and says is so easy and so natural.

HAR.   Some men's verses seem so to the unskilful, but labour i' the one
and affectation in the other to the judicious plainly appear.

Y. BELL.   I never heard him accused of affectation before.
　　Enter DORIMANT *and stares upon her*

HAR.   It passes on the easy town, who are favourably pleased in him
to call it humour.   *Exeunt* YOUNG BELLAIR *and* HARRIET

DOR.   'Tis she! It must be she – that lovely hair, that easy shape, those
wanton eyes, and all those melting charms about her mouth which
Medley spoke of; I'll follow the lottery,[35] and put in for a prize with
my friend Bellair.   *Exit* DORIMANT, *repeating*:
　　　　In love the victors from the vanquish'd fly;
　　　　They fly that wound, and they pursue that die.[36]
　　Enter YOUNG BELLAIR *and* HARRIET, *and after them*
　　DORIMANT, *standing at a distance*

Y. BELL.   Most people prefer High Park[37] to this place.

HAR.   It has the better reputation, I confess; but I abominate the dull
diversions there, the formal bows, the affected smiles, the silly by-

---

[32]*time* the period of King Charles I, executed in 1649.

[33]*in a fine taking* distressed.

[34]*apprehend* fear.

[35]*follow the lottery* take a chance.

[36]*In love . . . die* Edmund Waller, 'To a Friend, of the Different Success of their
Loves', *Poems*, I (London, 1901), pp. 102–03.

[37]*High Park* Hyde Park.

words and amorous tweers[38] in passing. Here one meets with a little conversation now and then.

Y. BELL.   These conversations have been fatal to some of your sex, madam.

HAR.   It may be so; because some who want temper[39] have been undone by gaming, must others who have it wholly deny themselves the pleasure of play?

DOR.   Trust me, it were unreasonable, madam.

Coming up gently and bowing to her

HAR.   Lord, who's this?   *She starts and looks grave*

Y. BELL.   Dorimant.

DOR.   Is this the woman your father would have you marry?

Y. BELL.   It is.

DOR.   Her name?

Y. BELL.   Harriet.

DOR.   I am not mistaken; she's handsome.

Y. BELL.   Talk to her; her wit is better than her face. We were wishing for you but now.

DOR.   (*To* HARRIET) Overcast with seriousness o' the sudden! A thousand smiles were shining in that face but now; I never saw so quick a change of weather.

HAR.   (*Aside*) I feel as great a change within, but he shall never know it.

DOR.   You were talking of play, madam; pray, what may be your stint?[40]

HAR.   A little harmless discourse in public walks, or at most an appointment in a box barefaced at the playhouse; you are for masks and private meetings where women engage for all they are worth, I hear.

DOR.   I have been used to deep play, but I can make one at small game when I like my gamester well.

HAR.   And be so unconcerned you'll ha' no pleasure in't.

DOR.   Where there is a considerable sum to be won, the hope of drawing people in makes every trifle considerable.

HAR.   The sordidness of men's natures, I know, makes 'em willing to flatter and comply with the rich, though they are sure never to be the better for 'em.

DOR.   'Tis in their power to do us good, and we despair not but at some time or other they may be willing.

HAR.   To men who have fared in this town like you, 'twould be a great

---

[38]*tweers* covert glances.   [39]*temper* moderation.
[40]*stint* upper limit in gambling.

mortification to live on hope; could you keep a Lent for a mistress?

DOR.   In expectation of a happy Easter, and though time be very precious, think forty days well lost to gain your favour.

HAR.   Mr Bellair! Let us walk, 'tis time to leave him; men grow dull when they begin to be particular.

DOR.   You're mistaken; flattery will not ensue, though I know you're greedy of the praises of the whole Mall.

HAR.   You do me wrong.

DOR.   I do not. As I followed you I observed how you were pleased when the fops cried: 'She's handsome, very handsome, by God, she is', and whispered aloud your name, the thousand several forms you put your face into; then, to make yourself more agreeable, how wantonly you played with your head, flung back your locks, and looked smilingly over your shoulder at 'em.

HAR.   I do not go begging the men's, as you do the ladies' good liking, with a sly softness in your looks and a gentle slowness in your bows as you pass by 'em. As thus, sir, – (*Acts him*) Is not this like you?

> *Enter* LADY WOODVILL *and* BUSY

Y. BELL.   Your mother, madam.

> *Pulls* HARRIET; *she composes herself*

LADY WOOD.   Ah, my dear child Harriet!

BUSY.   Now is she so pleased with finding her again she cannot chide her.

LADY WOOD.   Come away!

DOR.   'Tis now but high Mall, madam, the most entertaining time of all the evening.

HAR.   I would fain see that Dorimant, mother, you so cry out of for a monster; he's in the Mall, I hear.

LADY WOOD.   Come away then! The plague is here, and you should dread the infection.

Y. BELL.   You may be misinformed of the gentleman.

LADY WOOD.   Oh, no! I hope you do not know him! He is the prince of all the devils in the town, delights in nothing but in rapes and riots.

DOR.   If you did but hear him speak, madam, –

LADY WOOD.   Oh, he has a tongue, they say, would tempt the angels to a second fall.

> *Enter* SIR FOPLING *with his equipage, six footmen and a page*

SIR FOP.   Hey, Champagne, Norman, La Rose, La Fleur, La Tour, La Verdure! Dorimant! –

LADY WOOD.   Here, here he is among this rout; he names him. Come away, Harriet, come away.

> *Exeunt* LADY WOODVILL, HARRIET, BUSY *and* YOUNG BELLAIR

DOR.   This fool's coming has spoiled all. She's gone, but she has left a pleasing image of herself behind that wanders in my soul. It must not settle there.

SIR FOP.   What reverie is this? Speak, man.

DOR.   Snatch'd from myself, how far behind
           Already I behold the shore![41]

Enter MEDLEY

MED.   Dorimant, a discovery! I met with Bellair.

DOR.   You can tell me no news, sir; I know all.

MED.   How do you like the daughter?

DOR.   You never came so near truth in your life as you did in her description.

MED.   What think you of the mother?

DOR.   Whatever I think of her, she thinks very well of me, I find!

MED.   Did she know you?

DOR.   She did not; whether she does now or no, I know not. Here was a pleasant scene towards,[42] when in came Sir Fopling, mustering up his equipage, and at the latter end named me and frighted her away.

MED.   Loveit and Belinda are not far off; I saw 'em alight at St James's.[43]

DOR.   (*Whispers*) Sir Fopling, hark you, a word or two. Look you do not want assurance.

SIR FOP.   I never do on these occasions.

DOR.   Walk on, we must not be seen together. Make your advantage of what I have told you; the next turn you will meet the lady.

SIR FOP.   Hey – Follow me all.

Exeunt SIR FOPLING *and his equipage*

DOR.   Medley, you shall see good sport anon between Loveit and this Fopling.

MED.   I thought there was something toward by that whisper.

DOR.   You know a worthy principle of hers?

MED.   Not to be so much as civil to a man who speaks to her in the presence of him she professes to love.

DOR.   I have encouraged Fopling to talk to her tonight.

MED.   Now you are here she will go nigh to beat him.

DOR.   In the humour she's in, her love will make her do some very extravagant thing, doubtless.

MED.   What was Belinda's business with you at my Lady Townley's?

---

[41]*Snatch'd . . . shore* Edmund Waller, 'Of Loving at First Sight', *Poems*, i (London, 1901), p. 100.

[42]*towards* in prospect.

[43]*St James's* St James's Palace, near the west end of the Mall.

DOR.   To get me to meet Loveit here in order to an *éclaircissement*.⁴⁴ I
made some difficulty of it, and have prepared this *recontre* to make
good my jealousy.

MED.   Here they come!

    Enter LOVEIT, BELINDA *and* PERT

DOR.   I'll meet her and provoke her with a deal of dumb civility in
passing by, then turn short and be behind her when Sir Fopling sets
upon her –

                See how unregarded now
                That piece of beauty passes.⁴⁵

                        Exeunt DORIMANT *and* MEDLEY

BEL.   How wonderful respectfully he bowed!

PERT.   He's always over-mannerly when he has done a mischief.

BEL.   Methought indeed at the same time he had a strange despising
countenance.

PERT.   The unlucky⁴⁶ look, he thinks, becomes him.

BEL.   I was afraid you would have spoke to him, my dear.

LOV.   I would have died first; he shall no more find me the loving fool
he has done.

BEL.   You love him still!

LOV.   No.

PERT.   I wish you did not.

LOV.   I do not, and I will have you think so. What made you hale me
to this odious place, Belinda?

BEL.   I hate to be hulched up in a coach; walking is much better.

LOV.   Would we could meet Sir Fopling now!

BEL.   Lord, would you not avoid him?

LOV.   I would make him all the advances that may be.

BEL.   That would confirm Dorimant's suspicion, my dear.

LOV.   He is not jealous, but I will make him so, and be revenged a way
he little thinks on.

BEL.   (*Aside*) If she should make him jealous, that may make him fond
of her again; I must dissuade her from it. – Lord, my dear, this will
certainly make him hate you.

LOV.   'Twill make him uneasy, though he does not care for me; I
know the effects of jealousy on men of his proud temper.

BEL.   'Tis a fantastic remedy; its operations are dangerous and
uncertain.

LOV.   'Tis the strongest cordial we can give to dying love; it often

---

⁴⁴*éclaircissement* clarification.

⁴⁵*See . . . passes* John Suckling, Sonnet 1, *Fragmenta Aurea* (1646), p. 14.

⁴⁶*unlucky* mischievous.

brings it back when there's no sign of life remaining. But I design not so much the reviving his, as my revenge.

    Enter SIR FOPLING *and his equipage*

SIR FOP.   Hey! Bid the coachman send home four of his horses, and bring the coach to Whitehall;[47] I'll walk over the Park – Madam, the honour of kissing your fair hands is a happiness I missed this afternoon at my Lady Townley's.

LOV.   You were very obliging, Sir Fopling, the last time I saw you there.

SIR FOP.   The preference was due to your wit and beauty. Madam, your servant. There never was so sweet an evening.

BEL.   'T has drawn all the rabble of the town hither.

SIR FOP.   'Tis pity there's not an order made that none but the *beau monde* should walk here.

LOV.   'Twould add much to the beauty of the place. See what a sort[48] of nasty fellows are coming.

    Enter four[49] *ill-fashioned* FELLOWS, *singing*
        'Tis not for kisses alone, etc.[50]

LOV.   Foh! Their periwigs are scented with tobacco so strong –

SIR FOP.   It overcomes our pulvilio.[51] Methinks I smell the coffee-house they come from.

FIRST MAN.   Dorimant's convenient,[52] Madam Loveit.

SECOND MAN.   I like the oily buttock[53] with her.

THIRD MAN.   What spruce prig is that?

FIRST MAN.   A caravan[54] lately come from Paris.

SECOND MAN.   Peace, they smoke.[55]
        There's something else to be done, etc.

        All of them coughing;[56] *exeunt, singing*
    Enter DORIMANT *and* MEDLEY

DOR.   They're engaged.

MED.   She entertains him as if she liked him.

DOR.   Let us go forward, seem earnest in discourse, and show ourselves. Then you shall see how she'll use him.

---

[47]*Whitehall* the Palace, near St James's Park, burned in 1698.
[48]*sort* crowd.
[49]*four* In the 1676 edition, the Dramatis Personae gives three.
[50]*'Tis . . . alone* This line and 'There's . . . done' (9 lines below) are from an anonymous song 'Tell me no more you love', in *A New Collection of the Choicest Songs*, 1676.
[51]*pulvilio* scented powder.   [52]*convenient* mistress.
[53]*oily buttock* fat strumpet.   [54]*caravan* an object for plunder.
[55]*smoke* observe us.
[56]*coughing* Perhaps Loveit coughed when she referred to tobacco, and they imitate her.

BEL.   Yonder's Dorimant, my dear.

LOV.   (*Aside*) I see him, he comes insulting;[57] but I will disappoint him in his expectation. (*To* SIR FOPLING) I like this pretty nice humour of yours, Sir Fopling. [*To* BELINDA] With what a loathing eye he looked upon those fellows!

SIR FOP.   I sat near one of 'em at a play today, and was almost poisoned with a pair of cordovan[58] gloves he wears.

LOV.   Oh, filthy cordovan! How I hate the smell!

Laughs in a loud, affected way

SIR FOP.   Did you observe, madam, how their cravats hung loose an inch from their neck, and what a frightful air it gave 'em?

LOV.   Oh, I took particular notice of one that is always spruced up with a deal of dirty sky-coloured ribbon.

BEL.   That's one of the walking flageolets[59] who haunt the Mall o' nights.

LOV.   Oh, I remember him; he has a hollow tooth enough to spoil the sweetness of an evening.

SIR FOP.   I have seen the tallest walk the streets with a dainty pair of boxes neatly buckled on.

LOV.   And a little footboy at his heels pocket-high, with a flat cap, a dirty face –

SIR FOP.   And a snotty nose.

LOV.   Oh, odious! There's many of my own sex with that Holborn equipage trig[60] to Gray's Inn Walks,[61] and now and then travel hither on a Sunday.

MED.   She takes no notice of you.

DOR.   Damn her! I am jealous of a counterplot!

LOV.   Your liveries are the finest, Sir Fopling. – Oh, that page! That page is the prettily'st dressed. They are all Frenchmen?

SIR FOP.   There's one damned English blockhead among 'em; you may know him by his mien.

LOV.   Oh, that's he, that's he! What do you call him?

SIR FOP.   Hey! – I know not what to call him. –

LOVE.   What's your name?

FOOTMAN.   John Trott, madam.

SIR FOP.   Oh, insufferable! Trott, Trott, Trott! There's nothing so barbarous as the names of our English servants. What countryman are you, sirrah?

---

[57]*insulting* triumphant.

[58]*cordovan* leather, made in Cordova, Spain, from horsehide.

[59]*flageolets* musical instruments like flutes or recorders; the implication here is 'tall and thin'.

[60]*trig* trip.   [61]*Gray's Inn Walks* an unfashionable area.

FOOT.   Hampshire, sir.

SIR FOP.   Then Hampshire be your name. Hey, Hampshire!

LOV.   Oh, that sound! That sound becomes the mouth of a man of quality.

MED.   Dorimant, you look a little bashful on the matter.

[MEDLEY *and* DORIMANT *speak apart*]

DOR.   She dissembles better than I thought she could have done.

MED.   You have tempted her with too luscious a bait: she bites at the coxcomb.

DOR.   She cannot fall from loving me to that?

MED.   You begin to be jealous in earnest.

DOR.   Of one I do not love?

MED.   You did love her.

DOR.   The fit has long been over.

MED.   But I have known men fall into dangerous relapses when they have found a woman inclining to another.

DOR.   (*To himself*) He guesses the secret of my heart! I am concerned, but dare not show it lest Belinda should mistrust all I have done to gain her.

BEL.   (*Aside*) I have watched his look, and find no alteration there. Did he love her, some signs of jealousy would have appeared.

DOR.   I hope this happy evening, madam, has reconciled you to the scandalous Mall; we shall have you now hankering[62] here again.

LOV.   Sir Fopling, will you walk?

SIR FOP.   I am all obedience, madam.

LOV.   Come along then, and let's agree to be malicious on all the ill-fashioned things we meet.

SIR FOP.   We'll make a critique on the whole Mall, madam.

LOV.   Belinda, you shall engage[63] –

BEL.   To the reserve[64] of our friends, my dear.

LOV.   No, no exceptions –

SIR FOP.   We'll sacrifice all to our diversion.

LOV.   All, all.

SIR FOP.   All.

BEL.   All? Then let it be.

Exeunt SIR FOPLING, LOVEIT, BELINDA *and* PERT, *laughing*

MED.   Would you had brought some more of your friends, Dorimant, to have been witnesses of Sir Fopling's disgrace and your triumph!

DOR.   'Twere unreasonable to desire you not to laugh at me; but pray do not expose me to the town this day or two.

MED.   By that time you hope to have regained your credit?

---

[62]*hankering* loitering.   [63]*engage* participate.   [64]*reserve* exception.

DOR.   I know she hates Fopling, and only makes use of him in hope
to work me on again; had it not been for some powerful
considerations which will be removed tomorrow morning, I had
made her pluck off this mask and show the passion that lies panting
under.

Enter a FOOTMAN

MED.   Here comes a man from Bellair with news of your last
adventure.

DOR.   I am glad he sent him. I long to know the consequence of our
parting.

FOOT.   Sir, my master desires you to come to my Lady Townley's
presently, and bring Mr Medley with you. My Lady Woodvill and
her daughter are there.

MED.   Then all's well, Dorimant.

FOOT.   They have sent for the fiddles and mean to dance. He bid me
tell you, sir, the old lady does not know you, and [he] would have
you own yourself to be Mr Courtage. They are all prepared to
receive you by that name.

DOR.   That foppish admirer of quality, who flatters the very meat at
honourable tables and never offers love to a woman below a lady-
grandmother.

MED.   You know the character you are to act, I see.

DOR.   This is Harriet's contrivance – wild, witty, lovesome, beautiful and young! Come along, Medley.

MED.   This new woman would well supply the loss of Loveit.

DOR.   That business must not end so; before tomorrow's sun is set I
will revenge and clear it:

> And you and Loveit, to her cost, shall find
> I fathom all the depths of womankind.   *Exeunt*

Act Four

[SCENE ONE]

[LADY TOWNLEY'S *house*]

The scene opens with the fiddles playing a country dance
Enter DORIMANT [*and*] LADY WOODVILL, YOUNG BELLAIR
and MRS HARRIET, OLD BELLAIR *and* EMILIA, MR MEDLEY *and*
LADY TOWNLEY, *as having just ended the dance*

O. BELL. So, so, so, a smart bout, a very smart bout, adod!

LADY TOWN. How do you like Emilia's dancing, brother?

O. BELL. Not at all, not at all.

LADY TOWN. You speak not what you think, I am sure.

O. BELL. No matter for that; go, bid her dance no more, it don't become her, it don't become her. Tell her I say so. – (*Aside*) Adod, I love her.

DOR. (*To* LADY WOODVILL) All people mingle nowadays, madam, and in public places women of quality have the least respect showed 'em.

LADY WOOD. I protest you say the truth, Mr Courtage.

DOR. Forms and ceremonies, the only things that uphold quality and greatness, are now shamefully laid aside and neglected.

LADY WOOD. Well, this is not the women's age, let 'em think what they will. Lewdness is the business now; love was the business in my time.

DOR. The women indeed are little beholding to the young men of this age; they're generally only dull admirers of themselves, and make their court to nothing but their periwigs and their cravats, and would be more concerned for the disordering of 'em, though on a good occasion, than a young maid would be for the tumbling of her head or handkercher.[1]

LADY WOOD. I protest you hit 'em.

DOR. They are very assiduous to show themselves at court, well dressed, to the women of quality, but their business is with the stale mistresses of the town, who are prepared to receive their lazy addresses by industrious old lovers who have cast 'em off and made 'em easy.

[1] *handkercher* head or neck covering.

HAR. [*To* MEDLEY] He fits my mother's humour so well, a little more and she'll dance a kissing dance with him anon.

MED. Dutifully observed, madam.

DOR. They pretend to be great critics in beauty; by their talk you would think they liked no face, and yet can dote on an ill one, if it belong to a laundress or a tailor's daughter; they cry a woman's past her prime at twenty, decayed at four-and-twenty, old and insufferable at thirty.

LADY WOOD. Insufferable at thirty! That they are in the wrong, Mr Courtage, at five-and-thirty there are living proofs enough to convince 'em.

DOR. Ay, madam, there's Mrs Setlooks, Mrs Droplip, and my Lady Loud. Show me among all our opening buds a face that promises so much beauty as the remains of theirs.

LADY WOOD. The depraved appetite of this vicious age tastes nothing but green fruit and loathes it when 'tis kindly² ripened.

DOR. Else so many deserving women, madam, would not be so untimely neglected.

LADY WOOD. I protest, Mr Courtage, a dozen such good men as you would be enough to atone for that wicked Dorimant and all the under-debauchees of the town.

HARRIET, EMILIA, YOUNG BELLAIR, MEDLEY, *and* LADY TOWNLEY *break out into a laughter*

What's the matter there?

MED. A pleasant mistake, madam, that a lady has made occasions a little laughter.

O. BELL. Come, come, you keep 'em idle. They are impatient till the fiddles play again.

DOR. You are not weary, madam?

LADY WOOD. One dance more. I cannot refuse you, Mr Courtage.

They dance

After the dance, OLD BELLAIR *singing and dancing up to* EMILIA

EMIL. You are very active, sir.

O. BELL. Adod, sirrah, when I was a young fellow I could ha' capered up to my woman's gorget.³

DOR. You are willing to rest yourself, madam?

LADY TOWN. We'll walk into my chamber and sit down.

MED. Leave us Mr Courtage; he's a dancer, and the young ladies are not weary yet.

LADY WOOD. We'll send him out again.

---

²*kindly* naturally.
³*capered . . . gorget* kicked as high as my partner's neckpiece.

HAR.   If you do not quickly, I know where to send for Mr Dorimant.

LADY WOOD.   This girl's head, Mr Courtage, is ever running on that wild fellow.

DOR.   'Tis well you have got her a good husband, madam; that will settle it.

   Exeunt LADY TOWNLEY, LADY WOODVILL, *and* DORIMANT

O. BELL.   (*To* EMILIA) Adod, sweetheart, be advised, and do not throw thyself away on a young idle fellow.

EMIL.   I have no such intention, sir.

O. BELL.   Have a little patience; thou shalt have the man I spake of. Adod, he loves thee, and will make a good husband; but no words.

EMIL.   But, sir, –

O. BELL.   No answer. – Out a pize! Peace, and think on 'it.

  Enter DORIMANT

DOR.   Your company is desired within, sir.

O. BELL.   I go, I go. Good Mr Courtage, fare you well. (*To* EMILIA) Go, I'll see you no more.

EMIL.   What have I done, sir?

O. BELL.   You are ugly, you are ugly. Is she not, Mr Courtage?

EMIL.   Better words or I shan't abide you.

O. BELL.   Out a pize! Adod, what does she say? Hit her a pat for me there.   *Exit* OLD BELLAIR

MED.   You have charms for the whole family.

DOR.   You'll spoil all with some unseasonable jest, Medley.

MED.   You see I confine my tongue and am content to be a bare spectator, much contrary to my nature.

EMIL.   Methinks, Mr Dorimant, my Lady Woodvill is a little fond of you.

DOR.   Would her daughter were!

MED.   It may be you may find her so. Try her; you have an opportunity.

DOR.   And I will not lose it. Bellair, here's a lady has something to say to you.

Y. BELL.   I wait upon her. Mr Medley, we have both business with you.

DOR.   Get you all together then. – (*To* HARRIET) That demure curtsey is not amiss in jest, but do not think in earnest it becomes you.

HAR.   Affectation is catching, I find; from your grave bow I got it.

DOR.   Where had you all that scorn and coldness in your look?

HAR.   From nature, sir; pardon my want of art: I have not learnt those softnesses and languishings which now in faces are so much in fashion.

DOR. You need 'em not; you have a sweetness of your own, if you would but calm your frowns and let it settle.

HAR. My eyes are wild and wandering like my passions, and cannot yet be tied to rules of charming.

DOR. Women, indeed, have commonly a method of managing those messengers of love; now they will look as if they would kill, and anon they will look as if they were dying. They point and rebate⁴ their glances, the better to invite us.

HAR. I like this variety well enough, but hate the set face that always looks as it would say, 'Come, love me' – a woman who at plays makes the *doux yeux*⁵ to a whole audience and at home cannot forbear 'em to her monkey.

DOR. Put on a gentle smile and let me see how well it will become you.

HAR. I am sorry my face does not please you as it is, but I shall not be complaisant and change it.

DOR. Though you are obstinate, I know 'tis capable of improvement and shall do you justice, madam, if I chance to be at court when the critics of the circle⁶ pass their judgment; for thither you must come.

HAR. And expect to be taken in pieces, have all my features examined, every motion censured, and on the whole be condemned to be but pretty, or a beauty of the lowest rate. What think you?

DOR. The women, nay, the very lovers who belong to the drawing-room, will maliciously allow you more than that; they always grant what is apparent that they may the better be believed when they name concealed faults they cannot easily be disproved in.

HAR. Beauty runs as great a risk exposed at court as wit does on the stage, where the ugly and the foolish all are free to censure.

DOR. (*Aside*) I love her and dare not let her know it; I fear she has an ascendant o'er me and may revenge the wrongs I have done her sex. (*To her*) Think of making a party,⁷ madam; love will engage.

HAR. You make me start! I did not think to have heard of love from you.

DOR. I never knew what 'twas to have a settled ague yet, but now and then have had irregular fits.

HAR. Take heed! Sickness after long health is commonly more violent and dangerous.

DOR. (*Aside*) I have took the infection from her and feel the disease

---

⁴*rebate* blunt, a fencing term.	⁵*doux yeux* soft eyes.
⁶*circle* coterie.	⁷*making a party* mustering troops.

now spreading in me. (*To her*) Is the name of love so frightful that
you dare not stand it?

HAR. 'Twill do little execution out of your mouth on me, I am sure.

DOR. It has been fatal –

HAR. To some easy women, but we are not all born to one destiny. I
was informed you use to laugh at love and not make it.

DOR. The time has been, but now I must speak –

HAR. If it be on that idle subject, I will put on my serious look, turn
my head carelessly from you, drop my lip, let my eyelids fall and
hang half o'er my eyes – thus – while you buzz a speech of an hour
long in my ear, and I answer never a word. Why do you not begin?

DOR. That the company may take notice how passionately I make
advances of love and how disdainfully you receive 'em.

HAR. When your love's grown strong enough to make you bear being
laughed at, I'll give you leave to trouble me with it; till when, pray
forbear, sir.

    Enter SIR FOPLING *and others in masks*

DOR. What's here, masquerades?

HAR. I thought that foppery had been left off and people might have
been in private with a fiddle.

DOR. 'Tis endeavoured to be kept on foot still by some who find
themselves the more acceptable the less they are known.

Y. BELL. This must be Sir Fopling.

MED. That extraordinary habit[8] shows it.

Y. BELL. What are the rest?

MED. A company of French rascals whom he picked up in Paris and
has brought over to be his dancing equipage on these occasions.
Make him own himself; a fool is very troublesome when he
presumes he is incognito.

SIR FOP. (*To* HARRIET) Do you know me?

HAR. Ten to one but I guess at you.

SIR FOP. Are you women as fond of a vizard as we men are?

HAR. I am very fond of a vizard that covers a face I do not like, sir.

Y. BELL. Here are no masks, you see, sir, but those which came with
you; this was intended a private meeting, but because you look like a
gentleman, if you will discover yourself, and we know you to be
such, you shall be welcome.

SIR FOP. (*Pulling off his mask*) Dear Bellair.

MED. Sir Fopling! How came you hither?

SIR FOP. Faith, as I was coming late from Whitehall, after the King's

[8]*habit* attire.

couchée,[9] one of my people told me he had heard fiddles at my Lady Townley's, and –

DOR.   You need not say any more, sir.

SIR FOP.   Dorimant, let me kiss thee.

DOR.   (*Whispers*) Hark you, Sir Fopling.

SIR FOP.   Enough, enough – Courtage. A pretty kind of young woman[10] that, Medley; I observed her in the Mall; more *éveillée*[11] than our English women commonly are. Prithee, what is she?

MED.   The most noted coquette in town; beware of her.

SIR FOP.   Let her be what she will, I know how to take my measures; in Paris the mode is to flatter the prude, laugh at the faux-prude, make serious love to the demi-prude, and only rally with the coquette. Medley, what think you?

MED.   That for all this smattering of the mathematics, you may be out in your judgment at tennis.[12]

SIR FOP.   What a *coq-à-l'âne*[13] is this! I talk of women, and thou answer'st tennis.

MED.   Mistakes will be, for want of apprehension.

SIR FOP.   I am very glad of the acquaintance I have with this family.

MED.   My lady truly is a good woman.

SIR FOP.   Ah, Dorimant – Courtage, I would say – would thou hadst spent the last winter in Paris with me. When thou wert there, La Corneus and Sallyes[14] were the only habitudes[15] we had; a comedian would have been a *bonne fortune*. No stranger ever passed his time so well as I did some months before I came over. I was well received in a dozen families where all the women of quality used to visit; I have intrigues to tell thee more pleasant than ever thou read'st in a novel.

HAR.   Write 'em, sir, and oblige us women; our language wants such little stories.

SIR FOP.   Writing, madam, 's a mechanic part of wit; a gentleman should never go beyond a song or a billet.

HAR.   Bussy[16] was a gentleman.

---

[9]*couchée* evening reception.   [10]*young woman* i.e. Harriet.

[11]*éveillée* animated.

[12]*out . . . tennis* unable to count accurately the points won.

[13]*coq-à-l'âne* piece of nonsense.

[14]*La Corneus and Sallyes* These words may represent either a compositor's puzzlement whilst reading a manuscript or Etherege's hit at Fopling for pretending familiarity with French society ladies whom he did not in fact know. Mesdames Cornue and Selles were contemporary Parisian social and literary figures.

[15]*habitudes* acquaintances.

[16]*Bussy* Etherege's allusion is to Roger de Rabutin, Comte de Bussy, 1618–93, a popular writer, author of *Historie Amoureuse des Gaules*, 1666.

SIR FOP.   Who, d'Ambois?[17]

MED.   [*Aside*] Was there ever such a brisk blockhead?

HAR.   Not d'Ambois, sir, but Rabutin, he who writ *The Loves of France*.

SIR FOP.   That may be, madam; many gentlemen do things that are below 'em. Damn your authors, Courtage; women are the prettiest things we can fool away our time with.

HAR.   I hope ye have wearied yourself tonight at court, sir, and will not think of fooling with anybody here.

SIR FOP.   I cannot complain of my fortune there, madam. Dorimant, –

DOR.   Again!

SIR FOP.   Courtage, a pox on't! I have something to tell thee. When I had made my court within, I came out and flung myself upon the mat under the state[18] i' th' outward room i' the midst of half a dozen beauties who were withdrawn to jeer among themselves, as they called it.

DOR.   Did you know 'em?

SIR FOP.   Not one of 'em, by heavens! Not I. But they were all your friends.

DOR.   How are you sure of that?

SIR FOP.   Why, we laughed at all the town, spared nobody but yourself; they found me a man for their purpose.

DOR.   I know you are malicious to your power.[19]

SIR FOP.   And, faith, I had occasion to show it, for I never saw more gaping fools at a ball or on a Birthday.[20]

DOR.   You learned who the women were?

SIR FOP.   No matter; they frequent the drawing-room.

DOR.   And entertain themselves pleasantly at the expense of all the fops who come there.

SIR FOP.   That's their business. Faith, I sifted[21] 'em and find they have a sort of wit among them – *Pinches a tallow candle* Ah, filthy.

DOR.   Look, he has been pinching the tallow candle.

SIR FOP.   How can you breathe in a room where there's grease frying? Dorimant, thou art intimate with my lady; advise her for her own sake and the good company that comes hither, to burn wax lights.

---

[17]*d'Ambois* Sir Fopling naively identifies 'Bussy' as Bussy d'Ambois, the hero of George Chapman's play of this title (1607), revived in London in 1661 and *c.* 1675.
[18]*state* canopy.
[19]*to your power* to the limits of your ability.
[20]*Birthday* the celebration of King Charles II's birthday (29 May).
[21]*sifted* interrogated.

HAR.   What are these masquerades who stand so obsequiously at a distance?

SIR FOP.   A set of baladines²² whom I picked out of the best in France, and brought over with a *flutes douces* or two, my servants; they shall entertain you.

HAR.   I had rather see you dance yourself, Sir Fopling.

SIR FOP.   And I had rather do it – all the company knows it. But madam, –

MED.   Come, come, no excuses, Sir Fopling.

SIR FOP.   By heavens, Medley, –

MED.   Like a woman, I find you must be struggled with before one brings you to what you desire.

HAR.   (*Aside*) Can he dance?

EMIL.   And fence and sing too, if you'll believe him.

DOR.   He has no more excellence in his heels than in his head. He went to Paris a plain, bashful English blockhead, and is returned a fine, undertaking²³ French fop.

MED.   I cannot prevail.

SIR FOP.   Do not think it want of complaisance, madam.

HAR.   You are too well bred to want that, Sir Fopling. I believe it want of power.

SIR FOP.   By heavens, and so it is. I have sat up so damned late and drunk so cursed hard since I came to this lewd town that I am fit for nothing but low dancing now, a *courante*,²⁴ *bourrée*,²⁵ or a *menuet*;²⁶ but St André²⁷ tells me, if I will but be regular, in one month I shall rise again.   *Endeavours at a caper*
Pox on this debachery!

EMIL.   I have heard your dancing much commended.

SIR FOP.   It had the good fortune to please in Paris. I was judged to rise within an inch as high as the Basque²⁸ in an entry I danced there.

HAR.   [*Aside*] I am mightily taken with this fool. – Let us sit. Here's a seat, Sir Fopling.

---

²²*baladines* male theatrical dancers.

²³*undertaking* bold.

²⁴*courante* a running or gliding dance, without capers.

²⁵*bourrée* a rustic dance.

²⁶*menuet* a slow, stately dance.

²⁷*St André* a French dancer (Crowne's *Calisto*, 1675) and choreographer (Shadwell's *Psyche*, 1674).

²⁸*Basque* Probably an allusion to *le Basque sauteur*, an unnamed French dancer, noted for leaping, referred to in 'Les Amours de Madame de Montespan', in *La France Galante*, attributed to Roger Bussy-Rabutin (Paris, 1868, vol. II).

SIR FOP. At your feet, madam: I can be nowhere so much at ease. By your leave, gown.

HAR. *and* EMIL. Ah, you'll spoil it.

SIR FOP. No matter, my clothes are my creatures. I make 'em to make my court to you ladies. Hey, *qu'on commence!*[29] ([Trott] *dances*) To an English dancer, English motions. I was forced to entertain[30] this fellow, one of my set miscarrying.[31] Oh, horrid! Leave your damned manner of dancing and put on the French air. Have you not a pattern before you? Pretty well! Imitation in time may bring him to something.

> *After the dance, enter* OLD BELLAIR, LADY WOODVILL *and* LADY TOWNLEY

O. BELL. Hey, adod! What have we here, a mumming?[32]

LADY WOOD. Where's my daughter? Harriet?

DOR. Here, here, madam. I know not but under these disguises there may be dangerous sparks; I gave the young lady warning.

LADY WOOD. Lord, I am so obliged to you, Mr Courtage.

HAR. Lord, how you admire this man.

LADY WOOD. What have you to except[33] against him?

HAR. He's a fop.

LADY WOOD. He's not a Dorimant, a wild, extravagant fellow of the times.

HAR. He's a man made up of forms and commonplaces sucked out of the remaining lees of the last age.

LADY WOOD. He's so good a man that, were you not engaged –

LADY TOWN. You'll have but little night to sleep in.

LADY WOOD. Lord, 'tis perfect day.

DOR. (*Aside*) The hour is almost come I appointed Belinda, and I am not so foppishly in love here to forget: I am flesh and blood yet.

LADY TOWN. I am very sensible,[34] madam.

LADY WOOD. Lord, madam, –

HAR. Look, in what a struggle is my poor mother yonder!

Y. BELL. She has much ado to bring out the compliment.

DOR. She strains hard for it.

HAR. See, see, her head tottering, her eyes staring, and her under lip trembling.

DOR. (*Aside*) Now, now she's in the very convulsions of her civility.

---

[29]*qu'on commence* begin.   [30]*entertain* engage.
[31]*miscarrying* going astray.
[32]*mumming* a performance of a mummers' play.
[33]*except* object.   [34]*sensible* capable of delicate feeling.

'Sdeath, I shall lose Belinda. I must fright her[35] hence; she'll be an hour in this fit of good manners else. (*To* LADY WOODVILL) Do you not know Sir Fopling, madam?

LADY WOOD.   I have seen that face. O heav'n, 'tis the same we met in the Mall. How came he here?

DOR.   A fiddle in this town is a kind of fop-call; no sooner it strikes up but the house is besieged with an army of masquerades straight.

LADY WOOD.   Lord, I tremble, Mr Courtage; for certain Dorimant is in the company.

DOR.   I cannot confidently say he is not; you had best be gone. I will wait upon you; your daughter is in the hands of Mr Bellair.

LADY WOOD.   I'll see her before me. Harriet, come away.

Exeunt LADY WOODVILL *and* HARRIET

Y. BELL.   Lights! lights!

LADY TOWN.   Light down there.

O. BELL.   Adod, it needs not –

DOR.   Call my Lady Woodvill's coach to the door quickly.

   [*Exeunt* DORIMANT *and* YOUNG BELLAIR *with the other ladies*]

O. BELL.   Stay, Mr Medley, let the young fellows do that duty; we will drink a glass of wine together. 'Tis good after dancing. What mumming spark is that?

MED.   He is not to be comprehended in few words.

SIR FOP.   Hey, La Tour.

MED.   Whither away, Sir Fopling?

SIR FOP.   I have business with Courtage.

MED.   He'll but put the ladies into their coach and come up again.

O. BELL.   In the meantime I'll call for a bottle.   *Exit* OLD BELLAIR
   Enter YOUNG BELLAIR

MED.   Where's Dorimant?

Y. BELL.   Stolen home. He has had business waiting for him there all this night, I believe, by an impatience I observed in him.

MED.   Very likely. 'Tis but dissembling drunkenness, railing at his friends, and the kind soul will embrace the blessing and forget the tedious expectation.

SIR FOP.   I must speak with him before I sleep.

Y. BELL.   Emilia and I are resolved on that business.

MED.   Peace, here's your father.

   Enter OLD BELLAIR *and butler, with a bottle of wine*

O. BELL.   The women are all gone to bed. Fill, boy. Mr Medley, begin a health.

---

[35]*her* i.e. Lady Woodvill.

MED.   (*Whispers*) To Emilia.

O. BELL.   Out a pize! She's a rogue, and I'll not pledge you.

MED.   I know you will.

O. BELL.   Adod, drink it then.

SIR FOP.   Let us have the new *bachique*.

O. BELL.   Adod, that is a hard word; what does it mean, sir?

MED.   A catch or drinking song.

O. BELL.   Let us have it then.

SIR FOP.   Fill the glasses round, and draw up in a body. Hey, music!

They Sing

The pleasures of love and the joys of good wine
To perfect our happiness wisely we join.
We to beauty all day
Give the sovereign sway,
And her favourite nymphs devoutly obey.
At the plays we are constantly making our court,
And when they are ended we follow the sport
To the Mall and the Park,
Where we love till 'tis dark;
Then sparkling champagne
Puts an end to their reign;
It quickly recovers
Poor lanquishing lovers,
Makes us frolic and gay, and drowns all our sorrow;
But, alas, we relapse again on the morrow.
Let ev'ry man stand
With his glass in his hand,
And briskly discharge at the word of command.
Here's a health to all those
Whom tonight we depose.
Wine and beauty by turns great souls should inspire;
Present all together, and now, boys, give fire![36]

O. BELL.   Adod, a pretty business and very merry.

SIR FOP.   Hark you, Medley, let you and I take the fiddles and go waken Dorimant.

MED.   We shall do him a courtesy, if it be as I guess. For after the fatigue of this night, he'll quickly have his belly full, and be glad of an occasion to cry, 'Take away, Handy'.

Y. BELL.   I'll go with you, and there we'll consult about affairs, Medley.

---

[36]*The pleasures . . . fire* adapted from Thomas Shadwell, *Psyche* (1675), V, p. 70.

O. BELL. (*Looks on his watch*) Adod, 'tis six o'clock!

SIR FOP. Let's away then.

O. BELL. Mr Medley, my sister tells me you are an honest man, and adod I love you. Few words and hearty, that's the way with old Harry, old Harry.

SIR FOP. Light your *flambeaux*. Hey!

O. BELL. What does the man mean?

MED. 'Tis day, Sir Fopling.

SIR FOP. No matter. Our serenade will look the greater.

Exeunt omnes

SCENE TWO

DORIMANT'S *lodging. A table, a candle, a toilet, etc.,*
HANDY *tying up linen*

Enter DORIMANT *in his gown, and* BELINDA

DOR. Why will you be gone so soon?

BEL. Why did you stay out so late?

DOR. Call a chair, Handy.   [*Exit* HANDY]
What makes you tremble so.

BELL. I have a thousand fears about me. Have I not been seen, think you?

DOR. By nobody but myself and trusty Handy.

BEL. Where are all your people?

DOR. I have dispersed 'em on sleeveless[37] errands. What does that sigh mean?

BEL. Can you be so unkind to ask me? — Well, (*Sighs*) were it to do again —

DOR. We should do it, should we not?

BEL. I think we should; the wickeder man you to make me love so well. Will you be discreet now?

DOR. I will.

BEL. You cannot.

DOR. Never doubt it.

BEL. I will not expect it.

DOR. You do me wrong.

BEL. You have no more power to keep the secret than I had not to trust you with it.

DOR. By all the joys I have had and those you keep in store —

BEL. You'll do for my sake what you never did before —

---

[37]*sleeveless* meaningless.

DOR. By that truth thou hast spoken, a wife shall sooner betray herself to her husband –

BEL. Yet I had rather you should be false in this than in another thing you promised me.

DOR. What's that?

BEL. That you would never see Loveit more but in public places, in the Park, at court, and plays.

DOR. 'Tis not likely a man should be fond of seeing a damned old play when there is a new one acted.

BEL. I dare not trust your promise.

DOR. You may.

BEL. This does not satisfy me. You shall swear you never will see her more.

DOR. I will! A thousand oaths – By all –

BEL. Hold! You shall not, now I think on't better.

DOR. I will swear.

BEL. I shall grow jealous of the oath and think I owe your truth to that, not to your love.

DOR. Then, by my love! No other oath I'll swear.

Enter HANDY

HANDY. Here's a chair.

BEL. Let me go.

DOR. I cannot.

BEL. Too willingly, I fear.

DOR. Too unkindly feared. When will you promise me again?

BEL. Not this fortnight.

DOR. You will be better than your word.

BEL. I think I shall. Will it not make you love me less? (*Starting*) Hark, what fiddles are these? *Fiddles without*

DOR. Look out, Handy. *Exit* HANDY *and returns*

HANDY. Mr Medley, Mr Bellair, and Sir Fopling; they are coming up.

DOR. How got they in?

HANDY. The door was open for the chair.

BEL. Lord, let me fly –

DOR. Here, here, down the back stairs. I'll see you into your chair.

BEL. No, no, stay and receive 'em, and be sure you keep your word and never see Loveit more. Let it be a proof of your kindness.

DOR. It shall. Handy, direct her. Everlasting love go along with thee.

Kissing her hand

Exeunt BELINDA *and* HANDY

Enter YOUNG BELLAIR, MEDLEY *and* SIR FOPLING [*with his page*]

Y. BELL. Not abed yet!

MED. You have had an irregular fit,[38] Dorimant.

DOR. I have.

Y. BELL. And is it off already?

DOR. Nature has done her part, gentlemen; when she falls kindly to work, great cures are effected in little time, you know.

SIR FOP. We thought there was a wench in the case by the chair that waited. Prithee make us a *confidence*.

DOR. Excuse me.

SIR FOP. *Le sage*[39] Dorimant! Was she pretty?

DOR. So pretty she may come to keep her coach and pay parish duties if the good humour of the age continue.

MED. And be of the number of the ladies kept by public-spirited men for the good of the whole town.

SIR FOP. Well said, Medley.   SIR FOPLING *dancing by himself*.

Y. BELL. See, Sir Fopling dancing.

DOR. You are practising and have a mind to recover, I see.

SIR FOP. Prithee, Dorimant, why hast not thou a glass hung up here? A room is the dullest thing without one.

Y. BELL. Here is company to entertain you.

SIR FOP. But I mean in case of being alone. In a glass a man may entertain himself, –

DOR. The shadow of himself indeed.

SIR FOP. Correct the errors of his motions and his dress.

MED. I find, Sir Fopling, in your solitude you remember the saying of the wise man, and study yourself.

SIR FOP. 'Tis the best diversion in our retirements. Dorimant, thou art a pretty fellow, and wear'st thy clothes well, but I never saw thee have a handsome cravat. Were they made up like mine, they'd give another air to thy face. Prithee let me send my man to dress thee but one day. By heavens, an Englishman cannot tie a ribbon.

DOR. They are something clumsy-fisted.

SIR FOP. I have brought over the prettiest fellow that ever spread a toilet; he served some time under Merille,[40] the greatest *genie* in the world for a *valet de chambre*.

DOR. What, he who formerly belonged to the Duke of Candale?[41]

SIR FOP. The same, and got him his immortal reputation.

DOR. You've a very fine brandenburgh[42] on, Sir Fopling.

---

[38]*irregular fit* Dorimant referred, IV, i, p. 169, to intermittent illness caused by love or passion.

[39]*Le sage* discreet.

[40]*Merille valet de chambre* of the Duke of Orleans, 1670's.

[41]*Candale* 1627–58, a notably brave general in the French army.

[42]*brandenburgh* a woollen morning gown.

SIR FOP.   It serves to wrap me up after the fatigue of a ball.

MED.   I see you often in it, with your periwig tied up.

SIR FOP.   We should not always be in a set dress; 'tis more *en cavalier* to appear now and then in a *déshabillé*.

MED.   Pray, how goes your business with Loveit?

SIR FOP.   You might have answered yourself in the Mall last night. Dorimant, did you not see the advances she made me? I have been endeavouring at a song.

DOR.   Already!

SIR FOP.   'Tis my *coup d'essai*43 in English; I would fain have thy opinion of it.

DOR.   Let's see it.

SIR FOP.   Hey, page, give me my song. Bellair, here; thou hast a pretty voice, sing it.

Y. BELL.   Sing it yourself, Sir Fopling.

SIR FOP.   Excuse me.

Y. BELL.   You learnt to sing in Paris.

SIR FOP.   I did, of Lambert,44 the greatest master in the world; but I have his own fault, a weak voice, and care not to sing out of a *ruelle*.45

DOR.   A *ruelle* is a pretty cage for a singing fop, indeed.

YOUNG BELLAIR *reads the song*:

How charming Phyllis is, how fair!
    Ah, that she were as willing
To ease my wounded heart of care,
    And make her eyes less killing!
I sigh, I sigh, I languish now,
    And love will not let me rest;
I drive about the Park and bow,
    Still as46 I meet my dearest.

SIR FOP.   Sing it, sing it, man! It goes to a pretty new tune, which I am confident was made by Baptiste.47

MED.   Sing it yourself, Sir Fopling; he does not know the tune.

SIR FOP.   I'll venture.   SIR FOPLING *sings*

43*coup d'essai* first attempt.

44*Lambert* Michel Lambert, 1610–96, singer, musician, composer, master of music in the court of Louis XIV.

45*ruelle* a bedchamber *cum* reception room.

46*Still as* Whenever.

47*Baptiste* perhaps Jean Baptiste Lully, 1633–87, composer and director of music and opera in the court of Louis XIV.

DOR. Ay, marry, now 'tis something. I shall not flatter you, Sir Fopling; there is not much thought in't, but 'tis passionate and well-turned.

MED. After the French way.

SIR FOP. That I aimed at. Does it not give you a lively image of the thing? Slap down goes the glass,[48] and thus we are at it.

DOR. It does indeed. I perceive, Sir Fopling, you'll be the very head of the sparks who are lucky in compositions of this nature.

Enter SIR FOPLING'S FOOTMAN

SIR FOP. La Tour, is the bath ready?

FOOT. Yes, sir.

SIR FOP. *Adieu donc, mes chers.*

Exit SIR FOPLING [*with page and* FOOTMAN]

MED. When have you your revenge on Loveit, Dorimant?

DOR. I will but change my linen, and about it.

MED. The powerful considerations which hindered have been removed then?

DOR. Most luckily, this morning. You must along with me; my reputation lies at stake there.

MED. I am engaged to Bellair.

DOR. What's your business?

MED. Ma-tri-mony, an't like you.

DOR. It does not, sir.

Y. BELL. It may in time, Dorimant. What think you of Mrs Harriet?

DOR. What does she think of me?

Y. BELL. I am confident she loves you.

DOR. How does it appear?

Y. BELL. Why, she's never well but when she's talking of you; but then she finds all the faults in you she can. She laughs at all who commend you; but then she speaks ill of all who do not.

DOR. Women of her temper betray themselves by their over-cunning. I had once a growing love with a lady who would always quarrel with me when I came to see her, and yet was never quiet if I stayed a day from her.

Y. BELL. My father is in love with Emilia.

DOR. That is a good warrant for your proceedings; go on and prosper. I must to Loveit. Medley, I am sorry you cannot be a witness.

MED. Make her meet Sir Fopling again in the same place and use him ill before me.

DOR. That may be brought about, I think. I'll be at your aunt's anon and give you joy, Mr Bellair.

---

[48]*glass* i.e. of my coach; see the penultimate line of the song above.

Y. BELL.   You had best not think of Mrs Harriet too much; without
church security there's no taking up[49] there.

DOR.   I may fall into the snare too. But
                    The wise will find a difference in our fate;
                    You wed a woman, I a good estate.   *Exeunt*

SCENE THREE

                    [*The Mall, near* MRS LOVEIT'S *residence*]
          Enter the chair with BELINDA; *the* MEN *set it down and open it.*
                    BELINDA *starting*

BEL.   (*Surprised*) Lord, where am I? In the Mall? Whither have you
brought me?

FIRST CHAIR.   You gave us no directions, madam.

BEL.   (*Aside*) The fright I was in made me forget it.

FIRST CHAIR.   We use to carry a lady from the squire's hither.

BEL.   (*Aside*) This is Loveit. I am undone if she sees me. Quickly, carry
me away.

FIRST CHAIR.   Whither, an't like your honour?

BEL.   Ask no questions.

          Enter LOVEIT'S FOOTMAN

FOOT.   Have you seen my lady, madam?

BEL.   I am just come to wait upon her.

FOOT.   She will be glad to see you, madam. She sent me to you this
morning to desire your company, and I was told you went out by five
o'clock.

BEL.   (*Aside*) More and more unlucky!

FOOT.   Will you walk in, madam?

BEL.   I'll discharge my chair and follow. Tell your mistress I am here.

                              Exit FOOTMAN
                              Gives the CHAIRMEN *money*

Take this, and if ever you should be examined, be sure you say you
took me up in the Strand, over against the Exchange, as you will
answer it to Mr Dorimant.

CHAIRMEN.   We will, an't like your honour.

                              Exeunt CHAIRMEN

BEL.   Now to come off, I must on –
                    In confidence and lies some hope is left;
                    'Twere hard to be found out in the first theft.   *Exit*

[49]*taking up* taking possession.

Act Five

SCENE ONE

[MRS LOVEIT'S *residence*]

Enter MISTRESS LOVEIT *and* PERT, *her woman*

PERT.   Well, in my eyes Sir Fopling is no such despicable person.

LOV.   You are an excellent judge!

PERT.   He's as handsome a man as Mr Dorimant and as great a gallant.

LOV.   Intolerable! Is't not enough I submit to his impertinences, but I must be plagued with yours too?

PERT.   Indeed, madam –

LOV.   'Tis false, mercenary malice –

Enter her FOOTMAN

FOOT.   Mrs Belinda, madam, –

LOV.   What of her?

FOOT.   She's below.

LOV.   How came she?

FOOT.   In a chair. Ambling Harry brought her.

LOV.   He bring her! His chair stands near Dorimant's door, and always brings me from thence. Run and ask him where he took her up. Go! [*Exit* FOOTMAN] There is no truth in friendship neither. Women as well as men, all are false, or all are so to me at least.

PERT.   You are jealous of her too?

LOV.   You had best tell her I am; 'twill become the liberty you take of late. This fellow's bringing of her, her going out by five o'clock – I know not what to think.

Enter BELINDA

Belinda, you are grown an early riser. I hear.

BEL.   Do you not wonder, my dear, what made me abroad so soon?

LOV.   You do not use to be so.

BEL.   The country gentlewomen I told you of (Lord, they have the oddest diversions!) would never let me rest till I promised to go with them to the markets this morning to eat fruit and buy nosegays.

LOV.   Are they so fond of a filthy nosegay?

BEL.   They complain of the stinks of the town, and are never well but when they have their noses in one.

LOV.   There are essences and sweet waters.

BEL.   Oh, they cry out upon perfumes they are unwholesome; one of 'em was falling into a fit with the smell of these nerolii.[1]

LOV.   Methinks, in complaisance you should have had a nosegay too.

BEL.   Do you think, my dear, I could be so loathsome to trick myself up with carnations and stock-gillyflowers? I begged their pardon, and told them I never wore anything but orangeflowers and tuberose.[2] That which made me willing to go was a strange desire I had to eat some fresh nectarines.[3]

LOV.   And had you any?

BEL.   The best I ever tasted.

LOV.   Whence came you now?

BEL.   From their lodgings, where I crowded out of a coach and took a chair to come and see you, my dear.

LOV.   Whither did you send for that chair?

BEL.   'Twas going by empty.

LOV.   Where do these country gentlewomen lodge, I pray?

BEL.   In the Strand, over against the Exchange.

PERT.   That place is never without a nest of 'em; they are always, as one goes by, fleering[4] in balconies or staring out of windows.

Enter FOOTMAN

LOV.   (*Whispers to the* FOOTMAN) Come hither.

BEL.   (*Aside*) This fellow by her order has been questioning the chairmen – I threatened 'em with the name of Dorimant; if they should have told truth I am lost forever.

LOV.   In the Strand, said you?

FOOT.   Yes, madam, over against the Exchange.   *Exit* FOOTMAN

LOV.   [*Aside*] She's innocent, and I am much to blame.

BEL.   (*Aside*) I am so frighted my countenance will betray me.

LOV.   Belinda! What makes you look so pale?

BEL.   Want of my usual rest and jolting up and down so long in an odious hackney.

FOOTMAN *returns*

FOOT.   Madam, Mr Dorimant.   [*Exit* FOOTMAN]

LOV.   What makes him here?

---

[1] *nerolii* perfumes based on the essence of leaves of orange trees.

[2] *tuberose* fragrant white lily-like blooms from a tuberous plant recently introduced from the East Indies.

[3] *nectarines* reputed to be an indication of pregnancy. See the innuendos below and Webster, *The Duchess of Malfi*, II, i, 132–77, and Ford, *'Tis Pity She's a Whore*, III, iv, 3–9.

[4] *fleering* jeering.

BEL. (*Aside*) Then I am betrayed indeed! He's broke his word, and I love a man that does not care for me.

LOV. Lord, you faint, Belinda.

BEL. I think I shall; such an oppression here on the sudden.

PERT. She has eaten too much fruit, I warrant you.

LOV. Not unlikely!

PERT. 'Tis that lies heavy on her stomach.

LOV. Have her into my chamber, give her some surfeit-water,⁵ and let her lie down a little.

PERT. Come, madam. I was a strange devourer of fruit when I was young, so ravenous –   *Exit* BELINDA, PERT *leading her off*

LOV. Oh, that my love would be but calm awhile, that I might receive this man with all the scorn and indignation he deserves.

Enter DORIMANT

DOR. Now for a touch of Sir Fopling to begin with. Hey, page! Give positive order that none of my people stir. Let the *canaille*⁶ wait, as they should do. Since noise and nonsense have such powerful charms,

> I, that I may successful prove,
> Transform myself to what you love.⁷

LOV. If that would do, you need not change from what you are; you can be vain and loud enough.

DOR. But not with so good a grace as Sir Fopling. 'Hey, Hampshire'! Oh, that sound! That sound becomes the mouth of a man of quality.

LOV. Is there a thing so hateful as a senseless mimic?

DOR. He's a great grievance indeed to all who, like yourself, madam, love to play the fool in quiet.

LOV. A ridiculous animal, who has more of the ape than the ape has of the man in him.

DOR. I have as mean an opinion of a sheer mimic as yourself; yet were he all ape I should prefer him to the gay, the giddy, brisk, insipid, noisy fool you dote on.

LOV. Those noisy fools, however you despise 'em, have good qualities which weigh more (or ought at least) with us women than all the pernicious wit you have to boast of.

DOR. That I may hereafter have a just value for their merit, pray do me the favour to name 'em.

---

⁵*surfeit-water* a medicinal drink.
⁶*canaille* rabble.
⁷*I . . . love* Edmund Waller, 'To the Mutable Fair' (slightly modified), *Poems*, I (London, 1901), pp. 106–08.

LOV.   You'll despise 'em as the dull effects of ignorance and vanity; yet I care not if I mention some. First, they really admire us, while you at best but flatter us well.

DOR.   Take heed! Fools can dissemble too.

LOV.   They may, but not so artificially as you: there is no fear they should deceive us. Then they are assiduous, sir: they are ever offering us their service and always waiting on our will.

DOR.   You owe that to their excessive idleness. They know not how to entertain themselves at home, and find so little welcome abroad, they are fain to fly to you who countenance 'em as a refuge against the solitude they would be otherwise condemned to.

LOV.   Their conversation too diverts us better.

DOR.   Playing with your fan, smelling to your gloves, commending your hair, and taking notice how 'tis cut and shaded after the new way –

LOV.   Were it sillier than you can make it, you must allow 'tis pleasanter to laugh at others than to be laughed at ourselves, though never so wittily. Then though they want skill to flatter us, they flatter themselves so well they save us the labour. We need not take that care and pains to satisfy 'em of our love, which we so often lose on you.

DOR.   They commonly indeed believe too well of themselves, and always better of you than you deserve.

LOV.   You are in the right; they have an implicit faith in us which keeps 'em from prying narrowly into our secrets, and saves us the vexatious trouble of clearing doubts which your subtle and causeless jealousies every moment raise.

DOR.   There is an inbred falsehood in women which inclines 'em still to them whom they may most easily deceive.

LOV.   The man who loves above his quality does not suffer more from the insolent impertinence of his mistress than the woman who loves above her understanding does from the arrogant presumptions of her friend.

DOR.   You mistake the use of fools: they are designed for properties,[8] and not for friends. You have an indifferent[9] stock of reputation left yet. Lose it all like a frank gamester on the square;[10] 'twill then be time enough to turn rook[11] and cheat it up again on a good substantial bubble.[12]

LOV.   The old and the ill-favoured are only fit for properties indeed, but young and handsome fools have met with kinder fortunes.

---

[8]*properties* instruments.   [9]*indifferent* moderate.
[10]*square* gaming board.   [11]*rook* swindler.   [12]*bubble* dupe.

DOR.   They have, to the shame of your sex be it spoken; 'twas this, the thought of this, made me, by a timely jealousy, endeavour to prevent the good fortune you are providing for Sir Fopling; but against a woman's frailty all our care is vain.

LOV.   Had I not with a dear experience bought the knowledge of your falsehood, you might have fooled me yet. This is not the first jealousy you have feigned to make a quarrel with me and get a week to throw away on some such unknown inconsiderable slut as you have been lately lurking with at plays.

DOR.   Women, when they would break off with a man, never want th'address to turn the fault on him.

LOV.   You take a pride of late in using of me ill, that the town may know the power you have over me, which now (as unreasonably as yourself) expects that I (do me all the injuries you can) must love you still.

DOR.   I am so far from expecting that you should, I begin to think you never did love me.

LOV.   Would the memory of it were so wholly worn out in me that I did doubt it too! What made you come to disturb my growing quiet?

DOR.   To give you joy of your growing infamy.

LOV.   Insupportable! Insulting devil! This from you, the only author of my shame! This from another had been but justice, but from you 'tis a hellish and inhuman outrage. What have I done?

DOR.   A thing that puts you below my scorn and makes my anger as ridiculous as you have made my love.

LOV.   I walked last night with Sir Fopling.

DAR.   You did, madam, and you talked and laughed aloud, 'Ha, ha, ha'! – Oh, that laugh! That laugh becomes the confidence of a woman of quality.

LOV.   You who have more pleasure in the ruin of a woman's reputation than in the endearments of her love, reproach me not with yourself, and I defy you to name the man can lay a blemish on my fame.

DOR.   To be seen publicly so transported with the vain follies of that notorious fop, to me is an infamy below the sin of prostitution with another man.

LOV.   Rail on. I am satisfied in the justice of what I did; you had provoked me to't.

DOR.   What I did was the effect of a passion whose extravagances you have been willing to forgive.

LOV.   And what I did was the effect of a passion you may forgive if you think fit.

DOR.   Are you so indifferent grown?

LOV.   I am.

DOR.   Nay, then 'tis time to part. I'll send you back your letters you
have so often asked for. I have two or three of 'em about me.

LOV.   Give 'em me.

DOR.   You snatch as if you thought I would not – There! And may the
perjuries in 'em be mine if e'er I see you more.

Offers to go; she catches him

LOV.   Stay!

DOR.   I will not.

LOV.   You shall.

DOR.   What have you to say?

LOV.   I cannot speak it yet.

DOR.   Something more in commendation of the fool. Death, I want
patience. Let me go.

LOV.   (*Aside*) I cannot. I can sooner part with the limbs that hold him.
– I hate that nauseous fool, you know I do.

DOR.   Was it the scandal you were fond of then?

LOV.   You'd raised my anger equal to my love, a thing you ne'er could
do before, and in revenge I did – I know not what I did. Would you
would not think on't any more!

DOR.   Should I be willing to forget it, I shall be daily minded of it.
'Twill be a commonplace for all the town to laugh at me; and
Medley, when he is rhetorically drunk, will ever be declaiming on it
in my ears.

LOV.   'Twill be believed a jealous spite! Come, forget it.

DOR.   Let me consult my reputation; you are too careless of it.
(*Pauses*) You shall meet Sir Fopling in the Mall again tonight.

LOV.   What mean you?

DOR.   I have thought on it, and you must. 'Tis necessary to justify my
love to the world. You can handle a coxcomb as he deserves when
you are not out of humour, madam.

LOV.   Public satisfaction for the wrong I have done you! This is some
new device to make me more ridiculous.

DOR.   Hear me.

LOV.   I will not.

DOR.   You will be persuaded.

LOV.   Never.

DOR.   Are you so obstinate?

LOV.   Are you so base?

DOR.   You will not satisfy my love?

LOV.   I would die to satisfy that, but I will not, to save you from a
thousand racks, do a shameless thing to please your vanity.

DOR. Farewell, false woman!

LOV. Do! Go!

DOR. You will call me back again.

LOV. Exquisite fiend! I knew you came but to torment me.

Enter BELINDA *and* PERT

DOR. (*Surprised*) Belinda here!

BEL. (*Aside*) He starts and looks pale; the sight of me has touched his guilty soul.

PERT. 'Twas but a qualm, as I said, a little indigestion; the surfeit-water did it, madam, mixed with a little *mirabilis*.[13]

DOR. [*Aside*] I am confounded, and cannot guess how she came hither!

LOV. 'Tis your fortune, Belinda, ever to be here when I am abused by this prodigy of ill-nature.

BEL. I am amazed to find him here! How has he the face to come near you?

DOR. (*Aside*) Here is fine work towards! I never was at such a loss before.

BEL. One who makes a public profession of breach of faith and ingratitude; I loathe the sight of him.

DOR. (*Aside*) There is no remedy; I must submit to their tongues now, and some other time bring myself off as well as I can.

BEL. Other men are wicked, but then they have some sense of shame. He is never well but when he triumphs, nay, glories to a woman's face in his villainies.

LOV. You are in the right, Belinda; but methinks your kindness for me makes you concern yourself too much with him.

BEL. It does indeed, my dear. His barbarous carriage to you yesterday made me hope you ne'er would see him more, and the very next day to find him here again provokes me strangely; but, because I know you love him, I have done.

DOR. You have reproached me handsomely, and I deserve it for coming hither; but —

PERT. You must expect it, sir; all women will hate you for my lady's sake.

DOR. (*Aside*) Nay, if she begins too, 'tis time to fly; I shall be scolded to death else. [*To* BELINDA] I am to blame in some circumstances, I confess; but as to the main, I am not so guilty as you imagine. — [*Aloud*] I shall seek a more convenient time to clear myself.

LOV. Do it now! What impediments are here?

DOR. I want time, and you want temper.

[13]*mirabilis aqua mirabilis*, a medicinal drink made from wine and spices.

LOV.   These are weak pretences!

DOR.   You were never more mistaken in your life, and so farewell.

DORIMANT flings off

LOV.   Call a footman, Pert, quickly; I will have him dogged.

PERT.   I wish you would not, for my quiet and your own.

[Exit PERT]

LOV.   I'll find out the infamous cause of all our quarrels, pluck her mask off, and expose her barefaced to the world.

BEL.   (*Aside*) Let me but escape this time I'll never venture more.

LOV.   Belinda, you shall go with me.

BEL.   I have such a heaviness hangs on me with what I did this morning, I would fain go home and sleep, my dear.

LOV.   Death and eternal darkness! I shall never sleep again. Raging fevers seize the world, and make mankind as restless all as I am!

Exit LOVEIT

BEL.   I knew him false and helped to make him so. Was not her ruin enough to fright me from the danger? It should have been, but love can take no warning.   *Exit BELINDA*

SCENE TWO

LADY TOWNLEY'S *house*

Enter MEDLEY, YOUNG BELLAIR, LADY TOWNLEY, EMILIA, *and* CHAPLAIN

MED.   Bear up, Bellair, and do not let us see that repentance in thine we daily do in married faces.

LADY TOWN.   This wedding will strangely surprise my brother when he knows it.

MED.   Your nephew ought to conceal it for a time, madam. Since marriage has lost its good name, prudent men seldom expose their own reputations till 'tis convenient to justify their wives.

O. BELL.   (*Without*) Where are you all there? Out, adod, will nobody hear?

LADY TOWN.   My brother! Quickly, Mr Smirk,[14] into this closet.[15] You must not be seen yet. *He goes into the closet*

Enter OLD BELLAIR *and* LADY TOWNLEY'S *page*

[14] *Mr Smirk Mr Smirke; or The Divine in Mode*, by Andrew Marvell (writing as Andreas Rivetus, Jr), was published later in 1676, a ridiculing of the Anglican clergy and a defence of Dissenters.

[15] *closet* private room.

O. BELL.   Desire Mr Fourbe to walk into the lower parlour. I will be
with him presently. (*To* YOUNG BELLAIR) Where have you been, sir,
you could not wait on me today?

Y. BELL.   About a business.

O. BELL.   Are you so good at business? Adod, I have a business too
you shall despatch out of hand, sir. Send for a parson, sister; my
Lady Woodvill and her daughter are coming.

LADY TOWN.   What need you huddle up things thus?

O. BELL.   Out a pize! Youth is apt to play the fool, and 'tis not good it
should be in their power.

LADY TOWN.   You need not fear your son.

O. BELL.   He's been idling this morning, and, adod, I do not like him.
(*To* EMILIA) How dost thou do, sweetheart?

EMIL.   You are very severe, sir. Married in such haste!

O. BELL.   Go to, thou'rt a rogue, and I will talk with thee anon. Here's
my Lady Woodvill come.

    Enter LADY WOODVILL, HARRIET, *and* BUSY

Welcome, madam; Mr Fourbe's below with the writings.

LADY WOOD.   Let us down and make an end then.

O. BELL.   Sister, show the way. (*To* YOUNG BELLAIR, *who is talking
to* HARRIET) Harry, your business lies not there yet. Excuse him till
we have done, lady, and then, adod, he shall be for thee. Mr Medley,
we must trouble you to be a witness.

MED.   I luckily came for that purpose, sir.

Exeunt OLD BELLAIR, MEDLEY, YOUNG BELLAIR, LADY TOWNLEY
and LADY WOODVILL

BUSY.   What will you do, madam?

HAR.   Be carried back and mewed up in the country again, run away
here, anything rather than be married to a man I do not care for –
Dear Emilia, do thou advise me.

EMIL.   Mr Bellair is engaged, you know.

HAR.   I do; but know not what the fear of losing an estate may fright
him to.

EMIL.   In the desperate condition you are in you should consult with
some judicious man. What think you of Mr Dorimant?

HAR.   I do not think of him at all.

BUSY.   She thinks of nothing else, I am sure.

EMIL.   How fond your mother was of Mr Courtage!

HAR.   Because I contrived the mistake to make a little mirth, you
believe I like the man.

EMIL.   Mr Bellair believes you love him.

HAR.   Men are seldom in the right when they guess at a woman's
mind. Would she whom he loves loved him no better!

BUSY. (*Aside*) That's e'en well enough, on all conscience.

EMIL. Mr Dorimant has a great deal of wit.

HAR. And takes a great deal of pains to show it.

EMIL. He's extremely well-fashioned.

HAR. Affectedly grave or ridiculously wild and apish.

BUSY. You defend him still against your mother.

HAR. I would not, were he justly rallied,[16] but I cannot hear anyone undeservedly railed at.

EMIL. Has your woman learnt the song you were so taken with?

HAR. I was fond of a new thing; 'tis dull at second hearing.

EMIL. Mr Dorimant made it.

BUSY. She knows it, madam, and has made me sing it at least a dozen times this morning.

HAR. Thy tongue is as impertinent as thy fingers.

EMIL. You have provoked her.

BUSY. 'Tis but singing the song, and I shall appease her.

EMIL. Prithee do.

HAR. She has a voice will grate your ears worse than a catcall,[17] and dresses so ill she's scarce fit to trick up a yeoman's daughter on a holiday.

BUSY *sings*

As Amoret with Phyllis sat
    One evening on the plain,
And saw the charming Strephon wait
    To tell the nymph his pain,

The threat'ning danger to remove
    She whisper'd in her ear,
'Ah, Phyllis, if you would not love,
    This shepherd do not hear.

None ever had so strange an art
    His passion to convey
Into a list'ning virgin's heart,
    And steal her soul away.

Fly, fly betimes,[18] for fear you give
    Occasion for your fate'.
'In vain', said she, 'in vain I strive,
    Alas! 'tis now too late'.[19]

---

[16]*rallied* ridiculed.　　　[17]*cat-call* a whistle.　　　[18]*betimes* speedily.
[19]*As . . . late* The 1676 edition has 'Song by C.S.', presumably Sir Car Scroope (author of the Prologue), a translation from a French song.

Enter DORIMANT

DOR. 'Music so softens and disarms the mind' –

HAR. 'That not one arrow does resistance find'.[20]

DOR. Let us make use of the lucky minute then.

HAR. (*Aside, turning from* DORIMANT) My love springs with my blood into my face. I dare not look upon him yet.

DOR. What have we here, the picture of celebrated beauty giving audience in public to a declared lover?

HAR. Play the dying fop and make the piece complete, sir.

DOR. What think you if the hint were well improved: the whole mystery of making love pleasantly designed and wrought in a suit of hangings?[21]

HAR. 'Twere needless to execute fools in effigy who suffer daily in their own persons.

DOR. (*Aside to* EMILIA) Mistress Bride, for such I know this happy day has made you, –

EMIL. Defer the formal joy you are to give me and mind your business with her. – (*Aloud*) Here are dreadful preparations, Mr Dorimant, writings sealing, and a parson sent for.

DOR. To marry this lady?

BUSY. Condemned she is, and what will become of her I know not, without you generously engage in a rescue.

DOR. In this sad condition, madam, I can do no less than offer you my service.

HAR. The obligation is not great; you are the common sanctuary for all young women who run from their relations.

DOR. I have always my arms open to receive the distressed. But I will open my heart, and receive you where none yet did ever enter; you have filled it with a secret, might I but let you know it –

HAR. Do not speak it if you would have me believe it. Your tongue is so famed for falsehood 'twill do the truth an injury.

Turns away her head

DOR. Turn not away then, but look on me and guess it.

HAR. Did you not tell me there was no credit to be given to faces, that women nowadays have their passions as much at will as they have their complexions, and put on joy and sadness, scorn and kindness, with the same ease they do their paint and patches? Are they the only counterfeits?

---

[20]*Music . . . find* Edmund Waller, 'Of my Lady Isabella, Playing on the Lute', *Poems*, I (London, 1901), p. 90.

[21]*a suit of hangings* a set of wall-hangings.

DOR.   You wrong your own while you suspect my eyes. By all the hope I have in you, the inimitable colour in your cheeks is not more free from art than are the sighs I offer.

HAR.   In men who have been long hardened in sin, we have reason to mistrust the first signs of repentance.

DOR.   The prospect of such a heaven will make me persevere and give you marks that are infallible.

HAR.   What are those?

DOR.   I will renounce all the joys I have in friendship and in wine, sacrifice to you all the interest I have in other women –

HAR.   Hold! Though I wish you devout, I would not have you turn fanatic. Could you neglect these a while and make a journey into the country?

DOR.   To be with you, I could live there and never send one thought to London.

HAR.   Whate'er you say, I know all beyond High Park's a desert to you, and that no gallantry can draw you farther.

DOR.   That has been the utmost limit of my love, but now my passion knows no bounds, and there's no measure to be taken of what I'll do for you from anything I ever did before.

HAR.   When I hear you talk thus in Hampshire, I shall begin to think there may be some little truth enlarged upon.

DOR.   Is this all? Will you not promise me –

HAR.   I hate to promise! What we do then is expected from us, and wants much of the welcome it finds when it surprises.

DOR.   May I not hope?

HAR.   That depends on you and not on me, and 'tis to no purpose to forbid it.   *Turns to* BUSY

BUSY.   Faith, madam, now I perceive the gentleman loves you too; e'en let him know your mind, and torment yourselves no longer.

HAR.   Dost think I have no sense of modesty?

BUSY.   Think, if you lose this you may never have another opportunity.

HAR.   May he hate me (a curse that frights me when I speak it) if ever I do a thing against the rules of decency and honour!

DOR.   (*To* EMILIA) I am beholding to you for your good intentions, madam.

EMIL.   I thought the concealing of our marriage from her might have done you better service.

DOR.   Try her again.

EMIL.   What have you resolved, madam? The time draws near.

HAR.   To be obstinate, and protest against this marriage.

   Enter LADY TOWNLEY *in haste*

LADY TOWN. [*To* EMILIA] Quickly, quickly, let Mr Smirk out of the
closet. SMIRK *comes out of the closet*

HAR. A parson! [*To* DORIMANT] Had you laid him in here?

DOR. I knew nothing of him.

HAR. Should it appear you did, your opinion of my easiness may cost
you dear.

Enter OLD BELLAIR, YOUNG BELLAIR, MEDLEY *and* LADY
WOODVILL

O. BELL. Out a pize! The canonical hour[22] is almost past. Sister, is
the man of God come?

LADY TOWN. He waits your leisure.

O. BELL. By your favour, sir. Adod, a pretty spruce fellow! What
may we call him?

LADY TOWN. Mr Smirk, my Lady Bigot's chaplain.

O. BELL. A wise woman, adod, she is. The man will serve for the flesh
as well as the spirit. Please you, sir, to commission a young couple to
go to bed together i' God's name? Harry!

Y. BELL. Here, sir.

O. BELL. Out a pize! Without your mistress in your hand?

SMIRK. Is this the gentleman?

O. BELL. Yes, sir.

SMIRK. Are you not mistaken, sir?

O. BELL. Adod, I think not, sir.

SMIRK. Sure you are, sir.

O. BELL. You look as if you would forbid the banns, Mr Smirk; I
hope you have no pretension to the lady.

SMIRK. Wish him joy, sir! I have done him the good office today
already.

O. BELL. Out a pize! What do I hear?

LADY TOWN. Never storm, brother, the truth is out.

O. BELL. How say you, sir? Is this your wedding day?

Y. BELL. It is, sir.

O. BELL. And, adod, it shall be mine too. (*To* EMILIA) Give me thy
hand, sweetheart. What dost thou mean? Give me thy hand, I say.

EMILIA *and* YOUNG BELLAIR *kneel*

LADY TOWN. Come, come, give her your blessing; this is the woman
your son loved and is married to.

O. BELL. Ha! Cheated! Cozened! And by your contrivance, sister!

LADY TOWN. What would you do with her? She's a rogue, and you
can't abide her.

---

[22]*canonical hour* when marriages might then be legally performed, between
8.00 am and noon.

MED.   Shall I hit her a pat for you, sir?

O. BELL.   Adod, you are all rogues, and I never will forgive you.

[*Moves aside abruptly*]

LADY TOWN.   Whither? Whither away?

MED.   Let him go and cool awhile.

LADY WOOD.   (*To* DORIMANT) Here's a business broke out now, Mr Courtage. I am made a fine fool of.

DOR.   You see the old gentleman knew nothing of it.

LADY WOOD.   I find he did not. I shall have some trick put upon me if I stay in this wicked town any longer. Harriet, dear child, where art thou? I'll into the country straight.

O. BELL.   Adod, madam, you shall hear me first.

Enter LOVEIT *and* BELINDA

LOV.   Hither my man dogged him.

BEL.   Yonder he stands, my dear.

LOV.   I see him. – (*Aside*) And with him the face that has undone me! Oh, that I were but where I might throw out the anguish of my heart! Here it must rage within and break it.

LADY TOWN.   Mrs Loveit! Are you afraid to come forward?

LOV.   I was amazed to see so much company here in a morning. The occasion sure is extraordinary.

DOR.   (*Aside*) Loveit and Belinda! The devil owes me a shame today, and I think never will have done paying it.[23]

LOV.   Married! Dear Emilia, how am I transported with the news!

HAR.   (*To* DORIMANT) I little thought Emilia was the woman Mr Bellair was in love with; I'll chide her for not trusting me with the secret.

DOR.   How do you like Mrs Loveit?

HAR.   She's a famed mistress of yours, I hear.

DOR.   She has been, on occasion.

O. BELL.   (*To* LADY WOODVILL) Adod, madam, I cannot help it.

LADY WOOD.   You need make no more apologies, sir.

EMIL.   (*To* LOVEIT) The old gentleman's excusing himself to my Lady Woodvill.

LOV.   Ha, ha, ha! I never heard of anything so pleasant.

HAR.   (*To* DORIMANT) She's extremely overjoyed at something.

DOR.   At nothing. She is one of those hoiting[24] ladies who gaily fling themselves about and force a laugh when their aching hearts are full of discontent and malice.

LOV.   O heav'n, I was never so near killing myself with laughing. Mr Dorimant, are you a brideman?

[23]*The devil . . . it* proverbial, 'I shall be embarrassed forever'.
[24]*hoiting* noisy.

LADY WOOD.　Mr Dorimant! Is this Mr Dorimant, madam?

LOV.　If you doubt it, your daughter can resolve you, I suppose.

LADY WOOD.　I am cheated too, basely cheated.

O. BELL.　Out a pize! What's here? More knavery yet?

LADY WOOD.　Harriet! On my blessing, come away, I charge you.

HAR.　Dear mother, do but stay and hear me.

LADY WOOD.　I am betrayed, and thou art undone, I fear.

HAR.　Do not fear it. I have not, nor never will do anything against my duty; believe me, dear mother, do.

DOR.　(*To* LOVEIT) I had trusted you with this secret, but that I knew the violence of your nature would ruin my fortune, as now unluckily it has. I thank you, madam.

LOV.　She's an heiress, I know, and very rich.

DOR.　To satisfy you I must give up my interest wholly to my love. Had you been a reasonable woman, I might have secured 'em both and been happy.

LOV.　You might have trusted me with anything of this kind, you know you might. Why did you go under a wrong name?

DOR.　The story is too long to tell you now. Be satisfied; this is the business, this is the mask has kept me from you.

BEL.　(*Aside*) He's tender of my honour, though he's cruel to my love.

LOV.　Was it no idle mistress then?

DOR.　Believe me, a wife, to repair the ruins of my estate that needs it.

LOV.　The knowledge of this makes my grief hang lighter on my soul, but I shall never more be happy.

DOR.　Belinda, —

BEL.　Do not think of clearing yourself with me, it is impossible. Do all men break their words thus?

DOR.　Th'extravagant words they speak in love; 'tis as unreasonable to expect we should perform all we promise then, as do all we threaten when we are angry. When I see you next —

BEL.　Take no notice of me, and I shall not hate you.

DOR.　How came you to Mrs Loveit?

BEL.　By a mistake the chairmen made for want of my giving them directions.

DOR.　'Twas a pleasant one. We must meet again.

BEL.　Never.

DOR.　Never?

BEL.　When we do, may I be as infamous as you are false.

LADY TOWN.　Men of Mr Dorimant's character always suffer in the general opinion of the world.

MED.   You can make no judgment of a witty man from common fame, considering the prevailing faction, madam.

O. BELL.   Adod, he's in the right.

MED.   Besides, 'tis a common error among women to believe too well of them they know and too ill of them they don't.

O. BELL.   Adod, he observes well.

LADY TOWN.   Believe me, madam, you will find Mr Dorimant as civil a gentleman as you thought Mr Courtage.

HAR.   If you would but know him better –

LADY WOOD.   You have a mind to know him better? Come away! You shall never see him more.

HAR.   Dear mother, stay!

LADY WOOD.   I wo' not be consenting to your ruin.

HAR.   Were my fortune in your power, –

LADY WOOD.   Your person is.

HAR.   Could I be disobedient, I might take it out of yours and put it into his.

LADY WOOD.   'Tis that you would be at? You would marry this Dorimant?

HAR.   I cannot deny it. I would, and never will marry any other man.

LADY WOOD.   Is this the duty that you promised?

HAR.   But I will never marry him against your will.

LADY WOOD.   (*Aside*) She knows the way to melt my heart. (*To* HARRIET) Upon yourself light your undoing.

MED.   (*To* OLD BELLAIR) Come, sir, you have not the heart any longer to refuse your blessing.

O. BELL.   Adod, I ha' not – Rise, and God bless you both! Make much of her, Harry; she deserves thy kindness. (*To* EMILIA) Adod, sirrah, I did not think it had been in thee.

    Enter SIR FOPLING *and his* PAGE

SIR FOP.   'Tis a damned windy day! Hey, page, is my periwig right?

PAGE.   A little out of order, sir.

SIR FOP.   Pox o' this apartment! It wants an antechamber to adjust oneself in. (*To* LOVEIT) Madam, I came from your house, and your servants directed me hither.

LOV.   I will give order hereafter they shall direct you better.

SIR FOP.   The great satisfaction I had in the Mall last night has given me much disquiet since.

LOV.   'Tis likely to give me more than I desire.

SIR FOP.   [*Aside*] What the devil makes her so reserved? – Am I guilty of an indiscretion, madam?

LOV.   You will be of a great one if you continue your mistake, sir.

SIR FOP.   Something puts you out of humour.

LOV.   The most foolish, inconsiderable thing that ever did.

SIR FOP.   Is it in my power?

LOV.   To hang or drown it. Do one of 'em, and trouble me no more.

SIR FOP.   So *fière?*[25] *Serviteur, madame.* Medley, where's Dorimant?

MED.   Methinks the lady has not made you those advances today she did last night, Sir Fopling.

SIR FOP.   Prithee do not talk of her.

MED.   She would be a *bonne fortune.*

SIR FOP.   Not to me, at present.

MED.   How so?

SIR FOP.   An intrigue now would be but a temptation to me to throw away that vigour on one which I mean shall shortly make my court to the whole sex in a ballet.

MED.   Wisely considered, Sir Fopling.

SIR FOP.   No one woman is worth the loss of a cut[26] in a caper.

MED.   Not when 'tis so universally designed.

LADY WOOD.   Mr Dorimant, everyone has spoke so much in your behalf that I can no longer doubt but I was in the wrong.

LOV.   [*To* BELINDA] There's nothing but falsehood and impertinence in this world. All men are villains or fools. Take example from my misfortunes, Belinda; if thou wouldst be happy, give thyself wholly up to goodness.

HAR.   (*To* LOVEIT) Mr Dorimant has been your God Almighty long enough; 'tis time to think of another.

LOV.   [*Aside*] Jeered by her! – I will lock myself up in my house, and never see the world again.

HAR.   A nunnery is the more fashionable place for such a retreat, and has been the fatal consequence of many a *belle passion.*

LOV.   Hold, heart, till I get home. Should I answer, 'twould make her triumph greater.   *Is going out*

DOR.   Your hand, Sir Fopling.

SIR FOP.   Shall I wait upon you, madam?

LOV.   Legion of fools, as many devils take thee!   *Exit* LOVEIT

MED.   Dorimant, I pronounce thy reputation clear, and henceforward when I would know anything of woman, I will consult no other oracle.

SIR FOP.   Stark mad, by all that's handsome! Dorimant, thou hast engaged me in a pretty business.

DOR.   I have not leisure now to talk about it.

O. BELL.   Out a pize! What does this man of mode do here again?

[25]*fière* haughty.   [26]*cut* a leap in a dance, with feet twiddling.

LADY TOWN.   He'll be an excellent entertainment within, brother, and is luckily come to raise the mirth of the company.

LADY WOOD.   Madam, I take my leave of you.

LADY TOWN.   What do you mean, madam?

LADY WOOD.   To go this afternoon part of my way to Hartley.[27]

O. BELL.   Adod, you shall stay and dine first. Come, we will all be good friends, and you shall give Mr Dorimant leave to wait upon you and your daughter in the country.

LADY WOOD.   If his occasions bring him that way, I have now so good an opinion of him he shall be welcome.

HAR.   To a great rambling lone house that looks as it were not inhabited, the family's so small. There you'll find my mother, an old lame aunt, and myself, sir, perched up on chairs at a distance in a large parlour, sitting moping like three or four melancholy birds in a spacious volary.[28] Does not this stagger your resolution?

DOR.   Not at all, madam. The first time I saw you, you left me with the pangs of love upon me, and this day my soul has quite given up her liberty.

HAR.   This is more dismal than the country. Emilia, pity me who am going to that sad place. Methinks I hear the hateful noise of rooks already – kaw, kaw, kaw. There's music in the worst cry in London, 'My dill and cucumbers to pickle'.

O. BELL.   Sister, knowing of this matter, I hope you have provided us some good cheer.

LADY TOWN.   I have, brother, and the fiddles too.

O. BELL.   Let 'em strike up then; the young lady shall have a dance before she departs.   *Dance*
(*After the dance*) So, now we'll in and make this an arrant[29] wedding-day.
(*To the pit*) And if these honest gentlemen rejoice,
      Adod, the boy has made a happy choice.   *Exeunt omnes*

---

[27] *Hartley* probably Hartley Row, near Basingstoke, Hants.
[28] *volary* aviary.
[29] *arrant* complete.

THE EPILOGUE

BY MR DRYDEN[1]

Most modern wits such monstrous fools have shown,
They seem'd not of heav'n's making, but their own.
Those nauseous harlequins in farce may pass,
But there goes more to a substantial ass;
Something of man must be exposed to view,
That, gallants, it may more resemble you.
Sir Fopling is a fool so nicely writ,
The ladies would mistake him for a wit,
And when he sings, talks loud, and cocks,[2] would cry,
'Ay now, methinks he's pretty company!
So brisk, so gay, so travell'd, so refin'd,
As he took pains to graft upon his kind'.
True fops help nature's work, and go to school
To file and finish God A'mighty's fool.[3]
Yet none Sir Fopling him, or him, can call;
He's knight o' the shire,[4] and represents ye all.
From each he meets he culls whate'er he can,
Legion's his name, a people in a man:
His bulky folly gathers as it goes,
And, rolling o'er you, like a snowball grows.
His various modes from various fathers follow;

[1] *Dryden* a long-time friend of Etherege, whom Dryden described as 'gentle George' in *Macflecknoe*, 1682. The Epilogue was originally spoken by William Smith, who played Sir Fopling Flutter.

[2] *cocks* struts.

[3] *fool* Two contemporary manuscript versions of Dryden's Epilogue include after 'fool' the following couplet that sneers at Buckingham's *The Rehearsal*, 1671. This play, written over several years, included Mr Bayes, a satiric character sketch of Dryden:

> Labor to put in more, as Master Bayes
> Thrums in additions to his ten-years' plays.

[4] *knight o' the shire* a member of parliament.

One taught the toss,[5] and one the new French wallow,[6]
His sword-knot[7] this, his cravat this design'd,
And this the yard-long snake[8] he twirls behind.
From one, the sacred periwig he gain'd,
Which wind ne'er blew, nor touch of hat profan'd.
Another's diving bow he did adore,
Which with a shog[9] casts all the hair before;
Till he, with full decorum, brings it back,
And rises with a water-spaniel shake.
As for his songs (the ladies' dear delight),
Those sure he took from most of you who write.
Yet every man is safe from what he fear'd,
For no one fool is hunted from the herd.

[5]*toss* a fling of the head.
[6]*wallow* a rolling way of walking.
[7]*sword-knot* a ribbon tied on the hilt of a sword.
[8]*snake* a tail attached to a wig.   [9]*shog* shake.

John Dryden

ALL FOR LOVE

or

THE WORLD WELL-LOST

1678

All for Love,
or
The World Well-lost
a Tragedy,
as it is acted at the
Theatre Royal,
and written in imitation of Shakespeare's style.
By John Dryden, servant to His Majesty.

Facile est [enim] verbum aliquod ardens [ut ita dicam) notare
idque restinctis [iam] animorum incendiis irridere.
CICERO.[1]

In the Savoy:
Printed by Thomas Newcomb, for Henry Herringman,
at the Blue Anchor
in the Lower Walk of the New Exchange, 1678.

[1]It is certainly easy to censure some fiery word (if I may use the expression) and to laugh at it when the fever of the moment has subsided. Cicero, *Orator*, viii, 27.

BIOGRAPHY

Born in Aldwinkle, Northamptonshire in 1631; studied at Westminster School and at Trinity College, Cambridge, 1650–54. He was a
poet, playwright, essayist, translator, literary critic; Fellow of the
Royal Society, the first officially appointed Poet Laureate, Historio-
grapher Royal. Dryden was the author of twenty-five plays (*The
Indian Queen*, 1664; *The Conquest of Granada*, 1670, 1671;
Marriage à la Mode, 1671; *Aureng-Zebe*, 1675; *All for Love*, 1678),
poems (*Absalom and Achitophel*, 1681; *Mac Flecknoe, 1682; Religio
Laici*, 1682), and criticism (*Essay of Dramatic Poesy*, 1668). Died in
1700.

INTRODUCTION

To set this play in context some reference to *Antony and Cleopatra* (1607) must be made, because Dryden specifically acknowledged an indebtedness to Shakespeare. *All for Love* was also influenced by Samuel Daniel's *Tragedy of Cleopatra* (*c.* 1593), Thomas May's *The Tragedie of Cleopatra Queen of Aegypt* (1626), Nathaniel Lee's *The Rival Queens* (1676),[1] Charles Sedley's *Antony and Cleopatra* (1677), other dramatic retellings of the story and Plutarch's *Lives of Noble Grecians and Romans*.

Roman historians were under some pressure to depict Antony and Cleopatra unsympathetically, in order to give greater heroic stature to Octavius Caesar, the other triumvir. Thus it is now impossible to reconstruct their careers in detail or accurately. Cleopatra was Julius Caesar's mistress in 48 and 47 BC, and she attracted Antony in 41 BC, when he was forty-two and she twenty-eight years of age. After his third wife, Fulvia, died in 40 BC, Antony returned briefly to Rome to marry the recently widowed Octavia, the sister of Octavius Caesar. When Antony divorced Octavia in 32 BC Octavius was angered and defeated Antony at Actium in 31 BC. Within a year Antony and Cleopatra were besieged by Octavius in Alexandria. All that is known of their last days is Antony's receipt of an anonymous false message informing him of Cleopatra's suicide; he killed himself (1 August 30 BC), and Cleopatra brought her life to an end a few days later.

In his preface to *All for Love*, Dryden draws attention to 'the excellency of the moral' in the story. This may suggest that there is a moral lesson in the preoccupation with a love and passion that have destroyed a man and a woman old enough to have resisted the distractions

[1] This play has nothing to do with Cleopatra and Octavia; the subject matter is Alexander the Great and his two wives, Statira (played by Elizabeth Bowtell) and Roxana. Lee's and Sedley's plays were performed in London in February and March respectively 1677. *All for Love* was first staged in December of that year.

of the flesh; hence in Dryden's words, 'their ends were unfortunate'. Yet, for Dryden 'excellency' was also a commendation of a fiery intensity of love, a transcendental love that is sufficient to overcome a moralist's objection to the adulterous nature of the affair; with this emphasis, Dryden ignored the fact that in life both Antony and Cleopatra had other lovers.

Shakespeare, the best-known interpreter of the same segment of history, faced the same dilemma: giving tragic impact (and, by implication, sympathy, pity, tolerance as well as grandeur) to characters and events that could not easily, given the bare bones of the story, be commended for 'the excellency of the moral'. Shakespeare largely overcame the difficulty by making his hero and heroine world-shakers, lovers with truly heroic careers and importance and whose private passion had a very public aspect to it in any event.

Dryden's telling of the story, crowded into a single day after Antony's shaming defeat at Actium, concentrates on Antony and Cleopatra's obsessive personal relationship and on how much both apparently sacrificed in order to remain together. It is here that the playwright found a moral to be commended and a world well lost: their story, as time has proved, has transcended normal mortal love.

There is also great pathos in the self-delusion of both lovers. Antony's is more explicit:

> In thy embraces I would be beheld
> By heaven and earth at once,
> And make their envy what they meant their sport.
> (III, i, p. 258)

To him Cleopatra's love has made giving up the world worthwhile.

Dryden emphasised the treachery of trusted lieutenants who, with inadequate minds or souls, by devious manipulation precipitated the deaths of the lovers and gave their passionate love tragic overtones. By Act v they are helpless against forces beyond their control.

All for Love is commendably economical. It has only a dozen characters, no subplot, no humour, and, in keeping with the revived neo-classical unities, the action is limited to the final day in the dramatised lives of Antony and Cleopatra. Such a concentration allows one almost to forget that the romance endured for more than ten years. Antony's days of glory and the idyllic time of the 'transcendant passion' were evidently long past, and the play might logically have more funereal than triumphant overtones, as the lovers indecisively try to come to grips with their present ignominy of having to treat with Caesar.

Triumphant it is though as a celebration of the idea that *amor vincit omnia*. The first four acts balance conflicting forces: Antony's credulity, his vacillations, and his rejection of political, military, and marital responsibilities for Cleopatra's immediate magnetism. In the final act she is victorious in death, a triumph that Dryden makes more convincing through the treachery which drives Antony finally towards her and away from the Roman world of duty, rivalry and jealousy.

All for Love centres more on an infatuated Antony, his dilemmas and conflicts, than on Cleopatra. Antony is a 'shadow of an emperor', and there is much pathos in watching his universe contract scene by scene as, despite repeatedly revived noble intentions, he withdraws further into a private world. Ventidius, a stern and dedicated Roman, continually acts as Antony's conscience (although historically dead by this time), reminding him of political and military realities. Misunderstanding and betrayal ultimately drive Antony to the besieged mausoleum, having been earlier separated from Cleopatra by his conviction – too hurriedly arrived at – that she has been unfaithful with Dolabella. This scene in Act IV closely echoes Othello's belief in an *affaire de coeur* between Desdemona and Cassio (*Othello*, III, iii, 94ff.).[2]

Although Dryden gave Cleopatra some of his best lines and a considerable dynamism, she lacks the intensity and sexuality of Shakespeare's queen. His Cleopatra would never seriously have described herself as 'a silly, harmless, household dove'.[3] Whatever weaknesses she may have, however, Dryden's Cleopatra is unquestionably more desirable than her rival, the cold, self-pitying and virtuous Octavia, played in 1677 by Katherine Corey, aged (like Octavia) about forty-five, and associated with shrewish roles. Dryden brought Octavia, without historical justification, from Rome to Alexandria to remind Antony of his responsibilities and to make possible a dramatic confrontation with Cleopatra, 'that bad woman'.

The 'perjured villain' Alexas – significantly here a eunuch – acting with an Iago-like self-interest, aggravates the situation near the end of the lovers' careers with a lie about Cleopatra's suicide. (In Shakespeare's play the report was initiated jointly by Charmion and Cleopatra.) Part of the tragedy associated with Antony's circumstances and his death is transferred to Cleopatra, who demonstrates the ultimate loyalty: to die, like a true Roman, beside her betrayed

---

[2]Dryden could have seen *Othello* at the Theatre Royal, Drury Lane, performed by the King's Company in January 1674 or January 1676; the cast of the earlier production (and probably the later) included Charles Hart as Othello and Michael Mohun as Iago, the actors who played Antony and Ventidius in December 1677.

[3]Dryden may have written the part of Cleopatra with the actress Elizabeth Bowtell in mind. She was a pretty, gentle, child-like actress, about twenty-seven, who performed regularly in London with Dryden's stage Antony, Charles Hart. (She was Margery Pinchwife in *The Country Wife* two years earlier.)

lover. Even here Dryden has eroded Cleopatra's nobility: her elaborate preparations for death emphasise her romantic wish to join her dead partner; however, at that moment 'Caesar's at the gates'. Perhaps of equal importance in her mind is using the asps to cheat the victorious Octavius Caesar and avoid being taken ignominiously back to Rome, 'to be led in triumph through the streets'.

Dryden prepared the way for Antony's earlier decision to die at his own hand by making the world that he gives up one which he could easily relinquish. Ventidius, Dolabella and Octavia of course contribute to his dissatisfaction with the world, as does Octavius Caesar. Unseen, but constantly in the background, he is a continuing reminder to Antony of the ambitions he had once had. From the beginning of the play, Antony's self-indulgent and Herculean posturing elicits both sympathy and impatience. His romantic escapism ('[To] live in a shady forest's sylvan scene/Stretched at my length beneath some blasted oak/ . . . a murmuring brook/Runs at my foot') in Act I seems distinctly un-Roman.

Influenced by Thomas Rymer, Réné Le Bossu and Réné Rapin, Dryden saw morality and compassion as the foundations of tragic drama. In *All for Love* Dryden utilised blank verse for the first time as a playwright, adding to the 'naturalism', lyric beauty and flow of the play. The imagery skilfully relates to the sea, jewellery, commerce, childhood, ruin, jealousy and the passage of time.

All for Love is Dryden's best play, a concise, well-organised version, with an appeal to Restoration sentiment, of a story that has been popular for centuries. The play has penetrating psychological insights and moments of grandeur in language and action. It is a moving commentary on the power of emotion to direct destiny. *All for Love* also has a particular fascination for Western audiences today, which are distinguished by their growing tolerance for a man such as Antony, torn between love and duty.

BIBLIOGRAPHY

All for Love

G. R. Wasserman, *John Dryden*. New York, 1964.

L. P. Goggin, 'This Bow of Ulysses', in *Essays and Studies in Language and Literature*, ed. H. H. Pettit. Pittsburgh, 1964.

A. D. Hope, 'All for Love or Comedy as Tragedy', *The Cave and the Spring, Essays on Poetry*. Adelaide, 1965.

E. Miner, 'Drama of the Will: *All for Love*'. *Dryden's Poetry*. Bloomington, 1967.

B. King, ed., *Dryden's 'All for Love'*. Twentieth Century Interpretations. Englewood Cliffs, N. J., 1968.

D. W. Hughes, 'The Significance of *All for Love*'. *ELH*, 37 (December 1970), 540–63.

F. J. Kearful, '"'Tis Past Recovery": Tragic Consciousness in *All for Love*'. *Modern Language Quarterly*, 34 (September 1973), 227–46.

J. D. Canfield, 'The Jewel of Great Price: Mutability and Constancy in Dryden's *All for Love*'. *ELH*, 42 (Spring 1975), 38–61.

L. H. Martin, '*All for Love* and the Millenarian Tradition'. *Comparative Literature*, 27 (Fall 1975), 289–306.

C. Tracey, 'The Tragedy of *All for Love*'. *University of Toronto Quarterly*, 45 (Spring 1976), 186–99.

M. Yots, 'Dryden's *All for Love* on the Restoration Stage'. *Restoration and 18th Century Theatre Research*, 16 (May 1977), 1–10.

A. S. Fisher, 'Necessity and the Winter: the Tragedy of *All for Love*'. *Philological Quarterly*, 56 (Spring 1977), 183–203.

M. Novak, 'Criticism, Adaptation, Politics, and the Shakespearean Model of Dryden's *All for Love*'. *Studies in Eighteenth Century Culture*, 7 (1978), 375–87.

D. W. Hughes, '*Aphrodite katadyomeme*: Dryden's Cleopatra on the Cydnos'. *Comparative Drama*, 14 (Spring 1980), 35–45.

C. F. Levine, '*All for Love* and Book IV of *The Aeneid*: the Moral Predicament'. *Comparative Literature*, 33 (Summer 1981), 239–57.

N. Rabkin, *Shakespeare and the Problem of Meaning*. Chicago, 1981.

D. W. Hughes, 'Art and Life in *All for Love*'. *Studies in Philology*, 80 (Winter 1983), 84–107.

R. Salvaggio, *Dryden's Dualities*. Victoria, B. C., English Literary Studies, 1983.

H. M. Solomon, 'Tragic Reconciliation: an Hegelian Analysis of *All for Love*'. *Studies in Philology*, 81 (Spring 1984), 185–211.

J. A. Vance, 'Antony Bound: Fragmentation and Insecurity in *All for Love*'. *Studies in English Literature 1500–1900*, 26 (Summer 1986), 421–38.

R. L. King, '*Res et verba*: the Reform of Language in Dryden's *All for Love*'. *ELH*, 54 (Spring 1987), 45–61.

J. A. Winn, *John Dryden and his World*. New Haven, 1987.

L. Hughes-Hallett, *Cleopatra: Histories, Dreams and Distortions*. London, 1990.

L. Kloesel, 'The Play of Desire: Vulcan's Net and Other Stories of Passion in *All for Love*'. *The Eighteenth Century: Theory and Interpretation*, 31 (Fall 1990), 227–44.

TO THE RIGHT HONOURABLE
THOMAS, EARL OF DANBY,

Viscount Latimer, and Baron Osborne of Kiveton, in
Yorkshire; Lord High Treasurer of England, one of His
Majesty's Most Honourable Privy Council, and Knight of
the Most Noble Order of the Garter[1]

My Lord,

The gratitude of poets is so troublesome a virtue to great men that
you are often in danger of your own benefits, for you are threatened
with some epistle and not suffered to do good in quiet or to compound[2]
for their silence whom you have obliged. Yet, I confess, I neither am
nor ought to be surprised at this indulgence; for your Lordship has the
same right to favour poetry which the great and noble have ever had –
   Carmen amat, quisquis carmine digna gerit.[3]
There is somewhat of a tie in nature betwixt those who are born for
worthy actions and those who can transmit them to posterity, and
though ours be much the inferior part, it comes at least within the verge
of alliance; nor are we unprofitable members of the commonwealth
when we animate others to those virtues which we copy and describe
from you.

'Tis indeed their interest, who endeavour the subversion of govern-
ments, to discourage poets and historians, for the best which can
happen to them is to be forgotten. But such who, under kings, are the
fathers of their country, and by a just and prudent ordering of affairs
preserve it, have the same reason to cherish the chroniclers of their
actions as they have to lay up in safety the deeds and evidences of their
estates; for such records are their undoubted titles to the love and
reverence of after ages. Your Lordship's administration has already
taken up a considerable part of the English annals, and many of its
most happy years are owing to it.

His Majesty, the most knowing judge of men and the best master,

---

[1]*Danby* Thomas Osborne, 1631–1712; first Earl of Danby 1674; Charles II's
chief minister 1673–79, when he was impeached and imprisoned.

[2]*compound* bargain.

[3]*Carmen . . . gerit* Everyone loves poetry who does deeds worthy of poetry.
Claudian, [poem] 23, Preface, Book III, On Stilicho's Consulship', *Claudian*
(London, 1922), II, p. 39.

has acknowledged the ease and benefit he receives in the incomes of his treasury, which you found not only disordered, but exhausted. All things were in the confusion of a chaos, without form or method, if not reduced beyond it, even to annihilation; so that you had not only to separate the jarring elements, but (if that boldness of expression might be allowed me) to create them. Your enemies had so embroiled the management of your office that they looked upon your advancement as the instrument of your ruin. And as if the clogging of the revenue and the confusion of accounts, which you found in your entrance, were not sufficient, they added their own weight of malice to the public calamity by forestalling the credit which should cure it. Your friends on the other side were only capable of pitying, but not of aiding you; no further help or counsel was remaining to you but what was founded on yourself; and that indeed was your security, for your diligence, your constancy, and your prudence wrought more surely within when they were not disturbed by any outward motion. The highest virtue is best to be trusted with itself; for assistance only can be given by a genius superior to that which it assists; and 'tis the noblest kind of debt when we are only obliged to God and nature.

This then, my Lord, is your just commendation, that you have wrought out yourself a way to glory by those very means that were designed for your destruction. You have not only restored but advanced the revenues of your master without grievance to the subject; and, as if that were little yet, the debts of the exchequer, which lay heaviest both on the crown and on private persons, have by your conduct been established in a certainty of satisfaction, an action so much the more great and honourable because the case was without the ordinary relief of laws, above the hopes of the afflicted and beyond the narrowness of the treasury to redress, had it been managed by a less able hand.[4]

'Tis certainly the happiest and most unenvied part of all your fortune to do good to many while you do injury to none, to receive at once the prayers of the subject and the praises of the prince, and, by the care of your conduct, to give him means of exerting the chiefest (if any be the chiefest) of his royal virtues, his distributive justice to the deserving and his bounty and compassion to the wanting.

The disposition of princes towards their people cannot better be discovered than in the choice of their ministers, who, like the animal spirits betwixt the soul and body, participate somewhat of both natures and make the communication which is betwixt them. A king

[4] *You ... hand* After his appointment as Lord High Treasurer in 1673, Danby carefully pared expenditures (including Dryden's salary of £100), liquidated debts, and reduced pensions, etc., making the nation at least temporarily solvent.

who is just and moderate in his nature, who rules according to the laws, whom God made happy by forming the temper of his soul to the constitution of his government, and who makes us happy by assuming over us no other sovereignty than that wherein our welfare and liberty consists, a prince, I say, of so excellent a character and so suitable to the wishes of all good men, could not better have conveyed himself into his people's apprehensions than in your Lordship's person who so lively express the same virtues that you seem not so much a copy as an emanation of him. Moderation is doubtless an establishment of greatness, but there is a steadiness of temper which is likewise requisite in a minister of state, so equal a mixture of both virtues that he may stand like an isthmus betwixt the two encroaching seas of arbitrary power and lawless anarchy. The undertaking would be difficult to any but an extraordinary genius, to stand at the line and to divide the limits, to pay what is due to the great representative of the nation, and neither to enhance nor to yield up the undoubted prerogatives of the crown.

These, my Lord, are the proper virtues of a noble Englishman, as indeed they are properly English virtues, no people in the world being capable of using them but we who have the happiness to be born under so equal and so well-poised a government, a government which has all the advantages of liberty beyond a commonwealth and all the marks of kingly sovereignty, without the danger of a tyranny.

Both my nature, as I am an Englishman, and my reason, as I am a man, have bred in me a loathing to that specious name of a republic, that mock appearance of a liberty, where all who have not part in the government are slaves, and slaves they are of a viler note than such as are subjects of an absolute dominion. For no Christian monarchy is so absolute but 'tis circumscribed with laws; but when the executive power is in the law-makers, there is no further check upon them, and the people must suffer without a remedy because they are oppressed by their representatives. If I must serve, the number of my masters who were born my equals would but add to the ignominy of my bondage. The nature of our government, above all others, is exactly suited both to the situation of our country and the temper of the natives, an island being more proper for commerce and for defence than for extending its dominions on the Continent; for what the valour of its inhabitants might gain, by reason of its remoteness and the casualties of the seas, it could not easily preserve. And therefore neither the arbitrary power of one, in a monarchy, nor of many, in a commonwealth, could make us greater than we are.

'Tis true that vaster and more frequent taxes might be gathered when the consent of the people was not asked or needed, but this were only by conquering abroad to be poor at home, and the examples of our neighbours teach us that they are not always the happiest subjects whose kings extend their dominions farthest.⁵ Since therefore we cannot win by an offensive war, at least a land war, the model of our government seems naturally contrived for the defensive part, and the consent of a people is easily obtained to contribute to that power which must protect it. *Felices nimium, bona si sua norint, Angligenae!*⁶ And yet there are not wanting malcontents amongst us who, surfeiting themselves on too much happiness, would persuade the people that they might be happier by a change. 'Twas indeed the policy of their old forefather,⁷ when himself was fallen from the station of glory, to seduce mankind into the same rebellion with him by telling him he might yet be freer than he was; that is, more free than his nature would allow, or, if I may so say, than God could make him. We have already all the liberty which freeborn subjects can enjoy, and all beyond it is but licence. But if it be liberty of conscience which they pretend,⁸ the moderation of our church is such that its practice extends not to the severity of persecution, and its discipline is withal so easy that it allows more freedom to dissenters than any of the sects would allow to it.

In the meantime, what right can be pretended by these men to attempt innovations in church or state? Who made them the trustees or, to speak a little nearer their own language, the keepers of the liberty of England? If their call be extraordinary, let them convince us by working miracles; for ordinary vocation they can have none, to disturb the government under which they were born and which protects them. He who has often changed his party⁹ and always has made his interest the rule of it gives little evidence of his sincerity for the public good; 'tis manifest he changes but for himself and takes the people for tools to work his fortune. Yet the experience of all ages might let him know that they who trouble the waters first have seldom the benefit of the fishing; as they who began the late rebellion enjoyed not the fruit of their undertaking, but were crushed themselves by the usurpation of their own instrument.¹⁰ Neither is it enough for them to answer that they only intend a reformation of the government, but not the subversion of it. On such pretences all insurrections have been founded; 'tis striking at the root of power, which is obedience. Every remonstrance of private men has the seed of treason in it, and

---

⁵*examples . . . farthest* Louis XIV of France had recently annexed part of Flanders, Lorraine, and Franche-Comté.

⁶*Felices . . . Angligenae* Happy Englishmen, too happy should they come to know their blessings! – an adaptation of Virgil, *Georgics*, II, 458–59.

⁷*forefather* Satan.   ⁸*pretend* claim.

⁹*He . . . party* no doubt the first Earl of Shaftesbury.

¹⁰*they . . . instrument* The metaphor sums up the Cromwellian rebellion, 1645–48.

discourses which are couched in ambiguous terms are therefore the more dangerous because they do all the mischief of open sedition, yet are safe from the punishment of the laws.

These, my Lord, are considerations which I should not pass so lightly over had I room to manage them as they deserve, for no man can be so inconsiderable in a nation as not to have a share in the welfare of it; and if he be a true Englishman, he must at the same time be fired with indignation and revenge himself as he can on the disturbers of his country. And to whom could I more fitly apply myself than to your Lordship, who have not only an inborn but an hereditary loyalty? The memorable constancy and sufferings of your father,[11] almost to the ruin of his estate for the royal cause, were an earnest of that which such a parent and such an instituion would produce in the person of a son. But so unhappy an occasion of manifesting your own zeal in suffering for his present majesty,[12] the providence of God and the prudence of your administration will, I hope, prevent; that as your father's fortune waited on the unhappiness of his sovereign, so your own may participate of the better fate which attends his son. The relation which you have by alliance to the noble family of your lady[13] serves to confirm to you both this happy augury. For what can deserve a greater place in the English chronicle than the loyalty and courage, the actions and death, of the general of an army, fighting for his prince and country? The honour and gallantry of the Earl of Lindsey is so illustrious a subject that 'tis fit to adorn an heroic poem, for he was the proto-martyr of the cause and the type[14] of his unfortunate royal master.

Yet after all, my Lord, if I may speak my thoughts, you are happy rather to us than to yourself, for the multiplicity, the cares, and the vexations of your employment have betrayed you from yourself, and given you up into the possession of the public. You are robbed of your privacy and friends, and scarce any hour of your life you can call your own. Those who envy your fortune, if they wanted not good nature,

[11]*your father* Sir Edward Osborne, 1596–1647, deputy lieutenant-general under Charles I.

[12]*suffering . . . majesty* As Dryden wrote these words, in March 1678, Danby's efforts to negotiate a treaty with the Dutch had been foiled by successful French attacks on Ghent and Ypres, and England was close to war with France. At the same time, Parliament ordered the release from the Tower (27 February 1678)of Danby's enemy, the Earl of Shaftesbury.

[13]*Your lady* Danby was married to Bridget Bertie, the grand-daughter of the first Earl of Lindsey, 1582–1642, general-in-chief of the royalist forces, killed at the Battle of Edgehill in October 1642; Bridget was the daughter of the second Earl of Lindsey, *c.* 1608–66, an important royalist leader.

[14]*type* symbol.

might more justly pity it; and when they see you watched by a crowd of suitors, whose importunity it is impossible to avoid, would conclude, with reason, that you have lost much more in true content than you have gained by dignity, and that a private gentleman is better attended by a single servant than your Lordship with so clamorous a train. Pardon me, my Lord, if I speak like a philosopher on this subject; the fortune which makes a man uneasy cannot make him happy, and a wise man must think himself uneasy when few of his actions are in his choice.

This last consideration has brought me to another, and a very seasonable one for your relief, which is, that while I pity your want of leisure, I have impertinently detained you so long a time. I have put off my own business, which was my dedication, till 'tis so late that I am now ashamed to begin it, and therefore I will say nothing of the poem[15] which I present to you, because I know not if you are like to have an hour which, with a good conscience, you may throw away in perusing it; and for the author, I have only to beg the continuance of your protection to him who is,

My Lord,

Your Lordship's most obliged, most humble, and most obedient servant,

JOHN DRYDEN.

[15]*poem* i.e. play.

PREFACE

The death of Antony and Cleopatra is a subject which has been treated by the greatest wits of our nation, after Shakespeare; and by all so variously that their example has given me the confidence to try myself in this bow of Ulysses amongst the crowd of suitors;[1] and, withal, to take my own measures in aiming at the mark. I doubt not but the same motive has prevailed with all of us in this attempt; I mean the excellency of the moral. For the chief persons represented were famous patterns of unlawful love, and their end accordingly was unfortunate. All reasonable men have long since concluded that the hero of the poem ought not to be a character of perfect virtue, for then he could not, without injustice, be made unhappy; nor yet altogether wicked, because he could not then be pitied. I have therefore steered the middle course, and have drawn the character of Antony as favourably as Plutarch, Appian, and Dion Cassius[2] would give me leave; the like I have observed in Cleopatra.

That which is wanting to work up the pity to a greater height was not afforded me by the story; for the crimes of love which they both committed were not occasioned by any necessity or fatal ignorance, but were wholly voluntary; since our passions are, or ought to be, within our power. The fabric of the play is regular enough, as to the inferior parts of it, and the unities of time, place and action more exactly observed than perhaps the English theatre requires. Particularly, the action is so much one that it is the only of the kind without episode or underplot, every scene in the tragedy conducing to the main design, and every act concluding with a turn of it.

The greatest error in the contrivance seems to be in the person of Octavia, for, though I might use the privilege of a poet to introduce her into Alexandria, yet I had not enough considered that the compassion

[1] *bow of Ulysses* None of Penelope's suitors had the strength to shoot an arrow from Ulysses' bow; only the disguised hero, returned from twenty years of travel, was capable of doing so. *Odyssey*, Book XXI.

[2] *Plutarch, Appian, and Dion Cassius* All wrote about Rome and Romans.

she moved to herself and children was destructive to that which I
reserved for Antony and Cleopatra, whose mutual love, being founded
upon vice, must lessen the favour of the audience to them, when virtue
and innocence were oppressed by it. And though I justified Antony in
some measure, by making Octavia's departure to proceed wholly from
herself, yet the force of the first machine[3] still remained; and the
dividing of pity, like the cutting of a river into many channels, abated
the strength of the natural stream. But this is an objection which none
of my critics have urged against me, and therefore I might have let it
pass, if I could have resolved to have been partial to myself.

The faults my enemies have found are rather cavils concerning little
and not essential decencies, which a master of the ceremonies may
decide betwixt us. The French poets, I confess, are strict observers of
these punctilios. They would not, for example, have suffered
Cleopatra and Octavia to have met; or if they had met, there must have
only passed betwixt them some cold civilities, but no eagerness of
repartee, for fear of offending against the greatness of their characters
and the modesty of their sex. This objection I foresaw, and at the same
time condemned, for I judged it both natural and probable that
Octavia, proud of her new-gained conquest, would search out
Cleopatra to triumph over her, and that Cleopatra, thus attacked, was
not of a spirit to shun the encounter. And 'tis not unlikely that two
exasperated rivals should use such satire as I have put into their
mouths, for, after all, though the one were a Roman and the other a
queen, they were both women. 'Tis true, some actions, though natural,
are not fit to be represented, and broad obscenities in words ought in
good manners to be avoided; expressions therefore are a modest
clothing of our thoughts, as breeches and petticoats are of our bodies.
If I have kept myself within the bounds of modesty, all beyond it is but
nicety and affectation, which is no more but modesty depraved into a
vice. They betray themselves who are too quick of apprehension in
such cases, and leave all reasonable men to imagine worse of them than
of the poet.

Honest Montaigne goes yet further: *Nous ne sommes que cérémonie; la cérémonie nous emporte, et laissons la substance des choses.
Nous nous tenons aux branches et abandonnons le tronc et le corps.
Nous avons appris aux dames de rougir, oyans seulement nommer ce
qu'elles ne craignent aucunement à faire: nous n'osons appeller à droit
nos membres, et ne craignons pas de les employer à toute sorte de
débauche. La cérémonie nous defend d'exprimer par paroles les choses
licites et naturelles, et nous l'en croyons; la raison nous défend de n'en*

---

[3]*machine* device.

faire point d'illicites et mauvaises, et personne ne l'en croit.[4] My comfort is that by this opinion my enemies are but sucking critics, who would fain be nibbling 'ere their teeth are come.

Yet, in this nicety of manners does the excellency of French poetry consist: their heroes are the most civil people breathing, but their good breeding seldom extends to a word of sense. All their wit is in their ceremony; they want the genius which animates our stage, and therefore 'tis but necessary, when they cannot please, that they should take care not to offend. But as the civilest man in the company is commonly the dullest, so these authors, while they are afraid to make you laugh or cry, out of pure good manners make you sleep. They are so careful not to exasperate a critic that they never leave him any work; so busy with the broom, and make so clean a riddance that there is little left either for censure or for praise. For no part of a poem is worth our discommending where the whole is insipid; as when we have once tasted of palled wine, we stay not to examine it glass by glass. But while they affect to shine in trifles, they are often careless in essentials.

Thus their Hippolytus[5] is so scrupulous in point of decency that he will rather expose himself to death than accuse his stepmother to his father; and my critics I am sure will commend him for it. But we of grosser apprehensions are apt to think that this excess of generosity is not practicable but with fools and madmen. This was good manners with a vengeance, and the audience is like to be much concerned at the misfortunes of this admirable hero. But take Hippolytus out of his poetic fit, and I suppose he would think it a wiser part to set the saddle on the right horse, and choose rather to live with the reputation of a plain-spoken, honest man than to die with the infamy of an incestuous villain. In the meantime we may take notice that where the poet ought to have preserved the character as it was delivered to us by antiquity, when he should have given us the picture of a rough young man of the Amazonian strain, a jolly huntsman, and both by his profession and his early rising a mortal enemy to love, he has chosen to give him the turn of gallantry, sent him to travel from Athens to Paris, taught him to make love, and transformed the Hippolytus of Euripides into Monsieur Hippolyte.

[4]*Nous . . . croit* We are only convention; convention carries us away, and we abandon the essence of things. We hold onto the branches and neglect the trunk and the body. We have taught ladies to blush at the very mention of things that they by no means fear to do. We are not bold enough to describe our parts accurately, and yet we do not fear to make use of them in all kinds of debauchery. Convention forbids us to express in words things permitted and natural, and we obey it. Reason forbids us to do what is illicit and evil, and no one obeys it.

Montaigne, 'On Presumption', *Essays* (1580), Book II, Chapter 17.

[5]*Hippolytus* the hero of Euripides' *Hippolytus*, 428 BC; Racine's *Phèdre*, 1677, is a simplified and sentimental adaptation of the story.

I should not have troubled myself thus far with French poets but that I find our *Chedreux*[6] critics wholly form their judgments by them. But for my part, I desire to be tried by the laws of my own country, for it seems unjust to me that the French should prescribe here till they have conquered. Our little sonneteers who follow them have too narrow souls to judge of poetry. Poets themselves are the most proper, though I conclude not the only critics. But till some genius as universal as Aristotle shall arise, one who can penetrate into all arts and sciences without the practice of them, I shall think it reasonable that the judgment of an artificer in his own art should be preferable to the opinion of another man, at least where he is not bribed by interest or prejudiced by malice. And this, I suppose, is manifest by plain induction. For, first, the crowd cannot be presumed to have more than a gross instinct of what pleases or displeases them. Every man will grant me this; but then, by a particular kindness to himself, he draws his own stake[7] first, and will be distinguished from the multitude, of which other men may think him one. But if I come closer to those who are allowed for witty men, either by the advantage of their quality or by common fame, and affirm that neither are they qualified to decide sovereignly concerning poetry, I shall yet have a strong party of my opinion; for most of them severally will exclude the rest, either from the number of witty men, or at least of able judges. But here again they are all indulgent to themselves; and everyone who believes himself a wit – that is, every man – will pretend at the same time to a right of judging.

But to press it yet further, there are many witty men, but few poets; neither have all poets[8] a taste of tragedy. And this is the rock on which they are daily splitting. Poetry, which is a picture of nature, must generally please; but 'tis not to be understood that all parts of it must please every man; therefore is not tragedy to be judged by a witty man, whose taste is only confined to comedy. Nor is every man who loves tragedy a sufficient judge of it; he must understand the excellencies of it too, or he will only prove a blind admirer, not a critic. From hence it comes that so many satires[9] on poets and censures of their writings fly abroad. Men of pleasant conversation (at least esteemed so) and endued with a trifling kind of fancy, perhaps helped out with some

---

[6]*Chedreux* fashionable; Chedreux was a popular French wigmaker. Sir Fopling Flutter wore a Chedreux periwig. *The Man of Mode*, III, ii, p. 155.

[7]*stake* withdraws his own wager.

[8]*poets* i.e. playwrights.

[9]*satires* Here and elsewhere in the Preface Dryden hits at John Wilmot, second Earl of Rochester, 1647–80, who had criticised him, notably in *An Allusion to Horace, c.* 1674.

smattering of Latin, are ambitious to distinguish themselves from the herd of gentlemen, by their poetry –

Rarus enim ferme sensus communis in illa Fortuna.[10]

And is not this a wretched affectation, not to be contented with what fortune has done for them, and sit down quietly with their estates, but they must call their wits in question and needlessly expose their nakedness[11] to public view, not considering that they are not to expect the same approbation from sober men which they have found from their flatterers after the third bottle. If a little glittering in discourse has passed them on us for witty men, where was the necessity of undeceiving the world? Would a man who has an ill title to an estate, but yet is in possession of it, would he bring it of his own accord to be tried at Westminster? We who write, if we want the talent, yet have the excuse that we do it for a poor subsistence, but what can be urged in their defence who, not having the vocation of poverty to scribble, out of mere wantonness take pains to make themselves ridiculous?

Horace was certainly in the right where he said that 'No man is satisfied with his own condition'.[12] A poet is not pleased, because he is not rich, and the rich are discontented because the poets will not admit them of their number. Thus the case is hard with writers: if they succeed not, they must starve; and if they do, some malicious satire is prepared to level them for daring to please without their leave. But while they are so eager to destroy the fame of others, their ambition is manifest in their concernment; some poem of their own is to be produced, and the slaves are to be laid flat with their faces on the ground, that the monarch may appear in the greater majesty.

Dionysius[13] and Nero[14] had the same longings, but with all their power they could never bring their business well about. 'Tis true, they proclaimed themselves poets by sound of trumpet, and poets they were, upon pain of death to any man who durst call them otherwise. The audience had a fine time on't, you may imagine; they sat in a bodily fear and looked as demurely as they could, for it was a hanging matter to laugh unseasonably; and the tyrants were suspicious, as they had reason, that their subjects had 'em in the wind; so every man, in his own defence, set as good a face upon the business as he could. 'Twas

[10]*Rarus . . . fortuna* Certainly common sense is rare in that condition of life. Juvenal, *Satires*, VII, 73–74.

[11]*nakedness* perhaps an allusion to episodes of public nakedness by Charles Sedley and later the Earl of Rochester in the autumn of 1677.

[12]*No . . . condition* Horace, *Satires*, I, i, 1–3.

[13]*Dionysius c.* 431–367 BC, Tyrant of Syracuse, a would-be playwright; as a matter of diplomacy, he was once awarded a first prize.

[14]*Nero* AD 37–68, Roman emperor, vain and dissolute, ambitious to be an actor, painter, and poet.

known beforehand that the monarchs were to be crowned laureates; but when the show was over, and an honest man was suffered to depart quietly, he took out his laughter which he had stifled, with a firm resolution never more to see an emperor's play, though he had been ten years a-making it.

In the meantime the true poets were they who made the best markets, for they had wit enough to yield the prize with a good grace, and not contend with him who had thirty legions. They were sure to be rewarded if they confessed themselves bad writers, and that was somewhat better than to be martyrs for their reputation. Lucan's[15] example was enough to teach them manners, and after he was put to death for overcoming Nero, the emperor carried it without dispute for the best poet in his dominions. No man was ambitious of that grinning honour,[16] for if he heard the malicious trumpeter proclaiming his name before his betters, he knew there was but one way with him.[17] Maecenas[18] took another course, and we know he was more than a great man, for he was witty too, but finding himself far gone in poetry, which Seneca assures us was not his talent,[19] he thought it his best way to be well with Virgil and with Horace, that at least he might be a poet at the second hand; and we see how happily it has succeeded with him, for his own bad poetry is forgotten, and their panegyrics of him still remain. But they who should be our patrons are for no such expensive ways to fame; they have much of the poetry of Maecenas, but little of his liberality. They are for persecuting Horace and Virgil in the persons of their successors, for such is every man who has any part of their soul and fire, though in a less degree.

Some of their little zanies[20] yet go further, for they are persecutors even of Horace himself, as far as they are able, by their ignorant and vile imitations of him, by making an unjust use of his authority and turning his artillery against his friends. But how would he disdain to be copied by such hands! I dare answer for him, he would be more uneasy in their company than he was with Crispinus,[21] their forefather, in the Holy Way, and would no more have allowed them a place amongst the critics than he would Demetrius the mimic and Tigellius the buffoon:

[15]*Lucan c.* AD 39–65; an allusion to the legend that Lucan bested Emperor Nero in a poetry competition, and was later executed for supposed treason.

[16]*grinning honour* death, echoing Falstaff's words, 1 *Henry IV*, V, iii, 62.

[17]*but one way with him* a reference to Falstaff's death, *Henry V*, II, iii, 15–16.

[18]*Maecenas c.* 70–8 BC, poet, patron of literature; colleague of Antony until *c.* 36 BC, when he allied himself to Octavius as general and administrator.

[19]*talent* in *Ad Lucilium Epistolae Morales*, CXIV, *passim*.

[20]*zanies* mimics, attendants on clowns, mountebanks, etc.

[21]*Crispinus* a prototype of a bore; Horace, *Satires*, I, i, 120.

> *—Demetri, teque, Tigelli,*
> *Discipulorum inter jubeo plorare cathedras.*[22]

With what scorn would he look down on such miserable translators, who make doggerel of his Latin, mistake his meaning, misapply his censures, and often contradict their own! He is fixed as a landmark to set out the bounds of poetry,

> *—Saxum antiquum, ingens,—*
> *Limes agro positus, litem ut discerneret arvis.*[23]

But other arms than theirs and other sinews are required to raise the weight of such an author, and when they would toss him against their enemies,

> *Genua labant, gelidus concrevit frigore sanguis.*
> *Tum lapis ipse viri, vacuum per inane volutus,*
> *Nec spatium evasit totum nec pertulit ictum.*[24]

For my part, I would wish no other revenge, either for myself or the rest of the poets, from this rhyming judge of the twelve-penny gallery,[25] this legitimate son of Sternhold,[26] than that he would subscribe his name to his censure or (not to tax him beyond his learning) set his mark. For, should he own himself publicly, and come from behind the lion's skin,[27] they whom he condemns would be thankful to him, they whom he praises would choose to be condemned, and the magistrates whom he has elected would modestly withdraw from their employment, to avoid the scandal of his nomination. The sharpness of his satire, next to himself, falls most heavily on his friends, and they ought never to forgive him for commending them perpetually the wrong way, and sometimes by contraries.

If he have a friend whose hastiness in writing is his greatest fault, Horace would have taught him to have minced the matter, and to have called it readiness of thought and a flowing fancy; for friendship will allow a man to christen an imperfection by the name of some neighbour virtue:

[22]*Demetri . . . cathedras* Demetrius and you, Tigellius, I command you to go wail amongst the chairs of your female students. Horace, *Satires*, I, x, 90–91.

[23]*Saxum . . . arvis* He observed a huge ancient stone placed as the boundary of a field, that it might decide litigation about the ploughed lands. Virgil, *Aeneid*, XII, 897–98.

[24]*Genua . . . ictum* His limbs totter, his blood has congealed with cold; then the hero's stone itself, thrown through space, did not carry the distance nor strike its objective. Virgil, *Aeneid*, XII, 905–07.

[25]*twelve-penny gallery* the cheapest seats at the theatre.

[26]*Sternhold* Thomas Sternhold, 1500–49, a popular but undistinguished English poet, author of a metrical version of the Psalms, 1549, with later revisions.

[27]*lion's skin* In Aesop's fable an ass disguised himself as a lion, but was detected by his bray.

> *Vellem in amicitia sic erraremus; et isti*
> *Errori nomen virtus posuisset honestum.*[28]

But he would never have allowed him to have called a slow man hasty, or a hasty writer a slow drudge, as Juvenal explains it:

> —*Canibus pigris, scabieque vetusta*
> *Laeveibus, et siccae lambentibus ora lucernae,*
> *Nomen erit, Pardus, Tigris, Leo; si quid adhus est*
> *Quod fremit in terris violentius.*[29]

Yet Lucretius laughs at a foolish lover, even for excusing the imperfections of his mistress:

> *Nigra* μελίχροος *est, immunda et foetida* ἀχοσμος. . . .
> *Balba loqui non quit,* τραυλίξει; *muta pudens est,* etc.[30]

But to drive it *ad Aethiopem cygnum*[31] is not to be endured. I leave him to interpret this by the benefit of his French version on the other side, and without further considering him than I have the rest of my illiterate censors, whom I have disdained to answer because they are not qualified for judges. It remains that I acquaint the reader that I have endeavoured in this play to follow the practice of the ancients, who, as Mr Rymer[32] has judiciously observed, are and ought to be our masters. Horace likewise gives it for a rule in his art of poetry:

> —*Vos exemplaria Graeca*
> *Nocturna versate manu, versate diurna.*[33]

Yet, though their models are regular, they are too little for English tragedy, which requires to be built in a larger compass. I could give an instance in the *Oedipus Tyrannus*, which was the masterpiece of Sophocles, but I reserve it for a more fit occasion, which I hope to have hereafter. In my style I have professed to imitate the divine Shakespeare; which that I might perform more freely, I have disencumbered

---

[28]*Vellem . . . honestum* I could wish that we had made such an error in friendship, and that on such a mistake virtue had bestowed an honourable name. Horace, *Satires*, I, iii, 41–42.

[29]*Canibus . . . violentius* Lazy dogs, hairless with chronic mange, licking the edges of a dry lamp, shall be called 'Panther', 'Tiger', 'Lion', or whatever else in the world roars more fiercely. Juvenal, *Satires*, VIII, 34–37.

[30]*Nigra . . . est* A dark-skinned girl is called 'honey-coloured', the foul and filthy 'unadorned' . . . she who stammers and cannot speak 'lisps', the mute is 'bashful', etc. Lucretius, *De Rerum Natura*, IV, 1160, 1164.

[31]*ad Aethiopem cygnum* to call an Ethiopian a swan. This phrase and the reference to 'zanies' above allude to the Earl of Rochester's having posed as a mountebank near the Black Swan Inn, *c.* 1675.

[32]*Rymer* Thomas Rymer, 1641–1713, literary critic: *Tragedies of the Late Age* (1678) etc.

[33]*Vos . . . diurna* You must study your Greek models by day and by night. Horace, *Ars Poetica*, lines 268–69.

myself from rhyme. Not that I condemn my former way, but that this is more proper to my present purpose. I hope I need not to explain myself, that I have not copied my author servilely. Words and phrases must of necessity receive a change in succeeding ages, but 'tis almost a miracle that much of his language remains so pure, and that he who began dramatic poetry amongst us, untaught by any, and, as Ben Jonson tells us, without learning, should by the force of his own genius perform so much that in a manner he has left no praise for any who come after him. The occasion is fair, and the subject would be pleasant to handle the difference of styles betwixt him and Fletcher, and wherein, and how far they are both to be imitated. But since I must not be over-confident of my own performance after him, it will be prudence in me to be silent. Yet I hope I may affirm, and without vanity, that by imitating him I have excelled myself throughout the play; and particularly, that I prefer the scene betwixt Antony and Ventidius in the first act to anything which I have written in this kind.

PROLOGUE

What flocks of critics hover here today,
As vultures wait on armies for their prey,
All gaping for the carcass of a play!
With croaking notes they bode some dire event,
And follow dying poets by the scent.
Ours gives himself for gone; y'have watch'd your time:
He fights this day unarm'd – without his rhyme –
And brings a tale which often has been told,
As sad as Dido's[1] and almost as old.
His hero, whom you wits his bully call,
Bates of[2] his mettle and scarce rants at all.
He's somewhat lewd, but a well-meaning mind;
Weeps much, fights little, but is wond'rous kind.
In short, a pattern and companion fit
For all the keeping Tonies[3] of the pit.
I could name more: a wife, and mistress too,
Both (to be plain) too good for most of you,
The wife well-natur'd, and the mistress true.

   Now, poets, if your fame has been his care,
Allow him all the candour you can spare.
A brave man scorns to quarrel once a day,
Like hectors,[4] in at every petty fray.
Let those find fault whose wit's so very small,
They've need to show that they can think at all;
Errors, like straws, upon the surface flow;

---

[1] *Dido* the legendary foundress of Carthage, *c.* eighth century BC; she killed herself rather than marry the King of Libya.
[2] *Bates of* decreases.
[3] *the keeping Tonies* i.e. kept, supported simpletons (punning on 'Antony'), in the same sense as 'kept woman' or 'kept player' (*The Country Wife*, IV, iii, p. 71).
[4] *hectors* bullies.

He who would search for pearls must dive below.
Fops may have leave to level all they can,
As pygmies would be glad to lop a man.
Half-wits are fleas, so little and so light,
We scarce could know they live but that they bite.
But as the rich, when tir'd with daily feasts,
For change become their next poor tenant's guests,
Drink hearty draughts of ale from plain brown bowls,
And snatch the homely rasher from the coals;
So you, retiring from much better cheer,
For once may venture to do penance here.
And since that plenteous autumn now is past,
Whose grapes and peaches have indulg'd your taste,
Take in good part from our poor poet's board
Such rivell'd fruits as winter can afford.

PERSONS REPRESENTED

MARC ANTONY   Mr [Charles] Hart
VENTIDIUS, *his general*   Mr [Michael] Mohun
DOLABELLA, *his friend*   MR CLARKE[1]
ALEXAS, *the Queen's eunuch*   Mr [Cardell] Goodman
SERAPION, *priest of Isis*   Mr [Philip] Griffin
ANOTHER PRIEST [MYRIS]   Mr [John] Coysh
Servants to ANTONY
CLEOPATRA, *Queen of Egypt*   Mrs Boutell[2]
OCTAVIA, ANTONY'S *wife*   Mrs [Katherine] Corey

CHARMION ⎱
         ⎰ CLEOPATRA'S *maids*
IRAS ⎱

ANTONY'S TWO LITTLE DAUGHTERS

Scene: Alexandria

[1]Thomas Clark.
[2]Elizabeth Bowtell; she also played Margery Pinchwife, in *The Country Wife*.

ALL FOR LOVE

Act One

SCENE ONE

The Temple of Isis

Enter SERAPION, MYRIS, *priests of Isis*

SERAP.   Portents and prodigies are grown so frequent
   That they have lost their name. Our fruitful Nile
   Flow'd ere the wonted season, with a torrent
   So unexpected and so wondrous fierce
   That the wild deluge overtook the haste
   Ev'n of the hinds that watch'd it. Men and beasts
   Were borne above the tops of trees that grew
   On th'utmost margin of the water-mark.
   Then, with so swift an ebb the flood drove backward,
   It slipp'd from underneath the scaly herd;
   Here monstrous phocae[1] panted on the shore;
   Forsaken dolphins there with their broad tails
   Lay lashing the departing waves; hard by 'em,
   Sea-horses,[2] flound'ring in the slimy mud,
   Toss'd up their heads, and dash'd the ooze about 'em.
     Enter ALEXAS *behind them*
MYR.   Avert these omens, heav'n!
SERAP.   Last night, between the hours of twelve and one,
   In a lone aisle o'the temple while I walk'd,
   A whirlwind rose that, with a violent blast,
   Shook all the dome. The doors around me clapp'd;
   The iron wicket that defends the vault
   Where the long race of Ptolemies is laid
   Burst open and disclos'd the mighty dead.
   From out each monument, in order plac'd,
   An armed ghost starts up; the boy-king[3] last

---

[1]*phocae* seals.   [2]*Sea-horses* Hippopotami.
[3]*boy-king* Ptolemy XIV, co-ruler of Egypt with Cleopatra, his sister and wife, who is thought to have had him poisoned in 44 BC.

Rear'd his inglorious head. A peal of groans
Then follow'd, and a lamentable voice
Cried, 'Egypt is no more'! My blood ran back,
My shaking knees against each other knock'd;
On the cold pavement down I fell entranc'd,
And so unfinish'd left the horrid scene.

ALEX.   (*Showing himself*) And dream'd you this or did

                                                     invent the story,

To frighten our Egyptian boys withal
And train 'em up betimes in fear of priesthood?

SERAP.   My lord, I saw you not,
Nor meant my words should reach your ears; but what
I utter'd was most true.

ALEX.   A foolish dream,
Bred from the fumes of indigested feasts
And holy luxury.

SERAP.   I know my duty:
This goes no further.

ALEX.   'Tis not fit it should;
Nor would the times now bear it, were it true.
All southern, from yon hills, the Roman camp
Hangs o'er us black and threat'ning, like a storm
Just breaking on our heads.

SERAP.   Our faint Egyptians pray for Antony,
But in their servile hearts they own Octavius.

MYR.   Why then does Antony dream out his hours,
And tempts not fortune for a noble day
Which might redeem what Actium lost?

ALEX.   He thinks 'tis past recovery.

SERAP.   Yet the foe
Seems not to press the siege.

ALEX.   Oh, there's the wonder.
Maecenas and Agrippa,[4] who can most[5]
With Caesar, are his foes. His wife Octavia,
Driv'n from his house, solicits her revenge;
And Dolabella, who was once his friend,
Upon some private grudge now seeks his ruin;
Yet still war seems on either side to sleep.

SERAP.   'Tis strange that Antony, for some days past,

[4] *Agrippa* commander of the fleet under Octavius, and responsible for the defeat of
Antony at Actium, 31 BC.
[5] *can most* can achieve most.

Has not beheld the face of Cleopatra;
But here, in Isis'[6] temple, lives retir'd,
And makes his heart a prey to black despair.

ALEX. 'Tis true; and we much fear he hopes by absence
To cure his mind of love.

SERAP.   If he be vanquish'd
Or make his peace, Egypt is doom'd to be
A Roman province, and our plenteous harvests
Must then redeem the scarceness of their soil.
While Antony stood firm, our Alexandria
Rivall'd proud Rome (dominion's other seat),
And Fortune, striding like a vast Colossus,
Could fix an equal foot of empire here.

ALEX.   Had I my wish, these tyrants of all nature,
Who lord it o'er mankind, should perish, perish,
Each by the other's sword; but since our will
Is lamely follow'd by our pow'r we must
Depend on one, with him to rise or fall.

SERAP.   How stands the queen affected?

ALEX.   Oh, she dotes,
She dotes, Serapion, on this vanquish'd man,
And winds herself about his mighty ruins;
Whom would she yet forsake, yet yield him up,
This hunted prey, to his pursuer's hands,
She might preserve us all; but 'tis in vain –
This changes my designs, this blasts my counsels,
And makes me use all means to keep him here,
Whom I could wish divided from her arms,
Far as the earth's deep centre. Well, you know
The state of things; no more of your ill omens
And black prognostics; labour to confirm
The people's hearts.

    Enter VENTIDIUS, *talking aside with a* GENTLEMAN *of* ANTONY'S

SERAP.   These Romans will o'erhear us.
But who's that stranger? By his warlike port,
His fierce demeanour, and erected look,
He's of no vulgar note.

ALEX.   Oh, 'tis Ventidius,
Our emp'ror's great lieutenant in the East,
Who first showed Rome that Parthia[7] could be conquer'd.

---

[6]*Isis* the Egyptian moon-goddess.

[7]*Parthia* part of modern Iran, where Ventidius won important victories in 39 and
38 BC.

When Antony return'd from Syria last,
He left this man to guard the Roman frontiers.
SERAP.   You seem to know him well.
ALEX.   Too well. I saw him at Cilicia[8] first,
When Cleopatra there met Antony;
A mortal foe he was to us, and Egypt.
But – let me witness to the worth I hate –
A braver Roman never drew a sword;
Firm to his prince, but as a friend, not slave.
He ne'er was of his pleasures, but presides
O'er all his cooler hours and morning counsels.
In short, the plainness, fierceness, rugged virtue
Of an old true-stamp'd Roman lives in him.
His coming bodes I know not what of ill
To our affairs. Withdraw, to mark him better,
And I'll acquaint you why I sought you here,
And what's our present work.

They withdraw to a corner of the stage, and VENTIDIUS, *with
the other, comes forward to the front*

VENT.   Not see him, say you?
I say, I must, and will.
GENT.   He has commanded,
On pain of death, none should approach his presence.
VENT.   I bring him news will raise his drooping spirits,
Give him new life.
GENT.   He sees not Cleopatra.
VENT.   Would he had never seen her!
GENT.   He eats not, drinks not, sleeps not, has no use
Of anything but thought; or if he talks,
'Tis to himself, and then 'tis perfect raving.
Then he defies the world and bids it pass;
Sometimes he gnaws his lip and curses loud
The boy Octavius; then he draws his mouth
Into a scornful smile, and cries 'Take all,
The world's not worth my care'.
VENT.   Just, just his nature.
Virtue's his path, but sometimes 'tis too narrow
For his vast soul, and then he starts out wide
And bounds into a vice that bears him far

---

[8]*Cilicia* in southern Turkey; here Antony commanded Cleopatra to meet him in
41 BC, to explain her ineffectual role in the campaign to defeat Brutus and Cassius;
their meeting is described in III, i, p. 262–63.

From his first course and plunges him in ills;
But when his danger makes him find his fault,
Quick to observe, and full of sharp remorse,
He censures eagerly his own misdeeds,
Judging himself with malice to himself,
And not forgiving what as man he did,
Because his other parts are more than man.
He must not thus be lost.

ALEXAS *and the* PRIESTS *come forward*

ALEX.   You have your full instructions; now advance,
Proclaim your orders loudly.

SERAP.   Romans, Egyptians, hear the queen's command.
Thus Cleopatra bids: 'Let labour cease;
To pomp and triumphs give this happy day,
That gave the world a lord; 'tis Antony's'.
Live, Antony; and Cleopatra live!
Be this the general voice sent up to heav'n.
And every public place repeat this echo.

VENT.   (*Aside*) Fine pageantry!

SERAP.   Set out before your doors
The images of all your sleeping fathers,
With laurels crown'd; with laurels wreathe your posts,
And strew with flow'rs the pavement; let the priests
Do present⁹ sacrifice; pour out the wine,
And call the gods to join with you in gladness.

VENT.   Curse on the tongue that bids this general joy!
Can they be friends of Antony, who revel
When Antony's in danger? Hide, for shame,
You Romans, your great-grandsires' images,
For fear their souls should animate their marbles,
To blush at their degenerate progeny.

ALEX.   A love which knows no bounds to Antony
Would mark the day with honours, when all heaven
Labour'd for him, when each propitious star
Stood wakeful in his orb, to watch that hour
And shed his better influence. Her own birthday
Our queen neglected, like a vulgar fate
That pass'd obscurely by.

VENT.   Would it had slept,
Divided far from this, till some remote
And future age had call'd it out, to ruin

---

⁹*present* immediate.

Some other prince, not him!

ALEX.   Your emperor,
Though grown unkind, would be more gentle than
T'upbraid my queen for loving him too well.

VENT.   Does the mute sacrifice upbraid the priest?
He knows him not his executioner.
Oh, she has deck'd his ruin with her love,
Led him in golden bands to gaudy slaughter,
And made perdition pleasing. She has left him
The blank of what he was.
I tell thee, eunuch, she has quite unmann'd him.
Can any Roman see and know him now,
Thus alter'd from the lord of half mankind,
Unbent, unsinew'd, made a woman's toy,
Shrunk from the vast extent of all his honours,
And cramp'd within a corner of the world?
O Antony,
Thou bravest soldier, and thou best of friends!
Bounteous as nature, next to nature's God!
Couldst thou but make new worlds, so wouldst thou give 'em,
As bounty were thy being. Rough in battle,
As the first Romans when they went to war;
Yet after victory more pitiful
Than all their praying virgins left at home!

ALEX.   Would you could add to those more shining virtues
His truth to her who loves him.

VENT.   Would I could not!
But wherefore waste I precious hours with thee?
Thou art her darling mischief, her chief engine,
Antony's other fate. Go, tell thy queen
Ventidius is arriv'd, to end her charms.
Let your Egyptian timbrels play alone,
Nor mix effeminate sounds with Roman trumpets.
You dare not fight for Antony; go pray,
And keep your cowards' holiday in temples.

                    Exeunt ALEXAS *and* SERAPION
     Enter a SECOND GENTLEMAN *of* ANTONY

SECOND GENT.   The emperor approaches and commands,
On pain of death, that none presume to stay.

FIRST GENT.   I dare not disobey him.   *Going out with the other*

VENT.   Well, I dare.
But I'll observe him first unseen and find
Which way his humour drives. The rest I'll venture.   *Withdraws*

Enter ANTONY, *walking with a disturbed motion before he speaks*

ANT.   They tell me 'tis my birthday, and I'll keep it
    With double pomp of sadness.
    'Tis what the day deserves, which gave me breath.
    Why was I rais'd the meteor of the world,
    Hung in the skies, and blazing as I travell'd,
    Till all my fires were spent; and then cast downward
    To be trod out by Caesar?

VENT.   (*Aside*)   On my soul,
    'Tis mournful, wondrous mournful!

ANT.   Count thy gains.
    Now, Antony, wouldst thou be born for this?
    Glutton of fortune, thy devouring youth
    Has starv'd thy wanting age.

VENT.   (*Aside*)   How sorrow shakes him!
    So, now the tempest tears him up by the roots,
    And on the ground extends the noble ruin.

                         ANTONY *having thrown himself down*

    Lie there, thou shadow of an emperor;
    The place thou pressest on thy mother earth
    Is all thy empire now. Now it contains thee.
    Some few days hence and then 'twill be too large,
    When thou'rt contracted in thy narrow urn,
    Shrunk to a few cold ashes; then Octavia
    (For Cleopatra will not live to see it),
    Octavia then will have thee all her own,
    And bear thee in her widow'd hand to Caesar.
    Caesar will weep, the crocodile will weep,
    To see his rival of the universe
    Lie still and peaceful there. I'll think no more on't.

[ANT.]   Give me some music; look that it be sad.
    I'll soothe[10] my melancholy till I swell
    And burst myself with sighing. –   *Soft music*
    'Tis somewhat to my humour. Stay, I fancy
    I'm now turn'd wild, a commoner of nature;
    Of all forsaken, and forsaking all.
    Live in a shady forest's sylvan scene,
    Stretch'd at my length beneath some blasted oak.
    I lean my head upon the mossy bark,
    And look just of a piece as I grew from it;
    My uncomb'd locks, matted like mistletoe,

[10]*soothe* encourage.

Hang o'er my hoary face; a murmuring brook
Runs at my foot.

VENT.   Methinks I fancy
Myself there too.

ANT.   The herd come jumping by me,
And, fearless, quench their thirst while I look on,
And take me for their fellow-citizen.
More of this image, more; it lulls my thoughts.

Soft music again

VENT.   I must disturb him; I can hold no longer;

Stands before him

ANT.   (*Starting up*) Art thou Ventidius?

VENT.   Are you Antony?
I'm liker what I was than you to him
I left you last.

ANT.   I'm angry.

VENT.   So am I.

ANT.   I would be private; leave me.

VENT.   Sir, I love you,
And therefore will not leave you.

ANT.   Will not leave me?
Where have you learnt that answer? Who am I?

VENT.   My emperor, the man I love next heaven.
If I said more, I think 'twere scarce a sin;
You're all that's good and god-like.

ANT.   All that's wretched.
You will not leave me then?

VENT.   'Twas too presuming
To say I would not; but I dare not leave you,
And 'tis unkind in you to chide me hence
So soon, when I so far have come to see you.

ANT.   Now thou hast seen me, art thou satisfied?
For, if a friend, thou hast beheld enough,
And, if a foe, too much.

VENT.   Look, emperor, this is no common dew.   *Weeping*
I have not wept this forty year, but now
My mother comes afresh into my eyes;
I cannot help her softness.

ANT.   By heav'n, he weeps! Poor good old man, he weeps!
The big round drops course one another down
The furrows of his cheeks. — Stop them, Ventidius,
Or I shall blush to death; they set my shame,
That caus'd them, full before me.

VENT.   I'll do my best.

ANT.   Sure there's contagion in the tears of friends.
See, I have caught it too. Believe me, 'tis not
For my own griefs, but thine. — Nay, father!

VENT.   Emperor.

ANT.   Emperor! Why, that's the style of victory;
The conqu'ring soldier, red with unfelt wounds,
Salutes his general so; but never more
Shall that sound reach my ears.

VENT.   I warrant you —

ANT.   Actium, Actium! Oh! —

VENT.   It sits too near you.

ANT.   Here, here it lies, a lump of lead by day,
And, in my short, distracted nightly slumbers,
The hag that rides my dreams.

VENT.   Out with it; give it vent.

ANT.   Urge not my shame.
I lost a battle, —

VENT.   So has Julius done.

ANT.   Thou favour'st me, and speak'st not half thou think'st;
For Julius fought it out, and lost it fairly,
But Antony —

VENT.   Nay, stop not.

ANT.   Antony, —
Well, thou wilt have it — like a coward, fled,
Fled while his soldiers fought; fled first, Ventidius.
Thou long'st to curse me, and I give thee leave.
I know thou cam'st prepar'd to rail.

VENT.   I did.

ANT.   I'll help thee. — I have been a man, Ventidius.

VENT.   Yes, and a brave one, but —

ANT.   I know thy meaning.
But I have lost my reason, have disgrac'd
The name of soldier with inglorious ease.
In the full vintage of my flowing honours,
Sat still, and saw it press'd by other hands.
Fortune came smiling to my youth and woo'd it,
And purple greatness met my ripen'd years.
When first I came to empire, I was borne
On tides of people crowding to my triumphs;
The wish of nations and the willing world
Receiv'd me as its pledge of future peace;
I was so great, so happy, so belov'd,

Fate could not ruin me till I took pains
And work'd against my fortune, chid her from me,
And turn'd her loose; yet still she came again.
My careless days and my luxurious nights
At length have wearied her, and now she's gone,
Gone, gone, divorc'd forever. Help me, soldier,
To curse this madman, this industrious fool,
Who labour'd to be wretched. Prithee, curse me.

VENT.   No.

ANT.   Why?

VENT.   You are too sensible already
Of what you've done, too conscious of your failings;
And, like a scorpion, whipp'd by others first
To fury, sting yourself in mad revenge.
I would bring balm and pour it in your wounds,
Cure your distemper'd mind, and heal your fortunes.

ANT.   I know thou would'st.

VENT.   I will.

ANT.   Ha, ha, ha, ha!

VENT.   You laugh.

ANT.   I do, to see officious[11] love
Give cordials to the dead.

VENT.   You would be lost then?

ANT.   I am.

VENT.   I say you are not. Try your fortune.

ANT.   I have, to th'utmost. Dost thou think me desperate
Without just cause? No, when I found all lost
Beyond repair, I hid me from the world,
And learnt to scorn it here; which now I do
So heartily I think it is not worth
The cost of keeping.

VENT.   Caesar thinks not so;
He'll thank you for the gift he could not take.
You would be kill'd like Tully,[12] would you? Do,
Hold out your throat to Caesar, and die tamely.

ANT.   No, I can kill myself, and so resolve.

VENT.   I can die with you too, when time shall serve;
But fortune calls upon us now to live,
To fight, to conquer.

---

[11] *officious* zealous.

[12] *Tully* Marcus Tullius Cicero, 106–43 BC, orator, writer, administrator, supporter of Octavius; when ordered to be executed by Antony, Tully invited pursuing soldiers to behead him.

ANT.   Sure thou dream'st, Ventidius.
VENT.   No, 'tis you dream; you sleep away your hours
   In desperate sloth, miscall'd philosophy.
   Up, up, for honour's sake; twelve legions wait you,
   And long to call you chief. By painful journeys
   I led 'em, patient both of heat and hunger,
   Down from the Parthian marches to the Nile.
   'Twill do you good to see their sunburnt faces,
   Their scarr'd cheeks, and chopp'd[13] hands. There's virtue in 'em;[14]
   They'll sell those mangled limbs at dearer rates
   Than yon trim bands can buy.
ANT.   Where left you them?
VENT.   I said in Lower Syria.
ANT.   Bring 'em hither;
   There may be life in these.
VENT.   They will not come.
ANT.   Why didst thou mock my hopes with promis'd aids,
   To double my despair? They're mutinous.
VENT.   Most firm and loyal.
ANT.   Yet they will not march
   To succour me. O trifler!
VENT.   They petition
   You would make haste to head 'em.
ANT.   I'm besieg'd.
VENT.   There's but one way shut up. How came I hither?
ANT.   I will not stir.
VENT.   They would perhaps desire
   A better reason.
ANT.   I have never us'd[15]
   My soldiers to demand a reason of
   My actions. Why did they refuse to march?
VENT.   They said they would not fight for Cleopatra.
ANT.   What was't they said?
VENT.   They said they would not fight for Cleopatra.
   Why should they fight indeed, to make her conquer,
   And make you more a slave, to gain you kingdoms
   Which, for a kiss at your next midnight feast,
   You'll sell to her? Then she new-names her jewels,
   And calls this diamond such or such a tax;
   Each pendant in her ear shall be a province.
ANT.   Ventidius, I allow your tongue free licence

[13]*chopp'd* chapped.
[14]*'em* these soldiers.   [15]*us'd* been accustomed to have.

On all my others faults, but, on your life,
No word of Cleopatra; she deserves
More worlds than I can lose.

VENT.   Behold, you pow'rs,
To whom you have entrusted humankind,
See Europe, Afric, Asia, put in balance,
And all weigh'd down by one light, worthless woman!
I think the gods are Antonies and give,
Like prodigals, this nether world away
To none but wasteful hands.

ANT.   You grow presumptuous.

VENT.   I take the privilege of plain love to speak.

ANT.   Plain love! Plain arrogance, plain insolence!
Thy men are cowards, thou an envious traitor
Who, under seeming honesty, hast vented
The burden of thy rank, o'erflowing gall.
Oh that thou wert my equal, great in arms
As the first Caesar was, that I might kill thee
Without a stain to honour!

VENT.   You may kill me;
You have done more already: call'd me traitor.

ANT.   Art thou not one?

VENT.   For showing you yourself,
Which none else durst have done? But had I been
That name, which I disdain to speak again,
I needed not have sought your abject fortunes,
Come to partake your fate, to die with you.
What hindered me t'have led my conqu'ring eagles
To fill Octavius' bands? I could have been
A traitor then, a glorious, happy traitor,
And not have been so call'd.

ANT.   Forgive me, soldier;
I've been too passionate.

VENT.   You thought me false,
Thought my old age betray'd you. Kill me, sir;
Pray, kill me. Yet you need not; your unkindness
Has left your sword no work.

ANT.   I did not think so;
I said it in my rage. Prithee, forgive me.
Why didst thou tempt my anger, by discovery[16]
Of what I would not hear?

---

[16]*discovery* revelation.

VENT.   No prince but you
  Could merit that sincerity I us'd,
  Nor durst another man have ventur'd it;
  But you, ere love misled your wand'ring eyes,
  Were sure the chief and best of human race,
  Fram'd in the very pride and boast of nature,
  So perfect that the gods who form'd you wonder'd
  At their own skill, and cried – 'A lucky hit
  Has mended our design'. Their envy hind'red,
  Else you had been immortal and a pattern,
  When heav'n would work for ostentation's sake,
  To copy out again.

ANT.   But Cleopatra –
  Go on, for I can bear it now.

VENT.   No more.

ANT.   Thou dar'st not trust my passion, but thou may'st;
  Thou only lov'st, the rest have flatter'd me.

VENT.   Heav'n's blessing on your heart for that kind word!
  May I believe you love me? Speak again.

ANT.   Indeed I do. Speak this, and this, and this.   *Hugging him*
  Thy praises were unjust, but I'll deserve 'em,
  And yet mend all. Do with me what thou wilt;
  Lead me to victory! Thou know'st the way.

VENT.   And will you leave this –

ANT.   Prithee, do not curse her,
  And I will leave her; though, heav'n knows, I love
  Beyond life, conquest, empire, all but honour;
  But I will leave her.

VENT.   That's my royal master!
  And shall we fight?

ANT.   I warrant thee, old soldier.
  Thou shalt behold me once again in iron,
  And, at the head of our old troops that beat
  The Parthians, cry aloud, 'Come, follow me'!

VENT.   Oh, now I hear my emperor! In that word
  Octavius fell. Gods, let me see that day,
  And, if I have ten years behind, take all;
  I'll thank you for th'exchange.

ANT.   O Cleopatra!

VENT. Again?

ANT.   I've done. In that last sigh she went.
  Caesar shall know what 'tis to force a lover
  From all he holds most dear.

VENT.   Methinks you breathe
  Another soul, your looks are more divine.
  You speak a hero, and you move a god.
ANT.   Oh, thou hast fir'd me; my soul's up in arms
  And mans each part about me. Once again
  That noble eagerness of fight has seiz'd me,
  That eagerness with which I darted upward
  To Cassius'[17] camp. In vain the steepy hill
  Oppos'd my way; in vain a war of spears
  Sung round my head, and planted[18] all my shield;
  I won the trenches while my foremost men
  Lagg'd on the plain below.
VENT.   Ye gods, ye gods,
  For such another hour!
ANT.   Come on, my soldier,
  Our hearts and arms are still the same. I long
  Once more to meet our foes, that thou and I,
  Like Time and Death, marching before our troops,
  May taste fate to 'em; mow 'em out a passage,
    And, ent'ring where the foremost squadrons yield,
    Begin the noble harvest of the field.   *Exeunt*

[17]*Cassius* Antony and Cleopatra defeated Cassius and Brutus at Philippi in 42 BC.
[18]*planted* hid.

Act Two

[SCENE ONE]

[CLEOPATRA'S *palace*]

Enter CLEOPATRA, IRAS *and* ALEXAS

CLEO.   What shall I do, or whither shall I turn?
    Ventidius has o'ercome, and he will go.

ALEX.   He goes to fight for you.

CLEO.   Then he would see me ere he went to fight.
    Flatter me not; if once he goes, he's lost,
    And all my hopes destroy'd.

ALEX.   Does this weak passion
    Become a mighty queen?

CLEO.   I am no queen.
    Is this to be a queen, to be besieg'd
    By yon insulting Roman, and to wait
    Each hour the victor's chain? These ills are small;
    For Antony is lost, and I can mourn
    For nothing else but him. Now come, Octavius,
    I have no more to lose. Prepare thy bands;
    I'm fit to be a captive. Antony
    Has taught my mind the fortune of a slave.

IRAS.   Call reason to assist you.

CLEO.   I have none,
    And none would have. My love's a noble madness,
    Which shows the cause deserv'd it. Moderate sorrow
    Fits vulgar love, and for a vulgar man;
    But I have lov'd with such transcendent passion
    I soar'd at first quite out of reason's view,
    And now am lost above it. No, I'm proud
    'Tis thus. Would Antony could see me now
    Think you he would not sigh, though he must leave me?
    Sure he would sigh, for he is noble-natur'd
    And bears a tender heart; I know him well.
    Ah, no, I know him not; I knew him once,
    But now 'tis past.

IRAS.   Let it be past with you;

Forget him, madam.

CLEO. Never, never, Iras.
He once was mine; and once, though now 'tis gone,
Leaves a faint image of possession still.

ALEX. Think him inconstant, cruel, and ungrateful.

CLEO. I cannot. If I could, those thoughts were vain.
Faithless, ungrateful, cruel though he be,
I still must love him.

Enter CHARMION

Now, what news, my Charmion?
Will he be kind and will he not forsake me?
Am I to live or die? Nay, do I live
Or am I dead? For when he gave his answer,
Fate took the word, and then I liv'd or died.

CHAR. I found him, madam, –

CLEO. A long speech preparing?
If thou bring'st comfort, haste and give it me,
For never was more need.

IRAS. I know he loves you.

CLEO. Had he been kind, her eyes had told me so,
Before her tongue could speak it. Now she studies
To soften what he said; but give me death,
Just as he sent it, Charmion, undisguis'd,
And in the words he spoke.

CHAR. I found him, then,
Encompass'd round, I think, with iron statues,
So mute, so motionless his soldiers stood,
While awfully he cast his eyes about,
And ev'ry leader's hopes or fears survey'd;
Methought he look'd resolv'd, and yet not pleas'd.
When he beheld me struggling in the crowd.
He blush'd and bade, 'Make way'.

ALEX. There's comfort yet.

CHAR. Ventidius fix'd his eyes upon my passage
Severely, as he meant to frown me back,
And sullenly gave place. I told my message
Just as you gave it, broken and disorder'd;
I number'd in it all your sighs and tears,
And while I mov'd your pitiful request,
That you but only begg'd a last farewell,
He fetch'd an inward groan, and ev'ry time
I nam'd you, sigh'd as if his heart were breaking,
But shunn'd my eyes and guiltily look'd down.

He seem'd not now that awful Antony
Who shook an arm'd assembly with his nod,
But, making show as he would rub his eyes,
Disguis'd and blotted out a falling tear.

CLEO. Did he then weep? And was I worth a tear?
If what thou hast to say be not as pleasing,
Tell me no more, but let me die contented.

CHAR. He bid me say he knew himself so well
He could deny you nothing if he saw you,
And therefore –

CLEO. Thou wouldst say, he would not see me?

CHAR. And therefore begg'd you not to use a power
Which he could ill resist; yet he should ever
Respect you as he ought.

CLEO. Is that a word
For Antony to use to Cleopatra?
Oh, that faint word, 'respect'! How I disdain it!
Disdain myself for loving after it!
He should have kept that word for cold Octavia.
'Respect' is for a wife; am I that thing,
That dull, insipid lump, without desires,
And without pow'r to give them?

ALEX. You misjudge;
You see through love, and that deludes your sight;
As what is straight seems crooked through the water.
But I who bear my reason undisturb'd
Can see this Antony, this dreaded man,
A fearful slave who fain would run away
And shuns his master's eyes. If you pursue him,
My life on't, he still drags a chain along
That needs must clog his flight.

CLEO. Could I believe thee!

ALEX. By ev'ry circumstance I know he loves.
True, he's hard press'd, by int'rest and by honour;
Yet he but doubts and parleys and casts out
Many a long look for succour.

CLEO. He sends word
He fears to see my face.

ALEX. And would you more?
He shows his weakness who declines the combat,
And you must urge your fortune. Could he speak
More plainly? To my ears, the message sounds:
'Come to my rescue, Cleopatra, come;

Come, free me from Ventidius, from my tyrant;
See me, and give me a pretence to leave him'!
I hear his trumpets. This way he must pass.
Please you, retire a while; I'll work him first,
That he may bend more easy.

CLEO.   You shall rule me;
But all, I fear, in vain.   *Exit with* CHARMION *and* IRAS

ALEX.   I fear so too,
Though I conceal'd my thoughts to make her bold;
But 'tis our utmost means, and fate befriend it!   *Withdraws*
    Enter lictors with fasces,[1] *one bearing the eagle; then enter*
        ANTONY *with* VENTIDIUS, *followed by other commanders*

ANT.   Octavius is the minion of blind chance,
But holds from virtue nothing.

VENT.   Has he courage?

ANT.   But just enough to season him from coward.
Oh, 'tis the coldest youth upon a charge,
The most deliberate fighter! If he ventures
(As in Illyria once they say he did,
To storm a town), 'tis when he cannot choose,
When all the world have fix'd their eyes upon him;
And then he lives on that for seven years after;
But at a close revenge he never fails.

VENT.   I heard you challenged him.

ANT.   I did, Ventidius.
What think'st thou was his answer? 'Twas so tame! –
He said he had more ways than one to die;
I had not.

VENT.   Poor!

ANT.   He has more ways than one,
But he would choose them all before that one.

VENT.   He first would choose an ague or a fever.

ANT.   No, it must be an ague, not a fever;
He has not warmth enough to die by that.

VENT.   Or old age and a bed.

ANT.   Ay, there's his choice;
He would live, like a lamp, to the last wink,
And crawl upon the utmost verge of life.
O Hercules, why should a man like this,
Who dares not trust his fate for one great action,

---

[1] *lictors with fasces* attendants carrying symbols of authority, bound bundles of
rods, each bundle including an axe.

Be all the care of heav'n? Why should he lord it
O'er fourscore thousand men, of whom each one
Is braver than himself?
VENT.   You conquer'd for him.
Philippi knows it; there you shar'd with him
That empire which your sword made all your own.
ANT.   Fool that I was, upon my eagle's wings
I bore this wren,² till I was tired with soaring,
And now he mounts above me.
Good heav'ns, is this, is this the man who braves³ me,
Who bids my age make way, drives me before him
To the world's ridge, and sweeps me off like rubbish?
VENT.   Sir, we lose time; the troops are mounted all.
ANT.   Then give the word to march.
I long to leave this prison of a town,
To join thy legions, and in open field
Once more to show my face. Lead, my deliverer.
    Enter ALEXAS
ALEX.   Great emperor,
In mighty arms renown'd above mankind,
But, in soft pity to th'oppress'd, a god;
This message sends the mournful Cleopatra
To her departing lord.
VENT.   Smooth sycophant!
ALEX.   A thousand wishes and ten thousand prayers,
Millions of blessings wait you to the wars;
Millions of sighs and tears she sends you too,
And would have sent
As many dear embraces to your arms,
As many parting kisses to your lips;
But those, she fears, have wearied you already.
VENT.   (*Aside*) False crocodile!
ALEX.   And yet she begs not now you would not leave her;
That were a wish too mighty for her hopes,
Too presuming
For her low fortune and your ebbing love;
That were a wish for her more prosp'rous days,
Her blooming beauty and your growing kindness.
ANT.   [*Aside*] Well, I must man it out. – What would the queen?

---

²*wren* an allusion to the medieval tale of a flying competition amongst birds; a wren hid in the feathers of an eagle, enabling the tiny bird to fly slightly higher than other birds.
³*braves* defies.

ALEX.   First, to these noble warriors who attend
    Your daring courage in the chase of fame,
    Too daring, and too dang'rous for her quiet,
    She humbly recommends all she holds dear,
    All her own cares and fears, the care of you.
VENT.   Yes, witness Actium.
ANT.   Let him speak, Ventidius.
ALEX.   You, when his matchless valour bears him forward,
    With ardour too heroic, on his foes,
    Fall down, as she would do, before his feet;
    Lie in his way, and stop the paths of death.
    Tell him this god is not invulnerable,
    That absent Cleopatra bleeds in him;
    And, that you may remember her petition,
    She begs you wear these trifles as a pawn
    Which, at your wish'd return, she will redeem
                        Gives jewels to the commanders
    With all the wealth of Egypt.
    This to the great Ventidius she presents,
    Whom she can never count her enemy,
    Because he loves her lord.
VENT.   Tell her I'll none on't;
    I'm not asham'd of honest poverty;
    Not all the diamonds of the East can bribe
    Ventidius from his faith. I hope to see
    These and the rest of all her sparkling store
    Where they shall more deservingly be plac'd.
ANT.   And who must wear 'em then?
VENT.   The wrong'd Octavia.
ANT.   You might have spar'd that word.
VENT.   And he that bribe.
ANT.   But have I no remembrance?
ALEX.   Yes, a dear one;
    Your slave the queen —
ANT.   My mistress.
ALEX.   Then your mistress;
    Your mistress would, she says, have sent her soul,
    But that you had long since; she humbly begs
    This ruby bracelet, set with bleeding hearts,
    The emblems of her own, may bind your arm. *Presenting a bracelet*
VENT.   Now, my best lord, in honour's name I ask you,
    For manhood's sake and for your own dear safety,
    Touch not these poison'd gifts,
    Infected by the sender. Touch 'em not;

Myriads of bluest plagues lie underneath 'em,
And more than aconite⁴ has dipp'd the silk.
ANT. Nay, now you grow too cynical, Ventidius;
A lady's favours may be worn with honour.
What, to refuse her bracelet! On my soul,
When I lie pensive in my tent alone,
'Twill pass the wakeful hours of winter nights,
To tell these pretty beads upon my arm,
To count for every one a soft embrace,
A melting kiss at such and such a time:
And now and then the fury of her love,
When – And what harm's in this?
ALEX.   None, none, my lord,
But what's to her, that now 'tis past forever.
ANT. (*Going to tie it*) We soldiers are so awkward – Help me tie it.
ALEX. In faith, my lord, we courtiers too are awkward
In these affairs; so are all men indeed,
Even I, who am not one. But shall I speak?
ANT. Yes, freely.
ALEX.   Then, my lord, fair hands alone
Are fit to tie it; she who sent it can.
VENT. Hell, death! This eunuch pander ruins you.
You will not see her?

                    ALEXAS *whispers [to] an attendant, who goes out*
ANT.   But to take my leave.
VENT. Then I have wash'd an Aethiop.⁵ You're undone;
You're in the toils; you're taken; you're destroy'd.
Her eyes do Caesar's work.
ANT.   You fear too soon.
I'm constant to myself. I know my strength;
And yet she shall not think me barbarous neither,
Born in the depths of Afric. I am a Roman,
Bred to the rules of soft humanity.
A guest, and kindly us'd, should bid farewell.
VENT. You do not know
How weak you are to her, how much an infant.
You are not proof against a smile or glance;
A sigh will quite disarm you.
ANT.   See, she comes!
Now you shall find your error. – Gods, I thank you;

---

⁴*aconite* a poison derived from monkshood or wolfsbane.
⁵*wash'd an Aethiop* laboured in vain.

I form'd the danger greater than it was,
And now 'tis near, 'tis lessen'd.

VENT.   Mark the end yet.

Enter CLEOPATRA, CHARMION, *and* IRAS

ANT.   Well, madam, we are met.

CLEO.   Is this a meeting?
Then, we must part?

ANT.   We must.

CLEO.   Who says we must?

ANT.   Our own hard fates.

CLEO.   We make those fates ourselves.

ANT.   Yes, we have made 'em; we have lov'd each other
Into our mutual ruin.

CLEO.   The gods have seen my joys with envious eyes;
I have no friends in heav'n, and all the world,
As 'twere the bus'ness of mankind to part us,
Is arm'd against my love; ev'n you yourself
Join with the rest; you, you are arm'd against me.

ANT.   I will be justified in all I do
To late posterity, and therefore hear me.
If I mix a lie
With any truth, reproach me freely with it;
Else favour me with silence.

CLEO.   You command me,
And I am dumb.

VENT.   I like this well; he shows authority.

ANT.   That I derive my ruin
From you alone —

CLEO.   O heav'ns, I ruin you!

ANT.   You promis'd me your silence, and you break it
Ere I have scarce begun.

CLEO.   Well, I obey you.

ANT.   When I beheld you first, it was in Egypt,
Ere Caesar saw your eyes; you gave me love,
And were too young to know it. That I settl'd
Your father in his throne was for your sake;
I left th'acknowledgment for time to ripen.
Caesar stepp'd in, and with a greedy hand
Pluck'd the green fruit, ere the first blush of red,
Yet cleaving to the bough. He was my lord,
And was, beside, too great for me to rival;
But I deserv'd you first, though he enjoy'd you.
When, after, I beheld you in Cilicia,
An enemy to Rome, I pardon'd you.

CLEO. I cleared myself –
ANT.   Again you break your promise.
  I lov'd you still, and took your weak excuses,
  Took you into my bosom, stain'd by Caesar,
  And not half mine. I went to Egypt with you
  And hid me from the bus'ness of the world,
  Shut out inquiring nations from my sight,
  To give whole years to you.
VENT. (*Aside*) Yes, to your shame be't spoken.
ANT.   How I lov'd
  Witness ye days and nights, and all your hours
  That danc'd away with down upon your feet,
  As all your bus'ness were to count my passion!
  One day pass'd by, and nothing saw but love;
  Another came, and still 'twas only love.
  The suns were wearied out with looking on,
  And I untir'd with loving.
  I saw you ev'ry day, and all the day,
  And ev'ry day was still but as the first,
  So eager was I still to see you more.
VENT. 'Tis all too true.
ANT.   Fulvia, my wife, grew jealous,
  As she indeed had reason, rais'd a war
  In Italy, to call me back.
VENT.   But yet
  You went not.
ANT.   While within your arms I lay,
  The world fell mould'ring from my hands each hour,
  And left me scarce a grasp – I thank your love for't.
VENT. Well push'd; that last was home.
CLEO.   Yet may I speak?
ANT. If I have urg'd a falsehood, yes; else, not.
  Your silence says I have not. Fulvia died
  (Pardon, you gods, with my unkindness died);
  To set the world at peace, I took Octavia,
  This Caesar's sister; in her pride of youth,
  And flow'r of beauty, did I wed that lady,
  Whom blushing I must praise, because I left her.
  You call'd; my love obey'd the fatal summons;
  This rais'd the Roman arms; the cause was yours.
  I would have fought by land, where I was stronger;
  You hind'red it; yet, when I fought at sea,
  Forsook me fighting; and (O stain to honour!
  O lasting shame!) I knew not that I fled,

But fled to follow you.

VENT.   What haste she made to hoist her purple sails!
And, to appear magnificent in flight,
Drew half our strength away.

ANT.   All this you caus'd,
And would you multiply more ruins on me?
This honest man, my best, my only friend,
Has gather'd up the shipwreck of my fortunes.
Twelve legions I have left, my last recruits,
And you have watch'd the news, and bring your eyes
To seize them too. If you have aught to answer,
Now speak, you have free leave.

ALEX.   (*Aside*)   She stands confounded;
Despair is in her eyes.

VENT.   Now lay a sigh i'the way to stop his passage.
Prepare a tear, and bid it for his legions;
'Tis like they shall be sold.

CLEO.   How shall I plead my cause, when you, my judge,
Already have condemn'd me? Shall I bring
The love you bore me for my advocate?
That now is turn'd against me, that destroys me;
For love, once past, is, at the best, forgotten;
But oft'ner sours to hate. 'Twill please my lord
To ruin me, and therefore I'll be guilty.
But could I once have thought it would have pleas'd you,
That you would pry, with narrow searching eyes,
Into my faults, severe to my destruction,
And watching all advantages with care,
That serve to make me wretched? Speak, my lord,
For I end here. Though I deserv'd this usage,
Was it like you to give it?

ANT.   Oh, you wrong me
To think I sought this parting or desir'd
To accuse you more than what will clear myself
And justify this breach.

CLEO.   Thus low I thank you,
And, since my innocence will not offend,
I shall not blush to own it.

VENT. [*Aside*]   After this,
I think she'll blush at nothing.

CLEO.   You seem griev'd
(And therein you are kind) that Caesar first
Enjoy'd my love, though you deserv'd it better;
I grieve for that, my lord, much more than you,

For, had I first been yours, it would have sav'd
My second choice: I never had been his,
And ne'er had been but yours. But Caesar first,
You say, possess'd my love. Not so, my lord;
He first possess'd my person, you, my love;
Caesar lov'd me, but I lov'd Antony.
If I endur'd him after, 'twas because
I judg'd it due to the first name of men,
And, half constrain'd, I gave, as to a tyrant,
What he would take by force.

VENT.   O siren, siren!
Yet grant that all the love she boasts were true,
Has she not ruin'd you? I still urge that,
The fatal consequence.

CLEO.   The consequence indeed,
For I dare challenge him, my greatest foe,
To say it was design'd. 'Tis true, I lov'd you,
And kept you far from an uneasy wife, –
Such Fulvia was.
Yes, but he'll say you left Octavia for me;
And can you blame me to receive that love
Which quitted such desert, for worthless me?
How often have I wish'd some other Caesar,
Great as the first,[6] and as the second young,[7]
Would court my love, to be refus'd for you!

VENT. Words, words; but Actium, sir, remember Actium.

CLEO. Ev'n there, I dare his malice. True, I counsell'd
To fight at sea, but I betray'd you not.
I fled, but not to the enemy. 'Twas fear.
Would I had been a man, not to have fear'd!
For none would then have envied me your friendship,
Who envy me your love.

ANT.   We're both unhappy.
If nothing else, yet our ill fortune parts us.
Speak. Would you have me perish by my stay?

CLEO. If, as a friend, you ask my judgment, go;
If, as a lover, stay. If you must perish –
'Tis a hard word; but stay.

VENT. See now th'effects of her so boasted love!
She strives to drag you down to ruin with her;

---

[6]*the first* Gaius Julius Caesar, *c.* 100–44 BC.
[7]*the second young* Gaius Julius Caesar Octavianus (Emperor Augustus),
63 BC–AD 14, grand-nephew of Julius Caesar.

But could she 'scape without you, oh, how soon
Would she let go her hold, and haste to shore,
And never look behind!

CLEO.   Then judge my love by this.   *Giving* ANTONY *a writing*
                                   Could I have borne
A life or death, a happiness or woe
From yours divided, this had giv'n me means.

ANT.   By Hercules, the writing of Octavius!
I know it well: 'tis that proscribing hand,[8]
Young as it was, that led the way to mine,
And left me but the second place in murder.
See, see, Ventidius! Here he offers Egypt
And joins all Syria to it as a present,
So, in requital, she forsake my fortunes
And join her arms with his.

CLEO.   And yet you leave me!
You leave me, Antony, and yet I love you,
Indeed I do. I have refus'd a kingdom;
That is a trifle,
For I could part with life, with anything,
But only you. Oh, let me die but with you!
Is that a hard request?

ANT.   Next living with you,
'Tis all that heav'n can give.

ALEX.   (*Aside*)   He melts; we conquer.

CLEO.   No, you shall go; your int'rest calls you hence.
Yes, your dear int'rest pulls too strong for these
Weak arms to hold you here.   *Takes his hand*
                        Go; leave me, soldier
(For you're no more a lover), leave me dying;
Push me, all pale and panting, from your bosom,
And, when your march begins, let one run after,
Breathless almost for joy, and cry, 'She's dead'.
The soldiers shout; you then perhaps may sigh
And muster all your Roman gravity.
Ventidius chides, and straight your brow clears up,
As I had never been.

ANT.   Gods, 'tis too much,
Too much for man to bear.

CLEO.   What is't for me then,

---

[8]*proscribing hand* Octavius Caesar, Lepidus, and Antony drew up a list of
political enemies, many of whom were executed after the assassination of Julius
Caesar, 44 BC.

A weak, forsaken woman, and a lover?
Here let me breathe my last. Envy me not
This minute in your arms; I'll die apace,
As fast as e'er I can and end your trouble.
ANT. Die! Rather let me perish. Loos'ned nature
Leap from its hinges, sink the props of heav'n,
And fall the skies, to crush the nether world!
My eyes, my soul, my all!   *Embraces her*
VENT.   And what's this toy,
In balance with your fortune, honour, fame?
ANT. What is't, Ventidius? — It outweighs 'em all.
Why, we have more than conquer'd Caesar now;
My queen's not only innocent, but loves me.
This, this is she who drags me down to ruin!
'But, could she 'scape without me, with what haste
Would she let slip her hold and make to shore,
And never look behind'!
Down on thy knees, blasphemer as thou art,
And ask forgiveness of wrong'd innocence.
VENT. I'll rather die than take it. Will you go?
ANT. Go! Whither? Go from all that's excellent?
Faith, honour, virtue, all good things forbid
That I should go from her who sets my love
Above the price of kingdoms! Give, you gods,
Give to your boy, your Caesar,
This rattle of a globe to play withal,
This gewgaw world, and put him cheaply off;
I'll not be pleas'd with less than Cleopatra.
CLEO. She's wholly yours. My heart's so full of joy
That I shall do some wild extravagance
Of love in public, and the foolish world,
Which knows not tenderness, will think me mad.
VENT. O women, women, women! All the gods
Have not such pow'r of doing good to man,
As you of doing harm.   *Exit*
ANT.   Our men are arm'd.
Unbar the gate that looks to Caesar's camp;
I would revenge the treachery he meant me,
And long security makes conquest easy.
I'm eager to return before I go,
For all the pleasures I have known beat thick
On my remembrance. How I long for night,
   That both the sweets of mutual love may try,
   And triumph once o'er Caesar ere we die!   *Exeunt*

Act Three

[SCENE ONE]

[CLEOPATRA'S *throne room*]

At one door enter CLEOPATRA, CHARMION, IRAS, *and* ALEXAS, *a train of Egyptians, at the other* ANTONY *and Romans. The entrance on both sides is prepared by music, the trumpets first sounding on* ANTONY'S *part, then answered by timbrels, etc., on* CLEOPATRA'S. CHARMION *and* IRAS *hold a laurel wreath betwixt them. A dance of Egyptians. After the ceremony,* CLEOPATRA *crowns* ANTONY

ANT.   I thought how those white arms would fold me in,
And strain me close, and melt me into love;
So pleas'd with that sweet image, I sprung forwards,
And added all my strength to every blow.

CLEO.   Come to me, come, my soldier, to my arms!
You've been too long away from my embraces;
But when I have you fast and all my own,
With broken murmurs and with amorous sighs,
I'll say you were unkind and punish you,
And mark you red with many an eager kiss.

ANT.   My brighter Venus!

CLEO.   O my greater Mars!

ANT.   Thou join'st us well, my love!
Suppose me come from the Phlegraean plains,[1]
Where gasping giants lay, cleft by my sword,
And mountain tops par'd[2] off each other blow,
To bury those I slew. Receive me, goddess!
Let Caesar spread his subtle nets, like Vulcan[3]
In thy embraces I would be beheld
By heav'n and earth at once,
And make their envy what they meant their sport.

---

[1] *Phlegraean plains* in Macedonia, where Hercules and other gods overwhelmed the Gigantes.
[2] *par'd* sliced off in alternate blows.
[3] *Vulcan* This Ròman deity spread a net over the bed of his wife Venus and Mars, to capture them in adultery.

Let those who took us, blush; I would love on
With awful state, regardless of their frowns,
As their superior god.
There's no satiety of love in thee:
Enjoy'd, thou still art new; perpetual spring
Is in thy arms; the ripen'd fruit but falls,
And blossoms rise to fill its empty place,
And I grow rich by giving.

 Enter VENTIDIUS *and stands apart*

ALEX. Oh, now the danger's past, your general comes!
He joins not in your joys nor minds your triumphs;
But with contracted brows looks frowning on,
As envying your success.

ANT. Now, on my soul, he loves me, truly loves me;
He never flatter'd me in any vice,
But awes me with his virtue; ev'n this minute,
Methinks, he has a right of chiding me.
Lead to the temple. I'll avoid his presence;
It checks too strong upon me.   *Exeunt the rest*

   As ANTONY *is going*, VENTIDIUS *pulls him by the robe*

VENT.   Emperor!

ANT. (*Looking back*) 'Tis the old argument: I prithee, spare me.

VENT. But this one hearing, emperor.

ANT.   Let go
My robe, or, by my father Hercules, —

VENT. By Hercules his father,[4] that's yet greater,
I bring you somewhat you would wish to know.

ANT. Thou see'st we are observ'd; attend me here,
And I'll return.   *Exit*

VENT. I am waning in his favour, yet I love him;
I love this man who runs to meet his ruin.
And sure the gods, like me, are fond of him;
His virtues lie so mingl'd with his crimes,
As would confound their choice to punish one
And not reward the other.

 Enter ANTONY

ANT.   We can conquer,
You see, without your aid.
We have dislodg'd their troops;
They look on us at distance, and, like curs
'Scap'd from the lion's paws, they bay far off,

---

[4] *Hercules his father* Jupiter.

And lick their wounds, and faintly threaten war.
Five thousand Romans, with their faces upward,
Lie breathless on the plain.
VENT.   'Tis well; and he
Who lost 'em could have spar'd ten thousand more.
Yet if, by this advantage, you could gain
An easier peace, while Caesar doubts the chance
Of arms –
ANT.   Oh, think not on't, Ventidius!
The boy[5] pursues my ruin, he'll no peace;
His malice is considerate in advantage.
Oh, he's the coolest murderer! So staunch,
He kills and keeps his temper.
VENT.   Have you no friend
In all his army, who has power to move him?
Maecenas or Agrippa might do much.
ANT.   They're both too deep in Caesar's interests.
We'll work it out by dint of sword, or perish.
VENT.   Fain I would find some other.
ANT.   Thank thy love.[6]
Some four or five such victories as this
Will save thy further pains.
VENT.   Expect no more; Caesar is on his guard.
I know, sir, you have conquer'd against odds;
But still you draw supplies from one poor town,
And of Egyptians; he has all the world,
And at his back nations come pouring in
To fill the gaps you make. Pray, think again.
ANT.   Why dost thou drive me from myself, to search
For foreign aids? To hunt my memory
And range all o'er a waste and barren place,
To find a friend? The wretched have no friends.
Yet I had one, the bravest youth of Rome,
Whom Caesar loves beyond the love of women;
He could resolve his mind as fire does wax,
From that hard, rugged image melt him down,
And mould him in what softer form he pleas'd.
VENT.   Him would I see, that man of all the world;
Just such a one we want.
ANT.   He lov'd me too;
I was his soul; he liv'd not but in me.

[5]*boy* Octavius Caesar, aged thirty-four, twenty years younger than Antony.
[6]*Thank thy love* i.e. I thank thy love.

We were so clos'd within each other's breasts,
The rivets were not found that joined us first.
That does not reach us yet; we were so mix'd
As meeting streams, both to ourselves were lost;
We were one mass; we could not give or take
But from the same, for he was I, I he.

VENT. (*Aside*) He moves as I would wish him.

ANT.   After this,
I need not tell his name: 'twas Dolabella.

VENT. He's now in Caesar's camp.

ANT.   No matter where,
Since he's no longer mine. He took unkindly
That I forbade him Cleopatra's sight,
Because I fear'd he lov'd her: he confess'd
He had a warmth which, for my sake, he stifl'd;
For 'twere impossible that two, so one,
Should not have lov'd the same. When he departed,
He took no leave, and that confirm'd my thoughts.

VENT. It argues that he lov'd you more than her,
Else he had stay'd; but he perceiv'd you jealous,
And would not grieve his friend. I know he loves you.

ANT. I should have seen him then ere now.

VENT.   Perhaps
He has thus long been lab'ring for your peace.

ANT. Would he were here!

VENT.   Would you believe he lov'd you?
I read your answer in your eyes: you would.
Not to conceal it longer, he has sent
A messenger from Caesar's camp with letters.

ANT. Let him appear.

VENT.   I'll bring him instantly.
      Exit VENTIDIUS, *and re-enters immediately with* DOLABELLA

ANT. 'Tis he himself! Himself, by holy friendship!
                                    Runs to embrace him
Art thou return'd at last, my better half?
Come, give me all myself! Let me not live
If the young bridegroom, longing for his night,
Was ever half so fond.

DOLA.   I must be silent, for my soul is busy
About a nobler work: she's new come home,
Like a long-absent man, and wanders o'er
Each room, a stranger to her own, to look
If all be safe.

ANT.   Thou hast what's left of me;
For I am now so sunk from what I was,
Thou find'st me at my lowest watermark.
The rivers that ran in and rais'd my fortunes
Are all dried up or take another course.
What I have left is from my native spring;
I've still a heart that swells, in scorn of fate,
And lifts me to my banks.

DOLA.   Still you are lord of all the world to me.

ANT.   Why, then I yet am so; for thou art all.
If I had any joy when thou wert absent,
I grudg'd it to myself; methought I robb'd
Thee of thy part. But, O my Dolabella,
Thou hast beheld me other than I am.
Hast thou not seen my morning chambers fill'd
With sceptr'd slaves who waited to salute me?
With eastern monarchs who forgot the sun,
To worship my uprising? Menial kings
Ran coursing up and down my palace-yard,
Stood silent in my presence, watch'd my eyes,
And, at my least command, all started out
Like racers to the goal.

DOLA.   Slaves to your fortune.

ANT.   Fortune is Caesar's now, and what am I?

VENT.   What you have made yourself; I will not flatter.

ANT.   Is this friendly done?

DOLA.   Yes; when his end is so, I must join with him;
Indeed I must, and yet you must not chide;
Why am I else your friend?

ANT.   Take heed, young man.
How thou upbraid'st my love; the queen has eyes;
And thou too hast a soul. Canst thou remember
When, swell'd with hatred, thou beheld'st her first,
As accessory to thy brother's death?[7]

DOLA.   Spare my remembrance; 'twas a guilty day,
And still the blush hangs here.

ANT.   To clear herself,
For sending him no aid, she came from Egypt.
Her galley down the silver Cydnus row'd,
The tackling silk, the streamers wav'd with gold;

---

[7]*thy brother's death* Publius Cornelius Dolabella, *c.* 80–43 BC, besieged by Cassius at Laodicea, is said to have committed suicide in despair. Cleopatra had in fact sent him aid.

The gentle winds were lodg'd in purple sails.
Her nymphs, like Nereids, round her couch were plac'd;
Where she, another sea-born Venus, lay.
DOLA.   No more; I would not hear it.
ANT.   Oh, you must!
She lay, and leant her cheek upon her hand,
And cast a look so languishingly sweet,
As if, secure of all beholders' hearts,
Neglecting, she could take 'em; boys, like Cupids,
Stood fanning, with their painted wings, the winds
That play'd about her face. But if she smil'd,
A darting glory seem'd to blaze abroad,
That men's desiring eyes were never wearied,
But hung upon the object. To soft flutes
The silver oars kept time, and while they play'd,
The hearing gave new pleasure to the sight,
And both to thought. 'Twas heav'n or somewhat more;
For she so charm'd all hearts that gazing crowds
Stood panting on the shore and wanted breath
To give their welcome voice.[8]
Then, Dolabella, where was then thy soul?
Was not thy fury quite disarm'd with wonder?
Didst thou not shrink behind me from those eyes
And whisper in my ear, 'Oh, tell her not
That I accus'd her of my brother's death'?
DOLA.   And should my weakness be a plea for yours?
Mine was an age when love might be excus'd,
When kindly warmth, and when my springing youth
Made it a debt to nature. Yours –
VENT.   Speak boldly.
Yours, he would say, in your declining age,
When no more heat was left but what you forc'd,
When all the sap was needful for the trunk,
When it went down, then you constrain'd the course
And robb'd from nature to supply desire;
In you (I would not use so harsh a word)
'Tis but plain dotage.
ANT.   Ha!
DOLA.   'Twas urg'd too home.
But yet the loss was private that I made;
'Twas but myself I lost. I lost no legions;
I had no world to lose, no people's love.

---

[8]*voice* Compare Shakespeare, *Antony and Cleopatra* (1607), II, ii, 192–223.

ANT.   This from a friend?
DOLA.   Yes, Antony, a true one,
A friend so tender that each word I speak
Stabs my own heart before it reach your ear.
Oh, judge me not less kind, because I chide!
To Caesar I excuse you.
ANT.   O ye gods!
Have I then liv'd to be excus'd to Caesar?
DOLA.   As to your equal.
ANT.   Well, he's but my equal;
While I wear this⁹ he never shall be more.
DOLA.   I bring conditions from him.
ANT.   Are they noble?
Methinks thou shouldst not bring 'em else; yet he
Is full of deep dissembling, knows no honour
Divided from his int'rest. Fate mistook him;
For nature meant him for an usurer:
He's fit indeed to buy, not conquer kingdoms.
VENT.   Then, granting this,
What pow'r was theirs, who wrought so hard a temper
To honourable terms?
ANT.   It was my Dolabella or some god.
DOLA.   Nor I, nor yet Maecenas nor Agrippa;
They were your enemies; and I, a friend,
Too weak alone; yet 'twas a Roman's deed.
ANT.   'Twas like a Roman done. Show me that man
Who has preserv'd my life, my love, my honour;
Let me but see his face.
VENT.   That task is mine,
And, heav'n, thou know'st how pleasing.   *Exit* VENTIDIUS
DOLA.   You'll remember
To whom you stand oblig'd?
ANT.   When I forget it,
Be thou unkind, and that's my greatest curse.
My queen shall thank him too.
DOLA.   I fear she will not.
ANT.   But she shall do it. The queen, my Dolabella!
Hast thou not still some grudgings¹⁰ of thy fever?
DOLA.   I would not see her lost.
ANT.   When I forsake her,
Leave me, my better stars! For she has truth

⁹*this* a sword or other symbol of his high rank.
¹⁰*grudgings* slight symptoms.

Beyond her beauty. Caesar tempted her,
At no less price than kingdoms, to betray me,
But she resisted all; and yet thou chid'st me
For loving her too well. Could I do so?

DOLA. Yes, there's my reason.

Re-enter VENTIDIUS, *with* OCTAVIA, *leading* ANTONY'S TWO
    LITTLE DAUGHTERS

ANT.   Where? – Octavia there! *Starting back*

VENT. What, is she poison to you, a disease?
Look on her, view her well, and those she brings:
Are they all strangers to your eyes? Has nature
No secret call, no whisper they are yours?

DOLA. For shame, my lord, if not for love, receive 'em
With kinder eyes. If you confess a man,
Meet 'em, embrace 'em, bid 'em welcome to you.
Your arms should open, ev'n without your knowledge,
To clasp 'em in; your feet should turn to wings,
To bear you to 'em; and your eyes dart out
And aim a kiss ere you could reach the lips.

ANT. I stood amaz'd to think how they came hither.

VENT. I sent for 'em; I brought 'em in unknown
To Cleopatra's guards.

DOLA.   Yet, are you cold?

OCTAV. Thus long I have attended for my welcome,
Which, as a stranger, sure I might expect.
Who am I?

ANT.   Caesar's sister.

OCTAV.   That's unkind.
Had I been nothing more than Caesar's sister,
Know, I had still remain'd in Caesar's camp;
But your Octavia, your much injur'd wife,
Though banish'd from your bed, driv'n from your house,
In spite of Caesar's sister, still is yours.
'Tis true, I have a heart disdains your coldness,
And prompts me not to seek what you should offer;
But a wife's virtue still surmounts that pride.
I come to claim you as my own, to show
My duty first, to ask, nay beg, your kindness;
Your hand, my lord; 'tis mine, and I will have it.   *Taking his hand*

VENT. Do, take it; thou deserv'st it.

DOLA.   On my soul,
And so she does; she's neither too submissive
Nor yet too haughty; but so just a mean

Shows, as it ought, a wife and Roman too.
ANT. I fear, Octavia, you have begg'd my life.
OCTAV. Begg'd it, my lord?
ANT.   Yes, begg'd it, my ambassadress!
Poorly and basely begg'd it of your brother.
OCTAV. Poorly and basely I could never beg;
Nor could my brother grant.
ANT. Shall I, who to my kneeling slave could say,
'Rise up, and be a king', shall I fall down
And cry, 'Forgive me, Caesar'! Shall I set
A man, my equal, in the place of Jove,
As he could give me being? No; that word,
'Forgive', would choke me up
And die upon my tongue.
DOLA.   You shall not need it.
ANT. I will not need it. Come, you've all betray'd me, –
My friend too! – to receive some vile conditions.
My wife has bought me with her prayers and tears,
And now I must become her branded slave.
In every peevish mood, she will upbraid
The life she gave; if I but look awry,
She cries, 'I'll tell my brother'.
OCTAV.   My hard fortune
Subjects me still to your unkind mistakes,
But the conditions I have brought are such
You need not blush to take: I love your honour
Because 'tis mine; it never shall be said
Octavia's husband was her brother's slave.
Sir, you are free; free ev'n from her you loathe;
For, though my brother bargains for your love,
Makes me the price and cement of your peace,
I have a soul like yours; I cannot take
Your love as alms nor beg what I deserve.
I'll tell my brother we are reconcil'd;
He shall draw back his troops, and you shall march
To rule the East. I may be dropp'd at Athens;
No matter where. I never will complain,
But only keep the barren name of wife,
And rid you of the trouble.
VENT. Was ever such a strife of sullen honour!
                    [VENTIDIUS *and* DOLABELLA *speak apart*]
Both scorn to be oblig'd.
DOLA. Oh, she has touched him in the tender'st part;
See how he reddens with despite and shame,

To be outdone in generosity!
VENT.　See how he winks, how he dries up a tear
　　That fain would fall!
ANT.　Octavia, I have heard you, and must praise
　　The greatness of your soul,
　　But cannot yield to what you have propos'd:
　　For I can ne'er be conquer'd but by love,
　　And you do all for duty. You would free me,
　　And would be dropp'd at Athens; was't not so?
OCTAV.　It was, my lord.
ANT.　　　　　　　　　　Then I must be oblig'd
　　To one who loves me not, who to herself
　　May call me thankless and ungrateful man.
　　I'll not endure it, no.
VENT.　(*Aside*) I am glad it pinches there.
OCTAV.　Would you triumph o'er poor Octavia's virtue?
　　That pride was all I had to bear me up,
　　That you might think you ow'd me for your life,
　　And ow'd it to my duty, not my love.
　　I have been injur'd, and my haughty soul
　　Could brook but ill the man who slights my bed.
ANT.　Therefore you love me not.
OCTAV.　　　　　　　　　　Therefore, my lord,
　　I should not love you.
ANT.　　　　　　　　Therefore you would leave me?
OCTAV.　And therefore I should leave you – if I could.
DOLA.　Her soul's too great, after such injuries,
　　To say she loves; and yet she lets you see it.
　　Her modesty and silence plead her cause.
ANT.　O Dolabella, which way shall I turn?
　　I find a secret yielding in my soul;
　　But Cleopatra, who would die with me,
　　Must she be left? Pity pleads for Octavia,
　　But does it not plead more for Cleopatra?
VENT.　Justice and pity both plead for Octavia;
　　For Cleopatra, neither.
　　One would be ruin'd with you, but she first
　　Had ruin'd you; the other you have ruin'd,
　　And yet she would preserve you.
　　In everything their merits are unequal.
ANT.　O my distracted soul!
OCTAV.　　　　　　　　　Sweet heav'n compose it!
　　Come, come, my lord, if I can pardon you,

Methinks you should accept it. Look on these;
Are they not yours? Or stand they thus neglected,
As they are mine? Go to him, children, go;
Kneel to him, take him by the hand, speak to him;
For you may speak and he may own you too,
Without a blush; and so he cannot all
His children:[11] go, I say, and pull him to me,
And pull him to yourselves from that bad woman.
You, Agrippina, hang upon his arms,
And you, Antonia, clasp about his waist.
If he will shake you off, if he will dash you
Against the pavement, you must bear it, children;
For you are mine, and I was born to suffer.

Here the CHILDREN *go to him etc.*

VENT.   Was ever sight so moving? Emperor!
DOLA.   Friend!
OCTAV.   Husband!
BOTH CHILD.   Father!
ANT.   I am vanquish'd: take me,
   Octavia; take me, children; share me all.   *Embracing them*
   I've been a thriftless debtor to your loves,
   And run out much, in riot, from your stock;
   But all shall be amended.
OCTAV.   O blest hour!
DOLA.   O happy change!
VENT.   My joy stops at my tongue,
   But it has found two channels here for one,
   And bubbles out above.
ANT.   (*To* OCTAVIA) This is thy triumph; lead me where thou wilt,
   Ev'n to thy brother's camp.
OCTAV.   All there are yours.

   Enter ALEXAS *hastily*

ALEX.   The queen, my mistress, and yours –
ANT.   'Tis past.
   Octavia, you shall stay this night. Tomorrow
   Caesar and we are one.

   Exit, leading OCTAVIA; DOLABELLA *and the* CHILDREN *follow*

VENT.   There's news for you. Run, my officious eunuch,
   Be sure to be the first. Haste forward.
   Haste, my dear eunuch, haste.   *Exit*
ALEX.   This downright fighting fool, this thick-skull'd hero,

----

[11]*His children* Antony had three children by Cleopatra; in Roman eyes they were
illegitimate.

This blunt, unthinking instrument of death,
With plain dull virtue has outgone my wit.
Pleasure forsook my earliest infancy;
The luxury of others robb'd my cradle,
And ravish'd thence the promise of a man.
Cast out from nature, disinherited
Of what her meanest children claim by kind,
Yet greatness kept me from contempt; that's gone.
Had Cleopatra follow'd my advice,
Then he had been betray'd who now forsakes.
She dies for love, but she has known its joys.
Gods, is this just that I, who know no joys,
Must die because she loves?

    Enter CLEOPATRA, CHARMION, IRAS *and train*
O madam, I have seen what blasts my eyes!
Octavia 's here!

CLEO.   Peace with that raven's note.
I know it too, and now am in
The pangs of death.

ALEX.   You are no more a queen;
Egypt is lost.

CLEO.   What tell'st thou me of Egypt?
My life, my soul is lost! Octavia has him!
O fatal name to Cleopatra's love!
My kisses, my embraces now are hers,
While I – But thou hast seen my rival. Speak,
Does she deserve this blessing? Is she fair,
Bright as a goddess? And is all perfection
Confin'd to her? It is. Poor I was made
Of that coarse matter which, when she was finish'd,
The gods threw by for rubbish.

ALEX.   She's indeed a very miracle.

CLEO.   Death to my hopes, a miracle!

ALEX.   A miracle,   *Bowing*
I mean of goodness; for in beauty, madam,
You made all wonders cease.

CLEO.   I was too rash;
Take this in part of recompense. But, oh,   *Giving a ring*
I fear thou flatter'st me.

CHAR.   She comes! She's here!

IRAS.   Fly, madam, Caesar's sister!

CLEO.   Were she the sister[12] of the thund'rer Jove,
And bore her brother's lightning in her eyes,

[12]*sister* Juno.

Thus would I face my rival.
              Meets OCTAVIA *with* VENTIDIUS. OCTAVIA *bears up to her.*
              Their trains come up on either side
OCTAV.   I need not ask if you are Cleopatra;
    Your haughty carriage —
CLEO.   Shows I am a queen.
    Nor need I ask you who you are.
OCTAV.   A Roman:
    A name that makes and can unmake a queen.
CLEO.   Your lord, the man who serves me, is a Roman.
OCTAV.   He was a Roman till he lost that name,
    To be a slave in Egypt; but I come
    To free him thence.
CLEO.   Peace, peace, my lover's Juno.[13]
    When he grew weary of that household clog,
    He chose my easier bonds.
OCTAV.   I wonder not
    Your bonds are easy: you have long been practis'd
    In that lascivious art. He's not the first
    For whom you spread your snares: let Caesar witness.
CLEO.   I lov'd not Caesar; 'twas but gratitude
    I paid his love. The worst your malice can
    Is but to say the greatest of mankind
    Has been my slave. The next, but far above him
    In my esteem, is he whom law calls yours,
    But whom his love made mine.
OCTAV.   I would view nearer *Coming up close to her*
    That face which has so long usurp'd my right,
    To find th' inevitable charms that catch
    Mankind so sure, that ruin'd my dear lord.
CLEO.   Oh, you do well to search, for had you known
    But half these charms, you had not lost his heart.
OCTAV.   Far be their knowledge from a Roman lady,
    Far from a modest wife! Shame of our sex,
    Dost thou not blush to own those black endearments
    That make sin pleasing?
CLEO.   You may blush, who want[14] 'em.
    If bounteous nature, if indulgent heav'n
    Have giv'n me charms to please the bravest man,
    Should I not thank 'em? Should I be asham'd,

[13]*my lover's Juno* Cleopatra regards Octavia as the consort of her lover Jupiter, i.e. Antony.
[14]*want* lack.

And not be proud? I am, that he has lov'd me;
And, when I love not him, heav'n change this face
For one like that.
OCTAV.   Thou lov'st him not so well.
CLEO.   I love him better, and deserve him more.
OCTAV.   You do not, cannot. You have been his ruin.
Who made him cheap at Rome but Cleopatra?
Who made him scorn'd abroad but Cleopatra?
At Actium, who betray'd him? Cleopatra.
Who made his children orphans, and poor me
A wretched widow? Only Cleopatra.
CLEO.   Yet she who loves him best is Cleopatra.
If you have suffer'd, I have suffer'd more.
You bear the specious title of a wife
To gild your cause and draw the pitying world
To favour it; the world condemns poor me,
For I have lost my honour, lost my fame,
And stain'd the glory of my royal house,
And all to bear the branded name of mistress.
There wants but life, and that too I would lose
For him I love.
OCTAV.   Be't so, then; take thy wish.   *Exit with suis*[15]
CLEO.   And 'tis my wish,
Now he is lost for whom alone I lived.
My sight grows dim, and every object dances,
And swims before me, in the maze of death.
My spirits, while they were oppos'd, kept up;
They could not sink beneath a rival's scorn.
But now she's gone, they faint.
ALEX.   Mine have had leisure
To recollect their strength, and furnish counsel
To ruin her who else must ruin you.
CLEO.   Vain promiser!
Lead me, my Charmion; nay, your hand too, Iras.
My grief has weight enough to sink you both.
Conduct me to some solitary chamber
And draw the curtains round;
Then leave me to myself, to take alone
My fill of grief;
   There I till death will his unkindness weep,
   As harmless infants moan themselves asleep.   *Exeunt*

---

[15]*suis* train.

Act Four

[SCENE ONE]

[ANTONY'S *apartments*]

Enter ANTONY *and* DOLABELLA

DOLA.   Why would you shift it from yourself on me?
Can you not tell her you must part?

ANT.   I cannot.
I could pull out an eye and bid it go,
And t'other should not weep. O Dolabella,
How many deaths are in this word, 'Depart'!
I dare not trust my tongue to tell her so:
One look of hers would thaw me into tears,
And I should melt till I were lost again.

DOLA.   Then let Ventidius;
He's rough by nature.

ANT.   Oh, he'll speak too harshly;
He'll kill her with the news. Thou, only thou.

DOLA.   Nature has cast me in so soft a mould
That but to hear a story feign'd, for pleasure,
Of some sad lover's death moistens my eyes,
And robs me of my manhood. I should speak
So faintly, with such fear to grieve her heart,
She'd not believe it earnest.

ANT.   Therefore, therefore
Thou only, thou art fit. Think thyself me,
And when thou speak'st (but let it first be long),
Take off the edge from every sharper sound,
And let our parting be as gently made
As other loves begin. Wilt thou do this?

DOLA.   What you have said so sinks into my soul
That, if I must speak, I shall speak just so.

ANT.   I leave you then to your sad task. Farewell.
I sent her word to meet you.   *Goes to the door and comes back*
                              I forgot;
Let her be told I'll make her peace with mine;
Her crown and dignity shall be preserv'd,

If I have pow'r with Caesar. – Oh, be sure
To think on that.
DOLA.   Fear not, I will remember.
                ANTONY *goes again to the door and comes back*
ANT.   And tell her, too, how much I was constrain'd;
I did not this but with extremest force.
Desire her not to hate my memory,
For I still cherish hers. Insist on that.
DOLA.   Trust me, I'll not forget it.
ANT.   Then that's all. *Goes out and returns again*
Wilt thou forgive my fondness[1] this once more?
Tell her, though we shall never meet again,
If I should hear she took another love,
The news would break my heart. – Now I must go;
For every time I have return'd, I feel
My soul more tender, and my next command
Would be to bid her stay, and ruin both.   *Exit*
DOLA.   Men are but children of a larger growth,
Our appetites as apt to change as theirs,
And full as craving too, and full as vain;
And yet the soul, shut up in her dark room,
Viewing so clear abroad, at home sees nothing;
But, like a mole in earth, busy and blind,
Works all her folly up and casts it outward
To the world's open view. Thus I discover'd,
And blam'd the love of ruin'd Antony,
Yet wish that I were he, to be so ruin'd.
      Enter VENTIDIUS *above*
VENT.   Alone, and talking to himself? Concern'd too?
Perhaps my guess is right; he lov'd her once,
And may pursue it still.
DOLA.   O friendship, friendship!
Ill canst thou answer this; and reason, worse;
Unfaithful in th'attempt; hopeless to win,
And if I win, undone, mere madness all,
And yet th'occasion's fair. What injury
To him to wear the robe which he throws by?
VENT.   None, none at all. This happens as I wish,
To ruin her yet more with Antony.
      Enter CLEOPATRA, *talking with* ALEXAS; CHARMION, IRAS *on
      the other side*

[1]*fondness* foolishness.

DOLA.   She comes! What charms have sorrow on that face!
　Sorrow seems pleas'd to dwell with so much sweetness;
　Yet now and then a melancholy smile
　Breaks loose, like lightning in a winter's night,
　And shows a moment's day.
VENT.   If she should love him too! Her eunuch there?
　That porc'pisce[2] bodes ill weather. Draw, draw nearer,
　Sweet devil, that I may hear.
ALEX.   Believe me; try

　　　　DOLABELLA goes over to CHARMION *and* IRAS,
　　　　　　　seems to talk with them

　To make him jealous; jealousy is like
　A polish'd glass held to the lips when life's in doubt;
　If there be breath, 'twill catch the damp and show it.
CLEO.   I grant you jealousy's a proof of love,
　But 'tis a weak and unavailing med'cine;
　It puts out[3] the disease and makes it show,
　But has no pow'r to cure.
ALEX.   'Tis your last remedy, and strongest too.
　And then this Dolabella, who so fit
　To practise on? He's handsome, valiant, young,
　And looks as he were laid for nature's bait,
　To catch weak women's eyes.
　He stands already more than half suspected
　Of loving you. The least kind word or glance
　You give this youth will kindle him with love;
　Then, like a burning vessel set adrift,
　You'll send him down amain before the wind,
　To fire the heart of jealous Antony.
CLEO.   Can I do this? Ah, no; my love's so true
　That I can neither hide it where it is
　Nor show it where it is not. Nature meant me
　A wife, a silly, harmless, household dove,
　Fond without art, and kind without deceit;
　But Fortune, that has made a mistress of me,
　Has thrust me out to the wide world, unfurnish'd
　Of falsehood to be happy.
ALEX.   Force yourself.
　Th'event will be, your lover will return,
　Doubly desirous to possess the good
　Which once he fear'd to lose.

---

[2]*porc'pisce* porcus piscus, porpoise.　　　[3]*puts out* brings out.

CLEO.   I must attempt it,
  But oh, with what regret!

                 Exit ALEXAS. *She comes up to* DOLABELLA

VENT.   So, now the scene draws near; they're in my reach.

CLEO.   (*To* DOL.) Discoursing with my women! Might not I
  Share in your entertainment?

CHAR.   You have been
  The subject of it, madam.

CLEO.   How![4] And how?

IRAS.   Such praises of your beauty!

CLEO.   Mere poetry.
  Your Roman wits, your Gallus and Tibullus,[5]
  Have taught you this from Cytheris and Delia.

DOLA.   Those Roman wits have never been in Egypt;
  Cytheris and Delia else had been unsung.
  I, who have seen – had I been born a poet,
  Should choose a nobler name.

CLEO.   You flatter me.
  But 'tis your nation's vice; all of your country
  Are flatterers and all false. Your friend's like you.
  I'm sure he sent you not to speak these words.

DOLA.   No, madam; yet he sent me –

CLEO.   Well, he sent you –

DOLA.   Of a less pleasing errand.

CLEO.   How less pleasing?
  Less to yourself or me?

DOLA.   Madam, to both;
  For you must mourn, and I must grieve to cause it.

CLEO.   You, Charmion, and your fellow, stand at distance.
  (*Aside*) Hold up, my spirits. – Well, now your mournful matter!
  For I'm prepar'd, perhaps can guess it too.

DOLA.   I wish you would, for 'tis a thankless office,
  To tell ill news; and I, of all your sex,
  Most fear displeasing you.

CLEO.   Of all your sex,
  I soonest could forgive you, if you should.

VENT.   (*Aside*) Most delicate advances! Woman, woman!
  Dear, damn'd, inconstant sex!

CLEO.   In the first place,

---

[4] *How* Indeed.

[5] *Gallus and Tibullus* Roman poets, first century BC, who wrote about their mistresses, Cytheris and Delia.

I am to be forsaken; is't not so?

DOLA.   I wish I could not answer to that question.

CLEO.   Then pass it o'er because it troubles you;
I should have been more griev'd another time.
Next, I'm to lose my kingdom – Farewell, Egypt!
Yet, is there any more?

DOLA.   Madam, I fear
Your too-deep sense of grief has turn'd your reason.

CLEO.   No, no, I'm not run mad; I can bear fortune,
And love may be expell'd by other love,
As poisons are by poisons.

DOLA.   You o'erjoy me, madam,
To find your griefs so moderately borne.
You've heard the worst; all are not false like him.

CLEO.   No; heav'n forbid they should.

DOLA.   Some men are constant.

CLEO.   And constancy deserves reward, that's certain.

DOLA.   Deserves it not, but give it leave to hope.

VENT.   (*Aside*) I'll swear thou hast my leave. I have enough.
But how to manage this! Well, I'll consider.   *Exit*

DOLA.   I came prepar'd
To tell you heavy news, news which I thought
Would fright the blood from your pale cheeks to hear;
But you have met it with a cheerfulness
That makes my task more easy; and my tongue,
Which on another's message was employ'd,
Would gladly speak its own.

CLEO.   Hold, Dolabella.
First tell me, were you chosen by my lord
Or sought you this employment?

DOLA.   He pick'd me out, and as his bosom friend
He charg'd me with his words.

CLEO.   The message then
I know was tender, and each accent smooth,
To mollify that rugged word, 'Depart'.

DOLA.   Oh, you mistake. He chose the harshest words;
With fiery eyes and with contracted brows,
He coin'd his face in the severest stamp,
And fury shook his fabric like an earthquake;
He heav'd for vent and burst like bellowing Aetna
In sounds scarce human: 'Hence away forever;
Let her begone, the blot of my renown,
And bane of all my hopes!

All the time of this speech, CLEOPATRA *seems more and more concerned, till she sinks quite down*

Let her be driv'n, as far as men can think,
From man's commerce! She'll poison to the centre'.

CLEO. Oh, I can bear no more!

DOLA. Help, help! O wretch! O cursed, cursed wretch!
What have I done?

CHAR. Help, chafe her temples, Iras.

IRAS. Bend, bend her forward quickly.

CHAR. Heav'n be prais'd,
She comes again.

CLEO. Oh, let him not approach me.
Why have you brought me back to this loath'd being,
Th'abode of falsehood, violated vows,
And injur'd love? For pity, let me go;
For, if there be a place of long repose,
I'm sure I want it. My disdainful lord
Can never break that quiet nor awake
The sleeping soul with hollowing in my tomb
Such words as fright her hence. – Unkind, unkind!

DOLA. (*Kneeling*) Believe me, 'tis against myself I speak;
That sure desires belief. I injur'd him;
My friend ne'er spoke those words. Oh, had you seen
How often he came back, and every time
With something more obliging and more kind,
To add to what he said! What dear farewells!
How almost vanquish'd by his love he parted,
And lean'd to what unwillingly he left!
I, traitor as I was, for love of you
(But what can you not do, who made me false?)
I forg'd that lie; for whose forgiveness kneels
This self-accus'd, self-punish'd criminal.

CLEO. With how much ease believe me what we wish!
Rise, Dolabella. If you have been guilty,
I have contributed, and too much love
Has made me guilty too.
Th'advance of kindness which I made was feign'd,
To call back fleeting love by jealousy,
But 'twould not last. Oh, rather let me lose
Than so ignobly trifle with his heart.

DOLA. I find your breast fenc'd round from human reach,
Transparent as a rock of solid crystal,
Seen through, but never pierc'd. My friend, my friend,

What endless treasure hast thou thrown away
And scatter'd, like an infant, in the ocean
Vain sums of wealth, which none can gather thence!
CLEO.   Could you not beg
An hour's admittance to his private ear?
Like one who wanders through long barren wilds,
And yet foreknows no hospitable inn
Is near to succour hunger, eats his fill
Before his painful march.
So would I feed a while my famish'd eyes
Before we part; for I have far to go,
If death be far, and never must return.

                        VENTIDIUS [*approaches*] *with* OCTAVIA, *behind*
VENT.   From hence you may discover – O sweet, sweet!
Would you indeed? The pretty hand in earnest?
DOLA.   (*Takes her hand*) I will, for this reward, Draw it not back.
'Tis all I e'er will beg.
VENT.   They turn upon us.
OCTAV.   What quick eyes has guilt!
VENT.   Seem not to have observ'd 'em, and go on.
        They enter
DOLA.   Saw you the emperor, Ventidius?
VENT.   No.
I sought him, but I heard that he was private,
None with him but Hipparchus, his freedman.
DOLA.   Know you his bus'ness?
VENT.   Giving him instructions
And letters to his brother Caesar.
DOLA.   Well,
He must be found.   *Exeunt* DOLABELLA *and* CLEOPATRA
OCTAV.   Most glorious impudence!
VENT.   She look'd, methought,
As she would say, 'Take your old man, Octavia;
Thank you, I'm better here'. Well, but what use
Make we of this discovery?
OCTAV.   Let it die.
VENT.   I pity Dolabella; but she's dangerous.
Her eyes have pow'r beyond Thessalian[6] charms
To draw the moon from heav'n; for eloquence,
The sea-green sirens taught her voice their flatt'ry;

---

[6]*Thessalian* Thessaly, Greece, was reputed to be a centre of witchcraft.

And, while she speaks, night steals upon the day,
Unmark'd of those that hear. Then she's so charming,
Age buds at sight of her and swells to youth.
The holy priests gaze on her when she smiles,
And with heav'd hands, forgetting gravity,
They bless her wanton eyes. Ev'n I, who hate her,
With a malignant joy behold such beauty,
And, while I curse, desire it. Antony
Must needs have some remains of passion still,
Which may ferment into a worse relapse,
If now not fully cur'd. I know, this minute,
With Caesar he's endeavouring her peace.

OCTAV.   You have prevail'd. But for a further purpose   *Walks off*
I'll prove how he will relish this discovery.
What, make a strumpet's peace! It swells my heart;
It must not, shall not be.

VENT.   His guards appear.
Let me begin, and you shall second me.

   Enter ANTONY

ANT.   Octavia, I was looking you, my love.
What, are your letters ready? I have giv'n
My last instructions.

OCTAV.   Mine, my lord, are written.

ANT.   Ventidius.   *Drawing him aside*

VENT.   My lord?

ANT.   A word in private –
When saw you Dolabella?

VENT.   Now, my lord,
He parted hence, and Cleopatra with him.

ANT.   Speak softly. – 'Twas by my command he went,
To bear my last farewell.

VENT.   (*Aloud*)   It look'd indeed
Like your farewell.

ANT.   More softly. – My farewell?
What secret meaning have you in those words
Of 'My farewell'? He did it by my order.

VENT.   (*Aloud*) Then he obey'd your order. I suppose
You bid him do it with all gentleness,
All kindness, and all – love.

ANT.   How she mourn'd,
The poor forsaken creature!

VENT.   She took it as she ought; she bore your parting
As she did Caesar's, as she would another's,

Were a new love to come.

ANT. (*Aloud*)   Thou dost belie her,
Most basely and maliciously belie her.

VENT. I thought not to displease you; I have done.

OCTAV. You seemed disturb'd, my lord.   *Coming up*

ANT.   A very trifle.
Retire, my love.

VENT.   It was indeed a trifle.
He sent –

ANT. (*Angrily*) No more. Look how thou disobey'st me;
Thy life shall answer it.

OCTAV.   Then 'tis no trifle.

VENT. (*To* OCTAVIA) 'Tis less, a very nothing. You too saw it,
As well as I, and therefore 'tis no secret.

ANT. She saw it!

VENT.   Yes. She saw young Dolabella –

ANT. Young Dolabella!

VENT.   Young, I think him young,
And handsome too, and so do others think him.
But what of that? He went by your command,
Indeed 'tis probable, with some kind message;
For she receiv'd it graciously; she smil'd;
And then he grew familiar with her hand,
Squeez'd it, and worried it with ravenous kisses;
She blush'd, and sigh'd, and smil'd, and blush'd again.
At last she took occasion to talk softly,
And brought her cheek up close and lean'd on his;
At which, he whisper'd kisses back on hers,
And then she cried aloud that constancy
Should be rewarded.

OCTAV.   This I saw and heard.

ANT. What woman was it whom you heard and saw
So playful with my friend?
Not Cleopatra?

VENT.   Ev'n she, my lord.

ANT.   My Cleopatra?

VENT. Your Cleopatra,
Dolabella's Cleopatra, every man's Cleopatra.

ANT. Thou liest.

VENT.   I do not lie, my lord.
Is this so strange? Should mistresses be left,
And not provide against a time of change?
You know she's not much us'd to lonely nights.

ANT. I'll think no more on't.
  I know 'tis false, and see the plot betwixt you.
  You needed not have gone this way, Octavia.
  What harms it you that Cleopatra's just?
  She's mine no more. I see, and I forgive.
  Urge it no further, love.

OCTAV.   Are you concern'd
  That she's found false?

ANT.   I should be, were it so;
  For, though 'tis past, I would not that the world
  Should tax my former choice, that I lov'd one
  Of so light note; but I forgive you both.

VENT. What has my age deserv'd that you should think
  I would abuse your ears with perjury?
  If heav'n be true, she's false.

ANT.   Though heav'n and earth
  Should witness it, I'll not believe her tainted.

VENT. I'll bring you, then, a witness
  From hell to prove her so.

                    Seeing ALEXAS *just entering, and starting back*
                        Nay, go not back;
  For stay you must and shall.

ALEX.   What means my lord?

VENT. To make you do what most you hate, speak truth.
  You are of Cleopatra's private counsel,
  Of her bed-counsel, her lascivious hours;
  Are conscious of each nightly change she makes,
  And watch her, as Chaldeans do the moon,
  Can tell what signs she passes through, what day.

ALEX. My noble lord!

VENT.   My most illustrious pander,
  No fine set speech, no cadence, no turn'd periods,
  But a plain homespun truth is what I ask.
  I did myself o'erhear your queen make love
  To Dolabella. Speak; for I will know,
  By your confession, what more pass'd betwixt 'em;
  How near the bus'ness draws to your employment,
  And when the happy hour.

ANT. Speak truth, Alexas; whether it offend
  Or please Ventidius, care not. Justify
  Thy injur'd queen from malice; dare his worst.

OCTAV. (*Aside*) See how he gives him courage, how he fears
  To find her false and shuts his eyes to truth,

Willing to be misled!

ALEX. As far as love may plead for woman's frailty,
Urg'd by desert and greatness of the lover,
So far, divine Octavia, may my queen
Stand ev'n excus'd to you for loving him
Who is your lord; so far, from brave Ventidius,
May her past actions hope a fair report.

ANT. 'Tis well and truly spoken. Mark, Ventidius.

ALEX. To you, most noble emperor, her strong passion
Stands not excus'd, but wholly justified.
Her beauty's charms alone, without her crown,
From Ind[7] and Meroe[8] drew the distant vows
Of sighing kings, and at her feet were laid
The sceptres of the earth, expos'd on heaps,
To choose where she would reign.
She thought a Roman only could deserve her,
And, of all Romans, only Antony;
And, to be less than wife to you, disdain'd
Their lawful passion.

ANT.   'Tis but truth.

ALEX. And yet, though love and your unmatch'd desert
Have drawn her from the due regard of honour,
At last heav'n open'd her unwilling eyes
To see the wrongs she offer'd fair Octavia,
Whose holy bed she lawlessly usurp'd.
The sad effects of this improsperous war
Confirm'd those pious thoughts.

VENT. (*Aside*)   Oh, wheel you there?
Observe him now; the man begins to mend,
And talk substantial reason. — Fear not, eunuch;
The emperor has giv'n thee leave to speak.

ALEX. Else had I never dar'd t'offend his ears
With what the last necessity has urg'd
On my forsaken mistress; yet I must not
Presume to say her heart is wholly alter'd.

ANT. No, dare not for thy life, I charge thee dare not
Pronounce that fatal word!

OCTAV. (*Aside*) Must I bear this? Good heav'n, afford me patience.

VENT. On, sweet eunuch; my dear half-man, proceed.

ALEX. Yet Dolabella

---

[7] *Ind* India.
[8] *Meroe* an ancient city, now ruined, in northern Sudan.

Has lov'd her long; he, next my god-like lord,
Deserves her best; and should she meet his passion,
Rejected as she is by him she lov'd —

ANT.   Hence from my sight, for I can bear no more!
Let furies drag thee quick to hell; let all
The longer damn'd have rest; each torturing hand
Do thou employ till Cleopatra comes;
Then join thou too, and help to torture her!

Exit ALEXAS, *thrust out by* ANTONY

OCTAV.   'Tis not well;
Indeed, my lord, 'tis much unkind to me
To show this passion, this extreme concernment,
For an abandon'd, faithless prostitute.

ANT.   Octavia, leave me; I am much disorder'd.
Leave me, I say.

OCTAV.   My lord!

ANT.   I bid you leave me.

VENT.   Obey him, madam; best withdraw a while,
And see how this will work.

OCTAV.   Wherein have I offended you, my lord,
That I am bid to leave you? Am I false
Or infamous? Am I a Cleopatra?
Were I she,
Base as she is, you would not bid me leave you,
But hang upon my neck, take slight excuses,
And fawn upon my falsehood.

ANT.   'Tis too much,
Too much, Octavia; I am press'd with sorrows
Too heavy to be borne, and you add more.
I would retire and recollect what's left
Of man within, to aid me.

OCTAV.   You would mourn
In private for your love, who has betray'd you.
You did but half return to me; your kindness
Linger'd behind with her. I hear, my lord,
You make conditions for her,
And would include her treaty. Wondrous proofs
Of love to me!

ANT.   Are you my friend, Ventidius?
Or are you turn'd a Dolabella too,
And let this fury loose?

VENT.   Oh, be advis'd,
Sweet madam, and retire.

OCTAV. Yes, I will go, but never to return.
You shall no more be haunted with this fury.
My lord, my lord, love will not always last,
When urg'd with long unkindness and disdain.
Take her again whom you prefer to me;
She stays but to be call'd. Poor cozen'd man!
Let a feign'd parting give her back your heart,
Which a feign'd love first got; for injur'd me,
Though my just sense of wrongs forbid my stay,
My duty shall be yours.
To the dear pledges of our former love
My tenderness and care shall be transferr'd,
And they shall cheer, by turns, my widow'd nights.
So, take my last farewell, for I despair
To have you whole, and scorn to take you half.   *Exit*
VENT. I combat heav'n, which blasts my best designs.
My last attempt must be to win her back,
But oh, I fear in vain.   *Exit*
ANT. Why was I fram'd with this plain, honest heart,
Which knows not to disguise its griefs and weakness,
But bears its workings outward to the world?
I should have kept the mighty anguish in,
And forc'd a smile at Cleopatra's falsehood;
Octavia had believ'd it, and had stay'd.
But I am made a shallow-forded stream,
Seen to the bottom, all my clearness scorn'd,
And all my faults expos'd. See where he comes,
    Enter DOLABELLA
Who has profan'd the sacred name of friend,
And worn it into vileness!
With how secure a brow and specious form
He gilds the secret villain! Sure that face
Was meant for honesty, but heav'n mismatch'd it,
And furnish'd treason out with nature's pomp,
To make its work more easy.
DOLA.   O my friend!
ANT. Well, Dolabella, you perform'd my message?
DOLA. I did, unwillingly.
ANT.   Unwillingly?
Was it so hard for you to bear our parting?
You should have wish'd it.
DOLA.   Why?
ANT.   Because you love me.

And she receiv'd my message with as true,
With as unfeign'd a sorrow as you brought it?
DOLA.   She loves you, ev'n to madness.
ANT.   Oh, I know it.
You, Dolabella, do not better know
How much she loves me. And should I
Forsake this beauty, this all-perfect creature?
DOLA.   I could not, were she mine.
ANT.   And yet you first
Persuaded me. How come you alter'd since?
DOLA.   I said at first I was not fit to go.
I could not hear her sighs and see her tears,
But pity must prevail, and so perhaps
It may again with you, for I have promis'd
That she should take her last farewell: And, see,
She comes to claim my word.

    Enter CLEOPATRA

ANT.   False Dolabella!
DOLA.   What's false, my lord?
ANT.   Why, Dolabella's false,
And Cleopatra's false, both false and faithless.
Draw near, you well-join'd wickedness, you serpents,
Whom I have in my kindly bosom warm'd
Till I am stung to death.
DOLA.   My lord, have I
Deserv'd to be thus us'd?
CLEO.   Can heav'n prepare
A newer torment? Can it find a curse
Beyond our separation?
ANT.   Yes, if fate
Be just, much greater; heav'n should be ingenious
In punishing such crimes. The rolling stone⁹
And gnawing vulture¹⁰ were slight pains, invented
When Jove was young, and no examples known
Of mighty ills; but you have ripen'd sin
To such a monstrous growth 'twill pose the gods
To find an equal torture. Two, two such –
Oh, there's no further name – two such – to me,
To me, who lock'd my soul within your breasts,

⁹*rolling stone* Sisyphus's punishment in Hades was rolling a stone uphill, which
immediately rolled down again.
¹⁰*gnawing vulture* Tityus had vultures gnawing eternally at his liver.

Had no desires, no joys, no life, but you.
When half the globe was mine, I gave it you
In dowry with my heart; I had no use,
No fruit of all, but you; a friend and mistress
Was what the world could give. O Cleopatra,
O Dolabella, how could you betray
This tender heart, which with an infant fondness
Lay lull'd betwixt your bosoms, and there slept,
Secure of injur'd faith?

DOLA.   If she has wronged you,
Heav'n, hell, and you revenge it.

ANT.   If she wrong'd me,
Thou wouldst evade thy part of guilt; but swear
Thou lov'st not her.

DOLA.   Not so as I love you.

ANT.   Not so? Swear, swear, I say, thou dost not love her.

DOLA.   No more than friendship will allow.

ANT.   No more?
Friendship allows thee nothing; thou art perjur'd —
And yet thou didst not swear thou lov'dst her not;
But not so much, no more. O trifling hypocrite,
Who dar'st not own to her thou dost not love,
Nor own to me thou dost! Ventidius heard it;
Octavia saw it.

CLEO.   They are enemies.

ANT.   Alexas is not so. He, he confess'd it.
He, who, next hell, best knew it, he avow'd it.
(*To* DOLABELLA) Why do I seek a proof beyond yourself?
You whom I sent to bear my last farewell
Return'd to plead her stay.

DOLA.   What shall I answer?
If to have lov'd be guilt, then I have sinn'd;
But if to have repented of that love
Can wash away my crime, I have repented.
Yet, if I have offended past forgiveness,
Let not her suffer; she is innocent.

CLEO.   Ah, what will not a woman do who loves?
What means will she refuse to keep that heart
Where all her joys are plac'd? 'Twas I encourag'd,
'Twas I blew up the fire that scorch'd his soul,
To make you jealous, and by that regain you.
But all in vain. I could not counterfeit;
In spite of all the dams my love broke o'er,

And drown'd my heart again. Fate took th'occasion,
And thus one minute's feigning has destroy'd
My whole life's truth.

ANT.   Thin cobweb arts of falsehood,
Seen and broke through at first!

DOLA.   Forgive your mistress.

CLEO.   Forgive your friend.

                              You have convinc'd[11] yourselves;

ANT.   You plead each other's cause. What witness have you
That you but meant to raise my jealousy?

CLEO.   Ourselves, and heav'n.

ANT.   Guilt witnesses for guilt. Hence, love and friendship!
You have no longer place in human breasts;
These two have driv'n you out. Avoid my sight!
I would not kill the man whom I [have] lov'd,
And cannot hurt the woman. But avoid me;
I do not know how long I can be tame,
For, if I stay one minute more, to think
How I am wrong'd, my justice and revenge
Will cry so loud within me that my pity
Will not be heard for either.

DOLA.   Heav'n has but
Our sorrow for our sins, and then delights
To pardon erring man. Sweet mercy seems
Its darling attribute, which limits justice,
As if there were degrees in infinite,
And infinite would rather want perfection
Than punish to extent.

ANT.   I can forgive
A foe, but not a mistress and a friend.
Treason is there in its most horrid shape,
Where trust is greatest, and the soul resign'd
Is stabb'd by its own guards. I'll hear no more;
Hence from my sight forever!

CLEO.   How! Forever?
I cannot go one moment from your sight,
And must I go forever?
My joys, my only joys, are centr'd here:
What place have I to go to? My own kingdom?
That I have lost for you. Or to the Romans?
They hate me for your sake. Or must I wander

---

[11]*convinc'd* convicted.

The wide world o'er, a helpless, banish'd woman,
Banish'd for love of you, banish'd from you?
Ay, there's the banishment! Oh, hear me, hear me,
With strictest justice, for I beg no favour,
And if I have offended you, then kill me,
But do not banish me.

ANT.   I must not hear you.
I have a fool within me takes your part,
But honour stops my ears.

CLEO.   For pity hear me!
Would you cast off a slave who follow'd you,
Who crouch'd beneath your spurn? — He has no pity!
See, if he gives one tear to my departure,
One look, one kind farewell. O iron heart!
Let all the gods look down and judge betwixt us,
If he did ever love!

ANT.   No more. Alexas!

DOLA.   A perjur'd villain!

ANT.   (*To* CLEOPATRA)   Your Alexas, yours.

CLEO.   Oh, 'twas his plot, his ruinous design,
T'engage you in my love by jealousy.
Hear him; confront him with me; let him speak.

ANT.   I have, I have.

CLEO.   And if he clear me not —

ANT.   Your creature! One who hangs upon your smiles,
Watches your eye, to say or to unsay
Whate'er you please! I am not to be mov'd.

CLEO.   Then must we part? Farewell, my cruel lord!
Th'appearance is against me, and I go,
Unjustified, forever from your sight.
How I have lov'd, you know; how yet I love,
My only comfort is, I know myself.
I love you more, ev'n now you are unkind,
Than when you lov'd me most; so well, so truly,
I'll never strive against it, but die pleas'd,
To think you once were mine.

ANT.   Good heav'n, they weep at parting!
Must I weep too? That calls 'em innocent.
I must not weep, and yet I must, to think
That I must not forgive.
Live, but live wretched; 'tis but just you should,
Who made me so. Live from each other's sight;
Let me not hear you meet. Set all the earth

And all the seas betwixt your sunder'd loves;
View nothing common but the sun and skies.
Now, all take several ways,
   And each your own sad fate, with mine, deplore;
   That you were false, and I could trust no more.   *Exeunt severally*

Act Five

[SCENE ONE]

[CLEOPATRA'S *apartments*]

Enter CLEOPATRA, CHARMION *and* IRAS

CHAR.   Be juster, heav'n; such virtue punish'd thus
Will make us think that chance rules all above,
And shuffles, with a random hand, the lots
Which man is forc'd to draw.

CLEO.   I could tear out these eyes that gain'd his heart
And had not pow'r to keep it. O the curse
Of doting on, ev'n when I find it dotage!
Bear witness, gods, you heard him bid me go;
You whom he mock'd with imprecating[1] vows
Of promis'd faith! – I'll die; I will not bear it.
You may hold me –

                        She pulls out her dagger and they hold her
But I can keep my breath;[2] I can die inward
And choke this love.

        Enter ALEXAS

IRAS.   Help! Oh, Alexas, help!
The queen grows desperate; her soul struggles in her,
With all the agonies of love and rage,
And strives to force its passage.

CLEO.   Let me go.
Art thou there, traitor? – Oh,
Oh, for a little breath to vent my rage;
Give, give me way, and let me loose upon him!

ALEX.   Yes, I deserve it, for my ill-tim'd truth.
Was it for me to prop
The ruins of a falling majesty,
To place myself beneath the mighty flaw,
Thus to be crush'd and pounded into atoms
By its o'erwhelming weight? 'Tis too presuming

---

[1] *imprecating* imploring.
[2] *keep my breath* hold my breath, until my life ends.

For subjects to preserve that wilful pow'r
Which courts its own destruction.

CLEO.   I would reason
More calmly with you. Did not you o'errule
And force my plain, direct, and open love
Into these crooked paths of jealousy?
Now, what's th'event?³ Octavia is remov'd,
But Cleopatra's banish'd. Thou, thou villain,
Hast push'd my boat to open sea, to prove,
At my sad cost, if thou canst steer it back.
It cannot be; I'm lost too far; I'm ruin'd.
Hence, thou impostor, traitor, monster, devil! —
I can no more; thou and my griefs have sunk
Me down so low that I want voice to curse thee.

ALEX.   Suppose some shipwreck'd seaman near the shore,
Dropping and faint with climbing up the cliff,
If from above some charitable hand
Pull him to safety, hazarding himself
To draw the other's weight; would he look back
And curse him for his pains? The case is yours;
But one step more, and you have gain'd the height.

CLEO.   Sunk, never more to rise.

ALEX.   Octavia's gone, and Dolabella banish'd.
Believe me, madam, Antony is yours.
His heart was never lost, but started off
To jealousy, love's last retreat and covert,
Where it lies hid in shades, watchful in silence,
And list'ning for the sound that calls it back.
Some other, any man ('tis so advanc'd),
May perfect this unfinish'd work, which I
(Unhappy only to myself) have left
So easy to his hand.

CLEO.   Look well thou do't; else —

ALEX.   Else what your silence threatens. — Antony
Is mounted up the Pharos,⁴ from whose turret
He stands surveying our Egyptian galleys
Engag'd with Caesar's fleet. Now death or conquest!
If the first happen, fate acquits my promise;
If we o'ercome, the conqueror is yours.   *A distant shout within*

³*event* outcome.
⁴*Pharos* the lighthouse at Alexandria, built *c.* 280 BC, reputed to have been 800
feet (270 metres) high.

CHAR.   Have comfort, madam. Did you mark that shout?

                                  Second shout nearer

IRAS.   Hark! they redouble it.

ALEX.   'Tis from the port.
  The loudness shows it near. Good news, kind heav'ns!

CLEO.   Osiris⁵ make it so!

    Enter SERAPION

SERAP.   Where, where's the queen?

ALEX.   How frightfully the holy coward stares
  As if not yet recover'd of the assault,
  When all his gods, and, what's more dear to him,
  His offerings were at stake!

SERAP.   Oh, horror, horror!
  Egypt has been; our latest hour has come;
  The queen of nations from her ancient seat
  Is sunk forever in the dark abyss;
  Time has unroll'd her glories to the last,
  And now clos'd up the volume.

CLEO.   Be more plain.
  Say whence thou com'st, though fate is in thy face,
  Which from thy haggard eyes looks wildly out,
  And threatens ere thou speak'st.

SERAP.   I came from Pharos;
  From viewing (spare me, and imagine it)
  Our land's last hope, your navy —

CLEO.   Vanquish'd?

SERAP.   No;
  They fought not.

CLEO.   Then they fled.

SERAP.   Nor that. I saw,
  With Antony, your well-appointed fleet
  Row out; and thrice he wav'd his hand on high,
  And thrice with cheerful cries they shouted back.
  'Twas then false Fortune, like a fawning strumpet
  About to leave the bankrupt prodigal,
  With a dissembl'd smile would kiss at parting
  And flatter to the last; the well-tim'd oars,
  Now dipp'd from every bank, now smoothly run
  To meet the foe; and soon indeed they met,
  But not as foes. In few,⁶ we saw their caps

---

⁵*Osiris* an Egyptian divinity, the husband of Isis.
⁶*in few* In brief.

On either side thrown up; th'Egyptian galleys,
Receiv'd like friends, pass'd through, and fell behind
The Roman rear; and now they all come forward
And ride within the port.

CLEO.   Enough, Serapion;
I've heard my doom. This needed not, you gods.
When I lost Antony, your work was done;
'Tis but superfluous malice. Where's my lord?
How bears he this last blow?

SERAP.   His fury cannot be express'd by words.
Thrice he attempted headlong to have fall'n
Full on his foes, and aim'd at Caesar's galley;
Withheld, he raves on you, cries he's betray'd.
Should he now find you —

ALEX.   Shun him; seek your safety
Till you can clear your innocence.

CLEO.   I'll stay.

ALEX.   You must not. Haste you to your monument,
While I make speed to Caesar.

CLEO.   Caesar! No,
I have no business with him.

ALEX.   I can work him
To spare your life, and let this madman perish.

CLEO.   Base, fawning wretch! Wouldst thou betray him too?
Hence from my sight! I will not hear a traitor;
'Twas thy design brought all this ruin on us.
Serapion, thou art honest; counsel me;
But haste, each moment's precious.

SERAP.   Retire. You must not yet see Antony.
He who began this mischief,
'Tis just he tempt the danger; let him clear you,
And, since he offer'd you his servile tongue,
To gain a poor precarious life from Caesar,
Let him expose that fawning eloquence,
And speak to Antony.

ALEX.   O heav'ns, I dare not;
I meet my certain death!

CLEO.   Slave, thou deserv'st it.
Not that I fear my lord, will I avoid him;
I know him noble; when he banish'd me
And thought me false, he scorn'd to take my life;
But I'll be justified, and then die with him.

ALEX.   Oh, pity me and let me follow you.

CLEO.   To death, if thou stir hence. Speak, if thou canst,
　　Now for thy life, which basely thou wouldst save,
　　While mine I prize at – this! Come, good Serapion.
　　　　　　　Exeunt CLEOPATRA, SERAPION, CHARMION *and* IRAS
ALEX.   Oh that I less could fear to lose this being,
　　Which, like a snowball in my coward hand,
　　The more 'tis grasp'd, the faster melts away.
　　Poor reason, what a wretched aid art thou!
　　For still, in spite of thee,
　　These two long lovers, soul and body, dread
　　Their final separation. Let me think.
　　What can I say to save myself from death?
　　No matter what becomes of Cleopatra.
ANT.   (*Within*) Which way? Where?
VENT.   (*Within*)   This leads to the monument.
ALEX.   Ah me, I hear him, yet I'm unprepar'd;
　　My gift of lying's gone,
　　And this court-devil, which I so oft have rais'd,
　　Forsakes me at my need. I dare not stay,
　　Yet cannot far go hence.   *Exit*
　　　Enter ANTONY *and* VENTIDIUS
ANT.   O happy Caesar, thou hast men to lead;
　　Think not 'tis thou hast conquer'd Antony;
　　But Rome has conquer'd Egypt. I'm betray'd.
VENT.   Curse on this treach'rous train!
　　Their soil and heav'n infect 'em all with baseness,
　　And their young souls come tainted to the world
　　With the first breath they draw.
ANT.   Th'original villain sure no god created;
　　He was a bastard of the sun by Nile,7
　　Ap'd into man, with all his mother's mud
　　Crusted about his soul.
VENT.   The nation is
　　One universal traitor, and their queen
　　The very spirit and extract of them all.
ANT.   Is there yet left
　　A possibility of aid from valour?
　　Is there one god unsworn to my destruction,
　　The least unmortgag'd hope? For, if there be,
　　Methinks I cannot fall beneath the fate
　　Of such a boy as Caesar.

7*by Nile* Legend had it that living creatures were generated by Nile mud.

The world's one half is yet in Antony,
And from each limb of it that's hew'd away,
The soul comes back to me.[8]

VENT.　　　　　　　　　　There yet remain
Three legions in the town. The last assault
Lopp'd off the rest; if death be your design –
As I must wish it now – these are sufficient
To make a heap about us of dead foes,
An honest pile for burial.

ANT.　　　　　　　　　They're enough.
We'll not divide our stars, but side by side
Fight emulous,[9] and with malicious eyes
Survey each other's acts. So every death
Thou giv'st, I'll take on me as a just debt
And pay thee back a soul.

VENT.　　Now you shall see I love you. Not a word
Of chiding more. By my few hours of life,
I am so pleas'd with this brave Roman fate
That I would not be Caesar, to outlive you.
When we put off this flesh and mount together,
I shall be shown to all th'ethereal crowd:
Lo, this is he who died with Antony!

ANT.　　Who knows but we may pierce through all their troops,
And reach my veterans yet? Tis worth the 'tempting,
T'o'erleap this gulf of fate,
And leave our wond'ring destinies behind.

　　　Enter ALEXAS, *trembling*

VENT.　　See, see, that villain!
See Cleopatra stamp'd upon that face,
With all her cunning, all her arts of falsehood!
How she looks out through those dissembling eyes!
How he has set his count'nance for deceit,
And promises a lie before he speaks!
Let me despatch him first.　　　　　　　　　　*Drawing*

ALEX.　　　　　　　　Oh, spare me, spare me!

ANT.　　Hold; he's not worth your killing. – On thy life,
Which thou mayst keep because I scorn to take it,
No syllable to justify thy queen;
Save thy base tongue its office.

---

[8]*one half . . . to me* After the defeat of Lepidus in 36 BC, Octavius and Antony
divided the Roman empire between them; 'I may lose parts of my share of the world;
however, I still possess my own soul'.

[9]*emulous* in rivalry.

ALEX.   Sir, she is gone,
Where she shall never be molested more
By love or you.
ANT.   Fled to her Dolabella!
Die, traitor! I revoke my promise! Die!   *Going to kill him*
ALEX.   Oh, hold, she is not fled.
ANT.   She is. My eyes
Are open to her falsehood; my whole life
Has been a golden dream of love and friendship,
But now I wake, I'm like a merchant rous'd
From soft repose to see his vessel sinking,
And all his wealth cast over. Ungrateful woman,
Who follow'd me but as the swallow summer,
Hatching her young ones in my kindly beams,
Singing her flatt'ries to my morning wake;
But now my winter comes, she spreads her wings,
And seeks the spring of Caesar.
ALEX.   Think not so;
Her fortunes have in all things mix'd with yours.
Had she betray'd her naval force to Rome,
How easily might she have gone to Caesar,
Secure by such a bribe!
VENT.   She sent it first,
To be more welcome after.
ANT.   'Tis too plain;
Else would she have appear'd to clear herself.
ALEX.   Too fatally she has; she could not bear
To be accus'd by you, but shut herself
Within her monument, look'd down and sigh'd,
While from her unchang'd face the silent tears
Dropp'd as they had not leave, but stole their parting.
Some undistinguish'd words she inly murmur'd;
At last she rais'd her eyes, and with such looks
As dying Lucrece[10] cast —
ANT.   My heart forebodes —
VENT.   All for the best. Go on.
ALEX.   She snatch'd her poniard,
And, ere we could prevent the fatal blow,
Plung'd it within her breast, then turn'd to me:
'Go, bear my lord', said she, 'my last farewell,

---

[10]*Lucrece* a Roman noblewoman, sixth century BC; according to legend, after being raped by Tarquinius Sextus, she took her own life.

And ask him if he yet suspect my faith'.
More she was saying, but death rush'd betwixt.
She half pronounc'd your name with her last breath,
And buried half within her.

VENT.   Heav'n be prais'd!

ANT.   Then art thou innocent, my poor dear love,
And art thou dead?
Oh, those two words! Their sound should be divided:
Hadst thou been false, and died; or hadst thou liv'd,
And hadst been true – But innocence and death!
This shows not well above. Then what am I,
The murderer of this truth, this innocence?
Thoughts cannot form themselves in words so horrid
As can express my guilt!

VENT.   Is't come to this? The gods have been too gracious,
And thus you thank 'em for it!

ANT.   (To ALEXAS)   Why stay'st thou here?
Is it for thee to spy upon my soul
And see its inward mourning? Get thee hence;
Thou art not worthy to behold what now
Becomes a Roman emperor to perform.

ALEX.   (Aside) He loves her still;
His grief betrays it. Good! The joy to find
She's yet alive completes the reconcilement.
I've sav'd myself and her. But, oh, the Romans!
Fate comes too fast upon my wit,
Hunts me too hard, and meets me at each double.[11]   Exit

VENT.   Would she had died a little sooner though,
Before Octavia went; you might have treated.[12]
Now 'twill look tame, and would not be receiv'd.
Come, rouse yourself, and let's die warm together.

ANT.   I will not fight; there's no more work for war.
The bus'ness of my angry hours is done.

VENT.   Caesar is at your gates.

ANT.   Why, let him enter;
He's welcome now.

VENT.   What lethargy has crept into your soul?

ANT.   'Tis but a scorn of life and just desire
To free myself from bondage.

VENT.   Do it bravely.

ANT.   I will, but not by fighting. O Ventidius,

---

[11]*double* doubling back.   [12]*treated* negotiated.

What should I fight for now? My queen is dead.
I was but great for her; my pow'r, my empire,
Were but my merchandise to buy her love,
And conquer'd kings, my factors. Now she's dead,
Let Caesar take the world, –
An empty circle, since the jewel's gone
Which made it worth my strife; my being's nauseous,
For all the bribes of life are gone away.

VENT.	Would you be taken?

ANT.	Yes, I would be taken,
But as a Roman ought, dead, my Ventidius,
For I'll convey my soul from Caesar's reach,
And lay down life myself. 'Tis time the world
Should have a lord and know whom to obey.
We two have kept its homage in suspense
And bent the globe, on whose each side we trod,
Till it was dented inwards. Let him walk
Alone upon't; I'm weary of my part.
My torch is out, and the world stands before me
Like a black desert at th'approach of night;
I'll lay me down and stray no further on.

VENT.	I could be griev'd,
But that I'll not outlive you. Choose your death,
For I have seen him in such various shapes,
I care not which I take. I'm only troubl'd,
The life I bear is worn to such a rag,
'Tis scarce worth giving. I could wish, indeed,
We threw it from us with a better grace;
That, like two lions taken in the toils,
We might at least thrust out our paws and wound
The hunters that enclose us.

ANT.	I have thought on it.
Ventidius, you must live.

VENT.	I must not, sir.

ANT.	Wilt thou not live, to speak some good of me,
To stand by my fair fame, and guard th'approaches
From the ill tongues of men?

VENT.	Who shall guard mine,
For living after you?

ANT.	Say I command it.

VENT.	If we die well, our deaths will speak themselves
And need no living witness.

ANT.	Thou hast lov'd me.

And fain I would reward thee. I must die;
Kill me, and take the merit of my death,
To make thee friends with Caesar.

VENT.   Thank your kindness.
You said I lov'd you, and in recompense
You bid me turn a traitor. Did I think
You would have us'd me thus, that I should die
With a hard thought of you?

ANT.   Forgive me, Roman.
Since I have heard of Cleopatra's death,
My reason bears no rule upon my tongue,
But lets my thoughts break all at random out.
I've thought better; do not deny me twice.

VENT.   By heav'n I will not.
Let it not be t'outlive you.

ANT.   Kill me first,
And then die thou; for 'tis but just thou serve
Thy friend before thyself.

VENT.   Give me your hand.
We soon shall meet again. Now, farewell, emperor!   *Embrace*
Methinks that word's too cold to be my last;
Since death sweeps all distinctions, farewell, friend!
That's all —
I will not make a bus'ness of a trifle,
And yet I cannot look on you and kill you;
Pray turn your face.

ANT.   I do. Strike home, be sure.

VENT.   Home as my sword will reach.   *Kills himself*

ANT.   Oh, thou mistak'st!
That wound was none of thine; give it me back;
Thou robb'st me of my death.

VENT.   I do indeed;
But think 'tis the first time I e'er deceiv'd you,
If that may plead my pardon. — And you, gods,
Forgive me, if you will, for I die perjur'd,
Rather than kill my friend.   *Dies*

ANT.   Farewell! Ever my leader, ev'n in death!
My queen and thou have got the start of me,
And I'm the lag of honour. — Gone so soon?
Is Death no more? He us'd him carelessly,
With a familiar kindness; ere he knock'd,
Ran to the door, and took him in his arms,
As who should say, 'You're welcome at all hours,

A friend need give no warning'. Books had spoil'd him,
For all the learn'd are cowards by profession.
'Tis not worth
My further thought; for death, for aught I know,
Is but to think no more. Here's to be satisfied.
                                            Falls on his sword

I've miss'd my heart. O unperforming hand!
Thou never couldst have err'd in a worse time.
My fortune jades me to the last; and death,
Like a great man, takes state, and makes me wait
For my admittance. —   *Trampling within*
                    Some, perhaps, from Caesar.
If he should find me living, and suspect
That I played booty¹³ with my life! I'll mend
My work ere they can reach me.   *Rises upon his knees*
        Enter CLEOPATRA, CHARMION *and* IRAS
CLEO.   Where is my lord? Where is he?
CHAR.   There he lies,
And dead Ventidius by him.
CLEO.   My fears were prophets; I am come too late.
O that accurs'd Alexas!   *Runs to him*
ANT.   Art thou living?
Or am I dead before I knew, and thou
The first kind ghost that meets me?
CLEO.   Help me seat him.
Send quickly, send for help!   *They place him in a chair*
ANT.   I am answer'd.
We live both. Sit thee down, my Cleopatra;
I'll make the most I can of life, to stay
A moment more with thee.
CLEO.   How is it with you?
ANT.   'Tis as with a man
Removing in a hurry; all pack'd up,
But one dear jewel that his haste forgot;
And he, for that, returns upon the spur.¹⁴
So I come back for thee.
CLEO.   Too long, you heav'ns, you have been cruel to me;
Now show your mended faith, and give me back
His fleeting life!
ANT.   It will not be, my love;

---

¹³*played booty* deliberately to lose in a game in order to trick a victim later.
¹⁴*spur* impulse.

I keep my soul by force.
Say but thou art not false.

CLEO.   'Tis now too late
To say I'm true; I'll prove it, and die with you.
Unknown to me, Alexas feign'd my death,
Which, when I knew, I hasted to prevent
This fatal consequence. My fleet betray'd
Both you and me.

ANT.   And Dolabella —
CLEO.   Scarce
Esteem'd before he lov'd, but hated now.

ANT.   Enough. My life's not long enough for more.
Thou say'st thou wilt come after. I believe thee,
For I can now believe whate'er thou say'st,
That we may part more kindly.

CLEO.   I will come.
Doubt not, my life, I'll come, and quickly too.
Caesar shall triumph o'er no part of thee.

ANT.   But grieve not while thou stay'st
My last disastrous times;
Think we have had a clear and glorious day,
And heav'n did kindly to delay the storm
Just till our close of ev'ning. Ten years' love,
And not a moment lost, but all improv'd
To th'utmost joys. What ages have we liv'd?
And now to die each other's; and, so dying,
While hand in hand we walk in groves below,
Whole troops of lovers' ghosts shall flock about us,
And all the train be ours.

CLEO.   Your words are like the notes of dying swans,
Too sweet to last. Were there so many hours
For your unkindness, and not one for love?

ANT.   No, not a minute. — This one kiss — more worth
Than all I leave to Caesar.   *Dies*

CLEO.   Oh, tell me so again,
And take ten thousand kisses for that word.
My lord, my lord! Speak, if you yet have being;
Sign to me, if you cannot speak; or cast
One look! Do anything that shows you live.

IRAS.   He's gone too far to hear you;
And this you see, a lump of senseless clay,
The leavings of a soul.

CHAR.   Remember, madam,

He charg'd you not to grieve.
CLEO.   And I'll obey him.
I have not lov'd a Roman not to know
What should become his wife; his wife, my Charmion!
For 'tis to that high title I aspire,
And now I'll not die less. Let dull Octavia
Survive, to mourn him dead. My nobler fate
Shall knit our spousals with a tie too strong
For Roman laws to break.
IRAS.   Will you then die?
CLEO.   Why shouldst thou make that question?
IRAS.   Caesar is merciful.
CLEO.   Let him be so
To those that want his mercy; my poor lord
Made no such cov'nant with him, to spare me
When he was dead. Yield me to Caesar's pride?
What! To be led in triumph through the streets,
A spectacle to base plebeian eyes,
While some dejected friend of Antony's,
Close in a corner, shakes his head, and mutters
A secret curse on her who ruin'd him!
I'll none of that.
CHAR.   Whatever you resolve,
I'll follow, ev'n to death.
IRAS.   I only fear'd
For you, but more should fear to live without you.
CLEO.   Why, now, 'tis as it should be. Quick, my friends,
Dispatch; ere this, the town's in Caesar's hands.
My lord looks down concern'd and fears my stay,
Lest I should be surpris'd;
Keep him not waiting for his love too long.
You, Charmion, bring my crown and richest jewels;
With 'em, the wreath of victory I made
(Vain augury!) for him who now lies dead.
You, Iras, bring the cure of all our ills.
IRAS.   The aspics, madam?
CLEO.   Must I bid you twice? *Exit* CHARMION *and* IRAS
'Tis sweet to die when they would force life on me,
To rush into the dark abode of death,
And seize him first. If he be like my love,
He is not frightful, sure.
We're now alone, in secrecy and silence;
And is not this like lovers? I may kiss

These pale, cold lips; Octavia does not see me,
And, oh, 'tis better far to have him thus
Than see him in her arms. – Oh, welcome, welcome!
    Enter CHARMION *and* IRAS
CHAR. What must be done?
CLEO.   Short ceremony, friends;
  But yet it must be decent. First, this laurel
  Shall crown my hero's head; he fell not basely,
  Nor left his shield behind him. Only thou
  Couldst triumph o'er thyself, and thou alone
  Wert worthy so to triumph.
CHAR.   To what end
  These ensigns of your pomp and royalty?
CLEO.   Dull that thou art! Why, 'tis to meet my love
  As when I saw him first, on Cydnus' bank,
  All sparkling, like a goddess. So adorn'd,
  I'll find him once again; my second spousals
  Shall match my first in glory. Haste, haste, both,
  And dress the bride of Antony.
CHAR.   'Tis done.
CLEO.   Now seat me by my lord. I claim this place,
  For I must conquer Caesar too, like him,
  And win my share o'the world. Hail, you dear relics
  Of my immortal love!
  Oh, let no impious hand remove you hence,
  But rest forever here! Let Egypt give
  His death that peace which it denied his life.
  Reach me the casket.
IRAS.   Underneath the fruit
  The aspic lies.
CLEO.   (*Pulling aside the leaves*) Welcome, thou kind deceiver!
  Thou best of thieves, who, with an easy key,
  Dost open life, and, unperceiv'd by us,
  Ev'n steal us from ourselves, discharging so
  Death's dreadful office better than himself,
  Touching our limbs so gently into slumber
  That Death stands by, deceiv'd by his own image,
  And thinks himself but sleep.
SERAP. (*Within*)   The queen, where is she?
  The town is yielded, Caesar's at the gates.
CLEO.   He comes too late t'invade the rights of death.
  Haste, bare my arm, and rouse the serpent's fury.
                 Holds out her arm and draws it back
  Coward flesh,

Wouldst thou conspire with Caesar to betray me,
As thou wert none of mine? I'll force thee t'it,
And not be sent by him,
But bring, myself, my soul to Antony.
                          Turns aside and then shows her arm bloody
Take hence; the work is done.
SERAP.   (*Within*)   Break ope the door,
And guard the traitor well.
CHAR.   The next is ours.
IRAS.   Now, Charmion, to be worthy
Of our great queen and mistress.   *They apply the aspics*
CLEO.   Already, death, I feel thee in my veins.
I go with such a will to find my lord
That we shall quickly meet.
A heavy numbness creeps through every limb,
And now 'tis at my head; my eyelids fall
And my dear love is vanish'd in a mist.
Where shall I find him, where? Oh, turn me to him,
And lay me on his breast! – Caesar, thy worst;
Now part us if thou canst.   *Dies*
          IRAS *sinks down at her feet and dies*; CHARMION *stands*
                behind her chair, as dressing her head
        Enter SERAPION, *two* PRIESTS, ALEXAS *bound*, Egyptians
PRIEST.   Behold, Serapion,
What havoc death has made!
SERAP.   'Twas what I fear'd. –
Charmion, is this well done?
CHAR.   Yes, 'tis well done, and like a queen, the last
Of her great race. I follow her.   *Sinks down, dies*
ALEX.   'Tis true,
She has done well. Much better thus to die
Than live to make a holiday in Rome.
SERAP.   See, see how the lovers sit in state together,
As they were giving laws to half mankind.
Th'impression of a smile left in her face
Shows she died pleas'd with him for whom she liv'd,
And went to charm him in another world.
Caesar's just ent'ring; grief has now no leisure.
Secure that villain as our pledge of safety,
To grace th'imperial triumph. – Sleep, blest pair,
Secure from human chance, long ages out,
While all the storms of fate fly o'er your tomb;
        And fame to late posterity shall tell,
        No lovers liv'd so great, or died so well.
                                                    Exeunt

EPILOGUE

Poets, like disputants when reasons fail,
Have one sure refuge left, and that's to rail.
'Fop, coxcomb, fool', are thunder'd through the pit,
And this is all their equipage of wit.
We wonder how the devil this diff'rence grows
Betwixt our fools in verse, and yours in prose;
For, faith, the quarrel rightly understood,
'Tis civil war with their own flesh and blood.
The threadbare author hates the gaudy coat,
And swears at the gilt coach, but swears afoot;
For 'tis observ'd of every scribbling man,
He grows a fop as fast as e'er he can;
Prunes up, and asks his oracle, the glass,
If pink or purple best become his face.
For our poor wretch, he neither rails nor prays,
Nor likes your wit just as you like his plays;
He has not yet so much of Mr Bayes.[1]
He does his best, and if he cannot please,
Would quietly sue out[2] his writ of ease.[3]
Yet, if he might his own grand jury call,
By the fair sex he begs to stand or fall.
Let Caesar's pow'r the men's ambition move,
But grace you him who lost the world for love!
Yet if some antiquated lady say,
The last age is not copied in his play;
Heav'n help the man who for that face must drudge,
Which only has the wrinkles of a judge.

[1]*Bayes* a character in *The Rehearsal* (performed 1671) by George Villiers, second Duke of Buckingham (1628–87) and others, a satirical portrait of John Dryden. He later satirised Buckingham as Zimri in *Absolom and Achitophel*, 1681.

[2]*sue out* put in suit.

[3]*writ of ease* a certificate of discharge from employment.

Let not the young and beauteous join with those;
For should you raise such numerous hosts of foes,
Young wits and sparks he to his aid must call;
'Tis more than one man's work to please you all.

Thomas Otway

VENICE PRESERVED
(1682)

Venice Preserved,
or
A Plot Discovered.
a tragedy,
as it is acted at the Duke's Theatre
Written by Thomas Otway.

London,
printed for Joseph Hindmarsh,
at the sign of the Black Bull,
over against the Royal Exchange in Cornhill,
1682

BIOGRAPHY

Thomas Otway was born in Sussex on 3 March 1652; he was educated at Winchester College and Christ Church, Oxford. He was briefly an unsuccessful actor and an army officer 1678–79. John Dryden was a good friend. For the last ten years of his life he had an unrequited passion for the actress Elizabeth Barry, who played Belvidera in *Venice Preserved* (1682 and later) and major roles in other Otway plays. His best plays are *The Orphan*, 1680, a domestic tragedy; *The Soldier's Fortune*, 1681, a comedy; and *Venice Preserved*, 1682, a tragedy. Otway died in poverty in 1685.

INTRODUCTION

Venice Preserved has enjoyed three centuries of stage performance, evidence of a continuing appeal to the varying tastes of many audiences. The tragedy incorporates several dilemmas, raising timeless questions about duty and friendship, parent-child relationships, the integrity of marriage, loyalty towards a corrupt, oppressive state, and the sanctity of an oath.

From the beginning of the play, weaknesses in the rebels are as apparent as corruption in the rulers of Venice whom they aim to overthrow. Pierre is a naive and self-centred idealist; the shallow, uxorious Jaffeir can be persuaded to break a solemn oath to his best male friend, and the opportunistic Renault attempts to rape Jaffeir's wife, Belvidera. Otway implies that Venice would not be significantly better off after a rebel victory. The quality of the present Venetian establishment is symbolised by the unattractive senators Priuli and Antonio, perhaps intended to ridicule the earlier enthusiasm of English whigs for Venice as a model republic.

The dilemma motif is developed in individual terms primarily through the masochistic Jaffeir, who is torn by conflicting loyalties: first to Belvidera and second, to his companion Pierre. Should Jaffeir remain loyal to his revolutionary comrade, who wishes to see every senator dead, or should he betray Pierre and his associates in order to save the lives of all the senators, at the behest of Belvidera? She is, of course, anxious about her father, Senator Priuli, whom Jaffeir has much reason to hate.

Out of this problem others evolve: Belvidera must choose between husband and father, Pierre between denunciation of Renault and a show of unity amongst the restless conspirators, and old Renault must consider his lust and his loyalty to Pierre. These and other conflicting demands create the dramatic tensions from which the tragedies of the three principal characters grow.

Otway incorporates in the play a tense commentary on marriage –

beginning with passionate young love opposed by an unforgiving father, who after three years still resents his daughter's having married without his approval. There seems to have been nothing truly objectionable about the suitor, particularly since the man had once saved the life of Priuli's only offspring; Jaffeir's social status evidently did not come up to the honour of the old man's house.

On the surface of the plot as developed in Act I, no conflict is apparent between Jaffeir's love for Belvidera and his friendship for Pierre; nor will many who read or see *Venice Preserved* in the present century object strenuously to Pierre's intention to overthrow a corrupt oligarchy. The idealism of both young men is quickly eroded: Jaffeir's antagonism towards the senate is strongly influenced by the fact that his much-resented father-in-law is a senator who has turned his own daughter and her husband out of their home. Pierre too has a personal motivation for his rebellion against the senate: another 'wretched old but itching senator', Antonio, has stolen his mistress Aquilina.

These episodes, building towards the planned overthrow of the senate, come to a climax in Act III with the appearance of Senator Antonio, the old man with whom Aquilina has a mercenary attachment; she puts up with his uncouth, perverse behaviour for the sake of his purses of gold. (He has made her his heir.) By this point, the centre of the play (III, ii), the way is prepared for the conspirators, headed by Pierre and joined by Jaffeir, to surprise the senate and kill them all. Now, by urging her husband to reveal the plot, Belvidera creates the terrible dilemma for Jaffeir. He wishes to keep the respect of Pierre (to whom he earlier vowed to participate in the insurrection, maintaining his idealistic loyalty to the cause even after he learns of Renault's attempted rape of his wife), but at the same time Jaffeir is anxious to retain Belvidera's love.

As the scene continues, Jaffeir's dilemma intensifies: if he reveals the conspiracy to the senate as Belvidera passionately requests, he will save both Antonio, whom Pierre hates, and his father-in-law, Priuli. Jaffeir could have retained some self-respect after his act of treachery had the senate remained bound to their word to free Pierre and the other conspirators; however, speaking for all the rebels, Pierre refuses to confess to the plot, inviting an 'honourable death', thus leaving the senate effectively no option but to punish the guilty. The apparent treachery of the senate leaves Jaffeir, overwhelmed with shame and chagrin, ready to consider killing his beloved Belvidera. To him the only compensation for his wrongdoing must be to cheat the state of punishment of Pierre by stabbing him and then committing suicide. The impression of tragic waste is reinforced by the appearance on stage of the distraught and dying Belvidera.

For the scholar or historian *Venice Preserved* is puzzling when seen as political allegory.[1] Thomas Otway's Tory and royalist sympathies were well known; thus it is plausible to recognise a parallel between the Venice of the play, threatened by rebellion, and England of the early 1680s, under attack by Whig dissidents. (*Venice Preserved* was first performed in February 1682.) The major political tensions in England then centred on the succession to the throne. Charles II had no legitimate offspring; consequently, there was every likelihood that he would be succeeded by his brother, James, Duke of York, a practising Catholic (he was briefly King James II, 1685–88).

This prospect dismayed many Englishmen and created a division between Tory supporters of Charles II (or heir-apparent James) and Whig promoters – led by the ruthless Anthony Ashley Cooper, first Earl of Shaftesbury – of James, Duke of Monmouth, an illegitimate, though Protestant, son of King Charles.

In both the dramatised seventeenth-century Venice and the real England of 1681–82 rebellious forces were very active. Amongst the followers of Pierre in the play, Otway included old Renault, described in the first Prologue as 'Turbulent, subtle, mischievous and bold, . . . Loves fumbling with a wench . . .', words that echo John Dryden's character study of Achitophel, i.e. the Earl of Shaftesbury, in *Absalom and Achitophel* (Part I, lines 150–213 ff.). The poem was published only a few months before Otway's play reached the stage (he and Dryden were good friends).

Although this oblique allusion and other references make it easy to see Renault as an allegorical portrait of Shaftesbury, the playwright complicates his allegory by identifying also Senator Antonio with Shaftesbury through obvious suggestions and parallels in the same Prologue and the drama. Antonio is, however, not one of the dissidents like Renault, but a senator, a member of the ruling clique, which at the end of the play endures, albeit chastened. The drama therefore creates the perplexing situation of Renault (representing Shaftesbury) plotting assiduously to overthrow Antonio (who also represents Shaftesbury).[2]

[1] In 1618 Venice had experienced a rebellion comparable to that in Otway's drama; however, his prologues, epilogues and allusions in the text make clear that the playwright had contemporary English parallels more prominently in mind.
[2] In '*Venice Preserv'd* Reconsidered' (*Tulane Studies in English*, I, 1949, pp. 81–118), Aline Mackenzie plausibly suggested that Senator Antonio was a late addition to the play, representing no more than Otway's effort near the end of 1681 to capitalise on a *cause célèbre* (the downfall of Shaftesbury) and to bring up to date a play that had already been constructed around a *general* political allegory. Many eighteenth-century productions of *Venice Preserved* omitted Antonio's 'Nicky-Nacky' scenes (III, i and part of V, i).

The most likely explanation for the seeming confusion is to consider that Otway's inconsistent intention was to show allegorically the rebels and the senate of Venice as two kinds of English Whigs (both strongly influenced by the Earl of Shaftesbury); the conspirators represent influential Whig private citizens, especially in the City of London, attacking the rulers of the nation, Charles II and his associates. The senate symbolises the Whig-dominated parliament, also opposed to the probable succession of James, Duke of York.

Otway's message is that both a corrupt aristocracy and any group of men plotting to overturn a government are destructive in nature (although the former, with good judgment and tolerance, is capable of improvement, as illustrated in the tolerance of the Duke and the later actions of Priuli). The playwright warns against extreme positions, self-interest and greed in any nation. Whilst he was writing the play during 1681, the Popish Plot of 1678 was still in English minds, and the Exclusion crisis (designed by the Whigs to prevent the Duke of York from succeeding to the throne) was at its peak. By February 1682 Shaftesbury had been in effect deposed (in November 1682 he fled to Holland, where he died in January 1683) and the immediate crisis had passed. The nation was stable for the time being, and it was safe for the Duke of York to return from exile in Scotland.

Otway wrote more than a political allegory, which might be of limited interest three centuries later. The tragedy of *Venice Preserved* centres on three participants in the unsuccessful rebellion. Jaffeir, Pierre and Belvidera meet their deaths as a result of potentially heroic but misguided actions and thereby engender our pity. A confusion of loyalty and self-interest leads to the destruction of Jaffeir and Pierre's hopes of destroying a decadent government. At his best Pierre protests nobly against the corrupt senate; yet his indignation has self-interested roots. Pierre elicits sympathy by determining to die rather than suffer the ignominy of confession, chains and public derision.

An unsentimental reader or viewer of *Venice Preserved* observes Jaffeir deteriorate from the point at which he yields to his wife's importunities to reveal the plot to the Duke and senate; however, he redeems himself by his late recognition that self-respect is possible by cheating the state of its opportunity to punish both Pierre and himself. Belvidera's extended dilemma comes to a tragic climax when she realises that she is partly responsible for the deaths of Jaffeir and Pierre; her life ends, like Ophelia's, in the pathos of an unhinged mind.

Partly through the influence of Restoration heroic plays, the tone of tragedy was changing, not only by the incorporation of a sentimental, melodramatic quality, reinforced by high rhetoric, but by a modification of the traditional elements of pity, fear and catharsis. At the end of this tragedy nothing has changed as a result of the heroes' efforts.[3] The tragic impact of the play derives from the destruction of characters who have struggled with conflicting interests, ultimately to achieve self-recognition. The misguided idealism which leads to their downfall stands in sharp contrast to the sordidness of the comic scenes, the violence of the main action and the ugliness of the imagery.

Otway's principal source was a novel, based on fact, by César Vischard, L'Abbé de Saint-Réal, *A Conspiracy of the Spaniards against the State of Venice* (1675, with a second English edition in 1679); the playwright magnified and modified the roles of Jaffeir, Pierre, and Renault, and he invented Belvidera to suit the purposes of his domestic tragedy. In addition Otway created Senator Antonio to play roles in both the private and the political drama.

---

[3] At the beginning of Act IV, ii, the Duke and senate have already congregated in the middle of the night, evidently called together by Priuli ('From unknown hands I had this warning'). Thus prepared and with guards nearby, they could have defeated the conspirators (Pierre's ten thousand supporters [II, iii] seem to have been mythical), making Jaffeir's message redundant and his traitorous action ironically unnecessary.

BIBLIOGRAPHY

Venice Preserved

A. M. Taylor, *Next to Shakespeare; Otway's 'Venice Preserv'd' and 'The Orphan' and their History on the London Stage*. Durham, N. C., 1950.

W. H. McBurney, 'Otway's Tragic Muse Debauched: Sensuality in *Venice Preserv'd*'. *Journal of English and Germanic Philology*, 58 (July 1959), 380–99.

R. Berman, 'Nature in *Venice Preserv'd*'. *ELH*, 36 (September 1969), 529–43.

B. Proffitt, 'Religious Symbolism in Otway's *Venice Preserv'd*'. *Papers on Language and Literature*, 7 (Winter 1971), 26–37.

D. W. Hughes, 'A New Look at *Venice Preserv'd*'. *Studies in English Literature 1500–1900*, 11 (1971), 437–57.

N. Rabkin, *Shakespeare and the Problem of Meaning*. Chicago, 1981.

J. Durant, '"Honour's Toughest Task": Family and State in *Venice Preserved*'. *Studies in Philology*, 71 (October 1974), 484–503.

K. P. Warner, *Thomas Otway*. Boston, 1982.

M. DePorte, 'Otway and the Straits of Venice'. *Papers on Language and Literature*, 18 (Summer 1982), 245–57.

D. Bywaters, 'Venice, its Senate, and its Plot in Otway's *Venice Preserv'd*'. *Modern Philology*, 80 (February 1983), 256–63.

K. M. Rogers, 'Masculine and Feminine Values in Restoration Drama: the Distinctive Power of *Venice Preserved*'. *Texas Studies in Literature and Language*, 27 (Winter 1985), 390–404.

H. M. Solomon, 'The Rhetoric of "Redressing Grievances": Court Propaganda as the Hermeneutical Key to *Venice Preserv'd*'. *ELH*, 53 (Summer 1986), 289–310.

J. Munns, '"Plain as the Light in the Cowcumber": a Note on the Conspiracy in Thomas Otway's *Venice Preserv'd*'. *Modern Philology*, 85 (August 1987), 54–7.

P. Harth, 'Political Interpretations of *Venice Preserv'd*'. *Modern Philology*, 85 (May 1988), 345–62.

EPISTLE DEDICATORY

TO HER GRACE THE DUCHESS OF PORTSMOUTH[1]

Madam:

Were it possible for me to let the world know how entirely your
Grace's goodness has devoted a poor man to your service, were there
words enough in speech to express the mighty sense I have of your
great bounty towards me, surely I should write and talk of it forever;
but your Grace has given me so large a theme and laid so very vast a
foundation that imagination wants stock to build upon it. I am as one
dumb when I would speak of it, and when I strive to write, I want a
scale of thought sufficient to comprehend the height of it.

Forgive me then, madam, if (as a poor peasant[2] once made a present
of an apple to an emperor) I bring this small tribute, the humble growth
of my little garden, and lay it at your feet. Believe it is paid you with the
utmost gratitude, believe that so long as I have thought to remember
how very much I owe your generous nature, I will ever have a heart that
shall be grateful for it too: your Grace, next heaven, deserves it amply
from me; that gave me life, but on a hard condition, till your extended
favour taught me to prize the gift, and took the heavy burden it was
clogged with from me: I mean hard fortune. When I had enemies that
with malicious power kept back and shaded me from those royal
beams, whose warmth is all I have, or hope to live by, your noble pity
and compassion found me, where I was far cast backward from my

---

[1] *Duchess of Portsmouth* Louise Renée de Kéroualle, 1649–1734, the French
mistress of Charles II, privately working with the Whigs in the hope that her son by
the king, Charles Lennox, might succeed to the throne. He is 'the young prince'
referred to at p. 316, line 11 below.

[2] *a poor peasant* i.e. an innocent cause of trouble. The emperor, Theodosius II, of
the eastern Roman empire, gave an apple to his wife; she made a gift of it to her
lover, who later offered the same apple to the emperor.

blessing, down in the rear of fortune, called me up, placed me in the shrine, and I have felt its comfort. You have in that restored me to my native right, for a steady faith and loyalty to my prince was all the inheritance my father left me, and however hardly my ill-fortune deal with me, 'tis what I prize so well that I ne'er pawned it yet, and hope I ne'er shall part with it.

Nature and fortune were certainly in league when you were born, and as the first took care to give you beauty enough to enslave the hearts of all the world, so the other resolved to do its merit justice, that none but a monarch fit to rule that world should e'er possess it, and in it he had an empire. The young prince you have given him, by his blooming virtues, early declares the mighty stock he came from; and as you have taken all the pious care of a dear mother and a prudent guardian to give him a noble and generous education, may it succeed according to his merits and your wishes.

May he grow up to be a bulwark to his illustrious father and a patron to his loyal subjects, with wisdom and learning to assist him, whenever called to his councils, to defend his right against the encroachments of republicans in his senates, to cherish such men as shall be able to vindicate the royal cause, that good and fit servants to the crown may never be lost for want of a protector. May he have courage and conduct, fit to fight his battles abroad and terrify his rebels at home; and that all these may be yet more sure, may he never, during the springtime of his years, when these growing virtues ought with care to be cherished in order to their ripening, may he never meet with vicious natures or the tongues of faithless, sordid, insipid flatterers to blast 'em. To conclude: may he be as great as the hand of fortune (with his honour) shall be able to make him, and may your Grace, who are so good a mistress and so noble a patroness, never meet with a less grateful servant than,

Madam,

Your Grace's entirely devoted creature,

THOMAS OTWAY.

PROLOGUE[1]

In these distracted times, when each man dreads
The bloody strategems of busy heads;
When we have fear'd three years[2] we know not what,
Till witnesses begin to die o' the rot,
What made our poet meddle with a plot?
Was't that he fancied, for the very sake
And name of plot, his trifling play might take?[3]
For there's not in't one inch-board[4] evidence,
But 'tis, he says, to reason plain and sense,
And that he thinks a plausible defence.
Were Truth by Sense and Reason to be tried,
Sure all our swearers might be laid aside.
No, of such tools our author has no need,
To make his plot or make his play succeed;
He of black bills[5] has no prodigious tales,
Or Spanish pilgrims[6] cast ashore in Wales.
Here's not one murder'd magistrate[7] at least,
Kept rank like ven'son for a City feast,

[1] *Prologue* The later prologues and epilogues may be found in Appendix A, pp. 659–69.

[2] *three years* The Popish Plot, instigated by Titus Oates, began in 1678; reverberations continued until his imprisonment in 1685 (*Venice Preserved* was first produced early in 1682).

[3] *take* be popular.

[4] *inch-board* i.e. solid, tangible. The allusion is to a board one inch thick.

[5] *black bills* battle weapons, like halberds or pikes.

[6] *Spanish pilgrims* A false rumour claimed that Jesuits intended to invade England via Wales with an Irish army disguised as Spanish pilgrims.

[7] *murder'd magistrate* Sir Edmund Berry Godfrey, 1621–1678, was murdered, apparently by followers of Titus Oates, at Somerset House, London; the culprits are said to have removed the body a few days later in a sedan chair.

Grown four days stiff, the better to prepare
And fit his pliant limbs to ride in chair.
Yet here's an army rais'd, though under ground,
But no man seen, nor one commission[8] found;
Here is a traitor too that's very old,
Turbulent, subtle, mischievous, and bold,
Bloody, revengeful, and, to crown his part,
Loves fumbling with a wench with all his heart;
Till after having many changes pass'd,
In spite of age (thanks heaven) is hang'd at last.
Next is a senator that keeps a whore,
In Venice none a higher office bore;
To lewdness every night the letcher ran,
Show me, all London, such another man,
Match him at Mother Creswold's[9] if you can.
O Poland,[10] Poland! Had it been thy lot,
T' have heard in time of this Venetian plot,
Thou surely chosen hadst one king from thence,
And honoured them as thou hast England since.

[8] *commission* Pope Innocent XI was reputed to have sent commissions to England to raise a rebel army.

[9] *Mother Creswold* or Creswell, a well-known procuress of London, popular amongst the Whigs.

[10] *Poland* Shaftesbury was said to have sought the throne of Poland in 1675.

DRAMATIS PERSONAE

DUKE OF VENICE | Mr D[avid] Williams
PRIULI, *father to* BELVIDERA,
  a senator | Mr Bowman[1]
ANTONIO, *a fine speaker in the
  senate* | Mr [Anthony] Leigh
JAFFEIR | Mr [Thomas] Betterton
PIERRE | Mr [William] Smith
RENAULT | Mr [John] Wiltshire
BEDAMORE | Mr Gillo[2]
SPINOSA | Mr [Thomas] Percival
THEODORE
ELIOT
REVILLIDO | *conspirators*
DURAND
MEZZANA
BRAMVEIL
TERNON
BRABE
RETROSI
BELVIDERA | Mrs [Elizabeth] Barry
AQUILINA | Mrs [Elizabeth] Currer
TWO WOMEN, *attendants on*
  BELVIDERA
TWO WOMEN, *servants to*
  AQUILINA
[TWO FOOTMEN]
THE COUNCIL OF TEN
OFFICER
GUARDS
FRIAR
EXECUTIONER *and* RABBLE.

[Scene: Venice.]

[1] John Boman.
[2] Thomas Gillow.

VENICE PRESERVED

Act One

SCENE ONE

[Near PRIULI'S *house]*

Enter PRIULI *and* JAFFEIR

PRIU.   No more! I'll hear no more; begone and leave.
JAFF.   Not hear me? By my sufferings but you shall!
  My lord, my lord! I'm not that abject wretch
  You think me. Patience! Where's the distance throws
  Me back so far but I may boldly speak
  In right, though proud oppression will not hear me!
PRIU.   Have you not wrong'd me?
JAFF.   Could my nature e'er
  Have brook'd injustice or the doing wrongs,
  I need not now thus low have bent myself
  To gain a hearing from a cruel father!
  Wrong'd you?
PRIU.   Yes, wrong'd me; in the nicest point,
  The honour of my house, you have done me wrong;
  You may remember (for I now will speak
  And urge its baseness), when you first came home
  From travel, with such hopes as made you look'd on
  By all men's eyes a youth of expectation.
  Pleas'd with your growing virtue, I receiv'd you,
  Courted, and sought to raise you to your merits.
  My house, my table, nay my fortune too,
  My very self, was yours; you might have us'd me
  To your best service. Like an open friend,
  I treated, trusted you, and thought you mine;
  When in requital of my best endeavours,
  You treacherously practis'd to undo me,
  Seduc'd the weakness of my age's darling,
  My only child, and stole her from my bosom:
  O Belvidera!
JAFF.   'Tis to me you owe her;

Childless you had been else, and in the grave,
Your name extinct, nor no more Priuli heard of.
You may remember, scarce five years are past,
Since in your brigandine you sail'd to see
The Adriatic wedded by our Duke,[1]
And I was with you. Your unskilful pilot
Dash'd us upon a rock; when to your boat
You made for safety, ent'red first yourself;
The affrighted Belvidera following next,
As she stood trembling on the vessel side,
Was by a wave wash'd off into the deep,
When instantly I plung'd into the sea,
And buffeting the billows to her rescue,
Redeem'd her life with half the loss of mine.
Like a rich conquest in one hand I bore her,
And with the other dash'd the saucy waves
That throng'd and press'd to rob me of my prize.
I brought her, gave her to your despairing arms;
Indeed you thank'd me, but a nobler gratitude
Rose in her soul, for from that hour she lov'd me,
Till for her life she paid me with herself.

PRIU.   You stole her from me, like a thief you stole her
At dead of night; that cursed hour you chose
To rifle me of all my heart held dear.
May all your joys in her prove false like mine;
A sterile fortune and a barren bed
Attend you both; continual discord make
Your days and nights bitter and grievous. Still
May the hard hand of a vexatious need
Oppress and grind you, till at last you find
The curse of disobedience all your portion.

JAFF.   Half of your curse you have bestow'd in vain;
Heav'n has already crown'd our faithful loves
With a young boy, sweet as his mother's beauty.
May he live to prove more gentle than his grandsire,
And happier than his father!

PRIU.   Rather live
To bait[2] thee for his bread, and din your ears

---

[1] *Adriatic . . . Duke* The Ascension Day ceremony during which the Doge threw a ring into the sea to symbolise the union of Venice and the Adriatic Sea. See IV, ii, p. 368.

[2] *bait* harass.

With hungry cries, whilst his unhappy mother
Sits down and weeps in bitterness of want.

JAFF.   You talk as if it would please you.

PRIU.   'Twould, by heav'n.
Once she was dear indeed; the drops that fell
From my sad heart when she forgot her duty,
The fountain of my life was not so precious;
But she is gone, and if I am a man
I will forget her.

JAFF.   Would I were in my grave!

PRIU.   And she too with thee;
For, living here, you're but my curs'd remembrancers
I once was happy.

JAFF.   You use me thus because you know my soul
Is fond of Belvidera. You perceive
My life feeds on her; therefore thus you treat me.
Oh, could my soul ever have known satiety!
Were I that thief, the doer of such wrongs
As you upbraid me with, what hinders me
But I might send her back to you with contumely,
And court my fortune where she would be kinder?

PRIU.   You dare not do't.

JAFF.   Indeed, my lord, I dare not.
My heart that awes me is too much my master.
Three years are past since first our vows were plighted,
During which time, the world must bear me witness,
I have treated Belvidera like your daughter,
The daughter of a senator of Venice;
Distinction, place, attendance, and observance,
Due to her birth, she always has commanded;
Out of my little fortune I have done this,
Because (though hopeless e'er to win your nature)
The world might see I lov'd her for herself,
Not as the heiress of the great Priuli.

PRIU.   No more!

JAFF.   Yes, all, and then adieu forever.
There's not a wretch that lives on common charity
But's happier than me, for I have known
The luscious sweets of plenty, every night
Have slept with soft content about my head,
And never wak'd but to a joyful morning;
Yet now must fall like a full ear of corn,
Whose blossom 'scap'd, yet's wither'd in the ripening.

PRIU.   Home and be humble, study to retrench;
Discharge the lazy vermin of thy hall,
Those pageants of thy folly,
Reduce the glittering trappings of thy wife
To humble weeds, fit for thy little state;
Then to some suburb cottage both retire;
Drudge, to feed loathsome life. Get brats and starve.
Home, home, I say.   *Exit* PRIULI

JAFF.   Yes, if my heart would let me —
This proud, this swelling heart — home I would go,
But that my doors are hateful to my eyes,
Fill'd and damm'd up with gaping creditors,
Watchful as fowlers when their game will spring;
I have now not fifty ducats in the world,
Yet still I am in love, and pleas'd with ruin.
O Belvidera! Oh, she is my wife,
And we will bear our wayward fate together,
But ne'er know comfort more.
      Enter PIERRE

PIERRE.   My friend, good morrow!
How fares the honest partner of my heart?
What, melancholy? Not a word to spare me?

JAFF.   I'm thinking, Pierre, how that damn'd starving quality
Call'd honesty got footing in the world.

PIERRE.   Why, pow'rful villainy first set it up,
For its own ease and safety; honest men
Are the soft, easy cushions on which knaves
Repose and fatten. Were all mankind villains,
They'd starve each other; lawyers would want practice,
Cut-throats rewards. Each man would kill his brother
Himself; none would be paid or hang'd for murder.
Honesty was a cheat invented first
To bind the hands of bold, deserving rogues,
That fools and cowards might sit safe in power,
And lord it uncontroll'd above their betters.

JAFF.   Then honesty is but a notion.

PIERRE.   Nothing else;
Like wit, much talk'd of, not to be defin'd.
He that pretends to most, too, has least share in't;
'Tis a ragged virtue. Honesty! No more on't.

JAFF.   Sure thou art honest?

PIERRE.   So indeed men think me,
But they're mistaken, Jaffeir; I am a rogue

As well as they,
A fine, gay, bold-fac'd villain, as thou seest me.
'Tis true, I pay my debts when they're contracted;
I steal from no man, would not cut a throat
To gain admission to a great man's purse
Or a whore's bed; I'd not betray my friend
To get his place or fortune; I scorn to flatter
A blown-up fool above me, or crush the wretch beneath me;
Yet, Jaffeir, for all this, I am a villain!

JAFF. A villain —

PIERRE.   Yes, a most notorious villain:
To see the suff'rings of my fellow-creatures,
And own myself a man; to see our senators
Cheat the deluded people with a show
Of liberty, which yet they ne'er must taste of;
They say by them our hands are free from fetters,
Yet whom they please they lay in basest bonds,
Bring whom they please to infamy and sorrow,
Drive us like wracks down the rough tide of power,
Whilst no hold's left to save us from destruction.
All that bear this are villains, and I one,
Not to rouse up at the great call of nature,
And check the growth of these domestic spoilers,
That make us slaves and tell us 'tis our charter.

JAFF. O Aquilina! Friend, to lose such beauty,
The dearest purchase of thy noble labours;
She was thy right by conquest, as by love.

PIERRE. O Jaffeir! I'd so fix'd my heart upon her
That wheresoe'er I fram'd a scheme of life
For time to come she was my only joy
With which I wish'd to sweeten future cares.
I fancied pleasures — none but one that loves
And dotes as I did can imagine like 'em —
When in the extremity of all these hopes,
In the most charming hour of expectation,
Then when our eager wishes soar the highest,
Ready to stoop and grasp the lovely game,
A haggard owl, a worthless kite of prey,
With his foul wings sail'd in and spoil'd my quarry.

JAFF. I know the wretch, and scorn him as thou hat'st him.

PIERRE. Curse on the common good that's so protected,
Where every slave that heaps up wealth enough
To do much wrong becomes a lord of right!

I, who believ'd no ill could e'er come near me,
Found in the embraces of my Aquilina
A wretched old but itching senator,
A wealthy fool that had bought out my title,
A rogue that uses beauty like a lambskin,
Barely to keep him warm. That filthy cuckoo too
Was in my absence crept into my nest,
And spoiling all my brood of noble pleasure.

JAFF.　Didst thou not chase him thence?

PIERRE.　　　　　　　　　　　　　　　　I did, and drove
The rank old bearded hirco³ stinking home.
The matter was complain'd of in the senate,
I summon'd to appear, and censur'd basely,
For violating something they call 'privilege'.
This was the recompense of my service;
Would I'd been rather beaten by a coward!
A soldier's mistress, Jaffeir, 's his religion;
When that's profan'd, all other ties are broken.
That even dissolves all former bonds of service,
And from that hour I think myself as free
To be the foe as e'er the friend of Venice.
Nay, dear revenge, whene'er thou call'st I'm ready.

JAFF.　I think no safety can be here for virtue,
And grieve, my friend, as much as thou to live
In such a wretched state as this of Venice,
Where all agree to spoil the public good,
And villains fatten with the brave man's labours.

PIERRE.　We have neither safety, unity, nor peace,
For the foundation's lost of common good.
Justice is lame as well as blind amongst us;
The laws (corrupted to their ends that make 'em)
Serve but for instruments of some new tyranny,
That every day starts up to enslave us deeper.
Now could this glorious cause but find out friends
To do it right! O Jaffeir, then might'st thou
Not wear these seals of woe upon thy face.
The proud Priuli should be taught humanity,
And learn to value such a son as thou art.
I dare not speak, but my heart bleeds this moment!

JAFF.　Curs'd be the cause, though I thy friend be part on't!
Let me partake the troubles of thy bosom,

³*hirco* goat.

For I am us'd to misery, and perhaps
May find a way to sweeten 't to thy spirit.
PIERRE.　Too soon it will reach thy knowledge –
JAFF.　　　　　　　　　　　　　　　　　Then from thee
Let it proceed. There's virtue in thy friendship
Would make the saddest tale of sorrow pleasing,
Strengthen my constancy, and welcome ruin.
PIERRE.　Then thou art ruin'd!
JAFF.　　　　　　　　　　　　That I long since knew;
I and ill-fortune have been long acquaintance.
PIERRE.　I pass'd this very moment by thy doors,
And found them guarded by a troop of villains;
The sons of public rapine were destroying.
They told me, by the sentence of the law
They had commission to seize all thy fortune,
Nay more, Priuli's cruel hand hath sign'd it.
Here stood a ruffian with a horrid face
Lording it o'er a pile of massy plate,
Tumbl'd into a heap for public sale;
There was another making villainous jests
At thy undoing; he had ta'en possession
Of all thy ancient most domestic ornaments,
Rich hangings, intermix'd and wrought with gold,
The very bed which on thy wedding night
Receiv'd thee to the arms of Belvidera,
The scene of all thy joys, was violated
By the coarse hands of filthy dungeon villains,
And thrown amongst the common lumber.
JAFF.　Now, thanks heav'n –
PIERRE.　Thank heav'n, for what?
JAFF.　　　　　　　　　　　　That I am not worth a ducat.
PIERRE.　Curse thy dull stars, and the worse fate of Venice,
Where brothers, friends, and fathers, all are false;
Where there's no trust, no truth; where innocence
Stoops under vile oppression, and vice lords it.
Hadst thou but seen, as I did, how at last
Thy beauteous Belvidera, like a wretch
That's doom'd to banishment, came weeping forth,
Shining through tears, like April suns in showers
That labour to o'ercome the cloud that loads 'em,
Whilst two young virgins, on whose arms she lean'd,
Kindly look'd up, and at her grief grew sad,
As if they catch'd the sorrows that fell from her.

Even the lewd rabble that were gather'd round
To see the sight stood mute when they beheld her,
Govern'd their roaring throats and grumbl'd pity.
I could have hugg'd the greasy rogues; they pleas'd me.
JAFF.   I thank thee for this story from my soul,
Since now I know the worst that can befall me.
Ah, Pierre, I have a heart that could have borne
The roughest wrong my fortune could have done me;
But when I think what Belvidera feels,
The bitterness her tender spirit tastes of,
I own myself a coward. Bear my weakness,
If throwing thus my arms about thy neck,
I play the boy, and blubber in thy bosom.
Oh, I shall drown thee with my sorrows!
PIERRE.   Burn!
First burn and level Venice to thy ruin.
What, starve like beggars' brats in frosty weather
Under a hedge, and whine ourselves to death!
Thou or thy cause shall never want assistance
Whilst I have blood or fortune fit to serve thee.
Command my heart; thou art every way its master.
JAFF.   No. There's a secret pride in bravely dying.
PIERRE.   Rats die in holes and corners, dogs run mad;
Man knows a braver remedy for sorrow:
Revenge! The attribute of gods, they stamp'd it
With their great image on our natures. Die!
Consider well the cause that calls upon thee,
And if thou art base enough, die then. Remember
Thy Belvidera suffers: Belvidera!
Die! Damn first! What, be decently interr'd
In a churchyard, and mingle thy brave dust
With stinking rogues that rot in dirty winding-sheets,
Surfeit-slain fools, the common dung o' the soil!
JAFF.   Oh!
PIERRE.   Well said. Out with 't; swear a little —
JAFF.   Swear!
By sea and air! By earth, by heaven and hell,
I will revenge my Belvidera's tears!
Hark thee, my friend: Priuli — is — a senator!
PIERRE.   A dog!
JAFF.   Agreed.
PIERRE.   Shoot him.
JAFF.   With all my heart.

No more. Where shall we meet at night?
PIERRE.   I'll tell thee:
   On the Rialto every night at twelve
   I take my evening's walk of meditation;
   There we two will meet, and talk of precious
   Mischief –
JAFF.   Farewell.
PIERRE.   At twelve.
JAFF.   At any hour. My plagues
   Will keep me waking.   *Exit* PIERRE
                     Tell me why, good heav'n,
   Thou mad'st me what I am, with all the spirit,
   Aspiring thoughts and elegant desires
   That fill the happiest man? Ah, rather why
   Didst thou not form me sordid as my fate,
   Base-minded, dull, and fit to carry burdens?
   Why have I sense to know the curse that's on me?
   Is this just dealing, Nature? Belvidera!
        Enter BELVIDERA [*with two attendants*]
   Poor Belvidera!
BELV.   Lead me, lead me, my virgins,
To that kind voice. My lord, my love, my refuge!
   Happy my eyes when they behold thy face;
   My heavy heart will leave its doleful beating
   At sight of thee, and bound with sprightful joys.
   Oh, smile, as when our loves were in their spring,
   And cheer my fainting soul.
JAFF.   As when our loves
   Were in their spring? Has then my fortune chang'd?
   Art thou not Belvidera, still the same,
   Kind, good, and tender, as my arms first found thee?
   If thou art alter'd, where shall I have harbour?
   Where ease my loaded heart? Oh, where complain?
BELV.   Does this appear like change or love decaying,
   When thus I throw myself into thy bosom,
   With all the resolution of a strong truth?
   Beats not my heart, as 'twould alarm thine
   To a new charge of bliss? I joy more in thee
   Than did thy mother when she hugg'd thee first,
   And bless'd the gods for all her travail past.
JAFF.   Can there in woman be such glorious faith?
   Sure all ill stories of thy sex are false.
   O woman, lovely woman! Nature made thee

To temper man; we had been brutes without you.
Angels are painted fair, to look like you;
There's in you all that we believe of heav'n,
Amazing brightness, purity and truth,
Eternal joy and everlasting love.

BELV.   If love be treasure, we'll be wondrous rich;
I have so much, my heart will surely break with't,
Vows cannot express it; when I would declare
How great's my joy, I am dumb with the big thought;
I swell, and sigh, and labour with my longing.
Oh, lead me to some desert wide and wild,
Barren as our misfortunes, where my soul
May have its vent; where I may tell aloud
To the high heav'ns and every list'ning planet,
With what a boundless stock my bosom's fraught!
Where I may throw my eager arms about thee,
Give loose to love with kisses, kindling joy,
And let off all the fire that's in my heart.

JAFF.   O Belvidera! Double I'm a beggar,
Undone by fortune, and in debt to thee;
Want, worldy want! That hungry, meagre fiend
Is at my heels, and chases me in view.
Canst thou bear cold and hunger? Can these limbs,
Fram'd for the tender offices of love,
Endure the bitter gripes of smarting poverty?
When banish'd by our miseries abroad
(As suddenly we shall be) to seek out
(In some far climate where our names are strangers)
For charitable succour; wilt thou then,
When in a bed of straw we shrink together,
And the bleak winds shall whistle round our heads,
Wilt thou then talk thus to me? Wilt thou then
Hush my cares thus, and shelter me with love?

BELV.   Oh, I will love thee, even in madness love thee.
Though my distracted senses should forsake me,
I'd find some intervals when my poor heart
Should 'suage itself and be let loose to thine.
Though the bare earth be all our resting place,
Its roots our food, some clift our habitation,
I'll make this arm a pillow for thy head;
As thou sighing liest, and swell'd with sorrow,
Creep to thy bosom, pour the balm of love
Into thy soul, and kiss thee to thy rest;

Then praise our God, and watch thee till the morning.
JAFF. Hear this, you heavens, and wonder how you made her!
Reign, reign, ye monarchs that divide the world;
Busy rebellion ne'er will let you know
Tranquillity and happiness like mine.
Like gaudy ships, th'obsequious billows fall
And rise again, to lift you in your pride;
They wait but for a storm and then devour you.
I, in my private bark, already wreck'd,
Like a poor merchant driven on unknown land,
That had by chance pack'd up his choicest treasure
In one dear casket, and sav'd only that:
   Since I must wander further on the shore,
   Thus hug my little, but my precious store;
   Resolv'd to scorn, and trust my fate no more.   *Exeunt*

Act Two

[SCENE ONE]

[AQUILINA'S *house*]

Enter PIERRE *and* AQUILINA

AQUIL. By all thy wrongs, thou'rt dearer to my arms
    Than all the wealth of Venice; prithee stay,
    And let us love tonight.
PIERRE.   No; there's fool,
    There's fool about thee. When a woman sells
    Her flesh to fools, her beauty's lost to me;
    They leave a taint, a sully where they've pass'd.
    There's such a baneful quality about 'em,
    E'en spoils complexions with their own nauseousness.
    They infect all they touch; I cannot think
    Of tasting anything a fool has pall'd.
AQUIL. I loathe and scorn that fool thou mean'st, as much
    Or more than thou canst, but the beast has gold
    That makes him necessary; power too,
    To qualify my character, and poise me
    Equal with peevish virtue that beholds
    My liberty with envy; in their hearts
    Are loose as I am, but an ugly power
    Sits in their faces, and frights pleasures from 'em.
PIERRE. Much good may't do you, madam, with your senator.
AQUIL. My senator! Why, canst thou think that wretch
    E'er fill'd thy Aquilina's arms with pleasure?
    Think't thou, because I sometimes give him leave
    To foil[1] himself at what he is unfit for,
    Because I force myself to endure and suffer him,
    Think'st thou I love him? No, by all the joys
    Thou ever gav'st me, his presence is my penance;
    The worst thing an old man can be's a lover,
    A mere *memento mori* to poor woman.
    I never lay by his decrepit side,

[1] *foil* defile.

But all that night I ponder'd on my grave.
PIERRE.   Would he were well sent thither!
AQUIL.   That's my wish too,
For then, my Pierre, I might have cause with pleasure
To play the hypocrite. Oh, how I could weep
Over the dying dotard, and kiss him too,
In hopes to smother him quite; then, when the time
Was come to pay my sorrows at his funeral,
For he has already made me heir to treasures
Would make me out-act a real widow's whining,
How could I frame my face to fit my mourning,
With wringing hands attend him to his grave,
Fall swooning on his hearse, take mad possession
Even of the dismal vault where he lay buried;
There like the Ephesian matron² dwell, till thou,
My lovely soldier, com'st to my deliverance;
Then throwing up my veil, with open arms
And laughing eyes, run to new-dawning joy.
PIERRE.   No more! I have friends to meet me here tonight,
And must be private. As you prize my friendship,
Keep up your coxcomb. Let him not pry nor listen,
Nor fisk about the house as I have seen him,
Like a tame mumping³ squirrel with a bell on;
Curs will be abroad to bite him if you do.
AQUIL.   What friends to meet? May I not be of your council?
PIERRE.   How!⁴ A woman ask questions out of bed?
Go to your senator, ask him what passes
Amongst his brethren; he'll hide nothing from you,
But pump not me for politics. No more!
Give order that whoever in my name
Comes here, receive admittance. So good night.
AQUIL.   Must we ne'er meet again? Embrace no more?
Is love so soon and utterly forgotten?
PIERRE.   As you henceforward treat your fool, I'll think on't.
AQUIL.   Curs'd be all fools, and doubly curs'd myself,
The worst of fools. I die if he forsakes me;
And how to keep him, heav'n or hell instruct me.   *Exeunt*

---

²*Ephesian matron* the widow of Ephesus who, in Petronius's *Satyricon* (Sections
111 and 112), weeps at her husband's tomb until a young soldier persuades her that
living is better than mourning.
³*mumping* munching.   ⁴*How* Indeed.

SCENE [TWO]

The Rialto

Enter JAFFEIR

JAFF. I am here, and thus, the shades of night around me,
I look as if all hell were in my heart,
And I in hell. Nay, surely 'tis so with me;
For every step I tread, methinks some fiend
Knocks at my breast, and bids it not be quiet.
I've heard how desperate wretches like myself
Have wander'd out at this dead time of night
To meet the foe of mankind in his walk.
Sure I'm so curs'd that, though of heav'n forsaken,
No minister of darkness cares to tempt me.
Hell, hell! Why sleepest thou?

Enter PIERRE

PIERRE. Sure I have stayed too long;
The clock has struck, and I may lose my proselyte.
Speak, who goes there?

JAFF.   A dog, that comes to howl
At yonder moon. What's he that asks the question?

PIERRE. A friend to dogs, for they are honest creatures
And ne'er betray their masters, never fawn
On any that they love not. Well met, friend.
Jaffeir!

JAFF. The same. O Pierre, thou art come in season;
I was just going to pray.

PIERRE.   Ah, that's mechanic;
Priests make a trade on't, and yet starve by it too.
No praying, it spoils business, and time's precious.
Where's Belvidera?

JAFF.   For a day or two
I've lodg'd her privately, till I see further
What fortune will do with me. Prithee, friend,
If thou wouldst have me fit to hear good counsel,
Speak not of Belvidera —

PIERRE.   Speak not of her?

JAFF. Oh, no!

PIERRE. Nor name her? May be I wish her well?

JAFF. Who well?

PIERRE.   Thy wife, thy lovely Belvidera;
I hope a man may wish his friend's wife well,

And no harm done!

JAFF.   You're merry, Pierre!

PIERRE.   I am so.
Thou shalt smile too, and Belvidera smile;
We'll all rejoice. Here's something to buy pins;
Marriage is chargeable.

JAFF.   I but half wish'd
To see the devil, and he's here already.
Well!
What must this buy, rebellion, murder, treason?
Tell me which way I must be damn'd for this.

PIERRE.   When last we parted, we had no qualms like these,
But entertain'd each other's thoughts like men
Whose souls were well acquainted. Is the world
Reform'd since our last meeting? What new miracles
Have happen'd? Has Priuli's heart relented?
Can he be honest?

JAFF.   Kind heav'n, let heavy curses
Gall his old age; cramps, aches, rack his bones,
And bitterest disquiet wring his heart;
Oh, let him live till life become his burden!
Let him groan under't long, linger an age
In the worst agonies and pangs of death,
And find its ease, but late.

PIERRE   Nay, couldst thou not
As well, my friend, have stretch'd the curse to all
The senate round, as to one single villain?

JAFF.   But curses stick not; could I kill with cursing,
By heav'n, I know not thirty heads in Venice
Should not be blasted; senators should rot
Like dogs on dunghills, but their wives and daughters
Die of their own diseases. Oh, for a curse
To kill with!

PIERRE.   Daggers, daggers are much better!

JAFF.   Ha!

PIERRE.   Daggers!

JAFF.   But where are they?

PIERRE.   Oh, a thousand
May be dispos'd in honest hands in Venice.

JAFF.   Thou talk'st in clouds.

PIERRE.   But yet a heart half wrong'd,
As thine has been, would find the meaning, Jaffeir.

JAFF.   A thousand daggers, all in honest hands;

And have not I a friend will stick one here?
PIERRE   Yes, if I thought thou wert not to be cherish'd
To a nobler purpose, I'd be that friend.
But thou hast better friends, friends whom thy wrongs
Have made thy friends, friends worthy to be called so.
I'll trust thee with a secret: there are spirits
This hour at work. But as thou art a man,
Whom I have pick'd and chosen from the world,
Swear that thou wilt be true to what I utter,
And when I have told thee that which only gods
And men like gods are privy to, then swear
No chance or change shall wrest it from my bosom.
JAFF.   When thou wouldst bind me, is there need of oaths?
(Greensickness girls lose maidenheads with such counters[5])
For thou'rt so near my heart that thou mayst see
Its bottom, sound its strength and firmness to thee.
Is coward, fool, or villain in my face?
If I seem none of these, I dare believe
Thou wouldst not use me in a little cause,
For I am fit for honour's toughest task;
Nor ever yet found fooling was my province;
And for a villainous, inglorious enterprise,
I know thy heart so well I dare lay mine
Before thee, set it to what point thou wilt.
PIERRE.   Nay, it's a cause thou wilt be fond of, Jaffeir,
For it is founded on the noblest basis,
Our liberties, our natural inheritance.
There's no religion, no hypocrisy in't;
We'll do the business, and ne'er fast and pray for't;
Openly act a deed the world shall gaze
With wonder at, and envy when it's done.
JAFF.   For liberty!
PIERRE.   For liberty, my friend!
Thou shalt be freed from base Priuli's tyranny,
And thy sequest'red fortunes heal'd again;
I shall be freed from opprobrious wrongs
That press me now and bend my spirit downward;
All Venice free, and every growing merit
Succeed to its just right. Fools shall be pull'd
From wisdom's seat; those baleful, unclean birds,
Those lazy owls, who (perch'd near fortune's top)

[5]*counters* tokens, substitutes for real coins.

Sit only watchful with their heavy wings
To cuff down new-fledg'd virtues that would rise
To nobler heights, and make the grove harmonious.
JAFF. What can I do?
PIERRE. Canst thou not kill a senator?
JAFF. Were there one wise or honest, I could kill him
For herding with that nest of fools and knaves.
By all my wrongs, thou talk'st as if revenge
Were to be had, and the brave story warms me.
PIERRE. Swear, then!
JAFF. I do, by all those glittering stars
And yond great ruling planet of the night;
By all good pow'rs above, and ill below;
By love and friendship, dearer than my life!
No pow'r or death shall make me false to thee.
PIERRE. Here we embrace, and I'll unlock my heart.
A council's held hard by, where the destruction
Of this great empire's hatching. There I'll lead thee!
But be a man, for thou'rt to mix with men
Fit to disturb the peace of all the world,
And rule it when it's wildest.
JAFF. I give thee thanks
For this kind warning. Yes, I will be a man,
And charge thee, Pierre, whene'er thou seest my fears
Betray me less, to rip this heart of mine
Out of my breast and show it for a coward's.
Come, let's begone, for from this hour I chase
All little thoughts, all tender human follies
Out of my bosom. Vengeance shall have room:
Revenge!
PIERRE. And liberty!
JAFF. Revenge! Revenge!

Exeunt

[SCENE THREE]

The scene changes to AQUILINA'S *house, the Greek courtesan*

Enter RENAULT
REN. Why was my choice ambition the first ground
A wretch can build on? It's indeed at distance
A good prospect, tempting to the view;
The height delights us, and the mountain top

Looks beautiful because it's nigh to heaven,
But we ne'er think how sandy's the foundation,
What storm will batter, and what tempest shake us!
Who's there?
    Enter SPINOSA
SPIN.   Renault, good morrow; for by this time
I think the scale of night has turn'd the balance,
And weighs up morning. Has the clock struck twelve?
REN.   Yes, clocks will go as they are set. But, man,
Irregular man's ne'er constant, never certain.
I've spent at least three precious hours of darkness
In waiting dull attendance; 'tis the curse
Of diligent virtue to be mix'd like mine,
With giddy tempers, souls but half resolv'd.
SPIN.   Hell seize that soul amongst us it can frighten!
REN.   What's then the cause that I am here alone?
Why are we not together?
    Enter ELIOT
                O sir, welcome!
You are an Englishman; when treason's hatching
One might have thought you'd not have been behindhand.
In what whore's lap have you been lolling?
Give but an Englishman his whore and ease,
Beef and a sea-coal[6] fire, he's yours forever.
ELIOT.   Frenchman, you are saucy.
REN.   How!
    Enter BEDAMORE *the Ambassador,* THEODORE, BRAINVEIL,
        DURAND, BRABE, REVILLIDO, MEZZANA, TERNON, RE-
        TROSI, *conspirators*
BEDA.   At difference, fie!
Is this a time for quarrels? Thieves and rogues
Fall out and brawl. Should men of your high calling,
Men separated by the choice of providence
From the gross heap of mankind, and set here
In this great assembly as in one great jewel,
T'adorn the bravest purpose it e'er smil'd on,
Should you like boys wrangle for trifles?
REN.   Boys!
BEDA.   Renault, thy hand!
REN.   I thought I'd given my heart

---

[6] *sea-coal* coal carried by sea or found at the edge of the sea, as distinct from charcoal.

Long since to every man that mingles here;
But grieve to find it trusted with such tempers
That can't forgive my froward age is weakness.

BEDA.   Eliot, thou once hadst virtue; I have seen
Thy stubborn temper bend with godlike goodness,
Not half thus courted; 'tis thy nation's glory
To hug the foe that offers brave alliance.
Once more embrace, my friends — we'll all embrace —
United thus, we are the mighty engine
Must twist this rooted empire from its basis!
Totters it not already?

ELIOT.   Would it were tumbling!

BEDA.   Nay, it shall down; this night we seal its ruin.

   Enter PIERRE

O Pierre, thou art welcome!
Come to my breast, for by its hopes thou look'st
Lovelily dreadful, and the fate of Venice
Seems on thy sword already. O my Mars!
The poets that first feign'd[7] a god of war
Sure prophesied of thee.

PIERRE.   Friends, was not Brutus
(I mean that Brutus who in open senate
Stabb'd the first Caesar that usurp'd the world)
A gallant man?

REN.   Yes, and Catiline[8] too,
Though story wrong his fame; for he conspir'd
To prop the reeling glory of his country.
His cause was good.

BEDA.   And ours as much above it,
As Renault thou art superior to Cethegus,[9]
Or Pierre to Cassius.[10]

PIERRE.   Then to what we aim at
When do we start? Or must we talk forever?

BEDA.   No, Pierre, the deed's near birth; fate seems to have set
The business up, and given it to our care.

[7]*feign'd* invented.

[8]*Catiline* Lucius Sergius Catilina, an unsuccessful politician and demagogue, executed for conspiracy 62 BC

[9]*Cethegus* conspirator, with Catiline, in an unsuccessful scheme to murder Cicero and other notables; executed 63 BC

[10]*Cassius* Gaius Cassius Longinus, military leader, statesman; Cassius with Brutus and others stabbed Julius Caesar 44 BC; they were amongst the conspirators defeated by Antony and Octavius 42 BC; Cassius committed suicide.

I hope there's not a heart nor hand amongst us
But is firm and ready.

ALL. All!
We'll die with Bedamore.

BEDA. O men
Matchless, as will your glory be hereafter,
The game is for a matchless prize, if won;
If lost, disgraceful ruin.

REN. What can lose it?
The public stock's a beggar; one Venetian
Trusts not another. Look into their stores
Of general safety: empty magazines,
A tatter'd fleet, a murmuring, unpaid army,
Bankrupt nobility, a harass'd commonalty,
A factious, giddy, and divided senate
Is all the strength of Venice. Let's destroy it;
Let's fill their magazines with arms to awe them,
Man out their fleet, and make their trade maintain it;
Let loose the murmuring army on their masters,
To pay themselves with plunder; lop their nobles
To the base roots, whence most of 'em first sprung;
Enslave the rout, whom smarting will make humble;
Turn out their droning senate, and possess
That seat of empire which our souls were fram'd for.

PIERRE. Ten thousand men are armed at your nod,
Commanded all by leaders fit to guide
A battle for the freedom of the world;
This wretched state has starv'd them in its service,
And by your bounty quicken'd, they're resolv'd
To serve your glory and revenge their own!
They've all their different quarters in this city,
Watch for th'alarm, and grumble 'tis so tardy.

BEDA. I doubt not, friend, but thy unwearied diligence
Has still kept waking, and it shall have ease;
After this night it is resolv'd we meet
No more, till Venice own us for her lords.

PIERRE. How lovely the Adriatic whore,
Dress'd in her flames, will shine! Devouring flames!
Such as shall burn her to the watery bottom
And hiss in her foundation.

BEDA. Now if any
Amongst us that owns this glorious cause,
Have friends or interest he'd wish to save,

Let it be told. The general doom is seal'd;
But I'd forego the hopes of a world's empire,
Rather than wound the bowels of my friend.

PIERRE.   I must confess you there have touch'd my weakness.
I have a friend; hear it, such a friend!
My heart was ne'er shut to him. Nay, I'll tell you,
He knows the very business of this hour;
But he rejoices in the cause and loves it;
We've chang'd a vow to live and die together,
And he's at hand to ratify it here.

REN.   How! All betray'd?

PIERRE.   No — I've dealt nobly with you;
I've brought my all into the public stock.
I had but one friend, and him I'll share amongst you!
Receive and cherish him; or if, when seen
And search'd, you find him worthless, as my tongue
Has lodg'd this secret in his faithful breast,
To ease your fears I wear a dagger here
Shall rip it out again, and give you rest.
Come forth, thou only good I e'er could boast of.

    Enter JAFFEIR *with a dagger*

BEDA.   His presence bears the show of manly virtue.

JAFF.   I know you'll wonder all, that thus uncall'd,
I dare approach this place of fatal counsels;
But I'm amongst you, and by heav'n it glads me
To see so many virtues thus united,
To restore justice and dethrone oppression.
Command this sword, if you would have it quiet,
Into this breast; but if you think it worthy
To cut the throats of reverend rogues in robes,
Send me into the curs'd assembl'd senate;
It shrinks not, though I meet a father there.
Would you behold this city flaming? Here's
A hand shall bear a lighted torch at noon
To the arsenal, and set its gates on fire.

REN.   You talk this well, sir.

JAFF.   Nay, by heav'n I'll do this.
Come, come, I read distrust in all your faces;
You fear me a villain, and indeed it's odd
To hear a stranger talk thus at first meeting
Of matters that have been so well debated;
But I come ripe with wrongs as you with counsels.
I hate this senate, am a foe to Venice;

A friend to none but men resolv'd like me,
To push on mischief. Oh, did you but know me,
I need not talk thus!
BEDA.   Pierre, I must embrace him;
My heart beats to this man as if it knew him.
REN.   I never lov'd these huggers.
JAFF.   Still I see
The cause delights me not. Your friends survey me,
As I were dangerous; but I come arm'd
Against all doubts, and to your trust will give
A pledge worth more than all the world can pay for.
My Belvidera! Ho, my Belvidera!
BEDA.   What wonder next?
JAFF.   Let me entreat you,
As I have henceforth hopes to call ye friends,
That all but the ambassador, [and] this
Grave guide of councils, with my friend that owns me,
Withdraw a while to spare a woman's blushes.
                    Exeunt all but BEDAMORE, RENAULT, JAFFEIR, PIERRE
BEDA.   Pierre, wither will this ceremony lead us?
JAFF.   My Belvidera! Belvidera!
    Enter BELVIDERA
BELV.   Who calls so loud at this late peaceful hour?
That voice was wont to come in gentler whispers,
And fill my ears with the soft breath of love;
Thou hourly image of my thoughts, where art thou?
JAFF.   Indeed 'tis late.
BELV.   Oh, I have slept and dreamt,
And dreamt again. Where hast thou been, thou loiterer?
Though my eyes clos'd, my arms have still been open'd,
Stretch'd every way betwixt my broken slumbers,
To search if thou wert come to crown my rest;
There's no repose without thee. Oh, the day
Too soon will break and wake us to our sorrow;
Come, come to bed and bid thy cares good night.
JAFF.   O Belvidera, we must change the scene
In which the past delights of life were tasted.
The poor sleep little; we must learn to watch
Our labours late, and early every morning,
Midst winter frosts, thin-clad and fed with sparing,
Rise to our toils, and drudge away the day.
BELV.   Alas, where am I? Whither is't you lead me?
Methinks I read distraction in your face!

Something less gentle than the fate you tell me.
You shake and tremble too! Your blood runs cold!
Heavens guard my love, and bless his heart with patience.

JAFF.   That I have patience, let our fate bear witness,
Who has ordain'd it so, that thou and I
(Thou the divinest good man e'er possess'd,
And I the wretched'st of the race of man)
This very hour, without one tear, must part.

BELV.   Part? Must we part? Oh, am I then forsaken?
Will my love cast me off? Have my misfortunes
Offended him so highly that he'll leave me?
Why drag you from me? Whither are you going?
My dear, my life, my love!

JAFF.   O friends, –

BELV.   Speak to me.

JAFF.   Take her from my heart;
She'll gain such hold else, I shall ne'er get loose.
I charge thee take her, but with tender'st care
Relieve her troubles and assuage her sorrows.

REN.   Rise, madam, and command amongst your servants!

JAFF.   To you, sirs, and your honours, I bequeath her,
And with her this, when I prove unworthy –   *Gives a dagger*
You know the rest – then strike it to her heart
And tell her he who three whole happy years
Lay in her arms, and each kind night repeated
The passionate vows of still-increasing love,
Sent that reward for all her truth and sufferings.

BELV.   Nay, take my life, since he has sold it cheaply;
Or send me to some distant clime your slave;
But let it be far off, lest my complainings
Should reach his guilty ears and shake his peace.

JAFF.   No, Belvidera, I've contriv'd thy honour.
Trust to my faith, and be but fortune kind
To me, as I'll preserve that faith unbroken,
When next we meet, I'll lift thee to a height
Shall gather all the gazing world about thee,
To wonder what strange virtue plac'd thee there.
But if we ne'er meet more –

BELV.   O thou unkind one,
Never meet more? Have I deserv'd this from you?
Look on me, tell me, speak, thou dear deceiver,
Why am I separated from thy love?
If I am false, accuse me; but if true,

Don't, prithee, don't in poverty forsake me,
But pity the sad heart that's torn with parting.
Yet hear me! Yet recall me —

     Exeunt RENAULT, BEDAMORE *and* BELVIDERA

JAFF.   O my eyes,
Look not that way, but turn yourselves awhile
Into my heart, and be wean'd all together.
My friend, where art thou?

PIERRE.   Here, my honour's brother.

JAFF. Is Belvidera gone?

PIERRE.   Renault has led her
Back to her own apartment; but, by heav'n,
Thou must not see her more till our work's over.

JAFF. No.

PIERRE. Not for your life.

JAFF.   O Pierre, wert thou but she,
How I could pull thee down into my heart,
Gaze on thee till my eye-strings crack'd with love,
Till all my sinews with its fire extended,
Fix'd me upon the rack of ardent longing;
Then swelling, sighing, raging to be bless'd,
Come like a panting turtle to thy breast,
On thy soft bosom, hovering, bill and play,
Confess the cause why last I fled away;
 Own 'twas a fault, but swear to give it o'er
 And never follow false ambition more.   *Exeunt ambo*[11]

[11]*ambo* both.

Act Three

[SCENE ONE]

[AQUILINA's *house*]

Enter AQUILINA *and her* MAID

AQUIL.   Tell him I am gone to bed; tell him I am not at home; tell him I've better company with me, or anything; tell him, in short, I will not see him, the eternal, troublesome, vexatious fool. He's worse company than an ignorant physician – I'll not be disturbed at these unseasonable hours.

MAID.   But, madam, he's here already, just entered the doors.

AQUIL.   Turn him out again, you unnecessary, useless, giddy-brained ass! If he will not begone, set the house afire and burn us both. I had rather meet a toad in my dish than that old hideous animal in my chamber tonight.

Enter ANTONIO

ANTO.   Nacky, Nacky, Nacky – how dost do, Nacky? Hurry durry. I am come, little Nacky; past eleven o'clock, a late hour; time in all conscience to go to bed, Nacky – Nacky, did I say? Ay, Nacky; Aquilina, lina, lina, quilina, quilina, quilina, Aquilina, Naquilina, Naquilina, Acky, Acky, Nacky, Nacky, Queen Nacky – Come let's to bed – you fubbs,[1] you pug[2] you – you little puss – purree tuzzey – I am a senator.

AQUIL.   You are a fool, I am sure.

ANTO.   May be so too, sweetheart. Never the worse senator for all that. Come, Nacky, Nacky, let's have a game at rump,[3] Nacky.

AQUIL.   You would do well, signor, to be troublesome here no longer, but leave me to myself. Be sober and go home, sir.

ANTO.   Home, Madonna!

AQUIL.   Ay, home, sir. Who am I?

ANTO.   Madonna, as I take it you are my – you are – thou art my little Nicky Nacky . . . that's all!

AQUIL.   I find you are resolved to be troublesome, and so to make short of the matter in few words, I hate you, detest you, loathe you, I am weary of you, sick of you – hang you, you are an old, silly,

---

[1]*fubbs* chubby person.   [2]*pug* doll.   [3]*game at rump* frolic.

impertinent, impotent, solicitous coxcomb, crazy in your head, and lazy in your body, love to be meddling with everything, and if you had not money, you are good for nothing.

ANTO. Good for nothing! Hurry, durry, I'll try that presently.[4] Sixty-one years old, and good for nothing; that's brave. – [*To the* MAID] Come, come, come, Mistress Fiddle-faddle, turn you out for a season; go turn out, I say, it is our will and pleasure to be private some moments – out, out when you are bid to. – (*Puts her out and locks the door*) Good for nothing, you say.

AQUIL. Why, what are you good for?

ANTO. In the first place, madam, I am old, and consequently very wise, very wise, Madonna; d'ye mark that? In the second place, take notice, if you please, that I am a senator, and when I think fit can make speeches, Madonna. Hurry durry, I can make a speech in the senate-house now and then would make your hair stand on end, Madonna.

AQUIL. What care I for your speeches in the senate-house? If you would be silent here, I should thank you.

ANTO. Why, I can make speeches to thee too, my lovely Madonna; for example: My cruel fair one; (*Takes out a purse of gold and at every pause shakes it*) since it is my fate that you should with your servant angry prove; though late at night, I hope 'tis not too late with this to gain reception for my love – There's for thee, my little Nicky Nacky. Take it, here take it. I say take it, or I'll throw it at your head. How now, rebel?

AQUIL. Truly, my illustrious senator, I must confess your honour is at present most profoundly eloquent indeed.

ANTO. Very well; come now, let's sit down and think upon't a little. Come sit I say. Sit down by me a little, my Nicky Nacky, ha! – (*Sits down*) Hurry durry, 'good for nothing' –

AQUIL. No, sir, if you please I can know my distance and stand.

ANTO. Stand? How? Nacky up and I down! Nay, then, let me exclaim with the poet,

> Show me a case more pitiful who can,
> A standing woman and a falling man.

Hurry durry! Not sit down? See this, ye gods! You won't sit down?

AQUIL. No, sir.

ANTO. Then look you now, suppose me a bull, a basan-bull,[5] the bull of bulls, or any bull. Thus up I get, and with my brows thus bent, I broo, I say I broo, I broo, I broo. You won't sit down, will you? I broo – (*Bellows like a bull and drives her about*)

---

[4]*presently* immediately.
[5]*basan-bull* notable for strength and ferocity; Psalms 22:12.

AQUIL.   Well, sir, I must endure this. (*She sits down*) Now your honour has been a bull, pray what beast will your worship please to be next?

ANTO.   Now I'll be a senator again and thy lover, little Nicky Nacky! (*He sits by her*) Ah toad, toad, toad, toad! Spit in my face a little, Nacky. Spit in my face prithee, spit in my face, never so little. Spit but a little bit – spit, spit, spit, spit when you are bid, I say; do prithee spit – now, now, now, spit. What, you won't spit, will you? Then I'll be a dog.

AQUIL.   A dog, my lord?

ANTO.   Ay, a dog, and I'll give thee this t'other purse to let me be a dog, and to use me like a dog a little. Hurry durry – I will – here 'tis.   *Gives the purse*

AQIUL.   Well, with all my heart. But let me beseech your dogship to play your tricks over as fast as you can, that you may come to stinking the sooner, and be turned out of doors as you deserve.

ANTO.   Ay, ay, no matter for that – that (*He gets under the table*) shan't move me – Now, bow wow wow, bow wow . . .
                                                 Barks like a dog

AQUIL.   Hold, hold, hold, sir, I beseech you. What is't you do? If curs bite, they must be kicked, sir. Do you see, kicked thus.

ANTO.   Ay, with all my heart. Do kick, kick on; now I am under the table, kick again – kick harder – harder yet. Bow wow wow, wow, bow! Od, I'll have a snap at thy shins. Bow wow wow, wow, bow! Od, she kicks bravely!

AQUIL.   Nay, then I'll go another way to work with you, and I think here's an instrument fit for the purpose. (*Fetches a whip and bell*) What, bite your mistress, sirrah? Out, out of doors, you dog, to kennel and be hanged! Bite your mistress by the legs, you rogue?
                                                 She whips him

ANTO.   Nay, prithee, Nacky, now thou art too loving. Hurry durry, od, I'll be a dog no longer.

AQUIL.   Nay, none of your fawning and grinning. But be gone, or here's the discipline. What, bite your mistress by the legs, you mongrel? Out of doors! Hout hout, to kennel, sirrah! Go.

ANTO.   This is very barbarous usage, Nacky, very barbarous. Look you, I will not go – I will not stir from the door, that I resolve. Hurry durry, what, shut me out?   *She whips him out*

AQUIL.   Ay, and if you come here any more tonight I'll have my footmen lug you, you cur. What, bite your poor mistress, Nacky, sirrah?

     Enter MAID

MAID.   Heavens, madam! What's the matter?

He howls at the door like a dog

AQUIL. Call my footmen hither presently.

Enter two footmen

MAID. They are here already, madam; the house is all alarmed with a strange noise that nobody knows what to make of.

AQUIL. Go all of you and turn that troublesome beast in the next room out of my house. If I ever see him within these walls again, without my leave for his admittance, you sneaking rogues, I'll have you poisoned all, poisoned, like rats; every corner of the house shall stink of one of you. Go, and learn hereafter to know my pleasure. So now for my Pierre:

> Thus when godlike lover was displeas'd,
> We sacrifice our fool and he's appeas'd.   *Exeunt*

[SCENE TWO]

[*A street in Venice*]

Enter BELVIDERA

BELV. I'm sacrific'd, I am sold, betray'd to shame!
Inevitable ruin has enclos'd me!
No sooner was I to my bed repair'd
To weigh, and (weeping) ponder my condition,
But the old hoary wretch, to whose false care
My peace and honour was entrusted, came
(Like Tarquin[6]) ghastly with infernal lust.
O thou, Roman Lucrece! Thou couldst find friends
To vindicate thy wrong,
I never had but one, and he's prov'd false;
He that should guard my virtue has betray'd it,
Left me, undone me! Oh that I could hate him!
Where shall I go, oh whither, whither wander?

Enter JAFFEIR

JAFF. Can Belvidera want a resting place
When these poor arms are open to receive her?
Oh, 'tis in vain to struggle with desires
Strong as my love to thee; for every moment
I am from thy sight, the heart within my bosom

---

[6]*Tarquin* Tarquinius Sextus, 6th century BC; he raped Lucrece, a Roman noble-woman.

Moans like a tender infant in its cradle
Whose nurse has left it. Come, and with the songs
Of gentle love persuade it to its peace.

BELV.   I fear the stubborn wanderer will not own me,
'Tis grown a rebel to be rul'd no longer,
Scorns the indulgent bosom that first lull'd it,
And like a disobedient child disdains
The soft authority of Belvidera.

JAFF.   There was a time –

BELV.   Yes, yes, there was a time
When Belvidera's tears, her cries, and sorrows
Were not despis'd; when if she chanc'd to sigh
Or look but sad – there was indeed a time
When Jaffeir would have ta'en her in his arms,
Eas'd her declining head upon his breast,
And never left her till he found the cause.
But let her now weep seas,
Cry till she rend the earth, sigh till she burst
Her heart asunder; still he bears it all,
Deaf as the wind, and as the rocks unshaken.

JAFF.   Have I been deaf? Am I that rock unmov'd,
Against whose root tears beat and sighs are sent?
In vain have I beheld thy sorrows calmly!
Witness against me, heav'ns, have I done this?
Then bear me in a whirlwind back again,
And let that angry dear one ne'er forgive me!
O thou too rashly censur'st of my love!
Couldst thou but think how I have spent this night,
Dark and alone, no pillow to my head,
Rest in my eyes, nor quiet in my heart,
Thou wouldst not, Belvidera, sure thou wouldst not
Talk to me thus, but like a pitying angel
Spreading thy wings come settle on my breast,
And hatch warm comfort there ere sorrows freeze it.

BELV.   Why, then, poor mourner, in what baleful corner
Hast thou been talking with that witch the night?
On what cold stone hast thou been stretch'd along,
Gathering the grumbling winds about thy head,
To mix with theirs the accents of thy woes!
Oh, now I find the cause my love forsakes me!
I am no longer fit to bear a share
In his concernments; my weak female virtue
Must not be trusted; 'tis too frail and tender.

JAFF.   O Portia,[7] Portia, what a soul was thine!
BELV.   That Portia was a woman, and when Brutus,
 Big with the fate of Rome (heav'n guard thy safety!)
 Conceal'd from her the labours of his mind,
 She let him see her blood was great as his,
 Flow'd from a spring as noble, and a heart
 Fit to partake his troubles, as his love.
 Fetch, fetch that dagger back, the dreadful dower
 Thou gav'st last night in parting with me; strike it
 Here to my heart, and as the blood flows from it
 Judge if it run not pure as Cato's daughter's.[8]
JAFF.   Thou art too good, and I indeed unworthy,
 Unworthy so much virtue; teach me how
 I may deserve such matchless love as thine,
 And see with what attention I'll obey thee.
BELV.   Do not despise me; that's the all I ask.
JAFF.   Despise thee! Hear me –
BELV.   O, thy charming tongue
 Is but too well acquainted with my weakness,
 Knows, let it name but love, my melting heart
 Dissolves within my breast, till with clos'd eyes
 I reel into thy arms, and all's forgotten.
JAFF.   What shall I do?
BELV.   Tell me! Be just, and tell me
 Why dwells that busy cloud upon thy face?
 Why am I made a stranger? Why that sigh,
 And I not know the cause? Why, when the world
 Is wrapp'd in rest, why chooses then my love
 To wander up and down in horrid darkness,
 Loathing his bed and these desiring arms?
 Why are these eyes bloodshot with tedious watching?
 Why starts he now and looks as if he wish'd
 His fate were finish'd? Tell me; ease my fears;
 Lest when we next time meet, I want the power
 To search into the sickness of thy mind,
 But talk as wildly then as thou look'st now.
JAFF.   O Belvidera!
BELV.   Why was I last night deliver'd to a villain?
JAFF.   Ha, a villain!

[7]*Portia* 85–42 BC, wife of Marcus Junius Brutus, said to have wounded herself to prove that she was worthy to share her husband's secrets.
 [8]*Cato's daughter's* i.e. Portia.

BELV.   Yes, to a villain! Why at such an hour
Meets that assembly all made up of wretches
That look as hell had drawn 'em into league?
Why, I in this hand, and in that a dagger,
Was I deliver'd with such dreadful ceremonies?
'To you, sirs, and to your honour I bequeath her,
And with her this, whene'er I prove unworthy –
You know the rest – then strike it to her heart'?9
Oh, why's that 'rest' conceal'd from me? Must I
Be made the hostage of a hellish trust?
For such I know I am; that's all my value?
But by the love and loyalty I owe thee,
I'll free thee from the bondage of these slaves;
Straight to the senate, tell 'em all I know,
All that I think, all that my fears inform me!

JAFF.   Is this the Roman virtue? This the blood
That boasts its purity with Cato's daughter's?
Would she have e'er betray'd her Brutus?

BELV.   No;
For Brutus trusted her. Wert thou so kind,
What would not Belvidera suffer for thee?

JAFF.   I shall undo myself and tell thee all.

BELV.   Look not upon me as I am a woman,
But as a bone, thy wife, thy friend, who long
Has had admission to thy heart, and there
Studied the virtues of thy gallant nature;
Thy constancy, thy courage and thy truth
Have been my daily lesson: I have learnt them,
Am bold as thou, can suffer or despise
The worst of fates for thee, and with thee share them.

JAFF.   O you divinest powers, look down and hear
My prayers, instruct me to reward this virtue!
Yet think a little ere thou tempt me further;
Think I have a tale to tell will shake thy nature,
Melt all this boasted constancy thou talk'st of
Into vile tears and despicable sorrows.
Then if thou shouldst betray me!

BELV.   Shall I swear?

JAFF.   No, do not swear. I would not violate
Thy tender nature with so rude a bond;
But as thou hopest to see me live my days

9*To . . . heart* See above II, iii, p. 343.

And love thee long, lock this within thy breast:
I've bound myself by all the strictest sacraments
Divine and human –

BELV.   Speak!

JAFF.   To kill thy father.

BELV.   My father!

JAFF.   Nay, the throats of the whole senate
Shall bleed, my Belvidera; he amongst us
That spares his father, brother, or his friend
Is damn'd. How rich and beauteous will the face
Of ruin look when these wide streets run blood;
I and the glorious partners of my fortune
Shouting and striding o'er the prostrate dead,
Still to new waste; whilst thou, far off in safety,
Smiling, shalt see the wonders of our daring,
And when night comes, with praise and love receive me.

BELV.   Oh!

JAFF.   Have a care, and shrink not even in thought!
For if thou dost –

BELV.   I know it, thou wilt kill me.
Do, strike thy sword into this bosom; lay me
Dead on the earth, and then thou wilt be safe.
Murder my father! Though his cruel nature
Has persecuted me to my undoing,
Driven me to basest wants, can I behold him
With smiles of vengeance, butcher'd in his age,
The sacred fountain of my life destroy'd?
And canst thou shed the blood that gave me being,
Nay, be a traiter too, and sell thy country?
Can thy great heart descend so vilely low,
Mix with hir'd slaves, bravoes, and common stabbers,
Nose-slitters, alley-lurking villains? Join
With such a crew and take a ruffian's wages
To cut the throats of wretches as they sleep?

JAFF.   Thou wrong'st me, Belvidera! I've engag'd
With men of souls, fit to reform the ills
Of all mankind. There's not a heart amongst them
But's as stout as death, yet honest as the nature
Of man first made, ere fraud and vice were fashions.

BELV.   What's he, to whose curs'd hands last night thou gav'st me?
Was that well done? Oh, I could tell a story
Would rouse thy lion heart out of its den
And make it rage with terrifying fury.

JAFF.   Speak on, I charge thee!
BELV.   O my love, if e'er
  Thy Belvidera's peace deserv'd thy care,
  Remove me from this place. Last night, last night –
JAFF.   Distract me not, but give me all the truth.
BELV.   No sooner wert thou gone, and I alone,
  Left in the pow'r of that old son of mischief;
  No sooner was I lain on my sad bed,
  But that vile wretch approach'd me, loose, unbutton'd,
  Ready for violation: then my heart
  Throbb'd with its fears. Oh, how I wept and sigh'd
  And shrunk and trembl'd; wish'd in vain for him
  That should protect me. Thou, alas, wert gone!
JAFF.   Patience, sweet heav'n, till I make vengeance sure!
BELV.   He drew the hideous dagger forth thou gav'st him
  And with upbraiding smiles, he said, 'Behold it;
  This is the pledge of a false husband's love',
  And in my arms then press'd, and would have clasp'd me;
  But with my cries I scar'd his coward heart,
  Till he withdrew and mutter'd vows to hell.
  These are thy friends! With these thy life, thy honour,
  Thy love, all's stak'd, and all will go to ruin.
JAFF.   No more. I charge thee keep this secret close.
  Clear up thy sorrows, look as if thy wrongs
  Were all forgot, and treat him like a friend,
  As no complaint were made. No more, retire.
  Retire, my life, and doubt not of my honour;
  I'll heal its failings and deserve thy love.
BELV.   Oh, should I part with thee, I fear thou wilt
  In anger leave me, and return no more.
JAFF.   Return no more! I would not live without thee
  Another night to purchase the creation.
BELV.   When shall we meet again?
JAFF.   Anon at twelve!
  I'll steal myself to thy expecting arms,
  Come like a travell'd dove and bring thee peace.
BELV.   Indeed!
JAFF.   By all our loves!
BELV.   'Tis hard to part;
  But sure no falsehood ever looked so fairly.
  Farewell – Remember twelve.   *Exit* BELVIDERA
JAFF.   Let heaven forget me
  When I remember not thy truth, thy love.

How curs'd is my condition, toss'd and jostl'd
From every corner; fortune's common fool,
The jest of rogues, an instrumental ass
For villains to lay loads of shame upon,
And drive about just for their ease and scorn.

    Enter PIERRE

PIERRE.   Jaffeir!

JAFF.   Who calls?

PIERRE.   A friend that could have wish'd
T' have found thee otherwise employ'd. What, hunt
A wife on the dull foil?[10] Sure a staunch husband
Of all hounds is the dullest! Wilt thou never,
Never be wean'd from caudles[11] and confections?
What feminine tale hast thou been listening to,
Of unair'd shirts, catarrhs and toothache got
By thin-sol'd shoes? Damnation! That a fellow
Chosen to be a sharer in the destruction
Of a whole people should sneak thus in corners
To ease his fulsome lusts and fool his mind!

JAFF.   May not a man then trifle out an hour
With a kind woman and not wrong his calling?

PIERRE.   Not in a cause like ours.

JAFF.   Then, friend, our cause
Is in a damn'd condition; for I'll tell thee,
That canker-worm called lechery has touch'd it,
'Tis tainted vilely. Wouldst thou think it, Renault
(That mortified, old withered winter rogue)
Loves simple fornication like a priest;
I found him out for watering[12] at my wife:
He visited her last night like a kind guardian.
Faith, she has some temptations, that's the truth on't!

PIERRE.   He durst not wrong his trust!

JAFF.   'Twas something late, though,
To take the freedom of a lady's chamber.

PIERRE.   Was she in bed?

JAFF.   Yes, faith, in virgin sheets
White as her bosom, Pierre, dish'd neatly up,
Might tempt a weaker appetite to taste.
Oh, how the old fox stunk, I warrant thee,

---

[10]*foil* the track of a hunted animal.
[11]*caudles* warm, medicinal drinks.
[12]*watering* salivating.

When the rank fit was on him!
PIERRE.   Patience guide me!
He us'd no violence?
JAFF.   No, no! Out on't, violence?
Play'd with her neck, brush'd her with his grey beard,
Struggl'd and touz'd, tickl'd her till she squeak'd a little
Maybe, or so – but not a jot of violence!
PIERRE.   Damn him!
JAFF.   Ay, so say I. But hush, no more on't.
All hitherto is well, and I believe
Myself no monster[13] yet, though no man knows
What fate he's born to. Sure 'tis near the hour
We all should meet for our concluding orders.
Will the ambassador be here in person?
PIERRE.   No. He has sent commission to that villain, Renault,
To give the executing charge.
I'd have thee be a man if possible,
And keep thy temper, for a brave revenge
Ne'er comes too late.
JAFF.   Fear not, I'm cool as patience.
Had he completed my dishonour, rather
Than hazard the success our hopes are ripe for,
I'd bear it all with mortifying virtue.
PIERRE.   He's yonder coming this way through the hall;
His thoughts seem full.
JAFF.   Prithee retire, and leave me
With him alone; I'll put him to some trial,
See how his rotten part will bear the touching.
PIERRE.   Be careful then.   *Exit* PIERRE
JAFF.   Nay, never doubt, but trust me.
What, be a devil, take a damning oath
For shedding native blood! Can there be a sin
In merciful repentance? O this villain!
   Enter RENAULT
REN.   [*Apart*] Perverse and peevish, what a slave is man,
To let his itching flesh thus get the better of him!
Dispatch the tool her husband – that were well. –
Who's there?
JAFF.   A man.
REN.   My friend, my near ally!
The hostage of your faith, my beauteous charge,

---

[13]*monster* cuckold.

Is very well.

JAFF.   Sir, are you sure of that?
Stands she in perfect health? Beats her pulse even,
Neither too hot nor cold?

REN.   What means that question?

JAFF.   Oh, women have fantastic constitutions,
Inconstant as their wishes, always wavering,
And ne'er fix'd. Was it not boldly done
Even at first sight to trust the thing I lov'd
(A tempting treasure too!) with youth so fierce
And vigorous as thine? But thou art honest.

REN.   Who dares accuse me?

JAFF.   Curs'd be him that doubts
Thy virtue; I have tried it and declare
Were I to choose a guardian of my honour
I'd put it into thy keeping, for I know thee.

REN.   Know me!

JAFF.   Ay, know thee. There's no falsehood in thee;
Thou look'st just as thou art. Let us embrace.
Now would'st thou cut my throat or I cut thine?

REN.   You dare not do't.

JAFF.   You lie, sir.

REN.   How!

JAFF.   No more.
'Tis a base world and must reform, that's all.

> *Enter* SPINOSA, THEODORE, ELIOT, REVILLIDO, DURAND,
> BRAINVEIL, *and the rest of the conspirators*

REN.   Spinosa, Theodore!

SPIN.   The same.

REN.   You are welcome!

SPIN.   You are trembling, sir.

REN.   'Tis a cold night indeed; I am aged,
Full of decay and natural infirmities.   PIERRE *re-enters*
We shall be warm, my friend, I hope, tomorrow.

PIERRE.   [*To* JAFFEIR] 'Twas not well done; thou shouldst have
                                                          strok'd him
And not have gall'd him.

JAFF.   [*To* PIERRE]   Damn him, let him chew on't.
Heav'n! Where am I? Beset with cursed fiends
That wait to damn me. What a devil's man,
When he forgets his nature. Hush, my heart.

REN.   My friends, 'tis late. Are we assembl'd all?
Where's Theodore?

THEO.   At hand.
REN.   Spinosa.
SPIN.   Here.
REN.   Brainveil.
BRAIN.   I'm ready.
REN.   Durand and Brabe.
DUR.   Command us,
We are both prepar'd!
REN.   Mezzana, Revillido,
Ternon, Retrosi. Oh, you are men, I find,
Fit to behold your fate and meet her summons.
Tomorrow's rising sun must see you all
Deck'd in your honours! Are the soldiers ready?
OMN.   All, all.
REN.   You, Durand, with your thousand must possess
St Mark's; you, captain, know your charge already:
'Tis to secure the ducal palace; you,
Brabe, with a hundred more must gain the Secque;[14]
With the like number Brainveil to the Procuralle.[15]
Be all this done with the least tumult possible,
Till in each place you post sufficient guards;
Then sheathe your swords in every breast you meet.
JAFF.   [*Aside*] O reverend cruelty, damn'd bloody villain!
REN.   During this execution, Durand, you
Must in the midst keep your battalia fast,
And, Theodore, be sure to plant the cannon
That may command the streets; whilst Revillido,
Mezzana, Ternon, and Retrosi guard you.
This done, we'll give the general alarm,
Apply petards,[16] and force the ars'nal gates;
Then fire the city round in several places,
Or with our cannon, if it dare resist,
Batter't to ruin. But above all I charge you
Shed blood enough, spare neither sex nor age,
Name nor condition; if there live a senator
After tomorrow, though the dullest rogue
That e'er said nothing, we have lost our ends;
If possible, let's kill the very name
Of senator, and bury it in blood.

---

[14]*Secque* the Mint.
[15]*Procuralle* a residence for procurators, high-ranking Venetian officials.
[16]*petards* small boxes, loaded with powder, used to blow open doors or gates.

JAFF. [*Aside*] Merciless, horrid slave! Ay, blood enough!
　　Shed blood enough, old Renault. How thou charm'st me!
REN.　　But one thing more, and then farewell till fate
　　Join us again, or separate us ever:
　　First, let's embrace; heav'n knows who next shall thus
　　Wing ye together. But let's all remember
　　We wear no common cause upon our swords;
　　Let each man think that on his single virtue
　　Depends the good and fame of all the rest,
　　Eternal honour or perpetual infamy.
　　Let's remember through what dreadful hazards
　　Propitious fortune hitherto has led us,
　　How often on the brink of some discovery
　　Have we stood tottering, and yet kept our ground
　　So well, the busiest searchers ne'er could follow
　　Those subtle tracks which puzzzl'd all suspicion;
　　You droop, sir.
JAFF.　　　　　　No. With a most profound attention
　　I've heard it all, and wonder at thy virtue.
REN.　　Though there be yet few hours 'twixt them and ruin,
　　Are not the senate lull'd in full security,
　　Quiet and satisfied, as fools are always?
　　Never did so profound repose forerun
　　Calamity so great; nay, our good fortune
　　Has blinded the most piercing of mankind,
　　Strengthen'd the fearful'st, charm'd the most suspectful,
　　Confounded the most subtle; for we live,
　　We live, my friends, and quickly shall our life
　　Prove fatal to these tyrants. Let's consider
　　That we destroy oppression, avarice,
　　A people nurs'd up equally with vices
　　And loathsome lusts, which nature most abhors,
　　And such as without shame she cannot suffer.[17]
JAFF.　　[*Aside*] O Belvidera, take me to thy arms
　　And show me where's my peace, for I have lost it.　　　*Exit* JAFFEIR
REN.　　Without the least remorse then let's resolve
　　With fire and sword t'exterminate these tyrants,
　　And when we shall behold those curs'd tribunals,
　　Stain'd by the tears and sufferings of the innocent,
　　Burning with flames rather from heav'n than ours,
　　The raging, furious, and unpitying soldier

[17]*suffer* endure.

Pulling his reeking dagger from the bosoms
Of gasping wretches, death in every quarter,
With all that sad disorder can produce,
To make a spectacle of horror; then,
Then let us call to mind, my dearest friends,
That there's nothing pure upon the earth,
That the most valu'd things have most alloys,
And that in change of all those vile enormities,
Under whose weight this wretched country labours,
The means are only in our hands to crown them.

PIERRE.   And may those powers above that are propitious
To gallant minds record this cause and bless it.

REN.   Thus happy, thus secure of all we wish for,
Should there, my friends, be found amongst us one
False to this glorious enterprise, what fate,
What vengeance were enough for such a villain?

ELIOT.   Death here without repentance, hell hereafter.

REN.   Let that be my lot, if as here I stand
Lifted by fate amongst her darling sons,
Though I'd one only brother, dear by all
The strictest ties of nature; though one hour
Had given us birth, one fortune fed our wants,
One only love, and that but of each other,
Still fill'd our minds. Could I have such a friend
Join'd in this cause, and had but ground to fear
Meant foul play, may this right hand drop from me,
If I'd not hazard all my future peace,
And stab him to the heart before you. Who
Would not do less? Wouldst not thou, Pierre, the same?

PIERRE.   You have singl'd me, sir, out for this hard question,
As if 'twere started only for my sake!
Am I the thing you fear? Here, here's my bosom,
Search it with all your swords! Am I a traitor?

REN.   No, but I fear your late commended friend
Is little less. Come, sirs, 'tis now no time
To trifle with our safety. Where's this Jaffeir?

SPIN.   He left the room just now in strange disorder.

REN.   Nay, there's danger in him. I observ'd him
During the time I took for explanation;
He was transported from most deep attention
To a confusion which he could not smother.
His looks grew full of sadness and surprise,
All which betray'd a wavering spirit in him

That labour'd with reluctancy and sorrow.
What's requisite for safety must be done
With speedy execution. He remains
Yet in our power; I for my own part wear
A dagger.

PIERRE.   Well?

REN.   And I could wish it –

PIERRE.   Where?

REN.   Buried in his heart.

PIERRE.   Away! We're yet all friends;
No more of this, 'twill breed ill blood amongst us.

SPIN.   Let us all draw our swords, and search the house,
Pull him from the dark hole where he sits brooding
O'er his cold fears, and each man kill his share of him.

PIERRE.   Who talks of killing? Who's he'll shed the blood
That's dear to me? Is't you, or you, or you, sir?
What, not one speak? How you stand gaping all
In your grave oracle, your wooden god there!
Yet not a word. – [*To* RENAULT] Then, sir, I'll tell you a secret;
Suspicion's but at best a coward's virtue!

REN.   A coward!   *Handles his sword*

PIERRE.   Put, put up thy sword, old man,
Thy hand shakes at it; come, let's heal this breach,
I am too hot; we yet may live friends.

SPIN.   Till we are safe, our friendship cannot be so.

PIERRE.   Again. Who's that?

SPIN.   'Twas I.

THEO.   And I.

REVILL.   And I.

ELIOT.   And all.

REN.   Who are on my side?

SPIN.   Every honest sword.
Let's die like men and not be sold like slaves.

PIERRE.   One such word more, by heav'n I'll to the senate
And hang ye all, like dogs in clusters.
Why peep your coward swords half out their shells?
Why do you not all brandish them like mine?
You fear to die, and yet dare talk of killing?

REN.   Go to thy senate and betray us; hasten,
Secure thy wretched life. We fear to die
Less than thou dar'st be honest.

PIERRE.   That's rank falsehood.
Fear'st not thou death? Fie, there's a knavish itch

In that salt blood, an utter foe to smarting.
Had Jaffeir's wife prov'd kind, he'd still been true.
Foh – how that stinks!
Thou die! Thou kill my friend, or thou, or thou,
Or thou, with that lean, wither'd, wretched face!
Away! Disperse all to your several charges,
And meet tomorrow where your honour calls you.
I'll bring that man whose blood you so much thirst for,
And you shall see him venture for you fairly –
Hence, hence, I say.   *Exit* RENAULT *angrily*

SPIN.   I fear we have been to blame;
And done too much.

THEO.   'Twas too far urg'd against the man you lov'd.

REVILL.   Here, take our swords and crush 'em with your feet.

SPIN.   Forgive us, gallant friend.

PIERRE.   Nay, now you've found
The way to melt and cast me as you will;
I'll fetch this friend and give him to your mercy.
Nay, he shall die if you will take him from me;
For your repose I'll quit my heart's jewel,
But would not have him torn away by villains
And spiteful villainy.

SPIN.   No. May you both
Forever live and fill the world with fame!

PIERRE.   Now you are too kind. Whence rose all this discord?
Oh, what a dangerous precipice have we 'scap'd!
How near a fall was all we had long been building!
What an eternal blot had stain'd our glories,
If one, the bravest and the best of men,
Had fallen a sacrifice to rash suspicion,
Butcher'd by those whose cause he came to cherish!
Oh, could you know him all as I have known him,
How good he is, how just, how true, how brave,
You would not leave this place till you had seen him,
Humbl'd yourselves before him, kiss'd his feet,
And gain'd remission for the worst of follies.
    Come but tomorrow all your doubts shall end,
    And to your loves me better recommend,
    That I've preserv'd your fame and sav'd my friend. *Exeunt omnes*

Act Four

[SCENE ONE]

[*Near the Senate House*]

Enter JAFFEIR *and* BELVIDERA

JAFF.   Where does thou lead me? Every step I move,
Methinks I tread upon some mangl'd limb
Of a rack'd friend. O my dear charming ruin,
Where are we wand'ring?

BELV.   To eternal honour;
To do a deed shall chronicle thy name
Among the glorious legends of those few
That have sav'd sinking nations. Thy renown
Shall be the future song of all the virgins,
Who by thy piety have been preserv'd
From horrid violation; every street
Shall be adorn'd with statues to thy honour,
And at thy feet this great inscription written,
'Remember him that propp'd the fall of Venice'.

JAFF.   Rather, remember him who after all
The sacred bonds of oaths and holier friendship,
In fond compassion to a woman's tears
Forgot his manhood, virtue, truth, and honour,
To sacrifice the bosom that reliev'd him.
Why wilt thou damn me?

BELV.   O inconstant man!
How will you promise? How will you deceive?
Do return back, replace me in my bondage,
Tell all thy friends how dangerously thou lov'st me,
And let thy dagger do its bloody office;
O that kind dagger, Jaffeir, how 'twill look
Stuck through my heart, drench'd in my blood to th' hilts!
Whilst these poor dying eyes shall with their tears
No more torment thee, then thou wilt be free;
Or if thou think'st it nobler, let me live
Till I am a victim to the hateful lust
Of that infernal devil, that old fiend

That's damn'd himself and would undo mankind.
Last night, my love —
JAFF.   Name, name it not again;
  It shows a beastly image to my fancy
  Will wake me into madness. O the villain
  That durst approach such purity as thine
  On terms so vile! Destruction, swift destruction
  Fall on my coward head, and make my name
  The common scorn of fools if I forgive him.
  If I forgive him, if I not revenge
  With utmost rage and most unstaying fury
  Thy sufferings, thou dear darling of my life, love.
BELV.   Delay no longer, then, but to the senate,
  And tell the dismal'st story e'er was utter'd;
  Tell 'em what bloodshed, rapines, desolations
  Have been prepar'd, how near's the fatal hour!
  Save thy poor country, save the reverend blood
  Of all its nobles, which tomorrow's dawn
  Must else see shed; save the poor tender lives
  Of all those little infants which the swords
  Of murderers are whetting for this moment;
  Think thou already hear'st their dying screams,
  Think that thou seest their sad, distracted mothers
  Kneeling before thy feet, and begging pity
  With torn, dishevell'd hair and streaming eyes,
  Their naked mangl'd breasts besmear'd with blood,
  And even the milk with which their fondl'd babes
  Softly they hush'd, dropping in anguish from 'em.
  Think thou seest this, and then consult thy heart.
JAFF.   Oh!
BELV.   Think too, if [that] thou lose this present minute,
  What miseries the next day bring upon thee.
  Imagine all the horrors of that night,
  Murder and rapine, waste and desolation,
  Confusedly ranging. Think what then may prove
  My lot! The ravisher may then come safe,
  And midst the terror of the public ruin
  Do a damn'd deed; perhaps to lay a train
  May catch thy life; then where will be revenge,
  The dear revenge that's due to such a wrong?
JAFF.   By all heaven's powers, prophetic truth dwells in thee,
  For every word thou speak'st strikes through my heart
  Like a new light, and shows it how't has wander'd;

Just what thou'st made me, take me, Belvidera,
And lead me to the place where I'm to say
This bitter lesson, where I must betray
My truth, my virtue, constancy, and friends.
Must I betray my friends? Ah, take me quickly,
Secure me well before that thought's renew'd;
If I relapse once more, all's lost forever.

BELV.   Hast thou a friend more dear than Belvidera?

JAFF.   No, thou'rt my soul itself; wealth, friendship, honour,
All present joys, and earnest of all future,
Are summ'd in thee. Methinks when in thy arms,
Thus leaning on thy breast, one minute's more
Than a long thousand years of vulgar hours.
Why was such happiness not given me pure?
Why dash'd with cruel wrongs and bitter wantings?
Come, lead me forward now, like a tame lamb
To sacrifice; thus in his fatal garlands,
Deck'd fine and pleas'd, the wanton skips and plays,
   Trots by the enticing, flattering priestess' side,
   And much transported with his little pride,
   Forgets his dear companions of the plain
   Till by her bound, he's on the altar lain,
   Yet then too hardly bleats, such pleasure's in the pain.
   Enter OFFICER *and six guards*

OFFIC.   Stand, who goes there?

BELV.   Friends.

JAFF.   Friends, Belvidera! Hide me from my friends.
By heaven, I'd rather see the face of hell
Than meet the man I love.

OFFIC.   But what friends are you?

BELV.   Friends to the senate and the state of Venice.

OFFIC.   My orders are to seize on all I find
At this late hour, and bring 'em to the council,
Who now are sitting.

JAFF.   Sir, you shall be obey'd.
Hold, brutes, stand off, none of your paws upon me.
Now the lot's cast, and fate do what thou wilt!   *Exeunt guarded*

SCENE [TWO]

The Senate House

Where appear sitting, the DUKE OF VENICE, PRIULI, ANTONIO *and eight other* SENATORS

DUKE. Antonio, Priuli, Senators of Venice,
 Speak. Why are we assembl'd here this night?
 What have you to inform us of concerns
 The State of Venice, honour, or its safety?

PRIU. Could words express the story I have to tell you,
 Fathers, these tears were useless, these sad tears
 That fall from my old eyes; but there is cause
 We all should weep, tear off these purple robes,
 And wrap ourselves in sackcloth, sitting down
 On the sad earth, and cry aloud to heaven.
 Heaven knows if yet there be an hour to come
 Ere Venice be no more!

ALL SENATORS.   How!

PRIU.   Nay, we stand
 Upon the very brink of gaping ruin.
 Within this city's formed a dark conspiracy,
 To massacre us all, our wives and children,
 Kindred and friends, our palaces and temples
 To lay in ashes; nay, the hour too, fix'd,
 The swords, for aught I know, drawn even this moment,
 And the wild waste begun. From unknown hands
 I had this warning; but if we are men
 Let's not be tamely butcher'd, but do something
 That may inform the world in after ages
 Our virtue was not ruin'd though we were.   *A noise without*
 Room, room, make room for some prisoners —

SECOND SENATOR. Let's raise the city.

  Enter OFFICER *and guard*

PRIU.   Speak there, what disturbance?

OFFIC. Two prisoners have the guard seiz'd in the streets,
 Who say they come to inform this reverend senate
 About the present danger.

  Enter JAFFIER *and* BELVIDERA *guarded*

ALL.   Give 'em entrance.
 Well, who are you?

JAFF.   A villain.

ANTO.   Short and pithy.
 The man speaks well.

JAFF.   Would every man that hears me
 Would deal so honestly and own his title.

DUKE. 'Tis rumour'd that a plot has been contriv'd
 Against this state, that you have a share in't too.

If you are a villain, to redeem your honour,
Unfold the truth and be restor'd with mercy.
JAFF.   Think not that I to save my life come hither,
I know its value better; but in pity
To all those wretches whose unhappy dooms
Are fix'd and seal'd. You see me here before you,
The sworn and covenanted foe of Venice;
But use me as my dealings may deserve
And I may prove a friend.
DUKE.   The slave capitulates;
Give him the tortures.
JAFF.   That you dare not do;
Your fears won't let you, nor the longing itch
To hear a story which you dread the truth of,
Truth which the fear of smart shall ne'er get from me.
Cowards are scar'd with threat'nings; boys are whipp'd
Into confessions, but a steady mind
Acts of itself, ne'er asks the body counsel.
'Give him the tortures'! Name but such a thing
Again, by heaven I'll shut these lips forever,
Not all your racks, your engines, or your wheels
Shall force a groan away — that you may guess at.
ANTO.   A bloody-minded fellow, I'll warrant,
A damn'd bloody-minded fellow.
DUKE.   Name your conditions.
JAFF.   For myself full pardon,
Besides the lives of two and twenty friends   *Delivers a list*
Whose names are here enroll'd; nay, let their crimes
Be ne'er so monstrous, I must have the oaths
And sacred promise of this reverend council,
That in a full assembly of the senate
The thing I ask be ratified. Swear this,
And I'll unfold the secrets of your danger.
ALL.   We'll swear.
DUKE.   Propose the oath.
JAFF.   By all the hopes
Ye have of peace and happiness hereafter,
Swear.
ALL.   We all swear.
JAFF.   To grant me what I've ask'd,
Ye swear.
ALL.   We swear.
JAFF.   And as ye keep the oath,

May you and your posterity be bless'd
Or curs'd forever.
ALL.   Else be curs'd forever.
JAFF.   Then here's the list, and with't the full disclose
Of all that threatens you.   *Delivers another paper*
                     Now fate, thou hast caught me.
ANTO.   Why, what a dreadful catalogue of cutthroats is here!
  I'll warrant you not one of these fellows but has a face like a
  lion. I dare not so much as read their names over.
DUKE.   Give orders that all diligent search be made
  To seize these men; their characters are public.
  The paper intimates their rendezvous
  To be at the house of a fam'd Grecian courtesan
  Called Aquilina; see that place secur'd.
ANTO.   What, my Nicky Nacky? Hurry durry, Nicky Nacky
  in the plot? I'll make a speech. Most noble senators,
  What headlong apprehension drives you on,
  Right noble, wise, and truly solid senators,
  To violate the laws and rights of nations?
  The lady is a lady of renown.
  'Tis true, she holds a house of fair reception,
  And though I say't myself, as many more
  Can say as well as I.
SECOND SENATOR. My lord, long speeches
  Are frivolous here, when dangers are so near us;
  We all well know your interest in that lady,
  The world talks loud on't.
ANTO.   Verily, I have done,
  I say no more.
DUKE.   But since he has declar'd
  Himself concern'd, pray, captain, take great caution
  To treat the fair one as becomes her character,
  And let her bedchamber be search'd with decency.
  You, Jaffeir, must with patience bear till morning
  To be our prisoner.
JAFF.   Would the chains of death
  Had bound me fast ere I had known this minute!
  I've done a deed will make my story hereafter
  Quoted in competition with all ill ones;
  The history of my wickedness shall run
  Down through the low traditions of the vulgar,
  And boys be taught to tell the tale of Jaffeir.
DUKE.   Captain, withdraw your prisoner.

JAFF.   Sir, if possible,
Lead me where my own thoughts themselves may lose me,
Where I may doze out what I've left of life,
Forget myself and this day's guilt and falsehood.
Cruel remembrance, how shall I appease thee!   *Exit guarded*
                                                    Noise without
VOICES.   More traitors! Room, room, make room there.
DUKE.   How's this? Guards!
Where are our guards? Shut up the gates, the treason's
Already at our doors.
      Enter OFFICER
OFFIC.   My lords, more traitors,
Seiz'd in the very act of consultation,
Furnish'd with arms and instruments of mischief.
Bring in the prisoners.
      Enter PIERRE, RENAULT, THEODORE, ELIOT, REVILLIDO, *and*
      other CONSPIRATORS, *in fetters, guarded*
PIERRE.   You, my lords and fathers
(As you are pleas'd to call yourselves) of Venice,
If you sit here to guide the course of justice,
Why these disgraceful chains upon the limbs
That have so often labour'd in your service?
Are these the wreaths of triumph ye bestow
On those that bring you conquests home and honours?
DUKE.   Go on; you shall be heard, sir.
ANTO.   And be hang'd too, I hope.
PIERRE.   Are these the trophies I've deserv'd for fighting
Your battles with confederated powers,
When winds and seas conspir'd to overthrow you,
And brought the fleets of Spain to your own harbours,
When you, great Duke, shrunk trembling in your palace,
And saw your wife, th'Adriatic, plough'd
Like a lewd whore by bolder prows than yours,
Stepp'd not I forth, and taught your loose Venetians
The task of honour and the way to greatness,
Rais'd you from your capitulating fears
To stipulate the terms of su'd-for peace?
And this my recompense? If I am a traitor,
Produce my charge, or show the wretch that's base enough
And brave enough to tell me I am a traitor.
DUKE.   Know you one Jaffeir?   *All the* CONSPIRATORS *murmur*
PIERRE.   Yes, and know his virtue.
His justice, truth, his general worth and sufferings

From a hard father taught me first to love him.
>   *Enter* JAFFEIR *guarded*
DUKE.   See him brought forth.
PIERRE.   My friend too bound! Nay then,
>   Our fate has conquer'd us, and we must fall.
>   Why droops the man whose welfare's so much mine
>   They're but one thing? These reverend tyrants, Jaffeir,
>   Call us all traitors. Art thou one, my brother?
JAFF.   To thee I am the falsest, veriest slave
>   That e'er betray'd a generous, trusting friend,
>   And gave up honour to be sure of ruin.
>   All our fair hopes which morning was to have crown'd
>   Has this curs'd tongue o'erthrown.
PIERRE.   So, then, all's over;
>   Venice has lost her freedom, I my life.
>   No more, farewell.
DUKE.   Say, will you make confession
>   Of your vile deeds and trust the senate's mercy?
PIERRE.   Curs'd be your senate, curs'd your constitution,
>   The curse of growing factions and division
>   Still vex your councils, shake your public safety,
>   And make the robes of government you wear
>   Hateful to you, as these base chains to me!
DUKE.   Pardon or death?
PIERRE.   Death, honourable death!
REN.   Death's the best thing we ask or you can give.
ALL CONSPIR.   No shameful bonds, but honourable death.
DUKE.   Break up the council. Captain, guard your prisoners.
>   Jaffeir, you're free, but these must wait for judgment.
>   *Exeunt all the* SENATORS
PIERRE.   Come, where's my dungeon? Lead me to my straw;
>   It will not be the first time I've lodg'd hard
>   To do your senate service.
JAFF.   Hold one moment.
PIERRE.   Who's he disputes the judgment of the senate?
>   Presumptuous rebel! On.   *Strikes* JAFFEIR
JAFF.   By heaven, you stir not.
>   I must be heard, I must have leave to speak;
>   Thou hast disgrac'd me, Pierre, by a vile blow;
>   Had not a dagger done thee nobler justice?
>   But use me as thou wilt, thou canst not wrong me,
>   For I am fallen beneath the basest injuries;
>   Yet look upon me with an eye of mercy,

With pity and with charity behold me.
Shut not thy heart against a friend's repentance,
But as there dwells a godlike nature in thee,
Listen with mildness to my supplications.

PIERRE.   What whining monk art thou, what holy cheat
That wouldst encroach upon my credulous ears
And cant'st thus vilely? Hence; I know thee not.
Dissemble and be nasty; leave me, hypocrite.

JAFF.   Not know me, Pierre?

PIERRE.   No, I know thee not. What art thou?

JAFF.   Jaffeir, thy friend, thy once-lov'd, valu'd friend!
Though now deservedly scorn'd and us'd most hardly.

PIERRE.   Thou Jaffeir! Thou my once-lov'd, valu'd friend?
By heavens, thou liest; the man so call'd my friend
Was generous, honest, faithful, just, and valiant,
Noble in mind, and in his person lovely,
Dear to my eyes and tender to my heart;
But thou a wretched, base, false, worthless coward,
Poor even in soul, and loathsome in thy aspect,
All eyes must shun thee, and all hearts detest thee.
Prithee avoid, nor longer cling thus round me
Like something baneful, that my nature's chill'd at.

JAFF.   I have not wrong's thee, by these tears I have not,
But still am honest, true, and hope too, valiant,
My mind still full of thee, therefore still noble;
Let not thy eyes then shun me, nor thy heart
Detest me utterly; oh, look upon me,
Look back and see my sad sincere submission!
How my heart swells, as even 'twould burst my bosom,
Fond of its gaol, and labouring to be at thee!
What shall I do, what say to make thee hear me?

PIERRE.   Hast thou not wrong'd me? Dar'st thou call thyself
Jaffeir, that once-lov'd, valu'd friend of mine,
And swear thou hast not wrong'd me? Whence these chains?
Whence the vile death which I may meet this moment?
Whence this dishonour, but from thee, thou false one?

JAFF.   All's true, yet grant one thing, and I've done asking.

PIERRE.   What's that?

JAFF.   To take thy life on such conditions
The council have propos'd; thou and thy friends
May yet live long, and to be better treated.

PIERRE.   Life! Ask my life? Confess! Record myself
A villain for the privilege to breathe,

And carry up and down this cursed city
A discontented and repining spirit,
Burdensome to itself a few years longer,
To lose it, may be, at last in a lewd quarrel
For some new friend, treacherous and false as thou art!
No, this vile world and I have long been jangling,
And cannot part on better terms than now,
When only men like thee are fit to live in't.

JAFF. By all that's just —

PIERRE.   Swear by some other powers,
For thou hast broke that sacred oath too lately.

JAFF. Then by that hell I merit, I'll not leave thee,
Till to thyself at least thou'rt reconcil'd,
However thy resentments deal with me.

PIERRE. Not leave me?

JAFF.   No, thou shalt not force me from thee.
Use me reproachfully, and like a slave,
Tread on me, buffet me, heap wrongs on wrongs
On my poor head; I'll bear it all with patience
Shall weary out thy most unfriendly cruelty,
Lie at thy feet and kiss 'em though they spurn me,
Till, wounded by my sufferings, thou relent,
And raise me to thy arms with dear forgiveness.

PIERRE. Art thou not —

JAFF.   What?

PIERRE.   A traitor?

JAFF.   Yes.

PIERRE.   A villain?

JAFF. Granted.

PIERRE.   A coward, a most scandalous coward,
Spiritless, void of honour, one who has sold
Thy everlasting fame for shameless life?

JAFF. All, all, and more, much more; my faults are numberless.

PIERRE. And wouldst thou have me live on terms like thine?
Base as thou art false —

JAFF.   No, 'tis to me that's granted.
The safety of thy life was all I aim'd at,
In recompense for faith and trust so broken.

PIERRE. I scorn it more because preserv'd by thee.
And as when first my foolish heart took pity
On thy misfortunes, sought thee in thy miseries,
Reliev'd thy wants, and rais'd thee from thy state
Of wretchedness in which thy fate had plung'd thee,

To rank thee in my list of noble friends;
All I receiv'd in surety for thy truth
Were unregarded oaths, and this, this dagger,
Given with a worthless pledge, thou since hast stol'n;
So I restore it back to thee again,
Swearing by all those powers which thou hast violated,
Never from this curs'd hour to hold communion,
Friendship or interest with thee, though our years
Were to exceed those limited the world.
Take it – farewell – for now I owe thee nothing.

JAFF.   Say thou wilt live, then.

PIERRE.   For my life, dispose it
Just as thou wilt, because 'tis what I'm tir'd with.

JAFF.   O Pierre!

PIERRE.   No more.

JAFF.   My eyes won't lose the sight of thee,
But languish after thine, and ache with gazing.

PIERRE.   Leave me. Nay, then, thus, thus, I throw thee from me,
And curses great as is thy falsehood catch thee.   *Exit*

JAFF.   Amen.
He's gone, my father, friend, preserver,
And here's the portion he has left me.   *Holds the dagger up*
This dagger, well rememb'red, with this dagger
I gave a solemn vow of dire importance,
Parted with this and Belvidera together;
Have a care, mem'ry, drive that thought no further;
No, I'll esteem it as a friend's last legacy,
Treasure it up within this wretched bosom,
Where it may grow acquainted with my heart,
That when they meet, they start not from each other.
So; now for thinking. A blow, call'd traitor, villain,
Coward, dishonourable coward! Fough!
Oh, for a long sound sleep, and so forget it!
Down, busy devil –

    Enter BELVIDERA

BELV.   Whither shall I fly,
Where hide me and my miseries together?
Where's now the Roman constancy I boasted?
Sunk into trembling fears and desperation,
Not daring now to look up to that dear face
Which us'd to smile even on my faults, but down
Bending these miserable eyes to earth,
Must move in penance, and implore much mercy.

JAFF.   Mercy! Kind heaven has surely endless stores
   Hoarded for thee of blessings yet untasted.
   Let wretches loaded hard with guilt as I am,
   Bow with the weight and groan beneath the burden,
   Creep with a remnant of that strength they've left,
   Before the footstool of that heaven they've injur'd.
   O Belvidera, I'm the wretched'st creature
   E'er crawl'd on earth; now if thou hast virtue, help me,
   Take me into thy arms, and speak the words of peace
   To my divided soul that wars within me,
   And raises every sense to my confusion.
   By heav'n, I'm tottering on the very brink
   Of peace, and thou art all the hold I've left.
BELV.   Alas, I know thy sorrows are most mighty;
   I know thou'st cause to mourn, to mourn, my Jaffeir,
   With endless cries and never-ceasing wailings,
   Thou'st lost —
JAFF.   Oh, I have lost what can't be counted,
   My friend too, Belvidera, that dear friend,
   Who, next to thee, was all my health rejoic'd in,
   Has us'd me like a slave, shamefully us'd me;
   'Twould break thy pitying heart to hear the story.
   What shall I do? Resentment, indignation,
   Love, pity, fear, and mem'ry, how I've wrong'd him
   Distract my quiet with the very thought on't,
   And tear my heart to pieces in my bosom.
BELV.   What has he done?
JAFF.   Thou'dst hate me, should I tell thee.
BELV.   Why?
JAFF.   Oh, he has us'd me — Yet, by heaven, I bear it!
   He has us'd me, Belvidera — but first swear
   That when I've told thee, thou'lt not loathe me utterly,
   Though vilest blots and stains appear upon me;
   But still at least with charitable goodness,
   Be near me in the pangs of my affliction,
   Not scorn me, Belvidera, as he has done.
BELV.   Have I then e'er been false that now I'm doubted?
   Speak, what's the cause I'm grown into distrust,
   Why thought unfit to hear my love's complainings?
JAFF.   Oh!
BELV.   Tell me.
JAFF.   Bear my failings, for they are many.
   O my dear angel! In that friend I've lost

All my soul's peace; for every thought of him
Strikes my sense hard, and deads it in my brains;
Wouldst thou believe it?

BELV.   Speak!

JAFF.   Before we parted,
Ere yet his guards had led him to his prison,
Full of severest sorrows for his suff'rings,
With eyes o'erflowing and a bleeding heart,
Humbling myself almost beneath my nature,
As at his feet I kneel'd, and su'd for mercy.
Forgetting all our friendship, all the dearness,
In which we've liv'd so many years together,
With a reproachful hand he dash'd a blow.
He struck me, Belvidera, by heaven, he struck me,
Buffeted, call'd me traitor, villain, coward!
Am I a coward? Am I a villain? Tell me.
Thou'rt the best judge, and mad'st me, if I am so.
Damnation! Coward!

BELV.   Oh, forgive him, Jaffeir;
And if his sufferings wound thy heart already,
What will they do tomorrow?

JAFF.   Hah!

BELV.   Tomorrow,
When thou shalt see him stretch'd in all the agonies
Of a tormenting and a shameful death,
His bleeding bowels, and his broken limbs,
Insulted o'er by a vile butchering villain,
What will thy heart do then? Oh, sure 'twill stream
Like my eyes now.

JAFF.   What means thy dreadful story?
Death, and tomorrow? Broken limbs and bowels!
Insulted o'er by a vile butchering villain!
By all my fears I shall start out to madness,
With barely guessing if the truth's hid longer.

BELV.   The faithless senators, 'tis they've decreed it:
They say according to our friend's request,
They shall have death and not ignoble bondage,
Declare their promis'd mercy all as forfeited,
False to their oaths and deaf to intercession;
Warrants are pass'd for public death tomorrow.

JAFF.   Death! Doom'd to die! Condemn'd unheard! Unpleaded!

BELV.   Nay, cruell'st racks and torments are preparing,
To force confessions from their dying pangs.

Oh, do not look so terribly upon me!
How your lips shake, and all your face disorder'd!
What means my love?
JAFF.   Leave me, I charge thee, leave me. Strong temptations
Wake in my heart.
BELV.   For what?
JAFF.   No more, but leave me.
BELV.   Why?
JAFF.   Oh, by heaven I love thee with that fondness
I would not have thee stay a moment longer
Near these curs'd hands; are they not cold upon thee?
Pulls the dagger half out of his bosom and puts it back again
BELV.   No. Everlasting comfort's in thy arms;
To lean thus on thy breast is softer ease
Than downy pillows deck'd with leaves of roses.
JAFF.   Alas, thou think'st not of the thorns 'tis fill'd with;
Fly ere they gall thee. There's a lurking serpent,
Ready to leap and sting thee to thy heart;
Art thou not terrified?
BELV.   No.
JAFF.   Call to mind
What thou hast done and whither thou hast brought me.
BELV.   Hah!
JAFF.   Where's my friend? My friend, thou smiling mischief?
Nay, shrink not, now 'tis too late; thou shouldst have fled
When thy guilt first had cause, for dire revenge
Is up and raging for my friend. He groans,
Hark how he groans, his screams are in my ears
Already. See, they've fix'd him on the wheel,
And now they tear him! Murder! Perjur'd senate!
Murder! Oh, hark thee, traitress, thou hast done this,
                                        Fumbling for his dagger
Thanks to thy tears and false persuading love.
How her eyes speak! O thou bewitching creature!
Madness cannot hurt thee. Come, thou little trembler,
Creep, even into my heart, and there lie safe;
'Tis thy own citadel. Ha! – Yet stand off;
Heaven must have justice, and my broken vows
Will sink me else beneath its reaching mercy.
I'll wink and then 'tis done –
BELV.   What means the lord
Of me, my life and love? What's in thy bosom
                              He draws the dagger, offers to stab her

Thou grasp'st at so? Nay, why am I thus treated?
What wilt thou do? Ah, do not kill me, Jaffeir;
Pity these panting breasts and trembling limbs
That us'd to clasp thee when thy looks were milder,
That yet hang heavy on my unpurg'd soul,
And plunge it not into eternal darkness.

JAFF.   No, Belvidera, when we parted last
I gave this dagger with thee as in trust
To be thy portion, if I e'er prove false.
On such condition was my truth believ'd,
But now 'tis forfeited and must be paid for.   *Offers to stab her again*

BELV.   (*Kneeling*) Oh, mercy!

JAFF.   Nay, no struggling.

BELV.   Now, then, kill me,
                    Leaps upon his neck and kisses him
While thus I cling about thy cruel neck,
Kiss thy revengeful lips and die in joys
Greater than any I can guess hereafter.

JAFF.   I am, I am a coward; witness't, heaven,
Witness it, earth, and every being witness;
'Tis but one blow; yet, by immortal love,
I cannot longer bear a thought to harm thee;
                    He throws away the dagger and embraces her
The seal of providence is sure upon thee,
And thou wert born for yet unheard-of wonders.
Oh, thou wert either born to save or damn me!
By all the power that's given thee o'er my soul,
By thy resistless tears and conquering smiles,
By the victorious love that still waits on thee,
Fly to thy cruel father; save my friend,
Or all our future quiet's lost forever.
Fall at his feet, cling round his reverend knees,
Speak to him with thy eyes, and with thy tears
Melt his hard heart, and wake dead nature in him;
Crush him in thy arms, and torture him with thy softness,
    Nor, till thy prayers are granted, set him free,
    But conquer him, as thou hast vanquish'd me.   *Exeunt ambo*

Act Five

[SCENE ONE]

[PRIULI'S *house*]

Enter PRIULI, *solus*

PRIU.   Why, cruel heaven, have my unhappy days
Been lengthen'd to this sad one? Oh, dishonour
And deathless infamy is fall'n upon me!
Was it my fault? Am I a traitor? No.
But then, my only child, my daughter, wedded;
There my best blood runs foul, and a disease
Incurable has seiz'd upon my memory,
To make it rot and stink to after ages.
Curs'd be the fatal minute when I got her;
Or would that I'd been anything but man,
And rais'd an issue which would ne'er have wrong'd me.
The miserablest creatures, man excepted,
Are not the less esteem'd, though their posterity
Degenerate from the virtues of their fathers;
The vilest beasts are happy in their offsprings,
While only man gets traitors, whores, and villains.
Curs'd be the names, and some swift blow from fate
Lay his head deep, where mine may be forgotten.

Enter BELVIDERA *in a long mourning veil*

BELV.   He's there, my father, my inhuman father,
That, for three years, has left an only child
Expos'd to all the outrages of fate
And cruel rain – Oh! –

PRIU.   What child of sorrow
Art thou that com'st thus wrapp'd in weeds of sadness,
And mov'st as if thy steps were towards a grave?

BELV.   A wretch who from the very top of happiness
Am fallen into the lowest depths of misery,
And want your pitying hand to raise me up again.

PRIU.   Indeed thou talk'st as thou hadst tasted sorrows;
Would I could help thee!

BELV.   'Tis greatly in your power.

The world, too, speaks you charitable, and I,
Who ne'er ask'd alms before, in that dear hope
Am come a-begging to you, sir.

PRIU.   For what?

BELV.   Oh, well regard me, is this voice a strange one?
Consider, too, when beggars once pretend
A case like mine, no little will content 'em.

PRIU.   What wouldst thou beg for?

BELV.   Pity and forgiveness; *Throws up her veil*
By the kind tender names of child and father,
Hear my complaints and take me to your love.

PRIU.   My daughter?

BELV.   Yes, your daughter, by a mother
Virtuous and noble, faithful to your honour,
Obedient to your will, kind to your wishes,
Dear to your arms; by all the joys she gave you,
When in her blooming years she was your treasure,
Look kindly on me; in my face behold
The lineaments of hers you've kiss'd so often,
Pleading the cause of your poor cast-off child.

PRIU.   Thou art my daughter?

BELV.   Yes – and you've oft told me,
With smiles of love and chaste paternal kisses,
I'd much resemblance of my mother.

PRIU.   Oh,
Hadst thou inherited her matchless virtues
I'd been too bless'd.

BELV.   Nay, do not call to memory
My disobedience, but let pity enter
Into your heart and quite deface the impression;
For could you think how mine's perplex'd, what sadness,
Fears and despairs distract the peace within me,
Oh, you would take me in your dear, dear arms,
Hover with strong compassion o'er your young one,
To shelter me with a protecting wing
From the black-gather'd storm, that's just, just breaking.

PRIU.   Don't talk thus.

BELV.   Yes, I must, and you must hear too.
I have a husband.

PRIU.   Damn him.

BELV.   Oh, do not curse him!
He would not speak so hard a word towards you
On any terms, howe'er he deal with me.

PRIU.   Hah, what means my child?

BELV.   Oh, there's but this short moment
  'Twixt me and fate, yet send me not with curses
  Down to my grave. Afford me one kind blessing
  Before we part; just take me in your arms,
  And recommend me with a prayer to heaven,
  That I may die in peace, and when I'm dead –

PRIU.   How my soul's catch'd!

BELV.   Lay me, I beg you, lay me
  By the dear ashes of my tender mother;
  She would have pitied me, had fate yet spar'd her.

PRIU.   By heaven, my aching heart forebodes much mischief;
  Tell me thy story, for I'm still thy father.

BELV.   No, I'm contented.

PRIU.   Speak.

BELV.   No matter.

PRIU.   Tell me.
  By yon blest heaven, my heart runs o'er with fondness.

BELV.   Oh!

PRIU.   Utter't.

BELV.   O my husband, my dear husband
  Carries a dagger in his once kind bosom,
  To pierce the heart of your poor Belvidera.

PRIU.   Kill thee?

BELV.   Yes, kill me. When he pass'd his faith
  And covenant, against your state and senate,
  He gave me up as hostage for his truth,
  With me a dagger and a dire commission
  Whene'er he fail'd, to plunge it through this bosom.
  I learnt the danger, chose the hour of love
  T'attempt his heart and bring it back to honour.
  Great love prevail'd and bless'd me with success:
  He came, confess'd, betray'd his dearest friends
  For promis'd mercy; now they're doom'd to suffer,
  Gall'd with remembrance of what then was sworn,
  If they are lost, he vows t'appease the gods
  With this poor life, and make my blood th'atonement.

PRIU.   Heavens!

BELV.   Think you saw what pass'd at our last parting;
  Think you beheld him like a raging lion,
  Pacing the earth and tearing up his steps,
  Fate in his eyes, and roaring with the pain
  Of burning fury; think you saw his one hand

Fix'd on my throat, while the extended other
Grasp'd a keen threat'ning dagger. Oh, 'twas thus
We last embrac'd, when, trembling with revenge,
He dragg'd me to the ground, and at my bosom
Presented horrid death, cried out, 'My friends,
Where are my friends'? swore, wept, rag'd, threaten'd, lov'd,
For he yet lov'd, and that dear love preserv'd me
To this last trial of a father's pity.
I fear not death, but cannot bear a thought
That that dear hand should do th'unfriendly office;
If I was ever then your care, now hear me:
Fly to the senate, save the promis'd lives
Of his dear friends, ere mine be made the sacrifice.

PRIU.   O my heart's comfort!

BELV.   Will you not, my father?
Weep not, but answer me.

PRIU.   By heaven, I will.
Not one of 'em but what shall be immortal.
Canst thou forgive me all my follies past,
I'll henceforth be indeed a father; never,
Never more thus expose, but cherish thee.
Dear as the vital warmth that feeds my life,
Dear as these eyes that weep in fondness o'er thee.
Peace to thy heart. Farewell.

BELV.   Go, and remember
'Tis Belvidera's life her father pleads for.   *Exeunt severally*

[SCENE TWO]

[*A Street in Venice*]

Enter ANTONIO

[ANTO.]   Hum, hum, ha, Signor Priuli, my Lord Priuli, my lord, my
lord, my lord. Now we lords love to call one another by our titles!
My lord, my lord, my lord. Pox on him, I am a lord as well as he, and
so let him fiddle. I'll warrant him he's gone to the senate-house, and
I'll be there too, soon enough for somebody. Od, here's a tickling
speech about the plot; I'll prove there's a plot with a vengeance.
Would I had it without book. Let me see.

   Most reverend Senators,

   That there is a plot, surely by this time no man that hath eyes or
understanding in his head will presume to doubt; 'tis as plain as the
light in the cucumber – no – hold there – cucumber does not come in

yet – 'tis as plain as the light in the sun, or as the man in the moon
even at noonday; it is indeed a pumpkin-plot, which, just as it was
mellow, we have gathered; and now we have gathered it, prepared
and dressed it, shall we throw it like a pickled cucumber out at the
window? No. That it is not only a bloody, horrid, execrable,
damnable and audacious plot, but it is, as I may so say, a saucy plot,
and we all know, most reverend fathers, that what is sauce for a
goose is sauce for a gander; therefore, I say, as those bloodthirsty
ganders of the conspiracy would have destroyed us geese of the
senate, let us make haste to destroy them, so I humbly move for
hanging.– Ha, hurry durry, I think this will do, though I was
something out at first about the sun and the cucumber.

   Enter AQUILINA

AQUIL.   Good morrow, Senator.
ANTO.   Nacky, my dear Nacky, morrow, Nacky. Od I am very brisk,
very merry, very pert, very jovial – haaaaa! Kiss me, Nacky; how
dost thou do, my little tory rory strumpet? Kiss me, I say, hussy, kiss
me.
AQUIL.   'Kiss me, Nacky'. Hang you, Sir Coxcomb, hang you, sir.
ANTO.   Hayty tayty, is it so indeed, with all my heart, faith? 'Hey then
up go we, faith, hey then up go we', dum dum derum dump.   *Sings*
AQUIL.   Signior.
ANTO.   Madonna.
AQUIL.   Do you intend to die in your bed?
ANTO.   About threescore years hence much may be done, my dear.
AQUIL.   You'll be hanged, signior.
ANTO.   Hanged, sweetheart? Prithee be quiet! Hanged quotha?
That's a merry conceit, with all my heart! Why, thou jok'st, Nacky,
thou art given to joking, I'll swear; well, I protest, Nacky, nay, I
must protest, and will protest that I love joking dearly, man. And I
love thee for joking, and I'll kiss thee for joking, and touse thee for
joking, and od, I have a devilish mind to take thee aside about that
business for joking too, od I have, and 'Hey then up go we', dum
dum derum dump.   *Sings*
AQUIL.   See you this, sir?   *Draws a dagger*
ANTO.   O Laud, a dagger! O Laud! It is naturally my aversion, I
cannot endure the sight on't. Hide it, for heaven's sake; I cannot
look that way till it be gone. Hide it, hide it, oh, oh, hide it!
AQUIL.   Yes, in your heart I'll hide it.
ANTO.   My heart? What, hide a dagger in my heart's blood?
AQUIL.   Yes, in thy heart, thy throat, thou pamper'd devil;
Thou hast help'd to spoil my peace, and I'll have vengeance
On thy curs'd life, for all the bloody senate,

The perjur'd, faithless senate. Where's my lord,
My happiness, my love, my god, my hero,
Doom'd by thy accursed tongue, amongst the rest,
T'a shameful wrack? By all the rage that's in me
I'll be whole years in murdering thee.

ANTO.   Why, Nacky,
Wherefore so passionate? What have I done? What's the matter, my
dear Nacky? Am not I thy love, thy happiness, thy lord, thy hero, thy
senator, and everything in the world, Nacky?

AQUIL.   Thou? Think'st thou, thou art fit to meet my joys,
To bear the eager clasps of my embraces?
Give me my Pierre or –

ANTO.   Why, he's to be hang'd, little Nacky,
Truss'd up for treason, and so forth, child.

AQUIL.   Thou liest. Stop down thy throat that hellish sentence,
Or 'tis thy last. Swear that my love shall live,
Or thou art dead.

ANTO.   Ahhhh.

AQUIL.   Swear to recall his doom,
Swear at my feet, and tremble at my fury.

ANTO.   I do. Now if she would but kick a little bit, one kick now.
Ahhhh.

AQUIL.   Swear or –

ANTO.   I do, by these dear fragrant foots
And little toes, sweet as, eeee my Nacky Nacky Nacky.

AQUIL.   How!

ANTO.   Nothing but untie thy shoe string a little, faith and troth,
that's all, that's all, as I hope to live, Nacky, that's all.

AQUIL.   Nay, then –

ANTO.   Hold, hold; thy love, thy lord, thy hero
Shall be preserv'd and safe.

AQUIL.   Or may this poniard
Rust in thy heart.

ANTO.   With all my soul.

AQUIL.   Farewell.   *Exit* AQUILINA

ANTO.   Adieu. Why, what a bloody-minded, inveterate, termagant
strumpet have I been plagued with! Ohhh yet more! Nay then I die, I
die, I am dead already.   *Stretches himself out*
         Enter JAFFEIR

JAFF.   Final destruction seize on all the world;
Bend down, ye heavens, and shutting round this earth,
Crush the vile globe into its first confusion;
Scorch it with elemental flames to one curs'd cinder,

And all us little creepers in't, call'd men,
Burn, burn to nothing! But let Venice burn
Hotter than all the rest; here kindle hell
Ne'er to extinguish, and let souls hereafter
Groan here, in all those pains which mine feels now.

    Enter BELVIDERA

BELV. My life –   *Meeting him*
JAFF.   My plague –   *Turning from her*
BELV.   Nay, then, I see my ruin
  If I must die!
JAFF.   No, death's this day too busy;
  Thy father's ill-tim'd mercy came too late.
  I thank thee for thy labours though and him too,
  But all my poor betray'd, unhappy friends
  Have summons to prepare for fate's black hour;
  And yet I live.
BELV.   Then be the next my doom.
  I see thou'st pass'd my sentence in thy heart,
  And I'll no longer weep or plead against it,
  But with the humblest, most obedient patience
  Meet thy dear hands, and kiss 'em when they wound me;
  Indeed I'm willing, but I beg thee do it
  With some remorse, and where thou giv'st the blow,
  View me with eyes of a relenting love,
  And show me pity, for 'twill sweeten justice.
JAFF. Show pity to thee?
BELV.   Yes, and when thy hands,
  Charg'd with my fate, come trembling to the deed,
  As thou hast done a thousand thousand dear times
  To this poor breast, when kinder rage has brought thee,
  When our sting'd hearts have leap'd to meet each other,
  And melting kisses seal'd our lips together,
  When joys have left me gasping in thy arms,
  So let my death come now, and I'll not shrink from't.
JAFF. Nay, Belvidera, do not fear my cruelty,
  Nor let the thoughts of death perplex thy fancy,
  But answer me to what I shall demand
  With a firm temper and unshaken spirit.
BELV. I will when I've done weeping –
JAFF.   Fie, no more on't –
  How long is't since the miserable day
  We wedded first –
BELV.   Ohhh!

JAFF.   Nay, keep in thy tears,
  Lest they unman me too.
BELV.   Heaven knows I cannot!
  The words you utter sound so very sadly
  These streams will follow –
JAFF.   Come, I'll kiss 'em dry, then.
BELV.   But was't a miserable day?
JAFF.   A curs'd one.
BELV.   I thought it otherwise, and you've oft sworn
  In the transporting hours of warmest love
  When sure you spoke the truth, you've sworn you bless'd it.
JAFF.   'Twas a rash oath.
BELV.   Then why am I not curs'd too?
JAFF.   No, Belvidera; by the eternal truth,
  I dote with too much fondness.
BELV.   Still so kind?
  Still then do you love me?
JAFF.   Nature in her workings
  Inclines not with more ardour to creation
  Than I do now towards thee; man ne'er was bless'd,
  Since the first pair first met, as I have been.
BELV.   Then sure you will not curse me.
JAFF.   No, I'll bless thee.
  I came on purpose, Belvidera, to bless thee.
  'Tis now, I think, three years we've liv'd together.
BELV.   And may no fatal minute ever part us,
  Till, reverend grown, for age and love, we go
  Down to one grave, as our last bed, together,
  There sleep in peace till an eternal morning.
JAFF.   When will that be?   *Sighing*
BELV.   I hope long ages hence.
JAFF.   Have I not hitherto (I beg thee tell me
  Thy very fears) us'd thee with tender'st love?
  Did e'er my soul rise up in wrath against thee?
  Did e'er I frown when Belvidera smil'd,
  Or, by the least unfriendly word, betray
  A bating passion? Have I ever wrong'd thee?
BELV.   No.
JAFF.   Has my heart, or have my eyes e'er wand'red
  To any other woman?
BELV.   Never, never.
  I were the worst of false ones should I accuse thee;
  I own I've been too happy, bless'd above

My sex's charter.

JAFF.   Did I not say I came
To bless thee?

BELV.   Yes.

JAFF.   Then hear me, bounteous heaven!
Pour down your blessings on this beauteous head,
Where everlasting sweets are always springing,
With a continual giving hand; let peace,
Honour, and safety always hover round her,
Feed her with plenty, let her eyes ne'er see
A sight of sorrow, nor her heart know mourning;
Crown all her days with joy, her nights with rest,
Harmless as her own thoughts, and prop her virtue
To bear the loss of one that too much lov'd,
And comfort her with patience in our parting.

BELV. How, parting, parting!

JAFF.   Yes, forever parting.
I have sworn, Belvidera, by yon heaven,
That best can tell how much I lose to leave thee,
We part this hour forever.

BELV.   Oh, call back
Your cruel blessings, stay with me and curse me!

JAFF. No, 'tis resolv'd.

BELV.   Then hear me too, just heaven,
Pour down your curses on this wretched head
With never-ceasing vengeance; let despair,
Danger or infamy, nay, all surround me;
Starve me with wantings, let my eyes ne'er see
A sight of comfort, nor my heart know peace,
But dash my days with sorrow, nights with horrors
Wild as my own thoughts now, and let loose fury
To make me mad enough for what I lose,
If I must lose him; if I must, I will not.
Oh, turn and hear me!

JAFF.   Now hold, heart, or never.

BELV. By all the tender days we've liv'd together,
By all our charming nights, and joys that crown'd 'em,
Pity my sad condition. Speak, but speak.

JAFF. Ohhh!

BELV.   By these arms that now cling round thy neck,
By this dear kiss and by ten thousand more,
By these poor streaming eyes —

JAFF.   Murder! Unhold me.   *Draws his dagger*

By the immoral destiny that doom'd me
To this curs'd minute, I'll not live one longer.
Resolve to let me go or see me fall –
BELV.   Hold, sir, be patient.
JAFF.   Hark, the dismal bell   *Passing bell tolls*
Tolls out for death; I must attend its call too,
For my poor friend, my dying Pierre expects me;
He sent a message to require I'd see him
Before he died, and take his last forgiveness.
Farewell forever.   *Going out, looks back at her*
BELV.   Leave thy dagger with me.
Bequeath me something. Not one kiss at parting?
O my poor heart, when wilt thou break?
JAFF.   Yet stay,
We have a child, as yet a tender infant.
Be a kind mother to him when I am gone,
Breed him in virtue and the paths of honour,
But let him never know his father's story;
I charge thee guard him from the wrongs my fate
May do his future fortune or his name.
Now – nearer yet –   *Approaching each other*
Oh, that my arms were riveted
Thus round thee ever! But my friends, my oath!
This and no more.   *Kisses her*
BELV.   Another, sure another,
For that poor little one you've ta'en care of,
I'll give't him truly.
JAFF.   So, now farewell.
BELV.   Forever?
JAFF.   Heavens knows forever. All good angels guard thee.   [*Exit*]
BELV.   All ill ones sure had charge of me this moment.
Curs'd be my days, and doubly curs'd my nights,
Which I must now mourn out in widow'd tears;
Blasted be every herb and fruit and tree,
Curs'd be the rain that falls upon the earth,
And may the general curse reach man and beast.
Oh, give me daggers, fire, or water!
How I could bleed, how burn, how drown, the waves
Huzzing and booming round my sinking head,
Till I descended to the peaceful bottom!
Oh, there's all quiet, here all rage and fury.
The air's too thin, and pierces my weak brain;
I long for thick, substantial sleep. Hell, hell,

Burst from the centre, rage and roar aloud,
If thou art half so hot, so mad as I am.
    Enter PRIULI *and servants*
Who's there?   *They seize her*
PRIU.   Run, seize and bring her safely home.
    Guard her as you would life. Alas, poor creature!
BELV.   What? To my husband then conduct me quickly.
    Are all things ready? Shall we die most gloriously?
    Say not a word of this to my old father.
    Murmuring streams, soft shades, and springing flowers,
    Lutes, laurels, seas of milk, and ships of amber.   *Exeunt*

[SCENE THREE]

[*The Rialto*]

*Scene opening discovers a scaffold and a wheel prepared for the
executing of* PIERRE; *then enter* OFFICERS, PIERRE *and guards, a*
FRIAR, *executioner, and a great rabble.*

OFFIC.   Room, room, there. Stand all by, make room for the
    prisoner.
PIERRE.   My friend not come yet?
FATHER.   Why are you so obstinate?
PIERRE.   Why you so troublesome, that a poor wretch
    Cannot die in peace,
    But you, like ravens, will be croaking round him?
FATHER.   Yet, heaven —
PIERRE.   I tell thee heaven and I are friends.
    I ne'er broke peace with't yet, by cruel murders,
    Rapine or perjury, or vile deceiving,
    But liv'd in moral justice towards all men;
    Nor am a foe to the most strong believers,
    Howe'er my own short-sighted faith confine me.
FATHER.   But an all-seeing judge —
PIERRE.   You say my conscience
    Must be mine accuser. I've search'd that conscience,
    And find no records there of crimes that scare me.
FATHER.   'Tis strange you should want faith.
PIERRE.   You want to lead
    My reason blindfold, like a hamper'd lion,
    Check'd of its nobler vigour; then, when baited
    Down to obedient tameness, make it couch,
    And show strange tricks which you call signs of faith.

So silly souls are gull'd and you get money.
Away, no more. Captain, I would hereafter
This fellow write no lies of my conversion,
Because he has crept upon my troubled hours.
    Enter JAFFEIR

JAFF. Hold! Eyes, be dry! Heart, strengthen me to bear
  This hideous sight, and humble me to take
  The last forgiveness of a dying friend,
  Betray'd by my vile falsehood, to his ruin.
  O Pierre!

PIERRE.   Yet nearer.

JAFF.   Crawling on my knees,
  And prostrate on the earth, let me approach thee:
  How shall I look up to thy injur'd face,
  That always used to smile with friendship on me?
  It darts an air of so much manly virtue
  That I, methinks, look little in thy sight,
  And stripes are fitter for me than embraces.

PIERRE. Dear to my arms, though thou'st undone my fame,
  I cannot forget to love thee. Prithee, Jaffeir,
  Forgive that filthy blow my passion dealt thee;
  I am now preparing for the land of peace,
  And fain would have the charitable wishes
  Of all good men, like thee, to bless my journey.

JAFF. Good! I am the vilest creature, worse than e'er
  Suffer'd the shameful fate thou art going to taste of.
  Why was I sent for to be us'd thus kindly?
  Call, call me villain, as I am, describe
  The foul complexion of my hateful deeds,
  Lead me to the rack, and stretch me in thy stead,
  I've crimes enough to give it its full load,
  And do it credit. Thou wilt but spoil the use on't,
  And honest men hereafter bear its figure
  About 'em, as a charm from treacherous friendship.

OFFIC. The time grows short, your friends are dead already.

JAFF. Dead!

PIERRE.   Yes, dead, Jaffeir; they've all died like men too,
  Worthy their character.

JAFF.   And what must I do?

PIERRE. O Jaffeir!

JAFF.   Speak aloud thy burden'd soul,
  And tell thy troubles to thy tortur'd friend.

PIERRE. Friend? Couldst thou yet be a friend, a generous friend,

I might hope comfort from thy noble sorrows.
Heav'n knows I want a friend.

JAFF.   And I a kind one,
That would not thus scorn my repenting virtue,
Or think when he is to die, my thoughts are idle.

PIERRE.   No! Live, I charge thee, Jaffeir.

JAFF.   Yes, I will live,
But it shall be to see thy fall reveng'd
At such a rate as Venice long shall groan for.

PIERRE.   Wilt thou?

JAFF.   I will, by heav'n.

PIERRE.   Then still thou'rt noble,
And I forgive thee. Oh, yet – shall I trust thee?

JAFF.   No; I've been false already.

PIERRE.   Dost thou love me?

JAFF.   Rip up my heart and satisfy thy doubtings.

PIERRE.   Curse on this weakness.   *He weeps*

JAFF.   Tears! Amazement! Tears!
I never saw thee melted thus before,
And know there's something lab'ring in thy bosom
That must have vent. Though I'm a villain, tell me.

PIERRE.   Seest thou that engine?   *Pointing to the wheel*

JAFF.   Why?

PIERRE.   Is't fit a soldier who has liv'd with honour,
Fought nations' quarrels, and been crown'd with conquest,
Be expos'd a common carcass on a wheel?

JAFF.   Hah!

PIERRE.   Speak! Is't fitting?

JAFF.   Fitting?

PIERRE.   Yes, is't fitting?

JAFF.   What's to be done?

PIERRE.   I'd have thee undertake
Something that's noble, to preserve my memory
From the disgrace that's ready to attaint it.

OFFIC.   The day grows late, sir.

PIERRE.   I'll make haste! O Jaffeir,
Though thou'st betray'd me, do me some way justice.

JAFF.   No more of that; thy wishes shall be satisfied.
I have a wife, and she shall bleed, my child too
Yield up his little throat, and all t'appease thee –
                   Going away, PIERRE *holds him*

PIERRE.   No – this – no more!   *He whispers* [to] JAFFEIR

JAFF.   Ha! Is't then so?

PIERRE.   Most certainly.
JAFF.   I'll do't.
PIERRE.   Remember.
OFFIC.   Sir.
PIERRE.   Come, now I'm ready.
                                    He and JAFFEIR *ascend the scaffold*
Captain, you should be a gentleman of honour;
Keep off the rabble that I may have room
To entertain my fate and die with decency.
Come!   *Takes off his gown,* EXECUTIONER *prepares to bind him*
FATHER.   Son!
PIERRE.   Hence, tempter.
OFFIC.   Stand off, priest.
PIERRE.   I thank you, sir.
(*To* JAFFEIR) You'll think on't?
JAFF.   'Twon't grow stale before tomorrow.
PIERRE.   Now, Jaffeir! Now I am going. Now.
                                    EXECUTIONER *having bound him*
JAFF.   Have at thee,
Thou honest heart, then – here –   *Stabs him*
And this is well too.   *Then stabs himself*
FATHER.   Damnable deed!
PIERRE.   Now thou hast indeed been faithful.
This was done nobly. We have deceiv'd the senate.
JAFF.   Bravely.
PIERRE.   Ha, ha, ha! – Oh, oh! –   *Dies*
JAFF.   Now, ye curs'd rulers,
Thus of the blood you've shed I make libation,
And sprinkle't mingling; may it rest upon you
And all your race; be henceforth peace a stranger
Within your walls; let plagues and famine waste
Your generations. O poor Belvidera!
Sir, I have a wife, bear this (*Giving dagger*) in safety to her,
A token that with my dying breath I bless'd her,
And the dear little infant left behind me.
I am sick – I'm quiet –   JAFFEIR *dies*
OFFIC.   Bear this news to the senate,
And guard their bodies till there's further order.
Heav'n grant I die so well!   *Scene shuts upon them*

[SCENE FOUR]

[PRIULI's *house*]

Soft music. Enter BELVIDERA *distracted, led by two of her women,*
   PRIULI *and* SERVANTS

PRIU.   Strengthen her heart with patience, pitying heav'n.

BELV.   Come come come come come, nay, come to bed!
   Prithee my love. The winds, hark how they whistle,
   And the rain beats! Oh, how the weather shrinks me!
   You are angry now, who cares? Pish, no indeed.
   Choose then; I say you shall not go, you shall not;
   Whip your ill nature; get you gone then! Oh,   JAFFEIR's *ghost rises*
   Are you return'd? See, father, here he's come again!
   Am I to blame to love him? O thou dear one!   *Ghost sinks*
   Why do you fly me? Are you angry still, then?
   Jaffeir, where art thou? Father, why do you do thus?
   Stand off, don't hide him from me. He's here somewhere.
       Enter OFFICER *and others*
   Stand off, I say! What, gone? Remember't, tyrant!
   I may revenge myself for this trick one day.
   I'll do't – I'll do't! Renault's a nasty fellow.
   Hang him, hang him, hang him.

PRIU.   News, what news?   OFFICER *whispers* [*to*] PRIULI

OFFIC.   Most sad, sir.
   Jaffeir, upon the scaffold, to prevent
   A shameful death, stabb'd Pierre, and next himself;
   Both fell together.
       The ghosts of JAFFEIR *and* PIERRE *rise together, both bloody*

PRIU.   Daughter.

BELV.   Ha, look there!
   My husband bloody, and his friend too! Murder!
   Who has done this! Speak to me, thou sad vision,   *Ghosts sink*
   On these poor trembling knees I beg it. Vanish'd!
   Here they went down; oh, I'll dig, dig the den up.
   You shan't delude me thus. Ho, Jaffeir, Jaffeir,
   Peep up and give me but a look. I have him!
   I've got him, father. Oh, now how I'll smuggle[1] him!
   My love! My dear! My blessing! Help me, help me!
   They have hold on me and drag me to the bottom.
   Nay – now they pull so hard – farewell –   *She dies*

---

[1]*smuggle* cuddle, caress.

MAID.   She's dead.
  Breathless and dead.
PRIU.   Then guard me from the sight on't;
  Lead me into some place that's fit for mourning, ·
  Where the free air, light, and the cheerful sun
  May never enter. Hang it round with black,
  Set up one taper that may last a day,
  As long as I've to live, and there all leave me,
    Sparing no tears when you this tale relate,
    But bid all cruel fathers dread my fate.

Curtain falls. Exeunt omnes

EPILOGUE

The text is done, and now for application,
And when that's ended pass your approbation.
Though the conspiracy's prevented here,
Methinks I see another hatching there;
And there's a certain faction fain would sway,
If they had strength enough, and damn this play.
But this the author bade me boldly say:
If any take his plainness in ill part,
He's glad on't from the bottom of his heart;
Poets in honour of the truth should write,
With the same spirit brave men for it fight;
And though against him causeless hatreds rise,
And daily where he goes of late, he spies
The scowls of sullen and revengeful eyes;
'Tis what he knows with much contempt to bear,
And serves a cause too good to let him fear.
He fears no poison from an incens'd drab,
No ruffian's five-foot sword, nor rascal's stab;
Nor any other snares of mischief laid,
Not a Rose-Alley cudgel-ambuscade,[1]
From any private cause where malice reigns,
Or general pique all blockheads have to brains.
Nothing shall daunt his pen when truth does call,
No, not the picture-mangler[2] at Guildhall.
The rebel tribe, of which that vermin's one,

---

[1] *ambuscade* In 1679 John Dryden was beaten in Rose Alley by thugs said to have been hired by John Wilmot, second Earl of Rochester.

[2] *picture-mangler* A marginal note in the first edition of the play (1682) reads: 'The Rascal that cut the Duke of York's Picture'. The culprit was never apprehended, although a reward of £500 was offered. This portrait of James, Duke of York, does not now exist.

Have now set forward and their course begun;
And while that prince's figure they deface,
As they before had massacr'd the name,
Durst their base fears but look him in the face,
They'd use his person as they've us'd his fame;
A face, in which such lineaments they read
Of that great martyr's,[3] whose rich blood they shed,
That their rebellious hate they still retain,
And in his son would murder him again.
With indignation then, let each brave heart
Rouse and unite to take his injur'd part;
Till royal love and goodness call him home,
And songs of triumph meet him as he come;
Till heaven his honour and our peace restore,
And villains never wrong his virtue more.[4]

[3]*martyr* King Charles I, executed in 1649.
[4]The later prologues and epilogues to the play appear in Appendix A, pp. 659–69.

John Vanbrugh

THE PROVOKED WIFE

(1697)

The Provoked Wife
a comedy,
as it is acted at the New Theatre
in Little Lincoln's Inn Fields,
by the author [Sir John Vanbrugh] of a new comedy called
The Relapse, or Virtue in Danger.

London,
Printed by J. O. for R. Wellington
at the Lute in St Paul's Churchyard
and Sam. Briscoe in Covent Garden,
1697

BIOGRAPHY

Vanbrugh was born in London in 1664; the family moved to Chester c. 1667, perhaps as an aftermath of the Plague (1665) and/or The Great Fire (1666). After brief service in the army, he was imprisoned in France 1688–92. Vanbrugh wrote *The Relapse* in 1696 and *The Provoked Wife* in the following year. He also produced several dramatic adaptations; however, by 1700 he was active as an architect, with a diminishing interest in the theatre. His most notable surviving architectural designs are Castle Howard, Yorkshire, and Blenheim Palace, Oxfordshire.

Vanbrugh was an active Whig supporter and was a member of the Kit-Cat Club c. 1693–1717. He designed the Queen's Theatre, 1703, and held several important crown appointments. He was knighted in 1714 and married in 1719. At the time of his death in 1726 he left an unfinished comedy *A Journey to London*, which was rewritten by Colley Cibber and performed successfully in 1728 and subsequently as *The Provoked Husband*.

INTRODUCTION

Vanbrugh's second and last original play reveals a tentativeness in plot and theme which suggests that he never progressed beyond a dramatic apprenticeship. The drama is somewhat disjointed and incorporates many commonplace, predictable elements, but is distinguished for its vigour, pace and a few memorable character sketches. Amongst the conventional characters are an attractive, unmarried girl of considerable fortune, Belinda, and a handsome young man, significantly named Heartfree, who at the beginning of the action is 'a professed woman-hater'.

The union of these two is as inevitable as is the downfall of Belinda's rival, Lady Fanciful. Perhaps owing something to Mrs Loveit in *The Man of Mode* (1676), she is an exaggerated, though believable, illustration of the worst of female vanity, malice and affectation. Lady Fanciful's over-anxiety to capture Heartfree is self-defeating; Heartfree's cynicism evaporates as his love for Belinda grows, and at the end of the drama they anticipate an idyllic marriage, although Vanbrugh makes clear that Heartfree is a younger son with no money. These relationships are set, somewhat clumsily, in contrast to an existing marriage which is the centre of the play, that of Sir John and Lady Brute.

Neither the chains of unhappy wedlock nor a union of an uncouth husband and a virtuous wife were new to English drama.[1] Lady Brute is not, however, a commonplace heroine, but is very likeable and convincing in her impatience and vitality. It is characteristic of her high spirits that despite Sir John's uniform unpleasantness, she can tease and aggravate him, as she does in III, i. Despite such diversions and the pleasure that Lady Brute takes in her admirer Constant's devotion, her life is miserable, as is shown on the three occasions in two days when

---

[1] Vanbrugh's conception of the Brutes may have been influenced by Etherege's *She Would if She Could* (1668) and Otway's *The Soldier's Fortune* (1681).

her husband offers violence towards her (III, i; IV, iv; V, ii). Lady Brute's circumstances echo a familiar theme in other comedies of the Restoration period: the disadvantageous position of women in marriage. In other plays women found consolation in one or more lovers, but Lady Brute had too strong a sense of virtue to yield to Constant (as in IV, i).

Drunk or sober, Sir John is one of the most memorable boors in English literature. Understandably, David Garrick was attracted to the role; he revised the play and performed the part of Sir John with enthusiasm ninety-three times between 1744 and 1776. (The play has since been occasionally revived, at least seven times in the twentieth century.) With typical forthrightness Sir John gives his reasons for entering into this unsatisfactory marriage: 'I had a mind to lie with her, and she would not let me'. Neither could he seduce her without having 'hedged myself into forty quarrels with her relations, besides buying my pardon' (II, i). It gradually becomes increasingly evident that Sir John is both a bully and a coward; thus, even though late in Act V he is convinced of his wife's infidelity with Constant, thanks to Razor's fraudulent report, the husband determines to pocket his horns – 'if I don't, that goat there, that stallion, is ready to whip me though the guts'.

It is a major disappointment that Vanbrugh offered no solution to Lady Brute's problem. Indeed, he appears to have avoided the issue by filling much of Act V with the entertaining distractions of the Belinda-Heartfree romance and the implausible efforts of Lady Fanciful and Razor to frustrate it. Remarkably, all of Sir John and Lady Brute's dialogue in the *dénouement* concerns Belinda and Heartfree's problems; it is evident that Sir John is fundamentally unchanged and that Lady Brute's unhappy martyrdom will continue, with a partial consolation in the loyalty of Constant.

It must be appreciated, however, that the choices which Vanbrugh could offer Sir John and Lady Brute were limited. The dramatist would have been false to Lady Brute's fine character, to allow her simply to leave Sir John and turn to the waiting Constant. Divorce was then obtainable, but only with great difficulty, and although a formal separation was possible, it was not a satisfactory marital solution for a woman without independent means. (Lady Brute had married Sir John for money – I, i.) A husband could be compelled to provide for an estranged wife, but Sir John is unlikely to fulfil such an obligation. George Farquhar, who was to create a similar dramatic situation ten years later in *The Beaux Stratagem*, arranged a mutually agreed separation between Squire and Mrs Sullen, accompanied by the return of her substantial dowry.

The Provoked Wife has much variety in its dialogue. Sir John communicates with a rough vigour that includes frequent oaths, but surprisingly few sexual allusions; Lady Fanciful and Madamoiselle convey their affectations and pseudo-fastidiousness in a mixture of French and English; the language of the lovers has witty, ironically romantic overtones – 'I'm afraid he's too cold to warm himself by my fire'. Vanbrugh was exceptional amongst the creators of Restoration comedy in his casual attitude towards dramatic chronology and the traditional unity of time. Several days pass between the beginning and end of his earlier original play, *The Relapse* (1696); the action of *The Provoked Wife* occupies much of three days, with a large part of the second day left very vague.[2]

The realistic tone of much of the play is reflected in the simplicity of the language. There are intermittent similes and metaphors, several of them illustrative of Sir John's character: Lady Brute refers to him as 'a fiery dragon', he himself uses a few military images, and several metaphors are based on the cuckoldry motif. Razor's metaphor in Act v, as he is about to reveal secrets to Madamoiselle, is the most ingenious: 'The news is that cuckoldom in folio is newly printed, and matrimony in quarto is just going into the press. Will you buy any books, Madamoiselle?'

Contemporary comedies provoked the Reverend Jeremy Collier to voice stern criticism in *A Short View of the Immorality and Profaneness of the English Stage*, published in March 1698. After his close reading of *The Provoked Wife*, Collier objected to what he regarded as irreligious Biblical allusions (Razor's flippant references to Eve's having tempted Adam – v, ii) and to Vanbrugh's disguising the drunken Sir John Brute as a clergyman (IV, i and iii). In June of 1698 Vanbrugh offered a humourous and conciliatory reply, *A Short Vindication of 'The Relapse' and 'The Provok'd Wife'*. He defended the language and the morality of his plays, suggesting that *The Provoked Wife* tends to discourage vice and folly, and pointing out

---

[2] During the morning of the first day (said to be Sunday – III, ii), Sir John and Lady Brute wrangle; after a noon-time dinner he goes off to the Blue Posts. At night he and his drunken comrades terrorise the town, while Lady Brute and Belinda devise an assignation for the following evening with Heartfree and Constant in Spring Garden. Sir John spends the night in gaol, appearing before the justice early in the morning of the second day.

Vanbrugh gives no hint about what any of his characters do during this second day; Lady Brute, Belinda, Heartfree, and Constant meet that evening in Spring Garden, to be interrupted by Sir John, still drunk, and all proceed to the Brute house. The morning of the third day is occupied with explanations; soon Heartfree and Belinda are betrothed and Sir John and Lady Brute partially reconciled.

that in having Sir John Brute put on a clerical disguise, he ridicules the man and not the clergy.

In spite of Jeremy Collier and other moralistic critics of *The Provoked Wife*,[3] the play held the stage for much of the eighteenth century, undergoing repeated alterations, including the incorporation of additional songs. A study of successive editions issued during this period reveals a progressive bowdlerising of Vanbrugh's text, to soften the cynical overtones and to eliminate much of the vulgarity. Perhaps the most entertaining of the later editions is that of Mrs Elizabeth Inchbald, in *The British Theatre; or a Collection of Plays . . .* (1808).

Sir John Vanbrugh contributed two substantial modifications to the text. The episodes in which an inebriated Sir John disguises himself in a clergyman's cassock (IV, i and iii) were evidently thought to demean the clergy; hence, shortly before his death in 1726. the playwright conciliated popular taste by rewriting these scenes, first printed in a pirated Dublin edition of 1743. In the revised version of IV, i, Sir John dons a gown belonging to his wife; in IV, iii, as now modified, he appears drunkenly before the same obtuse justice and offers some amusing commonplaces of anti-feminist satire; this transvestite scene is longer and more entertaining than the original. The revisions appear as Appendix B, pp. 671–76.

[3] In 1701 the company at Lincoln's Inn Fields was charged at the Court of King's Bench with uttering profanities in *The Provoked Wife*, focussing again on Razor's speech in V, ii. The actors pleaded not guilty and repeatedly delayed appearing in court; they seem never to have been brought to trial.

BIBLIOGRAPHY

The Provoked Wife

B. Harris, *Sir John Vanbrugh*. London 1967.

M. Bingham, *Masks and Facades: Sir John Vanbrugh, the Man in his Setting*. London, 1974.

L. B. Faller, 'Between Jest and Earnest: the Comedies of Sir John Vanbrugh'. *Modern Philology*, 72 (August 1974), 17–29.

A. R. Huseboe, *Sir John Vanbrugh*. Boston, 1976.

G. M. Berkowitz, *Sir John Vanbrugh and the End of Restoration Tragedy*. Amsterdam, 1981.

M. Cordner, 'Anticlericalism in Vanbrugh's *The Provoked Wife*'. *Notes and Queries*, 226 (June 1981), 212–14.

M. Cordner, 'Vanbrugh's Lord Rake'. *Notes and Queries*, 226 (June 1981), 214–16.

K. Downes, *Sir John Vanbrugh, a Biography*. London, 1987.

PROLOGUE

SPOKEN BY MISTRESS BRACEGIRDLE.

Since 'tis the intent and business of the stage
To copy out the follies of the age,
To hold to every man a faithful glass,
And show him of what species he's an ass,
I hope the next that teaches in the school
Will show our author he's a scribbling fool.
And that the satire may be sure to bite,
Kind heav'n, inspire some venom'd priest to write,
And grant some ugly lady may indite.
For I would have him lash'd, by heav'ns, I would,
Till his presumption swam away in blood.
Three plays[1] at once proclaims a face of brass,
No matter what they are! That's not the case;
To write three plays, ev'n that's to be an ass.
But what I least forgive, he knows it too,
For to his cost he lately has known you.
Experience shows, to many a writer's smart,
You hold a court where mercy ne'er had part;
So much of the old serpent's sting you have,
You love to damn, as heav'n delights to save.
In foreign parts let a bold volunteer
For public good upon the stage appear,
He meets ten thousand smiles to dissipate his fear.
All tickle on th'adventuring young beginner,
And only scourge th'incorrigible sinner.
They touch indeed his faults, but with a hand
So gentle that his merit still may stand;

---

[1] *Three plays* Vanbrugh's *The Relapse* and *Aesop* (an adaptation) had been staged
earlier in the 1696–97 season.

Kindly they buoy the follies of his pen,
That he may shun 'em when he writes again.
But 'tis not so in this good-natur'd town;
All's one – an ox, a poet, or a crown,
Old England's play was always knocking down.

DRAMATIS PERSONAE

CONSTANT — Mr [John] Verbruggen

HEARTFREE — Mr Hudson[1]

SIR JOHN BRUTE — Mr [Thomas] Betterton

TREBLE, *a singing master* — Mr Bowman[2]

RAZOR, *valet de chambre*
  to SIR JOHN BRUTE — Mr [William] Bowen

JUSTICE OF THE PEACE — Mr [George] Bright

LORD RAKE ⎱ *companions to*
COL. BULLY ⎰ SIR JOHN BRUTE

CONSTABLE *and* WATCH

LADY BRUTE — Mrs [Elizabeth] Barry

BELINDA, *her niece* — Mrs [Anne] Bracegirdle

LADY FANCIFUL — Mrs Bowman[3]

MADAMOISELLE — Mrs [Elizabeth] Willis

CORNET *and* PIPE, *servants to*
  LADY FANCIFUL

[1] John Hodgson.   [2] John Boman.   [3] Elizabeth [Mrs John] Boman.

THE PROVOKED WIFE

Act One

SCENE [ONE]

SIR JOHN BRUTE'S *house*

Enter SIR JOHN, *solus*

SIR JOHN. What cloying meat is love, when matrimony's the sauce to it. Two years' marriage has debauched my five senses. Everything I see, everything I hear, everything I feel, everything I smell, and everything I taste, methinks has wife in't. No boy was ever so weary of his tutor, no girl of her bib, no nun of doing penance, nor old maid of being chaste, as I am of being married. Sure there's a secret curse entailed upon the very name of wife. My lady is a young lady, a fine lady, a witty lady, a virtuous lady, and yet I hate her. There is but one thing on earth I loathe beyond her: that's fighting. Would my courage come up but to a fourth part of my ill nature, I'd stand buff to her relations, and thrust her out of doors. But marriage has sunk me down to such an ebb of resolution, I dare not draw my sword, though even to get rid of my wife. But here she comes.

Enter LADY BRUTE

LADY B. Do you dine at home today, Sir John?

SIR JOHN. Why, do you expect I should tell you what I don't know myself?

LADY B. I thought there was no harm in asking you.

SIR JOHN. If thinking wrong were an excuse for impertinence, women might be justified in most things they say or do.

LADY B. I'm sorry I have said anything to displease you.

SIR JOHN. Sorrow for things past is of as little importance to me as my dining at home or abroad ought to be to you.

LADY B. My enquiry was only that I might have provided what you liked.

SIR JOHN. Six to four you had been in the wrong there again, for what I liked yesterday I don't like today, and what I like today, 'tis odds I mayn't like tomorrow.

LADY B. But if I had asked you what you liked?

SIR JOHN. Why then there would have been more asking about it than the thing was worth.

LADY B.   I wish I did but know how I might please you.

SIR JOHN.   Ay, but that sort of knowledge is not a wife's talent.

LADY B.   Whate'er my talent is, I'm sure my will has ever been to make you easy.

SIR JOHN.   If women were to have their wills, the world would be finely governed.

LADY B.   What reason have I given you to use me as you do of late? It once was otherwise. You married me for love.

SIR JOHN.   And you me for money. So you have your reward and I have mine.

LADY B.   What is it that disturbs you?

SIR JOHN.   A parson.

LADY B.   Why, what has he done to you?

SIR JOHN.   He has married me.   *Exit*

LADY B.   The devil's in the fellow, I think. I was told before I married him that thus 'twould be. But I thought I had charms enough to govern him, and that where there was an estate, a woman must needs be happy. So my vanity has deceived me, and my ambition has made me uneasy. But some comfort still: if one would be revenged of him, these are good times. A woman may have a gallant and a separate maintenance[1] too. The surly puppy! Yet he's a fool for't. For hitherto he has been no monster;[2] but who knows how far he may provoke me? I never loved him, yet I have been ever true to him, and that in spite of all the attacks of art and nature upon a poor weak woman's heart in favour of a tempting lover. Methinks so noble a defence as I have made should be rewarded with a better usage. Or who can tell? Perhaps a good part of what I suffer from my husband may be a judgment upon me for my cruelty to my lover. Lord, with what pleasure could I indulge that thought were there but a possibility of finding arguments to make it good. And how do I know but there may? Let me see. What opposes? My matrimonial vow? Why, what did I vow? I think I promised to be true to my husband. Well, and he promised to be kind to me. But he han't kept his word. Why then I'm absolved from mine. Ay, that seems clear to me. The argument's good between the king and the people; why not between the husband and the wife? Oh, but that condition was not expressed. No matter; 'twas understood. Well, by all I see, if I argue the matter a little longer with myself, I shan't find so many bugbears in the way as I thought I should. Lord, what fine notions of virtue do

---

[1]*maintenance* an allowance from an estranged husband.
[2]*monster* cuckold.

we women take up upon the credit of old foolish philosophers. Virtue's its own reward, virtue's this, virtue's that. Virtue's an ass, and a gallant's worth forty on't.

Enter BELINDA

Good morrow, dear cousin.[3]

BEL. Good morrow, madam. You look pleased this morning.

LADY B. I am so.

BEL. With what, pray?

LADY B. With my husband.

BEL. Drown husbands! For yours is a provoking fellow. As he went out just now I prayed him to tell me what time of day 'twas, and he asked me if I took him for the church clock, that was obliged to tell all the parish.

LADY B. He has been saying some good obliging things to me too. In short, Belinda, he has used me so barbarously of late that I could almost resolve to play the downright wife – and cuckold him.

BEL. That would be downright indeed.

LADY B. Why, after all, there's more to be said for't than you'd imagine, child. I know according to the strict statute law of religion, I should do wrong; but if there were a Court of Chancery[4] in heaven, I'm sure I should cast him.

BEL. If there were a House of Lords[5] you might.

LADY B. In either I should infallibly carry my cause. Why, he is the first aggressor, not I.

BEL. Ay, but you know we must return good for evil.

LADY B. That may be a mistake in the translation. Prithee be of my opinion, Belinda, for I'm positive I'm in the right; and if you'll keep up the prerogative of a woman, you'll likewise be positive you are in the right whenever you do anything you have a mind to. But I shall play the fool, and jest on till I make you begin to think I'm in earnest.

BEL. I shan't take the liberty, madam, to think of anything that you desire to keep a secret from me.

LADY B. Alas, my dear, I have no secrets. My heart could never yet confine my tongue.

BEL. Your eyes, you mean, for I am sure I have seen them gadding when your tongue has been locked up fast enough.

LADY B. My eyes gadding? Prithee after who, child?

BEL. Why, after one that thinks you hate him, as much as I know you love him.

---

[3] *cousin* in fact, her niece. 'Cousin' was then more casually used than now.

[4] *Court of Chancery* a court of equity.

[5] *House of Lords* the only possible earthly source of a divorce; in rare instances it could be obtained by means of a private bill in the Lords.

LADY B. Constant, you mean.

BEL. I do so.

LADY B. Lord, what should put such a thing into your head?

BEL. That which puts things into most people's heads, observation.

LADY B. Why, what have you observed, in the name of wonder?

BEL. I have observed you blush when you meet him, force yourself away from him, and then be out of humour with everything about you. In a word, never was poor creature so spurred on by desire and so reined in with fear.

LADY B. How strong is fancy!

BEL. How weak is woman.

LADY B. Prithee, niece, have a better opinion of your aunt's inclinations.

BEL. Dear aunt, have a better opinion of your niece's understanding.

LADY B. You'll make me angry.

BEL. You'll make me laugh.

LADY B. Then you are resolved to persist?

BEL. Positively.

LADY B. And all I can say —

BEL. Will signify nothing.

LADY B. Though I should swear 'twere false —

BEL. I should think it true.

LADY B. Then let us both forgive, (*Kissing her*) for we have both offended, I in making a secret, you in discovering it.

BEL. Good nature may do much, but you have more reason to forgive one than I have to pardon t'other.

LADY B. 'Tis true, Belinda, you have given me so many proofs of your friendship that my reserve has been indeed a crime. But that you may more easily forgive me, remember, child, that when our nature prompts us to a thing our honour and religion have forbid us, we would, were't possible, conceal even from the soul itself the knowledge of the body's weakness.

BEL. Well, I hope, to make your friend amends, you'll hide nothing from her for the future, though the body should still grow weaker and weaker.

LADY B. No. From this moment I have no more reserve; and for a proof of my repentance, I own, Belinda, I'm in danger. Merit and wit assault me from without, nature and love solicit me within, my husband's barbarous usage piques me to revenge, and Satan, catching at the fair occasion, throws in my way that vengeance which of all vengeance pleases women best.

BEL. 'Tis well Constant don't know the weakness of the fortifications, for o' my conscience he'd soon come on to the assault.

LADY B.   Ay, and I'm afraid carry the town too. But whatever you may have observed, I have dissembled so well as to keep him ignorant. So you see I'm no coquette, Belinda, and if you'll follow my advice you'll never be one either. 'Tis true, coquetry is one of the main ingredients in the natural composition of a woman, and I as well as others could be well enough pleased to see a crowd of young fellows ogling and glancing and watching all occasions to do forty foolish officious things; nay, should some of 'em push on, even to hanging or drowning, why, faith, if I should let pure woman alone, I should e'en be but too well pleased with't.

BEL.   I'll swear 'twould tickle me strangely.

LADY B.   But after all, 'tis a vicious practice in us to give the least encouragement but where we design to come to a conclusion. For 'tis an unreasonable thing to engage a man in a disease which we beforehand resolve we never will apply a cure to.

BEL.   'Tis true; but then a woman must abandon one of the supreme blessings of her life. For I am fully convinced no man has half that pleasure in possessing a mistress as a woman has in jilting a gallant.

LADY B.   The happiest woman then on earth must be our neighbour.[6]

BEL.   Oh, the impertinent composition! She has vanity and affectation enough to make her a ridiculous original,[7] in spite of all that art and nature ever furnished to any of her sex before her.

LADY B.   She concludes all men her captives, and whatever course they take, it serves to confirm her in that opinion.

BEL.   If they shun her, she thinks 'tis modesty, and takes it for a proof of their passion.

LADY B.   And if they are rude to her, 'tis conduct,[8] and done to prevent town talk.

BEL.   When her folly makes 'em laugh, she thinks they are pleased with her wit.

LADY B.   And when her impertinence makes 'em dull, concludes they are jealous of her favours.

BEL.   All their actions and their words she takes for granted aim at her.

LADY B.   And pities all other women because she thinks they envy her.

BEL.   Pray, out of pity to ourselves, let us find a better subject, for I am weary of this. Do you think your husband inclined to jealousy?

LADY B.   Oh, no. He does not love me well enough for that. Lord, how wrong men's maxims are. They are seldom jealous of their

[6]*our neighbour* Lady Fanciful.
[7]*original* an eccentric.   [8]*conduct* discretion.

wives unless they are very fond of 'em; whereas they ought to consider the woman's inclinations, for there depends their fate. Well, men may talk, but they are not so wise as we, that's certain.

BEL. At least in our affairs.

LADY B. Nay, I believe we should outdo 'em in the business of the state too, for methinks they do and undo, and make but mad work on't.

BEL. Why then don't we get into the intrigues of government as well as they?

LADY B. Because we have intrigues of our own that make us more sport, child. And so let's in and consider of 'em. *Exeunt*

SCENE [TWO]

LADY FANCIFUL'S *dressing room*

Enter LADY FANCIFUL, MADAMOISELLE, *and* CORNET

LADY F. How do I look this morning?

COR. Your ladyship looks very ill, truly.

LADY F. Lard, how ill-natured thou art, Cornet, to tell me so, though the thing should be true. Don't you know that I have humility enough to be but too easily out of conceit with myself? Hold the glass. I dare swear that will have more manners than you have. Madamoiselle, let me have your opinion too.

MADAM. My opinion pe, matam, dat your ladyship never look so well in your life.

LADY F. Well, the French are the prettiest obliging people. They say the most acceptable, well-mannered things, and never flatter.

MADAM. Your ladyship say great justice inteed.

LADY F. Nay, everything's just[9] in my house but Cornet. The very looking glass gives her the *dementi*.[10] But I'm almost afraid it flatters me, it makes me look so very engaging.

Looking affectedly in the glass

MADAM. Inteed, matam, your face pe hansomer den all de looking-glass in tee world, *croyez moi*.[11]

LADY F. But is it possible my eyes can be so languishing, and so very full of fire?

MADAM. Matam, if de glass was burning-glass, I believe your eyes set de fire in de house.

LADY F. You may take that nightgown, Madamoiselle. Get out of

---

[9]*just* correct.   [10]*dementi* lie.   [11]*croyez moi* believe me.

the room, Cornet; I can't endure you. This wench methinks does look so unsufferably ugly. *Exit* CORNET

MADAM. Everyting look ugly, matam, dat stand by your latyship.

LADY F. No, really, Madamoiselle, methinks you look mighty pretty.

MADAM. Ah, matam, de moon have no *éclat*¹² ven de sun appear.

LADY F. O pretty expression! Have you ever been in love, Madamoiselle?

MADAM. (*Sighing*) *Oui*, matam.

LADY F. And were you beloved again?

MADAM. (*Sighing*) No, matam.

LADY F. O ye gods, what an unfortunate creature should I be in such a case! But nature has made me nice¹³ for my own defence. I'm nice, strangely nice, Madamoiselle. I believe were the merit of whole mankind bestowed upon one single person, I should still think the fellow wanted¹⁴ something to make it worth my while to take notice of him. And yet I could love, were it possible to have a thing made on purpose for me; for I'm not cruel, Madamoiselle, I'm only nice.

MADAM. Ah, matam, I wish I was fine gentleman for your sake. I do all de ting in de world to get leetel way into your heart. I make song, I make verse, I give you de serenade, I give great many present to Madamoiselle. I no eat, I no sleep, I be lean, I be mad, I hang myself, I drown myself. Ah, *ma chère dame, que je vous aimerais.*¹⁵ *Embracing her*

LADY F. Well, the French have strange, obliging ways with 'em. You may take those two pairs of gloves, Madamoiselle.

MADAM. Me humbly tank my sweet lady.

Enter CORNET

COR. Madam, here's a letter for your ladyship by the penny post.¹⁶

LADY F. Some new conquest, I'll warrant you. For, without vanity, I looked extremely clear last night when I went to the Park.¹⁷ [*Opens the letter*] Oh, agreeable. Here's a new song made of me. And ready set too. O thou welcome thing! (*Kissing it*) Call Pipe hither. She shall sing it instantly.

Enter PIPE

Here, sing me this new song, Pipe.

¹²*éclat* brilliance.   ¹³*nice* fastidious.
¹⁴*wanted* lacked.   ¹⁵*que . . . aimerais* how I should love you.
¹⁶*penny post* The first regular postal service in London (for a penny) was established in 1680.
¹⁷*Park* St James's Park, the most fashionable promenade.

SONG

I

Fly, fly, you happy shepherds, fly,
    Avoid Philira's charms.
The rigour of her heart denies
    The heaven that's in her arms.
Ne'er hope to gaze and then retire,
    Nor yielding, to be bless'd.
Nature, who form'd her eyes of fire,
    Of ice compos'd her breast.

II

Yet, lovely maid, this once believe
    A slave whose zeal you move:
The gods, alas, your youth deceive;
    Their heaven consists in love.
In spite of all the thanks you owe,
    You may reproach 'em this,
That where they did their form bestow
    They have denied their bliss.   *Exit* PIPE

LADY F.   Well, there may be faults, Madamoiselle, but the design is so very obliging, 'twould be a matchless ingratitude in me to discover[18] 'em.

MADAM.   *Ma foi*, matam, I tink de gentleman's song tell you de trute. If you never love, you never be happy. Ah, *que j'aime l'amour, moi.*
    Enter SERVANT *with another letter*

SERV.   Madam, here's another letter for your ladyship.

LADY F.   'Tis thus I am importuned every morning, Madamoiselle. Pray, how do the French ladies when they are thus *accablées*?[19]

MADAM.   Matam, dey never complain. *Au contraire*. When one Frense laty have got hundred lover, den she do all she can, to get hundred more.

LADY F.   Well, strike me dead, I think they have *le goût bon*. For 'tis an unutterable pleasure to be adored by all the men and envied by all the women. Yet I'll swear I'm concerned at the torture I give 'em. Lard, why was I formed to make the whole creation uneasy? But let me read my letter. (*Reads*) 'If you have a mind to hear of your faults instead of being praised for your virtues, take the pains to walk in the Green Walk in St. James's with your woman an hour hence. You'll there meet one who hates you for some things as he could love

---

[18]*discover* reveal.   [19]*accablées* overwhelmed.

you for others, and therefore is willing to endeavour your reformation. If you come to the place I mention, you'll know who I am; if you
don't, you never shall, so take your choice'. This is strangely familiar,
Madamoiselle. Now have I a provoking fancy to know who this
impudent fellow is.

MADAM.   Den take your scarf and your mask and go to de rendezvous.
De Frense laty do *justement comme ça.*

LADY F.   Rendezvous! What, rendezvous with a man, Madamoiselle?

MADAM.   Eh, *pourquoi non?*

LADY F.   What, and a man perhaps I never saw in my life?

MADAM.   *Tant mieux; c'est donc quelque chose de nouveau.*[20]

LADY F.   Why, how do I know what designs he may have? He may
intend to ravish me for aught I know.

MADAM.   Ravish? Bagatelle! I would fain see one impudent rogue
ravish madamoiselle, *oui, je le voudrais.*[21]

LADY F.   Oh, but my reputation, Madamoiselle, my reputation, ah,
ma chère réputation.

MADAM.   *Matam, quand on l'a une fois perdue, on n'en est plus
embarrassée.*[22]

LADY F.   Fie, Madamoiselle, fie! Reputation is a jewel.

MADAM.   *Qui coûte bien chère,*[23] matam.

LADY F.   Why sure, you would not sacrifice your honour to your
pleasure?

MADAM.   *Je suis philosophe.*

LADY F.   Bless me, how you talk! Why, what if honour be a burden,
Madamoiselle, must it not be borne?

MADAM.   *Chaqu'un à sa façon. Quand quelque chose m'incommode,
moi, je m'en défais, vite.*[24]

LADY F.   Get you gone, you little naughty Frenchwoman, you. I vow
and swear I must turn you out of doors if you talk thus.

MADAM.   Turn me out of doors? Turn yourself out of doors, and go see
what de gentleman have to say to you. *Tenez.* (*Giving her her things
hastily*) *Voilà votre écharpe, voilà votre coiffe, voilà votre masque,
violà tout.*[25] (*Calling within*) Hey, Mercure, Coquin,[26] call

[20]*Tant . . . nouveau* So much the better; it is something new.
[21]*Oui . . . voudrais* Yes, I should like that.
[22]*quand . . . embarrassée* When it is once lost, it is no longer an encumbrance.
[23]*Qui . . . chere* It is very precious.
[24]*Chaqu'un . . . vite* Each to his own taste. When something inconveniences me I
dispose of it quickly.
[25]*Tenez . . . tout* Wait. Here is your scarf, here is your hood, here is your mask,
here is everything.
[26]*Coquin* knave.

one chair for matam, and one oder for me. *Va t'en vite.* (*Turning to her lady and helping her on hastily with her things*) *Allons*, matam. *Dépêchez vous donc. Mon dieu, quelles scrupules!*[27]

LADY F. Well, for once, Madamoiselle, I'll follow your advice, out of the intemperate desire I have to know who this ill-bred fellow is. But I have too much delicatesse to make a practice on it.

MADAM. *Belle chose vraiment que la délicatesse, lorsqu'il s'agit de se divertir. À ça, vous voilà équipée, partons. He bien, qu'avez vous donc?*[28]

LADY F. *J'ai peur.*[29]

MADAM. *Je n'en ai point, moi.*[30]

LADY F. I dare not go.

MADAM. *Demeurez donc.*[31]

LADY F. *Je suis poltrone.*[32]

MADAM. *Tant pis pour vous.*[33]

LADY F. Curiosity's a wicked devil.

MADAM. *C'est une charmante sainte.*

LADY F. It ruined our first parents.

MADAM. *Elle a bien diverti leurs enfants.*

LADY F. *L'honneur est contre.*

MADAM. *Le plaisir est pour.*

LADY F. Must I then go?

MADAM. Must you go? Must you eat, must you drink, must you sleep, must you live? De nature bid you do one, de nature bid you do t'oder. *Vous me ferez enrager.*[34]

LADY F. But when reason corrects nature, Madamoiselle?

MADAM. *Elle est donc bien insolente. C'est sa soeur aînée.*[35]

LADY F. Do you then prefer your nature to your reason, Madamoiselle?

MADAM. *Oui da.*[36]

LADY F. *Pourquoi?*

MADAM. Because my nature make me merry, my reason make me mad.

LADY F. *Ah, la méchante française!*[37]

MADAM. *Ah, la belle anglaise!*   *Forcing her lady off*

---

[27]*Va . . . scruples* Go quickly. Let's go. Hurry then. My God, what scruples.

[28]*Belle . . . donc* Fastidiousness is truly fine when it's a matter of enjoying oneself. There, you are ready; let us go. So, what's wrong now?

[29]*J'ai peur* I am afraid.   [30]*Je . . . moi* I am not at all.

[31]*Demeurez donc* Stay then.   [32]*Je suis poltrone* I am a coward.

[33]*Tant . . . vous* So much the worse for you.

[34]*Vous . . . enrager* You will make me angry.

[35]*Elle . . . aînée* She [Reason] is very insolent. She is her older sister.

[36]*Oui da* Yes indeed.   [37]*Ah . . . française* Ah, wicked Frenchwoman.

Act Two

SCENE [ONE]

St. James's Park

Enter LADY FANCIFUL *and* MADAMOISELLE

LADY F. Well, I vow, Madamoiselle, I'm strangely impatient to know who this confident fellow is.

Enter HEARTFREE

Look, there's Heartfree. But sure it can't be him, he's a professed woman-hater. Yet who knows what my wicked eyes may have done?

MADAM. *Il nous approche*, madam.

LADY F. Yes, 'tis he. Now will he be most intolerably cavalier, though he should be in love with me.

HEART. Madam, I'm your humble servant. I perceive you have more humility and good nature than I thought you had.

LADY F. What you attribute to humility and good nature, sir, may perhaps be only due to curiosity. I had a mind to know who 'twas had ill manners enough to write that letter. *Throwing him his letter*

HEART. Well, and now I hope you are satisfied.

LADY F. I am so, sir. Goodbye to ye.

HEART. Nay, hold there. Though you have done your business, I han't done mine. By your ladyship's leave, we must have one moment's prattle together. Have you a mind to be the prettiest woman about town or not? How she stares upon me! What,[1] this passes for an impertinent question with you now, because you think you are so already.

LADY F. Pray, sir, let me ask you a question in my turn: by what right do you pretend to examine me?

HEART. By the same right that the strong govern the weak, because I have you in my power, for you cannot get so quickly to your coach but I shall have time enough to make you hear everything I have to say to you.

LADY F. These are strange liberties you take, Mr Heartfree.

HEART. They are so, madam, but there's no help for it; for know that I have a design upon you.

[1] *What* Indeed.

LADY F.   Upon me, sir?

HEART.   Yes, and one that will turn to your glory and my comfort, if you will be but a little wiser than you use to be.

LADY F.   Very well, sir.

HEART.   Let me see. Your vanity, madam, I take to be about some eight degrees higher than any woman's in the town, let t'other be who she will; and my indifference is naturally about the same pitch. Now could you find the way to turn this indifference into fire and flames, methinks your vanity ought to be satisfied; and this perhaps you might bring about upon pretty reasonable terms.

LADY F.   And, pray, at what rate would this indifference be bought off, if one should have so depraved an appetite to desire it?

HEART.   Why madam, to drive a Quaker's bargain,[2] and make but one word with you, if I do part with it, you must lay me down – your affectation.

LADY F.   My affectation, sir?

HEART.   Why, I ask you nothing but what you may very well spare.

LADY F.   You grow rude, sir. Come, Madamoiselle, 'tis high time to be gone.

MADAM.   *Allons, allons, allons.*

HEART.   (*Stopping 'em*) Nay, you may as well stand still, for hear me you shall, walk which way you please.

LADY F.   What mean you, sir?

HEART.   I mean to tell you that you are the most ungrateful woman upon earth.

LADY F.   Ungrateful? To who?

HEART.   To nature.

LADY F.   Why, what has nature done for me?

HEART.   What you have undone by art. It made you handsome; it gave you beauty to a miracle, a shape without a fault, wit enough to make 'em relish, and so turned you loose to your own discretion, which has made such work with you that you are become the pity of our sex and the jest of your own. There is not a feature in your face but you have found the way to teach it some affected convulsion; your feet, your hands, your very fingers' ends are directed never to move without some ridiculous air or other; and your language is a suitable trumpet to draw people's eyes upon the raree-show.[3]

MADAM.   (*Aside*) *Est ce qu'on fait l'amour en Angleterre comme ça?*

LADY F.   (*Aside*) Now could I cry for madness, but that I know he'd laugh at me for it.

HEART.   Now do you hate me for telling you the truth, but that's

---

[2] *Quaker's bargain* giving no alternatives.
[3] *raree-show* a peep-show carried in a box.

because you don't believe it is so; for were you once convinced of that, you'd reform for your own sake. But 'tis as hard to persuade a woman to quit anything that makes her ridiculous as 'tis to prevail with a poet to see a fault in his own play.

LADY F. Every circumstance of nice breeding must needs appear ridiculous to one who has so natural an antipathy to good manners.

HEART. But suppose I could find the means to convince you that the whole world is of my opinion, and that those who flatter and commend you do it to no other intent but to make you persevere in your folly that they may continue in their mirth.

LADY F. Sir, though you and all that world you talk of should be so impertinently officious as to think to persuade me I don't know how to behave myself, I should still have charity enough for my own understanding to believe myself in the right and all you in the wrong.

MADAM. *Le voilà mort.*⁴

Exeunt LADY FANCIFUL *and* MADAMOISELLE

HEART. (*Gazing after her*) There her single clapper⁵ has published the sense of the whole sex. Well, this once I have endeavoured to wash the blackamoor white, but henceforward I'll sooner undertake to teach sincerity to a courtier, generosity to an usurer, honesty to a lawyer, nay, humility to a divine, than discretion to a woman I see has once set her heart upon playing the fool.

Enter CONSTANT

'Morrow, Constant.

CON. Good morrow, Jack. What are you doing here this morning?

HEART. Doing? Guess if thou canst. Why, I have been endeavouring to persuade my Lady Fanciful that she's the foolishest woman about town.

CON. A pretty endeavour truly.

HEART. I have told her in as plain English as I could speak both what the town says of her and what I think of her. In short, I have used her as an absolute king would do magna charta.

CON. And how does she take it?

HEART. As children do pills: bite 'em, but can't swallow 'em.

CON. But, prithee, what has put it in your head, of all mankind, to turn reformer?

HEART. Why, one thing was, the morning hung upon my hands; I did not know what to do with myself. And another was, that as little as I care for women, I could not see with patience one that heaven has taken such wondrous pains about be so very industrious to make herself the jack pudding⁶ of the creation.

---

⁴*Le voilà mort* That has killed him.
⁵*clapper* tongue.   ⁶*jack pudding* buffoon.

CON. Well, now could I almost wish to see my cruel mistress make the selfsame use of what heaven has done for her, that so I might be cured of a disease that makes me so very uneasy; for love, love is the devil, Heartfree.

HEART. And why do you let the devil govern you?

CON. Because I have more flesh and blood than grace and self-denial. My dear, dear mistress! 'Sdeath, that so genteel a woman should be a saint, when religion's out of fashion!

HEART. Nay, she's much in the wrong truly, but who knows how far time and good example may prevail?

CON. Oh, they have played their parts in vain already. 'Tis now two years since that damned fellow her husband invited me to his wedding, and there was the first time I saw that charming woman, whom I have loved ever since, more than e'er a martyr did his soul. But she's cold, my friend, still cold as the northern star.

HEART. So are all women by nature, which makes 'em so willing to be warmed.

CON. Oh, don't profane the sex. Prithee think 'em all angels for her sake, for she's virtuous even to a fault.

HEART. A lover's head is a good accountable thing truly; he adores his mistress for being virtuous, and yet is very angry with her because she won't be lewd.

CON. Well, the only relief I expect in my misery is to see thee some day or other as deeply engaged as myself, which will force me to be merry in the midst of all my misfortunes.

HEART. That day will never come, be assured, Ned. Not but that I can pass a night with a woman, and for the time perhaps make myself as good sport as you can do. Nay, I can court a woman too, call her nymph, angel, goddess, what you please; but here's the difference 'twixt you and I: I persuade a woman she's an angel, she persuades you she's one. Prithee let me tell you how I avoid falling in love; that which serves me for prevention may chance to serve you for a cure.

CON. Well, use the ladies moderately then, and I'll hear you.

HEART. That using 'em moderately undoes us all; but I'll use 'em justly, and that you ought to be satisfied with. I always consider a woman, not as the tailor, the shoemaker, the tire-woman,[7] the sempstress, and – which is more than all that – the poet makes her, but I consider her as pure nature has contrived her, and that more strictly than I should have done our old Grandmother Eve, had I seen her naked in the Garden, for I consider her turned inside out.

---

[7] *tire-woman* lady's maid.

Her heart well examined, I find there pride, vanity, covetousness, indiscretion, but above all things, malice; plots eternally aforging to destory one another's reputations, and as honestly to charge the levity of men's tongues with the scandal; hourly debates how to make poor gentlemen in love with 'em, with no other intent but to use 'em like dogs when they have done; a constant desire of doing more mischief, and an everlasting war waged against truth and good nature.

CON. Very well, sir, an admirable composition truly.

HEART. Then for her outside, I consider it merely as an outside. She has a thin tiffany covering over just such stuff as you and I are made on. As for her motion, her mien, her airs, and all those tricks, I know they affect you mightily. If you should see your mistress at a coronation, dragging her peacock's train, with all her state and insolence about her, 'twould strike you with all the awful thoughts that heaven itself could pretend to from you; whereas I turn the whole matter into a jest, and suppose her strutting in the self-same stately manner with nothing on but her stays and her scanty quilted under-petticoat.

CON. Hold thy profane tongue, for I'll hear no more.

HEART. What, you'll love on then?

CON. Yes, to eternity.

HEART. Yet have you no hopes at all?

CON. None.

HEART. Nay, the resolution may be discreet enough. Perhaps you have found out some new philosophy, that love's like virtue, its own reward; so you and your mistress will be as well content at a distance as others that have less learning are in coming together.

CON. No, but if she should prove kind at last, my dear Heartfree!

Embracing him

HEART. Nay, prithee don't take me for your mistress, for lovers are very troublesome.

CON. Well, who knows what time may do?

HEART. And just now he was sure time could do nothing.

CON. Yet not one kind glance in two years is somewhat strange.

HEART. Not strange at all. She don't like you, that's all the business.

CON. Prithee don't distract me.

HEART. Nay, you are a good handsome young fellow. She might use you better. Come, will you go see her? Perhaps she may have changed her mind. There's some hopes as long as she's a woman.

CON. Oh, 'tis in vain to visit her. Sometimes to get a sight of her, I visit that beast her husband, but she certainly finds some pretence to quit the room as soon as I enter.

HEART. It's much she don't tell him you have made love to her too, for that's another good-natured thing usual amongst women, in which they have several ends. Sometimes 'tis to recommend their virtue, that they may be lewd with the greater security. Sometimes 'tis to make their husbands fight in hopes they may be killed, when their affairs require it should be so. But more commonly 'tis to engage two men in a quarrel, that they may have the credit of being fought for; and if the lover's killed in the business, they cry, 'Poor fellow, he had ill luck', and so they go to cards.

CON. Thy injuries to women are not to be forgiven. Look to't if ever thou dost fall into their hands.

HEART. They can't use me worse than they do you, that speak well of 'em. Oho! Here comes the knight.

     Enter SIR JOHN BRUTE

HEART. Your humble servant, Sir John.

SIR JOHN. Servant, sir.

HEART. How does all your family?

SIR JOHN. Pox o' my family.

CON. How does your lady? I han't seen her abroad a good while.

SIR JOHN. Do? I don't know how she does, not I. She was well enough yesterday; I han't been at home tonight.

CON. What, were you out of town?

SIR JOHN. Out of town? No, I was drinking.

CON. You are a true Englishman, don't know your own happiness. If I were married to such a woman, I would not be from her a night for all the wine in France.

SIR JOHN. Not from her? Oons, what a time should a man have of that?

HEART. Why, there's no division, I hope?

SIR JOHN. No, but there's a conjunction,[8] and that's worse. A pox o' the parson. Why the plague don't you two marry? I fancy I look like the devil to you.

HEART. Why, you don't think you have horns, do you?

SIR JOHN. No. I believe my wife's religion will keep her honest.[9]

HEART. And what will make her keep her religion?

SIR JOHN. Persecution; and therefore she shall have it.

HEART. Have a care, knight; women are tender things.

SIR JOHN. And yet, methinks, 'tis a hard matter to break their hearts.

CON. Fie, fie! You have one of the best wives in the world, and yet you seem the most uneasy husband.

---

[8]*conjunction* a term from astrology; two planets seeming to come close to one another could be a force for good or ill; here the latter.
[9]*honest* chaste.

SIR JOHN. Best wives! The woman's well enough; she has no vice that I know of, but she's a wife, and – damn a wife! If I were married to a hogshead of claret, matrimony would make me hate it.

HEART. Why did you marry then? You were old enough to know your own mind.

SIR JOHN. Why did I marry? I married because I had a mind to lie with her, and she would not let me.

HEART. Why did not you ravish her?

SIR JOHN. Yes, and so have hedged myself into forty quarrels with her relations, besides buying my pardon. But more than all that, you must know I was afraid of being damned in those days, for I kept sneaking, cowardly company, fellows that went to church, said grace to their meat, and had not the least tincture of quality about 'em.

HEART. But I think you are got into a better gang now.

SIR JOHN. Zoons, sir, my Lord Rake and I are hand and glove. I believe we may get our bones broke together tonight. Have you a mind to share a frolic?

CON. Not I truly. My talent lies to softer exercises.

SIR JOHN. What, a down bed and a strumpet? A pox of venery, I say. Will you come and drink with me this afternoon?

CON. I can't drink today, but we'll come and sit an hour with you if you will.

SIR JOHN. Phugh! Pox! Sit an hour! Why can't you drink?

CON. Because I'm to see my mistress.

SIR JOHN. Who's that?

CON. Why, do you use to tell?

SIR JOHN. Yes.

CON. So won't I.

SIR JOHN. Why?

CON. Because 'tis a secret.

SIR JOHN. Would my wife knew it, 'twould be no secret long.

CON. Why, do you think she can't keep a secret?

SIR JOHN. No more than she can keep Lent.

HEART. Prithee tell it her to try, Constant.

SIR JOHN. No, prithee don't, that I mayn't be plagued with it.

CON. I'll hold you a guinea you don't make her tell it you.

SIR JOHN. I'll hold you a guinea I do.

CON. Which way?

SIR JOHN. Why, I'll beg her not to tell it me.

HEART. Nay, if anything does it, that will.

CON. But do you think, sir –

SIR JOHN.   Oons, sir, I think a woman and a secret are the two
impertinentest themes in the universe. Therefore, pray, let's hear no
more of my wife nor your mistress. Damn 'em both with all my heart,
and everything else that daggles[10] a petticoat, except four generous
whores, with Betty Sands[11] at the head of 'em, who were drunk with
my Lord Rake and I ten times in a fortnight.   *Exit* SIR JOHN
CON.   Here's a dainty fellow for you. And the veriest coward too. But
his usage of his wife makes me ready to stab the villain.
HEART.   Lovers are short-sighted; all their senses run into that of
feeling. This proceeding of his is the only thing on earth can make your
fortune. If anything can prevail with her to accept a gallant, 'tis his ill
usage of her, for women will do more for revenge than they'll do for
the gospel. Prithee take heart. I have great hopes for you, and since I
can't bring you quite off of her, I'll endeavour to bring you quite on,
for a whining lover is the damned'st companion upon earth.
CON.   My dear friend, flatter me a little more with these hopes; for
whilst they prevail I have heaven within me and could melt with joy.
HEART.   Pray, no melting yet. Let things go further first. This
afternoon perhaps we shall make some advance. In the meanwhile,
let's go dine at Locket's[12] and let hope get you a stomach.   *Exeunt*

SCENE [TWO]

LADY FANCIFUL'S *house*

Enter LADY FANCIFUL *and* MADAMOISELLE

LADY F.   Did you ever see anything so importune, Madamoiselle?
MADAM.   Inteed, matam, to say de trute, he want leetel good breeding.
LADY F.   Good breeding? He wants to be caned, Madamoiselle. An
insolent fellow! And yet let me expose my weakness: 'tis the only man
on earth I could resolve to dispense my favours on, were he but a fine
gentleman. Well, did men but know how deep an impression a fine
gentleman makes in a lady's heart, they would reduce all their studies
to that of good breeding alone.
     Enter CORNET

[10]*daggles* trails through mud, etc.
[11]*Betty Sands* 1667–99, prostitute, orange-seller at Theatre Royal, Drury Lane,
mistress of Peter the Great during his visit to England in 1698. See Alexander Smith,
'Betty Sands and the C—— of Muscovy', *The School of Venus*, 1716, vol. I,
pp. 185–92. [A. Coleman, 'Five Notes on *The Provok'd Wife*', *Notes and Queries*,
XVI (August 1969), pp. 298–300.]
[12]*Locket's* a famous ordinary at Spring Garden, near Charing Cross; the
proprietor was Adam Locket.

COR.   Madam, here's Mr Treble. He has brought home the verses your ladyship made and gave him to set.

LADY F.   Oh, let him come in, by all means. [*Exit* CORNET] Now, Madamoiselle, am I going to be unspeakably happy.

Enter TREBLE

So Mr Treble, you have set my little dialogue?

TREBLE.   Yes, madam, and I hope your ladyship will be pleased with it.

LADY F.   Oh, no doubt on't, for really, Mr Treble, you set all things to a wonder. But your music is in particular heavenly when you have my words to clothe in't.

TREBLE.   Your words themselves, madam, have so much music in 'em they inspire me.

LADY F.   Nay, now you make me blush, Mr Treble. But pray let's hear what you have done.

TREBLE.   You shall, madam.

[*Enter* MRS PIPE]

A Song to be sung between a man and a woman [TREBLE *and* MRS PIPE]

> *Man.*   Ah, lovely nymph, the world's on fire;
>   Veil, veil those cruel eyes.
> *Woman.* The world may then in flames expire,
>   And boast that so it dies.
> *Man.*   But when all mortals are destroy'd,
>   Who then shall sing your praise?
> *Woman.* Those who are fit to be employ'd:
>   The gods shall altars raise.

TREBLE.   How does your ladyship like it, madam?

LADY F.   Rapture, rapture, Mr Treble, I'm all rapture! O wit and art, what power you have when joined! I must needs tell you the birth of this little dialogue, Mr Treble. Its father was a dream, and its mother was the moon. I dreamt that by an unanimous vote I was chosen queen of that pale world and that the first time I appeared upon my throne all my subjects fell in love with me. Just then I waked, and seeing pen, ink and paper lie idle upon the table, I slid into my morning gown, and writ this impromptu.

TREBLE.   So I guess the dialogue, madam, is supposed to be between your majesty and your first minister of state.

LADY F.   Just. He as minister advises me to trouble my head about the welfare of my subjects, which I as sovereign find a very impertinent proposal. But is the town so dull, Mr Treble, it affords us never another new song?

TREBLE.   Madam, I have one in my pocket came out but yesterday, if your ladyship pleases to let Mrs Pipe sing it.

LADY F.   By all means. Here, Pipe. Make what music you can of this song here.

SONG

I

> Not an angel dwells above
> Half so fair as her I love.
>   Heaven knows how she'll receive me;
> If she smiles, I'm blest indeed,
> If she frowns, I'm quickly freed.
>   Heaven knows she ne'er can grieve me.

II

> None can love her more than I;
> Yet she ne'er shall make me die,
>   If my flame can never warm her.
> Lasting beauty I'll adore;
> I shall never love her more,
>   Cruelty will so deform her.

Exit PIPE

LADY F.   Very well. This is Heartfree's poetry without question.

TREBLE.   Won't your ladyship please to sing yourself this morning?

LADY F.   O Lord, Mr Treble, my cold is still so barbarous to refuse me that pleasure. He, he, hem.

TREBLE.   I'm very sorry for it, madam. Methinks all mankind should turn physician for the cure on't.

LADY F.   Why truly, to give mankind their due, there's few that know me but have offered their remedy.

TREBLE.   They have reason, madam, for I know nobody sings so near a cherubin as your ladyship.

LADY F.   What I do I owe chiefly to your skill and care, Mr Treble. People do flatter me indeed that I have a voice and a *je-ne-sais-quoi* in the conduct of it that will make music of anything. And truly I begin to believe so, since what happened t'other night. Would you think it, Mr Treble, walking pretty late in the Park, for I often walk late in the Park, Mr Treble, a whim took me to sing 'Chevy Chase',[13] and would you believe it, next morning I had three copies of verses and six billets-doux at my levee[14] upon it.

---

[13]'*Chevy Chase*' a famous, but in 1697 old-fashioned, sixteenth-century ballad about the fatal rivalry and battle between the Earl of Northumberland and Earl Douglas with their forces.

[14]*levee* morning reception.

TREBLE. And without all dispute you deserved as many more. Madam, are there any further commands for your ladyship's humble servant?

LADY F. Nothing more at this time, Mr Treble. But I shall expect you here every morning for this month, to sing my little matter there to me. I'll reward you for your pains.

TREBLE. O Lord, madam –

LADY F. Good morrow, sweet Mr Treble.

TREBLE. Your ladyship's most obedient servant.   *Exit* TREBLE
 Enter SERVANT

SERV. Will your ladyship please to dine yet?

LADY F. Yes, let 'em serve.   *Exit* SERVANT
 Sure this Heartfree has bewitched me, Madamoiselle. You can't imagine how oddly he mixed himself in my thoughts during my rapture e'en now. I vow 'tis a thousand pities he is not more polished. Don't you think so?

MADAM. Matam, I think it so great pity dat if I was in your ladyship place I take him home in my house. I lock him up in my closet, and I never let him go till I teach him everyting dat fine laty expect from fine gentleman.

LADY F. Why truly, I believe I should soon subdue his brutality, for without doubt he has a strange penchant to grow fond of me, in spite of his aversion to the sex, else he would ne'er have taken so much pains about me. Lord, how proud would some poor creatures be of such a conquest? But I, alas, I don't know how to receive as a favour what I take to be so infinitely my due. But what shall I do to new-mould him, Madamoiselle? For till then he's my utter aversion.

MADAM. Matam, you must laugh at him in all de place dat you meet him, and turn into de ridicule all he say and all he do.

LADY F. Why truly, satire has been ever of wondrous use to reform ill manners. Besides 'tis my particular talent to ridicule folks. I can be severe, strangely severe, when I will, Madamoiselle. Give me the pen and ink. I find myself whimsical. I'll write to him. (*Sitting down to write*) Or I'll let it alone and be severe upon him that way. (*Rising up again*) Yet active severity is better than passive. (*Sitting down*) 'Tis as good let alone too, for every lash I give him, perhaps he'll take for a favour. (*Rising*) Yet 'tis a thousand pities so much satire should be lost. (*Sitting*) But if it should have a wrong effect upon him 'twould distract me. (*Rising*) Well, I must write though after all. (*Sitting*) Or I'll let it alone, which is the same thing. (*Rising*)

MADAM. *La voilà determinée!*[15]   *Exeunt*

---

[15]*La voilà determinée* Look, she's quite determined.

Act Three

SCENE [ONE]

[SIR JOHN BRUTE'S *house*]

Scene opens; SIR JOHN, LADY BRUTE *and* BELINDA *rising from the table* [*with servants in attendance*]

SIR JOHN. (*To a servant*) Here, take away the things; I expect company. But first bring me a pipe; I'll smoke.

[*Servant leaves and returns*]

LADY B. Lord, Sir John, I wonder you won't leave that nasty custom.

SIR JOHN. Prithee don't be impertinent.

BEL. (*To* LADY BRUTE) I wonder who those are he expects this afternoon.

LADY B. [*To* BELINDA] I'd give the world to know. Perhaps 'tis Constant; he comes here sometimes. If it does prove him, I'm resolved I'll share the visit.

BEL. We'll send for our work and sit here.

LADY B. He'll choke us with his tobacco.

BEL. Nothing will choke us when we are doing what we have a mind to. Lovewell!

Enter LOVEWELL

LOVE. Madam.

LADY B. Here, bring my cousin's work and mine hither.

Exit LOVEWELL *and re-enters with their work* [*she leaves*]

SIR JOHN. Why, pox, can't you work somewhere else?

LADY B. We shall be careful not to disturb you, sir.

BEL. Your pipe would make you too thoughtful, uncle, if you were left alone. Our prittle-prattle will cure your spleen.

SIR JOHN. Will it so, Mrs Pert? Now I believe it will so increase it, I shall take my own house for a paper mill.[1] *Sitting and smoking*

LADY B. (*To* BELINDA *aside*) Don't let's mind him; let him say what he will.

SIR JOHN. A woman's tongue a cure for the spleen! Oons! – (*Aside*) If a man had got the headache, they'd be for applying the same remedy.

[1] *paper mill* i.e. a very noisy place.

LADY B. You have done a great deal, Belinda, since yesterday.

BEL. Yes, I have worked very hard. How do you like it?

LADY B. Oh, 'tis the prettiest fringe in the world. Well, cousin, you have the happiest fancy. Prithee advise me about altering my crimson petticoat.

SIR JOHN. A pox o' your petticoat! Here's such a prating a man can't digest his own thoughts for you.

LADY B. (*Aside*) Don't answer him. – Well, what do you advise me?

BEL. Why, really I would not alter it at all. Methinks 'tis very pretty as it is.

LADY B. Ay, that's true. But you know one grows weary of the prettiest things in the world when one has had 'em long.

SIR JOHN. Yes, I have taught her that.

BEL. [*To* LADY BRUTE] Shall we provoke him a little?

LADY B. [*To* BELINDA] With all my heart. Belinda, don't you long to be married?

BEL. Why, there are some things in't I could like well enough.

LADY B. What do you think you should dislike?

BEL. My husband, a hundred to one else.

LADY B. O ye wicked wretch! Sure you don't speak as you think.

BEL. Yes, I do; especially if he smoked tobacco.

He looks earnestly at 'em

LADY B. Why, that many times takes off worse smells.

BEL. Then he must smell very ill indeed.

LADY B. So some men will, to keep their wives from coming near 'em.

BEL. Then those wives should cuckold 'em at a distance.

He rises in a fury, throws his pipe at 'em, and drives 'em out. As they run off, CONSTANT *and* HEARTFREE *enter.* LADY BRUTE *runs against* CONSTANT

SIR JOHN. Oons, get you gone upstairs, you confederating strumpets you, or I'll cuckold you with a vengeance.

LADY B. O Lord, he'll beat us, he'll beat us! Dear, dear Mr Constant, save us. *Exeunt* LADY BRUTE *and* BELINDA

SIR JOHN. I'll cuckold you, with a pox.

CON. Heavens, Sir John, what's the matter?

SIR JOHN. Sure if woman had been already created, the devil, instead of being kicked down into hell, had been married.

HEART. Why, what new plague have you found now?

SIR JOHN. Why, these two gentlewomen did but hear me say I expected you here this afternoon, upon which they presently resolved to take up the room, o' purpose to plague me and my friends.

CON. Was that all? Why, we should have been glad of their company.

SIR JOHN. Then I should have been weary of yours, for I can't relish both together. They found fault with my smoking tobacco too, and said men stunk. But I have a good mind to say something.

CON. No, nothing against the ladies, pray.

SIR JOHN. Split² the ladies! Come, will you sit down? Give us wine, fellow. You won't smoke?

CON. No, nor drink neither, at this time. I must ask your pardon.

SIR JOHN. What, this mistress of yours runs in your head. I'll warrant it's some such squeamish minx as my wife, that's grown so dainty of late she finds fault even with a dirty shirt.

HEART. That a woman may do, and not be very dainty neither.

SIR JOHN. Pox o' the women, let's drink. Come, you shall take one glass, though I send for a box of lozenges to sweeten your mouth after it.

CON Nay, if one glass will satisfy you, I'll drink it without putting you to that expense.

SIR JOHN. Why, that's honest. Fill some wine, sirrah. So, here's to you, gentlemen. A wife's the devil. To your being both married.

They drink

HEART. Oh, your most humble servant, sir.

SIR JOHN. Well, how do you like my wine?

CON. 'Tis very good indeed.

HEART. 'Tis admirable.

SIR JOHN. Then give us t'other glass.

CON. No, pray excuse us now. We'll come another time and then we won't spare it.

SIR JOHN. This one glass and no more. Come, it shall be your mistresses' health, and that's a great compliment from me, I assure you.

CON. And 'tis a very obliging one to me. So give us the glasses.

SIR JOHN. So. Let her live.

HEART. And be kind.　　　　　　　　SIR JOHN *coughs in the glass*

CON. What's the matter? Does't go the wrong way?

SIR JOHN. If I had love enough to be jealous, I should take this for an ill omen. For I never drank my wife's health in my life but I puked in the glass.

CON. Oh, she's too virtuous to make a reasonable man jealous.

SIR JOHN. Pox of her virtue. If I could but catch her adulterating, I might be divorced from her by law.

²*Split* Tear apart.

HEART.   And so pay her a yearly pension to be a distinguished cuckold.

   Enter SERVANT

SERV.   Sir, there's my Lord Rake, Colonel Bully, and some other gentlemen at the Blue Posts[3] desire your company.

SIR JOHN.   Cods so, we are to consult about playing the devil tonight.

HEART.   Well, we won't hinder business.

SIR JOHN.   Methinks I don't know how to leave you though. But for once I must make bold. Or, look you, maybe the conference mayn't last long; so if you'll wait here half an hour or an hour – if I don't come then, why then, I won't come at all.

HEART.   (*To* CONSTANT *aside*) A good modest proposition truly.

CON.   [*To* HEARTFREE] But let's accept on't however. Who knows what may happen?

HEART.   Well, sir, to show you how fond we are of your company, we'll expect[4] your return as long as we can.

SIR JOHN.   Nay, maybe I mayn't stay at all; but business, you know, must be done. So, your servant. Or, hark you, if you have a mind to take a frisk with us, I have an interest with my lord; I can easily introduce you.

CON.   We are much beholding to you, but for my part I'm engaged another way.

SIR JOHN.   What? To your mistress, I'll warrant. Prithee leave your nasty punk to entertain herself with her own lewd thoughts, and make one with us tonight.

CON.   Sir, 'tis business that is to employ me.

HEART.   And me. And business must be done, you know.

SIR JOHN.   Ay, women's business, though the world were consumed for't!   *Exit* SIR JOHN [*and* SERVANT]

CON.   Farewell, beast. And now, my dear friend, would my mistress be but as complaisant as some men's wives, who think it a piece of good breeding to receive the visits of their husband's friends in his absence.

HEART.   Why, for your sake I could forgive her, though she should be so complaisant to receive something else in his absence. But what way shall we invent to see her?

CON.   Oh, ne'er hope it. Invention will prove as vain as wishes.

   Enter LADY BRUTE *and* BELINDA

HEART.   What do you think now, friend?

CON.   I think I shall swoon.

HEART.   I'll speak first then, whilst you fetch breath.

---

[3] *Blue Posts* an inn in the Haymarket.   [4] *expect* await.

LADY B. We think ourselves obliged, gentlemen, to come and return you thanks for your knight-errantry. We were just upon being devoured by the fiery dragon.

BEL. Did not his fumes almost knock you down, gentlemen?

HEART. Truly, ladies, we did undergo some hardships, and should have done more, if some greater heroes than ourselves hard by had not diverted him.

CON. Though I'm glad of the service you are pleased to say we have done you, yet I'm sorry we could do it no other way than by making ourselves privy to what you would perhaps have kept a secret.

LADY B. For Sir John's part, I suppose he designed it no secret, since he made so much noise. And for myself, truly I am not much concerned, since 'tis fallen only into this gentleman's hands and yours, who, I have many reasons to believe, will neither interpret nor report anything to my disadvantage.

CON. Your good opinion, madam, was what I feared I never could have merited.

LADY B. Your fears were vain then, sir, for I am just to everybody.

HEART. Prithee, Constant, what is't you do to get the ladies' good opinions, for I'm a novice at it?

BEL. Sir, will you give me leave to instruct you?

HEART. Yes, that I will with all my soul, madam.

BEL. Why then, you must never be slovenly, never be out of humour, fare well and cry roast meat,⁵ smoke tobacco, nor drink but when you are a-dry.

HEART. That's hard.

CON. Nay, if you take his bottle from him, you'll break his heart, madam.

BEL. Why, is it possible the gentleman can love drinking?

HEART. Only by way of antidote.

BEL. Against what, pray?

HEART. Against love, madam.

LADY B. Are you afraid of being in love, sir?

HEART. I should if there were any danger of it.

LADY B. Pray, why so?

HEART. Because I always had an aversion to being used like a dog.

BEL. Why truly, men in love are seldom used better.

LADY B. But was you never in love, sir?

HEART. No, I thank heaven, madam.

BEL. Pray, where got you your learning then?

HEART. From other people's expense.

⁵*cry roast meat* boast about good fortune (proverbial).

BEL.   That's being a sponger, sir, which is scarce honest. If you'd buy some experience with your own money, as 'twould be fairlier got, so 'twould stick longer by you.

    Enter FOOTMAN

FOOT.   Madam, here's my Lady Fanciful to wait upon your ladyship.

LADY B.   Shield me, kind heaven! What an inundation of impertinence is here coming upon us!

    Enter LADY FANCIFUL, *who runs first to* LADY BRUTE, *then to* BELINDA, *kissing 'em*

LADY F.   My dear Lady Brute, and sweet Belinda! Methinks 'tis an age since I saw you.

LADY B.   Yet 'tis but three days. Sure you have passed your time very ill, it seems so long to you.

LADY F.   Why really, to confess the truth to you, I am so everlastingly fatigued with the addresses of unfortunate gentlemen, that were it not for the extravagancy of the example, I should e'en tear out these wicked eyes with my own fingers, to make both myself and mankind easy. What think you on't, Mr Heartfree, for I take you to be my faithful adviser?

HEART.   Why truly, madam, I think – every project that is for the good of mankind ought to be encouraged.

LADY F.   Then I have your consent, sir?

HEART.   To do whatever you please, madam.

LADY F.   You had a much more limited complaisance this morning, sir. Would you believe it, ladies? The gentleman has been so exceeding generous to tell me of above fifty faults in less time than it was well possible for me to commit two of 'em.

CON.   Why truly, madam, my friend there is apt to be something familiar with the ladies.

LADY F.   He is indeed, sir, but he's wondrous charitable with it; he has the goodness to design a reformation, even down to my fingers' ends. 'Twas thus, I think, sir, you would have had 'em stand. (*Opening her fingers in an awkward manner*) My eyes too he did not like. How was't you would have directed 'em? Thus, I think. (*Staring at him*) Then there was something amiss in my gait too; I don't know well how 'twas, but as I take it he would have had me walk like him. Pray, sir, do me the favour to take a turn or two about the room, that the company may see you. He's sullen, ladies, and won't. But, to make short, and give you as true an idea as I can of the matter, I think 'twas much about this figure in general he would have moulded me to. (*She walks awkwardly about, staring and looking ungainly, then changes on a sudden to the extremity of her usual affectation*) But I was an obstinate woman, and could not resolve to make myself mistress of his heart by growing as awkward as his fancy.

Here CONSTANT *and* LADY BRUTE *talk together apart*

HEART.   Just thus women do when they think we are in love with 'em, or when they are so with us.

LADY F.   'Twould, however, be less vanity for me to conclude the former than you the latter, sir.

HEART.   Madam, all I shall presume to conclude is that if I were in love, you'd find the means to make me soon weary on't.

LADY F.   Not by over-fondness, upon my word, sir. But pray, let's stop here, for you are so much governed by instinct I know you'll grow brutish at last.

BEL.   (*Aside*) Now am I sure she's fond of him. I'll try to make her jealous. – Well, for my part, I should be glad to find somebody would be so free with me that I might know my faults and mend 'em.

LADY F.   Then pray let me recommend this gentleman to you. I have known him for some time and will be surety for him that, upon a very limited encouragement on your side, you shall find an extended impudence on his.

HEART.   I thank you, madam, for your recommendation. But, hating idleness, I'm unwilling to enter into a place where I believe there would be nothing to do. I was fond of serving your ladyship because I knew you'd find me constant employment.

LADY F.   I told you he'd be rude, Belinda.

BEL.   Oh, a little bluntness is a sign of honesty, which makes me always ready to pardon it. So, sir, if you have no other exceptions to my service but the fear of being idle in't, you may venture to 'list[6] yourself. I shall find you work, I warrant you.

HEART.   Upon those terms I engage, madam, and this, with your leave, I take for earnest.   *Offering to kiss her hand*

BEL.   Hold there, sir, I'm none of your earnest givers. But if I'm well served, I give good wages and pay punctually.

HEARTFREE *and* BELINDA *seem to continue talking familiarly*

LADY F.   (*Aside*) I don't like this jesting between 'em. Methinks the fool begins to look as if he were in earnest; but then he must be a fool indeed. Lard, what a difference there is between me and her! (*Looking at* BELINDA *scornfully*) How I should despise such a thing if I were a man! What a nose she has, what a chin, what a neck! Then her eyes, and the worst kissing lips in the universe. No, no, he can never like her, that's positive; yet I can't suffer 'em together any longer. – Mr Heartfree, do you know that you and I must have no

[6]*'list* enlist.

quarrel for all this? I can't forbear being a little severe now and then. But women, you know, may be allowed anything.

HEART.   Up to a certain age, madam.

LADY F.   Which I am not yet past, I hope.

HEART.   (*Aside*) Nor never will, I dare swear.

LADY F.   (*To* LADY BRUTE) Come, madam, will your ladyship be witness to our reconciliation?

LADY B.   You agree then at last?

HEART.   (*Slightingly*) We forgive.

LADY F.   (*Aside*) That was a cold, ill-natured reply.

LADY B.   Then there's no challenges sent between you?

HEART.   Not from me, I promise. – (*Aside to* CONSTANT) But that's more than I'll do for her, for I know she can as well be damned as forbear writing to me.

CON.   [*To* HEARTFREE] That I believe. But I think we had best be going lest she should suspect something and be malicious.

HEART.   [*To* CONSTANT] With all my heart.

CON.   Ladies, we are your humble servants. I see Sir John is quite engaged. 'Twould be in vain to expect him. Come, Heartfree.

Exit CONSTANT

HEART.   Ladies, your servant. – (*To* BELINDA) I hope, madam, you won't forget our bargain: I'm to say what I please to you.

BEL.   Liberty of speech entire, sir.   *Exit* HEARTFREE

LADY F.   (*Aside*) Very pretty truly. But how the blockhead went out, languishing at her, and not a look toward me. Well, churchmen may talk, but miracles are not ceased. For 'tis more than natural such a rude fellow as he and such a little impertinent as she should be capable of making a woman of my sphere uneasy. But I can bear her sight no longer. Methinks she's grown ten times uglier than Cornet. I must go home and study revenge. – (*To* LADY BRUTE) Madam, your humble servant. I must take my leave.

LADY B.   What, going already, madam?

LADY F.   I must beg you'll excuse me this once. For really I have eighteen visits to return this afternoon, so you see I'm importuned by the women as well as the men.

BEL.   (*Aside*) And she's quits with 'em both.

LADY F.   (*Going*) Nay, you shan't go one step out of the room.

LADY B.   Indeed, I'll wait upon you down.

LADY F.   No, sweet Lady Brute; you know I swoon at ceremony.

LADY B.   Pray give me leave.

LADY F.   You know I won't.

LADY B.   Indeed I must.

LADY F.   Indeed you shan't.

LADY B.   Indeed I will.

LADY F.   Indeed you shan't.

LADY B.   Indeed I will.

LADY F.   Indeed you shan't. Indeed, indeed, indeed you shan't.

> *Exit* LADY FANCIFUL *running. They follow*
> *Re-enter* LADY BRUTE *sola*

LADY B.   This impertinent woman has put me out of humour for a fortnight. What an agreeable moment has her foolish visit interrupted. Lord, how like a torrent love flows into the heart when once the sluice of desire is opened! Good gods, what a pleasure there is in doing what we should not do!

> *Re-enter* CONSTANT

Ha, here again?

CON.   Though the renewing my visit may seem a little irregular, I hope I shall obtain your pardon for it, madam, when you know I only left the room lest the lady who was here should have been as malicious in her remarks as she's foolish in her conduct.

LADY B.   He who has discretion enough to be tender of a woman's reputation carries a virtue about him may atone for a great many faults.

CON.   If it has a title to atone for any, its pretensions must needs be strongest where the crime is love. I therefore hope I shall be forgiven the attempt I have made upon your heart, since my enterprise has been a secret to all the world but yourself.

LADY B.   Secrecy indeed in sins of this kind is an argument of weight to lessen the punishment, but nothing's a plea for a pardon entire without a sincere repentance.

CON.   If sincerity in repentance consist in sorrow for offending, no cloister ever enclosed so true a penitent as I should be. But I hope it cannot be reckoned an offence to love where 'tis a duty to adore.

LADY B.   'Tis an offence, a great one, where it would rob a woman of all she ought to be adored for, her virtue.

CON.   Virtue? Virtue, alas, is no more like the thing that's called so than 'tis like vice itself. Virtue consists in goodness, honour, gratitude, sincerity, and pity, and not in peevish, snarling, strait-laced chastity. True virtue, wheresoe'er it moves, still carries an intrinsic worth about it, and is in every place and in each sex of equal value. So is not continence, you see, that phantom of honour, which men in every age have so condemned, they have thrown it amongst the women to scrabble for.

LADY B.   If it be a thing of so very little value, why do you so earnestly recommend it to your wives and daughters?

CON.   We recommend it to our wives, madam, because we would keep 'em to ourselves. And to our daughters, because we would dispose of 'em to others.

LADY B. 'Tis then of some importance it seems, since you can't dispose of 'em without it.

CON. That importance, madam, lies in the humour of the country, not in the nature of the thing.

LADY B. How do you prove that, sir?

CON. From the wisdom of a neighb'ring nation in a contrary practice. In monarchies things go by whimsy, but commonwealths weigh all things in the scale of reason.

LADY B. I hope we are not so very light a people to bring up fashions without some ground.

CON. Pray, what does your ladyship think of a powdered coat for deep mourning?

LADY B. I think, sir, your sophistry has all the effect that you can reasonably expect it should have: it puzzles, but don't convince.

CON. I'm sorry for it.

LADY B. I'm sorry to hear you say so.

CON. Pray, why?

LADY B. Because if you expected more from it, you have a worse opinion of my understanding than I desire you should have.

CON. (*Aside*) I comprehend her. She would have me set a value upon her chastity that I may think myself the more obliged to her when she makes me a present of it. – (*To her*) I beg you will believe I did but rally, madam. I know you judge too well of right and wrong to be deceived by arguments like those. I hope you'll have so favourable an opinion of my understanding too to believe the thing called virtue has worth enough with me to pass for an eternal obligation where'er 'tis sacrificed.

LADY B. It is, I think, so great a one as nothing can repay.

CON. Yes, the making the man you love your everlasting debtor.

LADY B. When debtors once have borrowed all we have to lend, they are very apt to grow very shy of their creditors' company.

CON. That, madam, is only when they are forced to borrow of usurers and not of a generous friend. Let us choose our creditors, and we are seldom so ungrateful to shun 'em.

LADY B. What think you of Sir John, sir? I was his free choice.

CON. I think he's married, madam.

LADY B. Does marriage then exclude men from your rule of constancy?

CON. It does. Constancy's a brave, free, haughty, generous agent that cannot buckle to the chains of wedlock. There's a poor, sordid slavery in marriage that turns the flowing tide of honour and sinks us to the lowest ebb of infamy. 'Tis a corrupted soil; ill nature, avarice, sloth, cowardice and dirt are all its product.

LADY B. Have you no exceptions to this general rule, as well as to t'other?

CON. Yes, I would, after all, be an exception to it myself if you were free in power and will to make me so.

LADY B. Compliments are well placed where 'tis impossible to lay hold on 'em.

CON. I would to heaven 'twere possible for you to lay hold on mine, that you might see it is no compliment at all. But since you are already disposed on beyond redemption to one who does not know the value of the jewel you have put into his hands, I hope you would not think him greatly wronged, though it should sometimes be looked on by a friend who knows how to esteem it as he ought.

LADY B. If looking on't alone would serve his turn, the wrong perhaps might not be very great.

CON. Why, what if he should wear it now and then a day, so he gave good security to bring it home again at night?

LADY B. Small security, I fancy, might serve for that. One might venture to take his word.

CON. Then where's the injury to the owner?

LADY B. 'Tis an injury to him if he think it one. For if happiness be seated in the mind, unhappiness must be so too.

CON. Here I close with you, madam, and draw my conclusive argument from your own position: if the injury lie in the fancy, there needs nothing but secrecy to prevent the wrong.

LADY B. (*Going*) A surer way to prevent it is to hear no more arguments in its behalf.

CON. (*Following her*) But madam, –

LADY B. But, sir, 'tis my turn to be discreet now, and not suffer too long a visit.

CON. (*Catching her hand*) By heaven, you shall not stir till you give me hopes that I shall see you again, at some more convenient time and place.

LADY B. I give you just hopes enough (*Breaking from him*) to get loose from you, and that's all I can afford you at this time.

Exit running

CON. (*Solus*) Now by all that's great and good, she is a charming woman. In what ecstasy of joy she has left me! For she gave me hope. Did she not say she gave me hope? Hope? Ay. What hope? Enough to make me let her go. Why, that's enough in conscience. Or no matter how 'twas spoke. Hope was the word. It came from her, and it was said to me.

Enter HEARTFREE

Ha, Heartfree, thou hast done me noble service in prattling to the young gentlewoman without there. Come to my arms, thou venerable bawd, and let me squeeze thee (*Embracing him eagerly*) as a new pair of stays does a fat country girl when she's carried to court to stand for a maid of honour.

HEART. Why, what the devil's all this rapture for?

CON. Rapture? There's ground for rapture, man. There's hopes, my Heartfree, hopes, my friend.

HEART. Hopes? Of what?

CON. Why, hopes that my lady and I together – for 'tis more than one body's work – should make Sir John a cuckold.

HEART. Prithee, what did she say to thee?

CON. Say? What did she not say? She said that, says she, she said – Zoons, I don't know what she said. But she looked as if she said everything I'd have her; and so if thou'lt go to the tavern, I'll treat thee with anything that gold can buy. I'll give all my silver amongst the drawers, make a bonfire before the door, say the plenipos have signed the peace,[7] and the Bank of England's grown honest.[8]

Exeunt

[SCENE TWO]

[*The Blue Posts*]

Scene opens: LORD RAKE, SIR JOHN, *etc., at a table drinking.*
[*Servants in attendance*]

ALL. Huzza!

LORD RAKE. Come, boys. Charge again. So. Confusion to all order. Here's liberty of conscience!

ALL. Huzza!

LORD RAKE. I'll sing you a song I made this morning to this purpose.

SIR JOHN. 'Tis wicked, I hope.

COL. BULLY. Don't my lord tell you he made it?

SIR JOHN. Well then, let's ha't.

LORD RAKE *sings*

I

What a pother of late

---

[7]*peace* The Treaty of Ryswick, concluding the War of the Grand Alliance, was not in fact signed until 20 September 1697; *The Provoked Wife* first reached the stage in mid April 1697.

[8]*honest* The Bank of England, founded in 1694, was still somewhat suspect, partly because of a run on it in 1696.

Have they kept in the state
    About setting our consciences[9] free.
A bottle has more
Dispensation[10] in store
    Than the king and the state can decree.

II

When my head's full of wine,
I o'erflow with design
    And know no penal laws[11] that can curb me.
Whate'er I devise
Seems good in my eyes,
    And religion ne'er dares to disturb me.

III

No saucy remorse
Intrudes in my course,
    Nor impertinent notions of evil.
So there's claret in store,
In peace I've my whore,
    And in peace I jog on to the devil.

ALL SING.   'So there's claret', etc.

LORD RAKE.   (*Repeats*) 'And in peace I jog on to the devil'. Well, how
    do you like it, gentlemen?

ALL.   Oh, admirable!

SIR JOHN.   I would not give a fig for a song that is not full of sin and
    impudence.

LORD RAKE.   Then my muse is to your taste. But drink away. The night
    steals upon us; we shall want time to be lewd in. Hey, page, sally out,
    sirrah, and see what's doing in the camp; we'll beat up their quarters
    presently.[12]

PAGE.   I'll bring your lordship an exact account.   *Exit*

LORD RAKE.   Now let the spirit of clary[13] go round. Fill me a brimmer.
    Here's to our forlorn hope.[14] Courage, knight, victory attends you.

SIR JOHN.   And laurels shall crown me. Drink away and be damned.

---

[9]*consciences* The Tolerance Act of 1689 allowed nonconformists a greater
freedom of worship according to their consciences.

[10]*Dispensation* A power to dispense with the established laws was claimed by
both Charles II and James II.

[11]*penal laws* restrictions on the activities of Roman Catholics.

[12]*presently* immediately.

[13]*clary* a sweet liquor made from wine, clarified honey, etc.

[14]*forlorn hope* a group of soldiers chosen to begin an attack.

LORD RAKE. Again, boys! T'other glass, and damn morality.

SIR JOHN. (*Drunk*) Ay, damn morality and damn the watch, and let the constable be married.

ALL. Huzza!

Re-enter PAGE

LORD RAKE. How are the streets inhabited, sirrah?

PAGE. My lord, it's Sunday night; they are full of drunken citizens.

LORD RAKE. Along then, boys, we shall have a feast.

COL. BULLY. Along, noble knight.

SIR JOHN. Ay, along, Bully. And he that says Sir John Brute is not as drunk and as religious as the drunkest citizen of 'em all – is a liar and the son of a whore.

COL. BULLY. Why, that was bravely spoke, and like a free-born Englishman.

SIR JOHN. What's that to you, sir, whether I am an Englishman or a Frenchman?

COL BULLY. Zoons, you are not angry, sir?

SIR JOHN. Zoons, I am angry, sir. For if I am a free-born Englishman, what have you to do, even to talk of my privileges?

LORD RAKE. Why prithee, knight, don't quarrel here. Leave private animosities to be decided by daylight. Let the night be employed against the public enemy.

SIR JOHN. My lord, I respect you because you are a man of quality. But I'll make that fellow know I am within a hair's breadth as absolute about my privileges as the King of France is by his prerogative. He by his prerogative takes money where it is not his due; I by my privilege refuse paying it where I owe it. Liberty and property and old England, huzza!

Exit SIR JOHN *reeling, all following him*

SCENE [THREE]

LADY BRUTE's *bedchamber*

Enter LADY BRUTE *and* BELINDA

LADY B. Sure, it's late, Belinda. I begin to be sleepy.

BEL. Yes, 'tis near twelve. Will you go to bed?

LADY B. To bed, my dear? And by that time I'm fallen into a sweet sleep, or perhaps a sweet dream, which is better and better, Sir John will come home, roaring drunk, and be overjoyed he finds me in a condition to be disturbed.

BEL. Oh, you need not fear him; he's in for all night. The servants say he's gone to drink with my Lord Rake.

LADY B. Nay, 'tis not very likely indeed such suitable company should part presently. What hogs men turn, Belinda, when they grow weary of women!

BEL.   And what owls they are whilst they are fond of 'em!

LADY B.   But that we may forgive well enough because they are so upon our accounts.

BEL.   We ought to do so indeed, but 'tis a hard matter. For when a man is really in love, he looks so unsufferably silly that though a woman liked him well enough before, she had then much ado to endure the sight of him. And this I take to be the reason why lovers are so generally ill used.

LADY B.   Well, I own now I'm well enough pleased to see a man look like an ass for me.

BEL.   Ay, I'm pleased he should look like an ass too; that is, I'm pleased with myself for making him look so.

LADY B.   Nay, truly, I think if he'd find some other way to express his passion 'twould be more to his advantage.

BEL.   Yes, for then a woman might like his passion and him too.

LADY B.   Yes, Belinda, after all, a woman's life would be but a dull business if 'twere not for men, and men that can look like asses too. We should never blame fate for the shortness of our days; our time would hang wretchedly upon our hands.

BEL.   Why, truly, they do help us off with a good share on't. For were there no men in the world, o' my conscience I should be no longer a-dressing than I'm a-saying my prayers. Nay, though it were Sunday; for you know that one may go to church without stays on.

LADY B.   But don't you think emulation might do something? For every woman you see desires to be finer than her neighbour.

BEL.   That's only that the men may like her better than her neighbour. No, if there were no men, adieu fine petticoats; we should be weary of wearing 'em.

LADY B.   And adieu plays; we should be weary of seeing 'em.

BEL.   Adieu Hyde Park; the dust would choke us.

LADY B.   Adieu St. James's; walking would tire us.

BEL.   Adieu London; the smoke would stifle us.

LADY B.   And adieu going to church, for religion would ne'er prevail with us.

BOTH.   Ha, ha, ha, ha, ha!

BEL.   Our confession is so very hearty, sure we merit absolution.

LADY B.   Not unless we go through with't and confess all. So prithee, for the ease of our consciences, let's hide nothing.

BEL.   Agreed.

LADY B.   Why then, I confess that I love to sit in the forefront of a box. For if one sits behind, there's two acts gone perhaps before one's found out. And when I am there, if I perceive the men whispering and looking upon me, you must know I cannot for my life forbear thinking they talk to my advantage. And that sets a thousand little tickling vanities on foot.

BEL.   Just my case for all the world, but go on.

LADY B.   I watch with impatience for the next jest in the play that I may laugh and show my white teeth. If the poet has been dull, and the jest be long a-coming, I pretend to whisper one to my friend, and from thence fall into a short discourse in which I take occasion to show my face in all humours: brisk, pleased, serious, melancholy, languishing. Not that what we say to one another causes any of these alterations, but –

BEL.   Don't trouble yourself to explain, for if I'm not mistaken, you and I have had some of these necessary dialogues before now, with the same intention.

LADY B.   Why, I'll swear, Belinda, some people do give strange agreeable airs to their faces in speaking. Tell me true: did you never practise in the glass?

BEL.   Why, did you?

LADY B.   Yes, faith, many a time.

BEL.   And I too, I own it. Both how to speak myself, and how to look when others speak. But my glass and I could never yet agree what face I should make when they come blurt out with a nasty thing in a play. For all the men presently look upon the women, that's certain; so laugh we must not, though our stays burst for't, because that's telling truth and owning we understand the jest. And to look serious is so dull, when the whole house is a-laughing.

LADY B.   Besides, that looking serious does really betray our knowledge in the matter as much as laughing with the company would do. For if we did not understand the thing we should naturally do like other people.

BEL.   For my part I always take that occasion to blow my nose.

LADY B.   You must blow your nose half off then at some plays.

BEL.   Why don't some reformer or other beat the poet for't?

LADY B.   Because he is not so sure of our private approbation as of our public thanks. Well, sure there is not upon earth so impertinent a thing as women's modesty.

BEL.   Yes, men's fantasque,[15] that obliges us to it. If we quit our modesty they say we lose our charms, and yet they know that very modesty is affectation, and rail at our hypocrisy.

LADY B.   Thus one would think 'twere a hard matter to please 'em,

---

[15] *fantasque* whim.

niece. Yet our kind Mother Nature has given us something that makes amends for all: let our weakness be what it will, mankind will still be weaker, and whilst there is a world, 'tis woman that will govern it. But prithee, one word of poor Constant before we go to bed, if it be but to furnish matter for dreams. I dare swear he's talking of me now, or thinking of me at least, though it be in the middle of his prayers.

BEL. So he ought, I think, for you were pleased to make him a good round advance today, madam.

LADY B. Why, I have e'en plagued him enough to satisfy any reasonable woman; he has besieged me these two years to no purpose.

BEL. And if he besieged you two years more he'll be well enough paid, so he had the plundering of you at last.

LADY B. That may be; but I'm afraid the town won't be able to hold out much longer, for to confess the truth to you, Belinda, the garrison begins to grow mutinous.

BEL. Then the sooner you capitulate the better.

LADY B. Yet methinks I would fain stay a little longer, to see you fixed too, that we might start together, and see who could love longest. What think you if Heartfree should have a month's mind[16] to you?

BEL. Why, faith, I could almost be in love with him for despising that foolish, affected Lady Fanciful, but I'm afraid he's too cold ever to warm himself by my fire.

LADY B. Then he deserves to be froze to death. Would I were a man for your sake, my dear rogue.   *Kissing her*

BEL. You'd wish yourself a woman again for your own, or the men are mistaken. But if I could make a conquest of this son of Bacchus and rival his bottle, what should I do with him? He has no fortune; I can't marry him, and sure you would not have me commit fornication.

LADY B. Why, if you did, child, 'twould be but a good friendly part; if 'twere only to keep me in countenance whilst I commit — you know what.

BEL. Well, if I can't resolve to serve you that way, I may perhaps some other, as much to your satisfaction. But pray, how shall we contrive to see these blades again quickly?

LADY B. We must e'en have recourse to the old way: make 'em an appointment 'twixt jest and earnest; 'twill look like a frolic, and that, you know's a very good thing to save a woman's blushes.

---

[16]*month's mind* strong inclination.

BEL.   You advise well; but where shall it be?

LADY B.   In Spring Garden.[17] But they shan't know their women till their women pull off their masks, for a surprise is the most agreeable thing in the world, and I find myself in a very good humour, ready to do 'em any good turn I can think on.

BEL.   Then pray write 'em the necessary billet, without further delay.

LADY B.   Let's go into your chamber then, and whilst you say your prayers I'll do it, child.   *Exeunt*

[17]*Spring Garden* pleasure gardens established *c.* 1654 at Vauxhall, London.

Act Four

SCENE [ONE]

Covent Garden

Enter LORD RAKE, SIR JOHN *etc., with swords drawn*

LORD RAKE. Is the dog dead?

COL. BULLY. No, damn him, I heard him wheeze.

LORD RAKE. How the witch his wife howled!

COL. BULLY. Ay, she'll alarm the watch presently.

LORD RAKE. Appear, knight, then. Come, you have a good cause to fight for; there's a man murdered.

SIR JOHN. Is there? Then let his ghost be satisfied; for I'll sacrifice a constable to it presently, and burn his body upon his wooden chair.

Enter a TAILOR, *with a bundle under his arm*

COL. BULLY. How now? What have we got here? A thief?

TAILOR. No, an't please you, I'm no thief.

LORD RAKE. That we'll see presently. Here, let the general examine him.

SIR JOHN. Ay, ay, let me examine him, and I'll lay a hundred pound I find him guilty in spite of his teeth – for he looks – like a – sneaking rascal. Come, sirrah, without equivocation or mental reservation, tell me of what opinion you are and what calling, for by them – I shall guess at your morals.

TAILOR. An't please you, I'm a dissenting journeyman tailor.

SIR JOHN. Then, sirrah, you love lying by your religion and theft by your trade. And so, that your punishment may be suitable to your crimes – I'll have you first gagged – and then hanged.

TAILOR. Pray, good worthy gentlemen, don't abuse me. Indeed, I'm an honest man and a good workman, though I say it that should not say it.

SIR JOHN. No words, sirrah, but attend your fate.

LORD RAKE. Let me see what's in that bundle.

TAILOR. An't please you, it's the doctor of the parish's gown.[1]

LORD RAKE. The doctor's gown! Hark you, knight, you won't stick at abusing the clergy, will you?

[1] *gown* For the rewriting of the remainder of this scene, see Appendix B, pp. 671–72.

SIR JOHN.   No, I'm drunk, and I'll abuse anything – but my wife, and her I name – with reverence.

LORD RAKE.   Then you shall wear this gown whilst you charge the watch, that though the blows fall upon you, the scandal may light upon the church.

SIR JOHN.   A generous design – by all the gods. Give it me.

Takes the gown and puts it on

TAILOR.   O dear gentlemen, I shall be quite undone if you take the gown.

SIR JOHN.   Retire, sirrah, and since you carry off your skin – go home and be happy.

TAILOR.   (*Pausing*) I think I had e'en as good follow the gentleman's friendly advice, for if I dispute any longer, who knows but the whim may take him to case[2] me? These courtiers are fuller of tricks than they are of money; they'll sooner cut a man's throat than pay his bill.

Exit

SIR JOHN.   So, how d'ye like my shapes now?

LORD RAKE.   This will do to a miracle. He looks like a bishop going to the holy war. But to your arms, gentlemen, the enemy appears.

Enter CONSTABLE *and* WATCH

WATCH.   Stand! Who goes there? Come before the constable.

SIR JOHN.   The constable's a rascal – and you are the son of a whore.

WATCH.   A good civil answer for a parson, truly.

CONST.   Methinks, sir, a man of your coat might set a better example.

SIR JOHN.   Sirrah, I'll make you know – there are men of my coat can set as bad examples – as you can do, you dog you.

SIR JOHN *strikes the* CONSTABLE. *They knock him down, disarm him and seize him.* LORD RAKE, *etc., run away*

CONST.   So, we have secured the parson, however.

SIR JOHN.   Blood and blood – and blood!

WATCH.   Lord have mercy upon us! How the wicked wretch raves of blood. I'll warrant he has been murdering somebody tonight.

SIR JOHN.   Sirrah, there's nothing got by murder but a halter. My talent lies towards drunkenness and simony.[3]

WATCH.   Why, that now was spoke like a man of parts, neighbour. It's pity he should be so disguised.[4]

SIR JOHN.   You lie. I am not disguised, for I am drunk barefaced.

WATCH.   Look you there again. This is a mad parson, Mr Constable; I'll lay a pot of ale upon's head, he's a good preacher.

CONST.   Come, sir, out of respect to your calling I shan't put you into the roundhouse,[5] but we must secure you in our drawing-room till morning, that you may do no mischief. So come along.

---

[2]*case* skin.   [3]*simony* buying and selling ecclesiastical preferments.
[4]*disguised* drunk.   [5]*roundhouse* lockup.

SIR JOHN. You may put me where you will, sirrah, now you have overcome me; but if I can't do mischief, I'll think of mischief – in spite of your teeth, you dog you. *Exeunt*

SCENE [TWO]

HEARTFREE'S *bedchamber*

Enter HEARTFREE, *solus*

HEART. What the plague ails me? Love? No, I thank you for that; my heart's rock still. Yet 'tis Belinda that disturbs me, that's positive. Well, what of all that? Must I love her for being troublesome? At that rate I might love all the women I meet, egad. But hold. Though I don't love her for disturbing me, yet she may disturb me because I love her. Ay, that may be, faith. I have dreamt of her, that's certain. Well, so I have of my mother; therefore, what's that to the purpose? Ay, but Belinda runs in my mind waking. And so does many a damned thing that I don't care a farthing for. Methinks though, I would fain be talking to her, and yet I have no business. Well, am I the first man that has had a mind to do an impertinent thing?

Enter CONSTANT

CON. How now, Heartfree? What makes you up and dressed so soon? I thought none but lovers quarrelled with their beds. I expected to have found you snoring, as I used to do.

HEART. Why, faith, friend, 'tis the care I have of your affairs that makes me so thoughtful. I have been studying all night how to bring your matter about with Belinda.

CON. With Belinda?

HEART. With my lady, I mean. And, faith, I have mighty hopes on't. Sure you must be very well satisfied with her behaviour to you yesterday.

CON. So well that nothing but a lover's fears can make me doubt of success. But what can this sudden change proceed from?

HEART. Why, you saw her husband beat her, did you not?

CON. That's true. A husband is scarce to be borne upon any terms, much less when he fights with his wife. Methinks she should e'en have cuckolded him upon the very spot, to show that after the battle she was master of the field.

HEART. A council of war of women would infallibly have advised her to't. But, I confess, so agreeable a woman as Belinda deserves a better usage.

CON. Belinda again?

HEART. My lady, I mean. What a pox makes me blunder so today? (*Aside*) A plague of this treacherous tongue.

CON. Prithee look upon me seriously, Heartfree. Now answer me directly. Is it my lady or Belinda employs your careful thoughts thus?

HEART. My lady or Belinda?

CON. In love, by this light, in love!

HEART. In love?

CON. Nay, ne'er deny it; for thou'lt do it so awkwardly 'twill but make the jest sit heavier about thee. My dear friend, I give thee much joy.

HEART. Why, prithee, you won't persuade me to it, will you?

CON. That she's mistress of your tongue, that's plain, and I know you are so honest a fellow, your tongue and heart always go together. But how? But how the devil? Pha! Ha, ha, ha!

HEART. Heyday! Why sure you don't believe it in earnest?

CON. Yes, I do, because I see you deny it in jest.

HEART. Nay, but look you, Ned – a – deny in jest – a – gadzooks, you know I say – a – when a man denies a thing in jest – a –

CON. Pha, ha, ha, ha, ha!

HEART. Nay, then we shall have it. What, because a man stumbles at a word? Did you never make a blunder?

CON. Yes, for I am in love; I own it.

HEART. Then so am I. (*Embracing him*) Now laugh till thy soul's glutted with mirth, but, dear Constant, don't tell the town on't.

CON. Nay then, 'twere almost pity to laugh at thee, after so honest a confession. But tell us a little, Jack. By what new-invented arms has this mighty stroke been given?

HEART. E'en by that unaccountable weapon called *je ne sais quoi*. For everything that can come within the verge of beauty, I have seen it with indifference.

CON. So in few words then: the *je ne sais quoi* has been too hard for the quilted petticoat.

HEART. Egad, I think the *je ne sais quoi* is in the quilted petticoat. At least 'tis certain I ne'er think on't without – a – a *je ne sais quoi* in every part about me.

CON. Well, but have all your remedies lost their virtue? Have you turned her inside out yet?

HEART. I dare not so much as think on't.

CON. But don't the two years' fatigue I have had discourage you?

HEART. Yes, I dread what I foresee, yet cannot quit the enterprise. Like some soldiers whose courage dwells more in their honour than in their nature, on they go, though the body trembles at what the soul makes it undertake.

CON. Nay, if you expect your mistress will use you as your profanations against her sex deserve, you tremble justly. But how do you intend to proceed, friend?

HEART. Thou know'st I'm but a novice. Be friendly and advise me.

CON. Why, look you then. I'd have you – serenade and a – write a song – go to church, look like a fool, be very officious, ogle, write, and lead out.[6] And who knows but in a year or two's time, you may be – called a troublesome puppy and sent about your business.

HEART. That's hard.

CON. Yet thus it oft falls out with lovers, sir.

HEART. Pox on me for making one of the number.

CON. Have a care. Say no saucy things. 'Twill but augment your crime, and if your mistress hears on't, increase your punishment.

HEART. Prithee say something then to encourage me. You know I helped you in your distress.

CON. Why then, to encourage you to perseverance, that you may be thoroughly ill-used for your offences, I'll put you in mind that even the coyest ladies of 'em all are made up of desires as well as we, and though they do hold out a long time, they will capitulate at last. For that thundering engineer, nature, does make such havoc in the town, they must surrender at long run or perish in their own flames.

Enter a FOOTMAN

FOOT. Sir, there's a porter without with a letter. He desires to give it into your own hands.

CON. Call him in. [*Exit* FOOTMAN]

Enter PORTER

What, Jo, is it thee?

PORTER. An't please you, sir, I was ordered to deliver this into your own hands by two well-shaped ladies at the New Exchange.[7] I was at your honour's lodgings, and your servants sent me hither.

CON. 'Tis well. Are you to carry any answer?

PORTER. No, my noble master. They gave me my orders, and whip they were gone, like a maidenhead at fifteen.

CON. Very well. There. *Gives him money*

PORTER. God bless your honour. *Exit*

CON. Now let's see what honest, trusty Jo has brought us. (*Reads*) 'If you and your playfellow can spare time from your business and devotions, don't fail to be at Spring Garden about eight in the evening. You'll find nothing there but women, so you need bring no

[6]*lead out* escort a lady.

[7]*New Exchange* a large, two-storeyed arcaded building, with shops, on the south side of the Strand, popular for promenades.

other arms than what you usually carry about you'. So, playfellow, here's something to stay your stomach till your mistress's dish is ready for you.

HEART.   Some of our old battered acquaintance. I won't go, not I.

CON.   Nay, that you can't avoid. There's honour in the case. 'Tis a challenge and I want a second.

HEART.   I doubt[8] I shall be but a very useless one to you, for I'm so disheartened by this wound Belinda has given me I don't think I shall have courage enough to draw my sword.

CON.   Oh, if that be all, come along. I'll warrant you find sword enough for such enemies as we have to deal withal.   *Exeunt*

SCENE [THREE][9]

At the JUSTICE'S *house*

Enter CONSTABLE, *etc., with* SIR JOHN

CONST.   Come along, sir. I thought to have let you slip this morning because you were a minister, but you are as drunk and as abusive as ever. We'll see what the justice of the peace will say to you.

SIR JOHN.   And you shall see what I'll say to the justice of the peace, sirrah.   *They knock at the door*

Enter SERVANT

CONST.   Pray acquaint his worship we have got an unruly parson here. We are unwilling to expose him, but don't know what to do with him.   *Exit*

SERV.   I'll acquaint my master.

SIR JOHN.   You – constable – what damned justice is this?

CONST.   One that will take care of you, I warrant you.

Enter JUSTICE

JUSTICE.   Well, Mr Constable, what's the disorder here?

CONST.   An't please your worship –

SIR JOHN.   Let me speak and be damned. I'm a divine and can unfold mysteries better than you can do.

JUSTICE.   Sadness, sadness, a minister so overtaken! Pray, sir, give the constable leave to speak, and I'll hear you very patiently, I assure you, sir, I will.

SIR JOHN.   Sir – you are a very civil magistrate. Your most humble servant.

CONST.   An't please your worship then. He has attempted to beat the watch tonight, and swore –

---

[8]*doubt* fear.
[9]*Scene 3* For the alternative version of this scene, see Appendix B, pp. 672–76.

SIR JOHN. You lie.

JUSTICE. Hold, pray, sir, a little.

SIR JOHN. Sir, your very humble servant.

CONST. Indeed, sir, he came at us without any provocation, called us whores and rogues, and laid us on with a great quarter-staff. He was in my Lord Rake's company. They have been playing the devil tonight.

JUSTICE. Hem – hem – pray, sir – May you be chaplain to my lord?

SIR JOHN. Sir – I presume – I may if I will.

JUSTICE. My meaning, sir, is, are you so?

SIR JOHN. Sir – you mean very well.

JUSTICE. He, hem – hem – Under favour, sir, pray answer me directly.

SIR JOHN. Under favour, sir – Do you use to answer directly when you are drunk?

JUSTICE. Good lack, good lack. Here's nothing to be got from him. Pray, sir, may I crave your name?

SIR JOHN. Sir – my name's – (*He hiccups*) Hiccup, sir.

JUSTICE. Hiccup? Doctor Hiccup. I have known a great many country parsons of that name, especially down in the fens. Pray where do you live, sir?

SIR JOHN. Here – and there, sir.

JUSTICE. Why, what a strange man is this? Where do you preach, sir? Have you any cure?[10]

SIR JOHN. Sir – I have – a very good cure – for a clap, at your service.

JUSTICE. Lord have mercy upon us!

SIR JOHN. (*Aside*) This fellow does ask so many impertinent questions I believe, egad, 'tis the justice's wife in the justice's clothes.

JUSTICE. Mr Constable, I vow and protest I don't know what to do with him.

CONST. Truly he has been but a troublesome guest to us all night.

JUSTICE. I think I had e'en best let him go about his business, for I'm unwilling to expose him.

CONST. E'en what your worship thinks fit.

SIR JOHN. Sir – not to interrupt Mr Constable, I have a small favour to ask.

JUSTICE. Sir, I open both my ears to you.

SIR JOHN. Sir, your very humble servant. I have a little urgent business calls upon me, and therefore I desire the favour of you to bring matters to a conclusion.

---

[10]*cure* parish.

JUSTICE.   Sir, if I were sure that business were not to commit more disorders, I would release you.

SIR JOHN.   None – by my priesthood.

JUSTICE.   Then, Mr Constable, you may discharge him.

SIR JOHN.   Sir, your very humble servant. If you please to accept of a bottle –

JUSTICE.   I thank you kindly sir, but I never drink in a morning. Goodbye to ye, sir, goodbye to ye.

SIR JOHN.   Goodbye t'ye, good sir.   *Exit* JUSTICE
So – now, Mr Constable, shall you and I go pick up a whore together?

CONST.   No, thank you, sir; my wife's enough to satisfy any reasonable man.

SIR JOHN.   (*Aside*) He, he, he, he, he! The fool's married then. – Well, you won't go?

CONST.   Not I, truly.

SIR JOHN.   Then I'll go by myself, and you and your wife may be damned.   *Exit*

CONST.   (*Gazing after him*) Why, God-a-mercy, parson!
                                        Exit CONSTABLE, *etc.*

SCENE [FOUR]

Spring Garden

CONSTANT *and* HEARTFREE *cross the stage. As they go off, enter* LADY FANCIFUL *and* MADAMOISELLE, *masked and dogging 'em*

CON.   So, I think we are about the time appointed. Let us walk up this way.   *Exeunt*

LADY F.   Good. Thus far I have dogged 'em without being discovered. 'Tis infallibly some intrigue that brings them to Spring Garden. How my poor heart is torn and wracked with fear and jealousy! Yet let it be anything but that flirt Belinda and I'll try to bear it. But if it prove her, all that's woman in me shall be employed to destroy her.
                          Exeunt after CONSTANT *and* HEARTFREE
        Re-enter CONSTANT *and* HEARTFREE. LADY FANCIFUL *and*
             MADAMOISELLE *still following at a distance*

CON.   I see no females yet that have anything to say to us. I'm afraid we are bantered.

HEART.   I wish we were, for I'm in no humour to make either them or myself merry.

CON.   Nay, I'm sure you'll make them merry enough if I tell 'em why you are dull. But prithee, why so heavy and sad before you begin to be ill-used?

HEART.   For the same reason, perhaps, that you are so brisk and well pleased; because both pains and pleasures are generally more considerable in prospect than when they come to pass.

Enter LADY BRUTE *and* BELINDA, *masked and poorly dressed*

CON.   How now, who are these? Not our game, I hope.

HEART.   If they are, we are e'en well enough served, to come hunting here, when we had so much better game in chase elsewhere.

LADY F.   (*To* MADAMOISELLE). So, those are their ladies, without doubt. But I'm afraid that doily stuff[11] is not worn for want of better clothes. They are the very shape and size of Belinda and her aunt.

MADAM.   So day be inteed, matam.

LADY F.   We'll slip into this close arbour, where we may hear all they say.   *Exeunt* LADY FANCIFUL *and* MADAMOISELLE

LADY B.   What, are you afraid of us, gentleman?

HEART.   Why, truly, I think we may, if appearance don't lie.

BEL.   Do you always find women what they appear to be, sir?

HEART.   No, forsooth, but I seldom find 'em better than they appear to be.

BEL.   Then the outside's best you think?

HEART.   'Tis the honestest.

CON.   Have a care, Heartfree; you are relapsing again.

LADY B.   Why, does the gentleman use to rail at women?

CON.   He has done formerly.

BEL.   I suppose he had very good cause for't. They did not use you so well as you thought you deserved, sir?

LADY B.   They made themselves merry at your expense, sir?

BEL.   Laughed when you sighed?

LADY B.   Slept while you were waking?

BEL.   Had your porter beat?

LADY B.   And threw your billets doux in the fire?

HEART.   Heyday, I shall do more than rail presently.

BEL.   Why, you won't beat us, will you?

HEART.   I don't know but I may.

CON.   What the devil's coming here? Sir John in a gown? And drunk, i' faith.

Enter SIR JOHN

SIR JOHN.   What a pox! Here's Constant, Heartfree — and two whores, egad. O you covetous rogues! What, have you never a spare punk for your friend? But I'll share with you.

He seizes both the women

---

[11]*doily stuff* a light, inexpensive woollen cloth, invented by Thomas Doyley, a late-seventeenth-century linen-draper in the Strand.

HEART. Why, what the plague have you been doing, knight?

SIR JOHN. Why, I have been beating the watch and scandalising the clergy.[12]

HEART. A very good account, truly.

SIR JOHN. And what do you think I'll do next?

CON. Nay, that no man can guess.

SIR JOHN. Why, if you'll let me sup with you, I'll treat both your strumpets.

LADY B. (*Aside*) O Lord, we are undone.

HEART. No, we can't sup together, because we have some affairs elsewhere. But if you'll accept of these two ladies, we'll be so complaisant to you to resign our right in 'em.

BEL. (*Aside*) Lord, what shall we do?

SIR JOHN. Let me see, their clothes are such damned clothes they won't pawn for the reckoning.[13]

HEART. Sir John, your servant. Rapture attend you.

CON. Adieu, ladies. Make much of the gentleman.

LADY B. Why sure you won't leave us in the hands of a drunken fellow to abuse us?

SIR JOHN. Who do you call a drunken fellow, you slut you? I'm a man of quality; the king has made me a knight.

HEART. Ay, ay, you are in good hands. Adieu, adieu. *Runs off*

LADY B. The devil's hands! Let me go, or I'll – For heaven's sake, protect us!

She breaks from him, runs to CONSTANT, *twitching off her mask and clapping it on again*

SIR JOHN. I'll devil you, you jade you. I'll demolish your ugly face.

CON. Hold a little, knight; she swoons.

SIR JOHN. I'll swoon her.

CON. Hey, Heartfree!

Re-enter HEARTFREE. BELINDA *runs to him and shows her face*

HEART. O heavens! My dear creature, stand there a little.

CON. Pull him off, Jack.

HEART. Hold, mighty man. Look you, sir, we did but jest with you. These are ladies of our acquaintance that we had a mind to frighten a little, but now you must leave us.

SIR JOHN. Oons, I won't leave you, not I.

HEART. Nay, but you must though, and therefore make no words on't.

SIR JOHN. Then you are a couple of damned uncivil fellows; and I hope your punks will give you sauce to your mutton.[14] *Exit*

[12]For the alternative speech, see Appendix B, p. 676.
[13]*reckoning* tavern bill.
[14]*give . . . mutton* make you pay a high price, i.e. give you a venereal disease.

LADY B.   Oh, I shall never come to myself again, I'm so frightened.

CON.   'Twas a narrow scape indeed.

BEL.   Women must have frolics, you see, whatever they cost 'em.

HEART.   This might have proved a dear one, though.

LADY B.   You are the more obliged to us for the risk we run upon your accounts.

CON.   And I hope you'll acknowledge something due to our knight-errantry, ladies. This is the second time we have delivered you.

LADY B.   'Tis true; and since we see fate has designed you for our guardians, 'twill make us the more willing to trust ourselves in your hands. But you must not have the worse opinion of us for our innocent frolic.

HEART.   Ladies, you may command our opinions in everything that is to your advantage.

BEL.   Then, sir, I command you to be of opinion that women are sometimes better than they appear to be.

LADY BRUTE *and* CONSTANT *talk apart*

HEART.   Madam, you have made a convert of me in everything. I'm grown a fool. I could be fond of a woman.

BEL.   I thank you, sir, in the name of the whole sex.

HEART.   Which sex nothing but yourself could ever have atoned for.

BEL.   Now has my vanity a devilish itch to know in what my merit consists.

HEART.   In your humility, madam, that keeps you ignorant it consists at all.

BEL.   One other compliment with that serious face, and I hate you forever after.

HEART.   Some women love to be abused. Is that it you would be at?

BEL.   No, not that neither. But I'd have men talk plainly what's fit for women to hear, without putting 'em either to a real or an affected blush.

HEART.   Why then, in as plain terms as I can find to express myself, I could love you even to — matrimony itself a'most, egad.

BEL.   Just as Sir John did her ladyship there. What think you? Don't you believe one month's time might bring you down to the same indifference, only clad in a little better manners perhaps. Well, you men are unaccountable things: mad till you have your mistresses, and then stark mad till you are rid of 'em again. Tell me honestly, is not your patience put to a much severer trial after possession than before?

HEART.   With a great many, I must confess, it is, to our eternal scandal; but I — Dear creature, do but try me.

BEL. That's the surest way indeed to know, but not the safest. (*To* LADY BRUTE) Madam, are not you for taking a turn in the Great Walk? It's almost dark; nobody will know us.

LADY B. Really I find myself something idle, Belinda. Besides, I dote upon this little odd private corner. But don't let my lazy fancy confine you.

CON. (*Aside*) So, she would be left alone with me. That's well.

BEL. Well, we'll take one turn and come to you again. (*To* HEARTFREE) Come, sir, shall we go pry into the secrets of the garden? Who knows what discoveries we may make?

HEART. Madam, I'm at your service.

CON. (*To* HEARTFREE *aside*) Don't make too much haste back, for — d'ye hear — I may be busy.

HEART. Enough.   *Exeunt* BELINDA *and* HEARTFREE

LADY B. Sure you think me scandalously free, Mr Constant. I'm afraid I shall lose your good opinion of me.

CON. My good opinion, madam, is like your cruelty, never to be removed.

LADY B. But if I should remove my cruelty, then there's an end of your good opinion.

CON. There is not so strict an alliance between 'em neither. 'Tis certain I should love you then better, if that be possible, than I do now; and where I love I always esteem.

LADY B. Indeed, I doubt you much. Why, suppose you had a wife, and she should entertain a gallant?

CON. If I gave her just cause, how could I justly condemn her?

LADY B. Ah, but you'd differ widely about just causes.

CON. But blows can bear no dispute.

LADY B. Nor ill manners much, truly.

CON. Then no woman upon earth has so just a cause as you have.

LADY B. Oh, but a faithful wife is a beautiful character.

CON. To a deserving husband, I confess it is.

LADY B. But can his faults release my duty?

CON. In equity, without doubt. And where laws dispense with equity, equity should dispense with laws.

LADY B. Pray let's leave this dispute, for you men have as much witchcraft in your arguments as women have in their eyes.

CON. But whilst you attack me with your charms, 'tis but reasonable I assault you with mine.

LADY B. The case is not the same. What mischief we do we can't help, and therefore are to be forgiven.

CON. Beauty soon obtains pardon, for the pain that it gives when it applies the balm of compassion to the wound. But a fine face and a hard heart is almost as bad as an ugly face and a soft one; both very troublesome to many a poor gentleman.

LADY B.   Yes, and to many a poor gentlewoman too, I can assure you. But, pray, which of 'em is it that most afflicts you?

CON.   Your glass and conscience will inform you, madam. But, for heaven's sake – for now I must be serious – if pity or gratitude can move you, (*Taking her hand*) if constancy and truth have power to tempt you, if love, if adoration can affect you, give me at least some hopes that time may do what you perhaps mean never to perform. 'Twill ease my sufferings, though not quench my flame.

LADY B.   Your sufferings eased, your flame would soon abate, and that I would preserve, not quench it, sir.

CON.   Would you preserve it, nourish it with favours; for that's the food it naturally requires.

LADY B.   Yet on that natural food 'twould surfeit soon, should I resolve to grant all that you would ask.

CON.   And in refusing all, you starve it. Forgive me, therefore, since my hunger rages, if I at last grow wild, and in my frenzy force at least this from you. (*Kissing her hand*) Or if you'd have my flame soar higher still, then grant me this and this and this and thousands more. (*Kissing first her hand, then her neck*) – (*Aside*) For now's the time; she melts into compassion.

LADY B.   (*Aside*) Poor coward virtue, how it shuns the battle. – O heavens, let me go!

CON.   Ay, go, ay. Where shall we go, my charming angel? Into this private arbour. Nay, let's lose no time; moments are precious.

LADY B.   And lovers wild. Pray, let us stop here, at least for this time.

CON.   'Tis impossible. He that has power over you can have none over himself.

LADY B.   Ah, I'm lost.

As he is forcing her into the arbour, LADY FANCIFUL *and* MADAMOI-SELLE *bolt out upon them and run over the stage*

LADY F.   Fie, fie, fie, fie, fie.

MADAM.   Fie, fie, fie, fie, fie.

CON.   Death and furies, who are these?

LADY B.   O heavens, I'm out of my wits! If they knew me, I'm ruined.

CON.   Don't be frightened. Ten thousand to one they are strangers to you.

LADY B.   Whatever they are, I won't stay here a moment longer.

CON.   Whither will you go?

LADY B.   Home, as if the devil were in me. Lord, where's this Belinda now?

     Enter BELINDA *and* HEARTFREE

Oh, it's well you are come. I'm so frightened my hair stands on end.
Let's be gone, for heaven's sake.

BEL.   Lord, what's the matter?

LADY B.   The devil's the matter! We are discovered. Here's a couple
of women have done the most impertinent thing. Away, away,
away, away, away!   *Exeunt running*

    Re-enter LADY FANCIFUL *and* MADAMOISELLE

LADY F.   Well, Madamoiselle, 'tis a prodigious thing how women can
suffer filthy fellows to grow so familiar with 'em.

MADAM.   Ah, matam, *il n'y a rien de si naturel.*[15]

LADY F.   Fie, fie, fie. But, oh my heart! O jealousy! O torture! I'm on
the rack. What shall I do? My lover's lost; I ne'er shall see him mine.
(*Pausing*) But I may be revenged, and that's the same thing. Ah,
sweet revenge! Thou welcome thought, thou healing balsam to my
wounded soul. Be but propitious on this one occasion, I'll place my
heaven in thee for all my life to come.

       To woman, how indulgent nature's kind.
       No blast of fortune long disturbs her mind.
       Compliance to her fate supports her still;
       If love won't make her happy, mischief will.   *Exeunt*

[15] *il n'y ... naturel* there is nothing so natural.

Act Five

SCENE [ONE]

LADY FANCIFUL'S *house*

Enter LADY FANCIFUL *and* MADAMOISELLE

LADY F.   Well, Madamoiselle, did you dog the filthy things?

MADAM.   *Oh, que oui,* matam.

LADY F.   And where are they?

MADAM.   *Au logis.*[1]

LADY F.   What, men and all?

MADAM.   *Tous ensemble.*

LADY F.   O confidence! What, carry their fellows to their own house?

MADAM.   *C'est que le mari n'y est pas.*[2]

LADY F.   No, so I believe truly. But he shall be there, and quickly too, if I can find him out. Well, 'tis a prodigious thing to see, when men and women get together, how they fortify one another in their impudence. But if that drunken fool her husband be to be found in e'er a tavern in town, I'll send him amongst 'em. I'll spoil their sport.

MADAM.   *En verité,* matam, *ce serait dommage.*[3]

LADY F.   'Tis in vain to oppose it, Madamoiselle; therefore, never go about it. For I am the steadiest creature in the world when I have determined to do mischief. So, come along.   *Exeunt*

SCENE [TWO]

SIR JOHN BRUTE'S *house*

Enter CONSTANT, HEARTFREE, LADY BRUTE, BELINDA and LOVEWELL

LADY B.   But are you sure you don't mistake, Lovewell?

LOVE.   Madam, I saw 'em all go into the tavern together, and my master was so drunk he could scarce stand.   [*Exit*]

LADY B.   Then, gentlemen, I believe we may venture to let you stay

---

[1] *Au logis* At home.
[2] *C'est . . . pas* It is because the husband isn't there.
[3] *En . . . dommage* Truly, madam, it would be a pity.

and play at cards with us for an hour or two, for they'll scarce part till morning.

BEL. I think 'tis pity they should ever part –

CON. The company that's here, madam.

LADY B. Then, sir, the company that's here must remember to part itself in time.

CON. Madam, we don't intend to forfeit your favours by an indiscreet usage of this. The moment you give us the signal we shan't fail to make our retreat.

LADY B. Upon those conditions then, let us sit down to cards.

Enter LOVEWELL

LOVE. O Lord, madam, here's my master just staggering in upon you. He has been quarrelsome yonder, and they have kicked him out of the company.

LADY B. Into the closet, gentlemen, for heaven's sake. I'll wheedle him to bed if possible. CONSTANT *and* HEARTFREE *run into the closet*
Enter SIR JOHN, *all dirt and bloody*
Ah, ah, he's all over blood.

SIR JOHN. What the plague does the woman – squall for? Did you never see a man in pickle before?

LADY B. Lord, where have you been?

SIR JOHN. I have been at – cuffs.

LADY B. I fear that is not all. I hope you are not wounded.

SIR JOHN. Sound as a roach, wife.

LADY B. I'm mighty glad to hear it.

SIR JOHN. You know – I think you lie.

LADY B. I know you do me wrong to think so then. For heaven's my witness, I had rather see my own blood trickle down than yours.

SIR JOHN. Then will I be crucified.

LADY B. 'Tis a hard fate I should not be believed.

SIR JOHN. 'Tis a damned atheistical age, wife.

LADY B. I am sure I have given you a thousand tender proofs how great my care is of you. Nay, spite of all your cruel thoughts I'll still persist, and at this moment, if I can, persuade you to lie down and sleep a little.

SIR JOHN. Why, – do you think I am drunk – you slut you?

LADY B. Heaven forbid I should! But I'm afraid you are feverish. Pray let me feel your pulse.

SIR JOHN. Stand off and be damned.

LADY B. Why, I see your distemper in your very eyes. You are all on fire. Pray go to bed. Let me entreat you.

SIR JOHN. Come, kiss me then.

LADY B. (*Kissing him*) There. Now go. – (*Aside*) He stinks like poison.

SIR JOHN.   I see it goes damnably against your stomach — and therefore — kiss me again.

LADY B.   Nay, now you fool me.

SIR JOHN.   Do't, I say.

LADY B.   (*Aside*) Ah, Lord have mercy upon me! — Well, there. Now will you go?

SIR JOHN.   Now, wife, you shall see my gratitude. You give me two kisses — I'll give you — two hundred.   *Kisses and tumbles her*

LADY B.   O Lord! Pray, Sir John, be quiet. — [*Aside*] Heavens, what a pickle am I in!

BEL.   (*Aside*) If I were in her pickle, I'd call my gallant out of the closet, and he should cudgel him soundly.

SIR JOHN.   So, now, you being as dirty and as nasty as myself, we may go pig together. But first I must have a cup of your cold tea,⁴ wife.   *Going to the closet*

LADY B.   [*Aside*] Oh, I'm ruined! — There's none there, my dear.

SIR JOHN.   I'll warrant you I'll find some, my dear.

LADY B.   You can't open the door; the lock's spoiled. I have been turning and turning the key this half hour to no purpose. I'll send for the smith tomorrow.

SIR JOHN.   There's ne'er a smith in Europe can open a door with more expedition than I can do. As for example — Pou! (*He bursts open the door with his foot*) How now? What the devil have we got here? Constant — Heartfree — and two whores again, egad. This is the worst cold tea — that ever I met with in my life.

     Enter CONSTANT *and* HEARTFREE

LADY B.   (*Aside*) O Lord, what will become of us?

SIR JOHN.   Gentlemen — I am your very humble servant — I give you many thanks — I see you take care of my family — I shall do all I can to return the obligation.

CON.   Sir, how oddly soever this business may appear to you, you would have no cause to be uneasy if you knew the truth of all things. Your lady is the most virtuous woman in the world, and nothing has passed but an innocent frolic.

HEART.   Nothing else, upon my honour, sir.

SIR JOHN.   You are both very civil⁵ gentlemen — and my wife there is a very civil gentlewoman; therefore I don't doubt that many civil things have passed between you. Your very humble servant.

LADY B.(*Aside to* CONSTANT) Pray be gone. He's so drunk he can't hurt you tonight, and tomorrow morning you shall hear from us.

---

⁴*cold tea* a contemporary euphemism for brandy. See Pope, *The Rape of the Lock*, III, 8.

⁵*civil* polite, decent, with a *double entendre*.

CON. I'll obey you, madam. Sir, when you are cool, you'll understand reason better. So then I shall take the pains to inform you. If
not, I wear a sword, sir, and so goodbye to you. Come along,
Heartfree.   [*Exeunt* CONSTANT *and* HEARTFREE]

SIR JOHN.   Wear a sword, sir? And what of all that, sir? He comes to
my house, eats my meat, lies with my wife, dishonours my family,
gets a bastard to inherit my estate, and when I ask a civil account of
all this – 'Sir', says he, 'I wear a sword'. Wear a sword, sir? 'Yes, sir',
says he, 'I wear a sword'. It may be a good answer at cross purposes,[6]
but 'tis a damned one to a man in my whimsical circumstance. 'Sir',
says he, 'I wear a sword'. (*To* LADY BRUTE) And what do you wear
now? Ha? Tell me. (*Sitting down in a great chair*) What, you are
modest and can't? Why then, I'll tell you, you slut you. You wear –
an impudent lewd face – a damned designing heart – and a tail – a
tail full of –   *He falls fast asleep snoring*

LADY B.   So, thanks to kind heaven, he's fast for some hours.

BEL.   'Tis well he is so, that we may have time to lay our story
handsomely; for we must lie like the devil to bring ourselves off.

LADY B.   What shall we say, Belinda?

BEL.   (*Musing*) I'll tell you. It must all light upon Heartfree and I.
We'll say he has courted me some time, but for reasons unknown to
us has ever been very earnest the thing might be kept from Sir John.
That therefore hearing him upon the stairs, he run into the closet,
though against our will, and Constant with him, to prevent jealousy.
And to give this a good impudent face of truth – that I may deliver
you from the trouble you are in – I'll e'en, if he pleases, marry him.

LADY B.   I'm beholding to you, cousin; but that would be carrying the
jest a little too far for your own sake. You know he's a younger
brother,[7] and has nothing.

BEL.   'Tis true, but I like him and have fortune enough to keep above
extremity. I can't say I would live with him in a cell upon love and
bread and butter, but I had rather have the man I love and a middle
state of life than that gentleman in the chair there and twice your
ladyship's splendour.

LADY B.   In truth, niece, you are in the right on't, for I am very uneasy
in my ambition. But perhaps, had I married as you'll do, I might have
been as ill-used.

BEL.   Some risk, I do confess; there always is. But if a man has the
least spark, either of honour or good nature, he can never use a
woman ill that loves him and makes his fortune both. Yet I must

[6]*cross purposes* a parlour game with mixed up questions and answers.

[7]*younger brother* Within the rules of primogeniture the elder or eldest son (or,
rarely, daughter) inherited the father's estate.

own to you some little struggling I still have with this teasing ambition of ours. For pride, you know, is as natural to a woman as 'tis to a saint. I can't help being fond of this rogue, and yet it goes to my heart to think I must never whisk to Hyde Park with above a pair of horses, have no coronet upon my coach, nor a page to carry up my train. But above all, that business of place[8] – Well, taking place is a noble prerogative.

LADY B. Especially after a quarrel.

BEL. Or of a rival. But pray say no more on't, for fear I change my mind. For o' my conscience, were't not for your affair in the balance, I should go near to pick up some odious man of quality yet, and only take poor Heartfree for a gallant.

LADY B. Then him you must have, however things go?

BEL. Yes.

LADY B. Why, we may pretend what we will, but 'tis a hard matter to live without the man we love.

BEL. Especially when we are married to the man we hate. Pray tell me, do the men of the town ever believe us virtuous when they see us do so?

LADY B. Oh no; nor indeed hardly, let us do what we will. They most of 'em think there is no such thing as virtue, considered in the strictest notions of it; and therefore when you hear 'em say such a one is a woman of reputation, they only mean she's a woman of discretion. For they consider we have no more religion than they have, nor so much morality. And between you and I, Belinda, I'm afraid the want of inclination seldom protects any of us.

BEL. But what think you of the fear of being found out?

LADY B. I think that never kept any woman virtuous long. We are not such cowards neither. No, let us once pass fifteen, and we have too good an opinion of our own cunning to believe the world can penetrate into what we would keep a secret. And in short, we cannot reasonably blame the men for judging of us by themselves.

BEL. But sure we are not so wicked as they are, after all.

LADY B. We are as wicked, child, but our vice lies another way. Men have more courage than we, so they commit more bold, impudent sins. They quarrel, fight, swear, drink, blaspheme, and the like. Whereas we, being cowards, only backbite, tell lies, cheat at cards, and so forth. But 'tis late. Let's end our discourse for tonight, and, out of an excess of charity, take a small care of that nasty drunken thing there. Do but look at him, Belinda.

BEL. Ah, 'tis a savoury dish.

[8] *place* rank.

LADY B. As savoury as 'tis, I'm cloyed with't. Prithee call the butler to take away.

BEL. Call the butler? Call the scavenger! (*To a servant within*) Who's there? Call Razor. Let him take away his master, scour him clean with a little soap and sand, and so put him to bed.

LADY B. Come, Belinda, I'll e'n lie with you tonight, and in the morning we'll send for our gentlemen to set this matter even.

BEL. With all my heart.

LADY B. [*To* SIR JOHN] Good night, my dear. *Making a low curtsey*

BOTH. Ha, ha, ha! *Exeunt*

    Enter RAZOR

RAZOR. My lady there's a wag, my master there's a cuckold. Marriage is a slippery thing. Women have depraved appetites. My lady's a wag. I have heard all, I have seen all, I understand all, and I'll tell all; for my little Frenchwoman loves news dearly. This story'll gain her heart or nothing will. (*To his master*) Come, sir, your head's too full of fumes at present to make room for your jealousy; but I reckon we shall have rare work with you when your pate's empty. Come, to your kennel, you cuckoldly drunken sot you. *Carries him out upon his back*

SCENE [THREE]

LADY FANCIFUL'S *house*

    Enter LADY FANCIFUL *and* MADAMOISELLE

LADY F. But why did not you tell me before, Madamoiselle, that Razor and you were fond?

MADAM. De modesty hinder me, matam.

LADY F. Why truly, modesty does often hinder us from doing things we have an extravagant mind to. But does he love you well enough yet to do anything you bid him? Do you think to oblige you he would speak scandal?

MADAM. Matam, to oblige your ladyship he shall speak blasphemy.

LADY F. Why then, Madamoiselle, I'll tell you what you shall do. You shall engage him to tell his master all that passed at Spring Garden. I have a mind he should know what a wife and a niece he has got.

MADAM. *Il le fera,*[9] matam.

    Enter a FOOTMAN, *who speaks to* MADAMOISELLE *apart*

[9] *Il le fera* He will do it.

FOOT. Madamoiselle, yonder's Mr Razor desires to speak with you.

MADAM. Tell him I come presently. *Exit* FOOTMAN
Razor be dare, matam.

LADY F. That's fortunate. Well, I'll leave you together. And if you find him stubborn, Madamoiselle – hark you – don't refuse him a few reasonable liberties to put him into humour.

MADAM. *Laissez-moi faire.*[10] *Exit* LADY FANCIFUL

RAZOR *peeps in, and seeing* LADY FANCIFUL *gone, runs to* MADAMOISELLE, *takes her about the neck and kisses her*
How now, confidence?

RAZOR. How now, modesty?

MADAM. Who make you so familiar, sirrah?

RAZOR. My impudence, hussy.

MADAM. Stand off, rogue-face.

RAZOR. Ah, Madamoiselle, great news at our house.

MADAM. Why, wat be de matter?

RAZOR. The matter? Why, uptails all's[11] the matter.

MADAM. *Tu te mocque de moi.*[12]

RAZOR. Now do you long to know the particulars – the time when, the place where, the manner how, but I won't tell you a word more.

MADAM. Nay, den dou kill me, Razor.

RAZOR. Come, kiss me then. *Clapping his hands behind him*

MADAM. Nay, pridee tell me.

RAZOR. Goodbye to ye. *Going*

MADAM. Hold, hold. I will kiss dee. *Kissing him*

RAZOR. So, that's civil. Why now, my pretty poll,[13] my goldfinch,[14] my little water wagtail,[15] you must know that – Come, kiss me again.

MADAM. I won't kiss dee no more.

RAZOR. Goodbye to ye.

MADAM. *Doucement.*[16] Dare. (*Kissing him*) *Es tu content?*

RAZOR. So, now I'll tell thee all. Why, the news is that cuckoldom in folio is newly printed, and matrimony in quarto is just going into the press. Will you buy any books, Madamoiselle?

MADAM. *Tu parle comme un libraire.*[17] De devil no understand dee.

RAZOR. Why, then, that I may make myself intelligible to a waiting-woman, I'll speak like a valet de chambre. My lady has cuckolded my master.

---

[10]*Laissez-moi faire* Leave it to me.
[11]*uptails all* great confusion; the name of an old song, c. 1610, and a card game.
[12]*Tu . . . moi* You make fun of me. [13]*poll* parrot.
[14]*goldfinch* slang, one who is well to do. [15]*wagtail* prostitute.
[16]*Doucement* Gently. [17]*Tu . . . libraire.* You talk like a bookseller.

MADAM. *Bon.*

RAZOR. Which we take very ill from her hands, I can tell her that. We can't yet prove matter of fact upon her.

MADAM. *N'importe.*[18]

RAZOR. But we can prove that matter of fact had like to have been upon her.

MADAM. *Oui da.*

RAZOR. For we have such bloody circumstances –

MADAM. *Sans doute.*

RAZOR. That any man of parts may draw tickling conclusions from 'em.

MADAM. *Fort bien.*

RAZOR. We have found a couple of tight, well-built gentlemen stuffed into her ladyship's closet.

MADAM. *Le diable!*

RAZOR. And I, in my particular person, have discovered a most damnable plot how to persuade my poor master that all this hide-and-seek, this will-in-the-wisp, has no other meaning than a Christian marriage for sweet Mrs Belinda.

MADAM. *Une mariage? Ah, les drôlesses!*[19]

RAZOR. Don't you interrupt me, hussy. 'Tis agreed, I say. And my innocent lady, to wriggle herself out at the back door of the business, turns marriage-bawd to her niece, and resolves to deliver up her fair body to be tumbled and mumbled by that young liquorish whipster, Heartfree. Now are you satisfied?

MADAM. No.

RAZOR. Right[20] woman, always gaping for more!

MADAM. Dis be all den, dat dou know?

RAZOR. All? Ay, and a good deal too, I think.

MADAM. Dou be fool, dou know noting. *Écoute, mon pauvre* Razor.[21] Dou see des two eyes? Des two eyes have see de devil.

RAZOR. The woman's mad.

MADAM. In Spring Garden dat rogue Constant met dy lady.

RAZOR. *Bon.*

MADAM. I'll tell dee no more.

RAZOR. Nay, prithee, my swan.

MADAM. Come, kiss me den.

> *Clapping her hands behind her, as he had done before*

RAZOR. I won't kiss you, not I.

---

[18]*N'importe* It doesn't matter.   [19]*drôlesses* strumpets.

[20]*Right* Promiscuous.

[21]*Écoute ... Razor* 'Listen, my dear Razor' (said with sarcasm).

MADAM.   Adieu.

RAZOR.   Hold. (*Gives her a hearty kiss*) Now proceed.

MADAM.   *À ça.*[22] I hide myself in one cunning place, where I hear all
and see all. First de drunken master come *mal à propos*;[23] but de sot
no know his own dear wife, so he leave her to her sport. Den de game
begin. (*As she speaks,* RAZOR *still acts the man and she the woman*)
De lover say soft ting. De lady look upon de ground. He take her by
de hand. She turn her head one oder way. Den he squeeze very hard.
Den she pull – very softly. Den he take her in his arm. Den she give
him leetel pat. Den he kiss her *tétons*.[24] Den she say, 'Pish, nay, see'.
Den he tremble. Den she – sigh. Den he pull her into de arbour. Den
she pinch him.

RAZOR.   Ay, but not so hard, you baggage you.

MADAM.   Den he grow bold. She grow weak. He tro her down. *Il
tombe dessus. Le diable assiste. Il emporte tout.*[25]

        RAZOR *struggles with her, as if he would throw her down*
Stand off, sirrah!

RAZOR.   You have set me afire, you jade you.

MADAM.   Den go to de river and quench dyself.

RAZOR.   What an unnatural harlot 'tis!

MADAM.   (*Looking languishingly on him*) Razor.

RAZOR.   Madamoiselle.

MADAM.   Dou no love me?

RAZOR.   Not love thee? More than a Frenchman does soup.

MADAM.   Den dou will refuse noting dat I bid dee?

RAZOR.   Don't bid me be damned then.

MADAM.   No. Only tell dy master all I have tell dee of dy laty.

RAZOR.   Why, you little malicious strumpet you! Should you like to
be served so?

MADAM.   Dou dispute den? Adieu.

RAZOR.   Hold. But why wilt thou make me to be such a rogue, my
dear?

MADAM.   *Voilà un vrai Anglais! Il est amoureux et cependant il veut
raisonner. Va t'en au diable.*[26]

RAZOR.   Hold once more. In hopes thou'lt give me up thy body, I
resign thee up my soul.

MADAM.   *Bon. Écoute donc:* If dou fail me, I never see dee more; if
dou obey me, *je m'abandonné à toi.*[27]

---

[22]*A ça* Well then.   [23]*mal à propos* at the wrong moment.
[24]*tétons* breasts.
[25]*Il . . . tout* He falls on top. The devil helps. He conquers all.
[26]*Voilà . . . diable* There's a real Englishman! He is in love and still he wants to
debate. Go to the devil.   [27]*je . . . toi* I shall give myself to you.

She takes him about the neck and gives him a smacking kiss, and exit

RAZOR. (*Licking his lips*) Not be a rogue? *Amor vincit omnia.* Exit

Enter LADY FANCIFUL *and* MADAMOISELLE

LADY F. Marry, say ye? Will the two things marry?

MADAM. *On le va faire,*[28] matam.

LADY F. Look you, Madamoiselle, in short, I can't bear it. No, I find I can't. If once I see 'em abed together, I shall have ten thousand thoughts in my head will make me run distracted. Therefore run and call Razor back immediately, for something must be done to stop this impertinent wedding. If I can but defer it four and twenty hours, I'll make such work about town with that little pert slut's reputation, he shall as soon marry a witch.

MADAM. (*Aside*) *La voilà bien intentionée!*[29]　　　　　　*Exeunt*

SCENE [FOUR]

CONSTANT'S *lodgings*

Enter CONSTANT *and* HEARTFREE

CON. But what dost think will come of this business?

HEART. 'Tis easier to think what will not come on't.

CON. What's that?

HEART. A challenge. I know the knight too well for that. His dear body will always prevail upon his noble soul to be quiet.

CON. But though he dare not challenge me, perhaps he may venture to challenge his wife.

HEART. Not if you whisper him in the ear, you won't have him do't, and there's no other way left that I see. For as drunk as he was, he'll remember you and I were where we should not be, and I don't think him quite blockhead enough yet to be persuaded we were got into his wife's closet only to peep in her prayer book.

Enter SERVANT, *with a letter*

SERV. Sir, here's a letter. A porter brought it.　　　　　　*Exit*

CON. O ho, here's instructions for us. (*Reads*) 'The accident that has happened has touched our invention to the quick. We would fain come off without your help, but find that's impossible. In a word, the whole business must be thrown upon a matrimonial intrigue between your friend and mine. But if the parties are not fond enough to go quite through with the matter, 'tis sufficient for our turn they own the design. We'll find pretences enough to break the match.

[28]*On . . . faire* That's being arranged
[29]*La . . . intentionée* There's good intentions indeed!

Adieu'. Well, woman for invention! How long would my blockhead have been a-producing this? Hey, Heartfree! What, musing, man? Prithee be cheerful. What say'st thou, friend, to this matrimonial remedy?

HEART. Why, I say it's worse than the disease.

CON. Here's a fellow for you! There's beauty and money on her side, and love up to the ears on his, and yet –

HEART. And yet, I think I may reasonably be allowed to boggle at marrying the niece, in the very moment that you are a-debauching the aunt.

CON. Why truly, there may be something in that. But have not you a good opinion enough of your own parts to believe you could keep a wife to yourself?

HEART. I should have, if I had a good opinion enough of hers to believe that she could do as much by me. For to do 'em right after all, the wife seldom rambles till the husband shows her the way.

CON. 'Tis true. A man of real worth scarce ever is a cuckold but by his own fault. Women are not naturally lewd; there must be something to urge 'em to it. They'll cuckold a churl out of revenge, a fool because they despise him, a beast because they loath him. But when they make bold with a man they once had a well-grounded value for, 'tis because they first see themselves neglected by him.

HEART. Nay, were I well assured that I should never grow Sir John, I ne'er should fear Belinda'd play my lady. But our weakness, thou know'st, my friend, consists in that very change we so impudently throw upon, indeed, a steadier and more generous sex.

CON. Why, faith, we are a little impudent in that matter; that's the truth on't. But this is wonderful, to see you grown so warm an advocate for those but t'other day you took so much pains to abuse.

HEART. All revolutions run into extremes. The bigot makes the boldest atheist, and the coyest saint the most extravagant strumpet. But prithee, advise me in this good and evil, this life and death, this blessing and cursing, that is set before me; shall I marry or die a maid?

CON. Why, faith, Heartfree, matrimony is like an army going to engage. Love's the forlorn hope, which is soon cut off; the marriage knot is the main body, which may stand buff a long, long time; and repentance is the rear-guard, which rarely gives ground as long as the main battle has a being.

HEART. Conclusion then: you advise me to whore on, as you do.

CON. That's not concluded yet. For though marriage be a lottery in which there are a wondrous many blanks, yet there is one inestimable lot in which the only heaven on earth is written. Would your kind fate but guide your hand to that, though I were wrapped in all that luxury itself could clothe me with, I still should envy you.

HEART.   And justly too; for to be capable of loving one doubtless is better than to possess a thousand. But how far that capacity's in me, alas I know not.

CON.   But would you know?

HEART.   I would so.

CON.   Matrimony will inform you. Come, one flight of resolution carries you to the land of experience, where in a very moderate time you'll know the capacity of your soul and your body both, or I'm mistaken.   *Exeunt*

SCENE [FIVE]

SIR JOHN BRUTE'S *house*

Enter LADY BRUTE *and* BELINDA

BEL.   Well, madam, what answer have you from 'em?

LADY B.   That they'll be here this moment. I fancy 'twill end in a wedding. I'm sure he's a fool if it don't. Ten thousand pound and such a lass as you are is no contemptible offer to a younger brother. But are not you under strange agitations? Prithee how does your pulse beat?

BEL.   High and low. I have much ado to be valiant. Sure it must feel very strange to go to bed to a man.

LADY B.   Um, it does feel a little odd at first, but it will soon grow easy to you.

Enter CONSTANT *and* HEARTFREE

LADY B.   Good morrow, gentlemen. How have you slept after your adventure?

HEART.   Some careful thoughts, ladies, on your accounts have kept us waking.

BEL.   And some careful thoughts on your own, I believe, have hindered you from sleeping. Pray how does this matrimonial project relish with you?

HEART.   Why, faith, e'en as storming towns does with soldiers, where the hopes of delicious plunder banishes the fear of being knocked on the head.

BEL.   Is it then possible, after all, that you dare think of downright lawful wedlock?

HEART.   Madam, you have made me so foolhardy I dare do anything.

BEL.   Then, sir, I challenge you, and matrimony's the spot where I expect you.

HEART. 'Tis enough; I'll not fail. – (*Aside*) So, now I am in for Hobbes's voyage,[30] a great leap in the dark.

LADY B. Well, gentlemen, this matter being concluded then, have you got your lessons ready? For Sir John is grown such an atheist of late he'll believe nothing upon easy terms.

CON. We'll find ways to extend his faith, madam. But, pray, how do you find him this morning?

LADY B. Most lamentably morose, chewing the cud after last night's discovery, of which, however, he had but a confused notion e'en now. But I'm afraid his valet de chambre has told him all, for they are very busy together at this moment. When I told him of Belinda's marriage, I had no other answer but a grunt; from which you may draw what conclusions you think fit. But to your notes, gentlemen, he's here.

Enter SIR JOHN *and* RAZOR

CON. Good morrow, sir.

HEART. Good morrow, Sir John. I'm very sorry my indiscretion should cause so much disorder in your family.

SIR JOHN. Disorders generally come from indiscretions, sir; 'tis no strange thing at all.

LADY B. I hope, my dear, you are satisfied there was no wrong intended you.

SIR JOHN. None, my dove.

BEL. If not, I hope my consent to marry Mr Heartfree will convince you. For as little as I know of amours, sir, I can assure you one intrigue is enough to bring four people together without further mischief.

SIR JOHN. And I know too that intrigues tend to procreation of more kinds than one. One intrigue will beget another as soon as beget a son or a daughter.

CON. I am very sorry, sir, to see you still seem unsatisfied with a lady whose more than common virtue, I am sure, were she my wife, should meet a better usage.

SIR JOHN. Sir, if her conduct has put a trick upon her virtue, her virtue's the bubble, but her husband's the loser.

CON. Sir, you have received a sufficient answer already to justify both her conduct and mine. You'll pardon me for meddling in your family affairs, but I perceive I am the man you are jealous of, and therefore it concerns me.

SIR JOHN. Would it did not concern me, and then I should not care who it concerned.

[30] *Hobbes's voyage* Thomas Hobbes translated Books IX-XII of Homer's *Odyssey* as *The Travels of Ulysses*, 1673, and several later editions.

CON.   Well, sir, if truth and reason won't content you, I know but one
way more which, if you think fit, you may take.

[Displays his sword]

SIR JOHN.   Lord, sir, you are very hasty; if I had been found at prayers
in your wife's closet, I should have allowed you twice as much time to
come to yourself in.

CON.   Nay, sir, if time be all you want, we have no quarrel.

SIR JOHN muses

HEART.   I told you how the sword would work upon him.

CON.   Let him muse; however, I'll lay fifty pound our foreman brings
us in not guilty.

SIR JOHN.   (*Aside*) 'Tis well, 'tis very well. In spite of that young jade's
matrimonial intrigue, I am a downright stinking cuckold. Here they
are. (*Putting his hand to his forehead*) Boo! Methinks I could butt
with a bull. What the plague did I marry her for? I knew she did not
like me; if she had, she would have lain with me, for I would have done
so because I liked her. But that's past, and I have her. And now what
shall I do with her? If I put my horns in my pocket, she'll grow
insolent; if I don't, that goat there, that stallion, is ready to whip me
through the guts. The debate then is reduced to this: shall I die a hero
or live a rascal? Why, wiser men than I have long since concluded that
a living dog is better than a dead lion. –(*To* CONSTANT *and* HEART-
FREE) Gentlemen, now my wine and passion are governable, I must
own I have never observed anything in my wife's course of life to back
me in my jealousy of her. But jealousy's a mark of love, so she need not
trouble her head about it, as long as I make no more words on't.

LADY FANCIFUL *enters disguised and addresses to* BELINDA *apart*

CON.   I am glad to see your reason rule at last. Give me your hand. I
hope you'll look upon me as you are wont.

SIR JOHN.   Your humble servant. – (*Aside*) A wheedling son of a
whore.

HEART.   And that I may be sure you are friends with me too, pray give
me your consent to wed your niece.

SIR JOHN.   Sir, you have it with all my heart, damn me if you han't. –
(*Aside*) 'Tis time to get rid of her. A young pert pimp, she'll make an
incomparable bawd in a little time.

Enter a servant, who gives HEARTFREE *a letter. [Servant exits]*

BEL.   [*To* LADY FANCIFUL] Heartfree your husband, say you? 'Tis
impossible.

LADY F.   Would to kind heaven it were! But 'tis too true, and in the
world there lives not such a wretch. I'm young, and either I have been
flattered by my friends as well as glass,[31] or nature has been kind and

---

[31]*glass* mirror.

generous to me. I had a fortune too was greater far than he could ever hope for. But with my heart, I am robbed of all the rest. I'm slighted and I'm beggared both at once. I have scarce a bare subsistence from the villain, yet dare complain to none, for he has sworn if e'er 'tis known I am his wife he'll murder me.   *Weeping*

BEL.   The traitor!

LADY F.   I accidentally was told he courted you. Charity soon prevailed upon me to prevent your misery; and, as you see, I'm still so generous even to him as not to suffer he should do a thing for which the law[32] might take away his life.   *Weeping*

BEL.   Poor creature, how I pity her.   *They continue talking aside*

HEART.   (*Aside*) Death and damnation! Let me read it again (*Reads*) 'Though I have a particular reason not to let you know who I am till I see you, yet you'll easily believe 'tis a faithful friend that gives you this advice. I have lain with Belinda. (Good!) I have a child by her, (Better and better!) which is now at nurse, (heaven be praised!) and I think the foundation laid for another. (Ha, old truepenny!)[33] No rack could have tortured this story from me, but friendship has done it. I heard of your design to marry her, and could not see you abused. Make use of my advice, but keep my secret till I ask you for't again. Adieu'.   *Exit* LADY FANCIFUL

CON.   (*To* BELINDA) Come, madam, shall we send for the parson? I doubt here's no business for the lawyer; younger brothers have nothing to settle but their hearts, and that I believe my friend here has already done very faithfully.

BEL.   (*Scornfully*) Are you sure, sir, there are no old mortgages upon it?

HEART.   (*Coldly*) If you think there are, madam, it mayn't be amiss to defer the marriage till you are sure they are paid off.

BEL.   (*Aside*) How the galled horse kicks! (*To* HEARTFREE) We'll defer it as long as you please, sir.

HEART.   The more time we take to consider on't, madam, the less apt we shall be to commit oversights. Therefore, if you please, we'll put it off for just nine months.

BEL.   Guilty consciences make men cowards. I don't wonder you want time to resolve.

HEART.   And they make women desperate. I don't wonder you were so quickly determined.

BEL.   What does the fellow mean?

HEART.   What does the lady mean?

---

[32]*law* Bigamy was punishable by death.
[33]*truepenny* good fellow (*Hamlet*, I, v, 150).

SIR JOHN. Zoons, what do you both mean?

HEARTFREE *and* BELINDA *walk chafing about*

RAZOR. (*Aside*) Here is so much sport going to be spoiled, it makes me ready to weep again. A pox o' this impertinent Lady Fanciful and her plots, and her Frenchwoman too. She's a whimsical, ill-natured bitch, and when I have got my bones broke in her service, 'tis ten to one but my recompense is a clap. I hear 'em tittering without still. Ecod, I'll e'en go lug 'em both in by the ears and discover the plot, to secure my pardon. *Exit* RAZOR

CON. Prithee explain, Heartfree.

HEART. A fair deliverance, thank my stars and my friend.

BEL. 'Tis well it went no further. A base fellow.

LADY B. What can be the meaning of all this?

BEL. What's his meaning I don't know, but mine is, that if I had married him, I had had no husband.

HEART. And what's her meaning I don't know, but mine is, that if I had married her, I had had wife enough.

SIR JOHN. Your people of wit have got such cramp[34] ways of expressing themselves, they seldom comprehend one another. Pox take you both, will you speak that you may be understood?

Enter RAZOR *in sackcloth, pulling in* LADY FANCIFUL *and* MADAMOISELLE

RAZOR. If they won't, here comes an interpreter.

LADY B. Heavens, what have we here?

RAZOR. A villain, but a repenting villain. Stuff which saints in all ages have been made of.

ALL. Razor!

LADY B. What means this sudden metamorphose?

RAZOR. Nothing, without my pardon.

LADY B. What pardon do you want?

RAZOR. *Imprimis*, your ladyship's, for a damnable lie made upon your spotless virtue and set to the tune of Spring Garden. (*To* SIR JOHN) Next, at my generous master's feet I bend, for interrupting his more noble thoughts with phantoms of disgraceful cuckoldom. (*To* CONSTANT) Thirdly, I to this gentleman apply, for making him the hero of my romance.[35] (*To* HEARTFREE) Fourthly, your pardon, noble sir, I ask for clandestinely marrying you, without either bidding of banns, bishop's licence, friends' consent, or your own knowledge. (*To* BELINDA) And lastly, to my good young lady's clemency I come, for pretending the corn was sowed in the ground before ever the plough had been in the field.

---

[34]*cramp* difficult to understand.　　[35]*romance* fiction.

SIR JOHN. (*Aside*) So that after all, 'tis a moot point whether I am a cuckold or not.

BEL. Well, sir, upon condition you confess all, I'll pardon you myself, and try to obtain as much from the rest of the company. But I must know then, who 'tis has put you upon all this mischief?

RAZOR. Satan and his equipage. Woman tempted me, lust weakened me, and so the devil overcame me. As fell Adam, so fell I.

BEL. Then pray, Mr Adam, will you make us acquainted with your Eve?

RAZOR. (*To* MADAMOISELLE) Unmask, for the honour of France.

ALL. Madamoiselle?

MADAM. Me ask ten tousand pardon of all de good company.

SIR JOHN. Why, this mystery thickens instead of clearing up. (*To* RAZOR) You son of a whore you, put us out of our pain.

RAZOR. One moment brings sunshine. (*Showing* MADAMOISELLE) 'Tis true, this is the woman that tempted me. But this is the serpent that tempted the woman. And if my prayers might be heard, her punishment for so doing should be like the serpent's of old. (*Pulls off* LADY FANCIFUL'S *mask*) She should lie upon her face all the days of her life.

ALL. Lady Fanciful!

BEL. Impertinent.

LADY B. Ridiculous.

ALL. Ha, ha, ha, ha, ha!

BEL. I hope your ladyship will give me leave to wish you joy, since you have owned your marriage yourself. Mr Heartfree, I vow 'twas strangely wicked in you to think of another wife when you had one already so charming as her ladyship.

ALL. Ha, ha, ha, ha, ha!

LADY F. (*Aside*) Confusion seize 'em as it seizes me.

MADAM. *Que le diable étouffe ce maraud de Razor.*[36]

BEL. Your ladyship seems disordered. A breeding qualm perhaps. Mr Heartfree, your bottle of Hungary water[37] to your lady. Why, madam, he stands as unconcerned as if he were your husband in earnest.

LADY F. Your mirth's as nauseous as yourself, Belinda. You think you triumph o'er a rival now. *Hélas, ma pauvre fille*, where'er I'm rival there's no cause for mirth. No, my poor wretch, 'tis from another principle I have acted. I knew that thing there would make

[36]*Que . . . Razor* Let the devil choke that scoundrel Razor.

[37]*Hungary water* used as a lotion or drunk as a restorative; made from rosemary flowers and spirit of wine. Reputed to have been first prepared for an unidentified queen of Hungary.

so perverse a husband and you so impertinent a wife, that lest your mutual plagues should make you both run mad, I charitably would have broke the match. He, he, he, he, he!

Exit laughing affectedly, MADAMOISELLE *following her*

MADAM. He, he, he, he, he!

ALL. Ha, ha, ha, ha, ha!

SIR JOHN. (*Aside*) Why now this woman will be married to somebody too.

BEL. Poor creature, what a passion she's in. But I forgive her.

HEART. Since you have so much goodness for her, I hope you'll pardon my offence too, madam.

BEL. There will be no great difficulty in that, since I am guilty of an equal fault.

HEART. Then pardons being passed on all sides, let's to church to conclude the day's work.

CON. But before you go, let me treat you, pray, with a song a new-married lady made within this week. It may be of use to you both.

SONG

I

When yielding first to Damon's flame,
　　I sunk into his arms
He swore he'd ever be the same
　　Then rifl'd all my charms.
But fond of what h'ad long desir'd,
　　Too greedy of his prey,
My shepherd's flame, alas, expir'd
　　Before the verge of day.

II

My innocence in lovers' wars
　　Reproach'd his quick defeat.
Confus'd, asham'd, and bath'd in tears,
　　I mourn'd his cold retreat.
At length, 'Ah, shepherdess', cried he,
　　'Would you my fire renew,
Alas, you must retreat like me,
　　I'm lost if you pursue'.

HEART. So, madam, now had the parson but done his business —

BEL. You'd be half weary of your bargain.

HEART. No sure, I might dispense with[38] one night's lodging.

---

[38]*dispense with* abstain from.

BEL. I'm ready to try, sir.

HEART. Then let's to church, and if it be our chance to disagree —

BEL. Take heed, the surly husband's fate you see. [*Exeunt*]

EPILOGUE

BY ANOTHER HAND

SPOKEN BY LADY BRUTE AND BELINDA

LADY B. No epilogue?

BEL.   I swear I know of none.

LADY B. Lord, how shall we excuse it to the town?

BEL. Why, we must e'en say something of our own.

LADY B. Our own! Ay, that must needs be precious stuff.

BEL. I'll lay my life they'll like it well enough.
Come, faith, begin.

LADY B.   Excuse me, after you.

BEL. Nay, pardon me for that. I know my cue.

LADY B. Oh, for the world, I would not have precedence.

BEL. O Lord!

LADY B.   I swear –

BEL.   Oh, fie!

LADY B.   I'm all obedience.
First then, know all, before our doom is fix'd,
The third day[1] is for us –

BEL.   Nay, and the sixth.

LADY B. We speak not from the poet now, nor is it
His cause – I want a rhyme –

BEL.   That we solicit.

LADY B. Then sure you cannot have the hearts to be severe
And damn us –

BEL.   Damn us? Let 'em if they dare.

LADY B. Why, if they should, what punishment remains?

BEL. Eternal exile from behind our scenes.

LADY B. But if they're kind, that sentence we'll recall.
We can be grateful –

---

[1] *third day* The profits from the third (and sometimes the sixth) performance of a play were usually the perquisite of the author. Occasionally a day's profits were assigned to the actors; there is a record of playwright Elkanah Settle's having contributed his third day's right to the actresses [*The London Stage* 1660–1800; Part I, 1660–1700 (Carbondale, Ill., 1965), p. LXXIX].

BEL.   And have wherewithal.
LADY B.   But at grand treaties, hope not to be trusted
Before preliminaries are adjusted.
BEL.   You know the time, and we appoint this place
Where, if you please, we'll meet and sign the peace.

William Congreve
THE WAY OF THE WORLD
(1700)

The Way of the World
a comedy,
as it is Acted
at the Theatre in Lincoln's Inn Fields,
by His Majesty's Servants.
Written by Mr Congreve.

Audire est opera pretium, procedere recte
Qui maechis non vultis —
— Metuat doti deprensa.
HORACE, *Satires* 2[1]

London,
Printed for Jacob Tonson,
within Gray's Inn Gate,
next Gray's Inn Lane,
1700.

[1] It is worth your while to listen, you who do not wish things to go well for adulterers. . . . She who is found out fears for her dowry. Horace, *Satires,* Book I, Satire 2, 37–38 . . . . 131.

BIOGRAPHY

William Congreve was born at Bardsey, Yorkshire, in 1670 and was educated at Kilkenny School, Trinity College, Dublin and (briefly) at the Middle Temple, London. He was a friend of William Wycherley and John Dryden. Congreve held several government appointments. He was the author of poetry, literary criticism, prose fiction (*Incognita*, 1692), a masque and several very popular plays: *The Old Bachelor*) 1693; *The Double Dealer*, 1693; *The Mourning Bride*, his only tragedy, 1697. His last play, *The Way of the World*, 1700, was not very enthusiastically received; financial independence and ill health led him to retire *c.* 1700. He joined with John Vanbrugh in building and managing the Queen's Theatre, Haymarket, *c.* 1703–05. Congreve died in 1729 and was buried in Westminster Abbey.

INTRODUCTION

Often claimed to be the best of all Restoration comedies and frequently staged, *The Way of the World* presents an array of complex relationships and illicit liaisons. The play demands the close attention of an audience, even though they are aided by Congreve's early introduction of the complications and rivalries, by the short time span of the action (little more than a single afternoon) and by the presentation of the characters in pairs.

The drama opens with two contrasting men, clearly not friends, finishing a game of cards. During their flippant, cynical dialogue Mirabell and Fainall arouse interest in all the important characters who will appear later. Mrs Millamant, whom Mirabell hopes to marry, is introduced at length before 'she comes i'faith full sail, with her fan spread and streamers out' in Act II. Her aunt, Lady Wishfort, who does not approve of Mirabell, is alluded to frequently enough during the first two acts to show that the outcome of the plot will depend on her whims and affections. Her appearance at the beginning of Act III is carefully prepared for, and no one will be disappointed at the sight of the ageing, *déshabillé* aristocrat, with her interest divided between a container of cosmetic and a bottle of brandy.

From the opening lines the audience is quickly caught up in the scintillating dialogue and the rapid movement of characters on and off stage. Their names immediately suggest certain attitudes: 'Millamant' and 'Mirabell', approbation; 'Fainall', Marwood', and 'Wishfort', distrust; 'Witwoud' and 'Petulant', amusement. This comedy of manners has rather fewer *doubles entendres* than earlier plays of the type.

In *The Way of the World* Congreve uses matrimony as a focal point for both plot and theme; in fact, only a few minor servants remain uninvolved in the marital game. One existing marriage and three under negotiation occupy central positions. The Fainall union had been entered into for the most pragmatic of reasons: Arabella Languish,

Lady Wishfort's daughter, needed a 'cover' during her liaison with Mirabell, and Mr Fainall needed her money. The prospective second marriage of widowed Lady Wishfort, 'full of the vigour of fifty-five', also involves sex and money. The marriage of Waitwell and Foible takes place off stage during the action. This wedding might be regarded as no more than a convenience in the execution of Mirabell's plot; yet Congreve took some trouble to give both servants vital, independent personalities. Foible's active imagination is revealed when she reports at length to Lady Wishfort what Mirabell is supposed to have said about her ('superannuated . . . frippery' . . . III, i).

The third marriage being arranged, that of Millamant and Mirabell, is, however, the essential subject of the play. Their courtship is, of course, beset with obstacles, amongst them suggestions that the hero is a libertine and a schemer, and that the heroine is a coquette. These flaws turn out to be only superficial, and the playwright stresses the sincerity and depth of feeling of which both Mirabell and Millamant are capable, in particular how Mirabell's genuine love for the girl is the primary motivation for his ruthless deception of Lady Wishfort in arranging her 'marriage' to Sir Rowland (really Waitwell).

Congreve unites the serious and the frivolous by approaching the young people's marriage through the apparently ridiculous exchange of conditions, the 'odious provisos' (IV, i). The lovers have already determined to be together and now seek only to explore degrees of mutual tolerance and respect, agreeing on forms of address, the right to privacy and the avoidance of affectations. It must be remembered that marriage was then an almost irrevocable step for a woman (see particularly *The Provoked Wife* and *The Beaux Stratagem*), and Millamant displays beneath her teasing banter a serious concern for her future. She can hardly be called a liberated woman, but her conditions represent a gesture towards independence. With them she tests Mirabell's character and is much relieved by his conciliatory tone and willingness to respond in kind.

Millamant's depth of character[1] is illustrated by her willingness to marry Sir Wilfull Witwoud, 'this flower of knighthood' (v, i), in order to save her aunt from disgrace. Millamant's 'pecquet of letters' is revealing of her temperament: 'I am persecuted with letters – I hate letters . . . they serve to pin up one's hair' (II, i). The bemused, pert tone of the dialogue which follows is in sharp contrast to the spirit of a similar episode in *The Provoked Wife* (I, ii); in that play the letters received in rapid succession by Lady Fanciful simply feed her profound vanity.

[1] The role of Millamant was probably written for the first actress who played the part, Mrs Bracegirdle, whom Congreve loved.

Mirabell and Millamant are in fact guilty of affectation, a subject which Congreve regarded seriously in *The Way of the World*. Unlike other affected characters, such as Petulant, Witwoud, and Lady Wishfort, the lovers rise above this failing. Affectation is a major source of Lady Wishfort's difficulties, reaching as far back in time as the pseudo-moral education she provided for her daughter Arabella (now Mrs Fainall). One would hardly expect either lady to profit much from the works of Bunyan, Prynne and Quarles in Lady Wishfort's library.

Lady Wishfort's pretentiousness is cleverly illustrated during Sir Rowland's pretended wooing, astutely acted by Waitwell in disguise. This episode is carefully prepared for by Lady Wishfort's conceits in her dressing-room: her fretting over cosmetics, ordering the brandy bottle to be hidden under the table and practising effective poses to impress Sir Rowland.[2] Congreve's brilliant portrait of Lady Wishfort is not wholly unsympathetic, despite his satire of her vanity, credulity and sexuality. His characterisation includes elements of pathos, as in the acknowledgement of the distressing effect of ageing ('I look like an old peeled wall'). He reveals a tolerance of her whims and something akin to admiration of her buoyancy and vitality.

The playwright seems in general to accept the formal, carefully-structured society he exploits in the drama. It is the exaggerations, the deviations from the norm, the threats to social stability, as portrayed by Fainall and Mrs Marwood, that concern Congreve most. The un-satisfactory Fainall marriage and the unreal romance of Lady Wishfort are ultimately left behind; the final memory of the play is a prospect of happiness in the match of Mirabell and Mallamant. The action has a more satisfying conclusion than earlier Restoration comedies. In this play only Fainall violates social decorum by drawing his sword, a 'bear-garden flourish' (v, i), on – of all people – his wife, and he behaves as uncouthly as Pinchwife in *The Country Wife*.

Significantly, it is the profligate Fainall who represents and persist-ently refers to 'the way of the world'. Congreve did not believe that this way was immutable, but that it was capable of improvement, as

---

[2] One of many contemporary plays that ridiculed female vanity was Thomas Shadwell's *Bury Fair* (1689). The following lines suggest that it had an influence on *The Way of the World*:

OLDWIT. ... You and your daughter are notorious for out-painting all the Christian jezebels in England.

LADY FANTAST. 'Tis false, rude fellow; we only use a wash and lay on a little red.

OLDWIT. No more does a wall; but you for your part are fain to fill up the chinks in your rivelled skin as house-painters do the cracks in wainscot with putty. Pox on't, you would by art appear a beauty, and are by nature a mere mummy. (II, i)

illustrated in the union of Millamant and Mirabell. Modern theatrical taste may be impatient with the complex plotting and the contrived *dénouement* of *The Way of the World*, but the play is undated in its perceptive exploration of social ambition and pretension, of marriage and money.

Congreve's characterisation of Mirabell illustrates well the changing tone of Restoration comedy. This anthology began with plays about the ruthless libertines Horner, in the *The Country Wife* (1675) and Dorimant, in *The Man of Mode* (1676). In *The Way of the World* (1700) the central figure is both more mature and tolerant; he is interested, of course, in sexual exploits, but lacks the sexual aggression and promiscuity of the earlier men. One can hardly applaud all of Mirabell's activities; yet if he were invited today to defend himself, he might cheerfully argue that for true love to win, it must occasionally be unscrupulous. His winning of Millamant is almost frustrated by Lady Wishfort's own passion and by Mrs Marwood's intensely jealous plotting.

The 'proviso scene' (IV, i) is intended to show a more relaxed relationship than in earlier comedies between single young men and women, now negotiating greater permanence and stability in marriage. (Dorimant and Harriet engage in a brief wooing scene in *The Man of Mode* [IV, i], but it is much more reserved and defensive than the one in *The Way of the World*.) Congreve has, however, certainly not neglected the pressures and power of sexuality, evident in Lady Wishfort, Mrs Marwood and Fainall.

One of the most enduring pleasures of *The Way of the World* is Congreve's facility with language. Incisively he uses unforgettable similes and metaphors to reveal Lady Wishfort – in her malapropisms, her affected use of a high style and her vigorous denunciation of her servants. He also provides us with revealing glimpses into the characters' personalities through passing remarks or minor incidents. We find out a great deal about Petulant when Witwoud confides to Mirabell his friend's former custom of calling for himself, in disguise, at a chocolate-house. Later, Witwoud states that Petulant made his mark on a document, an unjustifiable accusation of illiteracy. Millamant reveals that pinning up one's hair in love letters written in prose is wasted effort, but, as Mincing earnestly observes, hair done up in verse is 'so pure and so crips'. We are surprised by Lady Wishfort's unlikely ambition, at a moment of depression, to retire with Mrs Marwood 'to deserts and solitudes', to be shepherdesses. These and many other similar instances illustrate the marvellous energy and ingenuity of the language of Congreve's best play.

The Way of the World reveals few specific literary or dramatic influences. It inevitably echoes any number of dramas and narratives about marriage, the battle of the sexes and sophisticated society. Congreve may have been influenced by earlier plays dealing with a search for a spouse, especially those involving hesitations and tests. The dramatist seems to have been familiar with the plays of Molière, Shakespeare's *Much Ado about Nothing* (1600), Jonson's *Epicoene* (1609) and *The Devil is an Ass* (1616) and Otway's *The Soldier's Fortune* (1680). Lady Wishfort may owe something to Lady Woodvill in *The Man of Mode* (1676), and Lady Wishwell in Thomas Southerne's *The Maid's Last Prayer* (1693).

BIBLIOGRAPHY

The Way of the World

P. and M. Mueschke, *A New View of Congreve's 'Way of the World'*. Ann Arbor, 1958.

J. Gagen, 'Congreve's Mirabell and the Ideal of a Gentleman'. *PMLA*, 79B (September 1964), 422–7.

M. E. Novak, *William Congreve*. New York, 1971.

H. Love, *Congreve*. Oxford, 1974.

B. Corman, '*The Way of the World* and Morally Serious Comedy'. *University of Toronto Quarterly*, 44 (Spring 1975), 199–212.

S. Rosowski, 'Thematic Development in the Comedies of William Congreve'. *Studies in English Literature 1500–1900*, 16 (Summer 1976), 387–406.

A. L. Williams, *An Approach to Congreve*. New Haven, 1979.

P. Holland, *The Ornament of Action*. Cambridge, Eng., 1979.

P. Lyons, ed., *William Congreve, Comedies, a Casebook*. London, 1982.

H. Weber, 'The Rake-Hero in Wycherley and Congreve'. *Philological Quarterly*, 61 (1982), 143–60.

R. Braverman, 'Capital Relations and *The Way of the World*'. *ELH*, 52 (Spring 1985), 133–58.

H. Weber, 'Disguise and the Audience in Congreve'. *Modern Language Quarterly*, 46 (December 1985), 368–89.

R. W. F. Kroll, 'Discourse and Power in *The Way of the World*'. *ELH*, 53 (Winter 1986), 727–58.

E. Kraft, 'Why Didn't Mirabell Marry the Widow Languish?' *Restoration: Studies in English Literary Culture 1660–1700*, 13 (Spring 1989), 26–34.

A. Snider, 'Professing a Libertine in *The Way of the World*'. *Papers on Language and Literature*, 25 (Fall 1989), 376–97.

J. Peters, *Congreve, the Drama and the Printed Word*. Stanford, 1990.

D. Thomas, *William Congreve*. London, 1992.

A. Hoffman, *Congreve's Comedies*. Victoria, B. C., English Literary Studies, 1993.

[DEDICATION]

TO THE RIGHT HONOURABLE RALPH, EARL OF MONTAGUE,[1] &c.

My Lord,

Whether the world will arraign me of vanity or not, that I have presumed to dedicate this comedy to your Lordship, I am yet in doubt, though it may be it is some degree of vanity even to doubt it. One who has at any time had the honour of your Lordship's conversation cannot be supposed to think very meanly of that which he would prefer to your perusal; yet it were to incur the imputation of too much sufficiency to pretend to such a merit as might abide the test of your Lordship's censure.

Whatever value may be wanting to this play while yet it is mine will be sufficiently made up to it when it is once become your Lordship's; and it is my security that I cannot have over-rated it more by my dedication than your Lordship will dignify it by your patronage.

That it succeeded on the stage was almost beyond my expectation; for but little of it was prepared for that general taste which seems now to be predominant in the palates of our audience.

Those characters which are meant to be ridiculed in most of our comedies are of fools so gross that, in my humble opinion, they should rather disturb than divert the well-natured and reflecting part of an audience; they are rather objects of charity than contempt; and, instead of moving our mirth, they ought very often to excite our compassion.

This reflection moved me to design some characters which should appear ridiculous not so much through a natural folly (which is incorrigible, and therefore not proper for the stage) as through an affected wit; a wit, which at the same time that it is affected, is also false. As there is some difficulty in the formation of a character of this nature, so there is some hazard which attends the progress of its success upon the stage; for many come to a play so over-charged with criticism that they very often let fly their censure, when through their rashness they have mistaken their aim. This I had occasion lately to observe: for

[1] *Montague c.* 1638–1709, diplomat, ambassador, politician under Charles II, James II, and William III. Reputed to have been unscrupulous.

this play had been acted two or three days before some of these hasty judges could find the leisure to distinguish betwixt the character of a Witwoud and a Truewit.[2]

I must beg your Lordship's pardon for this disgression from the true course of this epistle; but that it may not seem altogether impertinent, I beg that I may plead the occasion of it, in part of that excuse of which I stand in need, for recommending this comedy to your protection. It is only by the countenance of your Lordship and the *few* so qualified that such who write with care and pains can hope to be distinguished; for the prostituted name of *poet* promiscuously levels all that bear it.

Terence,[3] the most correct writer in the world, had a Scipio[4] and a Laelius,[5] if not to assist him, at least to support him in his reputation; and notwithstanding his extraordinary merit, it may be their countenance was not more than necessary.

The purity of his style, the delicacy of his turns, and the justness of his characters were all of them beauties which the greater part of his audience were incapable of tasting. Some of the coarsest strokes of Plautus,[6] so severely censured by Horace,[7] were more likely to affect the multitude; such who come with expectation to laugh at the last act of a play, and are better entertained with two or three unseasonable jests than with the artful solution of the fable.

As Terence excelled in his performances, so had he great advantages to encourage his undertakings; for he built most on the foundations of Menander;[8] his plots were generally modelled and his characters ready drawn to his hand. He copied Menander, and Menander had no less light in the formation of his characters from the observations of Theophrastus,[9] of whom he was a disciple, but the immediate successor of Aristotle, the first and greatest judge of poetry. These were great models to design by; and the further advantage which Terence possessed, towards giving his plays the due ornaments of purity of style and justness of manners, was not less considerable from the freedom of

[2] *Truewit* a perceptive, unquestionably witty man; a major character in Jonson's *Epicoene*, 1609.

[3] *Terence* a Roman comic dramatist, *c*. 190–*c*. 159 BC.

[4] *Scipio* Publius Cornelius Scipio Aemilianus Africanus, the younger; 185–129 BC, distinguished soldier, orator, *littérateur*, patron of Terence.

[5] *Laelius* Gaius Laelius Sapiens, born *c*. 186 BC, consul, etc., lover of literature, friend of Terence.

[6] *Plautus* Roman comic dramatist, translator and adapter of Greek plays; *c*. 254–184 BC.

[7] *Horace* Roman poet, satirist, critic (*Ars Poetica, c*. 19 BC); 65–8 BC.

[8] *Menander* Greek comic dramatist, 342–291 BC.

[9] *Theophrastus* Greek writer; *Characters*, sketches of abnormal types, *c*. 300 BC, popular in England; *c*. 370–*c*. 288 BC.

conversation which was permitted him with Laelius and Scipio, two of the greatest and most polite men of his age. And indeed, the privilege of such a conversation is the only certain means of attaining to the perfection of dialogue.

If it has happened in any part of this comedy that I have gained a turn of style or expression more correct, or at least more corrigible, than in those which I have formerly written, I must, with equal pride and gratitude, ascribe it to the honour of your Lordship's admitting me into your conversation, and that of a society where everybody else was so well worthy of you, in your retirement last summer from the town;[10] for it was immediately after that this comedy was written. If I have failed in my performance, it is only to be regretted, where there were so many, not inferior either to a Scipio or a Laelius, that there should be one wanting equal in capacity to a Terence.

If I am not mistaken, poetry is almost the only art which has not yet laid claim to your Lordship's patronage. Architecture and painting, to the great honour of our country, have flourished under your influence and protection. In the meantime, poetry, the eldest sister of all arts and parent of most, seems to have resigned her birthright, by having neglected to pay her duty to your Lordship, and by permitting others of a later extraction to prepossess that place in your esteem to which none can pretend a better title. Poetry, in its nature, is sacred to the good and great; the relation between them is reciprocal, and they are ever propitious to it. It is the privilege of poetry to address to them, and it is their prerogative alone to give it protection.

This received maxim is a general apology for all writers who consecrate their labours to great men: but I could wish at this time that this address were exempted from the common pretence of all dedications, and that, as I can distinguish your Lordship even among the most deserving, so this offering might become remarkable by some particular instance of respect, which should assure your Lordship that I am, with all due sense of your extreme worthiness and humanity,

My Lord,

Your Lordship's most obedient and most obliged humble servant.

WILL. CONGREVE.

[10] *town* presumably to Montague's country estate, Broughton House, Broughton, Northamptonshire.

PROLOGUE

SPOKEN BY MR BETTERTON

Of those few fools who with ill stars are curs'd,
Sure scribbling fools called poets fare the worst:
For they're a sort of fools which fortune makes,
And after she has made 'em fools, forsakes.
With nature's oafs 'tis quite a diff'rent case,
For fortune favours all her idiot-race;
In her own nest the cuckoo eggs we find,
O'er which she broods to hatch the changeling kind.
No portion for her own she has to spare,
So much she dotes on her adopted care.

     Poets are bubbles,[1] by the town drawn in,
Suffer'd at first some trifling stakes to win;
But what unequal hazards do they run!
Each time they write they venture all they've won;
The squire that's butter'd[2] still is sure to be undone.
This author heretofore has found your favour,
But pleads no merit from his past behaviour.
To build on that might prove a vain presumption,
Should grants to poets made admit resumption;
And in Parnassus[3] he must lose his seat,
If that be found a forfeited estate.

     He owns, with toil he wrought the following scenes,
But if they're naught ne'er spare him for his pains:
Damn him the more, have no commiseration
For dulness on mature deliberation.
He swears he'll not resent one hiss'd-off scene,

---

  [1] *bubbles* dupes.
  [2] *butter'd* 1) flattered; 2) to gamble with repeatedly doubled stakes, i.e.
to depend over-heavily on one patron.
  [3] *Parnassus* a mountain in Greece where the muses lived.

Nor, like those peevish wits, his play maintain,
Who, to assert their sense, your taste arraign.
Some plot we think he has, and some new thought;
Some humour too, no farce; but that's a fault.
Satire he thinks you ought not to expect;
For so reform'd a town who dares correct?
To please this time has been his sole pretence;
He'll not instruct lest it should give offence.
Should he by chance a knave or fool expose,
That hurts none here; sure here are none of those.
In short, our play shall (with your leave to show it)
Give you one instance of a passive poet,
Who to your judgments yields all resignation;
So save or damn, after your own discretion.

DRAMATIS PERSONAE

FAINALL, *in love with* MRS MARWOOD	Mr [Thomas] Betterton
MIRABELL, *in love with* MRS MILLAMANT	Mr [John] Verbruggen
WITWOUD ⎱ *followers of*	Mr [William] Bowen
PETULANT ⎰ MRS MILLAMANT	Mr Bowman[1]
SIR WILFULL WITWOUD, *half-brother to* WITWOUD, *and nephew to* LADY WISHFORT[2]	Mr [Cave] Underhill
WAITWELL, *servant to* MIRABELL	Mr [George] Bright
LADY WISHFORT, *enemy to* MIRABELL, *for having falsely pretended love to her*	Mrs [Elinor] Leigh
MRS MILLAMANT, *a fine lady, niece to* LADY WISHFORT, *and loves* MIRABELL	Mrs [Anne] Bracegirdle
MRS MARWOOD, *friend to* MR FAINALL, *and likes* MIRABELL	Mrs [Elizabeth] Barry
MRS FAINALL, *daughter to* LADY WISHFORT *and wife to* FAINALL, *formerly friend to* MIRABELL	Mrs Bowman[3]
FOIBLE, *woman to* LADY WISHFORT	Mrs [Elizabeth] Willis
MINCING, *woman to* MRS MILLAMANT	Mrs Prince
[BETTY, *servant in a chocolate house*]	
[PEG, *servant to* LADY WISHFORT]	
Dancers, footmen and attendants	

Scene: London
The time equal to that of the presentation

[1] John Boman.
[2] A sister, now deceased, of Lady Wishfort, had married a man named Witwoud; they had a son Sir Wilfull Witwoud. His father remarried and had a son Anthony (Squire) Witwoud.   [3] Elizabeth (Mrs John) Boman.

THE WAY OF THE WORLD

Act One

SCENE ONE

A chocolate-house

MIRABELL *and* FAINALL, *rising from cards,* BETTY *waiting*

MIRA. You are a fortunate man, Mr Fainall.

FAIN. Have we done?

MIRA. What you please. I'll play on to entertain you.

FAIN. No, I'll give you your revenge another time, when you are not so indifferent; you are thinking of something else now, and play too negligently; the coldness of a losing gamester lessens the pleasure of the winner. I'd no more play with a man that slighted his ill fortune than I'd make love to a woman who undervalued the loss of her reputation.

MIRA. You have a taste extremely delicate and are for refining on your pleasures.

FAIN. Prithee, why so reserved? Something has put you out of humour.

MIRA. Not at all. I happen to be grave today, and you are gay; that's all.

FAIN. Confess, Millamant and you quarrelled last night after I left you; my fair cousin has some humours that would tempt the patience of a stoic. What, some coxcomb came in and was well received by her while you were by.

MIRA. Witwoud and Petulant, and — what was worse — her aunt, your wife's mother, my evil genius; or to sum up all in her own name, my old Lady Wishfort came in —

FAIN. Oh, there it is then! She has a lasting passion[1] for you, and with reason. — What, then my wife was there?

MIRA. Yes, and Mrs Marwood and three or four more, whom I never saw before. Seeing me, they all put on their grave faces, whispered one another, then complained aloud of the vapours, and after fell into a profound silence.

[1] *passion* anger.

FAIN.   They had a mind to be rid of you.

MIRA.   For which reason I resolved not to stir. At last the good old lady broke through her painful taciturnity with an invective against long visits. I would not have understood her, but Millamant joining in the argument, I rose and with a constrained smile told her I thought nothing was so easy as to know when a visit began to be troublesome; she reddened and I withdrew, without expecting[2] her reply.

FAIN.   You were to blame to resent what she spoke only in compliance with her aunt.

MIRA.   She is more mistress of herself than to be under the necessity of such a resignation.

FAIN.   What?[3] Though half her fortune depends upon her marrying with my lady's approbation?

MIRA.   I was then in such a humour that I should have been better pleased if she had been less discreet.

FAIN.   Now I remember, I wonder not they were weary of you; last night was one of their cabal-nights; they have 'em three times a week, and meet by turns, at one another's apartments, where they come together like the coroner's inquest, to sit upon the murdered reputations of the week. You and I are excluded; and it was once proposed that all the male sex should be excepted;[4] but somebody moved that to avoid scandal there might be one man of the community; upon which motion Witwoud and Petulant were enrolled members.

MIRA.   And who may have been the foundress of this sect? My Lady Wishfort, I warrant, who publishes her detestation of mankind, and full of the vigour of fifty-five, declares for a friend and ratafia;[5] and let posterity shift for itself, she'll breed no more.

FAIN.   The discovery of your sham addresses to her, to conceal your love to her niece, has provoked this separation. Had you dissembled better, things might have continued in the state of nature.

MIRA.   I did as much as man could, with any reasonable conscience. I proceeded to the very last act of flattery with her, and was guilty of a song in her commendation. Nay, I got a friend to put her into a lampoon, and compliment her with the imputation of an affair with a young fellow, which I carried so far that I told her the malicious town took notice that she was grown fat of a sudden; and when she lay in of a dropsy, persuaded her she was reported to be in labour. The devil's in't, if an old woman is to be flattered further, unless a

---

[2]*expecting* awaiting.   [3]*What* Indeed.
[4]*excepted* disbarred.   [5]*ratafia* a fruit-flavoured liqueur.

man should endeavour downright personally to debauch her; and that my virtue forbad me. But for the discovery of this amour, I am indebted to your friend, or your wife's friend, Mrs Marwood.

FAIN. What should provoke her to be your enemy, without she has made you advances which you have slighted? Women do not easily forgive omissions of that nature.

MIRA. She was always civil to me till of late; I confess I am not one of those coxcombs who are apt to interpret a woman's good manners to her prejudice, and think that she who does not refuse 'em everything can refuse 'em nothing.

FAIN. You are a gallant man, Mirabell; and though you may have cruelty enough not to satisfy a lady's longing, you have too much generosity not to be tender of her honour. Yet you speak with an indifference which seems to be affected and confesses you are conscious of a negligence.

MIRA. You pursue the argument with a distrust that seems to be unaffected and confesses you are conscious of a concern for which the lady is more indebted to you than is your wife.

FAIN. Fie, fie, friend, if you grow censorious I must leave you. I'll look upon the gamesters in the next room.

MIRA. Who are they?

FAIN. Petulant and Witwoud. – [*To* BETTY] Bring me some chocolate. [*Exit* FAINALL]

MIRA. Betty, what says your clock?

BET. Turned of the last canonical hour,[6] sir. *Exit*

MIRA How pertinently the jade answers me! (*Looking on his watch*) Ha, almost one a'clock!

[*Enter a* SERVANT]

Oh, you're come – Well, is the grand affair over? You have been something tedious.

SERV. Sir, there's such coupling at Pancras[7] that they stand behind one another, as 'twere in a country dance. Ours was the last couple to lead up; and no hopes appearing of dispatch, besides, the parson growing hoarse, we were afraid his lungs would have failed before it came to our turn; so we drove round to Duke's Place,[8] and there they were riveted in a trice.

MIRA. So, so, you are sure they are married.

___

[6]*canonical hour* when marriages might then be legally performed, between 8:00 a.m. and noon.

[7]*Pancras* St Pancras Church, outside the jurisdiction of the City; notable for irregular marriages.

[8]*Duke's Place* at St James's Church, Duke's Place, Aldgate; marriages were performed there without a licence.

SERV.   Married and bedded, sir; I am witness.

MIRA.   Have you the certificate?

SERV.   Here it is, sir.

MIRA.   Has the tailor brought Waitwell's clothes home, and the new liveries?

SERV.   Yes, sir.

MIRA.   That's well. Do you go home again, d'ye hear, and adjourn the consummation till further order. Bid Waitwell shake his ears, and Dame Partlet[9] rustle up her feathers, and meet me at one a'clock by Rosamond's Pond,[10] that I may see her before she returns to her lady; and as you tender your ears, be secret.   *Exit* SERVANT

Re-enter FAINALL [*and* BETTY]

FAIN.   Joy of your success, Mirabell; you look pleased.

MIRA.   Ay, I have been engaged in a matter of some sort of mirth, which is not yet ripe for discovery. I am glad this is not a cabal-night. I wonder, Fainall, that you who are married, and of consequence should be discreet, will suffer your wife to be of such a party.

FAIN.   Faith, I am not jealous. Besides, most who are engaged are women and relations; and for the men, they are of a kind too contemptible to give scandal.

MIRA.   I am of another opinion. The greater the coxcomb, always the more the scandal; for a woman who is not a fool can have but one reason for associating with a man who is one.

FAIN.   Are you jealous as often as you see Witwoud entertained by Millamant?

MIRA.   Of her understanding I am, if not of her person.

FAIN.   You do her wrong; for to give her her due, she has wit.

MIRA.   She has beauty enough to make any man think so, and complaisance enough not to contradict him who shall tell her so.

FAIN.   For a passionate lover, methinks you are a man somewhat too discerning in the failings of your mistress.

MIRA.   And for a discerning man, somewhat too passionate a lover; for I like her with all her faults; nay, like her for her faults. Her follies are so natural, or so artful, that they become her; and those affectations which in another woman would be odious, serve but to make her more agreeable. I'll tell thee, Fainall, she once used me with that insolence, that in revenge I took her to pieces; sifted her, and separated her failings; I studied 'em, and got 'em by rote. The catalogue was so large that I was not without hopes one day or other to hate her heartily; to which end I so used myself to think of 'em

---

[9]*Dame Partlet* i.e. Foible. The reference is to Pertelote, wife of the cock Chauntecleer in Chaucer, 'The Nun's Priest's Tale', *The Canterbury Tales*.

[10]*Rosamond's Pond* a small lake in St James's Park, later filled in, a trysting place.

that at length, contrary to my design and expectation, they gave me every hour less and less disturbance; till in a few days it became habitual to me to remember 'em without being displeased. They are now grown as familiar to me as my own frailties; and in all probability in a little time longer I shall like 'em as well.

FAIN.   Marry her, marry her! Be half as well acquainted with her charms as you are with her defects, and, my life on't, you are your own man again.

MIRA.   Say you so?

FAIN.   Ay, ay, I have experience. I have a wife, and so forth.

Enter MESSENGER

MESS.   Is one Squire Witwoud here?

BET.   Yes; what's your business?

MESS.   I have a letter for him, from his brother, Sir Wilfull, which I am charged to deliver into his own hands.

BET.   He's in the next room, friend. That way.   *Exit* MESSENGER

MIRA.   What, is the chief of that noble family in town, Sir Wilfull Witwoud?

FAIN.   He is expected today. Do you know him?

MIRA.   I have seen him. He promises to be an extraordinary person; I think you have the honour to be related to him.

FAIN.   Yes; he is half-brother to this Witwoud by a former wife, who was sister to my Lady Wishfort, my wife's mother. If you marry Millamant, you must call cousins too.

MIRA.   I had rather be his relation than his acquaintance.

FAIN.   He comes to town in order to equip himself for travel.

MIRA.   For travel! Why the man that I mean is above forty.

FAIN.   No matter for that. 'Tis for the honour of England that all Europe should know we have blockheads of all ages.

MIRA.   I wonder there is not an act of parliament to save the credit of the nation, and prohibit the exportation of fools.

FAIN.   By no means; 'tis better as 'tis. 'Tis better to trade with a little loss than to be quite eaten up with being overstocked.

MIRA.   Pray, are the follies of this knight-errant and those of the squire his brother anything related?

FAIN.   Not at all. Witwoud grows by the knight, like a medlar grafted on a crab.[11] One will melt in your mouth, and t'other set your teeth on edge; one is all pulp, and the other all core.

MIRA.   So one will be rotten before he be ripe, and the other will be rotten without ever being ripe at all.

---

[11]*crab* A medlar, a type of apple, was eaten when over-ripe; a crab apple is hard and tart.

FAIN. Sir Wilfull is an odd mixture of bashfulness and obstinacy.
But when he's drunk, he's as loving as the monster in *The Tempest*,[12]
and much after the same manner. To give t'other his due, he has
something of good nature and does not always want wit.

MIRA. Not always, but as often as his memory fails him and his
commonplace[13] of comparisons. He is a fool with a good memory and
some few scraps of other folks' wit. He is one whose conversation can
never be approved; yet it is now and then to be endured. He has indeed
one good quality: he is not exceptious; for he so passionately affects
the reputation of understanding raillery that he will construe an
affront into a jest, and call downright rudeness and ill language, satire
and fire.

FAIN. If you have a mind to finish his picture, you have an opportunity
to do it at full length. Behold the original.

 Enter WITWOUD

WIT. Afford me your compassion, my dears. Pity me, Fainall;
Mirabell, pity me.

MIRA. I do, from my soul.

FAIN. Why, what's the matter?

WIT. No letters for me, Betty?

BET. Did not the messenger bring you one but now, sir?

WIT. Ay, but no other?

BET. No, sir.

WIT. That's hard, that's very hard. A messenger, a mule, a beast of
burden! He has brought me a letter from the fool my brother, as heavy
as a panegyric in a funeral sermon, or a copy of commendatory verses
from one poet to another. And what's worse, 'tis as sure a forerunner
of the author as an epistle dedicatory.

MIRA. A fool, and your brother, Witwoud!

WIT. Ay, ay, my half-brother. My half-brother he is, no nearer, upon
honour.

MIRA. Then 'tis possible he may be but half a fool.

WIT. Good, good, Mirabell, *le drôle*! Good, good. Hang him, don't
let's talk of him. Fainall, how does your lady? Gad! I say anything in
the world to get this fellow out of my head. I beg pardon that I should
ask a man of pleasure and the town a question at once so foreign and
domestic. But I talk like an old maid at a marriage; I don't know what I
say. But she's the best woman in the world.

---

[12]*The Tempest* probably an allusion to Thomas Shadwell's popular opera (1674
and frequently revived), based on Shakespeare's *The Tempest*, as revised by
Davenant and Dryden, 1667. Cave Underhill, the interpreter of Sir Wilfull, also
played the monster Trinculo in the opera.

[13]*commonplace* i.e. a commonplace book.

FAIN. 'Tis well you don't know what you say, or else your commendation would go near to make me either vain or jealous.

WIT. No man in town lives well with a wife but Fainall. Your judgment, Mirabell?

MIRA. You had better step and ask his wife, if you would be credibly informed.

WIT. Mirabell.

MIRA. Ay.

WIT. My dear, I ask ten thousand pardons. Gad, I have forgot what I was going to say to you.

MIRA. I thank you heartily, heartily.

WIT. No, but prithee excuse me; my memory is such a memory.

MIRA. Have a care of such apologies, Witwoud; for I never knew a fool but he affected to complain, either of the spleen or his memory.

FAIN. What have you done with Petulant?

WIT. He's reckoning his money – my money it was. I have no luck today.

FAIN. You may allow him to win of you at play, for you are sure to be too hard for him at repartee: since you monopolise the wit that is between you, the fortune must be his of course.

MIRA. I don't find that Petulant confesses the superiority of wit to be your talent, Witwoud.

WIT. Come, come, you are malicious now, and would breed debates. Petulant's my friend, and a very honest fellow, and a very pretty fellow, and has a smattering – faith and troth – a pretty deal of an odd sort of a small wit. Nay, I'll do him justice. I'm his friend, I won't wrong him neither. And if he had but any judgment in the world, he would not be altogether contemptible. Come, come, don't detract from the merits of my friend.

FAIN. You don't take your friend to be over-nicely bred?

WIT. No, no, hang him, the rogue has no manners at all, that I must own – no more breeding than a bum-baily,[14] that I grant you. 'Tis pity, faith; the fellow has fire and life.

MIRA. What, courage?

WIT. Hum. Faith, I don't know as to that. I can't say as to that. Yes, faith, in a controversy he'll contradict anybody.

MIRA. Though 'twere a man whom he feared, or a woman whom he loved?

WIT. Well, well, he does not always think before he speaks. We have all our failings. You are too hard upon him, you are, faith. Let me excuse him. I can defend most of his faults, except one or two. One

[14]*bum-baily* a persistent bailiff.

he has, that's the truth on't; if he were my brother, I could not acquit
him – that indeed I could wish were otherwise.

MIRA.   Ay, marry, what's that, Witwoud?

WIT.   Oh, pardon me. Expose the infirmities of my friend? No, my
dear, excuse me there.

FAIN.   What, I warrant he's insincere, or 'tis some such trifle.

WIT.   No, no, what if he be? 'Tis no matter for that; his wit will excuse
that. A wit should no more be sincere than a woman constant. One
argues a decay of parts,[15] as t'other of beauty.

MIRA.   Maybe you think him too positive?

WIT.   No, no, his being positive is an incentive to argument, and
keeps up conversation.

FAIN.   Too illiterate?

WIT.   That! That's his happiness. His want of learning gives him the
more opportunities to shew his natural parts.[16]

MIRA.   He wants words.

WIT.   Ay, but I like him for that now; for his want of words gives me
the pleasure very often to explain his meaning.

FAIN.   He's impudent.

WIT.   No, that's not it.

MIRA.   Vain.

WIT.   No.

MIRA.   What, he speaks unseasonable truths sometimes, because he
has not wit enough to invent an evasion?

WIT.   Truths? Ha, ha, ha! No, no, since you will have it, – I mean, he
never speaks truth at all. That's all. He will lie like a chambermaid or
a woman of quality's porter. Now that is a fault.

     Enter COACHMAN

COACH.   Is Master Petulant here, mistress?

BET.   Yes.

COACH.   Three gentlewomen in a coach would speak with him.

FAIN.   O brave Petulant! Three!

BET.   I'll tell him.

COACH.   You must bring two dishes of chocolate and a glass of
cinnamon-water.   *Exeunt* [BETTY *and* COACHMAN]

WIT.   That should be for two fasting strumpets and a bawd troubled
with wind. Now you may know what the three are.

MIRA.   You are very free with your friend's acquaintance.

WIT.   Ay, ay, friendship without freedom is as dull as love without
enjoyment, or wine without toasting. But to tell you a secret, these
are trulls whom he allows coach-hire and something more, by the
week, to call on him once a day at public places.

---

[15]*parts* talents, abilities.   [16]*his natural parts* his simplicity.

MIRA. How![17]

WIT. You shall see he won't go to 'em because there's no more company here to take notice of him. Why this is nothing to what he used to do. Before he found out this way, I have known him call for himself –

FAIN. Call for himself? What dost thou mean?

WIT. Mean? Why he would slip you out of this chocolate-house, just when you had been talking to him – As soon as your back was turned, whip, he was gone, – then trip to his lodging, clap on a hood and scarf, and a mask, slap into a hackney-coach, and drive hither to the door again in a trice, where he would send in for himself; that I mean, call for himself, wait for himself; nay and what's more, not finding himself, sometimes leave a letter for himself.

MIRA. I confess this is something extraordinary. I believe he waits for himself now, he is so long a-coming. Oh, I ask his pardon.

Enter PETULANT [*and* BETTY]

BET. Sir, the coach stays.

PET. Well, well; I come. 'Sbud,[18] a man had as good be a professed midwife as a professed whoremaster at this rate. To be knocked up and raised at all hours, and in all places! Pox on 'em, I won't come. D'ye hear? Tell 'em I won't come. Let 'em snivel and cry their hearts out.

FAIN. You are very cruel, Petulant.

PET. All's one; let it pass. I have a humour to be cruel.

MIRA. I hope they are not persons of condition[19] that you use at this rate.

PET. Condition, condition's a dried fig if I am not in humour. By this hand, if they were your – a – a – your what-dee-call-'ems themselves, they must wait or rub off,[20] if I want appetite.

MIRA. What-dee-call-'ems! What are they, Witwoud?

WIT. Empresses, my dear. By your what-dee-call-'ems he means sultana queens.[21]

PET. Ay, Roxolanas.[22]

MIRA. Cry you mercy.

FAIN. Witwoud says they are –

PET. What does he say th'are?

WIT. I? Fine ladies, I say.

---

[17] *How* Indeed.
[18] *'Sbud* By God's blood.   [19] *condition* high rank.
[20] *rub off* make off, leave.   [21] *sultana queens* mistresses.
[22] *Roxolana* a former concubine, later wife of Solyman the Magnificent, in William Davenant's *The Siege of Rhodes*, 1656.

PET. Pass on, Witwoud. Harkee, by this light his relations: two co-heiresses his cousins, and an old aunt who loves catterwauling better than a conventicle.[23]

WIT. Ha, ha, ha; I had a mind to see how the rogue would come off. Ha, ha, ha! Gad, I can't be angry with him, if he had said they were my mother and my sisters.

MIRA. No!

WIT. No; the rogue's wit and readiness of invention charm me. Dear Petulant!

BET. They are gone, sir, in great anger.

PET. Enough, let 'em trundle. Anger helps complexion, saves paint.

FAIN. This continence is all dissembled; this is in order to have something to brag of the next time he makes court to Millamant, and swear he has abandoned the whole sex for her sake.

MIRA. Have you not left off your impudent pretensions there yet? I shall cut your throat sometime or other, Petulant, about that business.

PET. Ay, ay, let that pass. There are other throats to be cut.

MIRA. Meaning mine, sir?

PET. Not I. I mean nobody. I know nothing. But there are uncles and nephews in the world and they may be rivals. What then? All's one for that.

MIRA. How! Harkee, Petulant, come hither. Explain, or I shall call your interpreter.[24]

PET. Explain? I know nothing. Why, you have an uncle, have you not, lately come to town, and lodges by my Lady Wishfort's?

MIRA. True.

PET. Why that's enough. You and he are not friends, and if he should marry and have a child, you may be disinherited, ha?

MIRA. Where hast thou stumbled upon all this truth?

PET. All's one for that. Why then, say I know something.

MIRA. Come, thou art an honest fellow, Petulant, and shalt make love to my mistress; thou shalt, faith. What hast thou heard of my uncle?

PET. I? Nothing, I. If throats are to be cut, let swords clash. Snug's the word; I shrug and am silent.

MIRA. Oh, raillery, raillery. Come, I know thou art in the women's secrets. What, you're a cabalist; I know you stayed at Millamant's last night after I went. Was there any mention made of my uncle or me? Tell me. If thou hadst but good nature equal to thy wit,

---

[23]*conventicle* a clandestine meeting of Non-conformists.
[24]*interpreter* an ironic reference to Witwoud.

Petulant, Tony Witwoud, who is now thy competitor in fame, would show as dim by[25] thee as a dead whiting's eye by a pearl of orient. He would no more be seen by thee than Mercury[26] is by the sun. Come, I'm sure thou wo't tell me.

PET. If I do, will you grant me common sense then for the future?

MIRA. Faith, I'll do what I can for thee, and I'll pray that heaven may grant it thee in the meantime.

PET. Well, harkee.   [PETULANT *and* MIRABELL *talk apart*]

FAIN. Petulant and you both will find Mirabell as warm a rival as a lover.

WIT. Pshaw, pshaw. That she laughs at Petulant is plain. And for my part, but that it is almost a fashion to admire her, I should, harkee — to tell you a secret, but let it go no further — between friends, I shall never break my heart for her.

FAIN. How!

WIT. She's handsome, but she's a sort of an uncertain woman.

FAIN. I thought you had died for her.

WIT. Umh, no.

FAIN. She has wit.

WIT. 'Tis what she will hardly allow anybody else — Now, demme, I should hate that, if she were as handsome as Cleopatra. Mirabell is not so sure of her as he thinks for.

FAIN. Why do you think so?

WIT. We stayed pretty late there last night, and heard something of an uncle to Mirabell, who is lately come to town, and is between him and the best part of his estate. Mirabell and he are at some distance, as my Lady Wishfort has been told; and you know she hates Mirabell, worse than a Quaker hates a parrot,[27] or than a fishmonger hates a hard frost.[28] Whether this uncle has seen Mrs Millamant or not I cannot say, but there were items of such a treaty being in embryo; and if it should come to life, poor Mirabell would be in some sort unfortunately fobbed, i'faith.

FAIN. 'Tis impossible Millamant should hearken to it.

WIT. Faith, my dear, I can't tell; she's a woman and a kind of a humourist.[29]

MIRA. And this is the sum of what you could collect last night?

PET. The quintessence. Maybe Witwoud knows more; he stayed longer. Besides they never mind him; they say anything before him.

[25]*by* in comparison with.
[26]*Mercury* the planet closest to the sun.
[27]*parrot* because it is so talkative.
[28]*frost* because it makes his work difficult and unpleasant.
[29]*humourist* subject to humours or fancies, a faddist.

MIRA.   I thought you had been the greatest favourite.

PET.   Ay, *tête à tête*; but not in public, because I make remarks.

MIRA.   You do?

PET.   Ay, ay; pox, I'm malicious, man. Now he's soft, you know; they
are not in awe of him. The fellow's well bred; he's what you call a —
what-d'ye-call-'em — a fine gentleman, but he's silly withal.

MIRA.   I thank you. I know as much as my curiosity requires. Fainall,
are you for the Mall?

FAIN.   Ay, I'll take a turn before dinner.

WIT.   Ay, we'll all walk in the park; the ladies talked of being there.

MIRA.   I thought you were obliged to watch for your brother Sir
Wilfull's arrival.

WIT.   No, no. He comes to his aunt's, my Lady Wishfort. Pox on him,
I shall be troubled with him too. What shall I do with the fool?

PET.   Beg him³⁰ for his estate, that I may beg you afterwards, and so
have but one trouble with you both.

WIT.   O rare Petulant! Thou art as quick as fire in a frosty morning.
Thou shalt to the Mall with us, and we'll be very severe.³¹

PET.   Enough, I'm in a humour to be severe.

MIRA.   Are you? Pray then walk by yourselves. Let not us be
accessory to your putting the ladies out of countenance, with your
senseless ribaldry, which you roar out aloud as often as they pass by
you; and when you have made a handsome woman blush, then you
think you have been severe.

PET.   What, what? Then let 'em either show their innocence by not
understanding what they hear, or else show their discretion by not
hearing what they would not be thought to understand.

MIRA.   But hast not thou then sense enough to know that thou
ought'st to be most ashamed of thyself when thou hast put another
out of countenance?

PET.   Not I, by this hand. I always take blushing either for a sign of
guilt or ill breeding.

MIRA.   I confess you ought to think so. You are in the right, that you
may plead the error of your judgment in defence of your practice.

> Where modesty's ill manners, 'tis but fit
> That impudence and malice pass for wit.   *Exeunt*

---

³⁰*Beg him* to petition the Court of Wards for the custody of an incompetent
person.

³¹*severe* critical of everyone.

Act Two

SCENE ONE

St James's Park

Enter MRS FAINALL *and* MRS MARWOOD

MRS FAIN.   Ay, ay, dear Marwood, if we will be happy, we must find the means in ourselves and among ourselves. Men are ever in extremes, either doting or averse. While they are lovers, if they have fire and sense, their jealousies are insupportable; and when they cease to love (we ought to think at least) they loath. They look upon us with horror and distaste; they meet us like the ghosts of what we were, and as from such, fly from us.

MRS MAR.   True, 'tis an unhappy circumstance of life that love should ever die before us, and that the man so often should outlive the lover. But say what you will, 'tis better to be left than never to have been loved. To pass our youth in dull indifference, to refuse the sweets of life because they once must leave us, is as preposterous as to wish to have been born old, because we one day must be old. For my part, my youth may wear and waste, but it shall never rust in my possession.

MRS FAIN.   Then it seems you dissemble an aversion to mankind only in compliance to my mother's humour.

MRS MAR.   Certainly. To be free,[1] I have no taste of those insipid dry discourses, with which our sex of force must entertain themselves, apart from men. We may affect endearments to each other, profess eternal friendships, and seem to dote like lovers; but 'tis not in our natures long to persevere. Love will resume his empire in our breasts, and every heart, or soon or late, receive and readmit him as its lawful tyrant.

MRS FAIN.   Bless me, how have I been deceived! Why you profess[2] a libertine!

MRS MAR.   You see my friendship by my freedom. Come, be as sincere; acknowledge that your sentiments agree with mine.

MRS FAIN.   Never.

MRS MAR.   You hate mankind?

---

[1]*free* candid.   [2]*profess* speak like.

MRS FAIN.   Heartily, inveterately.

MRS MAR.   Your husband?

MRS FAIN.   Most transcendently; ay, though I say it, meritoriously.

MRS MAR.   Give me your hand upon it.

MRS FAIN.   There.

MRS MAR.   I join with you. What I have said has been to try you.

MRS FAIN.   Is it possible? Dost thou hate those vipers, men?

MRS MAR.   I have done hating 'em, and am now come to despise 'em.
The next thing I have to do is eternally to forget 'em.

MRS FAIN.   There spoke the spirit of an Amazon, a Penthesilea.[3]

MRS MAR.   And yet I am thinking sometimes to carry my aversion
further.

MRS FAIN.   How?

MRS MAR.   Faith by marrying. If I could but find one that loved me
very well and would be thoroughly sensible of ill usage, I think I
should do myself the violence of undergoing the ceremony.

MRS FAIN.   You would not make him a cuckold?

MRS MAR.   No, but I'd make him believe I did, and that's as bad.

MRS FAIN.   Why had not you as good do it?

MRS MAR.   Oh, if he should ever discover it, he would then know the
worst, and be out of his pain; but I would have him ever to continue
upon the rack of fear and jealousy.

MRS FAIN.   Ingenious mischief! Would thou wert married to
Mirabell.

MRS MAR.   Would I were.

MRS FAIN.   You change colour.

MRS MAR.   Because I hate him.

MRS FAIN.   So do I, but I can hear him named. But what reason have
you to hate him in particular?

MRS MAR.   I never loved him. He is, and always was, insufferably
proud.

MRS FAIN.   By the reason you give for your aversion, one would think
it dissembled, for you have laid a fault to his charge of which his
enemies must acquit him.

MRS MAR.   Oh, then it seems you are one of his favourable enemies.
Methinks you look a little pale, and now you flush again.

MRS FAIN.   Do I? I think I am a little sick o' the sudden.

MRS MAR.   What ails you?

MRS FAIN.   My husband. Don't you see him? He turned short upon
me unawares, and has almost overcome[4] me.

---

[3]*Penthesilea* queen of the Amazons; she aided the Trojans and was slain by
Achilles.

[4]*overcome* taken me by surprise.

Enter FAINALL *and* MIRABELL

MRS MAR.   Ha, ha, ha! He comes opportunely for you.

MRS FAIN.   For you, for he has brought Mirabell with him.

FAIN.   My dear.

MRS FAIN.   My soul.

FAIN.   You don't look well today, child.

MRS FAIN.   D'ye think so?

MIRA.   He is the only man that does, madam.

MRS FAIN.   The only man that would tell me so at least, and the only man from whom I could hear it without mortification.

FAIN.   O my dear, I am satisfied of your tenderness. I know you cannot resent anything from me, especially what is an effect of my concern.

MRS FAIN.   Mr Mirabell, my mother interrupted you in a pleasant relation⁵ last night: I would fain hear it out.

MIRA.   The persons concerned in that affair have yet a tolerable reputation; I am afraid Mr Fainall will be censorious.

MRS FAIN.   He has a humour more prevailing than his curiosity, and will willingly dispense with the hearing of one scandalous story, to avoid giving an occasion to make another by being seen to walk with his wife. This way, Mr Mirabell, and I dare promise you will oblige us both.   *Exeunt* MRS FAINALL *and* MIRABELL

FAIN.   Excellent creature! Well, sure if I should live to be rid of my wife, I should be a miserable man.

MRS MAR.   Ay!

FAIN.   For having only that one hope, the accomplishment of it, of consequence must put an end to all my hopes; and what a wretch is he who must survive his hopes! Nothing remains when that day comes, but to sit down and weep like Alexander, when he wanted⁶ other worlds to conquer.

MRS MAR.   Will you not follow 'em?

FAIN.   Faith, I think not.

MRS MAR.   Pray let us; I have a reason.

FAIN.   You are not jealous?

MRS MAR.   Of whom?

FAIN.   Of Mirabell.

MRS MAR.   If I am, is it inconsistent with my love to you that I am tender of your honour?

FAIN.   You would intimate then, as if there were a fellow-feeling between my wife and him.

MRS MAR.   I think she does not hate him to that degree she would be

---

⁵*relation* narration.   ⁶*wanted* lacked.

thought.

FAIN.   But he, I fear, is too insensible.[7]

MRS MAR.   It may be you are deceived.

FAIN.   It may be so. I do now begin to apprehend it.

MRS MAR.   What?

FAIN.   That I have been deceived, madam, and you are false.

MRS MAR.   That I am false! What mean you?

FAIN.   To let you know I see through all your little arts. Come, you both love him, and both have equally dissembled your aversion. Your mutual jealousies of one another have made you clash till you have both struck fire. I have seen the warm confession reddening on your cheeks and sparkling from your eyes.

MRS MAR.   You do me wrong.

FAIN.   I do not. 'Twas for my ease to oversee[8] and wilfully neglect the gross advances made him by my wife; that by permitting her to be engaged, I might continue unsuspected in my pleasures, and take you oftener to my arms in full security. But could you think, because the nodding husband would not wake, that e'er the watchful lover slept?

MRS MAR.   And wherewithal can you reproach me?

FAIN.   With infidelity, with loving another, with love of Mirabell.

MRS MAR.   'Tis false. I challenge you to show an instance that can confirm your groundless accusation. I hate him.

FAIN.   And wherefore do you hate him? He is insensible, and your resentment follows his neglect. An instance? The injuries you have done him are a proof, your interposing in his love. What cause had you to make discoveries of his pretended passion? To undeceive the credulous aunt, and be the officious obstacle of his match with Millamant?

MRS MAR.   My obligations to my lady urged me; I had professed a friendship to her, and could not see her easy nature so abused by that dissembler.

FAIN.   What, was it conscience then? 'Professed a friendship'! O the pious friendships of the female sex!

MRS MAR.   More tender, more sincere, and more enduring than all the vain and empty vows of men, whether professing love to us or mutual faith to one another.

FAIN.   Ha, ha, ha! You are my wife's friend too.

MRS MAR.   Shame and ingratitude! Do you reproach me? You, you upbraid me! Have I been false to her, through strict fidelity to you, and sacrificed my friendship to keep my love inviolate? And have

---

[7]*insensible* unaware.   [8]*oversee* overlook.

you the baseness to charge me with the guilt, unmindful of the merit? To you it should be meritorious that I have been vicious. And do you reflect that guilt upon me, which should lie buried in your bosom?

FAIN.   You misinterpret my reproof. I meant but to remind you of the slight account⁹ you once could make of strictest ties, when set in competition with your love to me.

MRS MAR.   'Tis false. You urged it with deliberate malice. 'Twas spoke in scorn, and I never will forgive it.

FAIN.   Your guilt, not your resentment, begets your rage. If yet you loved, you could forgive a jealousy; but you are stung to find you are discovered.

MRS MAR.   It shall be all discovered. You too shall be discovered; be sure you shall. I can but be exposed. If I do it myself, I shall prevent¹⁰ your baseness.

FAIN.   Why, what will you do?

MRS MAR.   Disclose it to your wife; own what has passed between us.

FAIN.   Frenzy!

MRS MAR.   By all my wrongs I'll do't. I'll publish to the world the injuries you have done me, both in my fame and fortune. With both I trusted you, you bankrupt in honour, as indigent of wealth.

FAIN.   Your fame I have preserved. Your fortune has been bestowed as the prodigality of your love would have it, in pleasures which we both have shared. Yet had not you been false, I had e'er this repaid it – 'tis true. Had you permitted Mirabell with Millament to have stolen their marriage, my lady had been incensed beyond all means of reconcilement. Millamant had forfeited the moiety¹¹ of her fortune, which then would have descended to my wife. And wherefore did I marry, but to make lawful prize of a rich widow's wealth, and squander it on love and you?

MRS MAR.   Deceit and frivolous pretence.

FAIN.   Death, am I not married? What's pretence? Am I not imprisoned, fettered? Have I not a wife? Nay, a wife that was a widow, a young widow, a handsome widow, and would be again a widow, but that I have a heart of proof, and something of a constitution to bustle through the ways of wedlock and this world. Will you yet be reconciled to truth and me?

MRS MAR.   Impossible. Truth and you are inconsistent. I hate you, and shall forever.

FAIN.   For loving you?

MRS MAR.   I loath the name of love after such usage, and next to the guilt with which you would asperse me, I scorn you most. Farewell.

---

⁹*account* consideration.   ¹⁰*prevent* anticipate.   ¹¹*moiety* half.

FAIN.   Nay, we must not part thus.

MRS MAR.   Let me go.

FAIN.   Come, I'm sorry.

MRS MAR.   I care not. Let me go. Break my hands, do. I'd leave 'em to get loose.

FAIN.   I would not hurt you for the world. Have I no other hold to keep you here?

MRS MAR.   Well, I have deserved it all.

FAIN.   You know I love you.

MRS MAR.   Poor dissembling! Oh, that – Well, it is not yet –

FAIN.   What? What is it not? What is it not yet? It is not yet too late.

MRS MAR.   No, it is not yet too late. I have that comfort.

FAIN.   It is, to love another.

MRS MAR.   But not to loath, detest, abhor mankind, myself, and the whole treacherous world.

FAIN.   Nay, this is extravagance. Come, I ask your pardon. No tears. I was to blame; I could not love you and be easy in my doubts. Pray, forbear. I believe you. I'm convinced I've done you wrong, and any way, every way will make amends. I'll hate my wife yet more, damn her; I'll part with her, rob her of all she's worth, and we'll retire somewhere, anywhere, to another world. I'll marry thee. Be pacified. 'Sdeath, they come! Hide your face, your tears. You have a mask; wear it a moment. This way, this way. Be persuaded. *Exeunt*
     Enter MIRABELL *and* MRS FAINALL

MRS FAIN.   They are here yet.

MIRA.   They are turning into the other walk.

MRS FAIN.   While I only hated my husband, I could bear to see him; but since I have despised him, he's too offensive.

MIRA.   Oh, you should hate with prudence.

MRS FAIN.   Yes, for I have loved with indiscretion.

MIRA.   You should have just so much disgust for your husband as may be sufficient to make you relish your lover.

MRS FAIN.   You have been the cause that I have loved without bounds, and would you set limits to that aversion, of which you have been the occasion? Why did you make me marry this man?

MIRA.   Why do we daily commit disagreeable and dangerous actions? To save that idol, reputation. If the familiarities of our loves had produced that consequence of which you were apprehensive, where could you have fixed a father's name with credit, but on a husband? I knew Fainall to be a man lavish[12] of his morals, an interested[13] and professing friend, a false and a designing lover; yet

---

[12]*lavish* extravagant.   [13]*interested* self-interested.

one whose wit and outward fair behaviour have gained a reputation with the town, enough to make that woman stand excused who has suffered herself to be won by his addresses. A better man ought not to have been sacrificed to the occasion; a worse had not answered to the purpose. When you are weary of him, you know your remedy.

MRS FAIN. I ought to stand in some degree of credit with you, Mirabell.

MIRA. In justice to you, I have made you privy to my whole design, and put it in your power to ruin or advance my fortune.

MRS FAIN. Whom have you instructed to represent your pretended uncle?

MIRA. Waitwell, my servant.

MRS FAIN. He is an humble servant[14] to Foible, my mother's woman, and may win her to your interest.

MIRA. Care is taken for that. She is won and worn by this time. They were married this morning.

MRS FAIN. Who?

MIRA. Waitwell and Foible. I would not tempt my servant to betray me by trusting him too far. If your mother, in hopes to ruin me, should consent to marry my pretended uncle, he might, like Mosca in *The Fox*, stand upon terms;[15] so I made him sure beforehand.

MRS FAIN. So, if my poor mother is caught in a contract, you will discover[16] the imposture betimes,[17] and release her by producing a certificate of her gallant's former marriage.

MIRA. Yes, upon condition that she consent to my marriage with her niece, and surrender the moiety of her fortune in her possession.

MRS FAIN. She talked last night of endeavouring at a match between Millamant and your uncle.

MIRA. That was by Foible's direction, and my instruction, that she might seem to carry it more privately.

MRS FAIN. Well, I have an opinion of your success, for I believe my lady will do anything to get an husband; and when she has this, which you have provided for her, I suppose she will submit to anything to get rid of him.

MIRA. Yes, I think the good lady would marry anything that resembled a man, though 'twere no more than what a butler could pinch out of a napkin.[18]

---

[14]*servant* suitor.

[15]*terms* to bargain, like Mosca, the parasite, in Jonson's *Volpone* (1606), v, iii, vii, and viii.

[16]*discover* reveal. [17]*betimes* before it is too late.

[18]*napkin* to shape a napkin in an ingenious way.

MRS FAIN.   Female frailty! We must all come to it, if we live to be old, and feel the craving of a false appetite when the true is decayed.

MIRA.   An old woman's appetite is depraved like that of a girl. 'Tis the green-sickness of a second childhood; and, like the faint offer of a latter spring, serves but to usher in the fall; and withers in an affected bloom.

MRS FAIN.   Here's your mistress.

Enter MRS MILLAMANT, WITWOUD, MINCING

MIRA.   Here she comes, i'faith, full sail, with her fan spread and streamers out, and a shoal of fools for tenders. Ha, no; I cry her mercy.

MRS FAIN.   I see but one poor empty sculler, and he tows her woman after him.

MIRA.   You seem to be unattended, madam; you used to have the *beau monde* throng after you, and a flock of gay fine perukes[19] hovering round you.

WIT.   Like moths about a candle. I had like to have lost my comparison for want of breath.

MILLA.   Oh, I have denied myself airs today. I have walked as fast through the crowd –

WIT.   As a favourite just disgraced, and with as few followers.

MILLA.   Dear Mr Witwoud, truce with your similitudes, for I am as sick of 'em –

WIT.   As a physician of a good air. I cannot help it, madam, though 'tis against myself.

MILLA.   Yet again! Mincing, stand between me and his wit.

WIT.   Do, Mrs Mincing, like a screen before a great fire. I confess I do blaze today. I am too bright.

MRS FAIN.   But, dear Millamant, why were you so long?

MILLA.   Long! Lord, have I not made violent haste? I have asked every living thing I met for you; I have enquired after you as after a new fashion.

WIT.   Madam, truce with your similitudes. No, you met her husband, and did not ask him for her.

MIRA.   By your leave, Witwoud, that were like enquiring after an old fashion, to ask a husband for his wife.

WIT.   Hum, a hit, a hit, a palpable hit;[20] I confess it.

MRS FAIN.   You were dressed before I came abroad.

MILLA.   Ay, that's true – Oh, but then I had – Mincing, what had I? Why was I so long?

MINC.   O mem, your la'ship stayed to peruse a pecquet of letters.

---

[19]*perukes* wigs.   [20]*hit Hamlet* I, ii, 295.

MILLA. Oh, ay, letters. I had letters. I am persecuted with letters. I hate letters. Nobody knows how to write letters, and yet one has 'em, one does not know why. They serve one to pin up one's hair.

WIT. Is that the way? Pray, madam, do you pin up your hair with all your letters? I find I must keep copies.

MILLA. Only with those in verse, Mr Witwoud. I never pin up my hair with prose. I fancy one's hair would not curl if it were pinned up with prose. I think I tried once, Mincing.

MINC. O mem, I shall never forget it.

MILLA. Ay, poor Mincing tift and tift all the morning.

MINC. Till I had the cremp in my fingers, I'll vow, mem. And all to no purpose. But when your la'ship pins it up with poetry, it sits so pleasant the next day as anything, and is so pure and so crips.

WIT. Indeed, so crips?

MINC. You're such a critic, Mr Witwoud.

MILLA. Mirabell, did you take exceptions last night? Oh, ay, and went away. Now I think on't, I'm angry. No, now I think on't, I'm pleased; for I believe I gave you some pain.

MIRA. Does that please you?

MILLA. Infinitely! I love to give pain.

MIRA. You would affect a cruelty which is not in your nature; your true vanity is in the power of pleasing.

MILLA. Oh, I ask your pardon for that. One's cruelty is one's power, and when one parts with one's cruelty, one parts with one's power; and when one has parted with that, I fancy one's old and ugly.

MIRA. Ay, ay, suffer your cruelty to ruin the object of your power, to destroy your lover; and then how vain, how lost a thing you'll be. Nay, 'tis true: you are no longer handsome when you've lost your lover; your beauty dies upon the instant. For beauty is the lover's gift; 'tis he bestows your charms; your glass is all a cheat. The ugly and the old, whom the looking-glass mortifies, yet after commendation can be flattered by it, and discover beauties in it; for that reflects our praises rather than your face.

MILLA. Oh, the vanity of these men! Fainall,[21] d'ye hear him? If they did not commend us, we were not handsome! Now you must know they could not commend one if one was not handsome. Beauty the lover's gift? Lord, what is a lover, that it can give? Why, one makes lovers as fast as one pleases, and they live as long as one pleases, and they die as soon as one pleases; and then if one pleases one makes more.

[21]*Fainall* i.e. Mrs Fainall.

WIT. Very pretty. Why you make no more of making of lovers, madam, than of making so many card-matches.[22]

MILLA. One no more owes one's beauty to a lover than one's wit to an echo. They can but reflect what we look and say; vain, empty things if we are silent or unseen, and want a being.

MIRA. Yet to those two vain, empty things, you owe two [of] the greatest pleasures of your life.

MILLA. How so?

MIRA. To your lover you owe the pleasure of hearing yourselves praised; and to an echo the pleasure of hearing yourselves talk.

WIT. But I know a lady that loves talking so incessantly she won't give an echo fair play; she has that everlasting rotation of tongue that an echo must wait till she dies, before it can catch her last words.

MILLA. Oh, fiction! Fainall,[23] let us leave these men.

MIRA. (*Aside to* MRS FAINALL) Draw off Witwoud.

MRS FAIN. Immediately. I have a word or two for Mr Witwoud.

Exeunt WITWOUD *and* MRS FAINALL

MIRA. I would beg a little private audience too. You had the tyranny to deny me last night, though you knew I came to impart a secret to you that concerned my love.

MILLA. You saw I was engaged.

MIRA. Unkind. You had the leisure to entertain a herd of fools, things who visit you from their excessive idleness, bestowing on your easiness[24] that time which is the encumbrance of their lives. How can you find delight in such society? It is impossible they should admire you; they are not capable. Or if they were, it should be to you as a mortification; for sure, to please a fool is some degree of folly.

MILLA. I please myself. Besides, sometimes to converse with fools is for my health.

MIRA. Your health! Is there a worse disease than the conversation of fools?

MILLA. Yes, the vapours. Fools are physic for it, next to assafoetida.[25]

MIRA. You are not in a course of fools?[26]

MILLA. Mirabell, if you persist in this offensive freedom, you'll displease me. I think I must resolve after all not to have you. We shan't agree.

[22]*card-matches* matches made of strips of cardboard dipped in melted sulphur.
[23]*Fainall* i.e. Mrs Fainall.   [24]*easiness* tolerance.
[25]*assafoetida* a resinous gum, an antispasmodic.
[26]*fools* Are you taking a cure consisting of association with fools?

MIRA.   Not in our physic, it may be.

MILLA.   And yet our distemper in all likelihood will be the same; for we shall be sick of one another. I shan't endure to be reprimanded nor instructed. 'Tis so dull to act always by advice, and so tedious to be told of one's faults − I can't bear it. Well, I won't have you, Mirabell, I'm resolved − I think. You may go. Ha, ha, ha! What would you give that you could help loving me?

MIRA.   I would give something that you did not know I could not help it.

MILLA.   Come, don't look grave then. Well, what do you say to me?

MIRA.   I say that a man may as soon make a friend by his wit, or a fortune by his honesty, as win a woman with plain-dealing and sincerity.

MILLA.   Sententious Mirabell! Prithee don't look with that violent and infexible wise face, like Solomon at the dividing of the child in an old tapestry hanging.

MIRA.   You are merry, madam, but I would persuade you for one moment to be serious.

MILLA.   What, with that face? No, if you keep your countenance, 'tis impossible I should hold mine. Well, after all, there is something very moving in a lovesick face. Ha, ha, ha! Well, I won't laugh. Don't be peevish. Heighho! Now I'll be melancholy, as melancholy as a watch-light.[27] Well, Mirabell, if ever you will win me, woo me now. Nay, if you are so tedious, fare you well. I see they are walking away.

MIRA.   Can you not find in the variety of your disposition one moment −

MILLA.   To hear you tell me Foible's married, and your plot like to speed? No.

MIRA.   But how you came to know it −

MILLA.   Unless by the help of the devil, you can't imagine; unless she should tell me herself. Which of the two it may have been, I will leave you to consider; and when you have done thinking of that, think of me.   *Exit [with* MINCING]

MIRA.   I have something more − Gone! Think of you? To think of a whirlwind, though 'twere in a whirlwind, were a case of more steady contemplation, a very tranquility of mind and mansion. A fellow that lives in a windmill has not a more whimsical dwelling than the heart of a man that is lodged in a woman. There is no point of the compass to which they cannot turn, and by which they are not turned; and by one as well as another, for motion, not method, is

---

[27]*watch-light* a slow-burning candle, for use at night.

their occupation. To know this, and yet continue to be in love, is to be made wise from the dictates of reason, and yet persevere to play the fool by the force of instinct. Oh, here come my pair of turtles. What, billing so sweetly? Is not Valentine's Day over with you yet?

 Enter WAITWELL *and* FOIBLE

Sirrah, Waitwell, why sure you think you were married for your own recreation, and not for my conveniency.

WAIT. Your pardon, sir. With submission, we have indeed been solacing in lawful delights, but still with an eye to business, sir. I have instructed her as well as I could. If she can take your directions as readily as my instructions, sir, your affairs are in a prosperous way.

MIRA. Give you joy, Mrs Foible.

FOIB. Oh, 'las, sir, I'm so ashamed. I'm afraid my lady has been in a thousand inquietudes for me. But I protest, sir, I made as much haste as I could.

WAIT. That she did indeed, sir. It was my fault that she did not make more.

MIRA. That I believe.

FOIB. But I told my lady as you instructed me, sir: that I had a prospect of seeing Sir Rowland your uncle, and that I would put her ladyship's picture in my pocket to show him, which I'll be sure to say has made him so enamoured of her beauty that he burns with impatience to lie at her ladyship's feet and worship the original.

MIRA. Excellent Foible! Matrimony has made you eloquent in love.

WAIT. I think she has profited, sir. I think so.

FOIB. You have seen Madam Millamant, sir?

MIRA. Yes.

FOIB. I told her, sir, because I did not know that you might find an opportunity; she had so much company last night.

MIRA. Your deligence will merit more. In the meantime –

                 Gives money

FOIB. O dear sir, your humble servant.

WAIT. Spouse. [WAITWELL *attempts to take the money from* FOIBLE]

MIRA. Stand off, sir, not a penny. Go on and prosper, Foible. The lease shall be made good and the farm stocked if we succeed.[28]

FOIB. I don't question your generosity, sir, and you need not doubt of success. If you have no more commands, sir, I'll be gone; I'm sure my lady is at her toilet, and can't dress till I come. (*Looking out*) Oh,

---

[28]*succeed* Mirabell has apparently offered them a farm and livestock as an incentive to participate in his scheme.

dear, I'm sure that was Mrs Marwood that went by in a mask. If she has seen me with you I'm sure she'll tell my lady. I'll make haste home and prevent her. Your servant, sir. B'w'y, Waitwell.

Exit FOIBLE

WAIT. Sir Rowland, if you please. The jade's so pert upon her preferment she forgets herself.

MIRA. Come, sir, will you endeavour to forget yourself and transform into Sir Rowland.

WAIT. Why, sir, it will be impossible I should remember myself. Married, knighted, and attended all in one day! 'Tis enough to make any man forget himself. The difficulty will be how to recover my acquaintance and familiarity with my former self, and fall from my transformation to a reformation into Waitwell. Nay, I shan't be quite the same Waitwell neither; for now I remember me, I'm married and can't be my own man again.

    Ay, there's the grief; that's the sad change of life,
    To lose my title, and yet keep my wife.   *Exeunt*

Act Three

SCENE ONE

A room in LADY WISHFORT'S *house*

LADY WISHFORT *at her toilet,* PEG *waiting*

LADY. Merciful, no news of Foible yet?

PEG. No, madam.

LADY. I have no more patience. If I have not fretted myself till I am pale again, there's no veracity in me. Fetch me the red – the red, do you hear, sweetheart? An arrant ash colour, as I'm a person![1] Look you how this wench stirs! Why dost thou not fetch me a little red? Didst thou not hear me, mopus?[2]

PEG. The red ratafia does your ladyship mean, or the cherry brandy?

LADY. Ratafia, fool? No, fool. Not the ratafia, fool. Grant me patience! I mean the Spanish paper,[3] idiot. Complexion, darling. Paint, paint, paint! Dost thou understand that, changeling,[4] dangling thy hands like bobbins before thee? Why dost thou not stir, puppet? Thou wooden thing upon wires!

PEG. Lord, madam, your ladyship is so impatient! I cannot come at the paint, madam. Mrs Foible has locked it up, and carried the key with her.

LADY. A pox take you both! Fetch me the cherry brandy then.

Exit PEG

I'm as pale and as faint, I look like Mrs Qualmsick, the curate's wife, that's always breeding. Wench, come! Come, wench! What art thou doing? Sipping? Tasting? Save thee, dost thou not know the bottle?

Enter PEG *with a bottle and china cup*

PEG. Madam, I was looking for a cup.

LADY. A cup, save thee! And what a cup hast thou brought! Dost thou take me for a fairy, to drink out of an acorn? Why didst thou not bring thy thimble? Hast thou ne'er a brass thimble clinking in thy pocket with a bit of nutmeg? I warrant thee. Come, fill, fill. So –

---

[1]*person* someone of consequence.   [2]*mopus* stupid.

[3]*Spanish paper* paper impregnated with rouge, made in Spain.

[4]*changeling* In folklore, fairies were said to steal an attractive child, leaving in exchange an ugly or stupid one.

again. (*One knocks*) See who that is, Set down the bottle first! Here, here, under the table. What, wouldst thou go with the bottle in thy hand, like a tapster? As I'm a person, this wench has lived in an inn upon the road, before she came to me, like Maritornes the Asturian in *Don Quixote*.[5] No Foible yet?

PEG.   No, madam, Mrs Marwood.

LADY.   Oh, Marwood; let her come in. Come in, good Marwood.

   Enter MRS MARWOOD

MRS MAR.   I'm surprised to find your ladyship in *déshabillé* at this time of day.

LADY.   Foible's a lost thing; has been abroad since morning, and never heard of since.

MRS MAR.   I saw her but now, as I came masked through the park, in conference with Mirabell.

LADY.   With Mirabell! You call my blood into my face, with mentioning that traitor. She durst not have the confidence. I sent her to negotiate an affair, in which if I'm detected I'm undone. If that wheedling villain has wrought upon Foible to detect me, I'm ruined. O my dear friend, I'm a wretch of wretches if I'm detected.

MRS MAR.   O madam, you cannot suspect Mrs Foible's integrity.

LADY.   Oh, he carries poison in his tongue that would corrupt integrity itself. If she has given him an opportunity, she has as good as put her integrity into his hands. Ah, dear Marwood, what's integrity to an opportunity? – Hark! I hear her. – [*To* PEG] Go, you thing, and send her in. (*Exit* PEG) – Dear friend, retire into my closet, that I may examine her with more freedom – You'll pardon me, dear friend; I can make bold with you. There are books over the chimney – Quarles[6] and Prynne,[7] and *The Short View of the Stage*,[8] with Bunyan's works to entertain you.   *Exit* MRS MARWOOD

   Enter FOIBLE

LADY.   O Foible, where hast thou been? What hast thou been doing?

FOIB.   Madam, I have seen the party.[9]

LADY.   But what hast thou done?

---

[5]*Quixote* Maritornes was a homely chambermaid, from Asturias, north-west Spain, in Cervantes' story (I, xvi). Thomas D'Urfey's play, *The History of Don Quixote*, 1694, was popular. See Part I; II, i.

[6]*Quarles* Francis Quarles, author of religious poetry and narratives; *Emblemes*, 1696.

[7]*Prynne* William Prynne, *Historio-Mastix. The Players Scourge . . .*, 1633 and many later editions; a 1006-page Puritan attack on the stage.

[8]*Stage* i.e. *A Short View of the Immorality and Profaneness of the English Stage*, 1698, by Jeremy Collier. He attacked Congreve's earlier plays; Chapter II, pp. 63–74.

[9]*the party* i.e. Sir Rowland.

FOIB. Nay, 'tis your ladyship has done, and are to do. I have only
promised. But a man so enamoured, so transported! Well, here it is
[*Passing a miniature to her*], all that is left, all that is not kissed
away. Well, if worshipping of pictures be a sin – poor Sir Rowland, I
say.

LADY. The miniature has been counted like.[10] But hast thou not
betrayed me, Foible? Hast thou not detected me to that faithless
Mirabell? What hadst thou to do with him in the park? Answer me,
has he got nothing out of thee?

FOIB. [*Aside*] So, the devil has been beforehand with me. What shall
I say? – Alas, madam, could I help it if I met that confident thing?
Was I in fault? If you had heard how he used me, and all upon your
ladyship's account, I'm sure you would not suspect my fidelity. Nay,
if that had been the worst, I could have borne; but he had a fling at
your ladyship too; and then I could not hold; but, i'faith, I gave him
his own.

LADY. Me? What did the filthy fellow say?

FOIB. O madam; 'tis a shame to say what he said, with his taunts and
his fleers, tossing up his nose. 'Humh,' says he, 'what, you are a-
hatching some plot,' says he, 'you are so early abroad, or catering,'
says he, 'ferreting for some disbanded officer, I warrant. Half pay is
but thin subsistence,' says he. 'Well, what pension does your lady
propose? Let me see,' says he, 'what, she must have come down[11]
pretty deep now, she's superannuated,' says he, 'and' –

LADY. Ods my life, I'll have him, I'll have him murdered! I'll have
him poisoned. Where does he eat? I'll marry a drawer to have him
poisoned in his wine! I'll send for Robin from Locket's[12] immediately!

FOIB. Poison him? Poisoning's too good for him. Starve him,
madam, starve him. Marry Sir Rowland, and get him disinherited.
Oh, you would bless yourself to hear what he said.

LADY. A villain! 'Superannuated!'

FOIB. 'Humh,' says he, 'I hear you are laying designs against me too,'
says he, 'and Mrs Millamant is to marry my uncle,' – he does not
suspect a word of your ladyship – 'but,' says he, 'I'll fit you for that. I
warrant you,' says he, 'I'll hamper you for that,' says he, 'you and
your old frippery[13] too,' says he, 'I'll handle you' –

---

10 *like* a good likeness.
11 *come down* pay a large sum to entice someone to be her husband.
12 *Locket's* a famous ordinary at Spring Garden, near Charing Cross; the
proprietor was Adam Locket.
13 *frippery* old clothes.

LADY. Audacious villain! Handle me! Would he durst! 'Frippery?' 'Old frippery!' Was there ever such a foul-mouthed fellow? I'll be married tomorrow; I'll be contracted tonight.

FOIB. The sooner the better, madam.

LADY. Will Sir Rowland be here, say'st thou? When, Foible?

FOIB. Incontinently,[14] madam. No new sheriff's wife expects the return of her husband after knighthood with that impatience in which Sir Rowland burns for the dear hour of kissing your ladyship's hands after dinner.

LADY. 'Frippery!' 'Superannuated frippery!' I'll frippery the villain. I'll reduce him to frippery and rags. A tatterdemallion. I hope to see him hung with tatters, like a Long-Lane penthouse,[15] or a gibbet-thief. A slander-mouthed railer! I warrant the spendthrift prodigal's in debt as much as the million lottery,[16] or the whole Court upon a birthday.[17] I'll spoil his credit with his tailor. Yes, he shall have my niece with her fortune, he shall!

FOIB. He! I hope to see him lodge in Ludgate[18] first, and angle into Blackfriars for brass farthings with an old mitten.

LADY. Ay, dear Foible. Thank thee for that, dear Foible. He has put me out of all patience. I shall never recompose my features to receive Sir Rowland with any economy of face.[19] This wretch has fretted me that I am absolutely decayed. Look, Foible.

FOIB. Your ladyship has frowned a little too rashly indeed, madam. There are some cracks discernible in the white varnish.

LADY. Let me see the glass. Cracks, say'st thou? Why, I am arrantly flayed. I look like an old peeled wall. Thou must repair me, Foible, before Sir Rowland comes, or I shall never keep up to my picture.

FOIB. I warrant you, madam, a little art once made your picture like you, and now a little of the same art must make you like your picture. Your picture must sit for you, madam.

LADY. But art thou sure Sir Rowland will not fail to come? Or will a not fail when he does come? Will he be importunate, Foible, and push? For if he should not be importunate – I shall never break decorums. I shall die with confusion, if I am forced to advance. Oh

[14]*Incontinently* Immediately.

[15]*penthouse* a covered stall in Long Lane, between West Smithfield and Barbican, where old clothes were sold.

[16]*lottery* a government scheme to raise £1,000,000 in 1694 by means of lottery tickets at £10 each. This sum was paid back, in instalments, over several years, and certain tickets won valuable cash prizes.

[17]*birthday* the extravagant celebration by the court of a royal birthday.

[18]*Ludgate* From Ludgate Prison prisoners lowered mittens on a string to beg for contributions from passersby.

[19]*face* the additional cost of cosmetics.

no, I can never advance – I shall swoon if he should expect advances. No, I hope Sir Rowland is better bred than to put a lady to the necessity of breaking her forms. I won't be too coy neither. I won't give him despair, but a little disdain is not amiss; a little scorn is alluring.

FOIB.   A little scorn becomes your ladyship.

LADY.   Yes, but tenderness becomes me best, a sort of a dyingness. You see that picture has a sort of a – Ha, Foible? – a swimmingness in the eyes. Yes, I'll look so. My niece affects it; but she wants features. Is Sir Rowland handsome? Let my toilet[20] be removed; I'll dress above. I'll receive Sir Rowland here. Is he handsome? Don't answer me. I won't know; I'll be surprised. I'll be taken by surprise.

FOIB.   By storm, madam. Sir Rowland's a brisk man.

LADY.   Is he? Oh, then he'll importune if he's a brisk man. I shall save decorums if Sir Rowland importunes. I have a mortal terror at the apprehension of offending against decorums. Nothing but importunity can surmount decorums. Oh, I'm glad he's a brisk man. Let my things be removed, good Foible.   *Exit*

    Enter MRS FAINALL

MRS FAIN.   O Foible, I have been in a fright lest I should come too late. That devil, Marwood, saw you in the park with Mirabell, and I'm afraid will discover it to my lady.

FOIB.   Discover what, madam?

MRS FAIN.   Nay, nay, put not on that strange face. I am privy to the whole design, and know that Waitwell, to whom thou wert this morning married, is to personate Mirabell's uncle, and as such, winning my lady, to involve her in those difficulties from which Mirabell only must release her, by his making his conditions to have my cousin and her fortune left to her own disposal.

FOIB.   O dear madam, I beg your pardon. It was not my confidence in your ladyship that was deficient; but I thought the former good correspondence between your ladyship and Mr Mirabell might have hindered his communicating this secret.

MRS FAIN.   Dear Foible, forget that.

FOIB.   O dear madam, Mr Mirabell is such a sweet, winning gentleman, but your ladyship is the pattern of generosity. Sweet lady, to be so good! Mr Mirabell cannot choose but be grateful. I find your ladyship has his heart still. Now, madam, I can safely tell your ladyship our success. Mrs Marwood had told my lady, but I warrant I managed myself. I turned it all for the better. I told my lady that Mr Mirabell railed at her. I laid horrid things to his charge, I'll

---

[20]*toilet* an elaborate decorated cloth for a dressing table.

vow; and my lady is so incensed that she'll be contracted to Sir Rowland tonight she says. I warrant I worked her up, that he may have her for asking for, as they say of a Welsh maidenhead.

MRS FAIN.   O rare Foible!

FOIB.   Madam, I beg your ladyship to acquaint Mr Mirabell of his success. I would be seen as little as possible to speak to him. Besides, I believe Madam Marwood watches me. She has a month's mind,[21] but I know Mr Mirabell can't abide her. – [*Calls*] John – Remove my lady's toilet. (*Enter footman and exit*) Madam, your servant. My lady is so impatient, I fear she'll come for me if I stay.

MRS FAIN.   I'll go with you up the back stairs, lest I should meet her.

Exeunt

Enter MRS MARWOOD

MRS MAR.   Indeed, Mrs Engine, is it thus with you? Are you become a go-between of this importance? Yes, I shall watch you. Why, this wench is the *passe partout*, a very master-key to everybody's strong box. My friend Fainall, have you carried it so swimmingly? I thought there was something in it; but it seems it's over with you. Your loathing is not from a want of appetite then, but from a surfeit. Else you could never be so cool to fall from a principal to be an assistant. To procure for him! A pattern of generosity, that I confess. Well, Mr Fainall, you have met with your match. O man, man! Woman, woman! The devil's an ass. If I were a painter, I would draw him like an idiot, a driveler with a bib and bells. Man should have his head and horns,[22] and woman the rest of him. Poor simple fiend! 'Madam Marwood has a month's mind, but he can't abide her'. 'Twere better for him you had not been his confessor in that affair, without you could have kept his counsel closer. I shall not prove another pattern of generosity and stalk for him, till he takes his stand to aim at a fortune. He has not obliged me to that, with those excesses of himself; and now I'll have none of him. Here comes the good lady, panting ripe, with a heart full of hope and a head full of care, like any chemist upon the day of projection.[23]

Enter LADY WISHFORT

LADY.   O dear Marwood, what shall I say for this rude forgetfulness? But my dear friend is all goodness.

MRS MAR.   No apologies, dear madam. I have been very well entertained.

---

[21]*month's mind* a strong inclination.

[22]*horns* the traditional emblem of the cuckold.

[23]*projection* the climax of an alchemist's attempt to transmute base metals into gold.

LADY.   As I'm a person, I am in a very chaos to think I should so
forget myself; but I have such an olio[24] of affairs, really I know not
what to do. – (*Calls*) Foible! I expect my nephew Sir Wilfull every
moment too. – Why, Foible! He means to travel for improvement.

MRS MAR.   Methinks Sir Wilfull should rather think of marrying than
travelling at his years. I hear he is turned of forty.

LADY.   Oh, he's in less danger of being spoiled by his travels. I am
against my nephew's marrying too young. It will be time enough
when he comes back and has acquired discretion to choose for
himself.

MRS MAR.   Methinks Mrs Millamant and he would make a very fit
match. He may travel afterwards. 'Tis a thing very usual with young
gentlemen.

LADY.   I promise you I have thought on't, and since 'tis your
judgment, I'll think on't again. I assure you I will; I value your
judgment extremely. On my word I'll propose it.

 Enter FOIBLE

LADY.   Come, come, Foible. I had forgot my nephew will be here
before dinner. I must make haste.

FOIB.   Mr Witwoud and Mr Petulant are come to dine with your
ladyship.

LADY.   Oh dear, I can't appear till I am dressed. Dear Marwood, shall
I be free with you again and beg you to entertain 'em? I'll make all
imaginable haste. Dear friend, excuse me.

       Exeunt LADY WISHFORT *and* FOIBLE
 Enter MRS MILLAMANT *and* MINCING

MILLA.   Sure never anything was so unbred as that odious man!
Marwood, your servant.

MRS MAR.   You have a colour. What's the matter?

MILLA.   That horrid fellow Petulant has provoked me into a flame. I
have broke my fan. Mincing, lend my yours. Is not all the powder
out of my hair?

MRS MAR.   No. What has he done?

MILLA.   Nay, he has done nothing; he has only talked. Nay, he has
said nothing neither; but he has contradicted everything that has
been said. For my part, I thought Witwoud and he would have
quarrelled.

MINC.   I vow, mem, I thought once they would have fit.

MILLA.   Well, 'tis a lamentable thing, I'll swear, that one has not the
liberty of choosing one's acquaintance as one does one's clothes.

MRS MAR.   If we had that liberty, we should be as weary of one set of

 [24]olio hotchpotch.

acquaintance, though never so good, as we are of one suit, though never so fine. A fool and a doily stuff[25] would now and then find days of grace,[26] and be worn for variety.

MILLA. I could consent to wear 'em, if they would wear alike; but fools never wear out. They are such *drap-de-Berry*[27] things without[28] one could give 'em to one's chambermaid after a day or two.

MRS MAR. 'Twere better so indeed. Or what think you of the playhouse? A fine, gay, glossy fool should be given there, like a new masking habit,[29] after the masquerade is over, and we have done with the disguise. For a fool's visit is always a disguise, and never admitted by a woman of wit, but to blind her affair with a lover of sense. If you would but appear barefaced now, and own Mirabell, you might as easily put off Petulant and Witwoud as your hood and scarf. And indeed 'tis time, for the town has found it; the secret is grown too big for the pretence. 'Tis like Mrs Primly's great belly; she may lace it down before, but it burnishes on her hips. Indeed, Millamant, you can no more conceal it than my Lady Strammel can her face, that goodly face, which in defiance of her Rhenish-wine tea,[30] will not be comprehended[31] in a mask.

MILLA. I'll take my death, Marwood, you are more censorious than a decayed beauty or a discarded toast;[32] Mincing, tell the men they may come up. My aunt is not dressing here. (*Exit* MINCING) Their folly is less provoking than your malice. 'The town has found it'. What has it found? That Mirabell loves me is no more a secret than it is a secret that you discovered it to my aunt, or than the reason why you discovered it is a secret.

MRS MAR. You are nettled.

MILLA. You're mistaken. Ridiculous!

MRS MAR. Indeed, my dear, you'll tear another fan if you don't mitigate those violent airs.

MILLA. Oh, silly! Ha, ha, ha! I could laugh immoderately. Poor Mirabell! His constancy to me has quite destroyed his complaisance for all the world beside. I swear I never enjoined it him to be so coy. If I

---

[25]*doily stuff* a light, inexpensive woollen cloth, invented by Thomas Doyley, a late-seventeenth-century linen-draper in the Strand.

[26]*days of grace* time allotted for repentance.

[27]*drap-de-Berry* a coarse woollen cloth originating in the province of Berry, France.

[28]*without* unless.   [29]*habit* ensemble.

[30]*Rhenish-wine tea* Used as a substitute for tea, Rhenish wine was believed to cure obesity.

[31]*comprehended* restrained.

[32]*discarded toast* someone once toasted, now ignored.

had the vanity to think he would obey me, I would command him to
show more gallantry. 'Tis hardly well-bred to be so particular on
one hand and so insensible on the other. But I despair to prevail, and
so let him follow his own way. Ha, ha, ha! Pardon me, dear creature,
I must laugh – ha, ha, ha! – though I grant you 'tis a little barbarous.
Ha, ha, ha!

MRS MAR.   What a pity 'tis, so much fine raillery, and delivered with
so significant gesture, should be so unhappily directed to miscarry.

MILLA.   Ha? Dear creature, I ask your pardon; I swear I did not mind
you.33

MRS MAR.   Mr Mirabell and you both may think it a thing
impossible, when I shall tell him, by telling you –

MILLA.   Oh dear, what? For it is the same thing, if I hear it. Ha, ha,
ha!

MRS MAR.   That I detest him, hate him, madam.

MILLA.   O madam, why so do I. And yet the creature loves me. Ha,
ha, ha! How can one forbear laughing to think of it? I am a sybil34 if I
am not amazed to think what he can see in me. I'll take my death, I
think you are handsomer, and within a year or two as young. If you
could but stay for me, I should overtake you; but that cannot be.
Well, that thought makes me melancholy. Now I'll be sad.

MRS MAR.   Your merry note may be changed sooner than you think.

MILLA.   D'ye say so? Then I'm resolved I'll have a song to keep up my
spirits.

Enter MINCING

MINC.   The gentlemen stay but to comb, madam, and will wait on
you.

MILLA.   Desire Mrs ——,35 that is in the next room, to sing the song I
would have learnt yesterday. You shall hear it, madam. Not that
there's any great matter in it, but 'tis agreeable to my humour.

SONG
*Set by Mr John Eccles,*36 *and sung by* MRS HODGSON37

I

Love's but the frailty of the mind,
When 'tis not with ambition join'd;
A sickly flame, which if not fed expires,
And feeding, wastes in self-consuming fires.

33*mind you* have you in mind.   34*sybil* prophetess.
35*Mrs* —— so in the first edition, 1700; the actress fills in the appropriate name.
36*John Eccles c.* 1668–1735; a popular composer.
37*Mrs Hodgson* a contemporary professional singer.

II

'Tis not to wound a wanton boy
Or am'rous youth that gives the joy;
But 'tis the glory to have pierc'd a swain,
For whom inferior beauties sigh'd in vain.

III

Then I alone the conquest prize,
When I insult a rival's eyes:
If there's delight in love, 'tis when I see
That heart which others bleed for, bleed for me.

Enter PETULANT *and* WITWOUD

MILLA. Is your animosity composed, gentlemen?

WIT. Raillery, raillery, madam. We have no animosity. We hit off a little wit now and then, but no animosity. The falling out of wits is like the falling out of lovers. We agree in the main, like treble and base. Ha, Petulant?

PET. Ay, in the main, but when I have a humour to contradict –

WIT. Ay, when he has a humour to contradict, then I contradict too. What, I know my cue. Then we contradict one another like two battledores,[38] for contradictions beget one another like Jews.

PET. If he says black's black – if I have a humour to say 'tis blue – let that pass – all's one for that. If I have a humour to prove it, it must be granted.

WIT. Not positively must, but it may, it may.

PET. Yes, it positively must, upon proof positive.

WIT. Ay, upon proof positive it must; but upon proof presumptive, it only may. That's a logical distinction now, madam.

MRS MAR. I perceive your debates are of importance and very learnedly handled.

PET. Importance is one thing and learning's another; but a debate's a debate, that I assert.

WIT. Petulant's an enemy to learning; he relies altogether on his parts.[39]

PET. No, I'm no enemy to learning; it hurts not me.

MRS MAR. That's a sign indeed it's no enemy to you!

PET. No, no, it's no enemy to anybody but them that have it.

MILLA. Well, an illiterate man's my aversion; I wonder at the impudence of any illiterate man to offer to make love.

WIT. That I confess I wonder at too.

---

[38]*battledores* the rackets used to hit the shuttlecocks.
[39]*parts* natural abilities.

MILLA.   Ah, to marry an ignorant that can hardly read or write.

PET.   Why should a man be the further from being married though
he can't read, any more than he is from being hanged? The
ordinary's⁴⁰ paid for setting the psalm, and the parish priest for
reading the ceremony. And for the rest which is to follow in both
cases, a man may do it without book – so all's one for that.

MILLA.   D'ye hear the creature? Lord, here's company, I'll be gone.

Exeunt MILLAMANT *and* MINCING

WIT.   In the name of Bartlemew and his fair,⁴¹ what have we here?

MRS MAR.   'Tis your brother, I fancy. Don't you know him?

WIT.   Not I. Yes, I think it is he – I've almost forgot him. I have not
seen him since the Revolution.

Enter SIR WILFULL WITWOUD, *in a country riding habit, and*
SERVANT *to* LADY WISHFORT

FOOT.   Sir, my lady's dressing. Here's company, if you please to
walk in, in the meantime.

SIR WIL.   Dressing! What, it's but morning here I warrant with you
in London; we should count it towards afternoon in our parts,
down in Shropshire. – Why then, belike my aunt han't dined yet,
ha, friend?

FOOT.   Your aunt, sir?

SIR WIL.   My aunt, sir, yes, my aunt, sir, and your lady, sir. Your
lady is my aunt, sir. Why, what, do'st thou not know me, friend?
Why then, send somebody here that does. How long hast thou
lived with thy lady, fellow, ha?

FOOT.   A week, sir; longer than anybody in the house, except my
lady's woman.

SIR WIL.   Why then, belike thou dost not know thy lady if thou
see'st her, ha, friend?

FOOT.   Why truly, sir, I cannot safely swear to her face in a morning,
before she is dressed. 'Tis like I may give a shrewd guess at her by
this time.

SIR WIL.   Well, prithee try what thou canst do. If thou canst not
guess, enquire her out, do'st hear, fellow? And tell her, her nephew,
Sir Wilfull Witwoud, is in the house.

FOOT.   I shall, sir.

SIR WIL.   Hold ye; hear me, friend. A word with you in your ear.
Prithee who are these gallants?

FOOT.   Really, sir, I can't tell. Here come so many here, 'tis hard to
know 'em all.   *Exit* SERVANT

⁴⁰*ordinary* the clergyman who attended a criminal before he was hanged.

⁴¹*fair* held on St Bartholomew's Day, 24 August, and a few days following, at
Smithfield, London.

SIR WIL.   Oons, this fellow knows less than a starling; I don't think a knows his own name.

MRS MAR.   Mr Witwoud, your brother is not behindhand in forgetfulness. I fancy he has forgot you too.

WIT.   I hope so. The devil take him that remembers first, I say.

SIR WIL.   Save you, gentlemen and lady.

MRS MAR.   For shame, Mr Witwoud; why won't you speak to him? – And you, sir.

WIT.   Petulant, speak.

PET.   And you, sir.

SIR WIL.   No offence, I hope.   *Salutes* MARWOOD

MRS MAR.   No, sure, sir.

WIT.   This is a vile dog, I see that already. 'No offence'! Ha, ha, ha! To him, to him, Petulant, smoke⁴² him.

PET.   It seems as if you had come a journey, sir; hem, hem.
                                        Surveying him round

SIR WIL.   Very likely, sir, that it may seem so.

PET.   No offence, I hope, sir.

WIT.   Smoke the boots, the boots. Petulant, the boots! Ha, ha, ha!

SIR WIL.   Maybe not, sir; thereafter as 'tis meant, sir.

PET.   Sir, I presume upon the information of your boots.

SIR WIL.   Why, 'tis like you may, sir: if you are not satisfied with the information of my boots, sir, if you will step to the stable, you may enquire further of my horse, sir.

PET.   Your horse, sir! Your horse is an ass, sir!

SIR WIL.   Do you speak by way of offence, sir?

MRS MAR.   The gentleman's merry, that's all, sir – [*Aside*] 'Slife, we shall have a quarrel betwixt an horse and an ass, before they find one another out. – You must not take anything amiss from your friends, sir. You are among your friends here, though it may be you don't know it. If I am not mistaken, you are Sir Wilfull Witwoud.

SIR WIL.   Right, lady. I am Sir Wilfull Witwoud, so I write myself. No offence to anybody, I hope. And nephew to the Lady Wishfort of this mansion.

MRS MAR.   Don't you know this gentleman, sir?

SIR WIL.   Hum! What, sure 'tis not – Yea, by'r Lady, but 'tis – 'Sheart, I know not whether 'tis or no – Yea, but 'tis, by the Wrekin!⁴³ Brother Anthony! What, Tony, i'faith! What, do'st thou not know me? By'r Lady, nor I thee, thou art so becravated, and so beperriwigged. 'Sheart, why do'st not speak? Art thou o'erjoyed?

WIT.   Odso, brother, is it you? Your servant, brother.

---

⁴²*smoke* take notice of.   ⁴³*Wrekin* a hill in Shropshire.

SIR WIL.   Your servant! Why yours, sir. Your servant again. 'Sheart, and your friend and servant to that – and a – (*Puff*) and a flapdragon[44] for your service, sir; and a hare's foot, and a hare's scut[45] for your service, sir, an you be so cold and so courtly!

WIT.   No offence, I hope, brother.

SIR WIL.   'Sheart, sir, but there is, and much offence. A pox, is this your Inns-o'-Court breeding, not to know your friends and your relations, your elders and your betters?

WIT.   Why, brother Wilfull of Salop, you may be as short as a Shrewsbury cake, if you please. But I tell you 'tis not modish to know relations in town. You think you're in the country, where great lubberly brothers slabber and kiss one another when they meet, like a call of sergeants.[46] 'Tis not the fashion here; 'tis not indeed, dear brother.

SIR WIL.   The fashion's a fool; and you're a fop, dear brother. 'Sheart, I've suspected this. By'r Lady, I conjectured you were a fop since you began to change the style of your letters, and write in a scrap of paper, gilt round the edges, no bigger than a subpaena. I might expect this when you left off 'Honoured Brother', and 'hoping you are in good health', and so forth – to begin with a 'Rat me,[47] knight, I'm so sick of a last night's debauch' – Ods heart, and then tell a familiar tale of a cock and a bull,[48] and a whore and a bottle, and so conclude. You could write news before you were out of your time,[49] when you lived with honest Pumplenose, the attorney of Furnival's Inn. You could entreat to be remembered then to your friends round the Wrekin. We could have gazettes then, and *Dawks's Letter*,[50] and *The Weekly Bill*,[51] till of late days.

PET.   'Slife, Witwoud, were you ever an attorney's clerk? Of the family of the Furnivals? Ha, ha, ha!

WIT.   Ay, ay, but that was but for a while. Not long, not long. Pshaw, I was not in my own power then. An orphan, and this fellow was my guardian. Ay, ay, I was glad to consent to that, man, to come to London. He had the disposal of me then. If I had not agreed to that, I might have been bound prentice to a felt-maker in Shrewsbury. This fellow would have bound me to a maker of felts!

[44]*flapdragon* a raisin dropped in flaming brandy.   [45]*scut* tail.

[46]*sergeants* a group of sergeants-at-law called to the bar at the same time.

[47]*Rat me* May God rot me.   [48]*bull* a preposterous story.

[49]*time* had completed your apprenticeship.

[50]*Dawks's Letter* a popular thrice-weekly newsletter, 1696–1716, printed with manuscript type.

[51]*The Weekly Bill* The Weekly Bills of Mortality for London, published, 1538–1837, by the Parish Clerks Company.

SIR WIL. 'Sheart, and better than to be bound to a maker of fops, where, I suppose, you have served your time, and now you may set up for yourself.

MRS MAR. You intend to travel, sir, as I'm informed.

SIR WIL. Belike I may, madam. I may chance to sail upon the salt seas, if my mind hold.

PET. And the wind serve.

SIR WIL. Serve or not serve, I shan't ask licence of you, sir, nor the weathercock your companion. I direct my discourse to the lady, sir. 'Tis like my aunt may have told you, madam. Yes, I have settled my concerns, I may say now, and am minded to see foreign parts. If an how that the peace[52] holds, whereby, that is, taxes abate.

MRS MAR. I thought you had designed for France at all adventures.

SIR WIL. I can't tell that; 'tis like I may, and 'tis like I may not. I am somewhat dainty in making a resolution, because when I make it I keep it. I don't stand shill I, shall I, then; if I say't, I'll do't. But I have thoughts to tarry a small matter in town, to learn somewhat of your lingo first, before I cross the seas. I'd gladly have a spice of your French, as they say, whereby to hold discourse in foreign countries.

MRS MAR. Here is an academy in town for that use.

SIR WIL. There is? 'Tis like there may.

MRS MAR. No doubt you will return very much improved.

WIT. Yes, refined,[53] like a Dutch skipper from a whale-fishing.

Enter LADY WISHFORT *and* FAINALL

LADY. Nephew, you are welcome.

SIR WIL. Aunt, your servant.

FAIN. Sir Wilfull, your most faithful servant.

SIR WIL. Cousin Fainall, give me your hand.

LADY. Cousin Witwoud, your servant; Mr Petulant, your servant. Nephew, you are welcome again. Will you drink anything after your journey, nephew, before you eat? Dinner's almost ready.

SIR WIL. I'm very well, I thank you, aunt; however, I thank you for your courteous offer. 'Sheart, I was afraid you would have been in the fashion too, and have remembered to have forgot your relations. Here's your cousin Tony; belike I mayn't call him brother for fear of offence.

LADY. Oh, he's a rallier, nephew. My cousin's a wit and your great wits always rally their best friends to choose.[54] When you have been abroad, nephew, you'll understand raillery better.

FAINALL *and* MRS MARWOOD *talk apart*

---

[52]*peace* The Peace of Ryswick, 1697, ended the War of the League of Augsburg between France and England. The War of the Spanish Succession began in 1701.
[53]*refined* i.e. unrefined.　　[54]*to choose* by choice.

SIR WIL.   Why then, let him hold his tongue in the meantime, and rail when that day comes.

Enter MINCING

MINC.   Mem, I come to acquaint your la'ship that dinner is impatient.

SIR WIL.   Impatient? Why then, belike it won't stay till I pull off my boots. Sweetheart, can you help me to a pair of slippers? My man's with his horses, I warrant.

LADY.   Fie, fie, nephew, you would not pull off your boots here. Go down into the hall. Dinner shall stay for you. My nephew's a little unbred; you'll pardon him, madam. Gentlemen, will you walk? Marwood, –

MRS MAR.   I'll follow you, madam, before Sir Wilfull is ready.

Manent MRS MARWOOD *and* FAINALL

FAIN.   Why then, Foible's a bawd, an arrant, rank, matchmaking bawd. And I, it seems, am a husband, a rank husband, and my wife a very arrant, rank wife, all in the way of the world. 'Sdeath, to be an anticipated cuckold, a cuckold in embryo! Sure I was born with budding antlers, like a young satyr or a citizen's child.⁵⁵ 'Sdeath, to be outwitted, to be outjilted – out-matrimonied! If I had kept my speed, like a stag, 'twere somewhat, but to crawl after, with my horns, like a snail, and be outstripped by my wife – 'tis scurvy wedlock.

MRS MAR.   Then shake it off. You have often wished for an opportunity to part, and now you have it. But first prevent their plot; the half of Millamant's fortune is too considerable to be parted with, to a foe, to Mirabell.

FAIN.   Damn him! That had been mine, had you not made that fond discovery.⁵⁶ That had been forfeited, had they been married. My wife had added lustre to my horns by that increase of fortune. I could have worn 'em tipped with gold, though my forehead had been furnished like a deputy-lieutenant's hall.

MRS MAR.   They may prove a cap of maintenance⁵⁷ to you still, if you can away with⁵⁸ your wife. And she's no worse than when you had her; I dare swear she had given up her game before she was married.

FAIN.   Hum! That may be; she might throw up her cards, but I'll be hanged if she did not put Pam⁵⁹ in her pocket.

---

⁵⁵*citizen's child* i.e. a bastard, the offspring of a London citizen who has been cuckolded by a gallant.

⁵⁶*fond discovery* foolish revelation.

⁵⁷*cap of maintenance* a cap with two horn-like points, a symbol of rank or importance.

⁵⁸*away with* endure.

⁵⁹*Pam* the knave or jack of clubs, the highest ranking card in five-card loo; i.e. Mrs Fainall may have a concealed winning card, Mirabell.

MRS MAR. You married her to keep you; and if you can contrive to
have her keep you better than you expected, why should you not
keep her longer than you intended?

FAIN. The means, the means.

MRS MAR. Discover to my lady your wife's conduct; threaten to
part with her. My lady loves her and will come to any composition
to save her reputation. Take the opportunity of breaking it just
upon the discovery of this imposture. My lady will be enraged
beyond bounds, and sacrifice niece and fortune and all at that
conjuncture. And let me alone to keep her warm. If she should flag
in her part, I will not fail to prompt her.

FAIN. Faith, this has an appearance.

MRS MAR. I'm sorry I hinted to my lady to endeavour a match
between Millamant and Sir Wilfull; that may be an obstacle.

FAIN. Oh, for that matter leave me to manage him; I'll disable him
for that. He will drink like a Dane; after dinner, I'll set his hand in.

MRS MAR. Well, how do you stand affected towards your lady?

FAIN. Why, faith, I'm thinking of it. Let me see. I am married
already, so that's over. My wife has played the jade with me; well,
that's over too. I never loved her, or if I had, why that would have
been over too by this time. Jealous of her I cannot be, for I am
certain; so there's an end of jealousy. Weary of her I am and shall
be. No, there's no end of that. No, no, that were too much to hope.
Thus far concerning my repose. Now for my reputation. As to my
own, I married not for it; so that's out of the question. And as to
my part in my wife's, why she had parted with hers before; so,
bringing none to me, she can take none from me. 'Tis against all
rule of play that I should lose to one who has not wherewithal to
stake.

MRS MAR. Besides, you forget, marriage is honourable.

FAIN. Hum! Faith, and that's well thought on. Marriage is honourable, as you say; and if so, wherefore should cuckoldom be a
discredit, being derived from so honourable a root?

MRS MAR. Nay, I know not; if the root be honourable, why not the
branches?[60]

FAIN. So, so; why this point's clear. Well, how do we proceed?

MRS MAR. I will contrive a letter which shall be delivered to my
lady at the time when that rascal who is to act Sir Rowland is with
her. It shall come as from an unknown hand; for the less I appear
to know of the truth, the better I can play the incendiary. Besides, I
would not have Foible provoked if I could help it, because, you

---

[60]*branches* the horns of the cuckold.

know, she knows some passages.[61] Nay, I expect all will come out,
but let the mine be sprung first, and then I care not if I'm discovered.

FAIN.   If the worst come to the worst, I'll turn my wife to grass. I have
already a deed of settlement of the best part of her estate, which I
wheedled out of her; and that you shall partake at least.

MRS MAR.   I hope you are convinced that I hate Mirabell. Now you'll
be no more jealous?

FAIN.   Jealous, no. By this kiss. Let husbands be jealous, but let the
lover still believe. Or if he doubt, let it be only to endear his pleasure
and prepare the joy that follows, when he proves his mistress true;
but let husbands' doubts convert to endless jealousy, or if they have
belief, let it corrupt to superstition and blind credulity. I am single,[62]
and will herd no more with 'em. True, I wear the badge, but I'll
disown the order. And since I take my leave of 'em, I care not if I
leave 'em a common motto to their common crest:

> All husbands must or pain or shame endure;
> The wise too jealous are, fools too secure.

Exeunt

[61] *some passages* i.e. the relationship between us.   [62] *single* solitary.

Act Four

SCENE ONE

Scene continues [at LADY WISHFORT'S *house]*

Enter LADY WISHFORT *and* FOIBLE

LADY. Is Sir Rowland coming, say'st thou, Foible? And are things in order?

FOIB. Yes, madam. I have put wax lights in the sconces, and placed the footmen in a row in the hall, in their best liveries, with the coachman and postilion to fill up the equipage.

LADY. Have you pulvilled¹ the coachman and postilion, that they may not stink of the stable when Sir Rowland comes by?

FOIB. Yes, madam.

LADY. And are the dancers and the music ready, that he may be entertained in all points with correspondence to his passion?

FOIB. All is ready, madam.

LADY. And – well, and how do I look, Foible?

FOIB. Most killing well, madam.

LADY. Well, and how shall I receive him? In what figure shall I give his heart the first impression? There is a great deal in the first impression. Shall I sit? No, I won't sit. I'll walk. Ay, I'll walk from the door upon his entrance, and then turn full upon him. No, that will be too sudden. I'll lie, ay, I'll lie down. I'll receive him in my little dressing-room; there's a couch. Yes, yes, I'll give the first impression on a couch. I won't lie neither, but loll and lean upon one elbow, with one foot a little dangling off, jogging in a thoughtful way. Yes, and then as soon as he appears, start, ay, start and be surprised, and rise to meet him in a pretty disorder. Yes. Oh, nothing is more alluring than a levee from a couch in some confusion. It shows the foot to advantage, and furnishes with blushes and re-composing airs beyond comparison. Hark! There's a coach.

FOIB. 'Tis he, madam.

LADY. Oh dear, has my nephew made his addresses to Millamant? I ordered him.

FOIB. Sir Wilfull is set in to drinking, madam, in the parlour.

¹*pulvilled* dusted with scented powder.

LADY.   Ods my life, I'll send him to her. Call her down, Foible; bring
her hither. I'll send him as I go. When they are together, then come to
me, Foible, that I may not be too long alone with Sir Rowland. *Exit*
    Enter MRS MILLAMANT *and* MRS FAINALL

FOIB.   Madam, I stayed here to tell your ladyship that Mr Mirabell
has waited this half hour for an opportunity to talk with you, though
my lady's orders were to leave you and Sir Wilfull together. Shall I
tell Mr Mirabell that you are at leisure?

MILLA.   No. What would the dear man have? I am thoughtful and
would amuse myself. Bid him come another time.

> There never yet was woman made,
> Nor shall, but to be curs'd.[2]
>   *Repeating and walking about*

That's hard!

MRS FAIN.   You are very fond of Sir John Suckling today, Millamant,
and the poets.

MILLA.   He? Ay, and filthy verses — so I am.

FOIB.   Sir Wilfull is coming, madam. Shall I send Mr Mirabell away?

MILLA.   Ay, if you please, Foible, send him away, or send him hither,
just as you will, dear Foible. I think I'll see him. Shall I? Ay, let the
wretch come.

> Thyrsis, a youth of the inspired train.[3]   *Repeating*

Dear Fainall, entertain Sir Wilfull. Thou hast philosophy to undergo
a fool; thou art married and hast patience. I would confer with my
own thoughts.

MRS FAIN.   I am obliged to you, that you would make me your proxy
in this affair, but I have business of my own.

    Enter SIR WILFULL

MRS FAIN.   O Sir Wilfull; you are come at the critical instant. There's
your mistress up to the ears in love and contemplation. Pursue your
point, now or never.

SIR WIL.   Yes, my aunt will have it so. I would gladly have been
encouraged with a bottle or two, because I'm somewhat wary at
first, before I am acquainted. (*This while* MILLAMANT *walks about
repeating to herself*) But I hope, after a time, I shall break my mind,
that is upon further acquaintance. So for the present, cousin, I'll take
my leave. If so be you'll be so kind to make my excuse, I'll return to
my company —

MRS FAIN.   Oh, fie, Sir Wilfull! What, you must not be daunted.

---

[2] *There . . . curs'd* John Suckling, Poem 63, 'Secular Poems', in *Non-Dramatic
Works* (Oxford, 1971), I, p. 61.

[3] *Thyrsis . . . train* Edmund Waller, 'The Story of Phoebus and Daphne, Applied',
Works, 1645, p. 32.

SIR WIL.   Daunted? No, that's not it. It is not so much for that; for if so be that I set on't, I'll do it. But only for the present; 'tis sufficient till further acquaintaince, that's all. Your servant.

MRS FAIN.   Nay, I'll swear you shall never lose so favourable an opportunity if I can help it. I'll leave you together and lock the door.

Exit

SIR WIL.   Nay, nay, cousin. I have forgot my gloves. What d'ye do? 'Sheart, a has locked the door indeed, I think. Nay, Cousin Fainall, open the door! Pshaw, what a vixen trick is this? Nay, now a has seen me too. Cousin, I made bold to pass through, as it were. I think this door's enchanted –

MILLA.   (*Repeating*)

I prithee spare me, gentle boy,
Press me no more for that slight toy.

SIR WIL.   Anan?4 Cousin, your servant.

MILLA.   'That foolish trifle of a heart' – Sir Wilfull!

SIR WIL.   Yes. Your servant. No offence, I hope, cousin.

MILLA.   (*Repeating*)

I swear it will not do its part,
Though thou dost thine, employ'st thy power and art.5
Natural, easy Suckling!

SIR WIL.   Anan? Suckling? No such suckling neither, cousin, nor stripling. I thank heaven, I'm no minor.

MILLA.   Ah, rustic, ruder than Gothic.6

SIR WIL.   Well, well, I shall understand your lingo one of these days, cousin. In the meanwhile I must answer in plain English.

MILLA.   Have you any business with me, Sir Wilfull?

SIR WIL.   Not at present, cousin. Yes, I made bold to see, to come and know if that how you were disposed to fetch a walk this evening; if so be that I might not be troublesome, I would have fought7 a walk with you.

MILLA.   A walk? What then?

SIR WIL.   Nay, nothing. Only for the walk's sake, that's all.

MILLA.   I nauseate walking; 'tis a country diversion. I loath the country and everything that relates to it.

SIR WIL.   Indeed! Hah! Look ye, look ye, you do? Nay, 'tis like you may. Here are choice of pastimes here in town, as plays and the like. That must be confessed indeed.

4*Anan* a rural expression, 'How's that'?
5*I prithee . . . art* Suckling, Poem 54, 'Secular Poems', in *Non-Dramatic Works* (Oxford, 1971), I, p. 51.
6*Gothic* barbaric.   7*fought* taken

MILLA.   *Ah l'étourdie!*⁸ I hate the town too.

SIR WIL.   Dear heart, that's much! Hah! That you should hate 'em
both! Hah! 'Tis like you may. There are some can't relish the town,
and others can't away with the country. 'Tis like you may be one of
those, cousin.

MILLA.   Ha, ha, ha! Yes, 'tis like I may. You have nothing further to
say to me?

SIR WIL.   Not at present, cousin. 'Tis like when I have an opportunity
to be more private, I may break my mind in some measure. I
conjecture you partly guess. However, that's as time shall try; but
spare to speak and spare to speed,⁹ as they say.

MILLA.   If it is of no great importance, Sir Wilfull, you will oblige me
to leave me. I have just now a little business –

SIR WIL.   Enough, enough, cousin. Yes, yes, all a case.¹⁰ When you're
disposed, when you're disposed. Now's as well as another time, and
another time as well as now. All's one for that. Yes, yes, if your
concerns call you, there's no haste; it will keep cold, as they say.
Cousin, your servant. I think this door's locked.

MILLA.   You may go this way, sir.

SIR WIL.   Your servant. Then with your leave I'll return to my
company.   *Exit*

MILLA.   Ay, ay. Ha, ha, ha!
        Like Phoebus sung the no less am'rous boy.

        Enter MIRABELL

MIRA.   Like Daphne she, as lovely and as coy.¹¹
    Do you lock yourself up from me, to make my search more
curious.¹² Or is this pretty artifice contrived to signify that here the
chase must end and my pursuit be crowned, for you can fly no further?

MILLA.   Vanity! No, I'll fly and be followed to the last moment.
Though I am upon the very verge of matrimony, I expect you should
solicit me as much as if I were wavering at the grate of a monastery,¹³
with one foot over the threshold. I'll be solicited to the very last, nay,
and afterwards.

MIRA.   What, after the last?

MILLA.   Oh, I should think I was poor and had nothing to bestow, if I
were reduced to an inglorious ease, and freed from the agreeable
fatigues of solicitation.

---

⁸*Ah l'étourdie* i.e. fool. Millamant was modelled in part on Melantha, in Dryden's
Marriage à la Mode (1673), who uses the phrase *étourdi bête* ('thoughtless fool').

⁹*spare . . . speed* proverbial: those frugal of speed don't get very far.

¹⁰*all a case* it doesn't matter.

¹¹*Like . . . coy* These two verses are also from the Waller poem quoted by
Millamant above, on p. 540.

¹²*curious* careful.   ¹³*monastery* i.e. nunnery.

MIRA.   But do not you know that when favours are conferred upon instant[14] and tedious solicitation, that they diminish in their value, and that both the giver loses the grace and the receiver lessens his pleasure?

MILLA.   It may be in things of common application, but never, sure, in love. Oh, I hate a lover that can dare to think he draws a moment's air independent on the bounty of his mistress. There is not so impudent a thing in nature as the saucy look of an assured man, confident of success. The pedantic arrogance of a very husband has not so pragmatical[15] an air. Ah, I'll never marry unless I am first made sure of my will and pleasure.

MIRA.   Would you have 'em both before marriage? Or will you be contented with the first now, and stay for the other till after grace?[16]

MILLA.   Ah, don't be impertinent. My dear liberty, shall I leave thee? My faithful solitude, my darling contemplation, must I bid you then adieu? Ay-h, adieu. My morning thoughts, agreeable wakings, indolent slumbers, all ye *douceurs*,[17] ye *sommeils du matin*,[18] adieu. I can't do't; 'tis more than impossible. Positively, Mirabell, I'll lie abed in a morning as long as I please.

MIRA.   Then I'll get up in a morning as early as I please.

MILLA   Ah, idle creature, get up when you will. And, d'ye hear, I won't be called names after I'm married; positively, I won't be called names.

MIRA.   Names?

MILLA.   Ay, as wife, spouse, my dear, joy, jewel, love, sweetheart, and the rest of that nauseous cant, in which men and their wives are so fulsomely familiar. I shall never bear that. Good Mirabell, don't let us be familiar or fond, nor kiss before folks, like my Lady Fadler and Sir Francis; nor go to Hyde Park together the first Sunday in a new chariot, to provoke eyes and whispers; and then never be seen there together again, as if we were proud of one another the first week and ashamed of one another ever after. Let us never visit together, nor go to a play together, but let us be very strange[19] and well-bred. Let us be as strange as if we had been married a great while, and as well-bred as if we were not married at all.

MIRA.   Have you any more conditions to offer? Hitherto your demands are pretty reasonable.

MILLA.   Trifles! – As liberty to pay and receive visits to and from whom I please, to write and receive letters, without interrogatories

---

[14]*instant* pressing.   [15]*pragmatical* dogmatic.
[16]*after grace* after the ritual of marriage.   [17]*douceurs* pleasures.
[18]*sommeils du matin* morning naps.   [19]*strange* reserved.

or wry faces on your part. To wear what I please, and choose conversation with regard only to my own taste. To have no obligation upon me to converse with wits that I don't like, because they are your acquaintance, or to be intimate with fools because they may be your relations. Come to dinner when I please, dine in my dressing-room when I'm out of humour, without giving a reason. To have my closet inviolate. To be sole empress of my tea-table, which you must never presume to approach without first asking leave. And lastly, wherever I am, you shall always knock at the door before you come in. These articles subscribed, if I continue to endure you a little longer, I may by degrees dwindle into a wife.

MIRA.   Your bill of fare is something advanced in this latter account. Well, have I liberty to offer conditions, that when you are dwindled into a wife, I may not be beyond measure enlarged into a husband?

MILLA.   You have free leave. Propose your utmost; speak and spare not.

MIRA.   I thank you. *Imprimis* then: I covenant that your acquaintance be general; that you admit no sworn confidante or intimate of your own sex; no she-friend to screen her affairs under your countenance and tempt you to make trial of a mutual secrecy. No decoy-duck to wheedle you a fop, scrambling to the play in a mask; then bring you home in a pretended fright, when you think you shall be found out, and rail at me for missing the play, and disappointing the frolic which you had to pick me up and prove my constancy.

MILLA.   Detestable *imprimis*! I go to the play in a mask!

MIRA.   *Item*: I article that you continue to like your own face as long as I shall; and while it passes current with me, that you endeavour not to new-coin it. To which end, together with all vizards[20] for the day, I prohibit all masks for the night, made of oiled skins and I know not what — hog's bones, hare's gall, pig-water, and the marrow of a roasted cat. In short, I forbid all commerce with the gentlewoman in what-d'ye-call-it Court. *Item*: I shut my doors against all bawds with baskets and pennyworths of muslin, china, fans, atlasses,[21] etc. *Item*: When you shall be breeding —

MILA.   Ah, name it not.

MIRA.   Which may be presumed, with a blessing on our endeavours —

MILLA.   Odious endeavours!

MIRA.   I denounce against all strait-lacing, squeezing for a shape till you mould my boy's head like a sugar-loaf, and instead of a man-child, make me father to a crooked billet. Lastly, to the dominion of the tea-table I submit, but with proviso that you exceed not in your

---

[20]*vizards* masks.   [21]*atlasses* an Oriental satin.

province, but restrain yourself to native and simple tea-table drinks, as tea, chocolate, and coffee. As likewise to genuine and authorised tea-table talk, such as mending of fashions, spoiling reputations, railing at absent friends, and so forth; but that on no account you encroach upon the men's prerogative, and presume to drink healths or toast fellows; for prevention of which, I banish all foreign forces, all auxiliaries to the tea-table, as orange brandy, all aniseed, cinnamon, citron, and Barbadoes waters,[22] together with ratafia and the most noble spirit of clary.[23] But for cowslip-wine, poppy-water, and all dormitives,[24] those I allow. – These provisos admitted, in other things I may prove a tractable and complying husband.

MILLA.   O horrid provisos! Filthy strong waters! I toast fellows, odious men! I hate your odious provisos.

MIRA.   Then we're agreed. Shall I kiss your hand upon the contract? And here comes one to be a witness to the sealing of the deed.

Enter MRS FAINALL

MILLA.   Fainall, what shall I do? Shall I have him? I think I must have him.

MRS FAIN.   Ay, ay, take him, take him. What should you do?

MILLA.   Well then – I'll take my death I'm in a horrid fright – Fainall, I shall never say it – Well, I think – I'll endure you.

MRS FAIN.   Fie, fie, have him, have him, and tell him so in plain terms, for I am sure you have a mind to him.

MILLA.   Are you? I think I have, and the horrid man looks as if he thought so too. Well, you ridiculous thing you, I'll have you – I won't be kissed, nor I won't be thanked. Here, kiss my hand though. So, hold your tongue now, and don't say a word.

MRS FAIN.   Mirabell, there's a necssity for your obedience; you have neither time to talk nor stay. My mother is coming; and in my conscience, if she should see you, would fall into fits, and maybe not recover time enough to return to Sir Rowland, who, as Foible tells me, is in a fair way to succeed. Therefore, spare your ecstasies for another occasion, and slip down the back stairs, where Foible waits to consult you.

MILLA.   Ay, go, go. In the meantime I suppose you have said something to please me.

MIRA.   I am all obedience.   *Exit*

MRS FAIN.   Yonder Sir Wilfull's drunk; and so noisy that my mother has been forced to leave Sir Rowland to appease him; but he answers her only with singing and drinking. What they may have done by this

[22]*Barbadoes-water* a cordial flavoured with orange and lemon peel.
[23]*clary* wine mixed with honey and spices.
[24]*dormitives* potions to encourage sleep.

time I know not, but Petulant and he were upon quarrelling as I came by.

MILLA.   Well, if Mirabell should not make a good husband, I am a lost thing, for I find I love him violently.

MRS FAIN.   So it seems; when you mind not what's said to you. If you doubt him, you had best take up with Sir Wilfull.

MILLA.   How can you name that superannuated lubber? Foh!

Enter WITWOUD *from drinking*

MRS FAIN.   So, is the fray made up, that you have left 'em?

WIT.   Left 'em? I could stay no longer. I have laughed like ten christ'nings. I am tipsy with laughing. If I had stayed any longer I should have burst. I must have been let out and pieced in the sides like an unsized camlet.[25] Yes, yes, the fray is composed; my lady came in like a *noli prosequi*,[26] and stopped the proceedings.

MILLA.   What was the dispute?

WIT.   That's the jest; there was no dispute. They could neither of 'em speak for rage, and so fell a-sputt'ring at one another like two roasting apples.

Enter PETULANT *drunk*

WIT.   Now, Petulant, all's over, all's well. Gad, my head begins to whim[27] it about. Why dost thou not speak? Thou art both as drunk and as mute as a fish.

PET.   Look you, Mrs Millamant, if you can love me, dear nymph, say it, and that's the conclusion. Pass on or pass off, that's all.

WIT.   Thou hast uttered volumes, folios, in less than *decimo sexto*,[28] my dear Lacedemonian.[29] Sirrah, Petulant, thou art an epitomiser of words.

PET.   Witwoud, you are an annihilator of sense.

WIT.   Thou art a retailer of phrases, and dost deal in remnants of remnants, like a maker of pincushions. Thou art in truth (metaphorically speaking) a speaker of shorthand.

PET.   Thou art (without a figure[30]) just one half of an ass, and Baldwin[31] yonder, thy half-brother, is the rest. A gemini[32] of asses split would make just four of you.

---

[25]*unsized camlet* an unstiffened wool and silk Oriental fabric.

[26]*noli prosequi* the giving up of a law suit before its conclusion.

[27]*whim* spin.

[28]*decimo sexto* a small book with leaves folded to one-sixteenth the size of a standard sheet of paper.

[29]*Lacedemonian* i.e. laconic.   [30]*figure* metaphor.

[31]*Baldwin* i.e. Boudewyn, the ass, who in the medieval story, climbed on his master's shoulders as his hound did and was beaten.

[32]*gemini* twins.

WIT.   Thou dost bite, my dear mustard-seed;[33] kiss me for that.

PET.   Stand off. I'll kiss no more males. I have kissed your twin yonder in a humour of reconciliation, till he (*Hiccup*) rises upon my stomach like a radish.

MILLA.   Eh! Filthy creature! What was the quarrel?

PET.   There was no quarrel. There might have been a quarrel.

WIT.   If there had been words enow between 'em to have expressed provocation, they had gone together by the ears like a pair of castanets.

PET.   You were the quarrel.

MILLA.   Me!

PET.   If I have a humour to quarrel, I can make less matters conclude premises. If you are not handsome, what then, if I have a humour to prove it? If I shall have my reward, say so; if not, fight for your face the next time yourself. I'll go sleep.

WIT.   Do. Wrap thyself up like a woodlouse, and dream revenge. And hear me, if thou canst learn to write by tomorrow morning, pen me a challenge. I'll carry it for thee.

PET.   Carry your mistress's monkey a spider! Go flea dogs, and read romances. I'll go to bed to my maid.   *Exit*

MRS FAIN.   He's horridly drunk. How came you all in this pickle?

WIT.   A plot, a plot, to get rid of the knight. Your husband's advice, but he sneaked off.

       Enter LADY WISHFORT *and* SIR WILFULL, *drunk*

LADY.   Out upon't, out upon't! At years of discretion, and comport yourself at this rantipole[34] rate!

SIR WIL.   No offence, aunt.

LADY.   Offence? As I'm a person, I'm ashamed of you. Foh! How you stink of wine! D'ye think my niece will ever endure such a borachio?[35] You're an absolute borachio!

SIR WIL.   Borachio!

LADY.   At a time when you should commence an amour and put your best foot foremost –

SIR WIL.   'Sheart, an you grutch me your liquor, make a bill. Give me more drink, and take my purse.   *Sings*

> Prithee fill me the glass
>   Till it laugh in my face,
> With ale that is potent and mellow;

---

[33]*mustard-seed* a sharp seasoning; a fairy in *A Midsummer Night's Dream*, III, i and IV, i.

[34]*rantipole* disorderly.

[35]*borachio* drunkard; a character in *Much Ado about Nothing*.

> He that whines for a lass
> Is an ignorant ass,
> For a bumper has not its fellow.

But if you would have me marry my cousin, say the word, and I'll do't. Wilfull will do't, that's the word. Wilfull will do't, that's my crest. My motto I have forgot.

LADY.   My nephew's a little overtaken, cousin, but 'tis with drinking your health. O' my word, you are obliged to him.

SIR WIL.   *In vino veritas*, aunt. If I drunk your health today, cousin, I am a borachio. But if you have a mind to be married, say the word, and send for the piper; Wilfull will do't. If not, dust it away, and let's have t'other round. Tony? Ods heart, where's Tony? Tony's an honest fellow, but he spits after a bumper, and that's a fault.   *Sings*

> We'll drink and we'll never ha' done, boys,
> Put the glass then around with the sun, boys;
> Let Apollo's example invite us,
> For he's drunk every night,
> And that makes him so bright,
> That he's able next morning to light us.

The sun's a good pimple,[36] an honest soaker. He has a cellar at your Antipodes. If I travel, aunt, I touch at your Antipodes. Your Antipodes are a good, rascally sort of topsy-turvy fellows. If I had a bumper, I'd stand upon my head and drink a health to 'em. A match or no match, cousin with the hard name? Aunt, Wilfull will do't. If she has her maidenhead, let her look to't; if she has not, let her keep her own counsel in the meantime, and cry out at the nine-months' end.

MILLA.   Your pardon, madam, I can stay no longer. Sir Wilfull grows very powerful. Egh! How he smells! I shall be overcome if I stay. Come, cousin.   *Exeunt* MILLAMANT *and* MRS FAINALL

LADY.   Smells! He would poison a tallow-chandler and his family. Beastly creature, I know not what to do with him. Travel, quoth a! Ay, travel, travel, get thee gone. Get thee but far enough, to the Saracens or the Tartars or the Turks, for thou art not fit to live in a Christian commonwealth, thou beastly pagan.

SIR WIL.   Turks, no; no Turks, aunt. Your Turks are infidels, and believe not in the grape. Your Mahometan, your Mussulman is a dry stinkard – no offence, aunt. My map says that your Turk is not so honest a man as your Christian. I cannot find by the map that your

---

[36]*pimple* boon companion.

mufti³⁷ is orthodox; whereby it is a plain case that orthodox is a hard word, aunt, and (*Hiccup*) Greek for claret.   *Sings*

> To drink is a Christian diversion,
> Unknown to the Turk or the Persian.
> Let Mahometan fools
> Live by heathenish rules,
> And be damn'd over tea cups and coffee.
> But let British lads sing,
> Crown a health to the king,
> And a fig for your sultan and sophy.

Ah, Tony!

Enter FOIBLE *and whispers* [*to*] LADY WISHFORT

LADY.   [*To* FOIBLE] Sir Rowland impatient? Good lack! What shall I do with this beastly tumbril?³⁸ — Go lie down and sleep, you sot, or as I'm a person, I'll have you bastinadoed with broomsticks. Call up the wenches.   *Exit* FOIBLE

SIR WIL.   Ahey? Wenches? Where are the wenches?

LADY.   Dear Cousin Witwoud, get him away, and you will bind me to you inviolably. I have an affair of moment that invades me with some precipitation. You will oblige me to all futurity.

WIT.   Come, knight. Pox on him! I don't know what to say to him. Will you go to a cock-match?

SIR WIL.   With a wench, Tony? Is she a shake-bag,³⁹ sirrah? Let me bite your cheek for that.

WIT.   Horrible! He has a breath like a bagpipe. Ay, ay, come. Will you march, my Salopian?

SIR WIL.   Lead on, little Tony. I'll follow thee, my Anthony, my Tantony.⁴⁰ Sirrah, thou sha't be my Tantony, and I'll be thy pig.
    — And a fig for your sultan and sophy.

          Exit singing, with WITWOUD

LADY.   This will never do. It will never make a match, at least before he has been abroad.

Enter WAITWELL, *disguised as for* SIR ROWLAND

Dear Sir Rowland, I am confounded with confusion at the retrospection of my own rudeness. I have more pardons to ask than the pope distributes in the year of jubilee.⁴¹ But I hope where there is likely to

---

³⁷*mufti* a Mohammedan priest.
³⁸*tumbril* dung cart.   ³⁹*shake-bag* lit., a fighting cock; i.e. lively.
⁴⁰*Tantony* St Anthony, AD 251–356, ascetic, hermit, patron saint of domestic animals, depicted as followed by a pig.
⁴¹*year of jubilee* a year, like 1700, in which the Pope granted a general remission of the punishments imposed for sins.

be so near an alliance, we may unbend the severity of decorum and dispense with a little ceremony.

WAIT.   My impatience, madam, is the effect of my transport, and till I have the possession of your adorable person, I am tantalised on the rack, and do but hang, madam, on the tenter[42] of expectation.

LADY.   You have excess of gallantry, Sir Rowland, and press things to a conclusion with a most prevailing vehemence. But a day or two for decency of marriage –

WAIT.   For decency of funeral, madam! The delay will break my heart; or if that should fail, I shall be poisoned. My nephew will get an inkling of my designs, and poison me; and I would willingly starve him before I die. I would gladly go out of the world with that satisfaction. That would be some comfort to me, if I could but live so long as to be revenged on that unnatural viper.

LADY.   Is he so unnatural, say you? Truly I would contribute much both to the saving of your life and the accomplishment of your revenge. Not that I respect[43] myself, though he has been a perfidious wretch to me.

WAIT.   Perfidious to you?

LADY.   O Sir Rowland, the hours that he has died away at my feet, the tears that he has shed, the oaths that he has sworn, the palpitations that he has felt, the trances and the tremblings, the ardors and the ecstasies, the kneelings and the risings, the heart-heavings and the hand-grippings, the pangs and the pathetic regards of his protesting eyes! Oh, no memory can register.

WAIT.   What, my rival! Is the rebel my rival? A dies.

LADY.   No, don't kill him at once, Sir Rowland; starve him gradually, inch by inch.

WAIT.   I'll do't. In three weeks he shall be bare-foot; in a month out at knees with begging an alms. He shall starve upward and upward, till he has nothing living but his head, and then go out in a stink like a candle's end upon a save-all.[44]

LADY.   Well, Sir Rowland, you have the way. You are no novice in the labyrinth of love; you have the clue. But as I am a person, Sir Rowland, you must not attribute my yielding to any sinister appetite or indigestion of widowhood, nor impute my complacency to any lethargy of continence. I hope you do not think me prone to any iteration[45] of nuptials –

WAIT.   Far be it from me –

---

[42]*tenter* a wooden drying framework.   [43]*respect* consider.
[44]*save-all* a dish with a central spike, designed to use up candle ends.
[45]*prone to iteration* eager for a repetition.

LADY. If you do, I protest I must recede. Or think that I have made a prostitution of decorums; but in the vehemence of compassion and to save the life of a person of so much importance –

WAIT. I esteem it so –

LADY. Or else you wrong my condescension –

WAIT. I do not, I do not –

LADY. Indeed you do.

WAIT. I do not, fair shrine of virtue.

LADY. If you think the least scruple of carnality was an ingredient –

WAIT. Dear madam, no. You are all camphire[46] and frankincense, all chastity and odour.[47]

LADY. Or that –
   Enter FOIBLE

FOIB. Madam, the dancers are ready, and there's one with a letter, who must deliver it into your own hands.

LADY. Sir Rowland, will you give me leave? Think favourably, judge candidly, and conclude you have found a person who would suffer racks in honour's cause, dear Sir Rowland, and will wait on you incessantly.[48]   *Exit*

WAIT. Fie, fie! What a slavery have I undergone! Spouse, hast thou any cordial? I want spirits.

FOIB. What a washy rogue art thou, to pant thus for a quarter of an hour's lying and swearing to a fine lady!

WAIT. Oh, she is the antidote to desire. Spouse, thou wilt fare the worse for't. I shall have no appetite to iteration of nuptials this eight and forty hours – By this hand, I'd rather be a chairman in the dog-days[49] than act Sir Rowland till this time tomorrow.
   Enter LADY WISHFORT *with a letter*

LADY. Call in the dancers. Sir Rowland, we'll sit, if you please, and see the entertainment.   *Dance*
   Now with your permission, Sir Rowland, I will peruse my letter. I would open it in your presence because I would not make you uneasy. If it should make you uneasy, I would burn it. Speak if it does. But you may see by the superscription it is like a woman's hand.

FOIB. (*To* WAITWELL) By heaven! Mrs Marwood's! I know it. My heart aches. Get it from her!

WAIT. A woman's hand? No, madam, that's no woman's hand; I see that already. That's somebody whose throat must be cut.

---

[46]*camphire* camphor, reputed to be an anaphrodisiac; Dryden, *The Spanish Friar* (1681), I, p. 14.
[47]*odour* sweet scent.   [48]*incessantly* immediately.
[49]*dog-days* a bearer of a sedan chair in the heat of summer.

LADY. Nay, Sir Rowland, since you give me a proof of your passion by your jealousy, I promise you I'll make a return, by a frank communication. You shall see it; we'll open it together. Look you here. (*Reads*) 'Madam, though unknown to you', – Look you there, 'tis from nobody that I know – 'I have that honour for your character that I think myself obliged to let you know you are abused. He who pretends to be Sir Rowland is a cheat and a rascal' – O heavens! What's this?

FOIB. [*Aside*] Unfortunate. All's ruined.

WAIT. How, how? Let me see, let me see! (*Reading*) 'A rascal, and disguised and suborned for that imposture', – O villainy! O villainy! – 'by the contrivance of' –

LADY. I shall faint, I shall die, I shall die! Oh!

FOIB. (*To* WAITWELL) Say 'tis your nephew's hand. Quickly! His plot. Swear, swear it.

WAIT. Here's a villain! Madam, don't you perceive it? Don't you see it?

LADY. Too well, too well. I have seen too much.

WAIT. I told you at first I knew the hand. A woman's hand? The rascal writes a sort of a large hand, your Roman hand. I saw there was a throat to be cut presently.[50] If he were my son, as he is my nephew, I'd pistol him.

FOIB. O treachery! But are you sure, Sir Rowland, it is his writing?

WAIT. Sure? Am I here? Do I live? Do I love this pearl of India? I have twenty letters in my pocket from him, in the same character.

LADY. How!

FOIB. Oh what luck it is, Sir Rowland, that you were present at this juncture! This was the business that brought Mr Mirabell disguised to Madam Millamant this afternoon. I thought something was contriving, when he stole by me and would have hid his face.

LADY. How, how! I heard the villain was in the house indeed, and now I remember, my niece went away abruptly when Sir Wilfull was to have made his addresses.

FOIB. Then, then, madam, Mr Mirabell waited for her in her chamber, but I would not tell your ladyship to discompose you when you were to receive Sir Rowland.

WAIT. Enough. His date is short.

FOIB. No, good Sir Rowland, don't incur the law.

WAIT. Law? I care not for the law. I can but die, and 'tis in a good cause. My lady shall be satisfied of my truth and innocence, though it cost me my life.

[50] *presently* immediately.

LADY. No, dear Sir Rowland, don't fight. If you should be killed I must never show my face, or hanged! Oh consider my reputation, Sir Rowland. No, you shan't fight. – I'll go in and examine my niece; I'll make her confess. I conjure you, Sir Rowland, by all your love, not to fight.

WAIT. I am charmed, madam; I obey. But some proof you must let me give you. I'll go for a black box which contains the writings of my whole estate, and deliver that into your hands.

LADY. Ay, dear Sir Rowland, that will be some comfort. Bring the black box.

WAIT. And may I presume to bring a contract to be signed this night? May I hope so far?

LADY. Bring what you will. But come alive, pray come alive. Oh, this is a happy discovery.

WAIT. Dead or alive I'll come, and married we will be in spite of treachery. Ay, and get an heir that shall defeat the last remaining glimpse of hope in my abandoned nephew. Come, my buxom widow.

> Ere long you shall substantial proof receive
> That I'm an arrant knight –

FOIB. [*Aside*] Or arrant knave. *Exeunt*

Act Five

SCENE ONE

[*Another room in* LADY WISHFORT'S *house*]

[*Enter*] LADY WISHFORT *and* FOIBLE

LADY. Out of my house, out of my house, thou viper, thou serpent that I have fostered; thou bosom traitress that I raised from nothing! Begone, begone, begone! Go, go! That I took from washing of old gauze and weaving of dead hair, with a bleak blue nose, over a chafing dish of starved embers and dining behind a traverse[1] rag, in a shop no bigger than a bird-cage! Go, go, starve again, do, do!

FOIB. Dear madam, I'll beg pardon on my knees.

LADY. Away! Out, out! Go set up for yourself again! Do! Drive a trade, do, with your threepennyworth of small ware flaunting upon a packthread, under a brandy-seller's bulk,[2] or against a dead[3] wall by a ballad-monger! Go, hang out an old frisoneer-gorget[4] with a yard of yellow colberteen[5] again, do. An old gnawed mask, two rows of pins and a child's fiddle, a glass necklace with the beads broken, and a quilted nightcap with one ear! Go, go, drive a trade! These were your commodities, you treacherous trull; this was the merchandise you dealt in when I took you into my house, placed you next myself, and made you governante[6] of my whole family! You have forgot this, have you, now you have feathered your nest?

FOIB. No, no, dear madam. Do but hear me. Have but a moment's patience. I'll confess all. Mr Mirabell seduced me. I am not the first he has wheedled with his dissembling tongue. Your ladyship's own wisdom has been deluded by him. Then how should I, a poor ignorant, defend myself? O madam, if you knew but what he promised me, and how he assured me your ladyship should come to no damage – or else the wealth of the Indies should not have bribed

[1]*traverse rag* a curtain on a cord across the back of a shop, intended to give privacy.
[2]*bulk* stall.
[3]*dead* unbroken.
[4]*frisoneer gorget* a neckpiece made of coarse woollen material.
[5]*colberteen* a cheap kind of lace.
[6]*governante* housekeeper.

me to conspire against so good, so sweet, so kind a lady as you have been to me!

LADY.   No damage? What, to betray me, to marry me to a cast serving-man? To make me a receptacle, an hospital for a decayed pimp? No damage? O thou frontless[7] impudence, more than a big-bellied actress.

FOIB.   Pray do but hear me, madam. He could not marry your ladyship, madam. No indeed. His marriage was to have been void in law, for he was married to me first, to secure your ladyship. He could not have bedded your ladyship, for if he had consummated with your ladyship, he must have run the risk of the law, and been put upon his clergy.[8] Yes indeed; I enquired of the law in that case before I would meddle or make.

LADY.   What, then I have been your property, have I? I have been convenient to you, it seems. While you were catering for Mirabell, I have been broker for you? What, have you made a passive bawd of me? This exceeds all precedent. I am brought to fine uses, to become a botcher[9] of second-hand marriages between Abigails and Andrews![10] I'll couple you! Yes, I'll baste you together, you and your Philander.[11] I'll Duke's Place[12] you, as I'm a person. Your turtle is in custody already. You shall coo in the same cage, if there be constable or warrant in the parish.   *Exit*

FOIB.   Oh that ever I was born! Oh that I was ever married! A bride! Ay, I shall be a Bridewell-bride.[13] Oh!

       Enter MRS FAINALL

MRS FAIN.   Poor Foible, what's the matter?

FOIB.   O madam, my lady's gone for a constable. I shall be had to a justice, and put to Bridewell to beat hemp. Poor Waitwell's gone to prison already.

MRS FAIN.   Have a good heart, Foible; Mirabell's gone to give security for him. This is all Marwood's and my husband's doing.

FOIB.   Yes, yes; I know it, madam. She was in my lady's closet, and overheard all that you said to me before dinner. She sent the letter to my lady, and, that missing effect, Mr Fainall laid this plot to arrest

---

[7]*frontless* shameless.

[8]*put upon his clergy* compelled to plead 'benefit of clergy', i.e. to claim the ability to read and write as a means of escaping punishment.

[9]*botcher* lit., a mender of old clothes.

[10]*Abigails and Andrews* comprehensive terms for maids and menservants.

[11]*Philander* i.e. lover.

[12]*Duke's Place* where Waitwell and Foible were married; Act I, i, p. 499.

[13]*Bridewell-bride* a London prison for women; their duties often included beating hemp.

Waitwell, when he pretended to go for the papers; and in the meantime Mrs Marwood declared all to my lady.

MRS FAIN. Was there no mention made of me in the letter? My mother does not suspect my being in the confederacy? I fancy Marwood has not told her, though she has told my husband.

FOIB. Yes, madam; but my lady did not see that part. We stifled the letter before she read so far. Has that mischievous devil told Mr Fainall of your ladyship then?

MRS FAIN. Ay, all's out, my affair with Mirabell, everything discovered. This is the last day of our living together, that's my comfort.

FOIB. Indeed, madam, and so 'tis a comfort if you knew all. He has been even[14] with your ladyship, which I could have told you long enough since, but I love to keep peace and quietness by my good will. I had rather bring friends together than set 'em at distance. But Mrs Marwood and he are nearer related than ever their parents thought for.

MRS FAIN. Say'st thou so, Foible? Canst thou prove this?

FOIB. I can take my oath of it, madam, so can Mrs Mincing. We have had many a fair word from Madam Marwood, to conceal something that passed in our chamber one evening when you were at Hyde Park, and we were thought to have gone a-walking. But we went up unawares, though we were sworn to secrecy too. Madam Marwood took a book and swore us upon it, but it was but a book of verses and poems. So long as it was not a Bible oath, we may break it with a safe conscience.

MRS FAIN. This discovery is the most opportune thing I could wish.

Enter MINCING

Now, Mincing?

MINC. My lady would speak with Mrs Foible, mem. Mr Mirabell is with her; he has set your spouse at liberty, Mrs Foible, and would have you hide yourself in my lady's closet till my old lady's anger is abated. Oh, my old lady is in a perilous passion at something Mr Fainall has said. He swears, and my old lady cries. There's a fearful hurricane, I vow. He says, mem, how that he'll have my lady's fortune made over to him, or he'll be divorced.

MRS FAIN. Does your lady or Mirabell know that?

MINC. Yes, mem, they have sent me to see if Sir Wilfull be sober, and to bring him to them. My lady is resolved to have him, I think, rather than lose such a vast sum as six thousand pound. Oh, come, Mrs Foible, I hear my old lady.

---

[14]*even* equal to Mrs Fainall, in the sense of his also having had an affair (with Mrs Marwood).

MRS FAIN. Foible, you must tell Mincing that she must prepare to vouch when I call her.

FOIB. Yes, yes, madam.

MINC. Oh yes, mem, I'll vouch anything for your ladyship's service, be what it will. *Exeunt* MINCING *and* FOIBLE
Enter LADY WISHFORT *and* MRS MARWOOD

LADY. O my dear friend, how can I enumerate the benefits that I have received from your goodness? To you I owe the timely discovery of the false vows of Mirabell; to you the detection of the imposter Sir Rowland. And now you are become an intercessor with my son-in-law, to save the honour of my house and compound[15] for the frailties of my daughter. Well, friend, you are enough to reconcile me to the bad world, or else I would retire to deserts and solitudes, and feed harmless sheep by groves and purling streams. Dear Marwood, let us leave the world, and retire by ourselves and be shepherdesses.

MRS MAR. Let us first dispatch the affair in hand, madam. We shall have leisure to think of retirement afterwards. Here is one who is concerned in the treaty.

LADY. O daughter, daughter, is it possible thou should'st be my child, bone of my bone, and flesh of my flesh, and, as I may say, another me, and yet transgress the most minute particle of severe virtue? Is it possible you should lean aside to iniquity, who have been cast in the direct mould of virtue? I have not only been a mould but a pattern for you, and a model for you, after you were brought into the world.

MRS FAIN. I don't understand your ladyship.

LADY. Not understand? Why, have you not been naught?[16] Have you not been sophisticated?[17] Not understand? Here I am ruined to compound for your caprices and your cuckoldoms. I must pawn my plate and my jewels, and ruin my niece, and all little enough –

MRS FAIN. I am wronged and abused, and so are you. 'Tis a false accusation, as false as hell, as false as your friend there, ay, or your friend's friend, my false husband.

MRS MAR. My friend, Mrs Fainall? Your husband my friend? What do you mean?

MRS FAIN. I know what I mean, madam, and so do you; and so shall the world at a time convenient.

MRS MAR. I am sorry to see you so passionate, madam. More temper[18] would look more like innocence. But I have done. I am sorry my zeal to serve your ladyship and family should admit of misconstruction, or make me liable to affronts. You will pardon me, madam, if I meddle no more with an affair in which I am not personally concerned.

---

[15]*compound* bargain.   [16]*naught* immoral.
[17]*sophisticated* corrupted.   [18]*temper* composure, restraint.

LADY. O dear friend, I am so ashamed that you should meet with such returns. – [*To* MRS FAINALL] You ought to ask pardon on your knees, ungrateful creature; she deserves more from you than all your life can accomplish. – [*To* MRS MARWOOD] Oh, don't leave me destitute in this perplexity. No, stick to me, my good genius.

MRS FAIN. I tell you, madam, you're abused. Stick to you? Ay, like a leech, to suck your best blood. She'll drop off when she's full. Madam, you sha'not pawn a bodkin, nor part with a brass counter in composition for me. I defy 'em all. Let 'em prove their aspersions. I know my own innocence and dare stand a trial.   *Exit*

LADY. Why, if she should be innocent, if she should be wronged after all, ha? I don't know what to think. And, I promise you, her education has been unexceptionable; I may say it, for I chiefly made it my own care to initiate her very infancy in the rudiments of virtue, and to impress upon her tender years a young odium and aversion to the very sight of men. Ay, friend, she would ha' shrieked if she had but seen a man till she was in her teens. As I'm a person, 'tis true. She was never suffered to play with a male child, though but in coats; nay, her very babies[19] were of the feminine gender. Oh, she never looked a man in the face but her own father or the chaplain, and him we made a shift to put upon her for a woman, by the help of his long garments and his sleek face, till she was going in her fifteen.[20]

MRS MAR. 'Twas much she should be deceived so long.

LADY. I warrant you, or she would never have borne to have been catechised by him, and have heard his long lectures against singing and dancing and such debaucheries, and going to filthy plays, and profane music-meetings, where the lewd trebles squeak nothing but bawdy, and the basses roar blasphemy. Oh, she would have swooned at the sight or name of an obscene playbook. And can I think, after all this, that my daughter can be naught? What, a whore? And thought it excommunication to set her foot within the door of a playhouse. O my dear friend, I can't believe it. No, no. As she says, let him prove it, let him prove it.

MRS MAR. Prove it, madam? What, and have your name prostituted in a public court? Yours and your daughter's reputation worried at the bar by a pack of bawling lawyers? To be ushered in with an 'Oyez' of scandal, and have your case opened by an old fumbling lecher in a quoif[21] like a man-midwife, to bring your daughter's infamy to light, to be a theme for legal punsters and quibblers by the statute, and become a jest against a rule of court, where there is no

[19]*babies* dolls.   [20]*fifteen* almost fifteen.
[21]*quoif* the white cap of a lawyer.

precedent for a jest in any record, not even in Doomsday Book; to discompose the gravity of the bench, and provoke naught interrogatories in more naughty law Latin; while the good judge, tickled with the proceeding, simpers under a grey beard, and fidges off and on his cushion as if he had swallowed cantharides[22] or sate upon cow-itch.[23]

LADY. Oh, 'tis very hard!

MRS MAR. And then to have my young revellers of the Temple[24] take notes, like prentices at a conventicle,[25] and after, talk it over again in commons[26] or before drawers in an eating-house.

LADY. Worse and worse.

MRS MAR. Nay, this is nothing. If it would end here, 'twere well. But it must after this be consigned by the shorthand writers to the public press, and from thence be transferred to the hands, nay, into the throats and lungs of hawkers, with voices more licentious than the loud flounder-man's,[27] or the woman that cries gray peas. And this you must hear till you are stunned; nay, you must hear nothing else for some days.

LADY. Oh, 'tis insupportable. No, no, dear friend; make it up, make it up. Ay, ay, I'll compound. I'll give up all, myself and my all, my niece and her all – anything, everything for composition.

MRS MAR. Nay, madam, I advise nothing, I only lay before you as a friend the inconveniencies which perhaps you have overseen.[28] Here comes Mr Fainall. If he will be satisfied to huddle up all in silence, I shall be glad. You must think I would rather congratulate than condole with you.

Enter FAINALL

LADY. Ay, ay, I do not doubt it, dear Marwood. No, no, I do not doubt it.

FAIN. Well, madam, I have suffered myself to be overcome by the importunity of this lady your friend, and am content you shall enjoy your own proper estate during life, on condition you oblige yourself never to marry, under such penalty as I think convenient.

LADY. Never to marry?

[22]*cantharides* Spanish fly, a dried beetle used as a diuretic, aphrodisiac, etc.
[23]*cow-itch* cowhage, a stinging plant, used as an anthelmintic.
[24]*Temple* undisciplined law students of the Inner Temple, London.
[25]*prentices at a coventicle* Apprentices of nonconformist merchants were obliged to attend Sunday services and write précis.
[26]*commons* the dining hall.
[27]*flounder-man* a London fish-vendor notable for his manner of calling his wares.
[28]*overseen* overlooked.

FAIN. No more Sir Rowlands. The next imposture may not be so timely detected.

MRS MAR. That condition, I dare answer, my lady will consent to without difficulty. She has already but too much experienced the perfidiousness of men. Besides, madam, when we retire to our pastoral solitude, we shall bid adieu to all other thoughts.

LADY. Ay, that's true; but in case of necessity; as of health or some such emergency —

FAIN. Oh, if you are prescribed marriage, you shall be considered. I will only reserve to myself the power to choose for you. If your physic be wholesome, it matters not who is your apothecary. Next, my wife shall settle on me the remainder of her fortune not made over already, and for her maintenance depend entirely on my discretion.

LADY. This is most inhumanly savage, exceeding the barbarity of a Muscovite husband.

FAIN. I learned it from his czarish majesty's[29] retinue, in a winter evening's conference over brandy and pepper, amongst other secrets of matrimony and policy, as they are at present practised in the northern hemisphere. But this must be agreed unto, and that positively. Lastly, I will be endowed, in right of my wife, with that six thousand pound which is the moiety of Mrs Millamant's fortune in your possession; and which she has forfeited (as will appear by the last will and testament of your deceased husband, Sir Jonathan Wishfort) by her disobedience in contracting herself against your consent or knowledge, and by refusing the offered match with Sir Wilfull Witwoud, which you, like a careful aunt, had provided for her.

LADY. My nephew was *non compos* and could not make his addresses.

FAIN. I come to make demands. I'll hear no objections.

LADY. You will grant me time to consider?

FAIN. Yes, while the instrument is drawing, to which you must set your hand till more sufficient deeds can be perfected, which I will take care shall be done with all possible speed. In the meanwhile, I will go for the said instrument, and till my return you may balance this matter in your own discretion.   *Exit* FAINALL

LADY. This insolence is beyond all precedent, all parallel. Must I be subject to this merciless villain?

---

[29]*czarish majesty* Peter the Great visited England in 1698, to study shipbuilding at Deptford; he and his uncouth suite leased John Evelyn's house, Sayes Court, doing £350 damage in less than a month.

MRS MAR. 'Tis severe indeed, madam, that you should smart for your daughter's wantonness.

LADY. 'Twas against my consent that she married this barbarian; but she would have him, though her year[30] was not out. – Ah, her first husband, my son[31] Languish, would not have carried it thus. Well, that was my choice; this is hers. She is matched now with a witness.[32] I shall be mad, dear friend; is there no comfort for me? Must I live to be confiscated at this rebel rate? Here come two more of my Egyptian plagues[33] too.

Enter MILLAMANT *and* SIR WILFULL

SIR WIL. Aunt, your servant.

LADY. Out, caterpillar! Call not me aunt. I know thee not.

SIR WIL. I confess I have been a little in disguise, as they say. 'Sheart, and I'm sorry for't. What would you have? I hope I committed no offence, aunt, and if I did I am willing to make satisfaction. And what can a man say fairer? If I have broke anything I'll pay for't, an it cost a pound. And so let that content for what's past, and make no more words. For what's to come, to pleasure you I'm willing to marry my cousin. So pray let's all be friends. She and I are agreed upon the matter before a witness.

LADY. How's this, dear niece? Have I any comfort? Can this be true?

MILLA. I am content to be a sacrifice to your repose, madam; and to convince you that I had no hand in the plot, as you were misinformed, I have laid my commands on Mirabell to come in person, and be a witness that I give my hand to this flower of knighthood; and for the contract that passed between Mirabell and me, I have obliged him to make a resignation of it, in your ladyship's presence. He is without, and waits your leave for admittance.

LADY. Well, I'll swear I am something revived at this testimony of your obedience, but I cannot admit that traitor. I fear I cannot fortify myself to support his appearance. He is as terrible to me as a Gorgon;[34] if I see him I fear I shall turn to stone, petrify incessantly.

MILLA. If you disoblige him he may resent your refusal, and insist upon the contract still. Then 'tis the last time he will be offensive to you.

[30]*her year* i.e. a year of mourning.

[31]*my son* i.e. son-in-law.

[32]*witness* and no mistake.

[33]*Egyptian plagues* Exodus 7–12.

[34]*Gorgon* one of three mythological sisters whose glance could turn anyone to stone.

LADY.   Are you sure it will be the last time? If I were sure of that —
Shall I never see him again?

MILLA.   Sir Wilfull, you and he are to travel together, are you not?

SIR WIL.   'Sheart, the gentleman's a civil gentleman, aunt; let him
come in. Why, we are sworn brothers and fellow travellers. We are
to be Pylades and Orestes,[35] he and I; he is to be my interpreter in
foreign parts. He has been overseas once already, and, with proviso
that I marry my cousin, will cross 'em once again, only to bear me
company. 'Sheart, I'll call him in. An I set on't once, he shall come in,
and see who'll hinder him.   *Exit*

MRS MAR.   This is precious fooling, if it would pass; but I'll know the
bottom of it.

LADY.   O dear Marwood, you are not going?

MRS MAR.   Not far, madam; I'll return immediately.   *Exit*

   Re-enter SIR WILFULL, *with* MIRABELL

SIR WIL.   Look up, man, I'll stand by you; 'sbud, an she do frown, she
can't kill you. Besides, harkee, she dare not frown desperately
because her face is none of her own. 'Sheart, an she should, her
forehead would wrinkle like the coat of a cream cheese, but mum for
that, fellow-traveller.

MIRA.   If a deep sense of the many injuries I have offered to so good a
lady, with a sincere remorse and a hearty contrition, can but obtain
the least glance of compassion, I am too happy. Ah, madam, there
was a time — but let it be forgotten. I confess I have deservedly
forfeited the high place I once held, of sighing at your feet. Nay, kill
me not, by turning from me in disdain. I come not to plead for
favour; nay, not for pardon. I am a suppliant only for your pity. I am
going where I never shall behold you more —

SIR WIL.   How, fellow-traveller! You shall go by yourself then.

MIRA.   Let me be pitied first, and afterwards forgotten. I ask no more.

SIR WIL.   By'r Lady, a very reasonable request, and will cost you
nothing, aunt. Come, come, forgive and forget, aunt. Why you
must, an you are a Christian.

MIRA.   Consider, madam, in reality. You could not receive much
prejudice. It was an innocent device, though I confess it had a face of
guiltiness; it was at most an artifice which love contrived; and errors
which love produces have ever been accounted venial. At least think
it is punishment enough that I have lost what in my heart I hold most
dear, that to your cruel indignation I have offered up this beauty,

---

[35]*Plyades and Orestes* i.e. devoted friends. Plyades assisted Orestes in avenging
the death of Agamemnon and, in some versions of the story, later married Orestes'
sister Electra.

and with her my peace and quiet, nay, all my hopes of future comfort.

SIR WIL. An he does not move me, would I might never be o' the quorum.[36] An it were not as good a deed as to drink, to give her to him again, I would I might never take shipping. Aunt, if you don't forgive quickly, I shall melt, I can tell you that. My contract went no further than a little mouth-glue[37] and that's hardly dry. One doleful sigh more from my fellow-traveller and 'tis dissolved.

LADY. Well, nephew, upon your account – Ah, he has a false insinuating tongue. Well, sir, I will stifle my just resentment at my nephew's request. I will endeavour what I can to forget, but on proviso that you resign the contract with my niece immediately.

MIRA. It is in writing and with papers of concern; but I have sent my servant for it, and will deliver it to you, with all acknowledgements for your transcendent goodness.

LADY. (*Aside*) Oh, he has witchcraft in his eyes and tongue. When I did not see him I could have bribed a villain to his assassination, but his appearance rakes the embers which have so long lain smothered in my breast.

Enter FAINALL *and* MRS MARWOOD

FAIN. Your date of deliberation, madam, is expired. Here is the instrument. Are you prepared to sign?

LADY. If I were prepared, I am not empowered. My niece exerts a lawful claim, having matched herself by my direction to Sir Wilfull.

FAIN. That sham is too gross to pass on me, though 'tis imposed on you, madam.

MILLA. Sir, I have given my consent.

MIRA. And, sir, I have resigned my pretensions.

SIR WIL. And, sir, I assert my right, and will maintain it in defiance of you, sir, and of your instrument. 'Sheart, an you talk of an instrument, sir, I have an old fox by my thigh shall hack your instrument of ram vellum to shreds, sir. It shall not be sufficient for a mittimus[38] or a tailor's measure;[39] therefore withdraw your instrument, sir, or, by'r Lady, I shall draw mine.

LADY. Hold, nephew, hold.

MILLA. Good Sir Wilfull, respite your valour.

FAIN. Indeed? Are you provided of your guard, with your single beefeater there? But I'm prepared for you, and insist upon my first proposal. You shall submit your own estate to my management and

---

[36]*quorum* one of a group of justices.
[37]*mouth-glue* an oral commitment.
[38]*mittimus* a warrant issued by a justice of the peace.
[39]*a tailor's measure* sometimes made of parchment.

absolutely make over my wife's to my sole use, as pursuant to the purport and tenor of this other covenant. [*To* MILLAMANT] I suppose, madam, your consent is not requisite in this case – nor, Mr Mirabell, your resignation, nor, Sir Wilfull, your right. You may draw your fox if you please, sir, and make a bear-garden flourish somewhere else, for here it will not avail. This, my Lady Wishfort, must be subscribed, or your darling daughter's turned adrift, like a leaky hulk, to sink or swim, as she and the current of this lewd town can agree.

LADY.   Is there no means, no remedy, to stop my ruin? Ungrateful wretch! Dost thou not owe thy being, thy subsistence, to my daughter's fortune?

FAIN.   I'll answer you when I have the rest of it in my possession.

MIRA.   But that you would not accept of a remedy from my hands – I own I have not deserved you should owe any obligation to me – or else perhaps I could advise –

LADY.   Oh what? What? To save me and my child from ruin, from want, I'll forgive all that's past; nay, I'll consent to anything to come, to be delivered from this tyranny.

MIRA.   Ay, madam; but that is too late; my reward is intercepted. You have disposed of her who only could have made me a compensation for all my services. But be it as it may, I am resolved I'll serve you. You shall not be wronged in this savage manner.

LADY.   How! Dear Mr Mirabell, can you be so generous at last? But it is not possible. Harkee, I'll break my nephew's match; you shall have my niece yet and all her fortune, if you can but save me from this imminent danger.

MIRA.   Will you? I take you at your word. I ask no more. I must have leave for two criminals to appear.

LADY.   Ay, ay, anybody, anybody.

MIRA.   Foible is one, and a penitent.

Enter MRS FAINALL, FOIBLE *and* MINCING

MIRABELL *and* LADY WISHFORT *go to* MRS FAINALL *and* FOIBLE
[*;they talk apart*]

MRS MAR.   (*To* FAINALL) O my shame! These corrupt things are brought hither to expose me.

FAIN.   If it must all come out, why, let 'em know it; 'tis but the way of the world. That shall not urge me to relinquish or abate one tittle of my terms. No, I will insist the more.

FOIB.   Yes indeed, madam, I'll take my Bible oath of it.

MINC.   And so will I, mem.

LADY.   O Marwood, Marwood, art thou false? My friend deceive me? Hast thou been a wicked accomplice with that profligate man?

MRS MAR. Have you so muıch ingratitude and injustice to give credit against your friend, to the aspersions of two such mercenary trulls?

MINC. Mercenary, mem? I scorn your words. 'Tis true we found you and Mr Fainall in the blue garret; by the same token, you swore us to secrecy upon Messalina's[40] poems. Mercenary? No. If we would have been mercenary, we should have held our tongues; you would have bribed us sufficiently.

FAIN. Go! You are an insignificant thing. Well, what are you the better for this? Is this Mr Mirabell's expedient? I'll be put off no longer. You thing, that was a wife, shall smart for this. I will not leave thee wherewithal to hide thy shame. Your body shall be naked as your reputation.

MRS FAIN. I despise you and defy your malice. You have aspersed me wrongfully. I have proved your falsehood. Go, you and your treacherous – I will not name it, but starve together, perish.

FAIN. Not while you are worth a groat indeed, my dear. Madam, I'll be fooled no longer.

LADY. Ah, Mr Mirabell, this is small comfort, the detection of this affair.

MIRA. Oh, in good time. Your leave for the other offender and penitent to appear, madam.

Enter WAITWELL *with a box of writings*

LADY. O Sir Rowland! Well, rascal?

WAIT. What your ladyship pleases. I have brought the black box at last, madam.

MIRA. Give it me. Madam, you remember your promise.

LADY. Ay, dear sir.

MIRA. Where are the gentlemen?

WAIT. At hand, sir, rubbing their eyes, just risen from sleep.

FAIN. 'Sdeath, what's this to me? I'll not wait your private concerns.

Enter PETULANT *and* WITWOUD

PET. How now? What's the matter? Whose hand's out?[41]

WIT. Heyday! What, are you all got together, like players at the end of the last act?

MIRA. You may remember, gentlemen, I once requested your hands as witnesses to a certain parchment.

WIT. Ay, I do. My hand I remember. Petulant set his mark.

MIRA. You wrong him. His name is fairly written, as shall appear. You do not remember, gentlemen, anything of what that parchment contained? *Undoing the box*

---

[40]*Messalina's* Mincing probably intended 'Miscellaneous'.
[41]*Whose hand's out* What's the trouble?

WIT.   No.

PET.   Not I. I writ; I read nothing.

MIRA.   Very well. Now you shall know. Madam, your promise.

LADY.   Ay, ay, sir, upon my honour.

MIRA.   Mr Fainall, it is now time that you should know that your
lady, while she was at her own disposal, and before you had by your
insinuations wheedled her out of a pretended settlement of the
greatest part of her fortune –

FAIN.   Sir! Pretended!

MIRA.   Yes, sir. I say that this lady, while a widow, having, it seems,
received some cautions respecting your inconstancy and tyranny of
temper, which from her own partial opinion and fondness of you she
could never have suspected, she did, I say, by the wholesome advice
of friends and of sages learned in the laws of this land, deliver this
same as her act and deed to me in trust, and to the uses within
mentioned. You may read if you please, (*Holding out the parchment*) though perhaps what is inscribed on the back may serve your
occasions.

FAIN.   Very likely, sir. What's here? Damnation! (*Reads*) 'A deed of
conveyance of the whole estate real of Arabella Languish, widow, in
trust to Edward Mirabell'. Confusion!

MIRA.   Even so, sir, 'tis the way of the world, sir, of the widows of the
world. I suppose this deed may bear an elder date than what you
have obtained from your lady.

FAIN.   Perfidious fiend! Then thus I'll be revenged!

                                Offers to run at MRS FAINALL

SIR WIL.   Hold, sir! Now you may make your bear-garden flourish
somewhere else, sir.

FAIN.   Mirabell, you shall hear of this, sir, be sure you shall. Let me
pass, oaf.   *Exit*

MRS FAIN.   Madam, you seem to stifle your resentment. You had
better give it vent.

MRS MAR.   Yes, it shall have vent, and to your confusion, or I'll perish
in the attempt.   *Exit*

LADY.   O daughter, daughter, 'tis plain thou hast inherited thy
mother's prudence.

MRS FAIN.   Thank Mr Mirabell, a cautious friend, to whose advice
all is owing.

LADY.   Well, Mr Mirabell, you have kept your promise, and I must
perform mine. First, I pardon for your sake Sir Rowland there and
Foible. The next thing is to break the matter to my nephew, and how
to do that –

MIRA.   For that, madam, give yourself no trouble. Let me have your
consent. Sir Wilfull is my friend; he has had compassion upon

lovers, and generously engaged a volunteer[42] in this action, for our service, and now designs to prosecute his travels.

SIR WIL. 'Sheart, aunt, I have no mind to marry. My cousin's a fine lady, and the gentleman loves her, and she loves him, and they deserve one another. My resolution is to see foreign parts. I have set on't, and when I'm set on't, I must do't. And if these two gentlemen would travel too, I think they may be spared.

PET. For my part, I say little. I think things are best off or on.[43]

WIT. Egad, I understand nothing of the matter. I'm in a maze yet, like a dog in a dancing-school.

LADY. Well, sir, take her, and with her all the joy I can give you.

MILLA. Why does not the man take me? Would you have me give myself to you over again?

MIRA. Ay, and over and over again; for I would have you as often as possibly I can. (*Kisses her hand*) Well, heaven grant I love you not too well; that's all my fear.

SIR WIL. 'Sheart, you'll have time enough to toy after you're married; or if you will toy now, let us have a dance in the meantime, that we who are not lovers may have some other employment besides looking on.

MIRA. With all my heart, dear Sir Wilfull. What shall we do for music?

FOIB. O sir, some that were provided for Sir Rowland's entertainment are yet within call.

A dance

LADY. As I am a person I can hold out no longer. I have wasted my spirits so today already that I am ready to sink under the fatigue, and I cannot but have some fears upon me yet that my son Fainall will pursue some desperate course.

MIRA. Madam, disquiet not yourself on that account. To my knowledge his circumstances are such he must of force comply. For my part, I will contribute all that in me lies to a reunion. (*To* MRS FAINALL) In the meantime, madam, let me before these witnesses restore to you this deed of trust. It may be a means, well managed, to make you live easily together.

> From hence let those be warn'd who mean to wed,
> Lest mutual falsehood stain the bridal bed;
> For each deceiver to his cost may find
> That marriage frauds too oft are paid in kind.

Exeunt omnes

---

[42]*engaged a volunteer* voluntarily committed his aid in the scheme.
[43]*off or on* of no concern to me.

EPILOGUE

After our epilogue this crowd dismisses,
I'm thinking how this play'll be pull'd to pieces.
But pray consider, ere you doom its fall,
How hard a thing 'twould be to please you all.
There are some critics so with spleen diseas'd
They scarcely come inclining to be pleas'd;
And sure he must have more than mortal skill
Who pleases anyone against his will.
Then all bad poets we are sure are foes,
And how their number's swell'd the town well knows;
In shoals, I've mark'd 'em judging in the pit,
Though they're on no pretence for judgment fit,
But that they have been damn'd for want of wit.
Since when they, by their own offences taught,
Set up for spies on plays and finding fault.
Others there are whose malice we'd prevent,
Such who watch plays with scurrilous intent,
To mark out who by characters are meant;
And though no perfect likeness they can trace,
Yet each pretends to know the copied face.
These with false glosses feed their own ill nature,
And turn to libel, what was meant a satire.
May such malicious fops this fortune find,
To think themselves alone the fools design'd,
If any are so arrogantly vain
To think they singly can support a scene,
And furnish fool enough to entertain;
For well the learn'd and the judicious know
That satire scorns to stoop so meanly low,
As any one abstracted fop to show.
For, as when painters form a matchless face,

They from each fair one catch some different grace,
And shining features in one portrait blend,
To which no single beauty must pretend;
So poets oft do in one piece expose
Whole *belles assemblées* of *coquettes* and *beaux*.

FINIS

George Farquhar

THE BEAUX STRATAGEM

1707

The Beaux Stratagem
a Comedy,
as it is acted
at the Queen's Theatre
in the Haymarket
by Her Majesty's Sworn Comedians.
Written by Mr Farquhar,
author of *The Recruiting Officer*.

London,
Printed for Bernard Lintott,
at the Cross Keys, next Nando's Coffee House
in Fleet Street.
[1707]

BIOGRAPHY

George Farquhar was born in Londonderry, Ireland, *c.* 1677; studied at Trinity College, Dublin (1694–96), and acted unsuccessfully in that city. He settled in London in 1697, where he wrote poetry, prose, and plays (*Love and a Bottle*, 1698; *The Constant Couple*, 1699). Three subsequent plays were not very successful; he married in 1703 and joined the army, serving principally as a recruiter in Lichfield and Shrewsbury, 1704–06. His most memorable plays followed: *The Recruiting Officer*, 1706, and *The Beaux Stratagem*, 1707. He died in poverty in May 1707.

INTRODUCTION

This is one of the few Restoration comedies set outside of London. Although the action takes place in Lichfield, Staffordshire, the metropolis is a significant part of the background. The young fortune-hunters, Aimwell and Archer, leave the capital with almost empty pockets, bringing to Lichfield their hard-headed city values. Later, when Mrs Sullen wants to punish her uncouth, insensitive husband, she wishes that they were in London (her former home) so that she could teach him how husbands should behave. Farquhar's intention was not primarily to establish contrasts or parallels between Lichfield and London, nor to draw satiric portraits of either, but to offer a lively, realistic commentary on human nature. *The Beaux Stratagem*, despite some conventional elements, is therefore less a comedy of manners than earlier plays of the period. Lady Bountiful illustrates well the changing tone of drama. Earlier Restoration comedies had no characters comparable to her; middle-aged or elderly women had been figures of fun or satire (Old Lady Squeamish, Lady Woodvill, Lady Wishfort). In *The Beaux Stratagem*, however, one observes Lady Bountiful's benevolence and is only amused by her unworldly innocence as she earnestly revives the love-wounded Aimwell from his feigned seizure (IV, i).

Hypocrisy dominates the stratagems of Archer and Aimwell as well as the marital problems of Squire and Mrs Sullen. Disguise is a major theme from the beginning, as the two opportunistic beaux hide their poverty behind the joint guise of a wealthy aristocrat and his servant. They share responsibility in fraudulence by an agreement to alternate roles as they move from town to town seeking a fortune.

Their questionable exploits in Lichfield begin with Aimwell's seemingly virtuous appearance in church;[1] his real motivation is to

[1] Important elements of the plot violate Christian principles or codes of conduct: a series of seductions, Sullen's distasteful treatment of his wife and two armed robberies. There are occasional reminders that much of the action takes place on Sunday.

create a favourable impression in the community, especially on any wealthy, susceptible girl. At the same time, Archer's scheme to seduce Cherry, the inn-keeper's daughter, is under way; to this end he uses flattery and insincere romantic words. Even the inn is ambivalent in nature. It appears to offer genuine hospitality, but is in reality the headquarters of the landlord's gang of thieves. The subplot, concerned with two robberies masterminded by Boniface and Gibbet, echoes the main plot, which also centres on the unscrupulous achievement of financial advantage. As in many other plays of that time, the names given to characters reveal their personalities: Boniface, Sullen, Bountiful, Archer, Aimwell – these last two inevitably the heart of the romantic activity.

In his portrayal of Squire and Mrs Sullen, Farquhar seriously analyses the hypocrisy of maintaining an unsuccessful marriage. A woman was then almost wholly dependent on the goodwill of her husband, as both this play and its partial dramatic source, *The Provoked Wife* (1697), illustrate. It was possible to obtain a formal marital separation through the ecclesiastical courts, but a divorce could be arranged only by a rare act of Parliament, accompanied by much expense and publicity.

Farquhar draws sympathy towards Mrs Sullen from her first appearance; the compassion of the audience diminishes briefly as she plans an *affaire d'amour* with Count Bellair (II, i), but Farquhar immediately makes it evident that she does so only to stir her obtuse husband into taking a greater interest in her. Squire Sullen spends surprisingly little time on stage; his uncouth behaviour is reported at length, but he makes only five appearances, three of them very brief. In contrast is the active role taken by his metaphorical brother, Sir John Brute in *The Provoked Wife*, who is on stage in nine episodes.

The morality of Mrs Sullen's subsequent interest in Archer also creates both criticism and compassion. She is certainly attracted to him, for obvious reasons, but following his aggressive wooing in the picture gallery, when Archer boldly proposes an inspection of her bedroom, she refuses him, guided by a sense of honour considerably more genuine than that of Lady Fidget and her associates in *The Country Wife*. Mrs Sullen's brief temptation towards sexual infidelity contributes to the realism of *The Beaux Stratagem*, as does the shrewd scheming, both sexual and financial, of Archer and Aimwell.

The subject of marriage is of great concern to Mrs Sullen's young, unmarried sister-in-law, Dorinda; her wooing by Aimwell parallels chronologically the attempted seduction of Mrs Sullen by Archer and the wrangles between the Sullens, creating contrasts and ironies. The love affairs of Aimwell and Archer reveal Farquhar's careful differentiation between the men. The former is more intense and somewhat more sincere in all his relationships, the latter more interested in casual sexual liaisons.

Aimwell proposes marriage to Dorinda (v, iv) in the guise of the rich Viscount Aimwell (who is, in fact, his unmarried elder brother), but almost immediately is impelled by conscience to confess his imposture. The remarkably opportune death in London of the true Viscount Aimwell is essentially a romantic or sentimental device, as it makes Thomas Aimwell truly a wealthy man and therefore worthy of Dorinda, herself the possessor of £10,000. Farquhar did not yield to the temptation to provide an equally romantic ending to Archer's tentative affair with Mrs Sullen. Indeed, the author left the conclusion to this phase of the play quite ambiguous.

In the final moments of Act v, Archer leads Mrs Sullen into a dance (at about 3.00 a.m.). This gesture may imply an extension of his relationship with the lady, now divorced in spirit, though not in fact, from her husband. Archer shrewdly imposes an obligation to him on Mrs Sullen. When the Squire refuses to return her dowry of £10,000, Archer offers to pay it to her (his friend the new Lord Aimwell having just given him that sum of money). In the event, Squire Sullen grudgingly agrees to return his wife's dowry; hence at the end of the play Archer has a large amount of money in hand and no real need to hand over any of it to Mrs Sullen. Also in Act v, prior to the dowry negotiations, Archer urges Aimwell to persuade Dorinda to employ Cherry as her maid. One may therefore imagine Archer, the eternal playboy, continuing indefinitely his efforts to seduce both Cherry and Mrs Sullen.

Farquhar's language in this play is distinguished by its naturalism and realism. There is little of the witty repartee that characterised many earlier Restoration comedies – *The Way of the World* (1700), for example. *The Beaux Stratagem* includes several down-to-earth people with Elizabethan antecedents: Boniface, Cherry, Gibbet and Hounslow. They contribute much to the lively action and the development of several humorous situations.

Autobiographical elements probably influenced the action and themes of *The Beaux Stratagem*. Farquhar spent some time in Lichfield (living at an inn) and Shrewsbury; his military duties in the latter city inspired *The Recruiting Officer*, 1706, and the author's interest in the difficulties of bringing a marital union to an end may have been prompted by his own marriage in 1703. The inference that it may have been unhappy is based on the tradition that his wife led him to believe that she had a substantial private income. John Milton's *The Doctrine and Discipline of Divorce* (1643), contributed many phrases and ideas to this play.[2]

[2]Martin A. Larson, 'The Influence of Milton's Divorce Tracts on Farquhar's *Beaux Stratagem*'. *PMLA*, 39 (March 1924), 174–178.

The popularity of *The Beaux Stratagem* throughout most of the eighteenth century was due in large part to David Garrick, who played the role of Archer approximately ninety-seven times between 1742 and 1776; he also acted the part of Scrub five times. The play is indebted to Richard Steele's *The Lying Lover* (1703) and was a major influence on Oliver Goldsmith's *She Stoops to Conquer* (1776), which Goldsmith acknowledges in a reference to Cherry by Kate Hardcastle, pretending to be a maid at an inn (III, i). *The Beaux Stratagem* has occasionally been revived during the past two centuries.

Farquhar's last play was first produced on 8 March 1707, and was subsequently modified. A 1728 edition, published, like the first edition of 1707, by Bernard Lintot, incorporates a footnote (III, iii, p. 45) stating that the part of Bellair was deleted after the first night's performance. Several references to him remained in the text, but his small contribution to III, iii was omitted, and his speeches in IV, iv were rewritten and given to Foigard. It cannot be proved that the dying Farquhar was responsible for these revisions, although Bellair was left off from all eighteenth-century cast lists after the first night. The revised lines from V, iv, as published in 1728, are printed as Appendix C, pp. 677–78.

BIBLIOGRAPHY

W. C. Connely, *Young George Farquhar*. London, 1949.

R. Berman, 'The Comedy of Reason'. *Texas Studies in Literature and Language*, 7 (Summer 1965), 161–68.

G. Farmer, *George Farquhar*. Writers and their Work Series. London, 1966.

E. Rothstein, *George Farquhar*. New York, 1967.

A. Roper, '*The Beaux Stratagem*: Image and Action,' in E. Miner, ed., *Seventeenth-Century Imagery; Essays on Uses of Figurative Language from Donne to Farquhar*. Berkeley, 1971.

E. N. James, *The Development of George Farquhar as a Comic Dramatist*. The Hague, 1972.

P. Lewis, '*The Beaux Stratagem* and *The Beggar's Opera*'. *Notes and Queries*, N.S. 28 (June 1981) 221–24.

E. N. James, *George Farquhar, a Reference Guide*. Boston, 1986.

S. L. Kimball, '"Ceres in her Harvest", the Exploded Myths of Womanhood in George Farquhar's *The Beaux Stratagem*'. *Restoration and Eighteenth Century Theatre Research*, 3 (1988), 1–9.

DRAMATIS PERSONAE

[THOMAS] AIMWELL	Mr [John] Mills
[FRANCIS] ARCHER	Mr [Robert] Wilks
Two gentlemen of broken fortunes, the first as master, and the second as servant	
COUNT BELLAIR, *a French officer, prisoner at Lichfield*	Mr Bowman[1]
[SQUIRE] SULLEN, *a country blockhead, brutal to his wife*	Mr [John] Verbruggen
[SIR CHARLES] FREEMAN, *a gentleman from London*	Mr Keen[2]
FOIGARD, *a priest, chaplain to the French officers*	Mr [William] Bowen
GIBBET, *a highwayman*	Mr [Colley] Cibber
HOUNSLOW BAGSHOT } *his companions*[3]	
[WILL] BONIFACE, *landlord of the inn*	Mr [William] Bullock
SCRUB, *servant to* MR SULLEN	Mr [Henry] Norris[4]
LADY BOUNTIFUL, *an old civil country gentlewoman that cures all her neighbours of all distempers, and foolishly fond of her son* [SQUIRE] SULLEN	Mrs [Mary] Powell
DORINDA, LADY BOUNTIFUL'S *daughter*	Mrs [Lucretia] Bradshaw
MRS SULLEN, LADY BOUNTIFUL'S *daughter-in-law*	Mrs [Anne] Oldfield

---

[1] John Boman.   [2] Theophilis Keene.
[3] Hounslow and Bagshot are areas near London then notorious for highway robbery.
[4] the younger actor with this name, 1665–1731.

GIPSY, *maid to the ladies*   Mrs Mills[5]
CHERRY, *the landlord's daughter in the*   Mrs [Margaret] Bicknell
  inn
COUNTRYMAN, COUNTRYWOMAN,
  tapster, servants and others.

Scene: Lichfield[6]

[5]Probably Margaret (Mrs John) Mills.
[6]In the earliest edition of the play, 1707, the following Advertisement follows the
Dramatis Personae:
  The reader may find some faults in this play, which my illness prevented the
  amending of, but there is great amends made in the representation, which cannot
  be matched, no more than the friendly and indefatigable care of Mr Wilks, to
  whom I chiefly owe the success of the play.
                                                    George Farquhar.
Robert Wilks, a friend who had urged the ill and impoverished dramatist to write
the play, performed the role of Archer from its opening, 8 March 1707, until his
death in 1732. (Farquhar was buried 23 May 1707.)

PROLOGUE

SPOKEN BY MR WILKS

When strife disturbs or sloth corrupts an age,
Keen satire is the business of the stage.
When the Plain Dealer[1] writ, he lash'd those crimes
Which then infested most the modish times.
But now, when faction sleeps and sloth is fled,
And all our youth in active fields are bred;[2]
When through Great Britain's fair extensive round,
The trumps of fame, the notes of Union[3] sound;
When Anna's sceptre[4] points the laws their course,
And her example gives her precepts force,
There scarce is room for satire; all our lays
Must be or songs of triumph or of praise.
But as in grounds best cultivated, tares
And poppies rise among the golden ears,
Our products so, fit for the field or school,
Must mix with nature's favourite plant – a fool:
A weed that has to twenty summers ran
Shoots up in stalk and vegetates to man.
Simpling[5] our author goes from field to field,
And culls such fools as may diversion yield;
And thanks to Nature, there's no want of those,
For, rain or shine, the thriving coxcomb grows.

[1] *Plain Dealer* William Wycherley, the author of the play of this name, first performed late in 1676.
[2] *bred* i.e. times have changed, and young men are now fighting in France in the War of the Spanish Succession, 1701–13.
[3] *Union* the Act of Union of the Parliaments of England and Scotland, 6 March 1707; this play was first produced 8 March 1707.
[4] *Anna's sceptre* Queen Anne reigned 1702–14.
[5] *Simpling* Gathering medicinal herbs.

Follies tonight we show ne'er lash'd before,
Yet such as nature shows you every hour;
Nor can the pictures give a just offence,
For fools are made for jests to men of sense.

THE BEAUX STRATAGEM

Act One

SCENE ONE

An inn

Enter BONIFACE *running*

BON.   Chamberlain! Maid! Cherry! Daughter Cherry! All asleep? All dead?

Enter CHERRY *running*

CHER.   Here, here! Why d'ye bawl so, father? D'ye think we have no ears?

BON.   You deserve to have none, you young minx! The company of the Warrington[1] coach has stood in the hall this hour, and nobody to show them to their chambers.

CHER.   And let 'em wait further; there's neither red-coat in the coach nor footman behind it.

BON.   But they threaten to go to another inn tonight.

CHER.   That they dare not, for fear the coachman should overturn them tomorrow. – Coming, coming! – Here's the London coach arrived.

Enter several people with trunks, bandboxes, and other luggage, and cross the stage

BON.   Welcome, ladies!

CHER.   Very welcome, gentlemen! Chamberlain, show the Lion and the Rose.[2]   *Exit with the company*

Enter AIMWELL *in a riding habit, and* ARCHER *as footman, carrying a portmantle*

BON.   This way, this way, gentlemen!

AIM.   [*To* ARCHER] Set down the things, go to the stable, and see my horses well rubbed.

ARCH.   I shall, sir.   *Exit*

AIM.   You're my landlord, I suppose?

BON.   Yes, sir, I'm old Will Boniface, pretty well known upon this road, as the saying is.

---

[1] *Warrington* a town 65 miles (*c.* 100 km.) north-west of Lichfield.
[2] *Lion and the Rose* the names of rooms at the inn.

AIM. O Mr Boniface, your servant!

BON. O sir, what will you honour please to drink, as the saying is?

AIM. I have heard your town of Lichfield much famed for ale; I think
I'll taste that.

BON. Sir, I have now in my cellar ten tun³ of the best ale in
Staffordshire; 'tis smooth as oil, sweet as milk, clear as amber, and
strong as brandy; and will be just fourteen year old the fifth day of
next March, old style.⁴

AIM. You're very exact, I find, in the age of your ale.

BON. As punctual, sir, as I am in the age of my children. I'll show you
such ale! – Here, tapster, broach number 1706,⁵ as the saying is. –
Sir, you shall taste my *Anno Domini* – I have lived in Lichfield, man
and boy, above eight-and-fifty years, and, I believe, have not
consumed eight-and-fifty ounces of meat.

AIM. At a meal, you mean, if one may guess your sense by your bulk.

BON. Not in my life, sir. I have fed purely upon ale; I have eat my ale,
drank my ale, and I always sleep upon ale.

   Enter tapster with a bottle and glass, and exit

Now, sir, you shall see! – (*Filling out a glass*) Your worship's health.
–[*Drinks*] Ha, delicious, delicious! Fancy it burgundy, only fancy it,
and 'tis worth ten shillings a quart.

AIM. (*Drinks*) 'Tis confounded strong!

BON. Strong! It must be so, or how should we be strong that drink it?

AIM. And have you lived so long upon this ale, landlord?

BON. Eight-and-fifty years, upon my credit, sir; but it killed my wife,
poor woman, as the saying is.

AIM. How came that to pass?

BON. I don't know how, sir. She would not let the ale take its natural
course, sir; she was for qualifying it every now and then with a
dram,⁶ as the saying is; and an honest gentleman that came this way
from Ireland made her a present of a dozen bottles of usquebaugh,
but the poor woman was never well after; but, howe'er, I was
obliged to the gentleman, you know.

AIM. Why, was it the usquebaugh that killed her?

BON. My Lady Bountiful said so. She, good lady, did what could be
done; she cured her of three tympanies,⁷ but the fourth carried her
off. But she's happy, and I'm contented, as the saying is.

³*tun* casks each holding about 250 gallons (*c.* 1150 litres).

⁴*old style* England did not adopt the Gregorian calendar, with a new year
beginning on 1 January, until 1752; on the Continent on 5 March it was already
1707, but it was 1706 in England until 25 March.

⁵1706 i.e. this year's ale.   ⁶*dram* a small quantity of spirits.

⁷*tympanies* tumours.

AIM.   Who's that Lady Bountiful you mentioned?

BON.   Ods my life, sir, we'll drink her health. – (*Drinks*) My Lady Bountiful is one of the best of women. Her last husband, Sir Charles Bountiful, left her worth a thousand pound a year; and I believe she lays out one half on't in charitable uses for the good of her neighbours. She cures rheumatisms, ruptures, and broken shins in men; green-sickness, obstructions, and fits of the mother[8] in women; the king's evil,[9] chincough,[10] and chilblains in children. In short, she has cured more people in and about Lichfield within ten years than the doctors have killed in twenty; and that's a bold word.

AIM.   Has the lady been any other way useful in her generation?

BON.   Yes, sir; she has a daughter by Sir Charles, the finest woman in all our country and the greatest fortune. She has a son too, by her first husband, Squire Sullen, who married a fine lady from London t'other day; if you please, sir, we'll drink his health.

AIM.   What sort of a man is he?

BON.   Why, sir, the man's well enough; says little, thinks less, and does – nothing at all, faith. But he's a man of a great estate and values nobody.

AIM.   A sportsman, I suppose?

BON.   Yes, sir, he's a man of pleasure; he plays at whisk[11] and smokes his pipe eight-and-forty hours together sometimes.

AIM.   And married, you say?

BON.   Ay, and to a curious[12] woman, sir. But he's a – he wants it here, sir.   *Pointing to his forehead*

AIM.   He has it there,[13] you mean?

BON.   That's none of my business; he's my landlord, and so a man, you know, would not – But, ecod, he's no better than – Sir, my humble service to you. – (*Drinks*) Though I value not a farthing what he can do to me; I pay him his rent at quarter-day; I have a good running-trade; I have but one daughter, and I can give her – but no matter for that.

AIM.   You're very happy, Mr Boniface. Pray, what other company have you in town?

BON.   A power of fine ladies; and then we have the French officers.[14]

---

[8]*mother* hysteria.

[9]*king's evil* scrofula. The custom of the ruler touching a victim to cure the disease died out only with the reign of Queen Anne.

[10]*chincough* whooping cough.

[11]*whisk* whist.

[12]*curious* clever.

[13]*He has it there* the sign of a cuckold, a pair of horns.

[14]*French officers* soldiers on parole, captured during the War of the Spanish Succession, 1701–13.

AIM. Oh, that's right, you have a good many of those gentlemen. Pray, how do you like their company?

BON. So well, as the saying is, that I could wish we had as many more of 'em; they're full of money, and pay double for everything they have. They know, sir, that we paid good round taxes for the taking of 'em, and so they are willing to reimburse us a little. One of 'em lodges in my house.

Re-enter ARCHER

ARCH. Landlord, there are some French gentlemen below that ask for you.

BON. I'll wait on 'em. – (*Aside to* ARCHER) Does your master stay long in town, as the saying is?

ARCH. I can't tell, as the saying is.

BON. Come from London?

ARCH. No.

BON. Going to London, mayhap?

ARCH. No.

BON. [*Aside*] An odd fellow this. – [*To* AIMWELL] I beg your worship's pardon; I'll wait on you in half a minute.   *Exit*

AIM. The coast's clear, I see. – Now, my dear Archer, welcome to Lichfield!

ARCH. I thank thee, my dear brother in iniquity.

AIM. Iniquity! Prithee, leave canting;[15] you need not change your style with your dress.

ARCH. Don't mistake me, Aimwell, for 'tis still my maxim that there is no scandal like rags nor any crime so shameful as poverty.

AIM. The world confesses it every day in its practice, though men won't own it for their opinion. Who did that worthy lord, my brother, single out of the side-box[16] to sup with him t'other night?

ARCH. Jack Handicraft, a handsome, well-dressed, mannerly, sharping rogue who keeps the best company in town.

AIM. Right! And, pray, who married my lady Manslaughter t'other day, the great fortune?

ARCH. Why, Nick Marrabone,[17] a professed pickpocket, and a good bowler;[18] but he makes a handsome figure and rides in his coach, that he formerly used to ride behind.

AIM. But did you observe poor Jack Generous in the Park last week?

[15]*canting* using hypocritical language.
[16]*side-box* a box at a theatre.
[17]*Marrabone* perhaps a variant of Marylebone. Marylebone Gardens, London, were notorious for thieves.
[18]*bowler* sportsman, used ironically.

ARCH. Yes, with his autumnal periwig, shading his melancholy face, his coat older than anything but its fashion, with one hand idle in his pocket, and with the other picking his useless teeth; and, though the Mall was crowded with company, yet was poor Jack as single and solitary as a lion in a desert.

AIM. And as much avoided, for no crime upon earth but the want of money.

ARCH. And that's enough. Men must not be poor; idleness is the root of all evil; the world's wide enough, let 'em bustle. Fortune has taken the weak under her protection, but men of sense are left to their industry.

AIM. Upon which topic we proceed, and, I think, luckily hitherto. Would not any man swear now that I am a man of quality and you my servant, when, if our intrinsic value were known —

ARCH. Come, come, we are the men of intrinsic value who can strike our fortunes out of ourselves, whose worth is independent of accidents in life or revolutions in government. We have heads to get money and hearts to spend it.

AIM. As to our hearts, I grant ye, they are as willing tits[19] as any within twenty degrees; but I can have no great opinion of our heads from the service they have done us hitherto, unless it be that they have brought us from London hither to Lichfield, made me a lord and you my servant.

ARCH. That's more than you could expect already. But what money have we left?

AIM. But two hundred pound.

ARCH. And our horses, clothes, rings, etc. Why, we have very good fortunes now for moderate people; and let me tell you that this two hundred pound, with the experience that we are now masters of, is a better estate than the ten thousand we have spent. Our friends, indeed, began to suspect that our pockets were low, but we came off with flying colours, showed no signs of want either in word or deed.

AIM. Ay, and our going to Brussels was a good pretence enough for our sudden disappearing; and, I warrant you, our friends imagine that we are gone a-volunteering.[20]

ARCH. Why, faith, if this prospect fails, it must e'en come to that. I am for venturing one of the hundreds, if you will, upon this knight-errantry; but, in case it should fail, we'll reserve t'other to carry us to some counter-scarp,[21] where we may die, as we lived, in a blaze.

[19]*tits* small horses.
[20]*a-volunteering* i.e. we have joined the army.
[21]*counterscarp* a part of a fortification.

AIM.   With all my heart; and we have lived justly, Archer; we can't
say that we have spent our fortunes, but that we have enjoyed 'em.

ARCH.   Right! So much pleasure for so much money. We have had
our pennyworths; and, had I millions, I would go to the same market
again. – O London, London! – Well, we have had our share, and let
us be thankful. Past pleasures, for aught I know, are best, such as we
are sure of; those to come may disappoint us.

AIM.   It has often grieved the heart of me to see how some inhuman
wretches murder their kind fortunes; those that, by sacrificing all to
one appetite, shall starve all the rest. You shall have some that live
only in their palates, and in their sense of tasting shall drown the
other four; others are only epicures in appearances, such who shall
starve their nights to make a figure a days, and famish their own to
feed the eyes of others. A contrary sort confine their pleasures to the
dark and contract their spacious acres to the circuit of a muff-string.

ARCH.   Right! But they find the Indies[22] in that spot where they
consume 'em, and I think your kind keepers[23] have much the best
on't, for they indulge the most senses by one expense. There's the
seeing, hearing, and feeling amply gratified; and some philosophers
will tell you that from such a commerce there arises a sixth sense that
gives infinitely more pleasure than the other five put together.

AIM.   And to pass to the other extremity, of all keepers I think those
the worst that keep their money.

ARCH.   Those are the most miserable wights[24] in being; they destroy
the rights of nature and disappoint the blessings of providence. Give
me a man that keeps his five senses keen and bright as his sword, that
has 'em always drawn out in their just order and strength, with his
reason as commander at the head of 'em, that detaches 'em by turns
upon whatever party of pleasure agreeably offers, and commands
'em to retreat upon the least appearance of disadvantage or danger.
For my part, I can stick to my bottle while my wine, my company,
and my reason hold good; I can be charmed with Sappho's singing
without falling in love with her face: I love hunting, but would not,
like Actaeon,[25] be eaten up by my own dogs; I love a fine house, but
let another keep it; and just so I love a fine woman.

AIM.   In that last particular you have the better of me.

ARCH.   Ay, you're such an amorous puppy that I'm afraid you'll spoil

[22]*the Indies* a source of riches.

[23]*kind keepers* men who support mistresses. (John Dryden, *The Kind Keeper or
Mr Limberham*, 1680).

[24]*wights* men.

[25]*Actaeon* As punishment for watching Artemis and her attendants bathing, he
was turned into a stag and killed by his dogs.

our sport; you can't counterfeit the passion without feeling it.

AIM. Though the whining part[26] be out of doors[27] in town, 'tis still in force with the country ladies; and let me tell you, Frank, the fool in that passion shall outdo the knave at any time.

ARCH. Well, I won't dispute it now; you command for the day, and so I submit. At Nottingham, you know, I am to be master.

AIM. And at Lincoln, I again.

ARCH. Then at Norwich I mount, which, I think, shall be our last stage; for, if we fail there, we'll embark for Holland, bid adieu to Venus, and welcome Mars.

AIM. A match! – Mum!

Re-enter BONIFACE

BON. What will your worship please to have for supper?

AIM. What have you got?

BON. Sir, we have a delicate piece of beef in the pot, and a pig at the fire.

AIM. Good supper-meat, I must confess. I can't eat beef, landlord.

ARCH. And I hate pig.

AIM. Hold your prating, sirrah! Do you know who you are?

BON. Please to bespeak something else; I have everything in the house.

AIM. Have you any veal?

BON. Veal! Sir, we had a delicate loin of veal on Wednesday last.

AIM. Have you got any fish or wildfowl?

BON. As for fish, truly, sir, we are an inland town, and indifferently provided with fish, that's the truth on't; and then for wildfowl – we have a delicate couple of rabbits.

AIM. Get me the rabbits fricasseed.[28]

BON. Fricasseed! Lard, sir, they'll eat much better smothered with onions.

ARCH. Pshaw! Damn your onions!

AIM. Again, sirrah! – Well, landlord, what you please. But hold, I have a small charge[29] of money, and your house is so full of strangers that I believe it may be safer in your custody than mine; for when this fellow of mine gets drunk he minds nothing. – Here, sirrah, reach me the strong-box.

ARCH. Yes, sir. – (*Aside*) This will give us a reputation.

Brings AIMWELL *the box*

AIM. Here, landlord; the locks are sealed down both for your security and mine; it holds somewhat above two hundred pound. If you doubt

---

[26]*whining part* the conventional complaining phase of a courtship.
[27]*out of doors* out of fashion.
[28]*fricasseed* cut up, stewed, and served in a sauce.
[29]*charge* sum.

it, I'll count it to you after supper. But be sure you lay it where I may have it at a minute's warning, for my affairs are a little dubious at present. Perhaps I may be gone in half an hour; perhaps I may be your guest till the best part of that be spent; and pray order your ostler to keep my horses always saddled. But one thing above the rest I must beg, that you would let this fellow have none of your *Anno Domini*, as you call it, for he's the most insufferable sot. – Here, sirrah, light me to my chamber.   *Exit, lighted by* ARCHER

BON.   Cherry! Daughter Cherry!

    Re-enter CHERRY

CHER.   D'ye call, father?

BON.   Ay, child, you must lay by this box for the gentleman; 'tis full of money.

CHER.   Money! All that money! Why, sure, father, the gentleman comes to be chosen parliament-man.³⁰ Who is he?

BON.   I don't know what to make of him; he talks of keeping his horses ready saddled, and of going perhaps at a minute's warning, or of staying perhaps till the best part of this be spent.

CHER.   Ay, ten to one, father, he's a highwayman.

BON.   A highwayman! Upon my life, girl, you have hit it, and this box is some new-purchased³¹ booty. Now, could we find him out, the money were ours.

CHER.   He don't belong to our gang.

BON.   What horses have they?

CHER.   The master rides upon a black.

BON.   A black! Ten to one the man upon the black mare; and since he don't belong to our fraternity, we may betray him with a safe conscience. I don't think it lawful to harbour any rogues but my own. Look'ee, child, as the saying is, we must go cunningly to work; proofs we must have. The gentleman's servant loves drink; I'll ply him that way, and ten to one loves a wench; you must work him t'other way.

CHER.   Father, would you have me give my secret for his?

BON.   Consider, child, there's two hundred pound to boot. – (*Ringing without*) Coming! coming! – Child, mind your business.³²   *Exit*

CHER.   What a rogue is my father! My father? I deny it. My mother was a good, generous, free-hearted woman, and I can't tell how far her good nature might have extended for the good of her children.

---

³⁰*parliament-man* i.e. he comes well provided with money in order to bribe his way into being elected to parliament.
³¹*new-purchased* newly obtained.
³²*business* sexual intercourse (colloquial).

This landlord of mine, for I think I can call him no more, would betray his guest, and debauch his daughter into the bargain – by a footman too!

Re-enter ARCHER

ARCH.   What footman, pray, mistress, is so happy as to be the subject of your contemplation?

CHER.   Whoever he is, friend, he'll be but little the better for't.

ARCH.   I hope so, for, I'm sure, you did not think of me.

CHER.   Suppose I had?

ARCH.   Why, then, you're but even with me; for the minute I came in, I was a-considering in what manner I should make love to you.

CHER.   Love to me, friend!

ARCH.   Yes, child.

CHER.   Child! Manners! If you kept a little more distance, friend, it would become you much better.

ARCH.   Distance! Good night, sauce-box. *Going*

CHER.   [*Aside*] A pretty fellow! I like his pride. – [*Aloud*] Sir, pray, sir, you see, sir, (ARCHER *returns*) I have the credit to be entrusted with your master's fortune here, which sets me a degree above his footman; I hope, sir, you an't affronted?

ARCH.   Let me look you full in the face, and I'll tell you whether you can affront me or no. 'Sdeath, child, you have a pair of delicate eyes, and you don't know what to do with 'em!

CHER.   Why, sir, don't I see everybody?

ARCH.   Ay, but if some women had 'em, they would kill everybody. Prithee, instruct me, I would fain make love to you, but I don't know what to say.

CHER.   Why, did you never make love to anybody before?

ARCH.   Never to a person of your figure, I can assure you, madam. My addresses have been always confined to people within my own sphere; I never aspired so high before. *Sings*

> But you look so bright,
> And are dress'd so tight[33]
> That a man would swear you're right,
> As arm was e'er laid over.
> Such an air
> You freely wear
> To ensnare,
> As makes each guest a lover!

[33]*tight* The remainder of this song was first printed in the fifth edition of the play, London, 1728, in Vol. II.

> Since then, my dear, I'm your guest,
> Prithee give me of the best
> Of what is ready drest:
> Since then, my dear, etc.

CHER.   (*Aside*) What can I think of this man? – [*Aloud*] Will you give me that song, sir?

ARCH.   Ay, my dear, take it while 'tis warm. (*Kisses her*) Death and fire! Her lips are honeycombs.

CHER.   And I wish there had been bees too, to have stung you for your impudence.

ARCH.   There's a swarm of Cupids, my little Venus, that has done the business much better.

CHER.   (*Aside*) This fellow is misbegotten as well as I. – [*Aloud*] What's your name, sir?

ARCH.   (*Aside*) Name! Egad, I have forgot it. – [*Aloud*] Oh, Martin.[34]

CHER.   Where were you born?

ARCH.   In St Martin's parish.

CHER.   What was your father?

ARCH.   St Martin's parish.

CHER.   Then, friend, good night.

ARCH.   I hope not.

CHER.   You may depend upon't.

ARCH.   Upon what?

CHER.   That you're very impudent.

ARCH.   That you're very handsome.

CHER.   That you're a footman.

ARCH.   That you're an angel.

CHER.   I shall be rude.

ARCH.   So shall I.

CHER.   Let go my hand.

ARCH.   Give me a kiss.   *Kisses her*

Call without. Cherry! Cherry!

CHER.   I'm – my father calls. You plaguy devil, how durst you stop my breath so? Offer to follow me one step, if you dare.   *Exit*

ARCH.   A fair challenge, by this light! This is a pretty fair opening of an adventure; but we are knight-errants, and so Fortune be our guide.   *Exit*

---

[34]*Martin* an appropriate choice of pseudonym; St Martin's parish, London, where Farquhar then lived, had a dubious reputation, an area where imitation jewellery was made.

Act Two

SCENE [ONE]

A gallery in LADY BOUNTIFUL'S *house*

Enter MRS SULLEN *and* DORINDA, *meeting*

DOR. Morrow, my dear sister;[1] are you for church this morning?

MRS SUL. Anywhere to pray; for heaven alone can help me. But I think, Dorinda, there's no form of prayer in the liturgy against bad husbands.

DOR. But there's a form of law in Doctors Commons;[2] and I swear, sister Sullen, rather than see you thus continually discontented, I would advise you to apply to that. For besides the part that I bear in your vexatious broils, as being sister to the husband, and friend to the wife, your example gives me such an impression of matrimony that I shall be apt to condemn my person to a long vacation all its life. But supposing, madam, that you brought it to a case of separation, what can you urge against your husband? My brother is, first, the most constant man alive.

MRS SUL. The most constant husband, I grant ye.

DOR. He never sleeps from you.

MRS SUL. No, he always sleeps with me.

DOR. He allows you a maintenance suitable to your quality.

MRS SUL. A maintenance! Do you take me, madam, for an hospital child,[3] that I must sit down and bless my benefactors for meat, drink, and clothes? As I take it, madam, I brought your brother ten thousand pound, out of which I might expect some pretty things called pleasures.

DOR. You share in all the pleasures that the country affords.

MRS SUL. Country pleasures! Racks and torments! Dost think, child, that my limbs were made for leaping of ditches and clambering over stiles, or that my parents, wisely foreseeing my future happiness in country pleasures, had early instructed me in the rural accomplishments of drinking fat[4] ale, playing at whisk, and smoking tobacco

---

[1] *sister* i.e. sister-in-law.

[2] *Doctors Commons* the College of Doctors of Civil Law, London; it directed divorce cases through the ecclesiastical courts.

[3] *hospital child* foundling.   [4] *fat* strong.

with my husband, or of spreading of plasters, brewing of diet drinks, and stilling⁵ rosemary water, with the good old gentlewoman my mother-in-law?

DOR.   I'm sorry, madam, that it is not more in our power to divert you; I could wish, indeed, that our entertainments were a little more polite or your taste a little less refined. But, pray, madam, how came the poets and philosophers that laboured so much in hunting after pleasure to place it at last in a country life?

MRS SUL.   Because they wanted money, child, to find out the pleasures of the town. Did you ever see a poet or philosopher worth ten thousand pound? If you can show me such a man, I'll lay you fifty pound you'll find him somewhere within the weekly bills.⁶ Not that I disapprove rural pleasures as the poets have painted them; in their landscape, every Phyllis has her Corydon, every murmuring stream and every flowery mead gives fresh alarms to love. Besides, you'll find that their couples were never married. But yonder I see my Corydon, and a sweet swain it is, heaven knows! Come, Dorinda, don't be angry; he's my husband and your brother; and, between both, is he not a sad brute?

DOR.   I have nothing to say to your part of him; you're the best judge.

MRS SUL.   O sister, sister, if ever you marry, beware of a sullen, silent sot, one that's always musing, but never thinks. There's some diversion in a talking blockhead, and since a woman must wear chains, I would have the pleasure of hearing 'em rattle a little. Now you shall see, but take this by the way. He came home this morning at his usual hour of four, wakened me out of a sweet dream of something else, by tumbling over the tea-table, which he broke all to pieces; after his man and he had rolled about the room, like sick passengers in a storm, he comes flounce into bed, dead as a salmon into a fishmonger's basket, his feet cold as ice, his breath hot as a furnace, and his hands and his face as greasy as his flannel nightcap. O matrimony! He tosses up the clothes with a barbarous swing over his shoulders, disorders the whole economy⁷ of my bed, leaves me half naked, and my whole night's comfort is the tuneable serenade of that wakeful nightingale, his nose! Oh, the pleasure of counting the melancholy clock by a snoring husband! But now, sister, you shall see how handsomely, being a well-bred man, he will beg my pardon.

   Enter SQUIRE SULLEN

SQUIRE SUL.   My head aches consumedly.

⁵*stilling* distilling.
⁶*weekly bills* i.e. dead. The Weekly Bills of Mortality for London were published, 1538–1837, by the Parish Clerks' Company.
⁷*economy* arrangement.

MRS SUL.   Will you be pleased, my dear, to drink tea with us this morning? It may do your head good.

SQUIRE SUL.   No.

DOR.   Coffee, brother?

SQUIRE SUL.   Pshaw!

MRS SUL.   Will you please to dress and go to church with me? The air may help you.

SQUIRE SUL.   Scrub!

  Enter SCRUB

SCRUB.   Sir!

SQUIRE SUL.   What day o' the week is this?

SCRUB.   Sunday, an't please your worship.

SQUIRE SUL.   Sunday! Bring me a dram; and d'ye hear, set out the venison pasty and a tankard of strong beer upon the hall table. I'll go to breakfast.   *Exit* SCRUB

DOR.   Stay, stay, brother, you shan't get off so; you were very naught[8] last night, and must make your wife reparation. Come, come, brother, won't you ask pardon?

SQUIRE SUL.   For what?

DOR.   For being drunk last night.

SQUIRE SUL.   I can afford it, can't I?

MRS SUL.   But I can't, sir.

SQUIRE SUL.   Then you may let it alone.

MRS SUL.   But I must tell you, sir, that this is not to be borne.

SQUIRE SUL.   I'm glad on't.

MRS SUL.   What is the reason, sir, that you use me thus inhumanly?

SQUIRE SUL.   Scrub!

  [*Enter* SCRUB]

SCRUB.   Sir!

SQUIRE SUL.   Get things ready to shave my head.

                              Exeunt SULLEN *and* SCRUB

MRS SUL.   Have a care of coming near his temples, Scrub, for fear you meet something there[9] that may turn the edge of your razor. Inveterate stupidity! Did you ever know so hard, so obstinate a spleen as his? O sister, sister, I shall never ha' good of the beast till I get him to town; London, dear London, is the place for managing and breaking a husband.

DOR.   And has not a husband the same opportunities there for humbling a wife?

MRS SUL.   No, no, child, 'tis a standing maxim in conjugal discipline

---

[8]*naught* badly behaved.
[9]*there* the horns of a cuckold.

that when a man would enslave his wife he hurries her into the country; and when a lady would be arbitrary with her husband, she wheedles her booby up to town. A man dare not play the tyrant in London because there are so many examples to encourage the subject to rebel. O Dorinda, Dorinda, a fine woman may do anything in London. O' my conscience, she may raise an army of forty thousand men.

DOR. I fancy, sister, you have a mind to be trying your power that way here in Lichfield; you have drawn the French count to your colours already.

MRS SUL. The French are a people that can't live without their gallantries.

DOR. And some English that I know, sister, are not averse to such amusements.

MRS SUL. Well, sister, since the truth must out, it may do as well now as hereafter; I think one way to rouse my lethargic, sottish husband is to give him a rival. Security begets negligence in all people, and men must be alarmed to make 'em alert in their duty. Women are like pictures, of no value in the hands of a fool, till he hears men of sense bid high for the purchase.

DOR. This might do, sister, if my brother's understanding were to be convinced into a passion for you, but I fancy there's a natural aversion on his side, and I fancy, sister, that you don't come much behind him, if you dealt fairly.

MRS SUL. I own it; we are united contradictions, fire and water, but I could be contented, with a great many other wives, to humour the censorious mob and give the world an appearance of living well with my husband, could I bring him but to dissemble a little kindness to keep me in countenance.

DOR. But how do you know, sister, but that, instead of rousing your husband by this artifice to a counterfeit kindness, he should awake in a real fury?

MRS SUL. Let him. If I can't entice him to the one, I would provoke him to the other.

DOR. But how must I behave myself between ye?

MRS SUL. You must assist me.

DOR. What, against my own brother?

MRS SUL. He's but half a brother, and I'm your entire friend. If I go a step beyond the bounds of honour, leave me; till then, I expect you should go along with me in everything. While I trust my honour in your hands, you may trust your brother's in mine. The count is to dine here today.

DOR. 'Tis a strange thing, sister, that I can't like that man.

MRS SUL. You like nothing; your time is not come. Love and death have their fatalities, and strike home one time or other; you'll pay for all one day, I warrant ye. But come, my lady's tea is ready, and 'tis almost church time. *Exeunt*

SCENE [TWO]

A room in BONIFACE'S *inn*

Enter AIMWELL *dressed, and* ARCHER

AIM. And was she the daughter of the house?

ARCH. The landlord is so blind as to think so, but I dare swear she has better blood in her veins.

AIM. Why dost think so?

ARCH. Because the baggage has a pert *je ne sais quoi*; she reads plays, keeps a monkey, and is troubled with vapours.

AIM. By which discoveries I guess that you know more of her.

ARCH. Not yet, faith. The lady gives herself airs, forsooth; nothing under a gentleman!

AIM. Let me take her in hand.

ARCH. Say one word more o' that, and I'll declare myself, spoil your sport there and everywhere else. Look ye, Aimwell, every man in his own sphere.

AIM. Right; and therefore you must pimp for your master.

ARCH. In the usual forms, good sir, after I have served myself. – But to our business. You are so well dressed, Tom, and make so handsome a figure that I fancy you may do execution in a country church; the exterior part strikes first, and you're in the right to make that impression favourable.

AIM. There's something in that which may turn to advantage. The appearance of a stranger in a country church draws as many gazers as a blazing star; no sooner he comes into the cathedral but a train of whispers runs buzzing round the congregation in a moment: 'Who is he? Whence comes he? Do you know him'? Then, I, sir, tips me the verger with half a crown; he pockets the simony[10] and inducts me into the best pew in the church. I pull out my snuff-box, turn myself round, bow to the bishop, or the dean, if he be the commanding-officer; single out a beauty, rivet both my eyes to hers, set my nose a-bleeding by the strength of imagination, and show the

---

[10]*simony* Aimwell alludes, with witty understatement, to the buying and selling of ecclesiastical preferments.

whole church my concern by my endeavouring to hide it. After the
sermon the whole town gives me to her for a lover, and by persuading
the lady that I am a-dying for her, the tables are turned, and she in
good earnest falls in love with me.

ARCH.   There's nothing in this, Tom, without a precedent; but instead
of riveting your eyes to a beauty, try to fix 'em upon a fortune; that's
our business at present.

AIM.   Pshaw! No woman can be a beauty without a fortune. Let me
alone, for I am a marksman.

ARCH.   Tom!

AIM.   Ay.

ARCH.   When were you at church before, pray?

AIM.   Um – I was there at the coronation.[11]

ARCH.   And how can you expect a blessing by going to church now?

AIM.   Blessing! Nay, Frank, I ask but for a wife.   *Exit*

ARCH.   Truly, the man is not very unreasonable in his demands.

Exit at the opposite door

    Enter BONIFACE *and* CHERRY

BON.   Well, daughter, as the saying is, have you brought Martin to
confess?

CHER.   Pray, father, don't put me upon getting anything out of a man;
I'm but young, you know, father, and I don't understand wheedling.

BON.   Young! Why, you jade, as the saying is, can any woman wheedle
that is not young? Your mother was useless at five-and-twenty. Not
wheedle! Would you make your mother a whore and me a cuckold, as
the saying is? I tell you, his silence confesses it, and his master spends
his money so freely and is so much a gentleman every manner of way
that he must be a highwayman.

    Enter GIBBET, *in a cloak*

GIB.   Landlord, landlord, is the coast clear?

BON.   O Mr Gibbet, what's the news?

GIB.   No matter, ask no questions, all fair and honourable. – Here, my
dear Cherry. (*Gives her a bag*) Two hundred sterling pounds, as good
as any that ever hanged or saved a rogue; lay 'em by with the rest. And
here – three wedding or mourning rings, 'tis much the same, you
know. Here, two silver-hilted swords; I took those from fellows that
never show any part of their swords but the hilts. Here is a diamond
necklace which the lady hid in the privatest place in the coach, but I
found it out. This gold watch I took from a pawnbroker's wife; it was
left in her hands by a person of quality; there's the arms upon the case.

CHER.   But who had you the money from?

---

[11]*coronation* Queen Anne was crowned 23 April 1702.

GIB.   Ah, poor woman, I pitied her; from a poor lady just eloped from her husband. She had made up her cargo and was bound for Ireland, as hard as she could drive; she told me of her husband's barbarous usage, and so I left her half a crown. But I had almost forgot, my dear Cherry, I have a present for you.

CHER.   What is't?

GIB.   A pot of ceruse,[12] my child, that I took out of a lady's underpocket.

CHER.   What,[13] Mr Gibbet, do you think that I paint?

GIB.   Why, you jade, your betters do; I'm sure the lady that I took it from had a coronet upon her handkerchief. Here, take my cloak, and go secure the premises.[14]

CHER.   I will secure 'em.   *Exit*

BON.   But, hark'ee, where's Hounslow and Bagshot?

GIB.   They'll be here tonight.

BON.   D'ye know of any other gentlemen o' the pad[15] on this road?

GIB.   No.

BON.   I fancy that I have two that lodge in the house just now.

GIB.   The devil! How d'ye smoke[16] 'em?

BON.   Why, the one is gone to church.

GIB.   That's suspicious, I must confess.

BON.   And the other is now in his master's chamber; he pretends to be servant to the other. We'll call him out and pump him a little.

GIB.   With all my heart.

BON.   Mr Martin, Mr Martin!
       Enter ARCHER, *combing a periwig and singing*

GIB.   The roads are consumed deep; I'm as dirty as Old Brentford[17] at Christmas. – A good pretty fellow that. Whose servant are you, friend?

ARCH.   My master's.

GIB.   Really?

ARCH.   Really.

GIB.   That's much. – The fellow has been at the bar by his evasions.[18] But pray, sir, what is your master's name?

ARCH.   'Tall, all, dall'! (*Sings and combs the periwig*) This is the most obstinate curl –

GIB.   I ask you his name.

---

[12]*ceruse* a cosmetic made from white lead.
[13]*What* Indeed.
[14]*premises* the stolen articles referred to above (a legal term).
[15]*pad* highwayman.   [16]*smoke* suspect.
[17]*Old Brentford* a town 8 miles (11 km.) west of London, reputedly muddy.
[18]*evasions* His subterfuges suggest that he has been in court, accused of a crime.

ARCH.   Name, sir? 'Tall, all, dall'! I never asked him his name in my
life. 'Tall, all, dall'!

BON.   [*Aside to* GIBBET] What think you now?

GIB.   [*Aside to* BONIFACE] Plain, plain, he talks now as if he were
before a judge. – [*To* ARCHER] But pray, friend, which way does
your master travel?

ARCH.   A-horseback.

GIB.   [*Aside*] Very well again; an old offender, right. – [*To* ARCHER]
But, I mean, does he go upwards or downwards?

ARCH.   Downwards, I fear, sir. 'Tall, all'!

GIB.   I'm afraid my fate will be a contrary way.¹⁹

BON.   Ha, ha, ha! Mr Martin, you're very arch. This gentleman is
only travelling towards Chester and would be glad of your
company, that's all. – Come, captain, you'll stay tonight, I suppose;
I'll show you a chamber. Come, captain.

GIB.   Farewell, friend!

ARCH.   Captain, your servant. – [*Exeunt* BONIFACE *and* GIBBET]
Captain! A pretty fellow! 'Sdeath, I wonder that the officers of the
army don't conspire to beat all scoundrels in red but their own.

   Re-enter CHERRY

CHER.   (*Aside*) Gone, and Martin here! I hope he did not listen; I
would have the merit of the discovery all my own, because I would
oblige him to love me. – [*Aloud*] Mr Martin, who was that man with
my father?

ARCH.   Some recruiting sergeant or whipped-out trooper,²⁰ I
suppose.

CHER.   [*Aside*] All's safe, I find.

ARCH.   Come, my dear, have you conned over the catechise²¹ I taught
you last night?

CHER.   Come, question me.

ARCH.   What is love?

CHER.   Love is I know not what, it comes I know not how, and goes I
know not when.

ARCH.   Very well, an apt scholar. (*Chucks her under the chin*) Where
does love enter?

CHER.   Into the eyes.

ARCH.   And where go out?

CHER.   I won't tell ye.

---

¹⁹*a contrary way* i.e. to be hanged.

²⁰*trooper* a soldier who has been flogged and dismissed.

²¹*catechise* The exchange that follows is almost identical to a dialogue between
Tom and Betty in *Love's Catechism*, London, 1707, compiled by George Farquhar.

ARCH. What are objects of that passion?

CHER. Youth, beauty, and clean linen.

ARCH. The reason?

CHER. The two first are fashionable in nature and the third at court.

ARCH. That's my dear. What are the signs and tokens of that passion?

CHER. A stealing look, a stammering tongue, words improbable, designs impossible, and actions impracticable.

ARCH. That's my good child; kiss me. What must a lover do to obtain his mistress?

CHER. He must adore the person that disdains him, he must bribe the chambermaid that betrays him, and court the footman that laughs at him. He must, he must –

ARCH. Nay, child, I must whip you if you don't mind your lesson: he must treat his –

CHER. Oh ay! – He must treat his enemies with respect, his friends with indifference, and all the world with contempt; he must suffer much and fear more; he must desire much and hope little; in short, he must embrace his ruin and throw himself away.

ARCH. Had ever man so hopeful a pupil as mine! – Come, my dear, why is love called a riddle?

CHER. Because, being blind, he leads those that see, and, though a child, he governs a man.

ARCH. Mighty well! And why is love pictured blind?

CHER. Because the painters, out of the weakness or privilege of their art, chose to hide those eyes that they could not draw.

ARCH. That's my dear little scholar; kiss me again. And why should love, that's a child, govern a man?

CHER. Because that a child is the end of love.

ARCH. And so ends love's catechism. And now, my dear, we'll go in and make my master's bed.

CHER. Hold, hold, Mr Martin! You have taken a great deal of pains to instruct me, and what d'ye think I have learnt by it?

ARCH. What?

CHER. That your discourse and your habit are contradictions, and it would be nonsense in me to believe you a footman any longer.

ARCH. 'Oons, what a witch it is!

CHER. Depend upon this, sir; nothing in this garb shall ever tempt me, for though I was born to servitude, I hate it. Own your condition,[22] swear you love me, and then –

ARCH. And then we shall go make the bed?

CHER. Yes.

---

[22]*condition* rank.

ARCH.   You must know then, that I am born a gentleman; my
education was liberal, but I went to London a younger brother,[23] fell
into the hands of sharpers who stripped me of my money. My
friends disowned me, and now my necessity brings me to what you
see.

CHER.   Then take my hand. Promise to marry me before you sleep,
and I'll make you master of two thousand pound.

ARCH.   How?

CHER.   Two thousand pound that I have this minute in my own
custody; so throw off your livery this instant, and I'll go find a
parson.

ARCH.   What said you? A parson?

CHER.   What, do you scruple?

ARCH.   Scruple? No, no, but – Two thousand pound, you say?

CHER.   And better.

ARCH.   [*Aside*] 'Sdeath, what shall I do? – [*Aloud*] But hark'ee, child,
what need you make me master of yourself and money, when you
may have the same pleasure out of me and still keep your fortune in
your hands?

CHER.   Then you won't marry me?

ARCH.   I would marry you, but –

CHER.   O sweet sir, I'm your humble servant; you're fairly caught!
Would you persuade me that any gentleman who could bear the
scandal of wearing a livery would refuse two thousand pound, let
the condition be what it would? No, no, sir. But I hope you'll pardon
the freedom I have taken, since it was only to inform myself of the
respect that I ought to pay you.   *Going*

ARCH.   [*Aside*] Fairly bit, by Jupiter! – [*Aloud*] Hold, hold! And have
you actually two thousand pound?

CHER.   Sir, I have my secrets as well as you; when you please to be
more open I shall be more free, and be assured that I have discoveries
that will match yours, be what they will. In the meanwhile, be
satisfied that no discovery I make shall ever hurt you, but beware of
my father!   *Exit*

ARCH.   So, we're like to have as many adventures in our inn as Don
Quixote had in his. Let me see – two thousand pound! If the wench
would promise to die when the money were spent, egad, one would
marry her; but the fortune may go off in a year ot two, and the wife
may live – Lord knows how long. Then, an innkeeper's daughter!
Ay, that's the devil. There my pride brings me off.

[23] *younger brother* i.e. with no prospect of an inheritance because of the laws of
primogeniture.

For whatsoe'er the sages charge on pride,
The angels' fall, and twenty faults beside;
On earth, I'm sure, 'mong us of mortal calling,
Pride saves man oft, and woman too, from falling.   *Exit*

Act Three

SCENE [ONE]

The gallery in LADY BOUNTIFUL'S *house*

Enter MRS SULLEN *and* DORINDA

MRS SUL. Ha, ha, ha, my dear sister, let me embrace thee! Now we are friends indeed, for I shall have a secret of yours as a pledge for mine. Now you'll be good for something; I shall have you conversable in the subjects of the sex.

DOR. But do you think that I am so weak as to fall in love with a fellow at first sight?

MRS SUL. Pshaw, now you spoil all. Why should not we be as free in our friendships as the men? I warrant you, the gentleman has got to his confidant already, has avowed his passion, toasted your health, called you ten thousand angels, has run over your lips, eyes, neck, shape, air, and everything, in a description that warms their mirth to a second enjoyment.

DOR. Your hand, sister, I an't well.

MRS SUL. [*Aside*] So, she's breeding already. – Come, child, up with it. Hem a little. So. Now tell me, don't you like the gentleman that we saw at church just now?

DOR. The man's well enough.

MRS SUL. Well enough! Is he not a demigod, a Narcissus, a star, the man i' the moon?

DOR. O sister, I'm extremely ill!

MRS SUL. Shall I send to your mother, child, for a little of her cephalic plaster[1] to put to the soles of your feet, or shall I send to the gentleman for something for you? Come, unlace your stays, unbosom yourself. The man is perfectly a pretty fellow; I saw him when he first came into church.

DOR. I saw him too, sister, and with an air that shone, methought, like rays about his person.

MRS SUL. Well said, up with it!

DOR. No forward coquette behaviour, no airs to set him off, no studied looks nor artful posture, but nature did it all –

[1] *cephalic plaster* a remedy for headache.

MRS SUL. Better and better! One touch more. Come!

DOR. But then his looks – did you observe his eyes?

MRS SUL. Yes, yes, I did. His eyes, well, what of his eyes?

DOR. Sprightly, but not wandering; they seemed to view, but never gazed on anything but me. And then his looks so humble were, and yet so noble that they aimed to tell me that he could with pride die at my feet, though he scorned slavery anywhere else.

MRS SUL. The physic² works purely! How d'ye find yourself now, my dear?

DOR. Hem! Much better, my dear. Oh, here comes our Mercury!³

Enter SCRUB

Well, Scrub, what news of the gentleman?

SCRUB. Madam, I have brought you a packet of news.

DOR. Open it quickly, come.

SCRUB. In the first place I enquired who the gentleman was: they told me he was a stranger. Secondly, I asked what the gentleman was; they answered and said that they never saw him before. Thirdly, I enquired what countryman he was; they replied, 'twas more than they knew. Fourthly, I demanded whence he came; their answer was, they could not tell. And, fifthly, I asked whither he went; and they replied, they knew nothing of the matter, – and this is all I could learn.

MRS SUL. But what do the people say? Can't they guess?

SCRUB. Why, some think he's a spy, some guess he's a mountebank,⁴ some say one thing, some another; but for my own part, I believe he's a Jesuit.

DOR. A Jesuit! Why a Jesuit?

SCRUB. Because he keeps his horses always ready saddled, and his footman talks French.

MRS SUL. His footman!

SCRUB. Ay, he and the count's footman were jabbering French like two intriguing ducks in a mill-pond ; and I believe they talked of me, for they laughed consumedly.

DOR. What sort of livery has the footman?

SCRUB. Livery! Lord, madam, I took him for a captain, he's so bedizzened with lace! And then he has tops to his shoes, up to his mid leg, a silver-headed cane dangling at his knuckles; he carries his hands in his pockets just so, (*Walks in the French air*) and has a fine long periwig tied up in a bag.⁵ – Lord, madam, he's clear another sort of man than I!

---

²*physic* medicine.   ³*Mercury* the messenger of the gods.
⁴*mountebank* charlatan.   ⁵*bag* a pouch to contain the back hair of a wig.

MRS SUL.   That may easily be. – But what shall we do now, sister?

DOR.   I have it! This fellow has a world of simplicity and some cunning; the first hides the latter by abundance. Scrub.

SCRUB.   Madam!

DOR.   We have a great mind to know who this gentleman is, only for our satisfaction.

SCRUB.   Yes, madam, it would be a satisfaction, no doubt.

DOR.   You must go and get acquainted with his footman and invite him hither to drink a bottle of your ale because you're butler today.

SCRUB.   Yes, madam, I am butler every Sunday.

MRS SUL.   O brave! Sister, o' my conscience, you understand the mathematics already. 'Tis the best plot in the world: your mother, you know, will be gone to church, my spouse will be got to the ale-house with his scoundrels, and the house will be our own. So we drop in by accident, and ask the fellow some questions ourselves. In the country, you know, any stranger is company, and we're glad to take up with the butler in a country dance, and happy if he'll do us the favour.

SCRUB.   O madam, you wrong me! I never refused your ladyship the favour in my life.

Enter GIPSY

GIP.   Ladies, dinner's upon table.

DOR.   Scrub, we'll excuse your waiting. Go where we ordered you.

SCRUB.   I shall.   *Exeunt*

SCENE [TWO]

The inn

Enter AIMWELL *and* ARCHER

ARCH.   Well, Tom, I find you're a marksman.

AIM.   A marksman! Who so blind could be as not discern a swan among the ravens?

ARCH.   Well, but hark'ee, Aimwell!

AIM.   Aimwell! Call me Oroondates,[6] Cesario,[7] Amadis,[8] all that romance can in a lover paint, and then I'll answer. O Archer! I read

---

[6]*Oroondates* the hero of La Calprenede's *Cassandra*, a romance published in France 1642–45 (10 vols.,) in England 1652.

[7]*Cesario* In *Twelfth Night* Viola disguises herself as Cesario.

[8]*Amadis* Amadis de Gaul, the hero of a popular fourteenth-century Spanish romance, first published in Spain in 1508, in England in 1567.

her thousands in her looks. She looked like Ceres[9] in her harvest: corn, wine and oil, milk and honey, gardens, groves, and purling streams played on her plenteous face.

ARCH.   Her face! Her pocket, you mean; the corn, wine, and oil lies there. In short, she has ten thousand pound, that's the English on't.

AIM.   Her eyes —

ARCH.   Are demi-cannons,[10] to be sure; so I won't stand their battery.[11]   *Going*

AIM.   Pray excuse me, my passion must have vent.

ARCH.   Passion! What a plague, d'ye think these romantic airs will do our business? Were my temper as extravagant as yours, my adventures have something more romantic by half.

AIM.   Your adventures!

ARCH.   Yes,

> The nymph that with her twice ten hundred pounds,
> With brazen engine[12] hot, and quoif[13] clear-starched,
> Can fire the guest in warming of the bed —

There's a touch[14] of sublime Milton for you, and the subject but an innkeeper's daughter! I can play with a girl as an angler does with his fish; he keeps it at the end of his line, runs it up the stream and down the stream, till at last he brings it to hand, tickles the trout, and so whips it into his basket.

Enter BONIFACE

BON.   Mr Martin, as the saying is, yonder's an honest fellow below, my Lady Bountiful's butler, who begs the honour that you would go home with him and see his cellar.

ARCH.   Do my *baisemains*[15] to the gentleman, and tell him I will do myself the honour to wait on him immediately.   *Exit* BONIFACE

AIM.   What do I hear?
> Soft Orpheus[16] play, and fair Toftida[17] sing!

ARCH.   Pshaw! Damn your raptures. I tell you, here's a pump going to be put into the vessel, and the ship will get into harbour, my life on't. You say there's another lady very handsome there?

AIM.   Yes, faith.

ARCH.   I'm in love with her already.

---

[9]*Ceres* the Roman corn-goddess.   [10]*demi-cannons* guns with a 6½" bore.
[11]*battery* attack.   [12]*brazen engine* warming pan.
[13]*quoif* coif, a close-fitting cap.   [14]*touch* imitation (in frivolous form).
[15]*baisemains* a kiss of the hands; respects.
[16]*Orpheus* In classical legend, the music of Orpheus' lyre made trees and rocks follow him.
[17]*Toftida* Mrs Katherine Tofts, *c.* 1680–1756; a notable soprano 1703–09, who performed in many popular operas.

AIM.   Can't you give me a bill¹⁸ upon Cherry in the meantime?

ARCH.   No, no, friend, all her corn, wine, and oil is engrossed¹⁹ to my
market. And once more I warn you to keep your anchorage clear of
mine, for if you fall foul of me, by this light you shall go to the
bottom! What, make prize of my little frigate, while I am upon the
cruise for you?

AIM.   Well, well, I won't.   *Exit* ARCHER
        Re-enter BONIFACE

Landlord, have you any tolerable company in the house? I don't care
for dining alone.

BON.   Yes, sir, there's a captain below, as the saying is, that arrived
about an hour ago.

AIM.   Gentlemen of his coat are welcome everywhere. Will you make
him a compliment from me and tell him I should be glad of his
company?

BON.   Who shall I tell him, sir, would –

AIM.   [*Aside*] Ha! That stroke was well thrown in! – [*Aloud*] I'm only
a traveller like himself, and would be glad of his company, that's all.

BON.   I obey your commands, as the saying is.   *Exit*
        Re-enter ARCHER

ARCH.   'Sdeath, I had forgot. What title will you give yourself?

AIM.   My brother's, to be sure; he would never give me anything else,
so I'll make bold with his honour this bout. You know the rest of
your cue.

ARCH.   Ay, ay.   [*Exit*]
        Enter GIBBET

GIB.   Sir, I'm yours.

AIM.   'Tis more than I deserve, sir, for I don't know you.

GIB.   I don't wonder at that, sir, for you never saw me before –(*Aside*)
I hope.

AIM.   And pray, sir, how came I by the honour of seeing you now?

GIB.   Sir, I scorn to intrude upon any gentleman, but my landlord –

AIM.   O sir, I ask your pardon; you're the captain he told me of?

GIB.   At your service, sir.

AIM.   What regiment, may I be so bold?

GIB.   A marching regiment, sir, an old corps.

AIM.   (*Aside*) Very old, if your coat be regimental. – [*Aloud*] You
have served abroad, sir?

GIB.   Yes, sir, in the plantations;²⁰ 'twas my lot to be sent into the
worst service. I would have quitted it indeed, but a man of honour,

---

¹⁸*bill* promissory note.   ¹⁹*engrossed* monopolised.
²⁰*plantations* i.e. as a transported criminal.

you know – Besides, 'twas for the good of my country that I should be abroad. Anything for the good of one's country – I'm a Roman²¹ for that.

AIM.   (*Aside*) One of the first, I'll lay my life. – [*Aloud*] You found the West Indies very hot, sir?

GIB.   Ay, sir, too hot for me.

AIM.   Pray, sir, han't I seen your face at Will's coffee-house?²²

GIB.   Yes, sir, and at White's²³ too.

AIM.   And where is your company now, captain?

GIB.   They an't come yet.

AIM.   Why, d'ye expect 'em here?

GIB.   They'll be here tonight, sir.

AIM.   Which way do they march?

GIB.   Across the country. – [*Aside*] The devil's in't, if I han't said enough to encourage him to declare! But I'm afraid he's not right; I must tack about.

AIM.   Is your company to quarter in Lichfield?

GIB.   In this house, sir.

AIM.   What, all?

GIB.   My company's but thin, ha, ha, ha! We are but three, ha, ha, ha!

AIM.   You're merry, sir.

GIB.   Ay, sir, you must excuse me, sir; I understand the world, especially the art of travelling. I don't care, sir, for answering questions directly upon the road, for I generally ride with a charge²⁴ about me.

AIM.   (*Aside*) Three or four, I believe.

GIB.   I am credibly informed that there are highwaymen upon this quarter; not, sir, that I could suspect a gentleman of your figure, but truly, sir, I have got such a way of evasion upon the road that I don't care for speaking truth to any man.

AIM.   [*Aside*] Your caution may be necessary. – [*Aloud*] Then I presume you're no captain?

GIB.   Not I, sir; 'Captain' is a good travelling name, and so I take it; it stops a great many foolish enquiries that are generally made about gentlemen that travel. It gives a man an air of something, and makes

---

²¹*Roman* a pseudo-virtuous claim that he was, like a true Roman, serving in the army, without pay, for his country's good.

²²*Will's coffee-house* in Bow Street, Covent Garden, popular with literary figures and playwrights.

²³*White's* a well known chocolate-house, founded in 1693; still extant as a private club in St James's Street.

²⁴*charge* a sum of money or a quantity of powder and shot, perhaps a purposeful ambiguity.

the drawers²⁵ obedient. And thus far I am a captain, and no farther.

AIM.   And pray, sir, what is your true profession?

GIB.   O sir, you must excuse me! Upon my word, sir, I don't think it safe to tell ye.

AIM.   Ha, ha, ha! Upon my word I commend you.

    Re-enter BONIFACE

Well, Mr Boniface, what's the news?

BON.   There's another gentleman below, as the saying is, that, hearing you were but two, would be glad to make the third man, if you would give him leave.

AIM.   What is he?

BON.   A clergyman, as the saying is.

AIM.   A clergyman! Is he really a clergyman or is it only his travelling name, as my friend the captain has it?

BON.   O sir, he's a priest and chaplain to the French officers in town.

AIM.   Is he a Frenchman?

BON.   Yes, sir, born at Brussels.

GIB.   A Frenchman, and a priest! I won't be seen in his company, sir; I have a value for my reputation, sir.

AIM.   Nay, but, captain, since we are by ourselves – Can he speak English, landlord?

BON.   Very well, sir; you may know him, as the saying is, to be a foreigner by his accent, and that's all.

AIM.   Then he has been in England before?

BON.   Never, sir; but he's a master of languages, as the saying is. He talks Latin; it does me good to hear him talk Latin.

AIM.   Then you understand Latin, Mr Boniface?

BON.   Not I, sir, as the saying is; but he talks it so very fast that I'm sure it must be good.

AIM.   Pray, desire him to walk up.

BON.   Here he is, as the saying is.

    Enter FOIGARD

FOI.   Save you, gentlemens, both.

AIM.   [*Aside*] A Frenchman! – [*To* FOIGARD] Sir, your most humble servant.

FOI.   Och, dear joy,²⁶ I am your most faithful shervant, and yours alsho.

GIB.   Doctor, you talk very good English, but you have a mighty twang of the foreigner.

FOI.   My English is very vell for the vords, but we foreigners, you know, cannot bring our tongues about the pronunciation so soon.

²⁵*drawers* servants at an inn.
²⁶*joy* darling (Irish).

AIM. (*Aside*) A foreigner! A downright Teague,[27] by this light! –
[*Aloud*] Were you born in France, doctor?

FOI. I was educated in France, but I was borned at Brussels;[28] I am a
subject of the King of Spain, joy.

GIB. What King of Spain, sir? Speak.

FOI. Upon my shoul, joy, I cannot tell you as yet.

AIM. Nay, captain, that was too hard upon the doctor; he's a
stranger.

FOI. Oh, let him alone, dear joy; I am of a nation that is not easily put
out of countenance.

AIM. Come, gentlemen, I'll end the dispute. – Here, landlord, is
dinner ready?

BON. Upon the table, as the saying is.

AIM. Gentlemen, pray – that door –

FOI. No, no, fait, the captain must lead.

AIM. No, doctor, the church is our guide.

GIB. Ay, ay, so it is.   *Exit* FOIGARD *foremost, the others follow*

SCENE [THREE]

The scene changes to a gallery in
LADY BOUNTIFUL'S *house*

Enter ARCHER *and* SCRUB *singing and hugging one another, the
latter with a tankard in his hand,* GIPSY *listening at a distance*

SCRUB. 'Tall, all, dall'! Come, my dear boy, let's have that song once
more.

ARCH. No, no, we shall disturb the family. But will you be sure to
keep the secret?

SCRUB. Pho, upon my honour, as I'm a gentleman.

ARCH. 'Tis enough. You must know then that my master is the Lord
Viscount Aimwell; he fought a duel t'other day in London, wounded
his man so dangerously that he thinks fit to withdraw till he hears
whether the gentleman's wounds be mortal or not. He never was in
this part of England before, so he chose to retire to this place, that's
all.

GIP. And that's enough for me.   *Exit*

27*Teague* Irishman; Teague was an Irish servant in Farquhar's *The Twin Rivals*,
1703.
28*Brussels* then a part of the Spanish Netherlands, claimed by Archduke Charles
of Austria and Philip, Duke of Anjou, grandson of Louis XIV of France. The issue
was not settled until 1713, when the area was ceded to Charles, by then Charles VI,
head of the Holy Roman Empire.

SCRUB.   And where were you when your master fought?

ARCH.   We never know of our masters' quarrels.

SCRUB.   No! If our masters in the country here receive a challenge, the first thing they do is to tell their wives; the wife tells the servants, the servants alarm the tenants, and in half an hour you shall have the whole county in arms.

ARCH.   To hinder two men from doing what they have no mind for! But if you should chance to talk now of my business?

SCRUB.   Talk! Ay, sir, had I not learned the knack of holding my tongue, I had never lived so long in a great family.

ARCH.   Ay, ay, to be sure, there are secrets in all families.

SCRUB.   Secrets! Ay, but I'll say no more. Come, sit down, we'll make an end of our tankard. Here –   [*Gives* ARCHER *the tankard*]

ARCH.   With all my heart. Who knows but you and I may come to be better acquainted, eh? Here's your ladies' healths; [*Drinks*] you have three, I think, and to be sure there must be secrets among 'em.

SCRUB.   Secrets! Ay, friend. – I wish I had a friend!

ARCH.   Am not I your friend? Come, you and I will be sworn brothers.

SCRUB.   Shall we?

ARCH.   From this minute. Give me a kiss. And now, brother Scrub –

SCRUB.   And now, brother Martin, I will tell you a secret that will make your hair stand on end. You must know that I am consumedly in love.

ARCH.   That's a terrible secret, that's the truth on't.

SCRUB.   That jade, Gipsy, that was with us just now in the cellar, is the arrantest whore that ever wore a petticoat, and I'm dying for love of her.

ARCH.   Ha, ha, ha! Are you in love with her person or her virtue, brother Scrub?

SCRUB.   I should like virtue best because it is more durable than beauty; for virtue holds good with some women long, and many a day after they have lost it.

ARCH.   In the country, I grant ye, where no woman's virtue is lost till a bastard be found.

SCRUB.   Ay, could I bring her to a bastard, I should have her all to myself; but I dare not put it upon that lay[29] for fear of being sent for a soldier. Pray brother, how do you gentlemen in London like that same Pressing Act?[30]

ARCH.   Very ill, brother Scrub; 'tis the worst that ever was made for us. Formerly I remember the good days, when we could dun our masters for our wages, and if they refused to pay us, we could have a warrant

---

29*put it upon that lay* take that tack.

30*Pressing Act* Impressment acts were passed in 1703, 1704, and 1705.

to carry 'em before a justice; but now if we talk of eating they have a warrant for us and carry us before three justices.

SCRUB. And to be sure we go, if we talk of eating, for the justices won't give their own servants a bad example. Now this is my misfortune – I dare not speak in the house, while that jade Gipsy dings about like a fury – Once I had the better end of the staff.

ARCH. And how comes the change now?

SCRUB. Why, the mother of all this mischief is a priest.

ARCH. A priest!

SCRUB. Ay, a damned son of a whore of Babylon,[31] that came over hither to say grace to the French officers and eat up our provisions. There's not a day goes over his head without a dinner or supper in this house.

ARCH. How came he so familiar in the family?

SCRUB. Because he speaks English as if he had lived here all his life and tells lies as if he had been a traveller from his cradle.

ARCH. And this priest, I'm afraid, has converted the affections of your Gipsy?

SCRUB. Converted! Ay, and perverted, my dear friend, for, I'm afraid, he has made her a whore and a papist. But this is not all: there's the French count and Mrs Sullen; they're in the confederacy, and for some private ends of their own, to be sure.

ARCH. A very hopeful family yours, brother Scrub! I suppose the maiden lady has her lover too?

SCRUB. Not that I know. She's the best on 'em, that's the truth on't; but they take care to prevent my curiosity, by giving me so much business that I'm a perfect slave. What d'ye think is my place in this family?

ARCH. Butler, I suppose.

SCRUB. Ah, Lord help you! I'll tell you. Of a Monday I drive the coach, of a Tuesday I drive the plough, on Wednesday I follow the hounds, a Thursday I dun the tenants, on Friday I go to market, on Saturday I draw warrants,[32] and a Sunday I draw beer.

ARCH. Ha, ha, ha! If variety be a pleasure in life, you have enough on't, my dear brother. But what ladies are those?

SCRUB. Ours, ours. That upon the right hand is Mrs Sullen, and the other is Mrs Dorinda. Don't mind 'em; sit still, man.

Enter MRS SULLEN *and* DORINDA

MRS SUL. I have heard my brother talk of my Lord Aimwell, but they

---

[31]*whore of Babylon* the Roman Catholic Church; from Revelations 17:5.
[32]*draw warrants* write authorisations.

say that his brother is the finer gentleman.

DOR. That's impossible, sister.

MRS SUL. He's vastly rich, but very close, they say.

DOR. No matter for that; if I can creep into his heart, I'll open his breast, I warrant him. I have heard say that people may be guessed at by the behaviour of their servants; I could wish we might talk to that fellow.

MRS SUL. So do I, for I think he's a very pretty fellow. Come this way; I'll throw out a lure for him presently.

> DORINDA *and* MRS SULLEN *walk a turn towards the opposite side of the stage*

ARCH. [*Aside*] Corn, wine, and oil indeed! But, I think, the wife has the greatest plenty of flesh and blood; she should be my choice. – Ay, ay, say you so! (MRS SULLEN *drops her glove*; ARCHER *runs, takes it up and gives to her*) Madam – your ladyship's glove.

MRS SUL. O sir, I thank you! – [*To* DORINDA] What a handsome bow the fellow has!

DOR. Bow! Why, I have known several footmen come down from London set up here for dancing-masters and carry off the best fortunes in the country.

ARCH. (*Aside*) That project, for aught I know, had been better than ours. – [*To* SCRUB] Brother Scrub, why don't you introduce me?

SCRUB. Ladies, this is the strange gentleman's servant that you saw at church today; I understood he came from London, and so I invited him to the cellar that he might show me the newest flourish in whetting my knives.

DOR. And I hope you have made much of him.

ARCH. Oh yes, madam, but the strength of your ladyship's liquor is a little too potent for the constitution of your humble servant.

MRS SUL. What, then you don't usually drink ale?

ARCH. No, madam. My constant drink is tea or a little wine and water. 'Tis prescribed me by the physician for a remedy against the spleen.[33]

SCRUB. Oh la! Oh la! A footman have the spleen!

MRS SUL. I thought that distemper had been only proper to people of quality.

ARCH. Madam, like all other fashions it wears out and so descends to their servants; though in a great many of us, I believe, it proceeds from some melancholy particles in the blood, occasioned by the stagnation of wages.

DOR. [*Aside to* MRS SULLEN] How affectedly the fellow talks! – [*To*

[33]*spleen* melancholy.

ARCHER] How long, pray, have you served your present master?

ARCH.   Not long; my life has been mostly spent in the service of the ladies.

MRS SUL.   And pray, which service do you like best?

ARCH.   Madam, the ladies pay best. The honour of serving them is sufficient wages; there is a charm in their looks that delivers a pleasure with their commands, and gives our duty the wings of inclination.

MRS SUL.   [*Aside*] That flight was above the pitch of a livery. – [*Aloud*] And, sir, would not you be satisfied to serve a lady again?

ARCH.   As a groom of the chamber, madam, but not as a footman.

MRS SUL.   I suppose you served as footman before.

ARCH.   For that reason I would not serve in that post again; for my memory is too weak for the load of messages that the ladies lay upon their servants in London. My Lady Howd'ye, the last mistress I served, called me up one morning, and told me, 'Martin, go to my Lady Allnight with my humble service. Tell her I was to wait on her ladyship yesterday, and left word with Mrs Rebecca that the preliminaries of the affair she knows of are stopped till we know the concurrence of the person that I know of, for which there are circumstances wanting which we shall accommodate at the old place; but that in the meantime there is a person about her ladyship that, from several hints and surmises, was accessory at a certain time to the disappointments that naturally attend things that to her knowledge are of more importance – '

MRS SUL., DOR.   Ha, ha, ha! Where are you going, sir?

ARCH.   Why, I han't half done! The whole howd'ye was about half an hour long; so I happened to misplace two syllables, and was turned off and rendered incapable.[34]

DOR.   [*Aside to* MRS SULLEN] The pleasantest fellow, sister, I ever saw! – [*To* ARCHER] But, friend, if your master be married, I presume you still serve a lady.

ARCH.   No, madam, I take care never to come into a married family. The commands of the master and mistress are always so contrary that 'tis impossible to please both.

DOR.   (*Aside*) There's a main point gained. My lord is not married, I find.

MRS SUL.   But I wonder, friend, that in so many good services, you had not a better provision made for you.

ARCH.   I don't know how, madam. I had a lieutenancy offered me three or four times, but that is not bread, madam; I live much better as I do.

SCRUB.   Madam, he sings rarely! I was thought to do pretty well here

---

[34]*incapable* disqualified.

in the country till he came, but alack a day, I'm nothing to my brother Martin.

DOR.   Does he? Pray, sir, will you oblige us with a song?

ARCH.   Are you for passion or humour?

SCRUB.   Oh le! He has the purest ballad about a trifle –

MRS SUL.   A trifle! Pray, sir, let's have it.

ARCH.   I'm ashamed to offer you a trifle, madam, but since you command me –

Sings to the tune of 'Sir Simon the King'[35]

A trifling song you shall hear,
Begun with a trifle and ended:[36]
All trifling people draw near,
And I shall be nobly attended.

Were it not for trifles, a few,
That lately have come into play,
The men would want something to do,
And the women want something to say.

What makes men trifle in dressing?
Because the ladies (they know)
Admire, by often possessing,
That eminent trifle, a beau.

When the lover his moments has trifled
The trifle of trifles to gain,
No sooner the virgin is rifled,
But a trifle shall part 'em again.

What mortal man would be able
At White's half an hour to sit?
Or who could bear a tea-table,
Without talking of trifles for wit?

The court is from trifles secure,
Gold keys[37] are not trifles, we see:
White rods[38] are no trifles, I'm sure,
Whatever their bearers may be.

---

[35]*Sir Simon the King* first published as 'Old Simon the King' in John Playford, *Musick's Recreation* . . ., 1652.

[36]*ended* Only the first two lines appear in the 1707 quarto. The remainder is supplied, like most of the song in Act I, from the fifth edition, Vol. II, 1728 (following Act V).

[37]*Gold keys* symbols of the Lord Chamberlain, who controlled the theatre.

[38]*White rods* symbols of high office, such as Lord High Treasurer, etc.

But if you will go to the place
Where trifles abundantly breed,
The levee[39] will show you His Grace[40]
Makes promises trifles indeed.

A coach with six footmen behind
I count neither trifle nor sin;
But, ye gods, how oft do we find
A scandalous trifle within.

A flask of champagne, people think it
A trifle, or something as bad:
But if you'll contrive how to drink it,
You'll find it no trifle, egad!

A parson's a trifle at sea,
A widow's a trifle in sorrow,
A peace is a trifle today;[41]
Who knows what may happen tomorrow?

A black coat a trifle may cloak,
Or to hide it the red may endeavour;
But if once the army is broke,[42]
We shall have more trifles than ever.

The stage is a trifle, they say,
The reason pray carry along,
Because at every new play
The house they with trifles so throng.

But with people's malice to trifle
And to set us all on a foot,
The author of this is a trifle,
And his song is a trifle to boot.

MRS SUL.   Very well, sir, we're obliged to you. – Something for a pair
    of gloves.   *Offering him money*

---

[39]*levee* morning reception.

[40]*His Grace . . .* probably a hit at the Duke of Ormond, Lord Lieutenant of
Ireland, who apparently promised aid to Farquhar in 1706, but forgot or ignored
him.

[41]*today* Farquhar ridicules the efforts of the Tories to bring about a peace with
France.

[42]*broke* disbanded (after the war is over).

ARCH.   I humbly beg leave to be excused. My master, madam, pays
me, nor dare I take money from any other hand, without injuring his
honour and disobeying his commands.

Exeunt ARCHER *and* SCRUB

DOR.   This is surprising! Did you ever see so pretty a well-bred
fellow?

MRS SUL.   The devil take him for wearing that livery!

DOR.   I fancy, sister, he may be some gentleman, a friend of my lord's,
that his lordship has pitched upon for his courage, fidelity, and
discretion, to bear him company in this dress, and who, ten to one,
was his second too.

MRS SUL.   It is so, it must be so, and it shall be so, for I like him.

DOR.   What, better than the count?

MRS SUL.   The count happened to be the most aggreeable man upon
the place, and so I chose him to serve me in my design upon my
husband, but I should like this fellow better in a design upon myself.

DOR.   But now, sister, for an interview with this lord and this
gentleman; how shall we bring that about?

MRS SUL.   Patience! You country ladies give no quarter if once you be
entered.43 Would you prevent44 their desires and give the fellows no
wishing-time? Look'ee, Dorinda, if my Lord Aimwell loves you or
deserves you, he'll find a way to see you, and there we must leave it.
My business comes now upon the tapis.45 Have you prepared your
brother?

DOR.   Yes, yes.

MRS SUL.   And how did he relish it?

DOR.   He said little, mumbled something to himself, promised to be
guided by me. But here he comes.

Enter SQUIRE SULLEN

SQUIRE SUL.   What singing was that I heard just now?

MRS SUL.   The singing in your head, my dear; you complained of it all
day.

SQUIRE SUL.   You're impertinent.

MRS SUL.   I was ever so since I became one flesh with you.

SQUIRE SUL.   One flesh! Rather two carcasses joined unnaturally
together.

MRS SUL.   Or rather a living soul coupled to a dead body.

DOR.   So, this is fine encouragement for me!

SQUIRE SUL.   Yes, my wife shows you what you must do.

MRS SUL.   And my husband shows you what you must suffer.

43*entered* engaged.   44*prevent* anticipate.
45*tapis* table-cloth; i.e. to be debated.

SQUIRE SUL. 'Sdeath, why can't you be silent?

MRS SUL. 'Sdeath, why can't you talk?

SQUIRE SUL. Do you talk to any purpose?

MRS SUL. Do you think to any purpose?

SQUIRE SUL. Sister, hark ye! – (*Whispers*) I shan't be home till it be late. *Exit*

MRS SUL. What did he whisper to ye?

DOR. That he would go round the back way, come into the closet, and listen as I directed him. But let me beg you once more, dear sister, to drop this project, for as I told you before, instead of awaking him to kindness, you may provoke him to a rage; and then who knows how far his brutality may carry him?

MRS SUL. I'm provided to receive him, I warrant you. But here comes the count. Vanish! *Exit* DORINDA

Enter COUNT BELLAIR[46]

Don't you wonder, Monsieur le Count, that I was not at church this afternoon?

COUNT BEL. I more wonder, madam, that you go dere at all, or how you dare to lift those eyes to heaven that are guilty of so much killing.

MRS SUL. If heaven, sir, has given to my eyes, with the power of killing, the virtue of making a cure, I hope the one may atone for the other.

COUNT BEL. Oh, largely, madam. Would your ladyship be as ready to apply the remedy as to give the wound. Consider, madam, I am doubly a prisoner; first to the arms of your general, then to your more conquering eyes. My first chains are easy; there a ransom may redeem me, but from your fetters I never shall get free.

MRS SUL. Alas, sir, why should you complain to me of your captivity, who am in chains myself? You know, sir, that I am bound, nay, must be tied up in that particular that might give you ease. I am like you, a prisoner of war, of war, indeed. I have given my parole of honour![47] Would you break yours to gain your liberty?

COUNT BEL. Most certainly I would, were I a prisoner among the Turks. Dis is your case; you're a slave, madam, slave to the worst of Turks, a husband.

MRS SUL. There lies my foible, I confess. No fortifications, no courage, conduct, nor vigilancy can pretend to defend a place where the cruelty of the governor forces the garrison to mutiny.

---

[46]*Count Bellair* After the first night the part of the count and this episode were omitted.

[47]*parole of honour* word of honour not to escape.

COUNT BEL.   And where de besieger is resolved to die before de place. Here will I fix (*Kneels*) – with tears, vows, and prayers assault your heart and never rise till you surrender; or if I must storm – Love and St Michael! And so I begin the attack.

MRS SUL.   Stand off! – (*Aside*) Sure he hears me not, and I could almost wish he did not! The fellow makes love very prettily. – [*Aloud*] But, sir, why should you put such a value upon my person, when you see it despised by one that knows it so much better?

COUNT BEL.   He knows it not, though he possesses it; if he but knew the value of the jewel he is master of, he would always wear it next his heart and sleep with it in his arms.

MRS SUL.   But since he throws me unregarded from him, –

COUNT BEL.   And one that knows your value well comes by and takes you up, is it not justice?   *Goes to lay hold of her*

Enter SQUIRE SULLEN *with his sword drawn*

SQUIRE SUL.   Hold, villain, hold!

MRS SUL.   (*Presenting a pistol*) Do you hold!

SQUIRE SUL.   What, murder your husband to defend your bully?[48]

MRS SUL.   Bully! For shame, Mr Sullen. Bullies wear long swords, the gentleman has none; he's a prisoner, you know. I was aware of your outrage and prepared this to receive your violence, and, if occasion were, to preserve myself against the force of this other gentleman.

COUNT BEL.   O madam, your eyes be bettre firearms than your pistol; they nevre miss.

SQUIRE SUL.   What, court my wife to my face?

MRS SUL.   Pray, Mr Sullen, put up; suspend your fury for a minute.

SQUIRE SUL.   To give you time to invent an excuse!

MRS SUL.   I need none.

SQUIRE SUL.   No, for I heard every syllable of your discourse.

COUNT BEL.   Ah, and begar, I tink the dialogue was vera pretty.

MRS SUL.   Then I suppose, sir, you heard something of your own barbarity.

SQUIRE SUL.   Barbarity! 'Oons, what does the woman call barbarity? Do I ever meddle with you?

MRS SUL.   No.

SQUIRE SUL.   As for you, sir, I shall take another time.

COUNT BEL.   Ah, begar, and so must I.

SQUIRE SUL.   Look'ee, madam, don't think that my anger proceeds from any concern I have for your honour, but for my own, and if you can contrive any way of being a whore without making me a cuckold, do it and welcome.

---

[48]*bully* a protector of prostitutes.

MRS SUL.   Sir, I thank you kindly. You would allow me the sin but rob me of the pleasure. No, no, I'm resolved never to venture upon the crime without the satisfaction of seeing you punished for't.

SQUIRE SUL.   Then will you grant me this, my dear? Let anybody else do you the favour but that Frenchman, for I mortally hate his whole generation.   *Exit*

COUNT BEL.   Ah, sir, that be ungrateful, for begar, I love some of yours. Madam, –   *Approaching her*

MRS SUL.   No, sir.

COUNT BEL.   No, sir! Garzoon, madam, I am not your husband.

MRS SUL.   'Tis time to undeceive you, sir. I believed your addresses to me were no more than an amusement, and I hope you will think the same of my complaisance; and to convince you that you ought, you must know that I brought you hither only to make you instrumental in setting me right with my husband, for he was planted to listen by my appointment.

COUNT BEL.   By your appointment?

MRS SUL.   Certainly.

COUNT BEL.   And so, madam, while I was telling twenty stories to part you from your husband, begar, I was bringing you together all the while.

MRS SUL.   I ask your pardon, sir, but I hope this will give you a taste of the virtue of the English ladies.

COUNT BEL.   Begar, madam, your virtue be vera great, but garzoon, your honeste be vera little.

Re-enter DORINDA

MRS SUL.   Nay, now, you're angry, sir.

COUNT BEL.   Angry! Fair Dorinda! (*Sings* 'Fair Dorinda',[49] *the opera tune, and addresses* DORINDA) Madam, when your ladyship want a fool, send for me. 'Fair Dorinda . . .', 'Revenge . . .' *etc.*

Exit [singing]

MRS SUL.   There goes the true humour of his nation: resentment with good manners, and the height of anger in a song! Well, sister, you must be judge, for you have heard the trial.

DOR.   And I bring in my brother guilty.

MRS SUL.   But I must bear the punishment. 'Tis hard, sister.

DOR.   I own it, but you must have patience.

MRS SUL.   Patience, the cant of custom. Providence sends no evil without a remedy. Should I lie groaning under a yoke I can shake off, I were accessory to my ruin, and my patience were no better than self-murder.

49*Fair Dorinda* a song in Owen Swiney's (or MacSwiney's) opera, *Camilla* (I, ix), published 1707. Farquhar referred slightingly to *Camilla* in his prose Epilogue to *The Recruiting Officer*, 1706.

DOR. But how can you shake off the yoke? Your divisions don't come within the reach of the law for a divorce.

MRS SUL. Law! What law can search into the remote abyss of nature? What evidence can prove the unaccountable disaffections of wedlock? Can a jury sum up the endless aversions that are rooted in our souls, or can a bench give judgment upon antipathies?

DOR. They never pretended, sister; they never meddle, but in case of uncleanness.

MRS SUL. Uncleanness! O sister, casual violation is a transient injury and may possibly be repaired, but can radical hatreds be ever reconciled? No, no, sister, nature is the first lawgiver, and when she has set tempers opposite, not all the golden links of wedlock nor iron manacles of law can keep 'em fast.

> Wedlock we own ordain'd by heaven's decree,
> But such as heaven ordain'd it first to be,
> Concurring tempers in the man and wife
> As mutual helps to draw the load of life.
> View all the works of providence above;
> The stars with harmony and concord move.
> View all the works of providence below,
> The fire, the water, earth, and air we know
> All in one plant agree to make it grow.
> Must man, the chiefest work of art divine,
> Be doom'd in endless discord to repine?
> No, we should injure heaven by that surmise;
> Omnipotence is just, were man but wise.   [*Exeunt*]

Act Four

SCENE [ONE]

[*The gallery in* LADY BOUNTIFUL'S *house*]

MRS SULLEN *discovered alone*

MRS SUL. Were I born an humble Turk, where women have no soul nor property, there I must sit contented. But in England, a country whose women are its glory, must women be abused? Where women rule, must women be enslaved? Nay, cheated into slavery, mocked by a promise of comfortable society into a wilderness of solitude! I dare not keep the thought about me. Oh, here comes something to divert me.

Enter a COUNTRYWOMAN

WOM. I come, an't please your ladyship – you're my Lady Bountiful, an't ye?

MRS SUL. Well, good woman, go on.

WOM. I have come seventeen long mail to have a cure for my husband's sore leg.

MRS SUL. Your husband! What, woman, cure your husband!

WOM. Ay, poor man, for his sore leg won't let him stir from home.

MRS SUL. There, I confess, you have given me a reason. Well, good woman, I'll tell you what you must do. You must lay your husband's leg upon a table, and with a chopping-knife you must lay it open as broad as you can; then you must take out the bone, and beat the flesh soundly with a rolling-pin; then take salt, pepper, cloves, and ginger, some sweet herbs, and season it very well; then roll it up like brawn, and put it into the oven for two hours.

WOM. Heavens reward your ladyship! – I have two little babies too that are piteous bad with the graips,[1] an't please ye.

MRS SUL. Put a little pepper and salt in their bellies, good woman.

Enter LADY BOUNTIFUL

I beg your ladyship's pardon for taking your business out of your hands; I have been a-tampering here a little with one of your patients.

LADY BOUN. Come, good woman, don't mind this mad creature; I am the person that you want, I suppose. What would you have, woman?

MRS SUL. She wants something for her husband's sore leg.

LADY BOUN. What's the matter with his leg, goody?

---

[1] *graips* cramps.

WOM.   It come first, as one might say, with a sort of dizziness in his foot, then he had a kind of laziness in his joints, and then his leg broke out, and then it swelled, and then it closed again, and then it broke out again, and then it festered, and then it grew better, and then it grew worse again.

MRS SUL.   Ha, ha, ha!

LADY BOUN.   How can you be merry with the misfortunes of other people?

MRS SUL.   Because my own make me sad, madam.

LADY BOUN.   The worst reason in the world, daughter; your own misfortunes should teach you to pity others.

MRS SUL.   But the woman's misfortunes and mine are nothing alike; her husband is sick, and mine, alas, is in health.

LADY BOUN.   What, would you wish your husband sick?

MRS SUL.   Not of a sore leg, of all things.

LADY BOUN.   Well, good woman, go to the pantry, get your bellyful of victuals, then I'll give you a receipt[2] of diet-drink for your husband. But d'ye hear, goody, you must not let your husband move too much.

WOM.   No, no, madam, the poor man's inclinable enough to lie still.

Exit

LADY BOUN.   Well, daughter Sullen, though you laugh, I have done miracles about the country here with my receipts.

MRS SUL.   Miracles indeed, if they have cured anybody; but I believe, madam, the patient's faith goes further toward the miracle than your prescription.

LADY BOUN.   Fancy helps in some cases; but there's your husband, who has as little fancy as anybody: I brought him from death's door.

MRS SUL.   I suppose, madam, you made him drink plentifully of ass's milk.

Enter DORINDA, *who runs to* MRS SULLEN

DOR.   News, dear sister! News, news!

Enter ARCHER, *running*

ARCH.   Where, where is my Lady Bountiful? Pray, which is the old lady of you three?

LADY BOUN.   I am.

ARCH.   O madam, the fame of your ladyship's charity, goodness, benevolence, skill and ability have drawn me hither to implore your ladyship's help in behalf of my unfortunate master, who is this moment breathing his last.

LADY BOUN.   Your master! Where is he?

---

[2]*receipt* recipe, prescription.

ARCH. At your gate, madam. Drawn by the appearance of your handsome house to view it nearer, and walking up the avenue within five paces of the courtyard, he was taken ill of a sudden with a sort of I-know-not-what, but down he fell, and there he lies.

LADY BOUN. Here, Scrub! Gipsy! All run, get my easy-chair down stairs, put the gentleman in it, and bring him in quickly! Quickly!

ARCH. Heaven will reward your ladyship for this charitable act.

LADY BOUN. Is your master used to these fits?

ARCH. Oh yes, madam, frequently; I have known him have five or six of a night.

LADY BOUN. What's his name?

ARCH. Lord, madam, he's a-dying! A minute's care or neglect may save or destroy his life.

LADY BOUN. Ah, poor gentleman! – Come, friend, show me the way; I'll see him brought in myself. *Exit with* ARCHER

DOR. O sister, my heart flutters about strangely! I can hardly forbear running to his assistance.

MRS SUL. And I'll lay my life he deserves your assistance more than he wants it. Did not I tell you that my lord would find a way to come at you? Love's his distemper, and you must be the physician. Put on all your charms, summon all your fire into your eyes, plant the whole artillery of your looks against his breast, and down with him.

DOR. O sister, I'm but a young gunner; I shall be afraid to shoot, for fear the piece should recoil and hurt myself.

MRS SUL. Never fear; you shall see me shoot before you, if you will.

DOR. No, no, dear sister; you have missed your mark so unfortunately that I shan't care for being instructed by you.

Enter AIMWELL *in a chair carried by* ARCHER *and* SCRUB, *and counterfeiting a swoon;* LADY BOUNTIFUL *and* GIPSY *following*

LADY BOUN. Here, here, let's see the hartshorn drops. – Gipsy, a glass of fair water! His fit's very strong. – Bless me, how his hands are clinched!

ARCH. For shame, ladies, what d'ye do? Why don't you help us? – (*To* DORINDA) Pray, madam, take his hand, and open it, if you can, whilst I hold his head. DORINDA *takes his hand*

DOR. Poor gentleman! – Oh, he has got my hand within his, and squeezes it unmercifully –

LADY BOUN. 'Tis the violence of his convulsion, child.

ARCH. O madam, he's perfectly possessed in these cases; he'll bite if you don't have a care.

DOR. Oh, my hand, my hand!

LADY BOUN.   What's the matter with the foolish girl? I have got his hand open, you see, with a great deal of ease.

ARCH.   Ay, but, madam, your daughter's hand is somewhat warmer than your ladyship's, and the heat of it draws the force of the spirits that way.

MRS SUL.   I find, friend, you're very learned in these sorts of fits.

ARCH.   'Tis no wonder, madam, for I'm often troubled with them myself; I find myself extremely ill at this minute.

Looking hard at MRS SULLEN

MRS SUL.   (*Aside*) I fancy I could find a way to cure you.

LADY BOUN.   His fit holds him very long.

ARCH.   Longer than usual, madam. – Pray, young lady, open his breast and give him air.

LADY BOUN.   Where did his illness take him first, pray?

ARCH.   Today at church, madam.

LADY BOUN.   In what manner was he taken?

ARCH.   Very strangely, my lady. He was of a sudden touched with something in his eyes which at the first he only felt, but could not tell whether 'twas pain or pleasure.

LADY BOUN.   Wind, nothing but wind!

ARCH.   By soft degrees it grew and mounted to his brain; there his fancy caught it, there formed it so beautiful and dressed it up in such gay, pleasing colours that his transported appetite seized the fair idea and straight conveyed it to his heart. That hospitable seat of life sent all its sanguine spirits forth to meet and opened all its sluicy gates to take the stranger in.

LADY BOUN.   Your master should never go without a bottle to smell to. – Oh, he recovers! The lavender-water, some feathers to burn under his nose, Hungary water[3] to rub his temples. – Oh, he comes to himself! – Hem a little, sir, hem. Gipsy, bring the cordial-water.

AIMWELL *seems to awake in amaze*

DOR.   How d'ye, sir?

AIM.   Where am I?   *Rising*

> Sure I have pass'd the gulf of silent death,
> And now I land on the Elysian shore!
> Behold the goddess of those happy plains,
> Fair Proserpine[4] – let me adore thy bright divinity.

Kneels to DORINDA *and kisses her hand*

MRS SUL.   So, so, so! I knew where the fit would end!

---

[3] *Hungary water* used as a lotion or drunk as a restorative; made from rosemary flowers and spirit of wine. Reputed to have been first prepared for an unidentified queen of Hungary.

[4] *Proserpine* or Persephone, queen of the underworld.

AIM. Eurydice[5] perhaps –
How could thy Orpheus keep his word,
And not look back upon thee?
No treasure but thyself could sure have bribed him
To look one minute off thee.

LADY BOUN. Delirious, poor gentleman!

ARCH. Very delirious, madam, very delirious.

AIM. Martin's voice, I think.

ARCH. Yes, my lord. How does your lordship?

LADY BOUN. 'Lord'! Did you mind that, girls?

[Aside to MRS SULLEN *and* DORINDA]

AIM. Where am I?

ARCH. In very good hands, sir. You were taken just now with one of your old fits under the trees, just by this good lady's house; her ladyship had you taken in and has miraculously brought you to yourself, as you see.

AIM. I am so confounded with shame, madam, that I can now only beg pardon and refer my acknowledgements for your ladyship's care till an opportunity offers of making some amends. I dare be no longer troublesome. Martin, give two guineas to the servants.

Going

DOR. Sir, you may catch cold by going so soon into the air; you don't look, sir, as if you were perfectly recovered.

Here ARCHER *talks to* LADY BOUNTIFUL *in dumb show*

AIM. That I shall never be, madam; my present illness is so rooted that I must expect to carry it to my grave.

MRS SUL. Don't despair, sir; I have known several in your distemper shake it off with a fortnight's physic.

LADY BOUN. Come, sir, your servant has been telling me that you're apt to relapse if you go into the air. Your good manners shan't get the better of ours; you shall sit down again sir. Come, sir, we don't mind ceremonies in the country. Here, sir, my service t'ye. You shall taste my water; 'tis a cordial, I can assure you, and of my own making. Drink it off, sir. – (AIMWELL *drinks*) And how d'ye find yourself now, sir?

AIM. Somewhat better, though very faint still.

LADY BOUN. Ay, ay, people are always faint after these fits. Come, girls, you shall show the gentleman the house. – 'Tis but an old family building, sir, but you had better walk about and cool by degrees than venture immediately into the air. You'll find some

---

[5]*Eurydice* Pluto permitted Orpheus to lead his wife, Eurydice, out of Hades, provided that he did not look back at her; he did so and lost her.

tolerable pictures. – Dorinda, show the gentleman the way. I must
go to the poor woman below.   *Exit*

DOR. This way, sir.

AIM. Ladies, shall I beg leave for my servant to wait on you, for he
understands pictures very well?

MRS SUL. Sir, we understand originals[6] as well as he does pictures, so
he may come along.

                    Exeunt all but SCRUB, AIMWELL *leading* DORINDA
        Enter FOIGARD

FOI. Save you, Master Scrub!

SCRUB. Sir, I won't be saved your way. I hate a priest, I abhor the
French, and I defy the devil. Sir, I'm a bold Briton, and will spill the
last drop of my blood to keep out popery and slavery.

FOI. Master Scrub, you would put me down in politics, and so I
would be speaking with Mrs Shipsy.

SCRUB. Good Mr Priest, you can't speak with her; she's sick, sir,
she's gone abroad, sir, she's – dead two months ago, sir.

        Re-enter GIPSY

GIP. How now, impudence! How dare you talk so saucily to the
doctor? – Pray, sir, don't take it ill, for the common people of
England are not so civil to strangers as –

SCRUB. You lie, you lie! 'Tis the common people that are civilest to
strangers.

GIP. Sirrah, I have a good mind to – Get you out, I say!

SCRUB. I won't.

GIP. You won't, sauce-box? – Pray, doctor, what is the captain's
name that came to your inn last night?

SCRUB. [*Aside*] The captain! Ah, the devil, there she hampers me
again. The captain has me on one side and the priest on t'other; so
between the gown and the sword, I have a fine time on't. But *Cedunt
arma togae*.[7]   *Going*

GIP. What, sirrah, won't you march?

SCRUB. No, my dear, I won't march, but I'll walk. – [*Aside*] And I'll
make bold to listen a little too.

                    Goes behind the side-scene[8] *and listens*

GIP. Indeed, doctor, the count has been barbarously treated, that's
the truth on't.

FOI. Ah, Mrs Gipsy, upon my shoul now, gra,[9] his complainings

---

[6]*originals* eccentrics, with a pun on 'works of art'.
[7]*Cedunt arma togae* Arms give precedence to the gown. Cicero, *Officia*, I, 22.
[8]*side-scene* narrow painted screens, in grooves, to hide the sides of the stage.
[9]*gra* dear (Irish).

would mollify the marrow in your bones and move the bowels of your commiseration! He veeps, and he dances, and he fistles, and he swears, and he laughs, and he stamps, and he sings; in conclusion, joy, he's afflicted *à la Française*, and a stranger would not know whider to cry or to laugh with him.

GIP. What would you have me do, doctor?

FOI. Noting, joy, but only hide the count in Mrs Sullen's closet when it is dark.

GIP. Nothing! Is that nothing? It would be both a sin and a shame, doctor.

FOI. Here is twenty louis d'ors,[10] joy, for your shame, and I will give you an absolution for the shin.

GIP. But won't that money look like a bribe?

FOI. Dat is according as you shall tauk it. If you receive the money beforehand, 'twill be, *logicè*, a bribe; but if you stay till afterwards, 'twill be only a gratification.[11]

GIP. Well, doctor, I'll take it *logicè*. But what must I do with my conscience, sir?

FOI. Leave dat wid me, joy; I am your priest, gra, and your conscience is under my hands.

GIP. But should I put the count into the closet –

FOI. Vel, is dere any shin for a man's being in a closhet? One may go to prayers in a closhet.

GIP. But if the lady should come into her chamber, and go to bed?

FOI. Vel, and is dere any shin in going to bed, joy?

GIP. Ay, but if the parties should meet, doctor?

FOI. Vel den, the parties must be responsible. Do you be gone after putting the count into the closhet and leave the shins wid themselves. I will come with the count to instruct you in your chamber.

GIP. Well, doctor, your religion is so pure! Methinks I'm so easy after an absolution and can sin afresh with so much security that I'm resolved to die a martyr to't. Here's the key of the garden door. Come in the back way when 'tis late; I'll be ready to receive you, but don't so much as whisper, only take hold of my hand; I'll lead you, and do you lead the count, and follow me. *Exeunt*

Enter SCRUB

SCRUB. What witchcraft now have these two imps of the devil been a-hatching here? 'There's twenty louis d'ors'; I heard that and saw the purse. – But I must give room to my betters. [*Exit*]

---

[10]*louis d'ors* French gold coins, each then worth approximately seventeen shillings.

[11]*gratification* gratuity.

Re-enter AIMWELL, *leading* DORINDA, *and making love in
      dumb show*, MRS SULLEN *and* ARCHER *following*

MRS SUL.   (*To* ARCHER) Pray, sir, how d'ye like that piece?

ARCH.   Oh, 'tis Leda![12] You find, madam, how Jupiter comes
disguised to make love –

MRS SUL.   But what think you there of Alexander's battles?

ARCH.   We only want a Le Brun,[13] madam, to draw greater battles
and a greater general of our own. The Danube, madam, would make
a greater figure in a picture than the Granicus;[14] and we have our
Ramillies to match their Arbela.[15]

MRS SUL.   Pray, sir, what head is that in the corner there?

ARCH.   O madam, 'tis poor Ovid in his exile.[16]

MRS SUL.   What was he banished for?

ARCH.   His ambitious love, madam. – (*Bowing*) His misfortune
touches me.

MRS SUL.   Was he successful in his amours?

ARCH.   There he has left us in the dark. He was too much a gentleman
to tell.

MRS SUL.   If he were secret, I pity him.

ARCH.   And if he were successful, I envy him.

MRS SUL.   How d'ye like that Venus over the chimney?

ARCH.   Venus! I protest, madam, I took it for your picture; but now I
look again, 'tis not handsome enough.

MRS SUL.   Oh, what a charm is flattery! If you would see my picture,
there it is over that cabinet. How d'ye like it?

ARCH.   I must admire anything, madam, that has the least resemblance of you. But, methinks, madam – (*He looks at the picture and*
MRS SULLEN *three or four times, by turns*) Pray, madam, who drew
it?

MRS SUL.   A famous hand, sir.

Here AIMWELL *and* DORINDA *go off*

ARCH.   A famous hand, madam! – Your eyes, indeed, are featured
there, but where's the sparking moisture, shining fluid, in which they

---

[12]*Leda* Jupiter, disguised as a swan, seduced Leda.

[13]*Le Brun* Charles Le Brun, 1619–90, distinguished French painter of scenes
based on battles of Alexander the Great.

[14]*Granicus* The Duke of Marlborough defeated a French and Bavarian army at
the Battle of Blenheim, 1704, on the left bank of the Danube; Alexander overcame
the Persians by the river Granicus in 334 BC.

[15]*Arbela* In 1706 Marlborough defeated the French at Ramillies, Belgium;
Alexander overwhelmed the Persians at Arbela, Iraq, in 331 BC.

[16]*exile* Publius Ovidus Naso, 43 BC–AD 18, a Roman poet (*Ars Amatoria*, etc.),
was banished in AD 1 as the result of some obscure scandal.

swim? The picture, indeed, has your dimples, but where's the swarm of killing Cupids that should ambush there? The lips too are figured out, but where's the carnation dew, the pouting ripeness that tempts the taste in the original?

MRS SUL. [*Aside*] Had it been my lot to have matched with such a man!

ARCH. Your breasts too. Presumptuous man! What, paint heaven! – Apropos, madam, in the very next picture is Salmoneus,[17] that was struck dead with lightning for offering to imitate Jove's thunder. I hope you served the painter so, madam.

MRS SUL. Had my eyes the power of thunder they should employ their lightning better.

ARCH. There's the finest bed in that room, madam. I suppose 'tis your ladyship's bedchamber.

MRS SUL. And what then, sir?

ARCH. I think the quilt is the richest that ever I saw. I can't at this distance, madam, distinguish the figures of the embroidery. Will you give me leave, madam?

MRS SUL. [*Aside*] The devil take his impudence! Sure, if I gave him an opportunity, he durst not offer[18] it! I have a great mind to try. (*Going; returns*) 'Sdeath, what am I doing? And alone, too! – Sister! Sister! *Runs out*

ARCH. I'll follow her close –
      For where a Frenchman durst attempt to storm,
      A Briton sure may well the work perform. *Going*
   Re-enter SCRUB

SCRUB. Martin, brother Martin!

ARCH. O brother Scrub, I beg your pardon; I was not a-going. Here's a guinea my master ordered you.

SCRUB. A guinea! Hi, hi, hi, a guinea! Eh, by this light it is a guinea! But I suppose you expect one-and-twenty shillings in change.

ARCH. Not at all; I have another for Gipsy.

SCRUB. A guinea for her! Faggot and fire for the witch! Sir, give me that guinea, and I'll discover[19] a plot.

ARCH. A plot!

SCRUB. Ay, sir, a plot, and a horrid plot! First, it must be a plot, because there's a woman in't; secondly, it must be a plot, because there's a priest in't; thirdly, it must be a plot, because there's French

---

[17]*Salmoneus* This son of Aeolus arrogantly ordered sacrifices to be made to himself and rashly imitated the thunder of Zeus, who killed him with a thunderbolt.
[18]*offer* attempt.
[19]*discover* reveal.

gold in't; and fourthly, it must be a plot, because I don't know what to make on't.

ARCH. Nor anybody else, I'm afraid, brother Scrub.

SCRUB. Truly, I'm afraid so too; for where there's a priest and a woman, there's always a mystery and a riddle. This I know, that here has been the doctor with a temptation in one hand and an absolution in the other, and Gipsy has sold herself to the devil; I saw the price paid down, my eyes shall take their oath on't.

ARCH. And is all this bustle about Gipsy?

SCRUB. That's not all. I could hear but a word here and there, but I remember they mentioned a count, a closet, a back door, and a key.

ARCH. The count! Did you hear nothing of Mrs Sullen?

SCRUB. I did hear some word that sounded that way, but whether it was Sullen or Dorinda, I could not distinguish.

ARCH. You have told this matter to nobody, brother?

SCRUB. Told! No, sir, I thank you for that; I'm resolved never to speak one word, pro nor con till we have a peace.

ARCH. You're i' the right, brother Scrub. Here's a treaty afoot between the count and the lady; the priest and the chambermaid are the plenipotentiaries. It shall go hard but I find a way to be included in the treaty. Where's the doctor now?

SCRUB. He and Gipsy are this moment devouring my lady's marmalade in the closet.

AIM. (*From without*) Martin! Martin!

ARCH. I come, sir. I come.

SCRUB. But you forget the other guinea, brother Martin.

ARCH. Here, I give it with all my heart.

SCRUB. And I take it with all my soul. – (*Exit* ARCHER) Ecod, I'll spoil your plotting, Mrs Gipsy, and if you should set the captain upon me, these two guineas will buy me off.   *Exit*

Re-enter MRS SULLEN *and* DORINDA, *meeting*

MRS SUL. Well, sister.

DOR. And well, sister.

MRS SUL. What's become of my lord?

DOR. What's become of his servant?

MRS SUL. Servant! He's a prettier fellow and a finer gentleman, by fifty degrees, than his master.

DOR. O' my conscience, I fancy you could beg that fellow at the gallows-foot![20]

MRS SUL. O' my conscience I could, provided I could put a friend of yours in his room.

---

[20]*gallows-foot* To beg a person was to appeal in court for his/her custody; it was once possible for a criminal to escape hanging if a woman volunteered to marry him.

DOR.   You desired me, sister, to leave you when you transgressed the bounds of honour.

MRS SUL.   Thou dear censorious country girl! What dost mean? You can't think of the man without the bedfellow, I find.

DOR.   I don't find anything unnatural in that thought; while the mind is conversant with flesh and blood it must conform to the humours of the company.

MRS SUL.   How a little love and good company improves a woman! Why, child, you begin to live; you never spoke before.

DOR.   Because I was never spoke to. My lord has told me that I have more wit and beauty than any of my sex, and truly I begin to think the man is sincere.

MRS SUL.   You're in the right, Dorinda; pride is the life of a woman, and flattery is our daily bread, and she's a fool that won't believe a man there, as much as she that believes him in anything else. But I'll lay you a guinea that I had finer things said to me than you had.

DOR.   Done! What did your fellow say to ye?

MRS SUL.   My fellow took the picture of Venus for mine.

DOR.   But my lover took me for Venus herself.

MRS SUL.   Common cant! Had my spark called me a Venus directly, I should have believed him a footman in good earnest.

DOR.   But my lover was upon his knees to me.

MRS SUL.   And mine was upon his tiptoes to me.

DOR.   Mine vowed to die for me.

MRS SUL.   Mine swore to die with me.[21]

DOR.   Mine spoke the softest moving things.

MRS SUL.   Mine had his moving things too.

DOR.   Mine kissed my hand ten thousand times.

MRS SUL.   Mine has all that pleasure to come.

DOR.   Mine offered marriage.

MRS SUL.   O Lard! D'ye call that a moving thing?

DOR.   The sharpest arrow in his quiver, my dear sister! Why, my ten thousand pounds may lie brooding here this seven years and hatch nothing at last but some ill-natured clown like yours. Whereas, if I marry my Lord Aimwell, there will be title, place, and precedence, the Park, the play, and the drawing-room, splendour, equipage, noise, and flambeaux. – 'Hey, my Lady Aimwell's servants there! – Lights, lights to the stairs! – My Lady Aimwell's coach put forward! – Stand by, make room for her ladyship'! – Are not these things moving? – What, melancholy of a sudden?

MRS SUL.   Happy, happy sister! Your angel has been watchful for

[21] *to die with me* to reach a sexual climax.

your happiness, whilst mine has slept regardless of his charge. Long smiling years of circling joys for you, but not one hour for me!

Weeps

DOR.   Come, my dear, we'll talk of something else.

MRS SUL.   O Dorinda, I own myself a woman, full of my sex, a gentle, generous soul, easy and yielding to soft desires, a spacious heart where love and all this train might lodge. And must the fair apartment of my breast be made a stable for a brute to lie in?

DOR.   Meaning your husband, I suppose?

MRS SUL.   Husband! No. Even husband is too soft a name for him. But, come, I expect my brother here tonight or tomorrow. He was abroad when my father married me; perhaps he'll find a way to make me easy.

DOR.   Will you promise not to make yourself easy in the meantime with my lord's friend?

MRS SUL.   You mistake me, sister. It happens with us as among the men, the greatest talkers are the greatest cowards, and there's a reason for it: those spirits evaporate in prattle which might do more mischief if they took another course. Though, to confess the truth, I do love that fellow, and if I met him dressed as he should be, and I undressed as I should be – look ye, sister, I have no supernatural gifts – I can't swear I could resist the temptation, though I can safely promise to avoid it, and that's as much as the best of us can do.

Exeunt

SCENE [TWO]

[*A room in* BONIFACE'S *inn*]

Enter AIMWELL *and* ARCHER *laughing*

ARCH.   And the awkward kindness of the good motherly old gentlewoman –

AIM.   And the coming easiness of the young one! 'Sdeath, 'tis pity to deceive her!

ARCH.   Nay, if you adhere to these principles, stop where you are.

AIM.   I can't stop, for I love her to distraction.

ARCH.   'Sdeath, if you love her a hair's-breadth beyond discretion, you must go no further.

AIM.   Well, well, anything to deliver us from sauntering away our idle evenings at White's, Tom's, or Will's, and be stinted to bare looking at our old acquaintance, the cards, because our impotent pockets can't afford us a guinea for the mercenary drabs.

ARCH.   Or be obliged to some purse-proud coxcomb for a scandalous bottle, where we must not pretend to our share of the discourse because we can't pay our club[22] o' the reckoning. Damn it, I had rather sponge upon Morris,[23] and sup upon a dish of bohea[24] scored[25] behind the door!

AIM. And there expose our want of sense by talking criticisms, as we should our want of money by railing at the government.

ARCH. Or be obliged to sneak into the side-box, and between both houses[26] steal two acts[27] of a play, and because we han't money to see the other three, we come away discontented and damn the whole five.

AIM. And ten thousand such rascally tricks had we outlived our fortunes among our acquaintance. But now, –

ARCH. Ay, now is the time to prevent all this. Strike while the iron is hot. This priest is the luckiest part of our adventure; he shall marry you and pimp for me.

AIM. But I should not like a woman that can be so fond of a Frenchman.

ARCH. Alas, sir, necessity has no law. The lady may be in distress; perhaps she has a confounded husband, and her revenge may carry her farther than her love. Egad, I have so good an opinon of her and of myself that I begin to fancy strange things, and we must say this for the honour of our women, and indeed of ourselves, that they do stick to their men as they do to their Magna Charta. If the plot lies as I suspect, I must put on the gentleman. – But here comes the doctor. I shall be ready.   *Exit*

Enter FOIGARD

FOI. Sauve you, noble friend.

AIM. O sir, your servant. Pray, doctor, may I crave your name?

FOI. Fat naam is upon me? My naam is Foigard, joy.

AIM. Foigard! A very good name[28] for a clergyman. Pray, Doctor Foigard, were you ever in Ireland?

FOI. Ireland! No, joy. Fat sort of plaace is dat saam Ireland? Dey say de people are catched dere when dey are young.

---

[22]*club* proportion.

[23]*Morris* probably the proprietor of Morris's coffee-house, the Strand.

[24]*bohea* black China tea, introduced *c.* 1700; tea drinking in England was first referred to in 1658.

[25]*scored* kept account of by chalk marks behind the door of an inn or coffee-house.

[26]*between both houses* i.e. at one or the other of the licenced theatres, the Queen's, Haymarket (where this play was performed in 1707), and the Drury Lane.

[27]*steal two acts* It was then possible to see part of a play before payment was demanded. See Farquhar, 'A Discourse upon Comedy in Reference to the English Stage', *Love and Business* (1702), p. 147.

[28]*name* i.e. 'a guardian of the faith'.

AIM.   And some of 'em when they are old. As for example: (*Takes*
FOIGARD *by the shoulder*) Sir, I arrest you as a traitor against the
government; you're a subject of England and this morning showed
me a commission by which you served as chaplain in the French
army. This is death by our law, and your reverence must hang for
it.

FOI.   Upon my shoul, noble friend, dis is strange news you tell me!
Fader Foigard a subject of England! De son of a burgomaster of
Brussels, a subject of England! Ubooboo –[29]

AIM.   The son of a bogtrotter in Ireland! Sir, your tongue will
condemn you before any bench in the kingdom.

FOI.   And is my tongue all your evidensh, joy?

AIM.   That's enough.

FOI.   No, no, joy, for I vill never spake English no more.

AIM.   Sir, I have other evidence. – Here, Martin!

    Re-enter ARCHER

You know this fellow?

ARCH.   (*In a brogue*) Saave you, my dear cussen, how does your
health?

FOI.   (*Aside*) Ah, upon my shoul dere is my countryman, and his
brogue will hang mine. – [*To* ARCHER] *Mynheer, Ick wet neat watt
hey zacht, Ick universton ewe neat, sacramant!*[30]

AIM.   Altering your language won't do, sir; this fellow knows your
person and will swear to your face.

FOI.   Faash! Fey, is dere a brogue upon my faash too?

ARCH.   Upon my soulvation dere ish, joy! – But cussen Mackshane,
vil you not put a remembrance upon me?

FOI.   (*Aside*) Macshane! By St Paatrick, dat ish my naam shure
enough!

AIM.   [*Aside to* ARCHER] I fancy, Archer, you have it.

FOI.   The devil hang you, joy! By fat acquaintance are you my
cussen?

ARCH.   Oh, de devil hang yourshelf, joy! You know we were little
boys togeder upon de school, and your foster-moder's son was
married upon my nurse's chister, joy, and so we are Irish cussens.

FOI.   De devil taake de relation! Vel, joy, and fat school was it?

ARCH.   I tinks it vas – aay – 'twas Tipperary.

FOI.   No, no, joy; it vas Kilkenny.

AIM.   That's enough for us – self-confession. Come, sir, we must
deliver you into the hands of the next magistrate.

----

[29]*Ubooboo* an Irish expletive.

[30]*sacrament* in inaccurate Flemish: 'Sir, I do not understand what you say; I do
not understand you, indeed'.

ARCH. He sends you to gaol, you're tried next assizes, and away you go swing into purgatory.

FOI. And is it so wid you, cussen?

ARCH. It vil be sho wid you, cussen, if you don't immediately confess the secret between you and Mrs Gipsy. Look'ee, sir, the gallows or the secret; take your choice.

FOI. The gallows! Upon my shoul, I hate that saam gallow, for it is a diseash dat is fatal to our family. Vel den, dere is nothing, shentlemens, but Mrs Shullen would spaak wid the count in her chamber at midnight, and dere is no haarm, joy, for I am to conduct the count to the plash myshelf.

ARCH. As I guessed. – Have you communicated the matter to the count?

FOI. I have not sheen him since.

ARCH. Right again! Why then, doctor, you shall conduct me to the lady instead of the count.

FOI. Fat, my cussen to the lady! Upon my shoul, gra, dat is too much upon the brogue.[31]

ARCH. Come, come, doctor; consider we have got a rope about your neck, and if you offer to squeak, we'll stop your windpipe, most certainly. We shall have another job for you in a day or two, I hope.

AIM. Here's company coming this way. Let's into my chamber and there concert our affairs further.

ARCH. Come, my dear cussen, come along. *Exeunt*

Enter BONIFACE, HOUNSLOW, *and* BAGSHOT *at one door,* GIBBET *at the opposite*

GIB. Well, gentlemen, 'tis a fine night for our enterprise.

HOUN. Dark as hell.

BAG. And blows like the devil. Our landlord here has showed us the window where we must break in and tells us the plate stands in the wainscot cupboard in the parlour.

BON. Ay, ay, Mr Bagshot, as the saying is, knives and forks, and cups and cans, and tumblers and tankards. There's one tankard, as the saying is, that's near upon as big as me; it was a present to the squire from his godmother and smells of nutmeg and toast like an East-India ship.

HOUN. Then you say we must divide at the stairhead?

BON. Yes, Mr Hounslow, as the saying is. At one end of that gallery lies my Lady Bountiful and her daughter, and at the other Mrs Sullen. As for the squire, –

[31]*upon the brogue* too much of a trick.

GIB.   He's safe enough, I have fairly entered him,[32] and he's more
than half seas over already. But such a parcel of scoundrels are got
about him now that, egad, I was ashamed to be seen in their
company.

BON.   'Tis now twelve, as the saying is. Gentlemen, you must set out
at one.

GIB.   Hounslow, do you and Bagshot see our arms fixed, and I'll come
to you presently.

HOUN., BAG.   We will.   *Exeunt*

GIB.   Well, my dear Bonny, you assure me that Scrub is a coward?

BON.   A chicken, as the saying is. You'll have no creature to deal with
but the ladies.

GIB.   And I can assure you, friend, there's a great deal of address and
good manners in robbing a lady; I am the most a gentleman that way
that ever travelled the road. But, my dear Bonny, this prize will be a
galleon, a Vigo[33] business. I warrant you we shall bring off three or
four thousand pounds.

BON.   In plate, jewels, and money, as the saying is, you may.

GIB.   Why then, Tyburn,[34] I defy thee! I'll get up to town, sell off my
horse and arms, buy myself some pretty employment in the
household,[35] and be as snug and as honest as any courtier of 'em all.

BON.   And what think you then of my daughter Cherry for a wife?

GIB.   Look'ee, my dear Bonny, 'Cherry is the Goddess I adore', as the
song goes, but it is a maxim that man and wife should never have it
in their power to hang one another, for if they should, the Lord have
mercy on 'um both!   *Exeunt*

[32] *entered him* introduced him (to drinking).

[33] *Vigo* At the Battle of Vigo (off the north-west coast of Spain) in 1702, the
English and Dutch fleets captured many French warships and several rich Spanish
treasure ships.

[34] *Tyburn* the usual place for public executions until 1783, near Marble Arch,
London.

[35] *household* i.e. the royal household.

Act Five

SCENE [ONE]

A room in BONIFACE'S *inn*

Knocking without, enter BONIFACE

BON. Coming, coming! A coach and six foaming horses at this time o' night! Some great man, as the saying is, for he scorns to travel with other people.

Enter SIR CHARLES FREEMAN

SIR CHAS. What, fellow, a public house, and abed when other people sleep?

BON. Sir, I an't abed, as the saying is.

SIR CHAS. Is Mr Sullen's family abed, think'ee?

BON. All but the squire himself, sir, as the saying is; he's in the house.

SIR CHAS. What company has he?

BON. Why, sir, there's the constable, Mr Gage the exciseman, the hunchbacked barber, and two or three other gentlemen.

SIR CHAS. [*Aside*] I find my sister's letters gave me the true picture of her spouse.

Enter SQUIRE SULLEN, *drunk*

BON. Sir, here's the squire.

SQUIRE SUL. The puppies left me asleep. – Sir!

SIR CHAS. Well, sir.

SQUIRE SUL. Sir, I am an unfortunate man – I have three thousand pounds a year, and I can't get a man to drink a cup of ale with me.

SIR CHAS. That's very hard.

SQUIRE SUL. Ay, sir; and unless you have pity upon me, and smoke one pipe with me, I must e'en go home to my wife, and I had rather go to the devil by half.

SIR CHAS. But I presume, sir, you won't see your wife tonight; she'll be gone to bed. You don't use to lie with your wife in that pickle?

SQUIRE SUL. What, not lie with my wife! Why, sir, do you take me for an atheist or a rake?

SIR CHAS. If you hate her, sir, I think you had better lie from her.

SQUIRE SUL. I think so too, friend, but I'm a justice of peace and must do nothing against the law.

SIR CHAS. Law! As I take it, Mr Justice, nobody observes law for law's sake, only for the good of those for whom it was made.

SQUIRE SUL. But if the law orders me to send you to gaol, you must lie there, my friend.

SIR CHAS. Not unless I commit a crime to deserve it.

SQUIRE SUL. A crime! 'Oons, an't I married?

SIR CHAS. Nay, sir, if you call marriage a crime, you must disown it for a law.

SQUIRE SUL. Eh! I must be acquainted with you, sir. But, sir, I should be very glad to know the truth of this matter.

SIR CHAS. Truth, sir, is a profound sea, and few there be that dare wade deep enough to find out the bottom on't. Besides, sir, I'm afraid the line of your understanding mayn't be long enough.

SQUIRE SUL. Look'ee, sir, I have nothing to say to your sea of truth, but if a good parcel of land can entitle a man to a little truth, I have as much as any he in the country.

BON. I never heard your worship, as the saying is, talk so much before.

SQUIRE SUL. Because I never met with a man that I liked before.

BON. Pray, sir, as the saying is, let me ask you one question: are not man and wife one flesh?[1]

SIR CHAS. You and your wife, Mr Guts, may be one flesh because ye are nothing else, but rational creatures have minds that must be united.

SQUIRE SUL. Minds!

SIR CHAS. Ay, minds, sir. Don't you think that the mind takes place of the body?

SQUIRE SUL. In some people.

SIR CHAS. Then the interest of the master must be consulted before that of his servant.

SQUIRE SUL. Sir, you shall dine with me tomorrow! – 'Oons, I always thought that we were naturally one.

SIR CHAS. Sir, I know that my two hands are naturally one, because they love one another, kiss one another, help one another in all the actions of life, but I could not say so much if they were always at cuffs.[2]

SQUIRE SUL. Then 'tis plain that we are two.

SIR CHAS. Why don't you part with her, sir?

SQUIRE SUL. Will you take her, sir?

SIR CHAS. With all my heart.

SQUIRE SUL. You shall have her tomorrow morning, and a venison pasty into the bargain.

---

[1] *flesh* The speeches that follow include paraphrases from Milton's divorce tracts.
[2] *cuffs* blows.

SIR CHAS.   You'll let me have her fortune too?

SQUIRE SUL.   Fortune! Why, sir, I have no quarrel at her fortune; I only hate the woman, sir, and none but the woman shall go.

SIR CHAS.   But her fortune, sir, –

SQUIRE SUL.   Can you play at whisk, sir?

SIR CHAS.   No, truly sir.

SQUIRE SUL.   Nor at all-fours?3

SIR CHAS.   Neither.

SQUIRE SUL.   (*Aside*) 'Oons, where was this man bred? – [*Aloud*] Burn me, sir! I can't go home; 'tis but two o'clock.

SIR CHAS.   For half an hour, sir, if you please; but you must consider 'tis late.

SQUIRE SUL.   Late! That's the reason I can't go to bed. – Come, sir!
Exeunt

Enter CHERRY, *runs across the stage, and knocks at* AIMWELL'S *chamber door. Enter* AIMWELL *in his nightcap and gown*

AIM.   What's the matter? You tremble, child; you're frighted.

CHER.   No wonder, sir. But, in short, sir, this very minute a gang of rogues are gone to rob my Lady Bountiful's house.

AIM.   How!4

CHER.   I dogged 'em to the very door and left 'em breaking in.

AIM.   Have you alarmed anybody else with the news?

CHER.   No, no, sir, I wanted to have discovered the whole plot and twenty other things to your man Martin, but I have searched the whole house and can't find him. Where is he?

AIM.   No matter, child. Will you guide me immediately to the house?

CHER.   With all my heart, sir. My Lady Bountiful is my godmother, and I love Mrs Dorinda so well –

AIM.   Dorinda! The name inspires me; the glory and the danger shall be all my own. – Come, my life, let me but get my sword.   *Exeunt*

SCENE [TWO]

The scene changes to a bedchamber in LADY BOUNTIFUL'S *house*

Enter MRS SULLEN *and* DORINDA *undressed; a table and lights*

DOR.   'Tis very late, sister; no news of your spouse yet?

MRS SUL.   No, I'm condemned to be alone till towards four, and then perhaps I may be executed5 with his company.

3*all-fours* a card game played by two people.
4*How* Indeed.   5*executed* inflicted.

DOR.   Well, my dear, I'll leave you to your rest; you'll go directly to bed, I suppose?

MRS SUL.   I don't know what to do. – Heigh-ho!

DOR.   That's a desiring sigh, sister.

MRS SUL.   This is a languishing hour, sister.

DOR.   And might prove a critical minute if the pretty fellow were here.

MRS SUL.   Here! What, in my bedchamber at two a'clock o' the morning, I undressed, the family asleep, my hated husband abroad, and my lovely fellow at my feet! – O gad, sister!

DOR.   Thoughts are free, sister, and them I allow you. – So, my dear, good night.

MRS SUL.   A good rest to my dear Dorinda! – [*Exit* DORINDA] Thoughts free! Are they so? Why, then suppose him here, dressed like a youthful, gay, and burning bridegroom, (*Here* ARCHER *steals out of the closet*) with tongue enchanting, eyes bewitching, knees imploring. – (*Turns a little o' one side and sees* ARCHER *in the posture she describes*) Ah! (*Shrieks, and runs to the other side of the stage*) Have my thoughts raised a spirit? – What are you, sir, a man or a devil?

ARCH.   A man, a man, madam.   *Rising*

MRS SUL.   How shall I be sure of it?

ARCH.   Madam, I'll give you demonstration this minute.

                                                        Takes her hand

MRS SUL.   What, sir, do you intend to be rude?

ARCH.   Yes, madam, if you please.

MRS SUL.   In the name of wonder, whence came ye?

ARCH.   From the skies, madam. I'm a Jupiter in love, and you shall be my Alcmena.[6]

MRS SUL.   How came you in?

ARCH.   I flew in at the window, madam. Your cousin Cupid lent me his wings, and your sister Venus opened the casement.

MRS SUL.   I'm struck dumb with admiration!

ARCH.   And I with wonder!   *Looks passionately at her*

MRS SUL.   What will become of me?

ARCH.   How beautiful she looks! The teeming jolly spring smiles in her blooming face, and when she was conceived her mother smelt to roses, looked on lilies –

        Lilies unfold their white, their fragrant charms,
        When the warm sun thus darts into their arms.

                                                        Runs to her

MRS SUL.   (*Shrieks*) Ah!

---

[6]*Alcmena* wife of Amphitrion, whose features Jupiter adopted in order to seduce her (Hercules was the son of Jupiter and Alcmena).

ARCH. 'Oons, madam, what d'ye mean? You'll raise the house.

MRS SUL. Sir, I'll wake the dead before I bear this! What, approach me with the freedom of a keeper! I'm glad on't; your impudence has cured me.

ARCH. If this be impudence, (*Kneels*) I leave to your partial self. No panting pilgrim, after a tedious, painful voyage, e'er bowed before his saint with more devotion.

MRS SUL. (*Aside*) Now, now, I'm ruined if he kneels! – [*Aloud*] Rise, thou prostrate engineer;⁷ not all thy undermining skill shall reach my heart. Rise, and know I am a woman without my sex. I can love to all the tenderness of wishes, sighs, and tears, but go no farther. Still, to convince you that I'm more than woman, I can speak my frailty, confess my weakness even for you, but –

ARCH. For me! *Going to lay hold on her*

MRS SUL. Hold, sir; build not upon that, for my most mortal hatred follows if you disobey what I command you now. Leave me this minute. – (*Aside*) If he denies I'm lost.

ARCH. Then you'll promise –

MRS SUL. Anything another time.

ARCH. When shall I come?

MRS SUL. Tomorrow. When you will.

ARCH. Your lips must seal the promise.

MRS SUL. Pshaw!

ARCH. They must, they must! (*Kisses her*) Raptures and paradise! And why not now, my angel? The time, the place, silence, and secrecy, all conspire. And the now conscious stars have preordained this moment for my happiness. *Takes her in his arms*

MRS SUL. You will not, cannot, sure.

ARCH. If the sun rides fast and disappoints not mortals of tomorrow's dawn, this night shall crown my joys.

MRS SUL. My sex's pride assist me!

ARCH. My sex's strength help me!

MRS SUL. You shall kill me first!

ARCH. I'll die with you. *Carrying her off*

MRS SUL. Thieves, thieves, murder!

Enter SCRUB *in his breeches, and one shoe*

SCRUB. Thieves, thieves, murder, popery!

ARCH. Ha, the very timorous stag will kill in rutting time.

Draws and offers to stab SCRUB

SCRUB. (*Kneeling*) Oh pray, sir, spare all I have, and take my life!

MRS SUL. (*Holding* ARCHER'S *hand*) What does the fellow mean?

⁷*engineer* plotter.

SCRUB. O madam, down upon your knees, your marrow-bones! He's one of 'um.

ARCH. Of whom?

SCRUB. One of the rogues – I beg your pardon, sir, one of the honest gentlemen that just now are broke into the house.

ARCH. How!

MRS SUL. I hope you did not come to rob me?

ARCH. Indeed I did, madam, but I would have taken nothing but what you might ha' spared, but your crying 'Thieves' has waked this dreaming fool, and so he takes 'em for granted.

SCRUB. Granted! 'Tis granted, sir; take all we have.

MRS SUL. The fellow looks as if he were broke out of Bedlam.[8]

SCRUB. 'Oons, madam, they're broke into the house with fire and sword! I saw them, heard them; they'll be here this minute.

ARCH. What, thieves!

SCRUB. Under favour, sir, I think so.

MRS SUL. What shall we do, sir?

ARCH. Madam, I wish your ladyship a good night.

MRS SUL. Will you leave me?

ARCH. Leave you! Lord, madam, did not you command me to be gone just now, upon pain of your immortal hatred?

MRS SUL. Nay, but pray, sir –   *Takes hold of him*

ARCH. Ha, ha, ha! Now comes my turn to be ravished. You see now, madam, you must use men one way or other; but take this by the way, good madam, that none but a fool will give you the benefit of his courage, unless you'll take his love along with it. How are they armed, friend?

SCRUB. With sword and pistol, sir.

ARCH. Hush! – I see a dark lantern coming through the gallery. Madam, be assured I will protect you or lose my life.

MRS SUL. Your life! No, sir, they can rob me of nothing that I value half so much; therefore now, sir, let me entreat you to be gone.

ARCH. No, madam, I'll consult my own safety for the sake of yours; I'll work by stratagem. Have you courage enough to stand the appearance of 'em?

MRS SUL. Yes, yes. Since I have 'scaped your hands, I can face anything.

ARCH. Come hither, brother Scrub! Don't you know me?

SCRUB. Eh, my dear brother, let me kiss thee.   *Kisses* ARCHER

ARCH. This way. Here.   ARCHER *and* SCRUB *hide behind the bed*

---

[8]*Bedlam* St Mary of Bethlehem, the insane asylum in London.

Enter GIBBET, *with a dark lantern in one hand and a pistol in the other*

GIB. Ay, ay, this is the chamber, and the lady alone.

MRS SUL. Who are you, sir? What would you have? D'ye come to rob me?

GIB. Rob you! Alack a day, madam, I'm only a younger brother, madam; and so, madam, if you make a noise, I'll shoot you through the head, but don't be afraid, madam. (*Laying his lantern and pistol upon the table*) These rings, madam. Don't be concerned, madam, I have a profound respect for you, madam. Your keys, madam. Don't be frighted, madam; I'm the most of a gentleman. (*Searching her pockets*) This necklace, madam. I never was rude to any lady; I have a veneration – for this necklace – (*Here* ARCHER *having come round and seized the pistol, takes* GIBBET *by the collar, trips up his heels, and claps the pistol to his breast*)

ARCH. Hold, profane villain, and take the reward of thy sacrilege!

GIB. Oh, pray, sir, don't kill me; I an't prepared.

ARCH. How many is there of 'em, Scrub?

SCRUB. Five-and-forty, sir.

ARCH. Then I must kill the villain, to have him out of the way.

GIB. Hold, hold, sir; we are but three, upon my honour.

ARCH. Scrub, will you undertake to secure him?

SCRUB. Not I, sir. Kill him, kill him!

ARCH. Run to Gipsy's chamber; there you'll find the doctor. Bring him hither presently. (*Exit* SCRUB, *running*) Come, rogue, if you have a short prayer, say it.

GIB. Sir, I have no prayer at all; the government has provided a chaplain to say prayers for us on these occasions.

MRS SUL. Pray, sir, don't kill him; you fright me as much as him.

ARCH. The dog shall die, madam, for being the occasion of my disappointment. – Sirrah, this moment is your last.

GIB. Sir, I'll give you two hundred pound to spare my life.

ARCH. Have you no more, rascal?

GIB. Yes, sir, I can command four hundred, but I must reserve two of 'em to save my life at the sessions.

Re-enter SCRUB, *with* FOIGARD

ARCH. Here, doctor, I suppose Scrub and you between you may manage him. Lay hold of him, doctor.

FOIGARD *lays hold of* GIBBET

GIB. What, turned over to the priest already! Look ye, doctor, you come before your time; I an't condemned yet, I thank ye.

FOI. Come, my dear joy, I vill secure your body and your shoul too; I vill make you a good Catholic and give you an absolution.

GIB.   Absolution! Can you procure me a pardon, doctor?

FOI.   No, joy.

GIB.   Then you and your absolution may go to the devil.

ARCH.   Convey him into the cellar, there bind him. Take the pistol, and if he offers to resist, shoot him through the head, and come back to us with all the speed you can.

SCRUB.   Ay, ay, come, doctor; do you hold him fast, and I'll guard him.
                                    Exit FOIGARD *with* GIBBET, SCRUB *following*

MRS SUL.   But how came the doctor –

ARCH.   In short, madam, – (*Shrieking without*) 'Sdeath, the rogues are at work with the other ladies. I'm vexed I parted with the pistol, but I must fly to their assistance. Will you stay here, madam, or venture yourself with me?

MRS SUL.   (*Taking him by the arm*) Oh, with you, dear sir, with you.
                                                                    Exeunt

SCENE [THREE]

Scene changes to another apartment in the same house

Enter HOUNSLOW, *dragging in* LADY BOUNTIFUL, *and* BAGSHOT, *haling in* DORINDA, *the rogues with swords drawn*

BAG.   Come, come, your jewels, mistress!

HOUN.   Your keys, your keys, old gentlewoman!
            Enter AIMWELL *and* CHERRY

AIM.   Turn this way, villains! I durst engage an army in such a cause.
                                                            He engages 'em both

DOR.   O madam, had I but a sword to help the brave man!

LADY BOUN.   There's three or four hanging up in the hall, but they won't draw. I'll go fetch one, however.   *Exit*
            Enter ARCHER *and* MRS SULLEN

ARCH.   Hold, hold, my lord! Every man his bird, pray.
                They engage man to man; HOUNSLOW *and* BAGSHOT *are thrown and disarmed*

CHER.   [*Aside*] What, the rogues taken! Then they'll impeach my father; I must give him timely notice.   *Runs out*

ARCH.   Shall we kill the rogues?

AIM.   No, no, we'll bind them.

ARCH.   Ay, ay. – (*To* MRS SULLEN, *who stands by him*) Here, madam, lend me your garter.

MRS SUL.   [*Aside*] The devil's in this fellow! He fights, loves, and banters, all in a breath. – [*Aloud*] Here's a cord that the rogues brought with 'em, I suppose.

ARCH. Right, right, the rogue's destiny, a rope to hang himself. Come, my lord – this is but a scandalous sort of an office (*Binding the rogues together*) if our adventures should end in this sort of hangman-work, but I hope there is something in prospect that –

    Enter SCRUB

ARCH. Well, Scrub, have you secured your Tartar?⁹

SCRUB. Yes, sir, I left the priest and him disputing about religion.

AIM. And pray carry these gentlemen to reap the benefit of the controversy.

        Delivers the prisoners to SCRUB, *who leads 'em out*

MRS SUL. Pray, sister, how came my lord here?

DOR. And pray, how came the gentleman here?

MRS SUL. I'll tell you the greatest piece of villainy –

        They talk in dumb show

AIM. I fancy, Archer, you have been more successful in your adventures than the housebreakers.

ARCH. No matter for my adventure, yours is the principal. Press her this minute to marry you, now while she's hurried between the palpitation of her fear and the joy of her deliverance, now while the tide of her spirits is at high flood. Throw yourself at her feet, speak some romantic nonsense or other, address her like Alexander in the height of his victory, confound her senses, bear down her reason, and away with her. The priest is now in the cellar and dare not refuse to do the work.

    Re-enter LADY BOUNTIFUL

AIM. But how shall I get off without being observed?

ARCHER. You a lover, and not find a way to get off! – Let me see, –

AIM. You bleed, Archer.

ARCH. 'Sdeath, I'm glad on't; this wound will do the business. I'll amuse the old lady and Mrs Sullen about dressing my wound, while you carry off Dorinda.

LADY BOUN. Gentlemen, could we understand how you would be gratified for the services –

ARCH. Come, come, my lady, this is no time for compliments; I'm wounded, madam.

LADY BOUN., MRS SUL. How, wounded!

DOR. I hope, sir, you have received no hurt.

AIM. None but what you may cure.   *Makes love in dumb show*

LADY BOUN. Let me see your arm, sir. I must have some powder-sugar to stop the blood. O me, an ugly gash. Upon my word, sir, you must go into bed.

---

⁹*Tartar* thief.

ARCH. Ay, my lady, a bed would do very well. – (*To* MRS SULLEN)
Madam, will you do me the favour to conduct me to a chamber?

LADY BOUN. Do, do, daughter, while I get the lint and the probe and
the plaster ready.

Runs out one way; AIMWELL *carries off* DORINDA *another*

ARCH. Come, madam, why don't you obey your mother's commands?

MRS SUL. How can you, after what is passed, have the confidence to
ask me?

ARCH. And if you go to that, how can you, after what is passed, have
the confidence to deny me? Was not this blood shed in your defence,
and my life exposed for your protection? Look ye, madam, I'm none
of your romantic fools that fight giants and monsters for nothing.
My valour is downright Swiss;[10] I'm a soldier of fortune and must be
paid.

MRS SUL. 'Tis ungenerous in you, sir, to upbraid me with your
services.

ARCH. 'Tis ungenerous in you, madam, not to reward 'em.

MRS SUL. How, at the expense of my honour!

ARCH. Honour! Can honour consist with ingratitude? If you would
deal like a woman of honour, do like a man of honour. D'ye think I
would deny you in such a case?

Enter a SERVANT

SERV. Madam, my lady ordered me to tell you that your brother is
below at the gate. [*Exit*]

MRS SUL. My brother! Heavens be praised! Sir, he shall thank you
for your services; he has it in his power.

ARCH. Who is your brother, madam?

MRS SUL. Sir Charles Freeman. You'll excuse me, sir; I must go and
receive him. [*Exit*]

ARCH. Sir Charles Freeman! 'Sdeath and hell, my old acquaintance!
Now unless Aimwell has made good use of his time, all our fair
machine goes souse into the sea like the Eddystone.[11] *Exit*

SCENE [FOUR]

Scene changes to the gallery in the same house

Enter AIMWELL *and* DORINDA

DOR. Well, well, my lord, you have conquered; your late generous

[10]*Swiss* Swiss soldiers sold their services as bodyguards, etc.

[11]*Eddystone* a lighthouse 13 miles (21 km.) off the coast of south Devon; built of
wood in 1699, it was destroyed by a storm in 1703.

action will, I hope, plead for my easy yielding, though I must own your lordship had a friend in the fort before.

AIM.   The sweets of Hybla[12] dwell upon her tongue! Here, doctor –
Enter FOIGARD *with a book*

FOI.   Are you prepared boat?[13]

DOR.   I'm ready. But first, my lord, one word. I have a frightful example of a hasty marriage in my own family; when I reflect upon't, it shocks me. Pray, my lord, consider a little –

AIM.   Consider! Do you doubt my honour or my love?

DOR.   Neither. I do believe you equally just as brave, and were your whole sex drawn out for me to choose, I should not cast a look upon the multitude if you were absent. But, my lord, I'm a woman; colours, concealments may hide a thousand faults in me; therefore know me better first. I hardly dare affirm I know myself in anything except my love.

AIM.   (*Aside*) Such goodness who could injure? I find myself unequal to the task of villain; she has gained my soul and made it honest like her own. I cannot, cannot hurt her. – [*Aloud*] Doctor, retire. (*Exit* FOIGARD) Madam, behold your lover and your proselyte,[14] and judge of my passion by my conversion. I'm all a lie, nor dare I give a fiction to your arms; I'm all counterfeit, except my passion.

DOR.   Forbid it, heaven, a counterfeit!

AIM.   I am no lord, but a poor needy man, come with a mean, a scandalous design to prey upon your fortune, but the beauties of your mind and person have so won me from myself that, like a trusty servant, I prefer the interest of my mistress to my own.

DOR.   Sure I have had the dream of some poor mariner, a sleepy image of a welcome port, and wake involved in storms! Pray, sir, who are you?

AIM.   Brother to the man whose title I usurped, but stranger to his honour or his fortune.

DOR.   Matchless honesty! Once I was proud, sir, of your wealth and title, but now am prouder that you want it. Now I can show my love was justly levelled and had no aim but love. – Doctor, come in.
Enter FOIGARD *at one door,* GIPSY *at another, who whispers* [*to*]
DORINDA
[*To* FOIGARD] Your pardon, sir, we sha' not want you now. – [*To* AIMWELL] Sir, you must excuse me: I'll wait on you presently.
Exit with GIPSY

FOI.   Upon my shoul now, dis is foolish.   *Exit*

---

[12]*Hybla* a town in Sicily, noted for its honey.
[13]*boat* i.e. both.   [14]*proselyte* convert.

AIM.   Gone, and bid the priest depart! It has an ominous look.
   Enter ARCHER
ARCH.   Courage, Tom! Shall I wish you joy?
AIM.   No.
ARCH.   'Oons, man, what ha' you been doing?
AIM.   O Archer, my honesty, I fear, has ruined me.
ARCH.   How?
AIM.   I have discovered myself.
ARCH.   Discovered, and without my consent? What, have I embarked
   my small remains in the same bottom with yours, and you dispose of
   all without my partnership?
AIM.   O Archer, I own my fault.
ARCH.   After conviction, 'tis then too late for pardon. You may
   remember, Mr Aimwell, that you proposed this folly. As you begun,
   so end it. Henceforth I'll hunt my fortune single – so farewell!
AIM.   Stay, my dear Archer, but a minute.
ARCH.   Stay! What, to be despised, exposed, and laughed at! No, I
   would sooner change conditions with the worst of the rogues we just
   now bound than bear one scornful smile from the proud knight that
   once I treated as my equal.
AIM.   What knight?
ARCH.   Sir Charles Freeman, brother to the lady that I had almost –
   but no matter for that; 'tis a cursed night's work, and so I leave you
   to make the best on't.   *Going*
AIM.   Freeman! – One word, Archer. Still I have hopes; methought
   she received my confession with pleasure.
ARCH.   'Sdeath, who doubts it?
AIM.   She consented after to the match, and still I dare believe she will
   be just.
ARCH.   To herself, I warrant her, as you should have been.
AIM.   By all my hopes she comes, and smiling comes!
   Re-enter DORINDA, *mighty gay*
DOR.   Come, my dear lord, I fly with impatience to your arms; the
   minutes of my absence were a tedious year. Where's this priest?
   Re-enter FOIGARD
ARCH.   'Oons, a brave girl!
DOR.   I suppose, my lord, this gentleman is privy to our affairs?
ARCH.   Yes, yes, madam, I'm to be your father.
DOR.   Come, priest, do your office.
ARCH.   Make haste, make haste, couple 'em any way. – (*Takes*
   AIMWELL'S *hand*) Come, madam, I'm to give you –
DOR.   My mind's altered; I won't.
ARCH.   Eh!

AIM.   I'm confounded!

FOI.   Upon my shoul, and sho is myshelf.

ARCH.   What's the matter now, madam?

DOR.   Look ye, sir, one generous action deserves another. This gentleman's honour obliged him to hide nothing from me; my justice engages me to conceal nothing from him. In short, sir, you are the person that you thought you counterfeited; you are the true Lord Viscount Aimwell, and I wish your lordship joy. – Now, priest, you may be gone; if my lord is pleased now with the match, let his lordship marry me in the face of the world.

AIM., ARCH.   What does she mean?

DOR.   Here's a witness for my truth.

Enter SIR CHARLES FREEMAN *and* MRS SULLEN

SIR CHAS.   My dear Lord Aimwell, I wish you joy.

AIM.   Of what?

SIR CHAS.   Of your honour and estate. Your brother died the day before I left London, and all your friends have writ after you to Brussels. Among the rest I did myself the honour.

ARCH.   Hark ye, sir knight, don't you banter now?

SIR CHAS.   'Tis truth, upon my honour.

AIM.   Thanks to the pregnant stars that formed this accident.

ARCH.   Thanks to the womb of time that brought it forth! Away with it!

AIM.   Thanks to my guardian angel that led me to the prize!

Taking DORINDA'S *hand*

ARCH.   And double thanks to the noble Sir Charles Freeman. – My lord, I wish you joy. – My lady, I wish you joy. – Egad, Sir Freeman, you're the honestest fellow living! 'Sdeath, I'm grown strange airy[15] upon this matter! – My lord, how d'ye? – A word, my lord. Don't you remember something of a previous agreement that entitles me to the moiety[16] of this lady's fortune, which I think will amount to five thousand pound?

AIM.   Not a penny, Archer; you would ha' cut my throat just now because I would not deceive this lady.

ARCH.   Ay, and I'll cut your throat again if you should deceive her now.

AIM.   That's what I expected; and to end the dispute, the lady's fortune is ten thousand pound; we'll divide stakes. Take the ten thousand pound or the lady.

DOR.   How, is your lordship so indifferent?

ARCH.   No, no, no, madam! His lordship knows very well that I'll

---

[15]*airy* gay.   [16]*moiety* half.

take the money; I leave you to his lordship, and so we're both provided for.

    Enter COUNT BELLAIR[17]

COUNT BEL. *Mesdames et Messieurs*, I am your servant trice humble! I hear you be rob here.

AIM. The ladies have been in some danger, sir.

COUNT BEL. And, begar, our inn be rob too!

AIM. Our inn! By whom?

COUNT BEL. By the landlord, begar! – Garzoon, he has rob himself and run away!

ARCH. Robbed himself!

COUNT BEL. Ay, begar, and me too of a hundre pound.

ARCH. A hundred pound?

COUNT BEL. Yes, that I owed him.

AIM. Our money's gone, Frank.

ARCH. Rot the money! My wench is gone. – [*To* COUNT BELLAIR] *Savez-vous quelquechose de Mademoiselle Cherry?*[18]

    Enter a COUNTRYMAN *with a strongbox and a letter*

COUN. Is there one Martin here?

ARCH. Ay, ay, who wants him?

COUN. I have a box here and letter for him.

ARCH. (*Taking the box*) Ha, ha, ha! What's here? Legerdemain! By this light, my lord, our money again! – But this unfolds the riddle. (*Opening the letter*) Hum, hum, hum! Oh, 'tis for the public good and must be communicated to the company. (*Reads*) 'Mr Martin: My father being afraid of an impeachment by the rogues that are taken tonight, is gone off, but if you can procure him a pardon, he'll make great discoveries that may be useful to the country. Could I have met you instead of your master tonight, I would have delivered myself into your hands, with a sum that much exceeds that in your strongbox, which I have sent you, with an assurance to my dear Martin that I shall ever be his most faithful friend till death. – Cherry Boniface'. There's a *billet doux* for you! As for the father, I think he ought to be encouraged. And for the daughter, pray, my lord, persuade your bride to take her into her service instead of Gipsy.

AIM. I can assure you, madam, your deliverance was owing to her discovery.

---

[17]*Count Bellair* After the first night, the role of the Count was omitted, as in Act III; his speeches, with modifications, were later given to Foigard, and the words of a few other actors were changed. The adaptations, taken from the 1728 edition of the play, appear in Appendix C, pp. 677–78.

[18]*Cherry* Do you know anything about Miss Cherry?

DOR. Your command, my lord, will do without the obligation. I'll take care of her.

SIR CHAS. This good company meets opportunely in favour of a design I have in behalf of my unfortunate sister. I intend to part her from her husband. Gentlemen, will you assist me?

ARCH. Assist you! 'Sdeath, who would not?

COUNT BEL. Assist! Garzoon, we all assist!

Enter SQUIRE SULLEN

SQUIRE SUL. What's all this? They tell me, spouse, that you had like to have been robbed.

MRS SUL. Truly, spouse, I was pretty near it, had not these two gentlemen interposed.

SQUIRE SUL. How came these gentlemen here?

MRS SUL. That's his way of returning thanks, you must know.

COUNT BEL. Garzoon, the question be apropos for all dat.

SIR CHAS. You promised last night, sir, that you would deliver your lady to me this morning.

SQUIRE SUL. Humph!

ARCH. 'Humph'! What do you mean by 'humph'? Sir, you shall deliver her. In short, sir, we have saved you and your family, and if you are not civil, we'll unbind the rogues, join with 'em, and set fire to your house. What does the man mean? Not part with his wife?

COUNT BEL. Ay, garzoon, de man no understan common justice.

MRS SUL. Hold, gentlemen, all things here must move by consent; compulsion would spoil us. Let my dear and I talk the matter over, and you shall judge it between us.

SQUIRE SUL. Let me know first who are to be our judges. Pray, sir, who are you?

SIR CHAS. I am Sir Charles Freeman, come to take away your wife.

SQUIRE SUL. And you, good sir?

AIM. Thomas, Viscount Aimwell, come to take away your sister.

SQUIRE SUL. And you, pray, sir?

ARCH. Francis Archer, esquire, come –

SQUIRE SUL. To take away my mother, I hope. Gentlemen, you're heartily welcome; I never met with three more obliging people since I was born! And now, my dear, if you please, you shall have the first word.

ARCH. And the last, for five pound!

MRS SUL. Spouse!

SQUIRE SUL. Rib![19]

MRS SUL. How long have we been married?

[19]*Rib* Scold.

SQUIRE SUL.   By the almanac, fourteen months; but by my account, fourteen years.

MRS SUL.   'Tis thereabout by my reckoning.

COUNT BEL.   Garzoon, their account will agree.

MRS SUL.   Pray, spouse, what did you marry for?

SQUIRE SUL.   To get an heir to my estate.

SIR CHAS.   And have you succeeded?

SQUIRE SUL.   No.

ARCH.   The condition fails of his side. Pray, madam, what did you marry for?

MRS SUL.   To support the weakness of my sex by the strength of his and to enjoy the pleasures of an agreeable society.

SIR CHAS.   Are your expectations answered?

MRS SUL.   No.

COUNT BEL.   A clear case, a clear case!

SIR CHAS.   What are the bars to your natural contentment?

MRS SUL.   In the first place, I can't drink ale with him.

SQUIRE SUL.   Nor can I drink tea with her.

MRS SUL.   I can't hunt with you.

SQUIRE SUL.   Nor can I dance with you.

MRS SUL.   I hate cocking²⁰ and racing.

SQUIRE SULLEN.   And I abhor ombre and piquet.²¹

MRS SUL.   Your silence is intolerable.

SQUIRE SUL.   Your prating is worse.

MRS SUL.   Have we not been a perpetual offence to each other, a gnawing vulture at the heart?

SQUIRE SUL.   A frightful goblin to the sight?

MRS SUL.   A porcupine to the feeling?

SQUIRE SUL.   Perpetual wormwood to the taste?

MRS SUL.   Is there on earth a thing we could agree in?

SQUIRE SUL.   Yes – to part.

MRS SUL.   With all my heart.

SQUIRE SUL.   Your hand.

MRS SUL.   Here.

SQUIRE SUL.   These hands joined us, these shall part us. Away!

MRS SUL.   North.

SQUIRE SUL.   South.

MRS SUL.   East.

SQUIRE SUL.   West, far as the poles asunder.

COUNT BEL.   Begar, the ceremony be vera pretty!

---

²⁰*cocking* cock-fighting.
²¹*ombre and piquet* popular card games.

SIR CHAS.   Now, Mr Sullen, there wants only my sister's fortune to make us easy.

SQUIRE SUL.   Sir Charles, you love your sister, and I love her fortune; every one to his fancy.

ARCH.   Then you won't refund?

SQUIRE SUL.   Not a stiver.[22]

ARCH.   Then I find, madam, you must e'en go to your prison again.

COUNT BEL.   What is the portion?

SIR CHAS.   Ten thousand pound, sir.

COUNT BEL.   Garzoon, I'll pay it, and she shall go home wid me.

ARCH.   Ha, ha, ha! French all over. Do you know, sir, what ten thousand pound English is?

COUNT BEL.   No, begar, not justement.

ARCH.   Why, sir, 'tis a hundred thousand livres.[23]

COUNT BEL.   A hundre tousand livres! Ah, garzoon, me canno' do't; your beauties and their fortunes are both too much for me.

ARCH.   Then I will. This night's adventure has proved strangely lucky to us all – for Captain Gibbet in his walk had made bold, Mr Sullen, with your study and escritoir, and had taken out all the writings of your estate, all the articles of marriage with this lady, bills, bonds, leases, receipts to an infinite value. I took 'em from him, and I deliver them to Sir Charles.   *Gives him a parcel of papers and parchments*

SQUIRE SUL.   How, my writings! My head aches consumedly. –Well, gentlemen, you shall have her fortune, but I can't talk. If you have a mind, Sir Charles, to be merry, and celebrate my sister's wedding and my divorce,[24] you may command my house, but my head aches consumedly. Scrub, bring me a dram.

ARCH.   (*To* MRS SULLEN) Madam, there's a country dance to the trifle that I sung today; your hand, and we'll lead it up.

Here a Dance

'Twould be hard to guess which of these parties is the better pleased, the couple joined or the couple parted; the one rejoicing in hopes of an untasted happiness and the other in their deliverance from an experienced misery.

> Both happy in their several states we find,
> Those parted by consent, and those conjoin'd.
> Consent, if mutual, saves the lawyer's fee;
> Consent is law enough to set you free.   [*Exeunt omnes*]

[22]*stiver* a small Dutch coin, of little value.

[23]*livres* French money of account; a livre was then equivalent to *c*. 9d.; 100,000 livres = £ 3750.

[24]*divorce* Used metaphorically; Sullen and his wife, now separated, were still legally married.

EPILOGUE[1]

If to our play your judgement can't be kind,
Let its expiring author[2] pity find;
Survey his mournful case with melting eyes,
Nor let the bard be damn'd before he dies.
Forbear, you fair, on his last scene to frown,
But his true exit with a plaudit crown;
Then shall the dying poet cease to fear
The dreadful knell, while your applause he hears.
At Leuctra[3] so the conqu'ring Theban died,
Claim'd his friends' praises, but their tears denied;
Pleas'd in the pangs of death he greatly thought
Conquest with loss of life but cheaply bought.
The difference this, the Greek was one would fight,
As brave, though not so gay, as Sergeant Kite;[4]
Ye sons of Will's,[5] what's that to those who write?
To Thebes alone the Grecian owed his bays;
You may the bard above the hero raise,
Since yours is greater than Athenian praise.

[1] *Epilogue* The edition of 1733 describes this Epilogue as written 'by Mr Smith, the author of *Phaedra and Hypolitis* [1707]'. This is the only play by Edmund Smith, 1672–1710, dilettante poet and scholar.

[2] *expiring author* When the play was first performed, 8 March 1707, Farquhar was mortally ill; he died, perhaps of tuberculosis, about two months later.

[3] *Leuctra* in Boeotia, Greece, where Epaminondas and his Theban army defeated the Spartans in 371 BC, but he did not in fact die there.

[4] *Sergeant Kite* the principal comic character in Farquhar's *The Recruiting Officer*, 1706.

[5] *sons of Will's* hangerson at Will's coffee-house, in Bow Street.

APPENDICES

A. Prologues and Epilogues to
VENICE PRESERVED

B. Lines revised in
THE PROVOKED WIFE

C. Rewritten lines in
THE BEAUX STRATAGEM

APPENDIX A

Prologues and Epilogues to
VENICE PRESERVED

Venice Preserved was first staged 9 February 1682 and published shortly afterward, with Thomas Otway's original Prologue and Epilogue (reproduced before and after the text of the play, pp. 317–18 and pp. 393–94). The play was performed again on 11 February and 21 April. For this third presentation, before James, Duke of York, Otway's friend John Dryden provided a new Prologue, and Otway wrote a new Epilogue (both poems were published separately in 1682). Yet another revival of the play occurred on 31 May, shortly after the Duchess of York returned from Scotland, with a third Prologue, by Dryden, and a third Epilogue, by Otway (and as before, both poems were published separately in 1682).

Prologues and Epilogues to
VENICE PRESERV'D

PROLOGUE [21 April 1682]

TO HIS ROYAL HIGHNESS [THE DUKE OF YORK]
Upon his first appearance at the Duke's Theatre
since his return from Scotland

Written by Mr Dryden   Spoken by Mr Smith[1]

In those cold regions which no summers cheer,
When brooding darkness covers half the year,
To hollow caves the shivering natives go;
Bears range abroad, and hunt in tracks of snow;
But when the tedious twilight wears away,
And stars grow paler at th'approach of day,
The longing crowds to frozen mountains run,
Happy who first can see the glimmering sun!
The surly savage offspring disappear,
And curse the bright successor of the year.
Yet, though rough bears in covert seek defence,
White foxes stay, with seeming innocence;
That crafty kind with daylight can dispense.
Still we are throng'd so full with Reynard's race,
That loyal subjects scarce can find a place;
Thus modest truth is cast behind the crowd;
Truth speaks too low, hypocrisy too loud.
Let 'em be first to flatter in success;
Duty can stay, but guilt has need to press.
Once, when true zeal the sons of God did call,
To make their solemn show at heaven's Whitehall,
The fawning devil appear'd among the rest,
And made as good a courtier as the best.
The friends of Job, who rail'd at him before,
Came cap in hand when he had three times more.
Yet late repentance may perhaps be true;
Kings can forgive if rebels can but sue:
A tyrant's pow'r in rigour is express'd,

[1] *Smith* William Smith, who played Pierre.

The father yearns in the true prince's breast.
We grant an o'ergrown Whig no grace can mend;
But most are babes that know not they offend.
The crowd, to restless motion still inclin'd,
Are clouds that rack according to the wind.
Driv'n by their chiefs, they storms of hailstones pour,
Then mourn, and soften to a silent shower.
O welcome to this much offending land
The prince that brings forgiveness in his hand!
Thus angels on glad messages appear;
Their first salute commands us not to fear.
Thus heav'n, that could constrain us to obey
(With rev'rence if we might presume to say)
Seems to relax the rights of sov'reign sway,
Permits to man the choice of good and ill,
And makes us happy by our own free will.

THE EPILOGUE

Written by Mr Otway to his play called Venice Preser-
ved, *or* A Plot Discovered; *spoken upon His Royal
Highness the Duke of York's coming to the theatre,
Friday, April 21, 1682*

When too much plenty, luxury, and ease
Had surfeited this isle to a disease,
When noisome blains[1] did its best parts o'erspread,
And on the rest their dire infection shed,
Our Great Physician, who the nature knew
Of the distemper and from whence it grew,
Fix'd for three kingdoms' quiet, Sir, on you.
He cast his searching eyes o'er all the frame,
And finding whence before one sickness[2] came,
How once before our mischiefs foster'd were,
Knew well your virtue and applied you there;
Where so your goodness, so your justice sway'd,
You but appear'd, and the wild plague was stay'd.
When from the filthy dunghill-faction bred,
New-form'd rebellion durst rear up its head,
Answer me all: who struck the monster dead?

  See, see, the injur'd prince, and bless his name,
Think on the martyr from whose loins he came;
Think on the blood was shed for you before,
And curse the parricides that thirst for more.
His foes are yours, then of their wiles beware;
Lay, lay him in your hearts and guard him there;
Where let his wrongs your zeal for him improve;
He wears a sword will justify your love,
With blood still ready for your good t'expend,
And has a heart that ne'er forgot his friend.

---

[1] *blains* inflamations.
[2] *sickness* i.e. a rebellion in Scotland. James, Duke of York, was there as a military
commander 1680–82.

His duteous loyalty before you lay,
And learn of him, unmurm'ring to obey.
Think what he'as borne, your quiet to restore;
Repent your madness and rebel no more.
No more let bout'feus³ hope to lead petitions,
Scriv'ners to be treas'rers; pedlars, politicians;
Nor ev'ry fool whose wife has tripp'd at court,
Pluck up a spirit, and turn rebel for't.
   In lands where cuckolds multiply like ours,
What prince can be too jealous of their powers,
Or can too often think himself alarm'd?
They're malcontents that ev'rywhere go arm'd;
And when the horned herd's together got,
Nothing portends a commonwealth like that.
   Cast, cast your idols off, your gods of wood,
Ere yet Philistines fatten with your blood;
Renounce your priests of Baal⁴ with amen-faces,
Your Wapping-feasts⁵ and your Mile-End⁶ high places;
Nail all your medals on the gallows post,
In recompense th'original was lost.
At these, illustrious repentance pay
In his kind hands your humble off'rings lay,
Let royal pardon be by him implor'd,
Th'attoning brother of your anger'd lord.
He only brings a medicine fit to assuage
A people's folly and rous'd monarch's rage;
An infant prince yet lab'ring in the womb,⁷
Fated with wond'rous happiness to come,
He goes to fetch the mighty blessing home.
Send all your wishes with him, let the air
With gentle breezes waft it safely here,
The seas, like what they'll carry, calm and fair.
Let the illustrious mother touch our land
Mildly, as hereafter may her son command;

---

   ³*bout'feus* troublemakers, incendiaries (lit., devices for setting off cannon).

   ⁴*priests of Baal* i.e. sanctimonious priests of false deities.

   ⁵*Wapping* in east London, then notorious for pirates.

   ⁶*Mile End* in east London, a militia training ground. This line of verse hints at Whig bribery; Shaftesbury derived much support from this area of London.

   ⁷*infant prince* The Duchess of York gave birth to a daughter, Princess Charlotte Mary, on 15 August 1682, who died 6 October 1682. Three earlier offspring had died. A son, James Francis Edward, was born in 1688 and became The Old Pretender.

While our glad monarch welcomes her to shore,
With kind assurance she shall part no more.
 Be the majestic babe then smiling born,
And all good signs of fate his birth adorn,
So live and grow, a constant pledge to stand
Of Caesar's love to an obedient land.

PROLOGUE TO THE DUCHESS
[OF YORK],
on her Return from Scotland
[Spoken on 31 May 1682]

WRITTEN BY MR DRYDEN

When factious rage to cruel exile drove
The queen of beauty and the court of love
The muses droop'd, with their forsaken arts,
And the sad cupids broke their useless darts.
Our fruitful plains to wilds and deserts turn'd,
Like Eden's face when banish'd man it mourn'd;
Love was no more when loyalty was gone,
The great supporter of his awful throne.
Love could no longer after beauty stay,
But wander'd northward to the verge of day,
As if the sun and he had lost their way.
But now th'illustrious nymph return'd again,
Brings every grace triumphant in her train;
The wond'ring nereids,[1] though they rais'd no storm,
Foreslow'd her passage to behold her form.
Some cried a Venus, some a Thetis pass'd;
But this was not so fair nor that so chaste.
Far from her sight flew faction, strife, and pride,
And envy did but look on her and died.
Whate'er we suffer'd from our sullen fate,
Her sight is purchas'd at an easy rate;
Three gloomy years against this day were set,
But this one mighty sum has clear'd the debt.
Like Joseph's dream,[2] but with a better doom,
The famine pass'd, the plenty still to come.
For her the weeping heav'ns become serene,
For her the ground is clad in cheerful green,

[1] *nereids* sea-nymphs, guardians of sailors, daughters of Nereus and Doria. Thetis (line 16), a nereid, became the mother of Achilles.
[2] *Joseph's dream* Genesis 42:09 *et seq.*

For her the nightingales are taught to sing,
And nature has for her delay'd the spring.
The muse resumes her long-forgotten lays,
And love restor'd, his ancient realm surveys,
Recalls our beauties, and revives our plays;
His waste dominions peoples once again,
And from her presence dates his second reign.
But awful charms on her fair forehead sit,
Dispensing what she never will admit.
Pleasing yet cold, like Cynthia's[3] silver beam,
The people's wonder and the poet's theme.
Distemper'd zeal, sedition, canker'd hate
No more shall vex the church and tear the state;
No more shall faction civil discords move,
Or only discords of too-tender love:
Discord like that of music's various parts,
Discord that makes the harmony of hearts,
Discord that only this dispute shall bring,
Who best shall love the Duke and serve the King.

[3]*Cynthia* Artemis, daughter of Zeus and Leto, a nature goddess of fertility, associated with the moon.

EPILOGUE TO HER ROYAL HIGHNESS
[the Duchess of York]
on her Return from Scotland
[Spoken on 31 May 1682]

WRITTEN BY MR OTWAY

All you who this day's jubilee attend
And every loyal muse's loyal friend
That come to treat your longing wishes here,
Turn your desiring eyes and feast 'em there.
Thus falling on your knees with me implore,
May this poor land ne'er lose that presence more.
But if there any in this circle be,
That come so curs'd to envy what they see,
From the vain fool that would be great too soon,
To the dull knave that writ the last lampoon,
Let such as victims to that beauty's fame,
Hang their vile blasted heads and die with shame.
Our mighty blessing is at last return'd,
The joy arriv'd for which so long we mourn'd;
From whom our present peace we expect increas'd,
And all our future generations bless'd.
Time have a care: bring safe the hour of joy
When some bless'd tongue proclaims a royal boy;
And when 'tis born, let nature's hand be strong,
Bless him with days of strength and make 'em long,
Till charg'd with honours we behold him stand,
Three kingdoms' banners waiting his command,
His father's conquering sword within his hand.
Then th'English lions in the air advance,
And with them roaring music to the dance,
Carry a *Quo Warranto*[1] into France.

[1] *Quo Warranto* Charles II, attempting to curb the power of municipal corporations, demanded that London surrender its charter. It refused, and Charles issued a *quo warranto* in January 1682; the city yielded only in October 1683.

APPENDIX B

Vanbrugh, *The Provoked Wife*.
Lines revised in the edition of 1743
(published in Dublin)

Act Four

SCENE [ONE] *continued*

(The original dialogue is at pp. 446–48 above)

TAILOR.   An't please you, it is my lady's short cloak and wrapping gown.

SIR JOHN.   What lady, you reptile you?

TAILOR.   My Lady Brute, your honour.

SIR JOHN.   My Lady Brute! My wife! The robe of my wife! With reverence let me approach it. The dear angel is always taking care of me in danger, and has sent me this suit of armour to protect me in this day of battle. On they go.

ALL.   O brave knight!

LORD RAKE.   Live Don Quixote the Second!

SIR JOHN.   Sancho, my squire, help me on with my armour.

TAILOR.   O dear gentleman, I shall be quite undone if you take the gown.

SIR JOHN.   Retire, sirrah, and since you carry off your skin, go home and be happy.

TAILOR.   [*Aside*] I think I'd e'en as good follow the gentleman's friendly advice, for if I dispute any longer, who knows but the whim may take 'em to case me? These courtiers are fuller of tricks than they are of money. They'll sooner break a man's bones than pay his bill.   *Exit*

SIR JOHN.   So, how do you like my shapes now?

LORD RAKE.   To a miracle! He looks like a queen of the Amazons. But to your arms, gentlemen! The enemy's upon their march. Here's the watch.

SIR JOHN.   Oons, if it were Alexander the Great at the head of his army, I would drive him into a horse pond.

ALL.   Huzza! O brave knight!

SIR JOHN.   See, here he comes with all his Greeks about him. Follow me, boys.

   Enter WATCH

FIRST WATCH.   Heyday! Who have we got here? Stand!

SIR JOHN.   Mayhap not.

FIRST WATCH.   What are you all doing here in the street at this time of night? And who are you, madam, that seem to be at the head of this noble crew?

SIR JOHN.   Sirrah, I am Bonduca, Queen of the Welshmen,[1] and with a leek as long as my pedigree I will destroy your Roman legion in an instant. Britons, strike home!

   Fights [with the WATCHMEN. *The others run away]*

FIRST WATCH.   So, we have got the queen, however. We'll make her pay well for her ransom. Come, madam, will your majesty please to walk before the constable?

SIR JOHN.   The constable's a rascal, and you are a son of a whore.

FIRST WATCH.   A most princely reply, truly. If this be her royal style, I'll warrant her maids of honour prattle prettily. But we'll teach you a little of our court dialect before we part with you, princess. Away with her to the roundhouse.

SIR JOHN.   Hands off, you ruffians! My honour's dearer to me than my life. I hope you won't be uncivil.

FIRST WATCH.   Away with her.

SIR JOHN.   Oh, my honour, my honour!   *Exeunt*

Act Four

[SCENE THREE]

Alternate to pp. 451–53 above

Enter CONSTABLE *and* WATCH *with* SIR JOHN *[in female garb]*

CONST.   Come, forsooth, come along, if you please. I once in

---

[1] *Bonduca . . . Welshmen* Bonduca or Boadicea, queen of the Iceni (of Norfolk and Suffolk) fought vigorously but unsuccessfully against the Romans, *c.* AD 60. She has no known association with Wales. Purcell's opera *Bonduca* was produced in 1696.

compassion thought to have seen you safe home this morning, but you have been so rampant and abusive all night I shall see what the justice of the peace will say to you.

SIR JOHN.   And you shall see what I'll say to the justice of peace.

WATCH *knocks. A* SERVANT *enters*

CONST.   Is Mr Justice at home?

SERV.   Yes.

CONST.   Pray acquaint his worship we have got an unruly woman here, and desire to know what he'll please to have done with her.

SERV.   I'll acquaint my master.   *Exit*

SIR JOHN.   Hark you, constable, what cuckoldly justice is this?

CONST.   One that will know how to deal with such romps as you are, I warrant you.

   Enter JUSTICE

JUSTICE.   Well, Mr Constable, what's the matter here?

CONST.   An't please your worship, this here comical sort of a gentlewoman has committed great outrages tonight. She has been frolicking with my Lord Rake and his gang. They have attacked the watch, and I hear there has been a gentleman killed. I believe 'tis they have done't.

SIR JOHN.   There may have been murder for aught I know, and 'tis a great mercy there has not been a rape too, for this fellow would have ravished me.

FIRST WATCH.   Ravish? I ravish? O lud! O lud! O lud! I ravish her? Why, please your honour, I heard Mr Constable say he believed she was little better than a mophrodite.

JUSTICE.   Why truly, she does seem to be a little masculine about the mouth.

FIRST WATCH.   Yes, and about the hands too, an't please your worship. I did but offer in mere civility to help her up the steps into our apartment, and with her grippen[2] fist – (Sir John *knocks him down*) Ay, just so, sir.

SIR JOHN.   I felled him to the ground like an ox.

JUSTICE.   Out upon this boisterous woman! Out upon her!

SIR JOHN.   Mr Justice, he would have been uncivil. It was in defence of my honour, and I demand satisfaction.

FIRST WATCH.   I hope your worship will satisy her honour in Bridewell.[3] That fist of hers will make an admirable hemp-beater.

SIR JOHN.   Sir, I hope you will protect me against that libidinous

[2] *grippen* clenched.
[3] *Bridewell* a prison near Fleet Street; beating hemp was a frequent punishment for female prisoners.

rascal. I am a woman of quality, and virtue too, for all I am in a sort of undress this morning.

JUSTICE. Why, she really has the air of a sort of a woman a little somethingish out of the common. Madam, if you expect I should be favourable to you, I desire I may know who you are.

SIR JOHN. Sir, I am anybody, at your service.

JUSTICE. Lady, I desire to know your name.

SIR JOHN. Sir, my name's Mary.

JUSTICE. Ay, but your surname, madam.

SIR JOHN. Sir, my surname's the very same as my husband's.

JUSTICE. A strange woman, this. Who is your husband, pray?

SIR JOHN. Why, Sir John.

JUSTICE. Sir John who?

SIR JOHN. Why, Sir John Brute.

JUSTICE. Is it possible, madam, you can be my Lady Brute?

SIR JOHN. That happy woman, sir, am I. Only a little in my merriment tonight.

JUSTICE. I'm concerned for Sir John.

SIR JOHN. Truly, so am I.

JUSTICE. I've heard he's an honest gentleman.

SIR JOHN. As ever drank.

JUSTICE. Good lack! Indeed, lady, I am sorry he should have such a wife.

SIR JOHN. Sir, I am sorry he has any wife at all.

JUSTICE. And so perhaps may he. I doubt you have not given him a very good taste of matrimony.

SIR JOHN. Taste, sir? I have scorned to stint him to a taste; I have given him a full meal of it.

JUSTICE. Indeed, I believe so. But pray, fair lady, may he have given you any occasion for this extraordinary conduct? Does he not use you well?

SIR JOHN. A little upon the rough sometimes.

JUSTICE. Ay, any man may be out of humour now and then.

SIR JOHN. Sir, I love peace and quiet, and when a woman don't find that at home, she's apt sometimes to comfort herself with a few innocent diversions abroad.

JUSTICE. I doubt he uses you but too well. Pray, how does he as to that weighty thing, money? Does he allow you what's proper of that?

SIR JOHN. Sir, I generally have enough to pay the reckoning, if this son of a whore the drawer would bring his bill.

JUSTICE. A strange woman, this. Does he spend a reasonable portion of his time at home, to the comfort of his wife and children?

SIR JOHN. Never gave his wife cause to repine at his being abroad in his life.

JUSTICE. Pray, madam, how may he be in the grand matrimonial point? Is he true to your bed?

SIR JOHN. Chaste? – [*Aside*] Oons, this fellow asks so many impertinent questions, egad, I believe it is the justice's wife in the justice's clothes.

JUSTICE. 'Tis a great pity he should have been thus disposed of. Pray, madam, and then I have done, what may be your ladyship's common method of life, if I may presume so far?

SIR JOHN. Why, sir, much like that of a woman of quality.

JUSTICE. Pray, how may you generally pass your time, madam? Your morning, for example.

SIR JOHN. Sir, like a woman of quality: I wake about two a'clock in the afternoon, I stretch, and then make a sign for my chocolate. When I have drank three cups, I slide down again upon my back, with my arms over my head, while two maids puts on my stockings; then, hanging upon their shoulders, I am trailed to my great chair, where I sit and yawn for my breakfast. If it don't come presently, I lie down upon my couch to say my prayers, while my maid reads me the playbills.

JUSTICE. Very well, madam.

SIR JOHN. When the tea is brought in I drink twelve regular dishes, with eight slices of bread and butter, and half an hour after, I send to the cook to know if the dinner is almost ready.

JUSTICE. Soh, madam.

SIR JOHN. By that time my head's half dressed, I hear my husband swearing himself into a state of perdition that the meat's all cold upon the table; to mend which I come down in an hour more, and have it sent back to the kitchen to be all dressed over again.

JUSTICE. Poor man.

SIR JOHN. When I have dined, and my idle servants are presumptuously set down at their ease to do so too, I call for my coach, go to visit fifty dear friends, of whom I hope I never shall find one at home while I shall live.

JUSTICE. So there's the morning and afternoon pretty well disposed of. Pray, madam, how do you pass your evenings?

SIR JOHN. Like a woman of spirit, sir, a great spirit. Give me a box and dice: seven's the main. Oons, sir, I set you a hundred pounds. Why, do you think women are married nowadays to sit at home and mend napkins? Sir, we have nobler ways of passing time.

JUSTICE. Mercy upon us, Mr Constable, what will this age come to?

CONST. What will it come to indeed, if such women as these are not set in the stocks?

SIR JOHN.   I have a little urgent business calls upon me, and therefore I desire the favour of you to bring matters to a conclusion.

JUSTICE.   Madam, if I were sure that business were not to commit more disorders, I would release you.

SIR JOHN.   None, by my virtue.

JUSTICE.   Then, Mr Constable, you may discharge her.

SIR JOHN.   Sir, your very humble servant. If you please to accept of a bottle –

JUSTICE.   I thank you kindly, madam, but I never drink in a morning. Goodbye, madam, goodbye to ye.

SIR JOHN.   Goodbye t'ye, good sir.   *Exit* JUSTICE
So now, Mr Constable, shall you and I go pick up a whore together?

CONST.   No, thank you, madam; my wife's enough to satisfy any reasonable man.

SIR JOHN.   (*Aside*) He, he, he, he, he! The fool is married then. – Well, you won't go?

CONST.   Not I, truly.

SIR JOHN.   Then I'll go by myself, and you and your wife may be damned.   *Exit*

CONST.   (*Gazing after him*) Why, God a mercy, my lady.   *Exeunt*

Act Four

SCENE [FOUR]

(p. 455)

SIR JOHN.   Why, I have been beating the watch and scandalising the women.

APPENDIX C

Rewritten lines in *The Beaux Stratagem* from the edition of 1728

The rewritten scene begins with Count Bellair's entrance in the 1707 edition p. 652 above. Speeches of characters other than Foigard are included below only if they differ from the 1707 version.

Enter FOIGARD

FOIG.   Arra, fait, de people do say you be all robbed, joy.

. . .

AIM.   The ladies have been in some danger, sir, as you saw.

FOIG.   Upon my shoul, our inn be rob too.

. . .

FOIG.   Upon my shalwation, our landlord has robbed himself and run away wid da money.

. . .

FOIG.   Ay, fait! And me too of a hundred pounds.

ARCH.   Robbed you of a hundred pound?

FOIG.   Yes, fait, honny, that I did owe to him.

. . .

FOIG.   Ay, upon my shoul, we'll all asshist.

. . .

FOIG.   Ay, but upon my conshience, de question be apropro, for all dat.

. . .

FOIG.   Arra, no part wid your wife? Upon my shoul, de man dosh not understand common shivility.

. . .

FOIG.   Upon my conscience, dere accounts vill agree.

. . .

FOIG.   Arra, honeys, a clear caase, a clear caase!

. . .

FOIG.   Upon my shoul, a very pretty sheremony.

. . .

ARCH.   What is her portion?

Foigard does not speak again. Some of Count Bellair's words are transferred to Archer, and the reviser has given this phase of the play an ending quite different from the original.

SIR CHARLES.   Ten thousand pound, sir.

. . .

ARCH.   I'll pay it. My lord, I thank him, has enabled me, and if the lady pleases, she shall go home with me. This night's adventure . . .

The dialogue to the end of the scene is the same as in the 1707 edition.

Wycherley, *The Country Wife*

I. Harry Horner persuades his physician, Dr Quack, to spread the (false) information that he is impotent. Sir Jasper Fidget, a self-important businessman, is delighted with this news, as he will now be able safely to trust Horner to entertain his wife and her friends, just as the young man had hoped. Horner's companions, Frank Harcourt, Dorilant, and Sparkish, ridicule their seemingly sexless friend. Jack Pinchwife has just come up to London from Hampshire to arrange for the dowry of his young sister Alithea, who is engaged to marry the foolish Master Sparkish. Knowing nothing of Horner's newly announced condition, Pinchwife, aged forty-nine, is very anxious to keep his young and pretty country wife isolated from the London beaux.

II. Margery Pinchwife, in the city for the first time, chafes within her husband's constraints, although he has taken her to a play the preceding afternoon, where she attracted the attention of an unidentified gallant. Sparkish rashly introduces his fiancée, Alithea, to Harcourt, who immediately falls in love with and woos her. She gives him no encouragement because she feels honour-bound to fulfill her commitment to Sparkish. Lady Fidget, Dainty Fidget, and Mrs Squeamish, restless society ladies, attempt to meet Margery Pinchwife, eager to introduce her to London society, much to her husband's annoyance. Sir Jasper attempts vigorously to persuade his wife to accept the eunuch Horner as a harmless companion. She demurs contemptuously until Horner confides to her that he is sexually able, when she concedes that he is 'a better man than I thought him'.

III. Margery Pinchwife learns that the gallant at the playhouse was Horner, who called at Pinchwife's lodgings, but was turned away by the jealous husband. He grudgingly agrees to take her, disguised as a boy, into town. Amongst his male friends Horner pretends to hate women. Harcourt admits his love for Alithea, and Sparkish encourages his rival to be on friendly terms with her, a foolish gesture that Alithea regards with impatience; she remains aloof from Harcourt. When Horner and Pinchwife meet in the Strand, Horner toys with the pretty young gentleman accompanying the country-man, plying the 'boy' with gifts, flattery, and kisses, to Margery's great pleasure.

IV. The next morning Alithea is to marry Sparkish; he unwittingly brings along Harcourt disguised as a parson to perform a fraudulent ceremony. Harcourt hopes that delaying Alithea's valid marriage may work to his advantage. Alithea immediately sees through the deception, although Sparkish cannot. She believes that this 'game' will only delay a valid marriage to Sparkish. Pinchwife tortures himself as he forces Margery to recount Horner's actions during the preceding evening. He then bullies his wife into writing a letter, in her own character, to Horner, rejecting his attentions. During Pinchwife's brief absence, Margery writes an affectionate letter to her gallant and cleverly switches the letters, whereupon Pinchwife takes the second epistle to Horner. In Horner's lodgings he and Lady Fidget are enjoying the preliminaries to a seduction when Sir Jasper enters. They persuade him that his wife is here merely to acquire a piece of Horner's fine collection of china, and she and Horner go into another room to examine it. Amongst the several people in the two rooms there is much sexual innuendo surrounding conversations about 'china'. As soon as the Fidget party leave, Lady Fidget being well satisfied with her 'china', Pinchwife arrives, carrying what he thinks is his wife's rejection of Horner's attentions. Horner reads Margery's love letter without revealing its nature, and Pinchwife tells him that the young gentleman of the earlier meeting was really his wife. Now Sparkish informs Pinchwife and Horner that Alithea 'denies her marriage'; however, Sparkish is rather complacent about it. At home Pinchwife discovers Margery writing another love letter to Horner; threatening her with his sword, the angry husband locks up his wife.

V. Margery persuades Pinchwife that she is writing to Horner on Alithea's behalf, telling her husband that, because his sister's marriage to Sparkish has failed to take place, Alithea is now in love with Horner. (The Pinchwifes do not yet know of Horner's reputed disability.) Pinchwife thinks it better that Horner should marry Alithea than perhaps seduce Margery; therefore he accedes to Margery's suggestion that Alithea should shyly go to Horner in a mask and cloak. Pinchwife is unaware that it is in fact a disguised Margery whom he leads to Horner. Margery has barely time to reveal her identity to him when Sir Jasper intrudes to forewarn Horner that Lady Fidget and her friends intend to organise a frolic and banquet at

Horner's apartment. Sparkish, having been told erroneously by Pinchwife that Alithea is about to marry Horner, now rejects a puzzled Alithea, leaving her free to marry Frank Harcourt.

Horner has only limited opportunity to make love to Margery before Lady Fidget and her friends set in motion a party at Horner's. After much drinking, they make candid disclosures about their sexual frustrations and Horner's true condition. Only after the party ends can Horner free Margery from another room and send her home. Soon everyone surrounds Horner to sort out the confusions: Alithea will marry Harcourt, and Lady Fidget will return to Sir Jasper with unsullied reputation after Quack lies assiduously to defend Horner's reputation as a eunuch. This scheme almost fails when Margery nearly blurts out the truth about Horner, but is commanded to shut up. She must return to Hampshire with Pinchwife, but is now a more sophisticated country wife than she was, and Horner, able to resume his pose as an unsexed man, will continue his sexual dalliance.

Etherege, *The Man of Mode*

I. Dorimant fastidiously dresses, aided by his servant Handy, and receives an orange-woman, a purveyor of gossip, who tells the young bachelor about a rich and handsome girl, Harriet, just arrived in London. They are interrupted by his shoemaker and his gossipy friend Medley, 'the very spirit of scandal'. Acting on the command of his new inamorata (Belinda), Dorimant is trying to conclude an affair with Loveit by picking a quarrel with her. Young Bellair learns that his father is coming to London to command him to marry Harriet, unaware that his son already loves Emilia.

II. Old Bellair, at fifty-five, is also much taken with Emilia, and Lady Townley, a London hostess, receives Medley in order to pick up town tattle. Loveit is annoyed at being ignored by Dorimant. Belinda, who is anxious to capture Dorimant firmly for herself, calls on Loveit, to inform her about Dorimant's mythical affair with another girl. Dorimant joins them, to aggravate Loveit and privately to make an assignation with Belinda.

III. Harriet's mother and Young Bellair's father urge them to marry, against their inclinations; to keep peace the young people pretend to love one another. During a period of idle talk at Lady Townley's home, Dorimant urges self-interested Belinda to help him to cast off Loveit. He accuses her of being attracted to Sir Fopling Flutter, just returned from Paris overloaded with French mannerisms and fashions. Harriet is attracted to Dorimant, despite his reputation as a seducer who 'delights in nothing but rapes and riots'.

Dorimant engineers a meeting in the Mall between Loveit and Sir Fopling, during which she flirts with him, making Dorimant jealous. Lady Woodvill, Harriet's protective mother, knows Dorimant only by reputation; therefore, at Harriet's suggestion, he will appear at Lady Townley's evening reception as 'Mr Courtage'.

IV. Mr Courtage ingratiates himself with Lady Townley and Lady Woodvill. Old Bellair, the life of the party, woos Emilia, and Dorimant talks to Harriet, unwilling to admit that he is falling in love with her. Sir Fopling makes a grand show of French fashions, versifying, and dancing. Dorimant slips out for an early-morning liaison with Belinda.

V. Belinda's chair men inadvertently carry her to Loveit's home; Belinda explains her early visit by saying that country visitors had forced sightseeing upon her. Dorimant calls, to break off with Loveit, leading Belinda to think that her lover is still involved with Loveit; hence, Belinda hides. Loveit, wanting to hold Dorimant, and Dorimant, eager to end the affair, quarrel; he is embarrassed when Belinda appears, and he leaves quickly.

Old Bellair orders his son to marry a reluctant Harriet immediately; Dorimant woos her. Old Bellair is much aggravated to learn that his son has married Emilia earlier that morning. Dorimant deals diplomatically with his former mistresses, closing no doors irretrievably, and resumes his wooing of Harriet, who conciliates her mother. Lady Woodvill is shocked to learn that the likeable Mr Courtage is really Dorimant. He vows fidelity to Harriet, and they will continue discussion of marriage during a visit to her home in Hampshire.

Dryden, *All for Love*

I. Antony, aloof from everyone, having recently been defeated at the Battle of Actium, 'makes his heart a prey to black despair'. Loyal Ventidius boldly accuses his commander of being a slave to Cleopatra, urging him to fight and conquer again, reminding him of past triumphs and glories.

II. Cleopatra passionately bemoans Antony's withdrawal from her. She conciliates her lover with gifts; he recalls that she was first the mistress of Julius Caesar, that he (Antony) left his wife Octavia for her, and that his enduring passion for Cleopatra caused him to join her in flight from the naval engagement at Actium. Cleopatra acknowledges that womanly fear prompted her withdrawal from Actium, and she wins Antony back by providing evidence that she refused Octavius Caesar's bribe to abandon Antony and to join forces with him. The reunion of the lovers persuades him to give up further serious military activity against Caesar.

III. Antony is proud of a victory over an army of Caesar; however, Antony's lieutenant Ventidius regards this as a minor skirmish unless it is followed up. He and Dolabella urge Antony to return to duty and responsibility; they bring in Octavia and two children. These three work on his 'distracted soul', persuading him to leave Cleopatra and make peace with Caesar. Cleopatra and Octavia meet briefly, competing sharply over who loves Antony the more.

IV. Antony deputises Dolabella to tell Cleopatra that her lover is leaving her, to return to duty. Dolabella attempts to comfort the distraught Cleopatra. Ventidius and Octavia, secretly observing this episode, believe Dolabella to be in love with Cleopatra and that she, with much self-interest, has responded to him. Ventidius and Octavia report their interpretation of the meeting to Antony, hoping to arouse his jealousy and drive the lovers further apart. Once Alexas, Cleopatra's servant, has reinforced the account of Dolabella's love for Cleopatra and her encouragement of it, Antony angrily rejects his apparently unfaithful mistress.

V. Antony determines to fight Octavius Caesar, despite Cleopatra's navy having gone over to the Romans, until Alexas, desperate to save himself, falsely reports to Antony that Cleopatra has fatally stabbed herself. Alexas believes that when Antony and Cleopatra are later joyously reunited, he will be rewarded. Now, however, Antony gives up: 'Let Caesar take the world'. As soon as faithful Ventidius kills himself, violating his and Antony's suicide pact, Antony 'falls on his sword'. Just in time, Cleopatra has searched him out, and in the few minutes before Antony's death they are reconciled. She then commands asps to be brought in, so that she may both join Antony in death and avoid being captured by the conquering Octavius Caesar.

Otway, *Venice Preserved*

I. Poverty-stricken Jaffeir is much aggrieved that his father-in-law, Priuli, a senator of Venice, refuses to accept his three-year-old marriage to Belvidera, despite their deep love for each other, the birth of a son, and Jaffeir's having once saved Belvidera's life in a shipwreck. Jaffeir is therefore easily persuaded by his friend Pierre to join in his rebellion against the corrupt state. Pierre is partially motivated by his anger towards Senator Antonio, whose wealth and power have tempted away Pierre's courtesan girlfriend Aquilina. Jaffeir is the more willing to join the rebels when he learns that Senator Priuli instigated the depredations of the bailiffs at Jaffeir and Belvidera's home, because of Jaffeir's debts.

II. Despite Antonio's intrusion in their relationship, Pierre and Aquilina remain on good terms, as he urges her to pry state secrets from the senile senator. Pierre persuades Jaffeir to swear loyalty to the insurgents, who are suspicious of the newcomer. They gather at midnight to affirm their dedication to the cause and doubtfully to accept Jaffeir as a comrade; he gives them Belvidera as a hostage to his faithfulness to the rebellion.

III. Old Antonio perversely urges Aquilina to spit on him, kick, and whip him; she contemptuously drives him out. The next morning Belvidera reveals to Jaffeir that her rebel guard Renault attempted to rape her. Resentful of Renault's actions, Jaffeir tells her the secret of his and others' commitment to kill all of the senators and take over the city. The quarreling rebels plan their bloodthirsty strategy, although Jaffeir is reluctant.

IV. Belvidera persuades Jaffeir to reveal the plot to the senate. He does so after it has agreed to pardon him and his twenty-two comrades. The conspirators are captured. Pierre, angered by Jaffeir's treachery, rejects his gestures of reconciliation. The senate revokes the pardon to the rebels, who are to be executed. The news deeply distresses Jaffeir, who holds Belvidera responsible for Pierre's imminent death. Jaffeir attempts to stab her, but, contrite and loving her still, he leaves her.

V. Priuli, reconciled to his daughter, promises, too late, to plead with the senate on behalf of Jaffeir and his friends. Antonio practises a disjointed speech to the senate and has his advances curtly rejected by Aquilina. Jaffeir vows to die with his comrades and sadly parts from Belvidera. Jaffeir and Pierre have an emotional farewell scene on the scaffold. Promising to stab Pierre, so that he will not have the ignominy of death like a common criminal, Jaffeir kills Pierre and then himself. As soon as Belvidera is told of Jaffeir's death, she goes mad and dies.

Vanbrugh, *The Provoked Wife*

I. Sir John Brute instigates an habitual morning wrangle with his wife. After he thunders off, Lady Brute draws sympathy for her unhappy situation from her unmarried companion and niece, Belinda. The much-provoked wife could be tempted to be unfaithful to her husband but for her marriage vows; she knows that the devoted Constant has long been in love with her. In another house a pert maid, Madamoiselle, attends the vain Lady Fanciful as she dresses for the day. One of her morning letters invites her to rendezvous in an hour with an unknown man who will tell her some of her faults. Irritated yet curious, Lady Fanciful, accompanied by Madamoiselle, determines to meet 'this impudent fellow'.

II. In St James's Park the women meet Heartfree, 'a professed woman-hater'. He tells Lady Fanciful some blunt truths about her vanity and affected behaviour before the ladies flounce away. Constant enters, to tell his cynical friend Heartfree about his own futile devotion to Lady Brute. Sir John Brute meets them, complaining loudly about the ties of matrimony, which he has endured for two years. Constant and Heartfree accept Sir John's invitation to go home with him to drink because Constant hopes to see Lady Brute; however, they refuse to join him, Lord Rake, and others for an evening's drunken 'frolic' in town. Beguiling the time with music and romantic songs, Lady Fanciful reiterates her resentment of Heartfree's behaviour; she admits, however, that she is attracted to him above all other men.

III. Whilst Sir John smokes after dinner, Lady Brute and Belinda tease and irritate him. He drives them out as Constant and Heartfree come in; the men drink briefly, Brute ridiculing Constant for his dedication to his (unnamed) mistress. After Sir John leaves to confer with Lord Rake at the Blue Posts, Constant, Heartfree, Lady Brute and Belinda talk, until Lady Fanciful joins them, with much self-dramatisation, and spars with Heartfree; she fears that he is attracted to Belinda. Constant avows his love to Lady Brute; however, she remains true to her principles, whilst giving him some hope for the future.

The drunken party at the inn concludes with Sir John and his comrades on the lookout for a good street brawl. At home Lady Brute and Belinda exchange confidences about the relationships of the former with her husband and with Constant, and they talk about social behaviour, particularly at a play when the actors 'come blurt out with a nasty thing' (i.e., a *double entendre* that ladies must pretend not to understand). The aunt and niece plan a masked assignation with their lovers at Spring Garden.

IV. In the street Sir John steals a parson's gown from a tailor; the knight and his friends brawl with the watch, and he is taken to the gaol. Heartfree, a younger brother, with neither a fortune nor the prospect of one, allows himself to fall in love (with Belinda) for the first time. He and Constant receive an anonymous letter inviting them to meet two women in the park the next morning. The men think that some of their 'old battered acquaintance' have sent the note. Early the following day the drunken 'parson' is brought before the magistrate and is discharged.

Constant and Heartfree go to Spring Garden, followed by the disguised Lady Fanciful and Madamoiselle, who hide before Lady Brute and Belinda, wearing masks, appear. These ladies and the men have barely met when Sir John, still inebriated and wearing the clerical gown, approaches. He attempts to molest the seeming strumpets, but Lady Brute and Belinda privately reveal themselves to their lovers, who send Sir John away. Belinda and Heartfree walk off, whilst Constant woos Lady Brute passionately, pushing her into an arbour. Lady Fanciful and Madamoiselle burst out of their hiding place, disrupting both trysts. Lady Fanciful is jealous and angry that Belinda has taken Heartfree.

V. Lady Fanciful, resenting the fact that Lady Brute and Belinda have invited their companions home, resolves to reveal everything to Sir John. Before she can put her plan into action, Sir John stumbles into his parlour, and the visitors hide in a closet, where Sir John discovers them. They leave promptly. Sir John passes out and is dragged to bed by a servant, Razor. The ladies devise a story, to satisfy Sir John, that Heartfree and Belinda are secretly engaged to be married; for that reason the men hid from him, fearing his objections.

Razor, who woos Madamoiselle, gives her an account of the events at Sir John's house the night before. Lady Fanciful urges her maid to persuade Razor to reveal everything to Sir John. A letter from Lady Brute to Constant informs him of Belinda's scheme; Constant then convinces Heartfree that he should marry Belinda. All four present a united front to the now-sober Sir John, who grudgingly accepts an apparent *fait accompli*.

Lady Fanciful, in disguise, tells Belinda that Heartfree is already married to this unidentified woman. As well, Lady Fanciful delivers a letter to Heartfree, as from a man who claims to have been intimate with Belinda. These statements seem to put paid to a marriage between Heartfree and Belinda. Suddenly repentant, Razor decides to reveal the work of the 'ill-natured bitch', Lady Fanciful, and her maid; he drags in both disguised women, tells his story, and unmasks the culprits. They leave chagrined, and Heartfree and Belinda resume their preparations for marriage. The relationship between Sir John and Lady Brute is unchanged, and Constant remains devoted to Lady Brute.

Congreve, *The Way of the World*

I. Edward Mirabell, a London gallant, tells Mr Fainall about tensions between himself and the girl whom he loves, Millamant. Mirabell has offended her aunt, Lady Wishfort, on whom Millamant depends for the use of half of her fortune, by rashly making 'sham addresses' to the widowed Lady, now fifty-five, in an attempt to conceal his wooing of her niece. Mirabell's deception was revealed by her ladyship's friend, Mrs Marwood, who would like to have Mirabell for herself. Mirabell has, for as yet obscure reasons, arranged a marriage between Waitwell (his servant) and an unidentified maid (Foible, a servant of Lady Wishfort). Sir Wilfull Witwoud, Lady Wishfort's nephew, has arrived from Shropshire, although he has not yet appeared; he is a half-brother to Anthony Witwoud, a man-about-town friend of Mirabell. Anthony Witwoud and Petulant, a pair of lackwits, reveal that Lady Wishfort is encouraging a match between her niece, Millamant, and Sir Wilfull, who is over forty.

II. Mrs Fainall, Lady Wishfort's daughter, and Mrs Marwood discuss their avowed aversion to men. When Mrs Fainall leaves with Mirabell, Mrs Marwood and Mr Fainall reveal their love affair, prompted principally by his pleasure in her wealth. As Mrs Fainall and Mirabell return, they refer to a romantic liaison of their own in the past; when she feared that she was pregnant, Mirabell arranged her marriage to Fainall, whom she now dislikes. Mirabell reveals that he has commanded Waitwell to disguise himself as Sir Rowland and quickly to woo and wed Lady Wishfort; then Mirabell plans to announce the deception, forcing Lady Wishfort to permit his marriage to her niece. (The fact that Waitwell is already married to Foible will invalidate his marriage to Lady Wishfort.) Millamant teases the devoted Mirabell, leaving him feeling as though he lives in a whirlwind.

III. Vain and impatient, Lady Wishfort prepares for Sir Rowland's arrival. Her willingness to receive him as a lover is intensified after Foible invents some rude remarks about her ladyship made by Mirabell. Preparations for dinner go forward, and Sir Wilfull joins the group. The sophisticated members of the company ridicule the country dress and manners of this alternative suitor for Millamant. Fainall and Marwood scheme to destroy surreptitiously Mirabell's hoped-for marriage to Millamant by sending an anonymous letter to Lady Wishfort exposing the false Sir Rowland.

IV. Sir Wilfull, a 'superannuated lubber', clumsily woos Millamant, and immediately after this episode Mirabell urges her to marry *him*; they spar happily with one another, each presenting a series of seemingly frivolous provisos, concluding with Millamant's make-believe condescension: 'I'll endure you'. A drunken Sir Wilfull now finds words to make his addresses to Millamant; she refuses him, thereby opposing her aunt's wish. This distraction briefly delays Sir Rowland's more articulate courting of Lady Wishfort. She is eager for the wedding to take place promptly, partly to revenge herself on her false suitor, Mirabell. When the Fainall-Marwood letter is delivered, Sir Rowland cleverly persuades Lady Wishfort that the disguised handwriting is that of Mirabell. Sir Rowland then pretends that he will seek out Mirabell, to fight a duel with him. Lady Wishfort dissuades him, in the interests of her reputation.

V. Marwood and Mrs Fainall have told everything to an angry and chagrined Lady Wishfort. Mr Fainall, believing himself to be in command of everyone and aided by Marwood, attempts to bully Lady Wishfort into signing over to him, first, the right to allow her to marry, and, second, both the residue of the fortune belonging to his wife and half that of Millamant. Lady Wishfort almost accedes to these harsh terms, in order to avoid the publicity of Fainall's threatened legal action.

Millamant is even willing to marry Sir Wilfull, so that she will not be guilty of violating Lady Wishfort's approval of any marriage her niece makes. Now Mirabell stages an impressive denouement: Marwood's affair with Fainall is revealed; Mirabell has long had a document that gives him control over Mrs Fainall's estate, thus enabling her freely to break with Fainall without penalty; Sir Wilfull will resign from the arrangement to marry Millamant; and, to conclude, Mirabell earns Lady Wishfort's grateful agreement that he should marry Millamant.

Farquhar, *The Beaux Stratagem*

I. Thomas Aimwell and Francis Archer, 'two gentlemen of broken fortunes', determined to live by their wits, have just arrived at an inn in Lichfield. They pick up local gossip from the landlord, Will Boniface, and learn about the aristocracy of the town: Lady Bountiful, her son, Squire Sullen, his wife, and the Lady's unmarried daughter, Dorinda. Archer, acting the part of Aimwell's servant, flirts with Boniface's daughter, Cherry.

II. Mrs Sullen complains to Dorinda about the barbarity of her uncouth husband, who, on appearance, lives up to the report. His wife considers providing him with a rival. Aimwell dresses impressively to make his first public appearance, at church. The inn is the headquarters for a gang of highwaymen. Boniface, Gibbet and Cherry try to wheedle information from Archer about his 'master' Aimwell. Archer continues to woo Cherry, much attracted by her claimed resources of £2,000.

III. Mrs Sullen and Dorinda are curious about the handsome young stranger who attended church service. At the inn Aimwell raves to Archer about the beautiful woman (Dorinda) whom he saw at church. Aimwell talks with Gibbet, who answers all questions ambiguously, and to Foigard, an Irishman masquerading as a French priest. Archer, now posing as footman to 'Viscount' Aimwell, has been invited by Scrub, Lady Bountiful's butler, to visit his kitchen, where they tipsily gossip and confide in each other. Mrs Sullen and Dorinda find excuses to get acquainted here with Archer, who sings to them. He craftily refuses a tip, leading the ladies to assume that he may be a gentleman in disguise. Mrs Sullen flirts with Count Bellair merely to provoke her husband to jealousy, hoping that he will be kind to her. This scheme fails.

IV. Mrs Sullen mopes about until, fortuitously, Aimwell is overcome with a feigned swoon at the gate of the Bountiful-Sullen home, a ruse to meet Dorinda. He is brought in in a chair, but Lady Bountiful's remedies are less efficacious than is holding Dorinda's hand. Archer and Mrs Sullen are attracted to one another. The men are invited to tour the house. Foigard bribes Gipsy, a maid, to hide Count Bellair, in love with Mrs Sullen, at night in her closet. Scrub observes these negotiations with Gipsy.

As Dorinda and Mrs Sullen lead the young men through the picture gallery, all indulge in flattery and love-making, Archer approaching Mrs Sullen more aggressively than she wishes. She leaves abruptly, having no real evidence that he is any more than a servant. Scrub reveals to Archer the night-time plot in train. Mrs Sullen and Dorinda argue over which of the men is the more attractive. Aimwell proposes marriage to Dorinda, who likes the idea of being 'Lady' Aimwell, and Mrs Sullen envies her prospective happiness. At their lodgings Aimwell and Archer congratulate each other on their successes. They trick Foigard into revealing his identity, whereupon he tells them about Bellair's midnight rendezvous. Boniface and his confederates plan to rob Lady Boniface's home.

V. Sir Charles Freeman, Mrs Sullen's brother, who has come from London to help to solve her matrimonial difficulties, meets Squire Sullen, drunk as usual, at the inn. Sullen is willing to return his wife to her brother, but not her fortune. Archer slips into Mrs Sullen's bedroom, makes passionate love to her (to which she half yields), and is about to carry her away when Scrub bursts in to announce that the house is full of thieves. Hounslow and Bagshot attempt to rob Lady Bountiful and Dorinda. Aimwell and Archer rescue them, the former taking Dorinda away to woo her, the latter using a small wound as a device to draw sympathy from Mrs Sullen; however, she remains aloof, referring emphatically to her honour.

Aimwell wins Dorinda and reveals that he is a poor man (a younger son) and an opportunist. This candour angers his partner, Archer. At this moment Aimwell learns that his older brother is dead; now Dorinda's suitor is 'the true Lord Viscount Aimwell', and she is indeed willing to marry him. Archer demands half of Dorinda's fortune, as per the men's earlier sharing agreement, whereupon Aimwell gives him the whole, £10,000, because, as a now-wealthy nobleman, he no longer needs his bride's wealth.

Cherry writes to Archer, whom she loves, sending his and Aimwell's money left at the inn and telling him that her father, implicated with the robbers, has fled. Sir Charles arranges for the formal severance of Squire and Mrs Sullen, with Archer and Gibbet cooperating, on her behalf, to get her wealth away from Sullen. Archer and Mrs Sullen lead off a country dance, to celebrate the Aimwell-Dorinda union and the Sullen separation.

DRAMA
IN EVERYMAN

The Oresteia
AESCHYLUS
*New translation of one of the
greatest Greek dramatic trilogies
which analyses the plays in
performance*
£5.99

**Everyman and Medieval
Miracle Plays**
edited by A. C. Cawley
*A selection of the most popular
medieval plays*
£4.99

Complete Plays and Poems
CHRISTOPHER MARLOWE
*The complete works of this great
Elizabethan in one volume*
£5.99

Restoration Plays
edited by Robert Lawrence
*Five comedies and two tragedies
representing the best of the
Restoration stage*
£7.99

**Female Playwrights of the
Restoration: Five Comedies**
edited by Paddy Lyons
*Rediscovered literary treasures
in a unique selection*
£5.99

**Plays, Prose Writings
and Poems**
OSCAR WILDE
*The full force of Wilde's wit
in one volume*
£4.99

**A Dolls House/The Lady from
the Sea/The Wild Duck**
HENRIK IBSEN
introduced by Fay Weldon
*A popular selection of Ibsen's
major plays*
£4.99

**The Beggar's Opera and
Other Eighteenth-Century Plays**
JOHN GAY et. al.
Including Goldsmith's She Stoops
To Conquer *and Sheridan's* The
School for Scandal, *this is a volume
which reflects the full scope of the
period's theatre*
£6.99

**Female Playwrights of the
Nineteenth Century**
edited by Adrienne Scullion
*The full range of female nineteenth-
century dramatic development*
£6.99

All books are available from your local bookshop or direct from:
Littlehampton Book Services Cash Sales, 14 Eldon Way, Lineside Estate,
Littlehampton, West Sussex BN17 7HE (*prices are subject to change*)

To order any of the books, please enclose a cheque (in sterling) made payable to
Littlehampton Book Services, or phone your order through with credit card details (Access,
Visa or Mastercard) on 01903 721596 (24 hour answering service) stating card number
and expiry date. (*Please add £1.25 for package and postage to the total of your order.*)

In the USA, for further information and a complete catalogue call 1-800-526-2778